PASCAL PROGRAMMING

A Spiral Approach

PASCAL PROGRAMMING

A Spiral Approach

Walter S. Brainerd
University of New Mexico
Los Alamos National Laboratory

Charles H. Goldberg
Trenton State College

Jonathan L. Gross
Columbia University

BOYD & FRASER PUBLISHING COMPANY
San Francisco

BOYD & FRASER COMPUTER SCIENCE SERIES

Tom Walker, **Sponsoring Editor**

© Copyright 1982 by Walter S. Brainerd, Charles H. Goldberg, and Jonathan L. Gross

Library of Congress number: 82-70213
ISBN: 0–87835–122–1

Cover Design by Walter Christiansen

1   2   3   4   ·   5   4   3   2

DEDICATION

To our parents:
      Scott and Verl Brainerd
      Ralph and Dorothy Goldberg
      Henrietta Light-Gross
      Nathan Gross

ACKNOWLEDGEMENTS

For their many ideas and contributions to the production of this book, the authors wish to thank Thomas Walker and Arthur Weisbach of Boyd & Fraser.

W.S.B.
C.H.G.
J.L.G.

ABOUT THE AUTHORS

Walter S. Brainerd (Ph.D. Purdue University) is Professor of Computer Science at the University of New Mexico and a staff member at the Los Alamos National Laboratory. His research is in theoretical computer science, and he is active in programming-language standardization.

Charles H. Goldberg (Ph.D. Princeton University) is currently a Visiting Professor of Mathematics at Princeton University, on leave from Trenton State College. His research interests include combinatorics, compilers, algorithms, numerical analysis, and geometric topology.

Jonathan L. Gross (Ph.D. Dartmouth College) is a Professor of Computer Science, Mathematics, and Mathematical Statistics at Columbia University. He has published research papers in mathematical modeling, graph theory, algorithms, anthropology and social organization, and topology. He has been an IBM Postdoctoral Fellow and an Alfred P. Sloan Fellow.

These three authors have previously written *FORTRAN 77 Programming* (Harper & Row, 1978) and *Introduction to Computer Programming* (Harper & Row, 1979). Gross and Brainerd have also written *Fundamental Programming Concepts* (Harper & Row, 1972). Brainerd has collaborated with L. H. Landweber to write *Theory of Computation* (Wiley–Interscience, 1974).

PREFACE

This book introduces computer programming in the language Pascal. It motivates and develops all of the concepts by careful analysis of practical examples. No prior background in computing or college mathematics is necessary.

The Rise of Pascal

The increasingly widespread adoption of Pascal is one of the most important trends in computer languages. The use of Pascal in commercial applications and personal computing is growing rapidly. Pascal compilers are often included in the initial software package for newly-announced computers. Leading departments of computer science now teach Pascal both to future computer scientists and in general introductory courses. The reason lies in three design principles of Pascal.

First, Pascal includes a broad range of the most useful programming constructs. The main kinds of decisions, loops, and data structures can all be programmed in Pascal in a natural way.

Second, Pascal encourages good programming practices such as top-down design and modularity. Mastering Pascal first will make you a better programmer in all the other languages you will ever learn.

Third, it is possible to give a complete description of Pascal syntax in a few pages. At the topmost level, the inside covers of this book provide a description of the general form of a Pascal program, Pascal data types, and Pascal statements. Appendix E fills in all the details. Thus, after you learn Pascal you can refresh yourself on any feature by referring to these summaries. Appendix C contains the syntax charts, an alternative form of language description, in brief format.

Our Presentation

This textbook includes about 200 complete programs and their execution printouts, enabling a beginner to examine in complete detail familiar applications such as credit cards, population growth, income taxes, and teaching arithmetic to a child. There are over 500 exercises, either for classroom assignment or for self-study, ranging in difficulty from routine to challenging.

Besides the technique of teaching by example, another important feature of the presentation is a reprise pedagogy—the "spiral" approach. Each important idea appears first in simple form. It is then explained carefully and developed in detail. It is reviewed again and again, each time with some new viewpoint. The first occurrence of a "loop," for instance, is in a simple program, early in Chapter 1, which averages some test scores. Loops are the main topic of Chapter 2, where close examination of loops includes their use in a program to compute gradepoint averages and in a program to predict the future population density in the State of New Jersey. The relationship of loops to subscripted variables is explored in Chapter 3. Explicit discussion of loops continues in Chapters 4 and 5 as well.

The style is consistently thoughtful of the beginner, anticipating and answering probable questions. Even in discussing a "hard" topic such as comparison of the efficiency of sorting or searching methods, examples are thoroughly worked out.

Classroom Tested Contents

The contents of this book have been tested in classrooms at the University of New Mexico, at Trenton State College, and at Columbia University. A variety of approaches worked out well. The thoroughness of the book and its presentation of complete examples allow an instructor to emphasize whatever seems appropriate, knowing that all of the essentials are fully covered. Moreover, the Pascal syntax reference guides on the inside covers and in Appendix E provide two levels of description of Pascal. These guides may prove useful when a student is writing programs.

How to Use This Book

Chapters 1, 2, 3, and 4 are the core for a one-semester introduction to programming in Pascal. Chapters 5, 6, and 7 are dependent on the earlier chapters, but independent of each other, aside from occasional remarks. Chapter 6 covers so many intermediate-level programming concepts and Pascal features that it alone provides enough material for at least half a semester of a course that emphasizes files and data structures. Some of the simulation applications in Chapter 7 can be presented immediately after Chapter 2 if an instructor chooses, since they use only programming language features from the first two chapters.

TABLE OF CONTENTS

1

BEGINNING TO PROGRAM A COMPUTER

A computer is a device for processing information in a wide variety of ways, both simple and complex. It can perform arithmetic, read, remember, transcribe, modify, and print information with amazing speed and accuracy. In fact, some computers can do more arithmetic in 1 second than a person can do in a lifetime, even if the person were to work 12 hours a day, every day, from birth to the age of 100. Moreover, the computer is unlikely to make even a single mistake in the process.

Computers are versatile, general purpose machines. The same computer that prepares a payroll one minute can also perform a scientific calculation or alphabetize a list of names the next minute. The versatility of computers is achieved by combining relatively simple basic operations such as reading, writing, and arithmetic into meaningful sequences called *programs*. Thus a computer can do as many different things as there are programs written for it.

This book is an introduction to *computer programming,* that is, the writing of computer programs. Accordingly, it discusses the things that computers can do from the point of view of how to direct a computer to do them. Besides providing a sound basis for those who would like to write programs, it is designed to satisfy the intellectual curiosity of persons who are familiar with computerized applications and would like to know how they work.

Computer programming is not a mysterious art practiced only by highly trained specialists after years of study and apprenticeship. As we shall see in this chapter, by using a suitable computer language, a person with no previous computer programming experience can write useful programs from the very beginning. Learning a computer language is like learning English, in the sense that it is not necessary to know the entire unabridged dictionary before anything meaningful can be said. In fact, using only a few dozen different words, one can communicate quite well with a computer.

It is possible to use a computer without knowing anything about computer programming. Indeed, many computer users do not write their own programs. Yet there are several reasons why a user could profit from at least some acquaintance with computer programming. To a user who writes programs, the potential uses of a computer are limited only by the user's ability, ingenuity, and experience in combining basic operations to achieve more complex goals. Of course, when an existing program can be found to perform a long or complex task, an experienced programmer does not hesitate to use it instead of writing a new version. There are programs called ''compilers'', ''assemblers'', and ''operating systems'' (see Section 1.4) that are used by nearly every programmer, although very few programmers ever write one.

Users who do not write programs, on the other hand, can only run the programs written by others. Sometimes exactly the right program can be found, but often the user must settle for a less than perfect match. Frequently, the most suitable program also contains a large number of unnecessary features and has a set of directions more difficult to master than a programming language. Moreover, while many programming languages remain stable for long periods of time and apply to many computers, even those produced by different manufacturers, only the very best applications programs provide a similar ease of use and stability.

Using someone else's program is like buying a sealed unit with a set of directions for its use. When the directions are complete and the unit does what it is supposed to, the results can be quite satisfactory. But when the directions are incomplete or vague, or when the unit doesn't seem to be doing what the instructions claim, or when it would be nice if it would do things just a little bit differently, then one cannot help wishing for some idea of what is going on inside.

Common programming languages such as Pascal, Fortran, Basic, PL/I, and Cobol are a compromise between the way people think and the way computers "think". Their introduction lightened the burden on programmers, who at one time were compelled to know minute details of a computer's internal operation. Part of the burden has been transferred to the computer, which must convert a program written in one of these languages into its own internal language before executing the program. However, before writing a program in Pascal, Basic, PL/I, or Cobol, it is still essential to analyze the application for computer solution.

Analyzing applications for computer solution is the universal part of computer programming, and it is the principal subject of this book. From a carefully written analysis, it is possible to write the details of a solution in any appropriate computer programming language. The programming language Pascal is used in this book. Programming details and debugging techniques are not neglected either. All programs in this book have been run on a computer.

The programming language Pascal was developed by Niklaus Wirth in Zurich. It is derived from the programming language Algol, developed in the late 1950s. In most respects, it is simpler than Algol, making it easier to learn; however, it contains excellent data structuring features not found in Algol. Pascal is implemented on a wide variety of computers and is a candidate for an American and international standard programming language.

We believe you should start reading and writing programs immediately. The objective of Chapter 1 is to convince a beginning programmer that it is possible to write and run meaningful programs with a minimum of fuss and bother. The very first section shows how to write programs to perform almost any sort of simple arithmetic computation and how to print both the problem statement and the answer. If a computer is available, we recommend that you begin to write and *run* programs modelled on our sample programs at this point. A short set of directions from the instructor or computer center or, better yet, a brief demonstration using the computer will show you how to enter and run a program at your local installation.

Section 1.2 plants the seeds of greater variety in your programs with variables, character strings, and arrays, but it is Section 1.3 that hits the jackpot by using a *loop* to produce more lines of output than there are statements in the program. With this breakthrough, the computer becomes an efficient processor of information and you can write some rather short programs that make the computer do rather large amounts of computation.

Section 1.4 shows how to run a program. It describes what it is like to enter a program either from punched cards or from a computer terminal and describes time sharing, an interesting topic of immediate applicability for readers who have access to a computer to run their programs. Section 1.4 supplements directions specific to the computer you will be using, which can be obtained only from your instructor or your local computer center.

Section 1.5 shows how to use if-statements to provide alternative computational paths for different values in the input data. It provides flexibility in a program. Section 1.6 introduces a major programming technique, programmer-defined procedures, with a simple example. Programmer-defined procedures are the natural tool to implement the modern top-down method of program design introduced in Chapter 2.

Section 1.7 places Pascal programs in a more general context. It contains a description of the characteristics of a computer, a bit of computer history, and a comparison of computers and hand calculators. Chapter 1 concludes with a chapter review, Section 1.8, as does every other chapter in this book.

The goals of Chapter 1 are twofold: first and foremost, to get you started writing and running meaningful Pascal programs as soon as possible, and second, to introduce most of the major programming techniques with complete yet simple examples. Chapter 1 should give a tantalizing sketch of what a computer can do. We will elaborate in subsequent chapters.

1.1 Programs That Calculate

Since computers are very good at arithmetic, one reasonable thing to learn first about computer programming is how to tell a computer to do the sort of arithmetic that otherwise might by done by hand or with the aid of a hand calculator. This section describes how to write programs to calculate and to print. Readers who want a historical perspective or an introduction to computers by way of desk calculators first may start with Section 1.7 and then return to Section 1.1 afterward.

Simple Calculations

The first example is a program that prints the result of an addition:

```
program calculation1 (output);
  begin
  writeln (84 + 13);
  end.
```

The program calculation1 tells the computer to add the numbers 84 and 13 and then to write the sum, which is 97. Thus, when the computer is told to run calculation1, it does precisely that. It adds the two numbers and writes their sum. The execution printout will look something like this with only minor variations from computer to computer.

```
run calculation1

97
```

A printed copy of a program is called a *program listing*. The four-line program calculation1 is listed above.

This example brings to mind five questions of immediate relevance.

1. How does the computer know that it is supposed to write the sum 97, and not the statement of the problem "84 + 13" instead?

2. What kinds of expressions may be written inside of the parentheses after the word "writeln" (which is an abbreviation for "write line")?

3. Just how much English is incorporated into the Pascal programming language? For example, are there any acceptable synonyms for the words "begin", "end", and "program", and the command "writeln"?

4. What is the meaning of the program name "calculation1"? Does it have to start with the word "calculation" to work properly?

5. How is a computer told what the program is and when to run it?

Printing Messages

The answer to question 1 is that, if you want the computer to print the exact typographic characters that you specify, you enclose them in apostrophes (or "single quotes"), as illustrated by the program printcharacters. The apostrophes are not printed.

```
program printcharacters (output);
  begin
  writeln ('84 + 13');
  end.
```

```
run printcharacters
```

```
84 + 13
```

In a Pascal program, a sequence of typographic characters enclosed in apostrophes represents a *character string*. A character string may contain alphabetic characters as well as numeric characters and other special characters such as punctuation marks and arithmetic symbols. For example, the program hello prints a largely alphabetic character string.

```
program hello (output);
  begin
  writeln ('Hello, I am a computer.');
  end.
run hello
```

```
Hello, I am a computer.
```

A happy combination of printing exact literal characters and printing a computed value produces the following easy-to-read output.

```
program calc1version2 (output);
  begin
  writeln ('84 + 13 = ',  84 + 13);
  end.
```

```
run calc1version2
```

```
84 + 13 =            97
```

In the program calc1version2 (calculation1 version 2), the list of items to be printed consists of two items, a character constant '84 + 13 = ' to be printed exactly as written, and an arithmetic expression whose value is first calculated and then printed. Thus, although the two items may look superficially identical, enclosing the character string in apostrophes means that it is to be *transcribed,* character for character, including the four blank characters (spaces, in ordinary typing), while the same expression written without apostrophes is to be *evaluated* so that the sum can be printed. As in English, commas are used to separate the items in a write list.

Constants: Character String, Real, and Integer

All of the numbers and character strings in the programs are examples of *constants*. There are several *types* of constants. A *character string constant* is a character string enclosed in apostrophes. A string of digits followed by a period, used as a decimal point, followed by another string of digits is called a *real constant*. The following are real constants.

13.5   0.1234567   123.45678   3.0   00.30

The following are not real constants in Pascal because there must be at least one digit before and at least one digit after the decimal point.

.1234567   3.   12345.   .0

An *integer constant* is a string consisting only of the digits 0 to 9, such as the following examples.

23   0   1234567

In Pascal, the distinction between integer type and real type constants is a matter of the appearance of a decimal point, not whether the number is whole or has a non-zero fractional part. There are some places in a Pascal program where an integer may appear, but a real number must not be used. For instance, it would make no sense to have a Pascal statement that says to repeat something 5.17 times. However, any place that a real number may be used, an integer may be used.

A *number* is a real constant or an integer constant. A *signed number* is a number, or a number preceded by a plus sign ("+") or a minus sign ("-"). A blank must never appear in a Pascal number. The following are examples of signed numbers.

-23.7955   -6   +7.42   +3453   0.7   1

Exponential Notation Versus Positional Notation

The usual way of writing real numbers, such as 32.17, 0.0021, or 384.41, is called *positional notation* because the place value of each digit is determined by its position relative to the decimal point. Since computers ordinarily store only a limited number of significant digits, there is another common representation of numbers to allow for very large or very small numbers.

A real or integer constant may be followed by the letter "e" and an integer to form a real constant written in exponential notation. The letter "e" is read as "times ten to the power" and the integer following the "e" is a power of ten to be multiplied by the number preceding the "e". This form, called the *exponential notation,* is useful for writing very large or very small numbers. For example, 2.3e5 is 2.3 times ten to the power 5, or 2.3 x 100000 = 230000. The integer power may have a minus or plus sign preceding it as in the real constant 2.3e-5, which is 2.3 times 10 to the power -5 or 2.3 x 0.00001 = 0.000023. Two more examples are 1e9, which is one billion, and 1e3, which is one one-thousandth. Blanks must never be written in a Pascal number.

Real values written as output appear in the exponential form unless the precision is specified using the decimals indicator, as described in Section 1.2.

Arithmetic Expressions

In answer to question 2, just about any arithmetic expression may appear within the parentheses of a writeln statement, and the computer will evaluate it and print the result. The Pascal notation for arithmetic operations conforms generally to ordinary notation, except in cases where the ordinary notation is difficult or impossible to type on standard computer input devices. Even when the notation is modified, as in calculation2, the evaluation is the usual one.

```
program calculation2 (output);
  begin
  writeln (8 * (12 * 3 - 143 / 11));
  end.
```

```
run calculation2
```

```
1.840000e+02
```

Two modifications of ordinary notation used in the program calculation2 are the asterisk (*) which means multiplication, and the slash (/) which means division. Thus the number 8 is to be multiplied by the expression in parentheses. Within the parentheses, the number 12 is multiplied by 3 to give 36. The term 143 / 11, which is written all on one line instead of the typographically more difficult method of typing the numerator over the denominator, has the value 13. Therefore the expression in parentheses has the value 36 − 13, which is 23. The product of 8 and 23 is 184, the answer. The answer is printed as a real number because the result of a division (/) is always real, even if both operands are type integer.

Warning: The asterisk denoting multiplication of the 8 by the expression in parentheses cannot be omitted, even though often it may be omitted in ordinary algebraic notation. On the other hand, the use of spacing around the values or the operators is unrestricted, and it may be chosen to improve the readability of the expression. Spaces must not be inserted within a number, however.

Pascal does not have an operator designating exponentiation. A simple way to raise numbers to an integer power is shown in the mortgage programs of Section 2.5 and a method for raising a number to other powers is described in Section 2.6.

As in ordinary algebra, the evaluation of a complicated expression with many parentheses begins with evaluation of a subexpression enclosed by an innermost pair of parentheses. In Pascal, as in algebra, multiplication and division are performed before addition or subtraction. It is always permissible, and often advisable, to insert parentheses to clarify the meaning of an arithmetic expression. The precedence rules as they apply in the absence of overriding parentheses are illustrated in the following example.

$$4 + 12 / 2 - 1 + 5 * 9$$
$$= 4 + 6 - 1 + 5 * 9 \qquad \text{first multiplications and divisions,}$$
$$= 4 + 6 - 1 + 45 \qquad \qquad \text{left to right}$$
$$= 10 - 1 + 45 \qquad \text{then additions and subtractions,}$$
$$= 9 + 45 \qquad \qquad \text{going from left to right}$$
$$= 54$$

Expressions involving repeated divisions are evaluated from left to right as shown below.

$$432 / 12 / 6 / 3$$
$$= 36 / 6 / 3 \qquad \text{leftmost division first}$$
$$= 6 / 3 \qquad \text{leftmost remaining division next}$$
$$= 2$$

but, as in algebra, it is a good practice to insert parentheses to distinguish this meaning more clearly from such other possible interpretations as

$$(432 / 12) / (6 / 3) \quad \text{and} \quad 432 / (12 / (6 / 3))$$

which have different values. Similarly, expressions involving a mixture of multiplications and divisions are evaluated from left to right. Thus

$$12 / 6 * 2$$
$$= 2 * 2 \qquad \text{leftmost operation first}$$
$$= 4$$

When the calculated expression 12 / (6 * 2) is desired, the parentheses must not be omitted.

Does A Computer Understand English?

The answer to question 3 is that a computer understands only as much English as it is programmed to understand. The similarity to English in a programming language represents a compromise between the convenience of the computer, whose native tongue is something called *machine language,* and the convenience of English-speaking programmers. In general, the more English-like properties possessed by a programming language, the more computational time and power required to translate a program into machine language for execution, so the more it costs to operate. Pascal is not much like English, but instead borrows much of its notation from mathematics.

Keywords

The instructions given to a computer must be precise, unambiguous, and complete. Thus, when English words are used in Pascal, they acquire a precise, unambiguous, technical meaning. For example, the word "program" means: "This is the beginning of a Pascal program" and the word "end" followed by a period means: "This is the end of a Pascal program".

An English word such as "program", "begin", or "end" used in a program for its precise, technical meaning is called a *keyword*. Program steps that use a keyword make sense on two different levels. First, using the technical meaning, they are precise and unambiguous directions to a computer. Second, using the ordinary meaning of the English word, they are understandable by people who speak English. It is a great convenience to programmers and an incalculable aid to clear thinking if the technical meaning of a keyword is consistent with the ordinary meaning. Every Pascal statement except an assignment statement (described in Section 1.2) and a request for execution of a procedure (described in Section 2.2) begins with a keyword.

The characters "writeln" do not form a Pascal keyword. Instead, the statements that have used this word are requests to execute a built-in procedure whose name is "writeln". For the same reasons that it is helpful to have keywords that direct a computer to do something corresponding to their English meaning, it is helpful to pick names for procedures and programs that reflect their function.

The Program Heading

Each Pascal program begins with a *program heading*. It consists of the keyword "program" followed by a program name of the programmer's choosing. The name must start with a letter and consist of letters and digits. In answer to question 4, the program name "calculation1" does not mean anything to the computer. Any other name following the rules would work just as well. However, the authors chose the program name "calculation1" because it is intended to mean *to persons who read the program* that this program is the first calculational program in the book.

Following the program name is a list of the names of the files used by the program. All a beginner needs to know about files is that any Pascal program that produces printed or displayed output using the procedures write or writeln must list the special output file named "output", and any program that accepts execution-time input from the standard input file (card reader, terminal, or prepared disk file) must list the special input file named "input". At a more advanced level, other files may be specified by the programmer.

The file names are separated by commas and enclosed in parentheses. The file names "input" and "output" are special in Pascal in that any read operation that does not name a file uses the file name "input". Similarly, any write operation that does not name a file uses the file named "output". Unless the programmer indicates differently when the program is run, the files named "input" and "output" refer to a standard input or output device, such as a card reader, terminal, or printer.

The Keywords Begin and End

The keywords "begin" and "end" are used to delimit a sequence of statements that are to be considered to belong together. Such a sequence of statements is called a *compound statement,* to be described in more detail in Section 1.3. In particular, all of the statements of a program are preceded by the keyword "begin" and are terminated by the keyword "end", thus making them one compound statement. The entire program is terminated with a period. There are no acceptable synonyms for the keywords "begin" or "end", or for that matter for any keywords in Pascal.

Running a Program

The answer to question 5, "How do you tell a computer to run a program?" is not given easily, since it depends very much on the computer being used. It also may depend on the type of device that is used to enter the program into the computer. Examples showing how to run a Pascal program on two machines using punched cards and using a computer terminal are shown in Section 1.4, but you should get instructions specific to the computer you will be using from your instructor or computer center. The simplest example is given by the program executions already shown. Once the program named "xxx" has been typed in at a terminal on the computer used to run the programs in this book, typing "run xxx" causes the program to run.

In order to run a Pascal program, it must be presented to the computer in a form the computer can accept. The two most common media for transmitting a program to a computer are punched cards and terminals. In addition to the Pascal program itself, other information must be presented with the program indicating such things as the name of the programmer and the programming language being used. The form required for this information varies widely from one computer installation to the next. At this point we recommend that you learn how to submit a program to the computer system that is available, and run at least one demonstration program to verify the procedures. Detailed instructions are available from an instructor, computer manuals, or computer center memoranda.

Regardless of the computer used or the media used to input the program to the computer, the form of a Pascal program is always the same. The entire program is considered to be one long string of characters. The parts of the program may be placed on lines in any way the programmer chooses as long as a new line is started only at a place in the program where a space may occur. However, it is usually considered good programming practice to begin each statement on a new line. If all of a statement will not fit on one line, then the statement may be continued on the next line.

Calculating an Average of Four Numbers

To further demonstrate the convenience of doing routine calculations on a computer using Pascal, this section closes with the program calculation3 for computing the average of four numbers.

```
program calculation3 (output);
  begin
  writeln ((92 + 72 + 83 + 89) / 4);
  end.
```

```
run calc3version2
```

```
The average is    8.40000000000000e+01
```

A second version of this program is named calc3version2. It identifies the answer by specifying a character string to be printed along with the computed answer.

```
program calc3version2 (output);
  begin
  writeln ('The average is ', (92 + 72 + 83 + 89) / 4);
  end.
```

```
run calc3version2
```

```
The average is    8.40000000000000e+01
```

Exercises

1. What computer output might be expected when the following program is run?

   ```
   program calculation4 (output);
     begin
     writeln ((201 + 55) * 4 - 2 * 10);
     end.
   ```

2. The program calculation5 uses a confusing sequence of arithmetic operations whose meaning would be clearer if written with parentheses. What computer output might be expected when it is run? Insert parentheses in the writeln statement in a way that does not change the value printed, but makes it easier to understand.

   ```
   program calculation5 (output);
     begin
     writeln (343 / 7 / 7 * 2);
     end.
   ```

3. What computer output might be expected when calculation6 is run?

   ```
   program calculation6 (output);
     begin
     writeln (2 * (3 * (5 - 3)));
     end.
   ```

4. Some computer programs have nothing to do with numerical computation. What computer output might be expected when the program wheeee is run?

```
program wheeee (output);
  begin
  writeln ('It is easy to do calculations on a computer.');
  end.
```

5. What computer output might be expected when the program powerof2 is run?

```
program powerof2 (output);
  begin
  writeln (2 * 2 * 2 * 2 * 2 * 2 * 2 * 2 * 2 * 2);
  end.
```

6. What computer output might be expected when the following program is run?

```
program simpleadd (output);
  begin
  writeln (1, ' and ', 1, ' makes ', 1 + 1);
  end.
```

7. Write a program to divide 125 by 16.
8. Write a program to add 5 squared and 12 squared.
9. Write a program to add the numbers 1, 2, 3, ..., 7.
10. Write a program to find the average of the numbers 1, 2, 3, ..., 10.
11. Write a program to print your name.
12. Write a program to compute how many seconds there are in a year.
13. Write a program to calculate the number of seconds in a year and to print the answer with appropriate alphabetic identifying information.
14. Write a program to print the division problem ''16,384 divided by 256'' and the answer to the problem.
15. Write a program to print your telephone number.
16. Write a program to print your address.
17. Write a program to print the Gettysburg address.
18. Convert the following type real numbers from positional notation to exponential notation.

    48.2613   -0.00241   38499.0
    0.2717   -55.0   7.000001

19. Convert the following type real numbers from exponential notation to positional notation.

    9.503e2   4.1679e+10   2.881e-5
    -4.421e2   -5.81e-2   7.000001e0

1.2 Variables, Input, and Output

One benefit of writing a computer program for doing a calculation rather than obtaining the answer using pencil and paper or a hand calculator is that when the same sort of problem arises again, the program already written can be applied to it. While this is not true of the programs in Section 1.1, this section tells how the use of *variables* gives the program the flexibility needed for such reuse.

The program add2 uses two variables named x and y. The first sample run shows how this new program could be used instead of the program calculation2 in Section 1.1 to add the numbers 84 and 13.

```
program add2 (input, output);
  var
    x, y : integer;
  begin
  read (x);
  writeln ('Input data  x: ', x);
  read (y);
  writeln ('Input data  y: ', y);
  writeln ('x + y = ', x + y);
  end.
```

```
run add2

Input data  x:          84
Input data  y:          13
x + y =            97
```

The program add2 tells the computer to read a number from an input device and call it x, then to read another number and call it y, and finally to print the value of x + y, identified as such. Two additional writeln statements that "echo" the values of the input data complete the program add2. During the execution of this program, the two numbers which are the values for x and y must be supplied to the computer, or the computer cannot complete the run.

The method used to provide input to the computer varies widely from one computer system to the next and, like the method of providing the program, can depend upon the type of input device being used. Most of the example programs in this book get their input from a file that is prepared prior to the running of the program. Section 1.4 gives directions for running a program using this technique. Section 1.4 also describes an alternative kind of operation, running a program interactively from a terminal. Your instructor will tell you what kind of system you have and how your programs are to be run.

Declarations of Variables

Every variable that is used in a Pascal program must be listed in a variable declaration that appears between the program heading and the keyword "begin" that signals the beginning of the executable part of the program. Variable declarations follow the keyword ''var'' (short for variable). A variable declaration consists of a list of variable names separated by commas, followed by a colon, and then by a type. The only types that have been discussed so far are real and integer. For example, if the variables q, t, and k are to be real variables in a program and the variables n and b are to be integer variables, then the following lines contain the necessary declarations.

```
var
  q, t, k : real;
  n, b : integer;
```

Semicolons separate variable declarations from each other and from the rest of the program.

Echo of Input Data

In Pascal, as well as most other programming languages, it is a good programming practice for the user to provide an *echo of the input data* using writeln statements, so that the output contains a record of the values used in the computation.

Rerunning a Program With Different Data

The program add2 contains such echoes whose importance is demonstrated immediately as we rerun the program using different input data. The echoes of input data help identify which answer goes with which problem. Other important uses of input echoes will appear later. In showing another sample run of the program add2, this time adding two different numbers, it is unnecessary to repeat the program listing since the program does not change; only the input data change.

```
run add2

Input data  x:          4
Input data  y:          7
x + y =          11
```

The final writeln command of add2 refers to the variables x and y. As the execution printout for the two sample runs shows, what actually is printed is the value of the character string constant 'x + y = ' followed by the value of the expression x + y at the moment the writeln command is executed.

The program add2reals is obtained from the program add2 simply by changing the keyword ''integer'' to the keyword ''real'', which causes the type of the variables x and y to be real. The program add2reals can be used to add two quantities that are not necessarily whole numbers. This execution of the program also illustrates that the input data values may be negative.

```
program add2reals (input, output);
  var
    x, y : real;
  begin
  read (x);
  writeln ('Input data  x: ', x);
  read (y);
  writeln ('Input data  y: ', y);
  writeln ('x + y = ', x + y );
  end.
run add2reals
Input data  x:    9.76000000000000e+01
Input data  y:   -1.29000000000000e+01
x + y =   8.47000000000000e+01
```

Roundoff

For reasons which we explain in Section 2.7, real quantities sometimes differ from their intended values by a small amount in the least significant digit. Perhaps you have already seen this in your own output. Often, the first hint that this has happened is a tell-tale sequence of 9's in the last decimal digits printed. For example, using the same program add2reals, the same input data, 97.6 and −12.9, but a different computer, the following output resulted:

```
run add2reals

Input data  x:    9.759999e+01
Input data  y:   -1.289999e+01
x + y =   8.469999e+01
```

The value of the variable x prints as 9.759999e+01 = 97.59999 although the value supplied in the input file is 97.6. The difference between the intended and calculated values, −0.00001 in this case, is called *roundoff* or *roundoff error*. It is normally of no consequence in practical calculations because virtually no measuring device is capable of distinguishing between such nearly equal values as 97.59999 and 97.6.

Similarly, the printed value of the variable y is 0.00001 too large at −12.89999 instead of −12.9. More peculiarly, the printed value of x + y is 84.69999, differing by 0.00001 from both the sum of the intended values and the sum of the printed values of x and y, a hint to the expert that the computer being used probably does not use decimal arithmetic for its internal calculations.

To oversimplify, roundoff shows up when more decimal digits are printed than are accurately calculated or represented in the computer. If the echoes of input data and the answer are rounded to 4 decimal places before printing, the calculated results will appear precisely as expected: 97.6000 + −12.9000 = 84.7000. On many computer systems, you rarely see any trace of roundoff, while on others, roundoff shows up in the first few calculations with reals. We mention roundoff at this point only to forewarn the beginner who sees it in output that roundoff is not a malfunction of the computer's hardware but a fact of life of real arithmetic on computers that can be cured easily by rounding printed answers.

Reading Several Values

The read command may be used to obtain values for several variables at a time, as shown in the program averageof4, which calculates the average of any four numbers supplied as data.

```
program averageof4 (input, output);
  var
    a, b, c, d : real;
  begin
  read (a, b, c, d);
  writeln ('Input data  a: ', a);
  writeln ('            b: ', b);
  writeln ('            c: ', c);
  writeln ('            d: ', d);
  writeln ('Average = ', (a + b + c + d) / 4)
  end.
```

```
run averageof4

Input data  a:    5.85000000000000e+01
            b:    6.00000000000000e+01
            c:    6.13000000000000e+01
            d:    5.70000000000000e+01
Average =    5.92000000000000e+01
```

As shown in the sample execution, the data are supplied to the variables in the order they are listed in the read command. Note that the four variables in the read statement are separated by commas. Although it is not required by Pascal, it is often desirable to put all input data for a read command on one line in the input file, thereby creating a correspondence between read commands and data lines. Execution of each read command reads data from the point in the input file where the previous read command finished. Thus, four separate read commands also could be used to read the variables a, b, c, and d, even if they were all on one input line. Pascal has another built-in procedure called "readln" that causes one complete line of input data to be read, even if there is more data on the line than required to determine values for the variables in the readln command. Four separate readln commands can by used only for reading data presented on four separate input lines.

Rules for Naming Variables

The variable names x and y are used in the program add2, and the variable names a, b, c, and d are used in averageof4. Single letters of the alphabet are acceptable variable names in Pascal. However, greater variety is desirable, both to improve the readability of programs and to provide for programs with more than 26 variables. Pascal has the following rules for naming variables:

1. The first character of any variable name must be a letter.

2. The remaining characters may be any mixture of letters or digits.

3. The name must not be a keyword. See Appendix A for a list of keywords.

These rules allow ordinary names like lisa, pamela, and julie to be used as variable names. They also allow ordinary English words such as sum, serendipity, and brains as variable names, and more technical-looking variable names such as x3j9, w3kt, and b52.

Blanks are important in Pascal programs. In particular, they must not appear in the middle of a Pascal variable name. Thus, box top is not a legal Pascal name, but boxtop is.

Note that the rules for naming variables are the same as the rules for naming programs. These same rules are applied to all names in a Pascal program. Other things that have names are constants, types, procedures, functions, and files.

Implicit in the first two rules is that characters other than letters and digits are not allowed in Pascal names. Arithmetic symbols must be excluded to prevent ambiguity. For example, if minus signs were allowed in variable names, there would be no way to decide whether a−1 was a single variable "a−one" or the result of subtracting the number 1 from the value of the variable a. Although some of the other characters available on computer input devices often could be allowed in names without causing ambiguity, some characters like the comma or decimal point have specific meaning, and it is simpler to exclude them all, since sufficient variety is already available. Tables 1.2.1 and 1.2.2 summarize what is and is not allowed in a name in Pascal.

In theory, a name may be any length, but some Pascal systems do not distinguish between different names if they have the same first eight characters. Therefore, it is unwise to use two different names whose first eight characters are the same.

Table 1.2.1   Acceptable Variable Names in Pascal.

lisa, pamela, julie	usual names
answer, number, nextvalue	English words
sitzmark, espirit, mucho	foreign words
x3j9, w3kt, yhvvqzt93x, expo67	mixed alphabetic and numeric

Table 1.2.2   Unacceptable Variable Names in Pascal.

6au8, 14u2	starting with a digit
e/l/o, many$, a-1	characters other than letters or digits
i o u, go home	blanks not allowed
begin, do, then	keywords

Assignment Statements

Another way to give a variable a value besides reading that value as input is to use an assignment statement. The program costofsandwich illustrates the use of assignment statements.

```
program costofsandwich (output);
{ computes the cost of a peanut butter and jelly
    sandwich using two slices of bread, 0.0625 jars
    of peanut butter, and 0.03125 jars of jelly  }
```

```
const
  loafofbread = 0.59;
  jarofpeanutbutter = 1.65;
  jarofjelly = 1.29;
  slicesperloaf = 16;

var
  sliceofbread, sandwich : real;

begin
sliceofbread := loafofbread / slicesperloaf;
sandwich := 2 * sliceofbread +
    0.0625 * jarofpeanutbutter +
    0.03125 * jarofjelly;
writeln ('A peanut butter and jelly sandwich costs $',
    sandwich);
writeln ('Prices are subject to change at any time');
writeln ('   without prior written notice.');
end.
```

```
run costofsandwich
```

```
A peanut butter and jelly sandwich costs $  2.17187500000000e-01
Prices are subject to change at any time
    without prior written notice.
```

The first statement in the executable part of the program costofsandwich is an assignment statement that assigns to the variable sliceofbread the value of an arithmetic expression that represents the cost of one slice of bread, obtained by dividing the cost of a loaf of bread by the number of slices of bread in the loaf. The next statement is also an assignment statement that assigns to the variable sandwich the cost of a peanut butter and jelly sandwich.

In Pascal the assignment operator is a colon followed by an equal sign (:=). This combination of symbols was chosen to suggest a left-pointing arrow, indicating that the value of the expression on the right is assigned to the variable on the left.

The program concludes with three separate writeln commands in order to produce three lines of output. The value printed represents a cost of approximately 22 cents (0.22 expressed in exponential notation). Methods of avoiding exponential notation in output are described at the close of this section.

Constant Declarations

The program costofsandwich illustrates another new feature, the constant declaration. A quantity whose value will not change during the entire execution of the program is called a *constant*. A constant is declared and given its value in a constant declaration that appears in a program after the program heading and before all variable declarations. Constant declarations begin with the keyword ''const'' (for constant) and consist of a constant name followed by an equal sign (=) followed by the constant's value, and ending with a semicolon. The name of the constant then may be used any place in the program that the constant value itself could be used. A constant may be a real number, an integer number, or a character string. Note that the equal sign (=) is used in constant declarations, the colon (:) is used in variable declarations, and a combination of the two (:=) is used in assignment statements.

There are two major differences between constant declarations and assignment statements. First, the value in a constant declaration must be a simple constant without arithmetic operations or other calculations implied, except that if the constant is real or integer, the constant may be preceded by a plus or minus sign. The integer value 16 for the constant slicesperloaf and the real value 0.58 for the constant loafofbread are examples. In the program costofsandwich, the values of the quantities sliceofbread and sandwich also never change, but it is not possible to give them values in constant declarations because arithmetic operations are used to compute their values. Second, the value of a constant is fixed by its declaration for the entire execution of the program. However, the value of a variable may change. This ability of variables to assume different values during an execution becomes important in the programs of Section 1.3.

It is good programming practice to declare quantities to be constants whenever that is possible. It allows the reader of the program to learn that the value corresponding to that name will never change when the program is running. It also allows the computer to provide a diagnostic message if the programmer inadvertently tries to change the value of the quantity using a read or assignment statement.

Perhaps the most important reason for using a constant declaration is that the program can be modified very easily if the particular value represented by the constant name needs to be changed. This will happen in the program costofsandwich when the price of any of the ingredients changes. When, for example, the price of a loaf of bread changes, the program can be updated by changing one single number in the program. The programmer can then be sure that the constant will be correct whenever it is used throughout the program.

Descriptive Names for Variables

The name of a variable should be chosen so that it describes what the value of the variable represents. The use of appropriate variable and constant names helps make the program costofsandwich almost completely self-explanatory. Some of the names might make their meaning even clearer if they were longer, such as costofajarofjelly in place of jarofjelly, but in a larger program in which the names were used often, one would quickly tire of writing such names.

Comments

An additional feature that also helps clarify a program for the reader is the use of comments. Any left brace ({) that occurs in a Pascal program, except one inside a character string, begins a comment. The comment is terminated by the next right brace (}). All characters that appear between the braces form the text of the comment. The explanations given in comments are reproduced every time a program is listed, but have absolutely no effect on the execution of the program. The comments in the program costofsandwich describe exactly what the program is supposed to do. This description makes it even easier for the reader to follow the rest of the program.

Important Rules About Assignment Statements

Beginners must accept that the Pascal statement

```
a : = b
```

(pronounced "a is set equal to b") means "Set the value of the variable a to whatever the value of the variable b is". It changes the value of a while leaving the value of the variable b fixed. It does not mean the same thing as

```
b : = a
```

whose execution changes the value of b while leaving the value of the variable a fixed. A statement such as

```
4.7 : = a
```

is absurd and unacceptable, because its left-hand side is a constant, whose value must not be changed.

The left-hand side of an assignment statement must be a variable (or as we will see later, an array element), and the right-hand side must be something whose value can be assigned to that variable. As described in Section 1.3, the right-hand side may involve the same variable that appears on the left-hand side.

The Statement Separator

A semicolon (;) is used to separate two consecutive statements. The keywords "begin" and "end" *are not statements* and thus do not need to be separated from the statements that occur between them. That is, no semicolon is required after the keyword "begin" or before the keyword "end". The semicolon also is used to separate the declarative parts of a program. It must occur between the program heading and the declarations and it is used to separate constant and variable declarations.

The semicolon is used to separate statements, and since separate statements usually go on separate lines, most semicolons appear at the ends of lines. However, it is important to remember that not every line should be terminated with a semicolon. The semicolon should appear only if what follows is another statement.

The Empty Statement

One of the legal Pascal statements consists of no characters at all. This statement has no effect on the execution of the program, but allows a semicolon to appear in places where the rule given above might indicate that it should not. For example, a semicolon may always be put between any statement and a following keyword "end". The effect is to insert an empty statement after the semicolon and before the keyword "end". Since an empty statement does not affect the program, no harm is done. There are, however, some places where a semicolon must not appear. A semicolon must never appear any place except at the end of a statement. This means, for example, that one must never appear just before the keyword "else" or just after the keywords "do" or "then". (See Sections 1.3 and 1.5.)

This book follows the style of putting a semicolon after each statement unless it is not allowed. Two benefits result. The first is that it is easier to put in a semicolon in all cases except those few that specifically forbid it. The second is that putting a semicolon after each statement makes it much easier to add another statement after the semicolon. If the semicolon were not there, then two lines would have to be changed-- the one containing the new statement, and the previous one to add the semicolon. Adopting the style of terminating most statements with a semicolon also makes it easier to delete a statement. For example, in the program costofsandwich, the last writeln command could be removed by simply removing one line, leaving the semicolon on the previous line. If it were necessary to add another writeln command at the end of the program, this also could be done without changing any lines already there.

Converting Meters to Inches

The program meterstoinches, which converts a length in meters to the same length expressed in inches, again illustrates how an appropriate choice of variable and constant names can enhance the readability of a program.

```
program meterstoinches (input, output);
{ converts length in meters to length in inches }

  const
    inchespermeter = 39.37;

  var
    meters, inches : real;

  begin
  read (meters);
  inches := meters*inchespermeter;
  writeln (meters, ' meters = ', inches, ' inches');
  end.
```

```
run meterstoinches

  2.00000000000000e+00 meters =    7.87400000000000e+01 inches
```

The assignment statement of the program meterstoinches tells the computer to assign to the variable inches the value obtained by multiplying the value of the variable meters by the constant named inchespermeter with value 39.37, the conversion factor rounded to two decimal places. Also notice that an extra space is inserted at the beginning and end of the messages in quotes to provide separation between the character strings and the numbers that precede or follow them.

The program meterstoinches also gives some indication why the rules for naming variables are not more flexible. If just any combination of characters were allowed as a variable name, then the assignment statement in meterstoinches might mean that the variable inches should be assigned the value of a variable called meters*inchespermeter. While it is clear to many persons that the context calls for multiplication of the variable meters by the conversion factor, it is extremely difficult to design a workable computer language with even this much sensitivity to the context of human experience. One simply cannot use a computer language in which the computer has to guess what a program means, and thus, to prevent confusion, variable names that look like arithmetic expressions cannot be allowed.

Character Data

Since computers can process alphabetic information as well as numeric information, computer languages provide for the manipulation of information in the form of character strings. The somewhat facetious program named "who" shows how this is done in Pascal.

```
program who (input, output);
  var
    whatsisname : packed array [1..20] of char;
    letter : integer;
  begin
  writeln ('Do I remember whatsisname?');
  write ('Of course, I remember ');
  for letter := 1 to 20 do
    read (whatsisname [letter]);
  writeln (whatsisname);
  end.
```

```
run who

Do I remember whatsisname?
Of course, I remember Roger Kaputnik
```

Character Data Type and Character String Variables

In addition to the data types integer and real, there is a character data type denoted by the keyword "char". A variable may be declared to be type character as illustrated in the following declaration.

```
var
  q23, c1, initial : char;
```

A variable of type character must have as its value *one single character*. A variable may be declared to be a *character string,* that is, a sequence of characters, by declaring it to be an *array* or *packed array* of characters. Arrays are discussed in detail in Chapter 3, but the declaration in the program who can be used as a model to declare a character string of the desired length. In this program the variable whatsisname is declared to be a character string of 20 characters by the declaration

```
var
  whatsisname : packed array [1..20] of char;
```

The variable name whatsisname refers to the whole character string or array. The individual characters that comprise the string are denoted whatsisname [1], whatsisname [2], whatsisname [3], ..., whatsisname [20].

Reading and Writing Character Strings

The value of a character string must be read *one character at a time*, usually by using a for-loop as illustrated in the program who.

```
for letter : = 1 to 20 do
  read (whatsisname [letter])
```

The for-loop serves as a convenient abbreviation for the 20 read statements

```
read (whatsisname [1]);
read (whatsisname [2]);
read (whatsisname [3]);
         .
         .
         .
read (whatsisname [20]);
```

each reading one character of the input string. Reading of character strings takes this form because what must appear within the parentheses of a read or readln command is a simple variable or array element, not a whole array of characters.

On the other hand, an entire character string may be written by putting its name in the write or writeln command as shown in the prgram who. It is also permissible, but less convenient, to use a loop similar to the input loop shown or to write each character individually.

Assignment of Character Values

A character or character string variable may be given a value consisting of a single character or string of characters, respectively. This may be done using an input statement, as described above, or by an assignment statement, as illustrated by the following examples.

```
var
  letter : char;
  name1, name2 : packed array [1..5] of char;
...
letter : = 'q';
name1 : = 'Julie';
name2 : = name1;
```

In a character assignment, the number of characters in the expression on the right hand side must be *exactly* the declared length of the character string on the left. It is also permissible to assign values to a character string variable character by character, but we will not do so until Chapter 5.

Arrays of Integers or Reals

Just as a collection of individual characters can be organized into a character string using an array, so collections of other types of data, such as integer data or real data, can be organized into arrays. For instance, suppose that the author of a popular textbook wants to write a program concerned with the number of copies his book sold in the years 1972 to 1983 and his royalties in those years. The declarations

```
sales : array [1972..1983] of integer;
royalty : array [1972..1973] of real;
```

would enable him to use the integer-valued quantities sales [1972], sales [1973], ..., sales [1983] and real-valued quantities royalty [1972], royalty [1973], ..., royalty [1983] in his program.

In the same way that a for-loop can tell the computer to read the letters of a character string one letter at a time, a for-loop can tell the computer to read the sales figures or royalties one year at a time, as follows:

```
for year := 1972 to 1983 do
  read (sales [year]);

for year := 1972 to 1983 do
  read (royalty [year]);
```

or better still

```
for year := 1972 to 1983 do
  read (sales [year], royalty [year]);
```

These fragmentary examples barely hint at the possible uses of for-loops in Pascal. It is the function of Chapter 1 to introduce most of the major programming tools and techniques and of Chapters 2-7 to explain them more fully. For example, loops are the major topic of Section 1.3 and of all of Chapter 2. Arrays reappear in Sections 2.1-2.3 and in all of Chapter 3. Character strings become important in Section 2.6 and in all of Chapter 5. Our expectation in Chapter 1 is that if you write statements similar to the ones in our examples, they will work, but we leave it to later chapters to delineate and exploit the full power of the statements and techniques we introduce here.

Formatting

The format of the output produced so far using the write and writeln commands has not always been satisfactory. For example, when a quantity of dollars is printed, usually it is not necessary to print decimal places past the pennies, and it is undesirable to print it in exponential form. Another problem is that values such as x = 1.0 and y = 2.5 might be printed as

$$1.00000000000000e+00 \qquad 2.49999999999999e+00$$

The next two subsections tell what to do if you are not satisfied with output in this form. A programmer may control the form of printed numerical values by using a *columns indicator* or a *decimals indicator*.

The Columns Indicator

In a write or writeln command, a numerical, character, or boolean value (described in Section 1.5) to be printed may be followed by a colon (:) and an integer expession that determines the number of columns used to print the value. If there are not enough columns to print the value, more columns are used than indicated. The following program shows how various values will appear when printed using different columns indicators. The columns used to print the values are separated by a vertical bar.

```
program format1 (output);
  const
    bar = '|';
    n = -999;
    x = 4.56;
    s = 'abcd';
  begin
  writeln (bar, n :1, bar, n :4, bar, n :5, bar, n :8, bar);
  writeln (bar, x :1, bar, x :4, bar, x :5, bar, x :8, bar);
  writeln (bar, s :1, bar, s :4, bar, s :5, bar, s :8, bar);
  end.
```

```
run format1

|-999|-999| -999|    -999|
| 4.6e + 00| 4.6e + 00| 4.6e + 00| 4.6e + 00|
|a| abcd| abcd|    abcd|
```

The Decimals Indicator

When printing a real value, it is also possible to indicate how many decimals are to be printed after the decimal point. This is done with a *decimals indicator* which is an integer valued expression that must be written after a columns indicator with a colon between the two indicators. Another effect of using a decimals indicator is that a real value will be printed using positional notation instead of exponential notation. For example, the statement

```
write ('|', 1.234567e2 :9 :2, '|')
```

will produce the output

```
|   123.46|
```

which is the value of 1.234567e2 expressed in positional notation and rounded to two decimal digits after the decimal point.

The program format2 shows how this same value will appear written using different combinations of columns and decimals indicators.

```
program format2 (output);
  const
    bar = '|';
    x = 1.234567e2;
  begin
  writeln (bar, x :1:1, bar, x :6:1, bar);
  writeln (bar, x :1:3, bar, x :9:3, bar);
  end.
```

```
run format2
```

```
| 123.5| 123.5|
| 123.457|   123.457|
```

Exercises

---

1. What is the output produced when the following program is run using the data given in the comments as input?

```
program subtract (input, output);
  var
    a, b : real;                    { data for Exercise 1 }
    begin                           { a = 27.93, b = 14.65 }
    read (a);
    writeln ('Input data  a: ', a :1:2);
    read (b);
    writeln ('Input data  b: ', b :1:2);
    writeln (a - b :1:2);
    end.
```

2. What does the printout for the following computational program look like? The data are in the comments.

```
program productof3 (input, output);
  var
    x, y, z : integer;              { data for Exercise 2 }
    begin                           { x = 3, y = 5, z = 7 }
    read (x, y, z);
    writeln ('Input data  x: ', x :1);
    writeln ('            y: ', y :1);
    writeln ('            z: ', z :1);
    writeln (x * y * z :1);
    end.
```

3. The program inchestofeet is similar to the program meterstoinches described in this section. What output is produced when it is run using 110 inches as the input value?

```
program inchestofeet (input, output);
   const
      inchesperfoot = 12.0;              { data for Exercise 3 }
   var                                   { inches = 110 }
      inches, feet : real;
   begin
   read (inches);
   feet := inches / inchesperfoot;
   writeln (inches :1:2, ' inches = ', feet :1:2, ' feet');
   end.
```

4. Write a program that reads two numbers, divides the first by the second, and then prints the result.

5. There are 453.6 grams in a pound and 1000 grams in a kilogram. Write a program that converts a weight in pounds into a "weight" in kilograms.

6. From each of the following groups, pick out which combinations of characters are and which are not permissible names in Pascal. For those that are not permissible, tell which rule is violated.

7eleven	svn 11	svn-11	seven11
two+2	six ft two	6ft2	
firstnumber	second number	3rdnumber	
john's	marysage	his/her	
1stname	last name	middleinitial	
time	minutes	seconds	hr:min

7. Which of the following are permissible names for variables in Pascal? Explain your answers. Are they desirable names for variables?

    ph   phd   ph.d.   doctor of philosophy

8. Both the variables in the program rhyme are assigned their values by constant declarations in the program. What does a computer print when this program is run?

```
program rhyme (output);
   const
      jack = 1;
      jill = 2;
   begin
   writeln (jack + jill, ' went up the hill.');
   end.
```

9. Discuss the program rhyme in Exercise 8 from the points of view of (a) clarity, (b) appropriateness of constant names, and (c) humor.

10. Modify the program costofsandwich to compute the cost using the current prices of the ingredients.

11. Modify the program costofsandwich to print the final answer as an ordinary dollars and cents amount $0.22 rounded to the nearest penny, thereby eliminating the objectionable exponential form of the output.

12. Write a program to compute and print the percent change in the cost of a peanut butter and jelly sandwich since this book was written. Also, have this program compute and print the percent increases in each of the ingredients.

13. Write a program to compute the average of any two numbers supplied as input data. The program should also identify the answer with an appropriate message.

14. What does the following program print? Its style is *not* recommended.

```
program
                        ugh  (
          output                    )
                         ;
                                  begin
      writeln
(
               12.0
                           +
34.6)end
```

1.3   Introduction to Loops

The value of a variable may change not only from one run to the next as a result of different values of the input data, but also during the course of a single run. The reassignment of new values to a variable during execution is a crucial feature of many programs, particularly of those containing a *loop,* which is a sequence of instructions to be executed repeatedly. In introducing a simple kind of loop, this section takes a closer look at the underlying nature of a variable in a computer program. Other kinds of loops are introduced in Chapter 2.

Calculating an Average of Many Numbers

Suppose an instructor wishes to find the average of the test scores that the 27 students in a class earned on their first examination. The instructor could write a program averageof27 similar to calculation3 of Section 1.1, but using 27 constants instead of 4.

However, if the instructor knows that there will be several more examinations during the semester, it might be desirable to write a program that can be used for subsequent examinations as well. The program averageof27 is modelled on the program averageof4 in Section 1.2. It uses variables instead of specific numbers written in the program, so that it can find the average of any 27 numbers. Recall that Pascal statements that do not fit on one line may be continued on subsequent lines.

```
program averageof27 (input, output);

  var
    a,b,c,d,e,f,g,h,i,j,k,l,m,n,o,p,q,r,s,t,
    u,v,w,x,y,z,aa : real;

  begin
  read (a,b,c,d,e,f,g,h,i,j,k,l,m,n,o,p,q,
      r,s,t,u,v,w,x,y,z,aa);
  writeln ((a + b + c + d + e + f + g + h + i + j + k + l + m + n + o +
      p + q + r + s + t + u + v + w + x + y + z + aa) / 27 :1:2);
  end.
```

```
run averageof27
```

```
 82.30
```

The fact that more than 26 variables are needed is no hardship since the name'of a variable can be more than one letter long. The absence of input echoes makes it impossible to tell whether 82.30 is indeed the correct answer, because it is impossible to tell what input data was used. Despite the extra trouble, input echoes would have been added if this program were not going to be replaced immediately with a better one.

Using a Loop to Calculate an Average

The previous program to find the average of 27 test scores does not exploit the basic repetitiveness of the process of adding the 27 test scores. The program avgof27version2, however, uses a Pascal for-statement of the simplest kind to reflect in the program the repetitiveness of the task. A side benefit is reducing the number of variables needed to two, namely sum and nextscore. Now it is reasonable to print the input data for the program.

```
program avgof27version2 (input, output);

  const
    numberofscores = 27;

  var
    count : integer;
    sum, nextscore : real;

  begin
  sum := 0;
  for count := 1 to numberofscores do
    begin
    read (nextscore);
    writeln ('Input data  nextscore: ', nextscore :7:2);
    sum := sum + nextscore;
    end; { for-loop }
  writeln ('Average test score = ', sum / numberofscores :1:2);
  end.
```

The first assignment statement of the program avgof27version2 gives the variable sum its initial value of zero. The next six lines, which comprise a for-statement, tell the computer to read and to add up the test scores, and the final writeln statement tells the computer to print the answer. The major new concept introduced in this program is that of a for-loop, the explanation of which occupies the next several pages. Loops are one of the most important concepts in computer programming.

Figure 1.3.1   Compound statement syntax chart.

Compound Statements

The for-statement in the program avgof27version2 contains our first example of the use of a compound statement other than the compound statements that comprise the complete executable portion of every Pascal program. Starting with the keyword "begin" and extending to the keyword "end", it forms the body of a for-loop executed 27 times, as specified by the for-loop heading

```
for count := 1 to numberofscores do
```

that precedes it. The form of a compound statement is

```
begin
<statement>;
<statement>;
.
.
.
<statement>
end
```

which means that as many statements as are needed may be included between the keywords "begin" and "end" as long as they are separated by semicolons. A semicolon is optional after the last statement before the keyword "end", because an invisible empty statement may be considered to follow it.

A compound statement itself is one kind of statement. This means that any of the statements in a compound statement may be compound itself. This sounds a bit strange at first, but it just means that statements may be used to construct more complex statements, and these more complex statements, in turn, may be used to build even more complex statements, and so on. In fact, the entire executable section of this and every other Pascal program is a compound statement.

⟨STATEMENT⟩

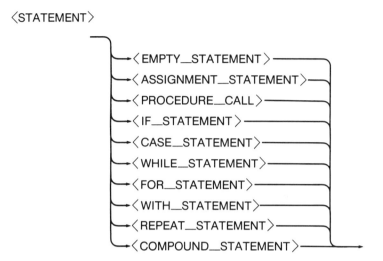

Figure 1.3.2   Statement syntax chart.

⟨FOR_STATEMENT⟩:

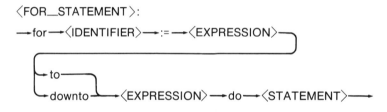

Figure 1.3.3   For-statement syntax chart.

Syntax Charts

The correct form of Pascal programs can be described using *syntax charts*. The syntax chart for a compound statement is shown in Figure 1.3.1.

Such a chart is sometimes called a "railroad" syntax chart because each correctly formed compound statement can be constructed by chugging along a path through the chart. Backing up is not permitted. Characters not enclosed in angle brackets (⟨⟩) must appear as written. Each name in angle brackets in the chart represents a syntactic construct whose form must be determined by examining another chart. For example, in order to understand from Figure 1.3.1 what a compound statement is in Pascal, it is necessary to look at the syntax chart that describes a Pascal statement. This chart is shown in Figure 1.3.2.

A syntactically correct Pascal statement can be formed in many ways. The empty statement is represented by the top path through the statement chart. Note that one of the possible statements is a compound statement, but that one of the parts of a compound statement is a statement. As we remarked earlier, this just means that statements can be grouped together to form compound statements, and that compound statements, in turn, can be used to build more complicated statements.

The precise definition of the correct form of each Pascal language construct is found in the set of syntax charts in Appendix C.

The For-Statement

The form of a for-statement is shown in Figure 1.3.3. The statement following a for-loop heading may be a simple statement, such as an assignment statement, or it may be a compound statement, as illustrated in the program avgof27version2. The for-loop heading and the simple or compound statement following the heading are considered to be one single statement, a *for-statement*.

The option of substituting the keyword "downto" for the keyword "to" in a for-statement is discussed in Section 2.5.

For-Variables

The variable in the for-statement is called the *for-variable*. The for-variable in the program avgof27version2 is count. For now, the type of the for-variable and the two expressions in the for-statement must be integer. They must not be real, but may be boolean (Section 1.5), character (Chapter 5), or a programmer-defined data type (Section 4.3).

It is the authors' policy to clarify the extent of a for-loop by the use of indentation. The statement (which may be compound) whose execution is controlled by the for-loop heading is indented two spaces more than the header line. This makes it possible to see at a glance which instructions are in the loop and which are not. It is a good programming practice to provide this visual redundancy so that finding the end of a loop does not depend solely on locating the keyword "end". Programs can be correct, although usually less readable, without the use of indentation.

Execution of a For-Loop

The for-loop of the program avgof27version2 is executed as if the 81 statements

```
read (nextscore);
writeln ('Input data  nextscore:', nextscore :7:2);
sum := sum + nextscore;
read (nextscore);
writeln ('Input data  nextscore:', nextscore :7:2);
sum := sum + nextscore;
read (nextscore);
writeln ('Input data  nextscore:', nextscore :7:2);
sum := sum + nextscore;

 .

 .

 .
read (nextscore);
writeln ('Input data  nextscore:', nextscore :7:2);
sum := sum + nextscore;
```

were written instead of the 6-line for-statement. Since the read and writeln commands
are executed 27 times, the execution printout is much longer than the actual program.

```
run avgof27version2

Input data  nextscore:    85.00
Input data  nextscore:    97.00
Input data  nextscore:    68.00
Input data  nextscore:    86.00
Input data  nextscore:    75.00
Input data  nextscore:    90.00
Input data  nextscore:    82.00
Input data  nextscore:   100.00
Input data  nextscore:    87.00
Input data  nextscore:    63.00
Input data  nextscore:    79.00
Input data  nextscore:    85.00
Input data  nextscore:    93.00
Input data  nextscore:    62.00
Input data  nextscore:    88.00
Input data  nextscore:    76.00
Input data  nextscore:    38.00
Input data  nextscore:    70.00
Input data  nextscore:    87.00
Input data  nextscore:    93.00
Input data  nextscore:    98.00
Input data  nextscore:    81.00
Input data  nextscore:    95.00
Input data  nextscore:    72.00
Input data  nextscore:    89.00
Input data  nextscore:    99.00
Input data  nextscore:    84.00
Average test score =   82.30
```

The echo of input data is extremely useful in checking that all the test scores were
entered correctly. In programs such as this, when a language is used that does not provide an automatic echo of input data, programmers often insert a write command immediately after each read command to provide this effect.

Increasing the Value of a Variable

The meaning of the assignment statement

```
sum := sum + nextscore
```

is: "Add the values of the variables sum and nextscore and assign their sum as the new
value of the variable sum". The value of the variable nextscore is not changed by this
statement. The assignment statement is not a mathematical equation in which the variable sum can be cancelled on both sides of the assignment operator to "solve" the assignment statement for the variable nextscore := 0. This distinction is emphasized by
using := as the assignment operator instead of the equal sign by itself (=) as is done in

some other programming languages. Each variable on the right of the assignment operator in an assignment statement has its value determined before execution of the instruction begins, while the variable on the left of the assignment operator designates which variable is to receive a new value.

Table 1.3.1 Values of the variables nextscore and sum during execution of the program avgof27version2 using data from the sample run.

NEXTSCORE	SUM	PASS THROUGH THE FOR LOOP
undefined	0.0	before the 1st pass
85.0	85.0	after the 1st pass
97.0	182.0	after the 2nd pass
68.0	250.0	after the 3rd pass
86.0	336.0	after the 4th pass
75.0	411.0	after the 5th pass
90.0	501.0	after the 6th pass
82.0	583.0	after the 7th pass
100.0	683.0	after the 8th pass
87.0	770.0	after the 9th pass
63.0	833.0	after the 10th pass
79.0	912.0	after the 11th pass
85.0	997.0	after the 12th pass
93.0	1090.0	after the 13th pass
62.0	1152.0	after the 14th pass
88.0	1240.0	after the 15th pass
76.0	1316.0	after the 16th pass
38.0	1354.0	after the 17th pass
70.0	1424.0	after the 18th pass
87.0	1511.0	after the 19th pass
93.0	1604.0	after the 20th pass
98.0	1702.0	after the 21st pass
81.0	1783.0	after the 22nd pass
95.0	1878.0	after the 23rd pass
72.0	1950.0	after the 24th pass
89.0	2039.0	after the 25th pass
99.0	2138.0	after the 26th pass
84.0	2222.0	after the 27th pass

Hand Simulation

To show in more detail how a for-loop works, we follow the steps, one at a time, that a computer performs during the execution of the program avgof27version2. Since the statements inside the loop are executed 27 times and the statements outside the loop are executed only once, almost all the steps of the execution correspond to instructions in the loop. Of particular interest are the changing values of the variables nextscore and sum. Following the steps in this manner is called *hand simulation* because one simulates by hand exactly the same computations a computer would do in executing the program. It is perfectly ethical to use a hand calculator to do the arithmetic when hand simulating a program.

The first statement of the program avgof27version2 assigns the variable sum its initial value of 0. The other variable nextscore does not yet have a value. The for-loop is then started. In each of the 27 repetitions of the loop, the computer reads a number and assigns that number to the variable nextscore. Then it prints an echo of the value read. Finally, it adds the value of nextscore to the current value of the variable sum to obtain a new value for the variable sum.

During the first pass through the repeated statements, the number 85.0 is read and assigned to the variable nextscore. The first echo of input data line

Input data nextscore: 85.00

of the printout confirms that the first number supplied as input data is indeed 85.0. Then the value 85.0 of nextscore is added to the current value, 0.0, of the variable sum to obtain a new sum 0.0 + 85.0 = 85.0, which is assigned as the new value for sum. Thus the values of the variables nextscore and sum after the first pass through the repeated instructions are 85.0 and 85.0 as shown in Table 1.3.1.

Since the end of the loop has been reached, but the body of the loop has been executed only once, the next instruction to be executed is not the final writeln statement, but the first statement of the repeated section of the loop, the read statement. Only after 27 passes through the loop is its execution completed and control transferred to the writeln statements after the keyword ''end''.

During the second pass through the repeated instructions, the number 97.0 is read and assigned to the variable nextscore. The previous value 85.0 for nextscore is thereby obliterated, since *a variable can have only one value assigned to it at any given time*. This is not a problem in the program avgof27version2 because, after the score 85.0 is added to the running total sum, there is no further use for the first test score in the computation. The assignment statement then directs the computer to add the current value 97.0 of nextscore to the current value 85.0 of sum to obtain the running total 182.0, which is assigned as the new value of sum. Again, the old value 85.0 of sum is lost. As shown in Table 1.3.1, the values of the variables nextscore and sum are, respectively, 97.0 and 182.0 after completion of pass 2 through the repeated steps.

During the third pass, the value 68.0 is read for nextscore, replacing the previous value 97.0. The new value for sum is then calculated as the current value 182.0 of sum plus the current value 68.0 of nextscore. Thus, for its new value, the variable sum is assigned 250.0, which is the sum of 182.0 and 68.0. The old value 182.0 is lost, of course.

The fourth through twenty-seventh passes proceed in much the same fashion with only the numbers and values changing. At this point, it is well to leave the arithmetic to the computer and to refer to Table 1.3.1 for a summary of the values assigned to the two variables nextscore and sum.

After 27 complete passes, the loop is not repeated and the computer execution proceeds to the final writeln statement. By then each of the test scores which were the successive values for the variable nextscore has already been added to accumulate their sum 2222.0, which is the final value of the variable sum. Thus when the final writeln statement specifies printing the expression sum / 27, the average 82.30 of all 27 test scores is printed.

A More General Program for Averaging

A slight modification of avgof27version2 produces a program avgofscores than can compute the average of any number of test scores.

```
program avgofscores (input, output);

  var
    enrollment, count : integer;
    sum, nextscore : real;

  begin
  read (enrollment);
  writeln ('Input data  enrollment: ', enrollment :1);
  sum := 0;
  for count := 1 to enrollment do
    begin
    read (nextscore);
    writeln ('Input data  nextscore: ', nextscore :7:2);
    sum := sum + nextscore;
    end; { for-loop }
  writeln;
  writeln ('Average test score = ', sum / enrollment :1:2);
  end.
```

The new feature in this program is that the number of times the for-loop is repeated is a variable. Of course, a value for this variable enrollment must be assigned
before the for-loop can be started. The statement

```
read (enrollment)
```

obtains this value from an input device before any of the test scores are read. Thus the
data for the more general program avgofscores must consist of a first number giving the
number of test scores to be averaged, and then an appropriate number of test scores.

The sample run of avgofscores uses only 6 scores to be averaged, although the program would work just as well with 60 or 600. It is a great convenience to be able to
test a program on a small number of data items, because the results can be checked
more easily by hand. The writeln command with no parentheses writes a blank line.

```
run avgofscores

Input data  enrollment: 6
Input data  nextscore:    82.00
Input data  nextscore:    78.00
Input data  nextscore:    93.00
Input data  nextscore:    91.00
Input data  nextscore:    52.00
Input data  nextscore:    72.00

Average test score =  78.00
```

The program avgofscores can be used by any instructor for a class of any size.
Even an instructor who does not know now to program can be told how to prepare input
data for avgofscores. The moral would seem to be that a special-purpose program can
be used only for a special purpose, while a somewhat more general-purpose program is
much more likely to be reusable.

A Word of Caution About Semicolons

Lest the beginner fall into the habit of terminating all lines with a semicolon, we caution again that a semicolon must not follow the keyword ''do'' in the for-statement of the program avgofscores. If this were done, it would be interpreted as separating an empty statement to be executed 27 times from the remainder of the program, the intended body of the for-loop, which would be executed once.

Exercises

---

1. For the following somewhat frivolous program, what does the computer print when it is run?

```
program happybirthday (output);
  const
    age = 12;
  var
    year : integer;
  begin
  for year := 1 to age do
    writeln ('Happy birthday to you!');
  end.
```

2. Modify the program avgof27version2 directly to produce a program to find the average of 6 test scores. How many statements of avgof27version2 must be changed?

3. Hand simulate the program written for Exercise 2 using the test scores 82.0, 78.0, 93.0, 91.0, 52.0, and 72.0 shown in the sample execution of the more general program avgofscores.

4. Discuss the relative merits of the following programs, all of which have exactly the same execution, except for the input echoes and identification of output.

```
program avgofscores (input, output);
  var
    enrollment, count : integer;
    sum, nextscore : real;
  begin
  read (enrollment);
  writeln ('Input data  enrollment: ', enrollment :1);
  sum := 0;
  for count := 1 to enrollment do
    begin
    read (nextscore);
    writeln ('Input data  nextscore: ', nextscore :7:2);
    sum := sum + nextscore;
    end; { for-loop }
  writeln;
  writeln ('Average test score = ', sum / enrollment :1:2);
  end.
```

```
program t (input, output);
   var
     c, n : integer;
     s, x : real;
   begin
   read (n);
   s := 0;
   for c := 1 to n do
     begin
     read (x);
     s := s + x;
     end;
   writeln ('Average test score = ', s / n);
   end.



program avg (input, output);
var c, n : integer; s, x : real;
begin
read (n); s := 0;
for c := 1 to n do begin
read (x); s := s + x; end;
writeln (s / n); end.



program confusing (input, output);

   var
     dinner, plate : integer;
     wine, abook : real;

   begin
   read (dinner);
   writeln ('Input data  dinner: ', dinner);
   wine := 0;
   for plate := 1 to dinner do
     begin
     read (abook);
     writeln ('Input data  abook: ', abook :7:2);
     wine := wine + abook;
     end;
   writeln ('A delightful meal = ', wine / dinner :1:2);
   end.
```

5. Modify the program happybirthday in Exercise 1 so that it accepts an age as input and prints out the birthday message that many times.

6. Write a program that computes the sum of an arbitrary number of items.

7. Write a program to print the following sentence 25 times: "I must not sleep in class."

8. Write a program that uses a for-loop to print the numbers from 1 to 10. Hint: Print the value of the for-variable.

9. Modify the program written for Exercise 8 to print the numbers from 1 to 100.

10. Modify the program written for Exercise 8 to read a number n as input and to print the numbers from 1 to n.

11. Write a program to print the numbers from 1 to 10 in a column, and their squares in a second column to the right. Hint: If the for-variable is named "number", the following writeln statement need be the only output statement in the program, unless column headings are printed also.

```
writeln (number, number * number)
```

1.4   Running and Debugging a Program

After writing a program, one might like to walk up to a computer, give it a handwritten copy, and command the computer, "run it". Running a program isn't too different from this, except that all communication from a user to a computer must be supplied in a form that the computer can read. In discussing such matters, this section provides a partial answer to the fourth question in Section 1.1, How is a computer told what the program is and when to run it?

Running a Program Using Punched Cards

One of the two computer "hardware" configurations for running a program that we consider in this section consists of a card reader, a central processing unit that does the computation, and a printer. An additional device called a keypunch, that is not connected to the computer, is used to punch information into the computer cards in a form the computer can read. We now describe how one might run the program add2 in Section 1.2 using this idealized computer configuration.

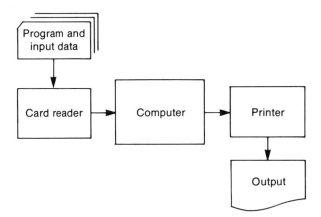

Figure 1.4.1   Flow of information for a simplified reader/printer computer configuration.

First, the keypunch is used to prepare the deck of computer cards containing the information shown below. This example illustrates the cards that are necessary to run a Pascal program on the Burroughs B7800 computer. They tell the computer what the program is and what to do with it. The control cards needed to run a Pascal program on some other machine would be different from the ones in this example, but some of the information required is similar.

```
?COMPILE ADD2 WITH PASCAL
?DATA
program add2 (input, output);
  var
    x, y : integer;
  begin
  read (x);
  writeln ('Input data  x: ', x);
  read (y);
  writeln ('Input data  y: ', y);
  writeln ('x + y = ', x + y );
  end.
?DATA
84 13
?END JOB
```

The first line indicates that a program named add2 is to be compiled (translated from Pascal into machine executable instructions) and then executed. The program is placed between the two DATA cards. These cards containing the program add2 are the input data for the compiler program. Each line of the program is punched on a separate card. The input data for the execution of the program add2 follow the second DATA card. The final card of the deck is an END JOB card.

The example given is one of the simplest possible. More complex situations may arise if it is necessary to specify the maximum execution time expected, which computer of a multiple processor installation is to be used, or possibly a user name or password.

To run a program with this computer configuration, the complete card deck shown above is placed in the card reader which reads the cards into the computer. The computer runs the program and prints the output on the printer. The flow of information is depicted in Figure 1.4.1.

Preparing Data Cards

Each read statement starts reading at the point in the input data where the previous read statement left off. Therefore, the two data values may be placed on the same card. If the two read statements were replaced by two readln statements, then the two data values would have to be placed on two separate cards. This is because the readln statement causes one entire line to be scanned even if all of the information on the line is not needed. Another input command following a readln command thus will always begin reading information from a new line.

Operating Systems

Control cards are actually instructions to the computer's *operating system,* one of the programs mentioned in the chapter introduction that nearly every programmer uses but very few ever write. The operating system is a complex program that controls the flow of information through the computer and schedules the use of the computer's hardware components. At any one computer installation, the characteristics of the operating system and the information required on its control cards may be regarded as characteristics of the computer. However, since an operating system is a program, it is possible to make modifications in the operating system, or to replace it with a new operating system, without replacing the computer. Different computer installations, even if they have exactly the same model of the same computer produced by the same manufacturer, may use different operating systems and consequently may require slightly different control cards.

The instructions on control cards are written in a language called an *operating system command language*. Unfortunately, operating system command languages are not standardized as are programming languages such as Pascal. Some installations might not require the equivalents of all the commands used in the preceding example. Others might require additional information on the control cards or additional control cards. Although a general idea of what command languages look like is useful, a programmer ordinarily learns specific details only for those commands required by the system being used. Upon arriving at a new installation, one of the first things a programmer needs to learn is a small amount of the control language used.

The Good Old Days of Computer Programming

There are programmers still young and active who can remember the good old days of personally reserving a whole computer, perhaps some time in the evening or after midnight. As recently as the early 1960s, it was common practice to place one's cards in the card reader, put one's feet up on the console, and sit back and watch the program run. At dinner time or a coffee break, the programmer shut the machine off for a rest and, upon returning suitably refreshed, turned the power back on. The programmer could stop the execution of a program to see what was happening, or step through a program one instruction at a time. He or she could examine any location in memory and make corrections from the console. In those days, programmers dealt directly with the computer and spoke the machine's own language. At least some of these programmers are happy that the recent trend toward minicomputers and microcomputers is bringing back the good old days.

Persons who had the opportunity to work so intimately with a computer did not soon forget the experience. Witness the dedication of Knuth's book [1] to the IBM 650 computer. Why then is it conceivable for a present-day programmer never to see an actual computer? The answer lies largely in the advances in electronic technology. With earlier machines whose computational speeds were slower, although still much faster than desk calculators or other computational devices, it was reasonable for a programmer to stop the machine, open up a program listing, scratch his or her head while trying to locate what needed changing, and enter a correction or change before resuming execution of the program.

However, as computational speeds increased by more than several thousand-fold, but there was no comparable increase in head scratching efficiency, a dozen complete programs could have been run while the computer was waiting for a programmer to make one correction. It became too expensive for a programmer to monitor the execution of a program or make corrections from the console, and so the programmer was asked to do thinking and head scratching in private, while machine operators took over

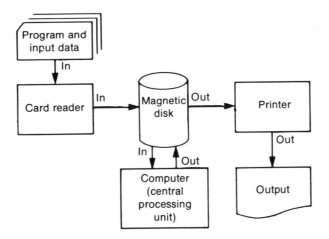

Figure 1.4.2 Flow of information in an efficient card-oriented computer system.

the job of shuttling the cards, printouts, and other data into and out of the machine as efficiently as possible. Computer programmers from the good old days welcomed the improvements in computer speed and power, but they began to feel that computer programming was becoming depersonalized.

Even certain machine operations suffered a similar fate. The input and output operations, such as card reading, printing, and reading of magnetic tape, to name a few, which are partly mechanical in nature, although speeded up substantially, still could not keep pace with the increases in electronic computational speeds. It became inefficient for the central processing unit, which performs the arithmetic and logical computations, to halt its operations while a card, or even a magnetic tape, was being read. The input and output operations were farmed out to satellite computers of limited computational ability, sometimes called "data channels", which signalled the central processing unit when the reading or writing was completed. This enabled the central processing unit to continue computing at the same time that data was being read or written.

Efficient Card-Oriented Systems

Considerations of this sort have guided the evolution of the typical card-oriented installation. The programmer submits the complete card deck, which is then copied into the highest-speed input device available, in order to be ready with minimum delay when it is that program's turn to be executed. The output is produced on the fastest available output device and is subsequently converted to printed form to be returned to the programmer. This flow of information, depicted in Figure 1.4.2, maximizes productive use of the extremely powerful and expensive central processing unit. If it is well designed, such a system can provide better service to the programmer than was possible with a slower machine. The programmer also has access to a larger, faster, more powerful machine which can handle problems too complex for smaller machines.

Time Sharing

The increased speed of computation which brought about separation of the computer programmer from the computer also can be used, paradoxically, to simulate the effect of giving each programmer a complete machine, by a process called time sharing. Imagine dining at a very well-run restaurant. You are met at the door and escorted immediately to a private booth from which no other diners can be seen. The waiter arrives with rolls and butter and fills the water glasses. He returns immediately with the menu and retires from sight to let you choose your dinner. When you are ready to order, he reappears to take your order. After a sufficient time for the preparation of each dish, the waiter returns to serve it. When the main course has been eaten, he returns in time to take dessert orders, et cetera. When the service is good enough (remember that no other tables can be seen), it is impossible to determine whether there are any other diners in the restaurant. It doesn't matter if the waiter takes menus to another table on his way to the kitchen, or takes orders from a third table while your dinner is being cooked. As long as the waiter responds relatively quickly whenever you need his services, for all intents and purposes you have his undivided attention.

Figure 1.4.3   A computer terminal.

In the analogous method of computer utilization, many users are connected simultaneously to a computer by means of relatively inexpensive input/output terminals. If the computational speeds of the central computer are sufficiently high so that no user needs all the computer's capabilities for very long, then each user has use of the computer almost as soon as she or he wants it. Thus each user has the illusion of being the only user and can program and operate from a terminal as though the computer were all his or her own. In addition, the capabilities of a much larger computer than could be reserved reasonably for one person's use are available when needed. This is called computer *time sharing*.

A second idealized computer hardware configuration consists of a computer and a combination input/output terminal to be used for time sharing. This configuration usually will have magnetic disk systems to store files. Some computer terminals look like typewriters, as depicted in Figure 1.4.3 (see also Figure 2.6.1). Other computer terminals use a television-type screen for output. In addition to the keyboard and typing or display mechanism, a terminal has circuitry to convert the characters typed on its keyboard into computer-readable form to transmit to a computer; conversely, it has circuitry to accept computer impulses and to convert them into typed or displayed characters for reading by the user.

Operating Systems for Time Sharing

With many users simultaneously connected to the computer, it is necessary to have a different kind of operating system than one used only for submitting programs using punched cards. Instead of scheduling jobs one at a time, the operating system must schedule many kinds of requests, from editing one line of a program to running a compiler or processing an input/output request from a running program. At many installations, the operating system also does the accounting for the installation. Accounting is more complicated in a time sharing system, because different users may be using different resources of the computer system at the same time.

When submitting programs using a punched card system, commands to the operating system are also punched on cards. When using a time sharing system, there are requests from a computer terminal that correspond to commands on a control card and there are also requests from the terminal that correspond to the card handling that might be done manually by the programmer in assembling a deck.

Editing a Program Using a Terminal

One of the programs that is usually available on a time sharing system is a *text editor*. This program allows a programmer at a terminal to build, change, and save files that could be programs, data files, or even operating system commands. The following is an editing session run on the UNIX operating system text editor, running on a Digital Equipment Corporation VAX 11/750. Although most text editors and operating systems have similar commands, it is rare to find two systems that agree on the abbreviations of the commands or the prompting character. In this example, information typed by the programmer is typed in lower case letters and responses and prompts typed by the computer are shown in upper case letters. Also, a few words of explanation appear to the right between the lines.

```
LOGIN: walt
PASSWORD: zounds
```
The user's name is "walt" and the password is "zounds". To protect the password, it will not appear when typed on most terminals.

```
% e add2.p
```
When this operating system is expecting a command to be typed by the user, it types the prompting character "%" and waits. The command "e" requests that the *editor* be run using a file called add2.p.

```
0 LINES
```
The system responds with the number of lines currently in the file.

```
a
```
The user indicates that some lines are to be *added*. The user then types the lines to be added.
```
program add2 (input, output);
   var
    x, y : integer;
  begin
  read (x);
  writeln ('Input data x: ', x);
   read (y);
  writeln ('Input data y: ', y);
  writeln ('x +y = ', x +y);
  end.
```
```
.
```
The period indicates the end of the lines to be added.
```
w
```
The user requests to *write* (save) the file called add2.p.
```
e add2.in
```
Now *edit* a file called add2.in, which will contain the input for add2.
```
0 LINES
a
```
Add a line to add2.in.
```
84 13
```
```
.
```
```
w
```
Write (save) the file add2.in.
```
q
```
Quit editing.
```
% run add2
```
This command says to execute the Pascal program add2.p, using input from the file add2.in and write the output into a file called add2.out. The commands to accomplish this have previously been placed in a file called "run" by the instructor.
```
% p add2.out
```
When execution of the program is complete, the system prompts with %. The programmer looks at the output file by *printing* add2.out.
```
Input data x:    84
Input data y:    13
x +y =   97
```

Once the editing process is completed, running a program from a terminal can be very similar to running a program using punched cards, except that the program and data are saved on system files instead of being read from the card reader. Also, the output is placed on a file (or written at the terminal) instead of being printed. Most of the programs in this book were run in this manner after being edited at a terminal.

Running a Program Interactively

A slightly different scheme involves using the computer terminal as the input and output media during program execution. Whenever a read command is executed in the program, the user is expected to type some input data at the terminal. Whenever a write command is executed, the data are written to the terminal. This mode of running a program is called *interactive execution*. In the example above showing the editing and execution of the program add2, the editor program was run interactively, but once the program add2 was edited, it was not itself run interactively. We now show how to run a Pascal program interactively.

When input data are expected from a terminal during an interactive execution of a program, it is a good programming practice to have the program send a *prompt*, which is an output message, giving the user at the terminal a clue as to what is supposed to be entered. A good way to provide such a prompt is to replace the write command that occurs after each read statement and shows the echo of input data with a prompt that occurs just before each read statement, as shown in the following editing session. To illustrate a few more features of the editor, the program name is changed to sub2 and the program is changed to one that subtracts two numbers.

```
% e add2.p
```
       Edit the Pascal program add2.
```
11 LINES
1s/add/sub
program sub2 (input, output);
```
       In line 1, *substitute* "sub" for "add". The resulting line is printed.
```
1,$s/+/-/g
```
       In lines 1 to the last line (indicated by $), *substitute* "−" for "+" *globally*, that is, everywhere it occurs, not just the first occurrence in each line. A global substitution is needed, because one line of the program has two plus signs. This time the changed lines are not printed.
```
6,8s/writeln/write
  write ('Input data y: ', y);
```
       In lines 6 through 8 *substitute* "write" for "writeln" and print the result of the last line changed. The line numbers 6 and 8 are known from the earlier listing of add2.
```
6s/, x
  write ('Input data x: ');
8s/, y
  write ('Input data y: ');
```
       In line 6 *substitute* no characters for ", x", that is, delete them. In line 8 delete the characters ", y".
```
6m4
8m6
```
       Move line 6 after line 4 and move line 8 after line 6.
```
1,$p
```
       Print all of the lines in the file.

```
program sub2 (input, output);
  var
    x, y : integer;
  begin
  write ('Input data x: ');
  read (x);
  write ('Input data y: ');
  read (y);
  writeln ('x − y = ', x − y);
  end.
w sub2.p
```

Write the result of editing as the file "sub2.p".

```
q
```

Quit editing.

```
% runi sub2
```

Run sub2 *interactively*, using the computer terminal for input and output. The commands for interactively running a Pascal program previously have been put in a file called "runi" by the instructor.

```
Input data x: 83
Input data y: 67
x − y =   16
```

What happens during interactive execution of the program sub2 is as follows. First the computer types "Input data x: " as directed by the first write statement and then pauses in the middle of the line to wait for the user to supply a value for x to complete execution of the read (x) statement. When the user types a value, 83, followed by the carriage return, execution resumes and the computer types "Input data y: " and pauses until the user supplies an input value to complete the read (y) statement. When a value, 67, and a carriage return are typed by the user, execution resumes again and the answer, 16, is written by the computer. For interactive execution no input file is prepared prior to execution and the output file is written on the terminal.

```
% logoff
```

The user is now logged off, but since the programs add2.p and sub2.p were saved in files on the system, they can be run another day without being retyped.

Scheduling Algorithms

An operating system serving several users may receive requests requiring as little as several millionths of a second or as much as several hours of processing time. The design of a satisfactory scheduling procedure is a complex task, very much the subject of active research and experimentation among computer scientists. In general terms, most scheduling algorithms provide for very short waiting times for requests demanding only a few central processing unit (CPU) cycles, and progressively longer waiting times for requests for greater usage. Thus a request to enter a single line of a program from a terminal may be processed almost immediately, while a request to run a program may wait from several seconds to several minutes and a request for a solid hour of computational time may have to wait until the end of the day or the end of the week.

Other factors are also taken into account. If a programmer is waiting at a terminal for the request to be completed, the priority may be higher than that given to a similar request when the programmer is not waiting. It is ordinarily more efficient to run several consecutive programs written in the same computer programming language, rather that to skip from one language to another. Thus some operating systems collect short jobs in the most popular programming languages over a period of perhaps 20 minutes and run the entire group at the end of the collection period. Such collection and deferred processing, called *batch processing,* ordinarily is unacceptable if the user is waiting at a terminal. Another consideration is how long a request has been waiting for action. Even at a busy computer installation, one does not want lower-priority requests to wait forever. A sophisticated scheduling algorithm may permit a lower-priority request that has been waiting a relatively long time eventually to be run ahead of higher-priority requests that have not been waiting nearly as long.

Requests specifying computer facilities already in use for another purpose or job must be delayed. Of course, the importance of the job must be taken into account. A business might want to be sure that its payroll program is run by Friday afternoon. A ''student program'' may or may not be given priority over an accounting or record keeping program, depending on whether the installation views its primary function as teaching programming or keeping records. Priorities may also vary with the time of day. Often shorter programs are given higher priority during ''prime hours'', and longer programs are given elevated priority at night.

Debugging

The practice of detecting and removing errors from a program is called *debugging.* Carefully rereading the program, or rereading selected parts of it, is an obvious first step. Hand simulation, described in the previous section, is a highly valuable technique. Another debugging method, to be elaborated upon later, is the insertion of write commands at carefully selected places in a program, to monitor the execution. In a large program, periodic monitoring can help localize the possible source of an error to a small enough region in the program so that critical rereading of that section is likely to turn up the error.

Discovering Mistakes in a Program

It may come as a rude surprise to a beginner, but the usual cause of a disappointing program execution is a mistake in the program. A programmer might mean to write one thing but accidentally write another, something like a slip of the tongue. Unfortunately, the computer executes the program it actually sees, not the one that would have made sense. For example, the program attemptavg contains a mistake of this kind.

```
program attemptavg (input, output);

  var
    enrollment, count : integer;
    sum, nextscore : real;

  begin
  read (enrollment);
  writeln ('Input data  enrollment: ', enrollment :1);
  sum := 0;
  for count := 1 to enrollment do
    begin
    read (nextscore);
    writeln ('Input data  nextscore: ', nextscore :7:2);
    sum := nextscore;
    end; { for }
  writeln;
  writeln ('Average test score = ', sum / enrollment :1:2);
  end.
```

```
run attemptavg

Input data  enrollment: 5
Input data  nextscore:    72.00
Input data  nextscore:    46.00
Input data  nextscore:    93.00
Input data  nextscore:    86.00
Input data  nextscore:    75.00

Average test score =   15.00
```

A programmer usually can determine whether or not there is an error in a program by carefully choosing test data and independently calculating what results to expect. The actual average of the five test scores in the illustrative test run is 74.4. The value 15 for the average test score shown in the execution printout is obviously wrong, because it is smaller than any of the supplied test scores.

In a program this short, there is not much room for an error to hide. Once one is known to exist, the programmer usually can find it by critically rereading the program. Moreover, examination of the echoes of input data in the execution output indicates that the value for enrollment was read correctly, as were each of the five test scores. Thus the loop was executed the correct number of times. Very little of the program is left to check for possible errors. In this case, the statement

```
sum := nextscore
```

should be changed to

```
sum := sum + nextscore
```

After making this change, which seems to explain the erroneous execution, the program should be rerun, first with the same test data and then with a representative range of reasonable test scores, including extreme values such as 100 and 0, if these are the limits of valid input data.

Mistakes in the Input Data

Even after exercising considerable care in writing a program, a programmer may sometimes still find the execution printout disappointing. After all, even a correct program cannot be expected to give correct results if there is a mistake in the input data. Consider what would happen if, during an execution of the program avgofscores in Section 1.3, the computer were supplied with data giving the test scores

45 98 77 64 38 86 53

but the first required data item giving the enrollment, seven students, were inadvertently omitted, a common kind of mistake.

```
run avgofscores
Input data   enrollment:  45
Input data   nextscore:    98.00
Input data   nextscore:    77.00
Input data   nextscore:    64.00
Input data   nextscore:    38.00
Input data   nextscore:    86.00
Input data   nextscore:    53.00
INPUT ERROR:   end of file reached
```

Because the sample execution printout contains clearly identified echoes of all input data, the cause of the erroneous program execution is not hard to find. The program avgofscores tells the computer that the first number it reads is the value for the variable enrollment. Accordingly, when the first number in the input data is 45, the computer anticipates 45 test scores in the data. When it finds only 6 more numbers, it is unable to continue with the program execution and prints an error message saying that it has run out of data, that is, that it has come to the end of the input file without having found all the numbers that it needs. The cure is simply to insert the enrollment data expected by the program in the input file before the 7 test scores.

Exercises

1. Under what circumstances might a programmer want to save a program for later execution rather that running it immediately?
2. What are the major differences between running a program from cards and running the same program from a terminal using prepared input files?
3. What are the major differences between running a program from a terminal using prepared input files and running the same program from a terminal interactively?
4. What is the purpose of an editing program?

5. (a) When a program is run interactively, why is it desirable to have a prompting message to the user printed before the user types an item of input data?

(b) What difficulties might occur if a computer program with a large number of read statements did not give sufficient information to the user in its prompting messages, or did not provide prompting messages at all?

6. (a) When running a program interactively, is an echo of input data desirable after the user has entered a piece of data in response to an input prompting message?

(b) Why are prompting messages superfluous when running a program from cards or from a terminal using prepared input files?

(c) Why is an echo of input data desirable when running a program from cards?

1.5   Decisions

The sequence of steps a computer follows in executing a program does not have to be the same every time the program is run. The computer is capable of choosing one of several computational alternatives. A company payroll is a familiar situation in which such a choice is necessary to handle the possibility that some of the employees work overtime, for which they are paid time and a half instead of straight time. Calculating income tax also requires a choice among alternative computational procedures, because the percentage of income to be paid as tax depends on the amount of taxable income.

In Section 1.3, the concept of a compound statement was introduced to describe a group of instructions whose execution is repeated several times as part of a for-statement. In this section, compound statements are used as parts of an if-statement to describe alternative sequences of instructions. The computer chooses one of the sequences depending on the results of a test or comparison. The form of the if-statement shows clearly the parallel sequences of steps the computer might take, depending on its decision.

Payroll Without Provision for Overtime

Before describing how to write a program involving a decision, we briefly consider a simple payroll program that does not have alternatives in the computational procedure. The program payroll1 computes the gross pay of a single hourly worker in the simplest possible way, as the product of the hourly rate and the number of hours worked.

```
program payroll1 (input, output);

  var
    hourlyrate, hoursworked, grosspay : real;

  begin
  read (hourlyrate, hoursworked);
  writeln ('Input data  hourlyrate: ', hourlyrate :1:2);
  writeln ('            hoursworked: ', hoursworked :1:2);
  grosspay := hourlyrate * hoursworked;
  writeln ('Gross pay = $', grosspay :1:2);
  end.
```

```
run payroll1

Input data  hourlyrate:   4.75
            hoursworked:  37.00
Gross pay = $ 175.75
```

The hourly rate of $4.75 must not be entered with a dollar sign, but simply as the number 4.75. The dollar sign appears in the printed output line for gross pay, only because it is part of the message within the apostrophes in the writeln command.

Payroll With Provision for Overtime

Among its many oversimplifications, the program payroll1 does not take into account the fact that hourly workers are usually paid at a higher rate for overtime hours. The program payroll2 provides for this possibility, calculating the gross pay by the simple formula above if the number of hours worked is 40 or fewer, but calculating gross pay by a slightly more complicated overtime pay procedure whenever the number of hours worked exceeds 40 hours. In a common overtime pay formula, the first 40 hours are paid at the worker's usual hourly rate, but the hours worked in excess of 40 hours are paid at 1 1/2 times the worker's rate. Note that as a good programming practice the value 40 is assigned to a constant so that if the traditional 40-hour work week is shortened to a 30-hour work week, this program can be modified easily to take this change into account. For similar reasons, the overtime pay factor 1.5 is also given a name.

```
program payroll2 (input, output);
  const
    regularhours = 40;
    otfactor = 1.5;

  var
    hourlyrate, hoursworked,
    grosspay : real;

  begin
  read and echo the input data
  if hoursworked > regularhours then
    compute grosspay by the overtime formula
  else
    compute grosspay by the regular formula;
  writeln ('Gross pay = $', grosspay :1:2);
  end.
```

The If-Statement

The computational alternatives in the program payroll2 are contained in the four-line if-statement that begins with the keyword ''if'' and ends with the semicolon just preceding the next writeln statement. The form of the if-statement is shown in the syntax chart of Figure 1.5.1. The chart shows that, like the for-statement, the if-statement is built using other statements. It is also possible to see from the syntax chart for the if-statement that the else-clause may be omitted, as will be discussed later in this section.

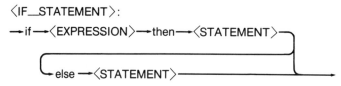

Figure 1.5.1   If-statement syntax chart.

Recall that a statement may be a compound statement, so that there may be many statements between the keywords ''then'' and ''else'' or after the keyword ''else'', provided they are bracketed by the keywords ''begin'' and ''end''. It is imperative that no semicolon be placed on the statement preceding the keyword ''else'', because a semicolon in this position would terminate the whole if-statement and indicate that there should be no else-clause following. See Exercise 9 for examples.

When the program payroll2 is executed, there are two possibilities. Either the computer executes a sequence of steps corresponding to the English language statement

```
compute grosspay by the overtime formula
```

or it executes a sequence of steps corresponding to the English language statement

```
compute grosspay by the regular formula
```

The first alternative is taken if the number of hours worked by the employee is more than 40, the number of regular hours; otherwise, the second alternative is taken.

The if-statement is terminated by the end of the statement that follows the keyword ''else''. In this case, the statement

```
compute grosspay by the regular formula
```

is part of the if-statement, but the statement

```
writeln ('Gross pay = $', grosspay :1:2);
```

is not part of the if-statement, but rather the first statement to be executed after completion of whichever alternative is taken in the if-statement. Thus, when an employee works more than 40 hours, the gross pay is computed by the overtime formula and then printed as output. On the other hand, when the employee works 40 or fewer hours, the gross pay is computed by the regular formula and then printed as output. The point is that the gross pay is printed whether or not the employee works overtime.

Indenting the parts of an If-Statement

The fact that the statement

```
compute grosspay by the overtime formula
```

is executed only if the condition ''hoursworked > regularhours'' is satisfied is emphasized visually by indenting it under the if-statement heading containing the keyword "if", the condition for its execution, and the keyword "then". The alternative calculation

```
compute grosspay by the regular formula
```

is indented under the keyword "else". The fact that the statement

```
writeln ('Gross pay = $', grosspay :1:2);
```

is not part of the if-statement is reinforced visually by the absence of indentation. This usage of indentation agrees with the usage for for-statements as presented in Section 1.3.

The entire if-statement is the complete thought that starts with the keyword "if". Thus the if-statement is more fully described as an if...then...else-statement. Expressed as an English sentence, a complete if-statement tells a computer, "If some condition is satisfied, then do one thing, otherwise do the other thing."

Table 1.5.1   Arithmetic comparison symbols. and their English equivalents.

>	is greater than
<	is less than
=	is equal to
>=	is greater than or equal to
<=	is less than or equal to
<>	is not equal to

Arithmetic Comparisons

A reasonable question to raise at this point is what sort of expressions are allowed as the condition following the keyword "if" in an if-statement. It is impossible to give a complete answer at this point, since what is permitted is called a "boolean expression" and many of the things allowed in such an expression are Pascal features that have not yet been introduced. However, the best short answer is that any if-test similar to one given as an example in this book is acceptable. If-tests like the first example given are sufficient for many purposes and, as more examples are given, the convenience and capabilities of if-statements will be expanded gradually. The syntax chart for boolean expressions may be found in Appendix C.

In the program payroll2, the if-test is a simple arithmetic comparison,

```
if hoursworked > regularhours then
```

The current value of the variable hoursworked is compared to the constant regularhours (which has the value 40) and the appropriate alternative is performed depending on the outcome of the comparison. There are five other arithmetic comparisons that may be used as well as greater than (>). Table 1.5.1 gives the Pascal symbol and the appropriate English phrase for each comparison.

For example, the if-test

```
if count = 100 then
```

is read: "If the value of the variable count is equal to 100, then ...". There is no reason why one side of the comparison must be a constant. Both sides are allowed to be variables.

```
if x < y then
```

is permissible, and the instructions immediately following this if-test are to be executed if the current value of the variable x is less than the current value of the variable y. When the comparison is changed to

```
if x <= y then
```

the conditionally executed instructions immediately following the if-test are performed not only when the value of x is less than the value of the variable y, but also when the value of x is equal to the value of y.

Arithmetic expressions also may be used in place of simple variables or numbers in the comparisons. Thus

```
if a + b < 10 then
if a + b < c + d then
if price * quantity > 75 then
if (first + last) / 2 = middle then
```

are all valid if-tests. Any expression that may be used in an arithmetic assignment statement also may be used in a comparison. However, it is rarely necessary or desirable to write overly long and complicated if-tests, which tend to be confusing.

Refining a Program

In the program payroll2, informal use of English in the three statements

```
read and echo the input data
compute grosspay by the overtime formula
compute grosspay by the regular formula
```

makes it easy for a person to see what the program does. Unfortunately, the computer cannot understand this informal usage. In order to obtain something the computer can understand, these two statements are *refined* into Pascal. This means replacing them by instructions in Pascal that direct a computer to do what these English language statements say to do. When we make this replacement, we often keep the informal English as a comment.

The first of these informal statements can be replaced with the three Pascal statements.

```
{ read and echo the input data }
read (hourlyrate, hoursworked);
writeln ('Input data  hourlyrate: ', hourlyrate);
writeln ('            hoursworked: ', hoursworked);
```

The formula for computing gross pay when there is overtime is based on the worker's usual hourly rate for the first 40 hours, but 1 1/2 times the usual hourly rate for overtime hours worked in excess of 40 hours. The English phrase

```
compute grosspay by the overtime formula
```

may be refined to the following Pascal compound statement:

```
begin  { compute the gross pay by the overtime formula }
regularpay := hourlyrate * regularhours;
otworked := hoursworked - regularhours;
otpay := otfactor * hourlyrate * otworked;
grosspay := regularpay + otpay;
end
```

It is perfectly reasonable for a single English sentence to be refined to several Pascal statements. The English sentence was used in the first place to postpone consideration of a mess of details.

It is also possible to refine the same English sentence to a single assignment statement:

```
grosspay := (hourlyrate * regularhours)
       + otfactor * hourlyrate * (hoursworked - regularhours)
```

Both refinements specify the same computation, performed in the same way, but the six-line computation using appropriate names for variables is more self-explanatory than the longer algebraic formula.

Substituting the first of these refinements, a compound statement, for the computation of gross pay with overtime, substituting the simple gross pay assignment statement used in payroll1 for the computation without overtime, and substituting the statements that read and echo the input data, refines the program payroll2 to a program in which no statement needs further refinement, because all statements are in Pascal, a language the computer can understand. Columns and decimals indicators have been used to improve the appearance of the output. Since the refined program is really the same program with more of the details spelled out, the same program name "payroll2" is used after refinement as before refinement.

Note that a semicolon must not follow the keyword "end" of the compound statement that forms the then-clause, nor may one follow the keywords "then", or "else". The results would be disastrous.

```
program payroll2 (input, output);

  const
    regularhours = 40;
    otfactor = 1.5;

  var
    hourlyrate, hoursworked,
        regularpay, otworked,
        otpay, grosspay : real;
```

```
begin
{ read and echo the input data }
read (hourlyrate, hoursworked);
writeln ('Input data  hourlyrate: ', hourlyrate :1:2);
writeln ('              hoursworked: ', hoursworked :1:2);
if hoursworked > regularhours then
  { compute grosspay by the overtime formula }
  begin
  regularpay := hourlyrate * regularhours;
  otworked := hoursworked - regularhours;
  otpay := otfactor * hourlyrate * otworked;
  grosspay := regularpay + otpay;
  end
else
  { compute grosspay by the regular formula }
  grosspay := hourlyrate * hoursworked;
writeln ('Gross pay = $', grosspay :1:2);
end.
```

```
run payroll2

Input data  hourlyrate:  4.75
            hoursworked:  46.00
Gross pay = $ 232.75
```

```
run payroll2

Input data  hourlyrate:  4.75
            hoursworked:  37.00
Gross pay = $ 175.75
```

Two sample executions are shown for payroll2, one for each alternative way of computing the gross pay. In the first sample execution, the input value for hoursworked is 46, which means that the overtime pay computation formula is used. In that formula, the hourly rate $4.75 is multiplied by the first 40 hours to obtain $190.00, the gross pay for the first 40 hours. To this is added the overtime pay for the last 6 hours, computed as 1.5 times the hourly rate times the number of hours in excess of 40. Since 1.5 times $4.75 per hour times 6 hours is $42.75, the overtime pay, the computed gross pay is $190.00 + $42.75 = $232.75, the printed answer.

The only interest in the second sample run is to show that, if the number of hours worked is less than 40, the program payroll2 computes the same gross pay as the simpler program payroll1. This is not very surprising, since the assignment that computes the overtime is exactly the same assignment statement used to compute the gross pay all the time in the program payroll1, which has no provision for overtime pay.

Omitting the Else-Clause

The if-statement of payroll2 is an example of a two-alternative decision. The computer is directed to calculate overtime pay if there is overtime, or to calculate regular pay if there is not. Decisions with two alternatives are the type most often encountered in programming.

Sometimes, no programming steps are required in one of the two alternatives of an if-statement. In the next program makexpositive, no action is needed if x is already positive. In this case, the else-clause of the if-statement may be omitted.

```
program makexpositive (input, output);

  var
    x : integer;

  begin
  read (x);
  writeln ('Input data  x: ', x :1);
  if x < 0 then
    x := -x;
  writeln ('Absolute value = ', x :1);
  end.
```

```
run makexpositive

Input data  x: -5
Absolute value = 5
```

```
run makexpositive

Input data  x: 7
Absolute value = 7
```

The executions above are easy to follow if one notes that $-(-5) = 5$. So when x is negative, $-x$ is positive, and this is what x is changed to before printing.

Multiple Alternatives, Income Tax

It is possible to handle situations in which there are more than two alternatives by means of a series of two-alternative if-statements. In the next example, a program incometax1 is written to compute the federal income tax for a single taxpayer according to Tax Rate Schedule X which applies to such taxpayers. The input is the person's taxable income, after all deductions and adjustments, and the output is both the tax due on that taxable income and the person's tax bracket, that is, the rate at which the last dollar earned is taxed. To avoid a very long program, only part of the complete Tax Rate Schedule X is incorporated into the program incometax1, so that this program cannot be used to compute the tax on incomes over $10,000. However, there is no difficulty in continuing the pattern of program steps to incorporate all of Tax Rate Schedule X, thus avoiding the limitation on applicable taxable incomes.

```
program incometax1 (input, output);

  var
    income, tax : real;
    bracket : integer;

  begin
  read (income);
  { find appropriate range and compute tax }
  if income = 0 then
    begin
    tax := 0;   bracket := 0;
    end;
  if (income > 0) and (income <= 500) then
    begin
    tax := 0.14 * income;   bracket := 14;
    end;
  if (income > 500) and (income <= 1000) then
    begin
    tax := 70 + 0.15 * (income - 500);   bracket := 15;
    end;
  if (income > 1000) and (income <= 1500) then
    begin
    tax := 145 + 0.16 * (income - 1000);   bracket := 16;
    end;
  if (income > 1500) and (income <= 2000) then
    begin
    tax := 225 + 0.17 * (income - 1500);   bracket := 17;
    end;
  if (income > 2000) and (income <= 4000) then
    begin
    tax := 310 + 0.19 * (income - 2000);   bracket := 19;
    end;
  if (income > 4000) and (income <= 6000) then
    begin
    tax := 690 + 0.21 * (income - 4000);   bracket := 21;
    end;
  if (income > 6000) and (income <= 8000) then
    begin
    tax := 1110 + 0.24 * (income - 6000);   bracket := 24;
    end;
  if (income > 8000) and (income <= 10000) then
    begin
    tax := 1590 + 0.25 * (income - 8000);   bracket := 25;
    end;
  { end of tax computation section }

  if income <= 10000 then
    begin
    writeln ('The tax on $', income :1:2, ' is $', tax :1:2);
    writeln ('This income is in the ', bracket :1, '% tax bracket.');
    end
```

```
else
  begin
  writeln ('Input data  income:', income :1:2);
  writeln ('Taxable income too high for this program');
  end;
end.
```

None of the if-statements in the tax computation section has an else-clause. If income lies in the indicated range for that if-test, then the variables tax and bracket are calculated by the formula in that if-statement. Otherwise, nothing is done in that if-statement. Note that, in every execution of the program, each of the if-tests is performed, but that the conditions describing the ranges for income have been written carefully to guarantee that only one range and one tax computation formula applies for each possible value of income less than or equal to $10,000.

To be more specific, let us look at a few sample executions of incometax1, in which the computer is supplied with a wide variety of different values as input for the variable income.

```
run incometax1

The tax on $ 100.00 is $ 14.00
This income is in the 14% tax bracket.


run incometax1

The tax on $ 1200.00 is $ 177.00
This income is in the 16% tax bracket.


run incometax1

The tax on $ 7500.00 is $ 1470.00
This income is in the 24% tax bracket.


run incometax1

Input data  income: 75000.00
Taxable income too high for this program
```

Consider the second run with a taxable income of $1200. The only condition in the tax computation section which this taxable income satisfies is

```
(income > 1000)  and  (income <= 1500)
```

Thus the tax is computed by the formula in that fourth statement:

```
tax := 145 + 0.16 * (income - 1000)
     = 145 + 0.16 * 200
     = 145 + 32
     = 177
```

The second assignment statement of the fourth if-statement assigns a tax bracket of 16 (percent) to the variable bracket. All of the other if-tests in the tax computation section are made, but none of the other conditions is satisfied and so no other action is taken for a taxable income of $1200.

The final if-test of the program controls the printout. Since the value of income is $1200, which is less than $10,000, the two sentences giving the tax and the tax bracket are printed.

In the last of the sample executions using a taxable income of $75,000, none of the conditions in the tax computation section is satisfied, and consequently tax and bracket are not assigned values at all. In this execution, the final if-test causes the computer to print a warning that the taxable income is too large for the program, instead of the usual printout giving the tax and tax bracket. It is good programming practice to warn the user when a situation occurs that the program is not designed to handle.

The Boolean Operators And, Or, and Not

The keywords "and", "or", and "not" may be used to specify conditions that cannot be described using only one comparison. In the program incometax1, most of the ranges for income are described by two comparisons. For example,

```
if (income > 1000) and (income <= 1500) then
if (income > 1500) and (income <= 2000) then
if (income > 2000) and (income <= 4000) then
```

Both comparisons must be true before the then-clause is executed. On the other hand, the program explainor below helps explain under what circumstances an if-test consisting of two conditions connected by the operator or is satisfied.

```
program explainor (input, output);
  var
    x, y : integer;

  begin
  read (x, y);
  writeln ('Input data  x: ', x :1);
  writeln ('            y: ', y :1);
  if (x = 0) or (y = 0) then
    writeln ('At least one of the variables x or y is zero.')
  else
    writeln ('Neither x nor y is zero.');
  end.
```

```
run explainor

Input data  x: 0
            y: 0
At least one of the variables x or y is zero.
```

```
run explainor

Input data  x: 0
            y: 1
At least one of the variables x or y is zero.


run explainor

Input data  x: 1
            y: 0
At least one of the variables x or y is zero.


run explainor

Input data  x: 1
            y: 1
Neither x nor y is zero.
```

As can be seen from the sample executions, the if-test is satisfied, and the writeln statement in the then-clause of the if-statement causes the computer to print "At least one of the variables x or y is zero." whenever x is zero or y is zero. If both x and y are zero, there are two reasons for printing the message. Only if x and y are both nonzero is the writeln statement in the else-clause executed to print the sentence "Neither x nor y is zero."

An important rule to remember is that in Pascal a comparison that is one of the operands of an "and" or "or" operation must be enclosed in parentheses to achieve the desired effect. This is because boolean operators are evaluated before comparison operators in the absence of parentheses.

The boolean operator "not" applied to a logical value changes it. If it is true, it becomes false; if it is false, it becomes true.

In expressions without parentheses, the "not" operator is applied first, then the "and" operator, and finally the "or" operator. Thus if a, b, and c are type boolean, the expression

```
a and not b or c
```

would be evaluated as if it were the expression

```
(a and (not b)) or c
```

If-Statements Inside a For-Loop

We close this section with three related examples of programs using if-statements. In each of the three applications, a test has been given to a class of 25 students. The test contains not only the regular questions which are marked normally, but also three bonus questions. The input data for all the programs consists of four items per student. The first item is a numerical test score for the regular questions. Each of the remaining three items is either the character R, for "right", or W, for "wrong", depending on which of the bonus questions are answered correctly. There is no partial credit for the bonus questions. Note that the comparison operator equals (=) may be used to compare two characters. It and the other comparison operators may be used to compare any two character strings of the same length (see Chapter 5).

```
program extra1 (input, output);
{ five extra points for each bonus question answered correctly }

  const
    numberofstudents = 25;
    right = 'R';

  var
    score, student : integer;
    bonus1, bonus2, bonus3 : char;

  begin
  for student := 1 to numberofstudents do
    begin
    writeln;
    read (score, bonus1, bonus2, bonus3);
    writeln ('Input data  score: ', score :1);
    writeln ('               bonus1: ', bonus1 :1);
    writeln ('               bonus2: ', bonus2 :1);
    writeln ('               bonus3: ', bonus3 :1);
    if bonus1 = right then
      score := score + 5;
    if bonus2 = right then
      score := score + 5;
    if bonus3 = right then
      score := score + 5;
    writeln ('Adjusted test score = ', score :1);
    end; { for-loop }
  end.
```

In the program extra1, the variable score is increased by 5 every time a bonus question is answered correctly. Thus an adjusted test score can be as much as 15 points higher than the score on the regular questions if all three bonus questions were answered correctly, or 5 or 10 points higher if only one or two of the bonus questions were answered correctly.

In the next example, the instructor has decided to adjust the regular test score only if all three bonus questions are answered correctly. No adjustment is to be made if only one or two bonus questions are answered correctly.

```
program extra2 (input, output);
{ five extra points if all three bonus questions answered correctly }

  const
    numberofstudents = 25;
    right = 'R';
```

```
var
  score, student : integer;
  bonus1, bonus2, bonus3 : char;

begin
for student := 1 to numberofstudents do
  begin
  writeln;
  read (score, bonus1, bonus2, bonus3);
  writeln ('Input data  score: ', score :1);
  writeln ('              bonus1: ', bonus1 :1);
  writeln ('              bonus2: ', bonus2 :1);
  writeln ('              bonus3: ', bonus3 :1);
  if (bonus1 = right) and (bonus2 = right)
      and (bonus3 = right) then
    score := score + 5;
  writeln ('Adjusted test score = ', score :1);
  end; { for-loop }
end.
```

The if-test has three comparisons separated by the keyword "and". Commas or other punctuation that might be used if this were an English sentence are not used in Pascal to set off the phrases of an if-test.

In the next example, test scores are to be adjusted by five points if any bonus question is answered correctly. There is no additional credit for a second or third bonus question that is also answered correctly.

```
program extra3 (input, output);
{ five extra points if at least one bonus question answered correctly }

  const
    numberofstudents = 25;
    right = 'R';

  var
    score, student : integer;
    bonus1, bonus2, bonus3 : char;

  begin
  for student := 1 to numberofstudents do
    begin
    writeln;
    read (score, bonus1, bonus2, bonus3);
    writeln ('Input data  score: ', score :1);
    writeln ('              bonus1: ', bonus1 :1);
    writeln ('              bonus2: ', bonus2 :1);
    writeln ('              bonus3: ', bonus3 :1);
    if (bonus1 = right) or (bonus2 = right) or
        (bonus3 = right) then
      score := score + 5;
    writeln ('Adjusted test score = ', score :1);
    end; { for-loop }
  end.
```

This program is identical to the previous program, except that the keywords "and" have been changed to "or". The regular test score thus is increased by five points if one, two, or three of the bonus questions are answered correctly and is unchanged only if none of the bonus questions is answered correctly.

Nested If-Statements

As further examples of the use of if-statements, we now show how to program the last two applications without using either the keyword "and" or the keyword "or" The programs become somewhat longer and probably less clear.

```
program extra2b (input, output);
{ five extra points if all three bonus questions answered correctly }

  const
    numberofstudents = 25;
    right = 'R';

  var
    score, student : integer;
    bonus1, bonus2, bonus3 : char;

  begin
  for student := 1 to numberofstudents do
    begin
    writeln;
    read (score, bonus1, bonus2, bonus3);
    writeln ('Input data  score: ', score :1);
    writeln ('                   bonus1: ', bonus1 :1);
    writeln ('                   bonus2: ', bonus2 :1);
    writeln ('                   bonus3: ', bonus3 :1);
    if bonus1 = right then
      if bonus2 = right then
        if bonus3 = right then
          score := score + 5;
    writeln ('Adjusted test score = ', score :1);
    end; { for-loop }
  end.
```

In this program, there are three if-statements, one *nested* within the next. They start on different lines, but each one ends after the assignment statement. None of these if-statements has an else-clause, so if any one of the three tests is not satisfied, that if-statement is completed without further action by the computer. More is said about the nesting of statements in Chapter 2. It suffices to say at this point that version 2 of this program is grammatically correct and executes properly, but it is more confusing than version 1, which is therefore preferred.

In order to eliminate the keyword "or" from the third application, a similar nesting of if-statements is necessary. This time the nesting occurs in the else-clause. That is, the statement following the keyword "else" is itself an if-statement.

```pascal
program extra3b (input, output);
{ five extra points if at least one bonus question answered correctly }

   const
     numberofstudents = 25;
     right = 'R';

   var
     score, student : integer;
     bonus1, bonus2, bonus3 : char;

   begin
   for student := 1 to numberofstudents do
     begin
     writeln;
     read (score, bonus1, bonus2, bonus3);
     writeln ('Input data  score: ', score :1);
     writeln ('              bonus1: ', bonus1 :1);
     writeln ('              bonus2: ', bonus2 :1);
     writeln ('              bonus3: ', bonus3 :1);
     if bonus1 = right then
       score := score + 5
     else
       if bonus2 = right then
         score := score + 5
       else
         if bonus3 = right then
           score := score + 5;
     writeln ('Adjusted test score = ', score :1);
     end; { for-loop }
   end.
```

By careful application of the rules, one can convince oneself that this program is actually correct. However, version 1 using the keyword "or" is clearly preferable. The program can be made a little clearer by writing the keyword "else" and the if-test following it on one line as described in Section 2.6, but even this does not make it as clear as version 1.

The Else Ambiguity

The following if-statement illustrates a point of possible confusion in the Pascal language.

```pascal
if x > 0 then
if y > 0 then
n := 1
else
n := 2
```

This statement intentionally has not been indented properly in order to raise the question: To which if-condition does the else belong? The answer is that an else-clause is part of the most recent if-statement that doesn't already have an else-clause. Thus the proper indentation is:

```
if x > 0 then
  if y > 0 then
    n := 1
  else
    n := 2
```

Suppose $x = y = -1$. The first if-test is false and the remainder of the statement is skipped, so that the value of n is not changed. Suppose $x = 1$ and $y = -1$. The first if-test is true, so the next if-statement is executed. Since y is not greater than 0, the else-clause is executed setting n equal to 2.

It is possible to force the else to go with the first if-statement in at least two ways. One is to use a begin-end pair of keywords to make the inner if-statement a single compound statement. The other way is to add another keyword "else" with an empty else-clause. The two resulting statements follow.

```
if x > 0 then
  begin
  if y > 0 then
    n := 1
  end
else
    n := 2
```

```
if x > 0 then
  if y > 0 then
    n := 1
  else
else
    n := 2
```

Each of the two statements above has been indented correctly to show its structure, but remember it is the text of the program that determines what is to be computed and the indentation has no effect whatsoever. With or without proper indentation, the begin-end version is probably clearer.

Exercises

---

1. On the first $25,900 of annual earnings an employee must pay 6.13 percent FICA tax (Social Security). Earnings beyond $25,900 are not subject to this tax. Write a program that computes the total FICA tax an employee must pay in a year, based on the amount of gross earnings supplied as input.

2. If a person works for two or more employers, each employer deducts 6.13 percent FICA tax. If a person earns a total of more than $25,900, it is possible that the total of all the FICA tax deductions by all employees will exceed $1,587.67

Table 1.5.2   New York State Tax Rate Schedule for Certain Persons

IF TAXABLE INCOME IS

OVER	BUT NOT OVER	THEN INCOME TAX IS		
$0	$1,000		2% of taxable income	
$1,000	$3,000	$20 plus	3% of excess over	$1,000
$3,000	$5,000	$80 plus	4% of excess over	$3,000
$5,000	$7,000	$160 plus	5% of excess over	$5,000
$7,000	$9,000	$260 plus	6% of excess over	$7,000
$9,000	$11,000	$380 plus	7% of excess over	$9,000
$11,000	$13,000	$520 plus	8% of excess over	$11,000
$13,000	$15,000	$680 plus	9% of excess over	$13,000
$15,000	$17,000	$860 plus	10% of excess over	$15,000
$17,000	$19,000	$1,060 plus	11% of excess over	$17,000
$19,000	$21,000	$1,280 plus	12% of excess over	$19,000
$21,000	$23,000	$1,520 plus	13% of excess over	$21,000
$23,000	$25,000	$1,780 plus	14% of excess over	$23,000
$25,000		$2,060 plus	15% of excess over	$25,000

(which is 6.13 percent of $25,900). The government then gives the person a tax credit equal to the difference between the total FICA deductions and $1,587.67. Write a program that accepts as input the gross earnings from each employer, computes the total FICA tax deducted, and computes the amount of the tax credit.

3. For nonresident married persons with income from New York State sources who elect to file a joint federal income tax return but separate New York State returns, Table 1.5.2 shows the progressive tax rate schedule on taxable income. Write a program that calculates for any taxable income supplied as input the New York State income tax according to this schedule.

4. The Enlightened Corporation is pleased when its employees enroll in college classes. It offers them an 80 percent rebate on the first $500 of tuition, a 60 percent rebate on the second $400, and a 40 percent rebate on the next $300. Write a program that computes the rebate for an amount of tuition supplied as input.

5. Write a bank account program that accepts as input a starting balance and then either a deposit (positive number) or a withdrawal (negative number). It prints the resulting balance if the second supplied number is either a positive number (a deposit) or a negative number (a withdrawal) that would not reduce the balance below zero. If the balance would be reduced below zero, the program prints the word "overdraft".

6. The Old Fashioned Department Store offers its cash customers a 7 percent discount but makes charge customers pay full price. Write a program that accepts as input a price and a mode of payment that is either "C" for cash or "P" for charge (plastic) and prints the price the customer will be asked to pay.

7. Modify the program written for Exercise 6 so that, if the mode of payment is neither "C" for cash nor "P" for charge, the program prints out "Mode of payment undecipherable, please reenter information."

8. Write a program that reads 25 numbers but prints only the numbers greater than 100.

9. To test your understanding of the placement of semicolons in a Pascal program, hand simulate the following programs exer9a to exer9f using the values 45, 75, and 95 in turn as input data for each program. Check your answers using a computer, if one that runs Pascal programs is available. Caution: These simulations are tricky, and to add to the challenge, some of these programs are syntactically incorrect and cannot be executed at all. See if you can tell which are incorrect before the computer gives you an error message.

```pascal
program exer9a (input, output);
  var
    x : integer;
  begin
  read (x);
  if x > 50 then
    if x > 90 then
      begin
      write ('Input data x = ', x :1);
      writeln (' is very high.')
      end
    else
      begin
      write ('Input data x = ', x :1);
      writeln (' is high.')
      end
  end.
```

```pascal
program exer9b (input, output);
  var
    x : integer;
  begin
  read (x);
  if x > 50 then
    if x > 90 then
      begin
      write ('Input data x = ', x :1);
      writeln (' is very high.');
      end
    else
      begin
      write ('Input data x = ', x :1);
      writeln (' is high.');
      end;
    end.
```

```
program exer9c (input, output);
  var
    x : integer;
  begin;
  read (x);
  if x > 50 then
    if x > 90 then
      begin;
      write ('Input data x = ', x :1);
      writeln (' is very high.');
      end
    else
      begin;
      write ('Input data x = ', x :1);
      writeln (' is high.');
      end;
    end.

program exer9d (input, output);
  var
    x : integer;
  begin
  read (x);
  if x > 50 then
    if x > 90 then
      begin
      write ('Input data x = ', x :1);
      writeln (' is very high.');
      end
    else;
      begin
      write ('Input data x = ', x :1);
      writeln (' is high.');
      end
    end.

program exer9e (input, output);
  var
    x : integer;
  begin
  read (x);
  if x > 50 then
    if x > 90 then
      begin
      write ('Input data x = ', x :1);
      writeln (' is very high.');
      end;
    else
      begin
      write ('Input data x = ', x :1);
      writeln (' is high.');
      end;
    end.
```

```
program exer9f (input, output);
  var
    x : integer;
  begin
  read (x);
  if x > 50 then;
    if x > 90 then
      begin
      write ('Input data x = ', x :1);
      writeln (' is very high.');
      end
    else
      begin
      write ('Input data x = ', x :1);
      writeln (' is high.');
      end
    end.
```

1.6   Programmer-Defined Procedures

Every program so far, and indeed every program in this book, uses the built-in procedures read, write, and writeln. They are by now familiar and easy to use. In fact, you may be wondering why they are called procedures instead of just garden-variety Pascal statements. A partial answer is that beneath their apparent simplicity lies a complex sequence of steps. The built-in procedure read must scan the sequence of input characters looking for digits, signs, decimal points, e's, and blanks; it must decide if the input number is in integer form, positional real form, or exponential real form; it must evaluate the number and convert it to an appropriate internal form; and it must store the value just computed in the proper place in memory. The procedures write and writeln do much the same steps, but in reverse, adding rounding and field spacing as well.

We mention this complexity only to make the point that using a built-in procedure in a Pascal program is a simple way to call for a possibly complex sequence of steps. You, as a writer of Pascal programs, never need to know about the details, some of which depend not only on Pascal but also on the details of the computer being used to run the programs. The designer of the Pascal system has taken care of the details once and for all.

Programmer-defined procedures work the same way: They provide a simple way to specify a possibly complex sequence of steps in a program. The only difference is that in this case, the programmer must supply the details. For example, suppose the instructor of Section 1.3 wishes to find the average test score in several classes. By making the averaging steps, that is, all the executable statments, of the program avgofscores into a programmer-defined procedure named avgoneclass (average one class), it is easy to write a main program to calculate the class average test scores for several classes as follows:

```
program avgofseveral (input, output);

  begin { main program to find the average test scores
          for several classes }
  read (numberofclasses);
  writeln ('Input data  numberofclasses: ', numberofclasses :1);
  for classcount := 1 to numberofclasses do
    begin
    writeln; writeln;
    avgoneclass;
    end; { for-loop }
  end. { avgofseveralclasses }
```

The dozen or so steps of the program avgofscores, which finds an average test
score for one class, become a single step, the procedure call avgoneclass, in the program avgofseveralclasses that averages test scores for several classes. *Programmer-
defined procedures enable a programmer to write a program in terms of larger conceptual units,* thus making it easier to keep one's mind on the forest instead of the individual trees.

```
program avgofseveral (input, output);

  var
    enrollment, count : integer;
    numberofclasses, classcount : integer;
    sum, nextscore : real;

  procedure avgoneclass;
    begin
    read (enrollment);
    writeln ('Input data  enrollment: ', enrollment :1);
    sum := 0;
    for count := 1 to enrollment do
      begin
      read (nextscore);
      writeln ('Input data  nextscore: ', nextscore :7:2);
      sum := sum + nextscore;
      end; { for-loop }
    writeln;
    writeln ('Average test score = ', sum / enrollment :1:2);
    end; { avgoneclass }

  begin { main program to find the average test scores
          for several classes }
  read (numberofclasses);
  writeln ('Input data  numberofclasses: ', numberofclasses :1);
  for classcount := 1 to numberofclasses do
    begin
    writeln; writeln;
    avgoneclass;
    end; { for-loop }
  end. { avgofseveralclasses }
```

```
run avgofseveral

Input data   numberofclasses: 3


Input data   enrollment:  6
Input data   nextscore:      73.00
Input data   nextscore:      68.00
Input data   nextscore:      94.00
Input data   nextscore:      88.00
Input data   nextscore:      75.00
Input data   nextscore:      79.00

Average test score =   79.50

Input data   enrollment:  2
Input data   nextscore:      76.00
Input data   nextscore:      83.00

Average test score =   79.50

Input data   enrollment:  4
Input data   nextscore:      99.00
Input data   nextscore:      77.00
Input data   nextscore:      64.00
Input data   nextscore:      73.00

Average test score =   78.25
```

The details of the programmer-defined procedure avgoneclass appear above the main begin-end block of the program avgofseveralclasses for the following reason. Pascal regards specifying the details of a programmer-defined procedure as a *definition* of the meaning of the procedure name. consistent with the Pascal policy that definitions and other declarations must precede their use in a program, the *procedure declaration for the programmer-defined procedure avgoneclass* is placed before the main program that calls for its execution. This placement makes good theoretical sense and simplifies the design of Pascal compilers, especially for smaller computers.

As we shall see in Section 2.1, the modern method of top-down design is based on planning the main program first and looking at the details later, so from this point of view it is clearer and more natural to put the highest level executive or "main" program first and the details later. The controversy is moot. If you want to write Pascal programs, you follow the Pascal rules. Pascal programmers simply learn to seek the main program near the end of the program listing.

Exercises

1. A test consists of three parts, each worth a maximum of 50 points. A student's grade on this test is the sum of the two highest point scores. Write a program avg3parts that reads the part scores for each student and finds the class average for

this test. Use a programmer-defined procedure getonescore to read the three part scores and to determine the test score for one student, so that these details do not appear in the main program.

2. An input file contains a list of one month's transaction for a checking account, represented as follows. First comes an integer, giving the number of transactions for the month. Next come pairs of entries, each consisting of a one-character transaction code and the amount of the transaction. Valid transaction codes are 'I' for initial balance brought forward from the previous month, 'C' for check, 'D' for deposit, and 'S' for service charge. Handle the processing for each transaction typ in a separate programmer-defined procedure, and let the main program decide which procedure to call. The program should print the final balance.

3. Modify the program in Exercise 3 so that it calculates the service charges. Service charges are $3 per month to maintain the account, 10 cents per check, and a $5 overdraft charge whenever a check brings the balance below $0.00.

4. The quadratic equation $ax^2 + b x + c = 0$ has two real roots, two complex roots, or one real root, depending on whether the quantity $b^2 - 4ac$ is positive, negative, or zero, repectively. Write a program to find and print the roots of any quadratic equation. Use a separate programmer-defined procedure for each of the three cases.

1.7   What Is A Computer?

These days, a great many devices are called computers, either by their manufacturers or by the general public. Since the kinds of computers discussed in this book are widely acclaimed as models of technological achievement, it is not surprising to find that many of the near and distant relatives are also called "computers" in order to proclaim their kinship. This section describes some computers and discusses the characteristic attributes and capabilities they share. It is essentially self-contained, and may be read before starting Section 1.1, if desired.

Ancient History

At one time, the word "computer" meant a person who performed arithmetic computations. In the eighteenth and nineteenth centuries, when knowledge of the basic arithmetic operations was far from universal, and proficiency in the more difficult operations of multiplication and division was quite rare, these human computers were in some demand, especially for computing the astronomical tables essential to navigation and the tables used in trade and insurance.

Unfortunately, it is not humanly possible to manipulate great volumes of numbers without error, and consequently the mathematical, astronomical, and navigational tables of the early 1800s contained a profusion of errors. Dionysius Lardner noted that, even the most carefully prepared and edited tables of his day might average one error per page, while less carefully prepared tables might have many more. Some of the errors were due to the human computers, but others entered later in the process, for instance in recopying the table for the printer, in typesetting, and even in the printing process itself. One remarkable error originated in Vlacq's table of logarithms, printed in Gouda in 1628 and recopied, often without acknowledgment, for

over 200 years thereafter. Two digits, one above the other on successive line of the
table, were interchanged. Lardner hypothesized that this error most probably occurred
when two adjacent pieces of type came loose from the printing matrix at the same
time during the printing of the table and were replaced by the pressman in the wrong
positions. All subsequent copies of the table contained this error, clearly not the
result of an arithmetic mistake.

The First Modern Computer

The first modern computer was Charles Babbage's Analytical Engine, designed in
1834 to eliminate these sources of error and thus produce perfectly accurate tables of
any description whatsoever. This fascinating device, unfortunately never built in its
entirety, preceded by over 100 years the first operational computer, the Mark I,
designed in 1939-1944 by Howard Aiken at Harvard. Yet all but one of the fundamental principles and capabilities of the modern computer are found in the design of
Babbage's Analytical Engine. What is even more remarkable is that of all the
features of the Analytical Engine, only one was even partially predated by any other
computational device. In 1671, Leibnitz designed a calculating machine that could
add, subtract, multiply, and divide, one original model of which may be found, still
in working condition, in the Niedersachsischen Landesbibliothek, Hannover, Ger-
many. However, Babbage's machine was completely automatic, while Leibnitz's
machine required additional human assistance in division because the carry mechanism
worked incompletely in reverse.

What Babbage got for his trouble was a reputation as a crank, the admiration of
the Countess of Lovelace, no financial support from the British government for construction of the Analytical Engine, and later an appointment from his alma mater,
Cambridge University, to the Lucasian Professorship of Mathematics, the chair once
held by Sir Isaac Newton.

Babbage was unable to construct his "engine" not because of its design or concept, but because of the state of the art of machining in his day. He was trying to
construct a machine with thousands of gears at a time when even the gears of most
clocks had to be hand-fitted to mesh properly. He contributed greatly to the art of
machining, devised a system of mechanical notation for representing moving
machinery, and wrote a pioneer work in a field now called operations research. He
devised a method for dating archeological sites using sequences of growth rings of
trees that was later rediscovered and used to great effect in the archeology of the
American Southwest. He published an excellent table of logarithms, hand-computed
and edited, and is credited with many inventions, great and small. His life and works
make interesting reading.

Characteristics of a Computer

Computers, from Babbage's Analytical Engine to the most modern computer,
have a great deal in common. Improvements in technology have continually changed
their size, speed, and physical appearance, but the fundamental principles on which
they are based have changed little. In the remainder of this section, we describe eight
attributes of computers that enable them to perform the applications of this book.

1. Automatic operation

2. Arithmetic

3. Input

4. Output

5. Memory

6. Programmability

7. Decisions in the instruction sequence

8. Modifiable memory references

Most computers also have a ninth attribute, a stored program, that improves their operation. Devices having only some of these attributes may still be used to perform the applications given in earlier chapters of this book.

Automatic Operation

The most fundamental principle in computer design from Babbage's time to the present is *automatic operation,* that is, the ability of a computer to operate as much as possible without human direction or assistance. According to Babbage's own account, the idea of performing repetitive computations by machine first came to him in the following way. On one occasion, his longtime friend, the scientist John Hershel, brought in some calculations done for the Astronomical Society by a (human) computer. In the course of their tedious checking, Hershel and Babbage found a number of errors, and at one point Babbage said, "I wish to God these calculations were executed by steam." by which he meant "automatically". If Babbage's metaphor seems strange to modern ears, it is because now, more than a century and a half later, steam power is no longer the new and innovative source of energy for industry and commerce it was then. Had he lived to see the invention of the vacuum tube and the transistor, Babbage might well have wished the calculations were executed by electronics, as indeed they are today.

The principle of requiring as little human assistance and direction as possible can be found in every aspect of computer design. In most instances, not only does accuracy improve with the elimination of unnecessary human intervention, but speed increases as well.

Arithmetic

The heart of Babbage's Analytical Engine is an apparatus called the "mill", capable of performing the four basic arithmetic operations-- entirely without human intervention once the numbers have been entered. Other devices for addition and subtraction that were suitably automatic had been built earlier, notably a device built by Pascal (after whom the programming language used in this book was named) to aid his father in collecting taxes, and Babbage's earlier Difference Engine. However, only Leibnitz's machine could perform multiplication without human assistance in the process, and none previously had been invented to perform division automatically.

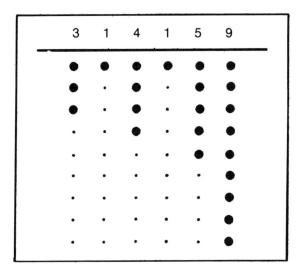

Figure 1.7.1   A number card for Babbage's Analytical Engine.

Modern computers still rely on the four arithmetic operations as the basis for numeric computing.

A working model of Babbage's mill, constructed from his drawings by the firm of R. W. Munro under the supervision of Babbage's son, Henry P. Babbage, works as well as Babbage had anticipated. With the main axis turning approximately once per second, the addition or subtraction of two 29-digit numbers takes approximately 1 second. Multiplication or division of 29-digit numbers requires up to 3 minutes, depending on the sum of the digits in the multiplier or quotient. The original mill is in the Science Museum, London.

Today, a battery-powered electronic hand calculator that performs these four basic arithmetic operations in fractions of a second can be purchased for less than the price of a book, but until recently a mechanical desk calculator with the same capabilities was at least as large as a typewriter, weighed twice as much, and cost several hundred dollars.

Another calculating aid superseded by the electronic hand calculator, the slide rule, is a portable arithmetic calculating device used extensively by scientists and engineers for nearly two centuries, until quite recently. It can do multiplication and division, but not addition or subtraction. Its operation is not very automatic, especially in the placing of the decimal point in the answer. Many slide rules also can calculate square and cube roots, trigonometric functions, logarithms, and powers. However, the answers are obtainable only to 3- or at most 4-digit accuracy as compared to the 8 to 10 digits provided by most electronic calculators. The slide rule is now obsolete. Its only advantage is that it has no batteries to run down.

Input

A computer or calculator must have some means of receiving information, the data of the problem, from its human operators. All operations supplying a computer with information are called *input*. Babbage's Analytical Engine had ''number cards'' for receiving information, an adaption of the pattern cards used by Jacquard in his automatic loom for weaving brocaded silk cloth. As shown in Figure 1.7.1, each column of a pasteboard number card had nine positions; no holes were punched for the digit 0, one hole for the digit 1, two holes for the digit 2, and so on. Thus each digit required a full column of the card for its representation in holes, and the number of digits encoded on a number card corresponded exactly to the number of columns on the card.

The modern computer punchcard is little changed from Babbage's number cards. Each column still represents 1 digit of input information in the most commonly used punchcard code, named for its inventor, Herman Hollerith. In the Hollerith code, each digit from 0 to 9 is encoded as a single punch in an appropriate position in the column. Alphabetic characters, requiring two holes per column, and other special characters such as punctuation marks, dollar signs, and arithmetic symbols requiring up to three holes punched per column are added to augment the simple numeric code. A standard Hollerith card contains 80 columns. Thus it is capable of encoding up to 80 digits, letters, or other characters of input information. Punchcards are still an important means of supplying information to a computer.

In contrast, when using most hand or desk calculators, input is accomplished by means of the entry keys. If two numbers are to be multiplied, each must first be entered into the machine by way of the entry keys before multiplication can begin.

The other major primary means of supplying input information to a computer is a typewriterlike computer terminal. Basically, these are electric typewriters equipped to encode electronically the letters and numbers that are typed and to transmit the encoded information directly to a computer. Like calculator keyboards, a computer terminal can supply input information only as fast as a person can type or press the keys. The use of computer terminals is also described in Section 1.4.

Much greater input speeds are possible using devices called magnetic tapes and magnetic disks. Many efficient operating systems accept input information entered from cards or terminals at whatever speeds these devices can manage and then recopy the input information onto magnetic disk or tape files for faster availability when the information is needed. As described in Section 1.4, many computer systems now support direct creation and editing of disk files from an interactive terminal, thereby providing great flexibility and convenience in the preparation of high speed input files. Similarly, calculated results that are to be reread at a later time as input data are written on magnetic disks and tapes, because of the higher reading and writing speeds of these devices. The use of magnetic disks and tapes is described in Chapter 6.

A wide variety of other computer input devices is less commonly used. Optical scanners can read carefully printed block letters and numerals at the present time and are sometimes used. Magnetic ink scanners are used to read account numbers on bank checks. Television cameras are used as input devices to analyze pictures transmitted from Mars and Jupiter, or to produce portraits on a printer. Thermocouples and other measuring instruments are used as input devices when a computer directly controls industrial processes. In fact, nearly any device capable of producing numeric or alphabetic information can probably be connected to a computer if there is good reason to do so.

Output

A computer must be able to communicate its answers back to the proposer of the problem. A common programming mistake often made by beginners in their first programs is the omission of a statement to print the answer. Since a computer does exactly as it is told, when such a program is run, the computer may compute the answer but never tells anyone what it is.

Any means of transcribing information held within a computer into a form external to the computer is called *output*. In computer terminology, one usually speaks of "writing" output, regardless of whether the result is printed, typed, displayed on a television screen, plotted, or encoded as tiny, inscrutable magnetic spots on a tape or disk.

Babbage was especially careful in designing the output for his Analytical Engine, because so many of the errors in the tables of his day were introduced after the computation. He provided for three types of ouput, a printing device capable of printing one or two copies of the results, a means for producing a stereotype mold from which printing plates for the tables could be made directly, and a mechanism for punching the numerical results of its computations into blank pasteboard cards for error-free rereading by the Analytical Engine. Great pains were taken in the design of these output features to ensure that no human error could intervene between the correct computation of the results and the final printing of the table.

At a modern computer installation, a principal form of output for human consumption is still the printed page. Direct computer typesetting has made a comeback in recent years with the complete computerization of the printing of several major newspapers. However, using modern photographic reproduction and printing processes, a computer text editing system that produces clean printed copy also can be used to provide error-free printing. The text of this book was produced this way.

Another form of computer output that dates back to Babbage is the punchcard. Babbage wanted his computer to be able to punch cards so that results, once calculated by the machine, could later be reentered into the machine without the consequent opportunities for error. This technique is still in use for bills sent through the mails. Customers are requested to return their prepunched billing card with their payment to minimize errors in crediting the payment. Similarly, most of the programs in this book were put in disk files, run, and then the program and output files were edited directly into the text to eliminate copying errors. Readable output that does not have to leave the computer center is usually written on magnetic tapes or disks.

In contrast, most desk calculators, especially those of the hand-held electronic variety, have only one form of output, visual display. A numerical answer is displayed in lights or other readable form, and the user must copy it onto paper if a more permanent record is desired. Persons who have had occasion to copy quantities of numbers, or even to copy notes from the blackboard in a technical course, know that this is a highly error-prone process. There is a practical limit to how many figures can be copied without making a mistake. Thus desk calculators become progressively less suitable as the volume of output information increases. A few desk calculators, and most adding machines, can provide a printed record of their calculations.

Many modern computers also have a provision for visual display. A television-type screen can be used to display several dozen lines of printing at the same time, or it can be used to produce other shapes for viewing. Used as an alternative to printing, this type of output can reduce substantially the amount of "hard" paper copy needed at a computer installation, an important conservation role. It is also important when computers are used to teach Chinese, Hebrew, Russian, or architectural drawing, all of which require shapes and characters not found in the usual English alphabet, and consequently not available on standard printers. Graphic displays, including diagrams, line drawings, and computer-generated cartoons can be produced in this way, and the result photographed for a more permanent record.

Other specialized output devices include plotters and electronic sound synthesizers for producing computer-generated or computer-processed music. For direct control of other machinery, output can be in the form of control impulses to that machinery, as is the case in airplane guidance systems, numerically controlled milling machines, and industrial process control.

Memory

In a computer or calculator, *memory* is the capacity to retain information and to recall that information later. Many simple hand calculators have no additional memory capacity beyond that required to retain the two numbers being added, subtracted, multiplied, or divided, and to produce the answer. Unless they are used in the very next step, intermediate results must be copied on paper and reentered later in the calculation. Thus the calculation

$(2 \times 3) / 4 = 6 / 4 = 1.5$

can be performed without recording the intermediate result 6, but the calculation of the expression

$(2 + 3) / (4 + 5)$

requires the recording of at.least one intermediate result on simple calculators. When intermediate results are retained by writing them on paper, it is jokingly called using the calculator's "paper memory", because it is a feature of the user and not of the calculator.

The most straightforward way to perform the intended calculation is to compute

$2 + 3 = 5$ which is recorded on paper
            or stored in the calculator
$4 + 5 = 9$ which is recorded on paper
            or stored in the calculator

and finally

$5 / 9 = 0.5555555556$ which is the answer

A standard trick, known to experienced users of desk calculators, is to compute and record the denominator first. Then the numerator does not have to be recorded, because it is used in the very next step when it is divided by the already calculated denominator to produce the answer. This trick also is used in efficient machine language programming of a computer.

In principle, the calculation

$(2.345678 + 3.456789) / (4.567890 + 5.678901)$

is similar to the previous example, because it involves the same sequence of arithmetic operations, but the penalty for having to copy and reenter a number and the probability of making a mistake are both increased by the larger number of digits in the intermediate results for the numerator and denominator. A large number of desk calculations can be made significantly easier by the addition of a small number of memory cells. For example, Table 1.7.1 shows the steps a person might follow to perform the harder calculations using a hand calculator that has an additional memory cell. The error-prone process of copying and reentering a number is replaced by use of the relatively error-free features called "store" (STO) and "recall" (RCL) on programmable calculators.

Table 1.7.1   A hand calculation that uses memory.

STEP	USER ACTION	DISPLAYED NUMBER
1	Enter 4.567890	4.56789
2	Add	
3	Enter 5.678901	5.678901
4	Equals	10.246791
5	Store displayed number	
6	Enter 2.345678	2.345678
7	Add	
8	Enter 3.456789	3.456789
9	Equals	5.802467
10	Divided by	
11	Recall stored number	10.246791
12	Equals	0.5662716259

Typical desk calculators include simple machines with no additional memory, more powerful calculators with 1 to 3 memory cells, calculators designed for statistical or financial use with 6 to 10 memory cells, and even calculators with several dozen memory cells, each capable of storing one piece of data with the same number of digits as handled by the rest of the calculator. For his Analytical Engine, Babbage wanted 1000 memory locations in what he called the "store", but this part of his computer was never built. Modern computers have thousands, and sometimes millions, of memory locations. With recent technological advances, the cost of manufacturing and operating large memories is dropping rapidly, and they are becoming more common.

The ease and speed with which a piece of information can be stored and recalled from a memory location may be different for different parts of a computer's memory. Many computers have a variety of different types and speeds of memory. At the slow end of the scale, the distinction between a computer storing a piece of information in a memory location, and a computer preserving the same piece of information by writing it on an output device such as a magnetic disk for eventual recall as input data, is almost imperceptible.

Programmability

Every hand or desk calculator has a set of basic operations which may be used individually or in meaningful combination to accomplish a desired computation. Typical basic operations include the four arithmetic operations-- addition, subtraction, multiplication, and division-- and the input operation of keying in a number. If a calculator has memory, the store and recall operations also are included. Many hand calculators also have more complex basic operations such as reciprocal (1/x), square root, logarithms, and trigonometric functions. With simpler hand calculators, although each basic operation is completed automatically, human direction is required to initiate each one.

Table 1.7.2   Raising 1.06 to the fifth power on a hand calculator.

STEP	USER ACTION	DISPLAYED NUMBER
1	Enter 1.06	1.06
2	Store displayed number	
3	Multiply by	
4	Recall store number	1.06
5	Equals	1.1236
6	Multiply by	
7	Recall stored number	1.06
8	Equals	1.191016
9	Multiply by	
10	Recall stored number	1.06
11	Equals	1.26247696
12	Multiply by	
13	Recall stored number	1.06
14	Equals	1.3382255776

A calculator is called *programmable* if meaningful sequences of basic operations can be selected in advance and then an entire preselected sequence of operations executed automatically. Usually, the entire preselected sequence of operations is stored in a special ''program memory'', so that the sequence, called a *program,* can be rerun easily, perhaps using different input data. Of course, input operations cannot be completely automatic if the only available form of input is a person using the entry keys.

For example, the operation of raising a number to the fifth power is useful in finding compound interest over a 5-year period, but it is not a basic operation on many hand calculators, just as there is no exponential operation in Pascal. On these machines, a number may be raised to the fifth power by multiplying it by itself five times. To raise 1.06 to the fifth power, the user might perform the sequence of basic operations shown in Table 1.7.2.

Table 1.7.3   A program for raising any number to the fifth power.

PROGRAM STEP	BASIC OPERATION
1	Halt for input (user must enter a number and resume program execution to complete this step)
2	Store displayed number
3	Multiply by
4	Recall stored number
5	Equals
6	Multiply by
7	Recall stored number
8	Equals
9	Multiply by
10	Recall stored number
11	Equals
12	Multiply by
13	Recall stored number
14	Equals
15	Halt so user can read the result

With the use of a nonprogrammable calculator, if it is also desired to raise 1.0625 to the fifth power, the same 14 steps shown in Table 1.7.2 must be repeated by the user, this time with the number 1.0625 entered in step 1. However, if the calculator is programmable, this sequence of basic operations can be made into a program by replacing the specific first step, ''Enter 1.06'', with a more general input request to enter any number. A program such as that in Table 1.7.3 can be stored in the program memory of a programmable hand calculator and easily run to raise any desired number to the fifth power.

Once this program has been entered and stored in the calculator's program memory, both of the desired calculations, raising 1.06 and 1.0625 to the fifth power, can be obtained as shown in Table 1.7.4.

As might be inferred from the title of this book, the computers that we talk about are programmable. The set of basic operations available on a computer is called that computer's *machine language*. A large number of the machine language instructions for most computers are variants of the basic arithmetic operations, the input and output operations, and the store and recall operations. When using computers that are sufficiently powerful to support a translator (compiler), one does not have to write programs in machine language.

Table 1.7.4   Using a program twice on a programmable hand calculator.

STEP	USER ACTION	DISPLAYED NUMBER
1	Start program	
2	Enter 1.06 and resume execution	1.06
		1.06
		1.1236
		1.06
		1.191016
		1.06
		1.26247696
		1.06
		1.3382255776
3	Start program	
4	Enter 1.0625 and resume execution	1.0625
		1.0625
		1.12890625
		1.0625
		1.199462891
		1.0625
		1.274429321
		1.0625
		1.354081154

Both the modern computer and Babbage's Analytical Engine are designed to allow the user to specify that nearly any sequence of basic operations whatsoever be performed. *Of course, this transfers the responsibility for ensuring that the sequence of computational steps produces a meaningful result from the designer of the machine to the designer of the program, the programmer.* This is what computer programming is all about: how to design sequences of computational steps so as to produce meaningful and useful results.

Probably the first computer programmer, aside from Babbage himself, was Ada Augusta, Countess of Lovelace, Babbage's longtime supporter and a knowledgeable mathematician in her own right. The new programming language ADA, developed by the Department of Defense, was named after her. She translated into English the first published description of the Analytical Engine, adding a set of translator's notes two and one-half times as long as the original article, in which she gave several computer programs for the Analytical Engine. These programs are equivalent to machine language programs for a modern computer or programmable hand calculator.

Decisions in the Instruction Sequence

Two important programming techniques, loops and alternative computational steps, stem from the ability of a computer to decide at preselected times during the execution of a program which instruction is to be performed next. It is a rare and straightforward computer program that does not use one or the other of these techniques.

A *loop* is a sequence of program steps that may be repeated more than once during a single running of a program. For example, if the same computations are to be performed on the data for each student in a class or each worker in a factory, it is a dreadfully inefficient use of both the programmer's time and the computer's memory to write the computational steps out in full as many times as they are needed. A loop is written instead. (See Section 1.3 and Chapter 2.)

The decision step in a loop can almost always be based on the answer to the question, Are we done? or Have the computational steps in the loop been executed a sufficient number of times? or a more specific inquiry of the same sort. If the computational steps in the loop have not been executed a sufficient number of times, the next thing the computer should do is to repeat them. If they have been executed the correct number of times, the computer should not repeat, but go on to the next instruction after the loop, perhaps to compute an average or to print summary totals, or even to stop if nothing else needs to be done by the program. Loops are the subject of Chapter 2 and are used extensively thereafter.

Alternative computational procedures use the same decision capability of a computer, but for a different purpose. Here the choice is not whether to repeat or not to repeat, but which computational procedure is to be performed next. It allows overtime pay to be calculated by a different formula than nonovertime pay, deposits to be handled differently from withdrawals and, in general, more logically complex procedures to be programmed.

Both Babbage's Analytical Engine and the modern computer or desk calculator can modify their sequence of operations without human intervention, based on the values of computed results or input data. The conditions under which this sequence modification is to take place must be specified in advance in the program, but it does not have to be known in advance which piece of input data or computed value will satisfy the conditions and thus cause an alternative sequence of steps to be performed.

On the other hand, an automatic device with a fixed sequence of operations is very limited. A kitchen clock is automatic and performs its fixed sequence of motions as long as power is supplied. An alarm clock, when certain of its wheels and hands are in the correct relative positions, can modify its usual sequence of motions and actions to include ringing a bell, sounding a buzzer, or turning on a radio. An alarm clock would be quite valueless if the sequence modification that sounds the alarm did not happen automatically but instead required the user to get up beforehand to turn the alarm on.

Table 1.7.5   Initializing 100 memory locations using a loop and index register.

STEP	INSTRUCTION
1	Retrieve the stored constant from memory
2	Put the number 1 in the index register
3	Add the number in the index register to 2000 to compute a memory location and then store the constant in the memory location just computed
4	Add 1 to the number in the index register
5	If the number in the index register does not exceed 100, then repeat starting at step 3; otherwise, continue with the rest of the program

---

Modifiable Memory References

The ability of the modern computer to modify the identities of the memory locations used by a program during the execution of that program has its value somewhat more deeply rooted in computational techniques than previously discussed capabilities, and thus its importance is correspondingly less evident to the novice at computing. More advanced features, the arrays in Chapter 3 and the functions and procedures with explicit arguments in Chapter 4, rely heavily on this ability. Nevertheless, the ability itself is not difficult to describe.

Suppose one wants to store the same constant in 100 consecutive memory locations, perhaps the constant 0 for numeric processing or the blank character for alphabetic processing. This could be done in 100 steps. However, when a computer has a hardware feature called an *index register*, the same procedure may be programmed, as shown in Table 1.7.5, in only five machine language steps as a loop.

The memory address in which the constant is stored whenever step 3 is executed consists of two parts. The address 2000 is the *base address* of the 100 consecutive memory location, and the number in the index register is a *relative address* that tells which one of the 100 memory locations is desired. The key principle that makes this program work is that it is possible to change the number in the index register using arithmetic operations, thereby changing the memory location specified in the "store" instruction in step 3. In Chapter 3, where this principle is used extensively in array processing, the name of the array or list corresponds to the base address in the example in Table 1.7.5, and the number in the index register corresponds to the subscript or index.

The other major use of modifiable memory address references, treated in Chapter 4, is to write general-purpose procedures to be used on several different variables. For example, in scientific problems, it is often necessary to compute a standard mathematical function such as the sine or the logarithm of many of the variables in a problem. In business problems, compound interest often has to computed for different principals, interest rate, and numbers of interest periods. These programs, called *functions* and *procedures with explicit arguments* are written in such as way that the locations of the variables on which they operate can be modified during a run to allow them to work on different variables each time their use is called for.

Modifiability of memory address references is the one important feature of the modern computer not possessed by Babbage's Analytic Engine. In Babbage's machine, although it is possible to reuse a sequence of operations to manipulate numbers stored in different memory locations, the identities of the memory locations themselves must be written out in full. In some computers, modification of memory address references is accomplished by machine language techniques called "indirect addressing", "instruction modification", and "hardware stacks", but a programmer using a higher-level language such as Pascal does not need to know how subscripts or procedures are translated into machine language. In fact, the main reason for having higher-level languages is to simplify programming by allowing the programmer to write in a language closer to the natural terminology of the problem and further from the peculiarities of machine language. Like Babbage's Analytical Engine, most programmable hand or desk calculators do not have memory address modification as a feature, but is a less serious loss because of their limited number of memory cells.

Stored Program

In order to run its programs rapidly and efficiently, a programmable calculator or computer must be able to locate and read its next instruction about as fast as a typical instruction is executed. Usually this means that a program, or as much of one as will fit, is stored in memory cells of the same general accessibility and speed as those used to store data. In most programmable calculators, the program memory is distinct from the data memory, but there are advantages in allowing the same memory cells to be used for either data or program steps, as is done in many computers. First, the computer's design is simplified because certain parts of the circuitry do not have to be duplicated for separate program and data memories. Second, short programs with a great deal of data and long programs with comparatively little data both can be run on the same computer without wasting valuable memory capacity. Third, there are additional opportunities for program modification, because the individual program steps, suitably encoded for storage in the same cells as data, can themselves be treated as data and modified arithmetically as though they were data. On some older computers without index registers, this was the only way that programs involving arrays and subscripts could be written in machine language. However, even the simplest microcomputers these days have features such as a stack or index registers, making it unneccessary to resort to this very undesirable technique.

Exercises

In Exercises 1 to 24, discuss which of the eight attributes of a computer described in this section are possessed by the device in question.

  1. A clock radio.
  2. A digital clock radio.
  3. A wristwatch.
  4. A digital wristwatch.

5. A bowl of Jello.

6. A desk calculator or hand calculator. Use the one you are most familiar with, if any.

7. A programmable hand calculator.

8. Babbage's Analytical Engine.

9. Babbage's earlier Difference Engine. A description can be found in Morrison and Morrison *Charles Babbage and his Calculating Engines*, Dover, N.Y. 1961.

10. A computer you have seen, or are using in conjunction with this book.

11. A player piano or music box.

12. An air conditioner.

13. A tape recorder.

14. A multichanger record player, that is, one that accepts more than one record at a time.

15. A slide projector. Answers may vary depending on the make and model.

16. A slide projector run by a tape recorder with synchronized sound.

17. A windup toy. Describe the toy you are analyzing.

18. The guidance system of a guided missile.

19. The automatic speed control mechanism in an automobile ("cruise control").

20. A Jacquard loom for weaving brocades.

21. An automatic exposure control camera or electronic flash unit.

22. A self-timing oven that can be set to turn itself on at any hour, cook for any number of hours, and turn itself off. Note: It does not open the oven door at the conclusion of the cooking cycle and remove the food, so the food continues to cook, or overcook, as the case may be, for some time after the oven turns itself off.

23. A telephone.

24. A central telephone switching office.

25. Write down an arithmetic calculation that requires two memory cells when performed on a hand or desk calculator.

26. Write down an arithmetic calculation that requires two intermediate results to be recorded for later use, but which can be performed on a desk calculator with only one memory cell without using pencil and paper. Hint: The two intermediate results need not be remembered simultaneously.

1.8   Chapter Review

The last section of each chapter in this book reviews some of the contents of the chapter. Typically, there is a recapitulation of programming concepts, of Pascal language features, and of general methods discussed in the chapter. Although some important topics are reviewed in detail, no attempt is made to include all the topics presented in the chapter or to review the topics in the order in which they appeared. The aim of a chapter review is an overview of the chapter.

What a Computer Can Do

Computers are machines for processing information. Although special input and output devices can be attached to a computer to enable it to monitor and control physical processes and machinery directly, the most important characteristic of a computer is the kind of processing of information that goes on inside a computer. Chapter 1 is an introduction to what a computer is, what it can do, and how one directs it to process information.

The Language Pascal

One thing a computer cannot do is to read minds. When a set of directions called a *computer program* is given to a computer to tell it what to do, the directions must be clear and unambiguous. Pascal is a language in which precise instructions can be given to a computer. Sample executions are shown for almost every program in this chapter and elsewhere in this book, because the ultimate test of correctness of a computer program is correct computer execution of that program.

Since Pascal emphasizes clarity of expression and program structure, a person who learns to read and write Pascal programs will write better programs in other programming languages than a person who concentrates on less important aspects of programming. Using a carefully written and documented Pascal program, a pregrammer can translate the program into any other suitable computer programming language.

Arithmetic Calculations

The bread and butter of computer information processing is simple arithmetic calculations. Most modern computers can do more arithmetic in a second that a person can do in a lifetime, and the computer is unlikely to make even a single mistake in the process. Many useful computer programs require only input, simple arithmetic calculations, and output. In Pascal, the commands read, readln, write, and writeln are used for input and output. An arithmetic assignment statement contains an arithmetic expression whose value is to be calculated and assigned to the variable on the left of the assignment operator (:=). The program distancetravelled illustrates how these kinds of statements are used in a computer program.

```
program distancetravelled (input, output);

  var
    speedinmph, timeinhours, distance : real;

  begin
  read (speedinmph);
  writeln ('Input data  speedinmph: ', speedinmph);
  read (timeinhours);
  writeln ('Input data  timeinhours: ', timeinhours);
  distance := speedinmph * timeinhours;
  writeln ('Distance traveled = ', distance, ' miles');
  end.
```

```
run distancetravelled

Input data   speedinmph:    5.50000000000000e+01
Input data   timeinhours:   1.50000000000000e+00
Distance traveled =    8.25000000000000e+01 miles


run distancetravelled

Input data   speedinmph:    4.26970000000000e+13
Input data   timeinhours:   7.20000000000000e+00
Distance traveled =    3.07418400000000e+14 miles
```

Below the program listing there appear two computer printouts from the sample executions of the program. The first read statement of the program distancetravelled tells a computer to obtain as input a value for the variable speedinmph (speed in miles per hour). It is a good practice to echo the input data with writeln statements unless the desired appearance of the output strictly prohibits it, perhaps when printing on business forms. The second read statement directs the computer to obtain as input a value for the variable timeinhours. Again, the value supplied as input is echoed. The assignment statement

```
distance := speedinmph * timeinhours
```

tells the computer that the variable distance is to be assigned as its value the computed product of the values of the variables speedinmph and timeinhours. The writeln statement tells the computer to print the character string

```
'Distance traveled = '
```

followed by the value of the variable distance, which is followed on the same line by the character string

```
'miles'
```

The printing of an alphabetic message to identify the calculated answer makes interpreting the printed answer easier. This becomes increasingly important as the number of printed answers increases.

The arithmetic operations available in Pascal are: addition ($+$), subtraction ($-$), multiplication ($*$), and division ($/$), and two other integer operators, div and mod, to be discussed in Section 2.6. Pascal has no exponentiation operator. Parentheses may be used to construct more complex arithmetic expressions.

Naming Variables and Programs

A computer does not understand English, but a suitable choice of names for variables often results in a program a person can understand easily, even a person who does not know programming. In Pascal, there are three rules governing the choice of names, including names of variables, names of programs, and names of things to be discussed later.

1. The first character of any name must be a letter.

2. The remaining characters of any name may be any mixture of letters and digits.

3. The name must not be a keyword. See Appendix A for a list of reserved words.

These rules are more or less standard in most programming languages, although some allow underscore characters or hyphens to make longer names more readable.

Data Types

In Pascal, each variable used in a program must be declared to have a data type which describes what kind of data that variable will hold during execution of the program. The types we have described so far are integer, real, and character, and arrays of integers, reals, and characters.

For-Loops

Most computational processes involve some degree of repetition of the same or similar sequences of processing steps. A *loop* is part of a program that is executed over and over again. A for-statement is one of the kinds of loops in Pascal, as illustrated in the program avgofscores, whose listing is reproduced from Section 1.3 with a new sample execution.

```
program avgofscores (input, output);

  var
    enrollment, count : integer;
    sum, nextscore : real;

  begin
  read (enrollment);
  writeln ('Input data  enrollment: ', enrollment :1);
  sum := 0;
  for count := 1 to enrollment do
    begin
    read (nextscore);
    writeln ('Input data  nextscore: ', nextscore :7:2);
    sum := sum + nextscore;
    end; { for-loop }
  writeln;
  writeln ('Average test score = ', sum / enrollment :1:2);
  end.
```

```
run avgofscores

Input data  enrollment: 2
Input data  nextscore:   91.00
Input data  nextscore:   85.00

Average test score =  88.00
```

Since the supplied value of the variable enrollment is 2 in the sample run, the sequence of three indented statements between the keywords "begin" and "end" that are part of the for-statement is executed twice before the computer moves on to the writeln statement immediately following the for-statement. The indentation is strictly for improving readability. What actually indicated the end of the loop to the computer is the keyword "end" that ends the compound statement within the for-statement.

Before execution of the loop, the assignment statement

```
sum  : = 0
```

initializes the value of the variable sum to zero. On each iteration of the body of the loop, the value of the variable sum is increased by whatever is supplied as the input value for the variable nextscore. Whereas the value of the variable nextscore is changed on successive iterations by the reading of new input values, the value of the variable sum is changed by computation, that is, by adding the value of nextscore to it.

If-Statements

The for-statement provides one way of building complex statements out of simpler ones. Another such statement is the if-statement, employed, for instance, in the program payroll2.

```
program payroll2 (input, output);

  const
    regularhours = 40;
    otfactor = 1.5;

  var
    hourlyrate, hoursworked,
        regularpay, otworked,
        otpay, grosspay : real;

  begin
  { read and echo the input data }
  read (hourlyrate, hoursworked);
  writeln ('Input data  hourlyrate: ', hourlyrate :1:2);
  writeln ('                hoursworked: ', hoursworked :1:2);
  if hoursworked > regularhours then
    { compute grosspay by the overtime formula }
    begin
    regularpay := hourlyrate * regularhours;
    otworked := hoursworked - regularhours;
    otpay := otfactor * hourlyrate * otworked;
    grosspay := regularpay + otpay;
    end
  else
    { compute grosspay by the regular formula }
    grosspay := hourlyrate * hoursworked;
  writeln ('Gross pay = $', grosspay :1:2);
  end.
```

There are two possibilities for execution of the if-statement in the program payroll2. If the number of hours an employee works is greater than 40, then the computer executes the four assignment statements in the compound statement following the keyword "then". Otherwise, the computer executes the single assignment statement following the keyword "else". As with for-statements, the indentation of statements is for the sake of appearance and readability. The computer is guided by the keywords "if", "then", "else", "begin", and "end".

Compound Statements

A compound statement consists of the keywords "begin" and "end" with an arbitrary number of statements in between. The statements in between must be separated by semicolons, and may, in turn, be compound statements. This allows arbitrarily complex for-loops, then-clauses, and else-clauses.

Refinement of Programs

The original form in which the program payroll2 is presented in Section 1.5 is displayed again also. Although it clearly describes to a person how to do the intended job, it is insufficiently refined for computer execution, because three lines are not yet written in the language Pascal.

```
program payroll2 (input, output);

  const
    regularhours = 40;
    otfactor = 1.5;

  var
    hourlyrate, hoursworked,
    grosspay : real;

  begin
  read and echo the input data
  if hoursworked > regularhours then
    compute grosspay by the overtime formula
  else
    compute grosspay by the regular formula;
  writeln ('Gross pay = $', grosspay :1:2);
  end.
```

Beyond its use in planning the executable Pascal program the unrefined program serves to explain the refined program. the informal English statement

```
compute grosspay by the overtime formula
```

tells immediately the purpose of the compound statement that replaces it in the refined program. Indeed, one should insert it as a comment in the refined program, and similarly for the informal English statement for the else-clause. The result of inserting these comments is the program payroll2 given above. In general, the refinement process might take several steps, each supplying more detail than its predecessor.

Detection of Errors

In spite of a programmer's best intentions, a program does not always run as it is intended. Thus a programmer must be adept not only at writing programs but also at systematically detecting and correcting errors. Ideally, a programmer tests every possibility for the flow of control during execution, usual and unusual cases alike, which may require several sets of carefully selected data. The programmer should know in advance what the outcome of a test should be and should plan the tests to check each branch of every if-statement.

If the execution printouts suggest the existence of an error, debugging begins with carefully rereading the program. If this does not reveal the error, then a programmer might hand simulate the execution of any portion of the program likely to contain the error, in order to uncover it. If it is unclear from the execution printout which branch of an if-statement was executed, then temporarily inserting write statements both before the if-test, to display the expressions to be compared, and in each branch of the if-statement, to verify the outcome of the if-test, may clear up the matter on the next run.

Syntax Charts

One of the favorable aspects of Pascal is that its rules can be described concisely by syntax charts. For instance, the syntax chart in Figure 1.8.1 shows exactly what is meant by a *name* in Pascal.

This kind of syntax chart used in this book is called "railroad normal form" or "railroad chart" because each path that a railroad train could take from the start to the finish of the chart, always going in the direction of the arrow, generates a syntactically correct Pascal name. The shortest path through the syntax chart shows that an name can be a single letter such as x. Slightly longer paths show that two letters such as pi or a letter followed by a digit such as j2 are correctly formed names that may be used for constants or variables.

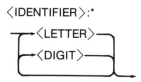

*An identifier must not be a reserved word.

Figure 1.8.1   Identifier (name) syntax chart.

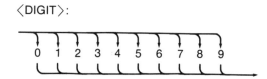

Figure 1.8.2   Digit syntax chart.

Terms in angle brackets (<>) in a syntax chart indicate items that are defined by other syntax charts. For example, the item <digit> that appears in the syntax chart for a Pascal name is defined by the syntax chart in Figure 1.8.2. Characters not in angle brackets, such as the ten digits 0 to 9 in alternative paths through the digit chart, must appear exactly as written in the syntactic item defined by the chart. A complete set of syntax charts for Pascal is given in Appendix C.

Programmer-Defined Procedures

Extensive use of programmer-defined procedures is a natural outgrowth of the modern method of *top-down program design*. Programs are planned at a high level in terms of large conceptual units or subtasks. Often these subtasks are complex enough that their details would obscure the overall organization of the main program. To maintain clarity of the main program, the subtasks are refined to single-line *procedure calls to programmer-defined procedures* instead of substituting all the details into the main program. To be sure, the task of describing the details does not go away. The details appear in *procedure declarations* that precede the main program. If the details of a programmer-defined procedure are themselves naturally expressed in terms of large conceptual units, a programmer-defined procedure may call still lower-level programmer-defined procedures to do the dirty work. Programmer-defined procedures allow a programmer to plan a program in terms of large conceptual units and still write executable Pascal programs showing this organization clearly.

2

LOOPS

It is hard to overestimate the importance of loops in computer programming. To be sure, most programs have individual blocks and subsections that are not themselves loops, and initialization sections that are not even contained in any larger loop, but you will hardly ever see a program written entirely without a loop. Without loops, each calculation, each manipulation, and each input or output operation performed by the computer must have a separate instruction. Without loops, even the largest computers could not store enough instructions to keep busy for even a minute.

The key to the efficient use of computers is simply to use at least some of the instructions in a program more than once, perhaps a large number of times. This invariably means a loop. The simplest loop structure, the for-loop, was introduced in Chapter 1 to indicate as early as possible the importance of repetition of instructions. The for-loop is not the most flexible loop structure, but it is easily explained, and it is just right for some purposes. In this chapter, we introduce other Pascal loop structures and loops with exits, and show how to use them to write efficient programs.

2.1   Top-Down Program Design

The descriptive method used in most of Chapter 1 is reversed in this section. Instead of starting with a program and explaining what it does and which problem it solves, this section starts with a problem and works toward producing a computer program to solve it. This is, of course, the usual situation when you attempt to solve a problem with the aid of a computer.

You have to be a little patient, because this section treats a somewhat larger problem than those solved by the programs in Chapter 1. It will take us this entire section to write and systematically refine the complete program, and the next section to polish it to a more satisfactory form. Also, because this section is your first introduction to *writing* a loop, the steps are explained in far greater detail than would be needed to describe the solution of this problem to a more experienced programmer. The problem concerns gradepoint averages for college students.

The Problem: Preparation of Grade Reports

South Mountain College is a liberal arts school with 1037 students presently enrolled. Although some administrative tasks are done by the computer, until recently each student's grade report was prepared by hand and typed. Gradepoint averages were computed on hand calculators and typed into the report as well. In the fall of

Name: Gordon Uchimata	Class: 1986	
Semester: Fall, 1983	GPA: 3.06	
Course	*Credits*	*Grade*
Computer Science 105	3	B
Japanese Sports 321	2	A
Parapsychology 294	4	A
Turkish Literature 308	5	C
Western Civilization 220	4	B

Figure 2.1.1   A grade report for a student at South Mountain College.

last year as a senior project, newly declared computer science major Rena Little prepared an analysis of the system then in effect and the extent to which it might be automated. We follow her analysis.

She observed that the registrar maintains a file of index cards prepared during registration, one for each student, with the student's roster of courses written on the card. This roster includes the name of each course and the number of credits that each course is worth. In most courses, the number of credits equals the number of hours per week that a course meets.

At the end of a semester, the instructors send copies of the grades to the registrar, and the registrar's assistants transfer the grades to these index cards. The grade reports are prepared from these index cards. For instance, Figure 2.1.1 shows a report for a student named Gordon Uchimata.

To calculate a gradepoint average (abbreviated GPA) at South Mountain College, the first step is to convert letter grades A, B, C, D, and F to the respective numerical values 4, 3, 2, 1, and 0, which are called number grades. The product of the number grade for a course and the number of credits is the student's gradepoint score in the course. For example, Gordon Uchimata has a gradepoint score of 3 x 3 = 9 in Computer Science 105 and a score of 2 x 4 = 8 in Japanese Sports 321. Overall, he earned a total gradepoint score of

$$3 \times 3 \ + \ 2 \times 4 \ + \ 4 \times 4 \ + \ 5 \times 2 \ + \ 4 \times 3 \ = \ 55$$

in the fall semester of 1983.

The gradepoint average is calculated by dividing the total gradepoint score by the total number of credits taken. Since Uchimata took

$$3 + 2 + 4 + 5 + 4 \ = \ 18$$

credits and earned 55 gradepoints, his GPA is

$$55 \ / \ 18 \ = \ 3.055555...$$

The gradepoint average is rounded to two decimal places and recorded on the grade report. As a first step toward automation, Rena Little suggested that the GPA calculation be done on a computer. We follow her suggestion and describe how a program to calculate gradepoint averages might be written.

How to Begin Writing a Program

We are faced with the task of constructing a program complex enough so that it might not be obvious where to begin programming. The methodology followed in this book, although almost all the programs in Chapter 1 were too simple in structure to need it, is called *successive refinement,* or *top-down programming.* Basically, this means to begin to write a program in a form understandable to humans, almost as though you were writing for a much smarter computer than you actually have available, a mythical computer that understands and can execute many more operations and processes than can reasonably be expected of a computer. Then you go back over the program, describing in more detail those processes that the available computer cannot understand. If some of the steps happen to be in a computer-executable language, so much the better. If not, the refinement process continues until they are. Since the ultimate objective is to write a program completely in some computer-executable language, called the *target language,* it is inevitable and desirable to chose phrases, even in parts of the program description that are not yet computer-executable, that resemble keywords and phrases of the target language, Pascal. This makes the task of converting preliminary descriptions into executable statements a little easier.

The first step is to write the main procedures of a program for solving the problem in a form understandable to humans, and even then perhaps only to humans familiar with gradepoint averaging procedures. For example, the following version of the program gradeptavg might be a suitable beginning.

```
program gradeptavg (input, output); { initial version }
{ calculates gradepoint average for one student }
  begin
  read the input data;
  convert letter grades to number grades;
  calculate the gradepoint average (gpa);
  print the output;
  end.
```

Although this initial version of the program might appear vague or even ambiguous because of its lack of detail, it is a small but definite step in the right direction. If we were writing this program for a computer smart enough to read and understand the preceding pages of this section, it would know that the input data consists of the information found on the registrar's index cards. It would know how to convert letter grades to number grades and to calculate a gradepoint average. And it would know what information belongs in the output and how to print it. Although it is easy to find humans who understand these instructions (for example, the clerical staff in the registrar's office), we do not expect to find a computer that will understand them without further elaboration of the details. We apply the terminology *refinement of a program* to the process of making the program's meaning more explicit by spelling out some of the steps in greater detail.

A First Refinement: Input and Output

In the absence of a supersmart computer that can execute the given initial version of the program gradeptavg, we *refine* the program by replacing one or more of its statements by other statements describing the same part of the procedure in greater detail.

Each refinement of a program is a little bit further along the way toward converting the program into a specified computer programming language. In this book, the target language is Pascal, so that, whenever possible, we use Pascal statements and constructions to refine program steps that are not yet computer-executable.

A good place to start refining a program is with the input and output statements. Such a refinement will make explicit exactly what answers we want the program to print and what input data must be supplied to the computer so that it has enough information to calculate these answers. In the process, we also will make explicit the names and types of some of the variables that appear in the input and output sections of the program.

In the output section, the most important thing we want printed is the gradepoint average for the student whose input data has been read. Since it is to be printed to two decimal places, a suitable choice in Pascal is a variable of type real, which can be rounded for printing with a decimals indicator in the write statement. We choose the abbreviated name gpa for this variable. It also is desirable to identify the gradepoint average output with the name of the student who earned it. A character string variable (an array of characters) is the natural Pascal type for a name. With these choices, the statement

```
print the output
```

of the initial version of the program may be refined to the following.

```
var
   gpa : real;
   name : packed array [1..namelength] of char;

{ print the output }
writeln (name);
writeln ('  Gradepoint average = ',  gpa :1:2);
```

Notice that the unrefined statement is retained as a comment describing the refined statement. As details begin to pile up, these comments will serve as a guide through the program, both for the original programmer and for anyone else reading it. For review purposes, we mention that a character string variable may be printed as a whole, but it is read one character at a time using a for-loop. The columns and decimals indicators (:1:2) for printing the value of gpa specify that the printed output will occupy at least one column and be rounded to two decimal places.

The input data necessary to prepare this output consists of the student's name, letter grades, and the number of credits associated with each letter grade. The names of the courses, the course numbers, and the instructors' names are irrelevant to the task of computing the gradepoint average. They could be read in and then ignored if it were convenient to prepare an input file with some of this information, and, indeed, in a fully automated system, there may be prepunched cards or magnetic disk records containing some of this extra information along with the information essential to the task at hand. Since calculation of gradepoint averages was the first task automated, and we will be preparing the input file specially for this program, we include only the essential information in the input file. A natural organization for the input data, illustrated with the grade data for Mr. Uchimata is as follows.

```
Gordon Uchimata
B 3
A 2
A 4
C 5
B 4
```

Temporarily ignoring the question of whether this file organization will increase the difficulty of writing the program, we chose a form that is natural to the user, and therefore easy to use and easy to check for errors in the input data. In contrast, the file organization

```
Gordon Uchimata
BAACB 3 2 4 5 4
```

is less congenial to the user, although equally good to the programmer, and will probably cause many more mistakes in preparing the input data.

The variables used in the input section are the student's name, a list of letter grades, and list of number of credits for the courses taken. Because arrays in Pascal are declared to have a fixed number of entries, and the number of courses taken by a student in a semester varies from student to student and from semester to semester, an additional integer variable nrcourses (number of courses) is introduced to hold the actual number of courses taken. With the addition of two ''index'' variables that point to positions in the arrays, the input statement

```
read the input data
```

may be refined as follows.

```
const
  maxcourses = 8;
  namelength = 30;

var
  name : packed array [1..namelength] of char;
  lettergrade : array [1..maxcourses] of char;
  credit : array [1..maxcourses] of integer;
  nrcourses, i, course : integer;

{ read the input data }
for i := 1 to namelength do
  read (name [i]);
readln;
writeln (name); { echo }
readln (nrcourses);
writeln (nrcourses :1, ' courses taken'); { echo }
writeln ('Input data:   grade  credit');
for course := 1 to nrcourses do
  begin
  readln (lettergrade [course], credit [course]);
  writeln (lettergrade [course] :17, credit [course] :8);
  end;
```

Two loops show up in this refinement. First, there is a simple for-loop to read the letters of the character string name, one at a time. The built-in procedure read is used in this loop so that successive characters will be taken from the same line of input. Second, there is a slightly more complicated for-loop to read the letter grades and credits, one pair at a time. On the first pass through this for-loop, the value of the variable course is 1, so values for lettergrade [1] and credit [1] are read. On the second pass, course is 2, so that values for lettergrade [2] and credit [2] are read, and so on. The procedure readln is used in this loop because each pair read is on a separate line in the input file.

Following good programming practice, *we echo all input data as it is read*. As a result, both the input and the output sections print the student's name. One of these could be dispensed with if we were so inclined. It doesn't matter much. The exact appearance of the output becomes important only when (see Exercise 4) the task is enlarged to printing the entire grade report for mailing to the student. Then, the output must look exactly like the report in Figure 2.1.1 unless someone can convince the registrar that a different format is desirable.

By inserting these details in the initial version of the program gradeptavg, we obtain the first refinement of the program.

```
program gradeptavg (input, output);
{ first refinement }

  const
    maxcourses = 8;
    namelength = 30;

  var
    gpa : real;
    name : packed array [1..namelength] of char;
    lettergrade : array [1..maxcourses] of char;
    credit : array [1..maxcourses] of integer;
    nrcourses, i, course : integer;

  begin
  { read the input data }
  for i := 1 to namelength do
    read (name [i]);
  readln;
  writeln (name); { echo }
  readln (nrcourses);
  writeln (nrcourses :1, ' courses taken'); { echo }
  writeln ('Input data:   grade  credit');
  for course := 1 to nrcourses do
    begin
    readln (lettergrade [course], credit [course]);
    writeln (lettergrade [course] :17, credit [course] :8);
    end;
  convert letter grades to number grades;
  calculate gradepoint average;
  { print the output }
  writeln (name);
  writeln ('  Gradepoint average = ', gpa :1:2);
  end.
```

Some final comments are in order before going on to the next refinement. First, we arbitrarily guessed that 8 was the maximum number of courses a student would take. We should ask the registrar to be on the safe side, and then perhaps add 1 or 2 because there are always exceptions. More seriously, we have made two programming choices that affect the preparation of the input data. The for-loop that reads the student's name demands at least 30 characters on the first line of input. Sufficient blanks must be added to any input name to make it at least 30 characters long. Additional blanks beyond 30 characters will be skipped by the readln statement. This is a considerable inconvenience to the preparer of input data that can can only be removed when we introduce while-loops in Section 2.3, so we will have to live with it for the present. Second, an additional piece of information, the number of courses taken, is now required in the input file. The preparer of the input data must count the number of courses and type this number in the input file between the student's name and the first letter grade. Again, there is a way to avoid this inconvenience, but it also uses a while-loop.

A Second Refinement: Converting Letter Grades to Number Grades

When the first refinement of a program is still not a program in the target language, the refinement process continues. In the current example, two statements remain to be refined; we tackle the first of these, converting letter grades to number grades.

The proper top-down approach to refining this statement is this: Whatever it is the computer does to convert one letter grade to a number grade must be done nrcourses times, once for each course taken. This insight produces the following refinement.

```
{ convert letter grades to number grades }
for course := 1 to nrcourses do
   convert the lettergrade for that course to a number grade
```

This is certainly a small step, but again in the right direction. It leaves us still with the major problem of how to convert one letter grade to a number grade. We wait until that step has been refined further before calling the result a second refinement of the program gradeptavg. There is no compelling criterion for determining when a refinement deserves a new number. If relatively little has changed, we wait; if much has changed, then we provide a new number. Many expert programmers would acknowledge fewer explicit stages of the refinement process than we show here for the instruction of a beginner. Indeed, with practice, a programmer can combine many of the small stages of refinement that we describe in such loving detail, without noticing the omission. Some experienced programmers even can write the entire final program from top to bottom in one pass. Beginners tend to improve most rapidly if they discipline themselves to go slowly at first.

The letter grade conversion problem resembles the graduated income tax problem in Section 1.5 in the sense that there are a number of alternative cases, each requiring a slightly different computation or treatment. In the letter grade conversion problem, the alternative cases correspond to the possible letter grades at South Mountain College, A, B, C, D, and F. No simple formula predicts the numeric equivalent of each of them. Even attempting a formula is bound to come to naught when such grades as P (pass), I (incomplete), and W (withdrawn) are introduced in the exercises. The solution applied in the income tax problem, a series of if-statements, works here as well, producing the following refinement.

```
{ convert letter grades to number grades }
for course := 1 to nrcourses do
  begin
  if lettergrade [course] = 'A' then
      numbergrade [course] := 4;
  if lettergrade [course] = 'B' then
      numbergrade [course] := 3;
  if lettergrade [course] = 'C' then
      numbergrade [course] := 2;
  if lettergrade [course] = 'D' then
      numbergrade [course] := 1;
  if lettergrade [course] = 'F' then
      numbergrade [course] := 0;
  end; { for-loop }
```

The keywords "begin" and "end" are necessary in this for-loop because the body of the loop is more that one simple statement. The keyword "end" that terminates the for-loop is followed by a comment indicating what construct it ends. It is a good practice to put a comment at the end of all reasonably long compound statements to indicate which statement is being concluded.

By substituting the details of the refined letter grade conversion step, we obtain the second refinement of the program gradeptavg. As before, we retain the original statement as a comment.

```
program gradeptavg (input, output);

  const
    maxcourses = 8;
    namelength = 30;

  var
    gpa : real;
    name : packed array [1..namelength] of char;
    lettergrade : array [1..maxcourses] of char;
    numbergrade : array [1..maxcourses] of integer;
    credit : array [1..maxcourses] of integer;
    nrcourses, i, course : integer;
  begin
  { read the input data }
  for i := 1 to namelength do
    read (name [i]);
  readln;
  writeln (name); { echo }
  readln (nrcourses);
  writeln (nrcourses :1, ' courses taken'); { echo }
  writeln ('Input data:   grade  credit');
  for course := 1 to nrcourses do
    begin
    readln (lettergrade [course], credit [course]);
    writeln (lettergrade [course] :17, credit [course] :8);
    end;
```

```
{ convert letter grades to number grades }
for course := 1 to nrcourses do
  begin
  if lettergrade [course] = 'A' then
      numbergrade [course] := 4;
  if lettergrade [course] = 'B' then
      numbergrade [course] := 3;
  if lettergrade [course] = 'C' then
      numbergrade [course] := 2;
  if lettergrade [course] = 'D' then
      numbergrade [course] := 1;
  if lettergrade [course] = 'F' then
      numbergrade [course] := 0;
  end; { for-loop }

calculate gradepoint average;
{ print the output }
writeln (name);
writeln ('  Gradepoint average = ', gpa :1:2);
end.
```

We make two final comments on the second refinement before completing the job by doing the third and final refinement. First, a new variable numbergrade is needed; it is an array of integers, one for each course taken. Second, the refinement of the letter grade conversion step is notably weak on treatment of likely errors in the input data. An input grade of G or W will cause no number grade to be assigned and probably will cause an error condition when later steps attempt to use the undefined number grade. The exercises discuss remedies.

Final Refinement: The Gradepoint Average Calculation

The last statement needing refinement is the gradepoint average calculation itself. The main idea is to divide the total number of gradepoints by the total number of credits to get the gradepoint average. Two new variables, totalgradepts and totalcredits, will be needed.

```
var
  totalgradepts, totalcredits : integer;
```

The overall strategy of the gradepoint calculation refines as follows.

```
{ calculate the gradepoint average }
calculate totalgradepts;
calculate totalcredits;
gpa := totalgradepts / totalcredits
```

All that remains is to refine the calculations of the two totals. We previously calculated a sum using a for-loop in the program avgofscores in Section 1.3 and can use much the same method here, except for omitting the statements dealing with reading and echoing the input data. Each total calculation begins by setting its total to zero, then using a for-loop to add contributions to the total, one by one, until all have been added. It takes longer to explain than to write, so we give the complete refinement of the gradepoint average calculation and let it explain itself.

```
{ calculate gradepoint average }
{ calculate total grade points }
totalgradepts := 0;
for course := 1 to nrcourses do
  totalgradepts := totalgradepts +
      numbergrade [course] * credit [course];
{ calculate total credits }
totalcredits := 0;
for course := 1 to nrcourses do
  totalcredits := totalcredits + credit [course];
gpa := totalgradepts / totalcredits;
```

It is an unsafe and unsound programming practice to assume that a numeric variable such as totalgradept or totalcredits, not previously assigned a value, has the value zero, even though this works for some languages on some computers. When it doesn't work, you would be lucky to have the computer merely stop the execution of the program. Otherwise, what could happen is that the computer might supply a number left over from an earlier calculation or even from the execution of someone else's program. The outcome might be the printing of false results.

All the refined details are now substituted for their less specific equivalents in the second refinement, and the result is the completely refined, executable Pascal program gradeptavg. A sample execution follows.

```
program gradeptavg (input, output);

  const
    maxcourses = 8;
    namelength = 30;

  var
    gpa : real;
    name : packed array [1..namelength] of char;
    lettergrade : array [1..maxcourses] of char;
    numbergrade : array [1..maxcourses] of integer;
    credit : array [1..maxcourses] of integer;
    nrcourses, i, course : integer;
    totalgradepts, totalcredits : integer;

  begin
  { read the input data }
  for i := 1 to namelength do
    read (name [i]);
  readln;
  writeln (name); { echo }
  readln (nrcourses);
  writeln (nrcourses :1, ' courses taken'); { echo }
  writeln ('Input data:    grade   credit');
  for course := 1 to nrcourses do
    begin
    readln (lettergrade [course], credit [course]);
    writeln (lettergrade [course] :17, credit [course] :8);
    end;
```

```
{ convert letter grades to number grades }
for course := 1 to nrcourses do
  begin
    if lettergrade [course] = 'A' then
        numbergrade [course] := 4;
    if lettergrade [course] = 'B' then
        numbergrade [course] := 3;
    if lettergrade [course] = 'C' then
        numbergrade [course] := 2;
    if lettergrade [course] = 'D' then
        numbergrade [course] := 1;
    if lettergrade [course] = 'F' then
        numbergrade [course] := 0;
  end; { for-loop }

{ calculate gradepoint average }
{ calculate total grade points }
totalgradepts := 0;
for course := 1 to nrcourses do
  totalgradepts := totalgradepts +
      numbergrade [course] * credit [course];

{ calculate total credits }
totalcredits := 0;
for course := 1 to nrcourses do
  totalcredits := totalcredits + credit [course];
gpa := totalgradepts / totalcredits;
{ print the output }
writeln (name);
writeln ('  Gradepoint average = ', gpa :1:2);
end.

run gradeptavg

Gordon Uchimata
5 courses taken
Input data:    grade    credit
                 B         3
                 A         2
                 A         4
                 C         5
                 B         4
Gordon Uchimata
  Gradepoint average = 3.06
```

Exercises

---

1. Modify the program gradeptavg so that it tests each letter grade in the input to see whether it is one of the allowable grades A, B, C, D, or F for which numeric equivalents are given. If one or more letter grades in the input file are in error, print an error message instead of a gradepoint average. Hint: Introduce a variable named errorcount.

2. Some schools use a grading scheme different from that of South Mountain College. For example, there may be grades of A+ and A-, B+ and B-, etc, in addition to the grades A, B, C, D, and F. Modify the program gradeptavg so that it computes gradepoint averages according to the system used at your school, if it differs from that of South Mountain College.

3. Modify the program gradeptavg to handle correctly grades of W (withdrawn), P (passing), and I (incomplete). Although their effects on the total number of credits accumulated toward a degree differ, all three grades W, P, and I have the same effect on the current semester's gradepoint average, that is, the courses for which they are given are to be excluded from the gradepoint average calculation. Hint: Use an array excludefromgpa [1..maxcourses] of type character or boolean to keep track of which courses are excluded.

4. Modify the program gradeptavg so that it prints the entire grade report form exactly as shown in Figure 2.1.1. Determine what additional data will have to be inserted in the input file and design a convenient format for entering the information.

5. Write a program that accepts as input the names, hourly pay rates, and number of hours worked of six employees and prints the gross pay of each. Be sure your program provides for an increased pay rate for overtime as in Section 1.5.

6. Modify the program of Exercise 5 so that it deducts a 6.13% social security tax from each worker and prints the gross pay, the social security tax, and the remaining take-home pay for each worker.

7. Modify the program of Exercise 5 so that it deducts a 15% income tax withholding on the amount of gross pay in excess of $100.

8. Modify the program of Exercise 7 so that it also asks for the number of exemptions per employee, and then excludes $100 for each exemption from the 15% deduction withheld for income tax.

9. The Enlightened Corporation is pleased when its employees enroll in college classes. It offers them an 80 percent rebate on the first $500 of tuition, a 60 percent rebate on the second $400, and a 40 percent rebate on the next $300. Write a program that computes the rebate on an amount of tuition supplied as input. The number of employees taking advantage of the tuition rebate program varies and will have to be an input parameter.

10. The government of Confiscation Island taxes your first $1000 of annual earnings at 1 percent, your second $1000 at 2 percent, your third $1000 at 3 percent, and so on. It takes everything you earn above $99,000, so no one earns more than that. Write a program that accepts your annual earnings as input and calculates your tax. If you earn $2500, for example, your tax is $45 = $1000 * 1% + $1000 * 2% + $500 * 3%. Test your program at 6 income levels in different tax brackets.

11. A month's transactions for a checking account are encoded as a sequence of numbers. Each positive number in this sequence represents the amount of a deposit. Each negative number represents the amount of a check. Write a program that accepts as input data the starting balance for the month, the number of transactions that occurred that month, and the sequence of transactions. The program is to compute the final balance for the account at the end of the month.

12. Modify the program for Exercise 11 so that, as each transaction is entered, the computer prints the type of transaction, that is, "deposit" or "check", the amount of the transaction, and the balance in the account after the transaction has been processed.

13. Modify the program for Exercise 11 so that it also counts and prints the number of checks.

14. Modify the program for Exercise 11 so that it prints a warning message "account overdrawn" if a transaction results in a balance of less than zero. The program should continue processing the rest of the checks and deposits for the month, even if the account is overdrawn.

15. Modify the program written for Exercise 14 so that a penalty of $3 is assessed whenever the processing of a check leaves the account overdrawn. Do not assess the penalty when the transaction is a deposit into an overdrawn account that does not bring the balance above zero.

16. Modify the program for Exercise 11 so that it assesses the account a penalty charge of $2 if the balance drops below $300 at any time during the month. This charge is to be assessed only once at most for a single month. Hint: One way is to use a variable called penalty whose value is zero if the account balance never dips below $300, and whose value is changed to $2 if the balance does go below $300.

17. Modify the program for Exercise 11 so that the account is assessed a penalty charge of $2 if the average balance during the month is less than $300. It is now necessary for each transaction card to have the day of the month of the transaction as well as the amount of the transaction. Only the final balance after the last transaction of a day is used in the average, and this balance is used for every succeeding day until the date of the next transaction.

    Would you prefer to have this kind of account rather than the one described in Exercise 16?

18. Modify the program for Exercise 11 so that the account is assessed a charge of 6 cents for each check and 3 cents for each deposit.

2.2   Refinement Using Procedures

Before introducing new loop structures in Section 2.3, we briefly resume the treatment begun in Section 1.6 of an important facility, *procedures* (also called *subroutines* in some programming languages), that can be used to clarify the structure of programs—especially those like the program gradeptavg in the previous section—that evolve through successive refinements. Besides writing programs that a computer can execute, an important goal for a programmer is to design programs a person can easily read and understand. Readable program listings play a substantial part in enabling someone to decide whether the computer is actually doing the job that is supposed to be done.

   Sometimes the aims of clarity and executability seem to lead a program in opposite directions. For instance, the early refinements of the program gradeptavg are easy to understand, so it would be nice to stop the refinement process, except that a computer cannot execute the instructions. On the other hand, the final refinement in the previous section is computer-executable, but its length alone makes it harder to comprehend all at once, because the details are in the way. Even the helpful comments tying the final version to the earlier refinements cannot completely overcome this handicap.

One resolution of this dilemma begins with the thought that instructions not in the target language may be regarded as executable statements for a much smarter computer. From this point of view, procedures provide a means of extending Pascal to include operations and processes that are not built-in, so that the available computer system can execute a clearer looking program. Other advantages of procedures will surface later. Of course, the available computer must be supplied with a program for these new operations and processes. If no one else has supplied the details in computer-executable form, the programmer must do so.

Upgrading the Problem

While we are at it, we may as well make the gradepoint average program calculate gradepoint averages for all 1037 students at South Mountain college in one run, rather than running the same program 1037 times to accomplish the same result. A first draft of the upgraded program allgradeptavgs showing few details is written easily.

```
program allgradeptavgs;
{ initial version
  const
    nrstudents = 1037;
  var
    student : integer;
  for student := 1 to nrstudents do
    process one student's gradepoint average;
  end. { allgradeptavgs }
```

Since we already know the major steps involved in processing one student's gradepoint average from Section 2.1, we pass immediately to a refinement of allgradeptavgs equivalent in detail to the initial version of the program gradeptavg in that section.

```
program allgradeptavgs;
{ first refinement }

  const
    nrstudents = 1037;

  var
    student : integer;
```

```
begin
for student := 1 to nrstudents do
  begin
  { process one student's gradepoint average }
  read the input;
  convert letter grades to number grades;
  calculate the gradepoint average (gpa);
  print the output;
  end; { for-loop }
end. { allgradeptavgs }
```

As a simple exercise in mimickry, devoid of new ideas, we wish to develop the second refinement of the program allgradeptavgs as follows: We could replace each of the four remaining unrefined statements by their more detailed counterparts, which already are given in Section 2.1. When we were finished, the body of the main for-loop obtained would be several dozen lines long and quite difficult to understand.

Instead, we now make each of the remaining unrefined steps a call to a programmer-defined procedure and retain the clarity of the first refinement by keeping the details out of the main program. The version of the program allgradeptavgs labelled "2nd refinement" shows the form of a procedure call and the placement of the procedure declarations within the main program, but still omits the details of the four programmer-defined procedures needed to make it an executable Pascal program.

```
program allgradeptavgs (input, output);
{ second refinement }
{ uses programmer-defined procedures to refine selected steps }

  const
    nrstudents = 1037;

  var
    student : integer;

  procedure readinput; { for one student }
    ... end; { readinput }

  procedure convertletterstonumbers;
    ... end; { convertletterstonumbers }

  procedure calculategpa; { gradepoint average }
    ... end; { calculategpa }

  procedure printoutput;
    ... end; { printoutput }
```

```
{ main program }
begin
for student : = 1 to nrstudents do
  begin
  { process one student's gradepoint average }
  readinput;
  convertletterstonumbers;
  calculategpa;
  printoutput;
  end; { for-loop }
end. { allgradeptavgs }
```

How to Call a Procedure

We recall from Section 1.6 how one *calls* a procedure: We issue a request to execute all of its steps by writing the procedure's name as a statement in a Pascal program. The body of the main for-loop of the second refinement consists of four procedure calls executed in sequence. Since these four procedures are not built in, their details must be supplied to the computer. The second refinement of the program allgradeptavgs indicates where the details are to be inserted, but does not yet indicate what these details are. What remains to be done to make the second refinement of the program allgradeptavgs into an executable Pascal program is to add all of the variable declarations from the program gradeptavg and to place the detailed refinements of the major steps, described at great length in Section 2.1, into the *procedure declarations* of the program allgradeptavgs.

The result, which would require another several pages of explanation and refinement if we had not already done all of the work in Section 2.1, is the final refinement of the program allgradeptavgs. The use of procedures has enabled us to retain the clarity of the main program.

```
program allgradeptavgs (input, output);
{ final refinement }
{ uses programmer-defined procedures to refine selected steps }

  const
    nrstudents = 1037;
    maxcourses = 8;
    namelength = 30;

  var
    student : integer;
    gpa : real;
    name : packed array [1..namelength] of char;
    lettergrade : array [1..maxcourses] of char;
    numbergrade : array [1..maxcourses] of integer;
    credit : array [1..maxcourses] of integer;
    nrcourses, i, course : integer;
    totalgradepts, totalcredits : integer;
```

```
procedure readinput; { for one student }
  begin
  for i := 1 to namelength do
    read (name [i]);
  readln;
  writeln (name); { echo }
  readln (nrcourses);
  writeln (nrcourses :1, ' courses taken'); { echo }
  writeln ('Input data:    grade   credit');
  for course := 1 to nrcourses do
    begin
    readln (lettergrade [course], credit [course]);
    writeln (lettergrade [course] :17, credit [course] :8);
    end; { for-loop }
  end; { readinput }

procedure convertletterstonumbers;
  begin
  for course := 1 to nrcourses do
    begin
    if lettergrade [course] = 'A' then
      numbergrade [course] := 4;
    if lettergrade [course] = 'B' then
      numbergrade [course] := 3;
    if lettergrade [course] = 'C' then
      numbergrade [course] := 2;
    if lettergrade [course] = 'D' then
      numbergrade [course] := 1;
    if lettergrade [course] = 'F' then
      numbergrade [course] := 0;
    end; { for-loop }
  end; { convertletterstonumbers }

procedure calculategpa; { gradepoint average }
  begin
  { calculate total grade points }
  totalgradepts := 0;
  for course := 1 to nrcourses do
    totalgradepts := totalgradepts +
        numbergrade [course] * credit [course];
  { calculate total credits }
  totalcredits := 0;
  for course := 1 to nrcourses do
    totalcredits := totalcredits + credit [course];
  gpa := totalgradepts / totalcredits;
  end; { calculategpa }

procedure printoutput;
  begin
  writeln (name);
  writeln ('  Gradepoint average = ', gpa :1:2);
  writeln; { blank line }
  end; { printoutput }
```

```
{ main program }
begin
for student := 1 to nrstudents do
  begin
  { process one student's gradepoint average }
  readinput;
  convertletterstonumbers;
  calculategpa;
  printoutput;
  end; { for-loop }
end. { allgradeptavgs }
```

For the following execution, the constant nrofstudents was changed to 3.

```
run allgradeptavgs

Gordon Uchimata
5 courses taken
Input data:    grade   credit
                 B        3
                 A        2
                 A        4
                 C        5
                 B        4
Gordon Uchimata
  Gradepoint average =  3.06

Jeanne Adams
3 courses taken
Input data:    grade   credit
                 A        4
                 B        3
                 A        5
Jeanne Adams
  Gradepoint average =  3.75

Tom Taylor
2 courses taken
Input data:    grade   credit
                 C        5
                 F        3
Tom Taylor
  Gradepoint average =  1.25
```

The Effect of Calling a Procedure

The effect of writing a procedure call such as readinput in the main program is the same as if the procedure call statement were replaced by all the executable statements in the procedure declaration for readinput. In Pascal, variables are known automatically by the same name in a main program as in a procedure called by that main program, unless otherwise specified as described in Chapter 4. The execution of the program allgradeptavgs would be exactly the same if written with procedures as shown or if written with the details of these procedures replacing the procedure calls as was done in Section 2.1. *The effect of using procedures is not one of eliminating details, but rather of moving them somewhere else.*

However, there are several important advantages obtained by using the main program-procedure approach to refinement. First, the calling program is not cluttered with details. If someone wants to know exactly how the grades are converted from letters to numbers, the procedure convertletterstonumbers can be examined carefully. But anyone who is interested only in the general organization of the grade point average program finds the main program much more readable than it would be with the details inserted. A second major advantage is that each of the major steps is now a separate procedure that can be programmed and debugged more or less independently of the main program. For programs of much larger size than this one, such independence becomes a very important factor. Each procedure can be assigned to a different programmer working simultaneously with the one preparing the main program, and the total calendar time to complete the project can be reduced.

Exercises

Exercises 1 through 11 are concerned with the following application. A library allows books to be borrowed for a period of 2 weeks and charges a fine of 5 cents a day for the first week a book is overdue, 10 cents a day for the second week, and 25 cents a day thereafter. The following program is for computing the amount of the fine, if any, on a borrowed book:

```
program libraryfine (input, output);
   begin
   read withdrawal and return dates;
   calculate number of days overdue;
   determine fine, if any;
   print fine or message saying that none is due;
   end.
```

1. Refine the program libraryfine to an executable Pascal program, using procedures and procedure calls for program steps that involve too much detail. An answer to this exercise is acceptable if the main program is entirely in Pascal, but some of the procedures still require further refinement. Exercises 2 to 8 give suggestions about how the procedures may be refined.

2. The amount of the fine on an overdue book depends only on the number of days the book is overdue. One way to calculate the number of days the book is overdue is based on numbering the days of a year from 1 for January 1 to 365 (or 366 in leap years) for December 31. For days in the same year, simple subtraction suffices to determine the number of days for which a book is borrowed. For borrowing periods that start in one year and end in another year, the formula is only slightly more complex.

Refine the procedure or program steps that determine this fine on an overdue book to an executable program. For this exercise, it is not necessary to refine the step that converts a month and day of the month to a day-of-the-year number from 1 to 365 (or 366), if it is done in a procedure. This is saved for Exercise 3.

Table 2.2.1   Converting a month and day of the month to a day of the year for ordinary (nonleap) years.

	MONTH	DAY OF THE YEAR
1	January	0 + day of the month
2	February	31 + day of the month
3	March	59 + day of the month
4	April	90 + day of the month
5	May	120 + day of the month
6	June	151 + day of the month
7	July	181 + day of the month
8	August	212 + day of the month
9	September	243 + day of the month
10	October	273 + day of the month
11	November	305 + day of the month
12	December	334 + day of the month

---

3. January 1 is the first day of the year, and December 31 is the 365th day of an ordinary year or the 366th day of a leap year. It is easy to convert a month and day of the month to a day of the year for ordinary years using the information contained in Table 2.2.1. For example, October 26 is the $273 + 26 = 299$th day of an ordinary year.

    Write a program to convert a given month and day of the month to a day of the year and refine it to an executable procedure. For this exercise, you may make the simplifying assumption that all years are ordinary years; that is, ignore leap years.

4. For the years from 1901 to 2099, any year that is exactly divisible by 4 (with remainder 0) is a leap year and has a twenty-ninth day in February. Improve the procedure written in Exercise 3 to work correctly for leap years also. If it is desired to refine this program to an executable Pascal procedure, the integer operator mod may be used. The value of the operator mod is the integer remainder when two integers are divided. Thus a year from 1901 to 2099 is a leap year if and only if

    year mod 4 = 0

5. Include a leap year correction in the procedure for Exercise 2.

6. Refine the procedure or program steps written for Exercise 1 that read the withdrawal date and the return date. You must make sure that all the information required to calculate the number of days overdue is obtained or calculated. Otherwise the program libraryfine will not work when all the procedures are included in the program. This is why the refinement of this step is saved for last. The answer to this exercise may be highly dependent on whether the procedure written for Exercise 3 to calculate the day of the year uses the full names January, February, and so on, or abbreviations such as Jan, Feb, and so on, for the months, or requires the month to be specified as a number from 1 to 12.

7. What effect would it have on the program libraryfine if the withdrawal and return dates were entered as numbers from 1 to 365 (or 366)? Are there any problems with this from the standpoint of a user of the program libraryfine?

8. What is the effect on the program libraryfine of entering the withdrawal and return dates as days of the century from 1 to 36525? Is this desirable?

9. The procedure described in Exercise 3 for ordinary years, and in Exercise 4 for leap years, for converting a month and day of the month into a day of the year from 1 to 365 (or 366) is a useful calculation in other applications besides library fines. Write a "driving" program whose sole purpose is to call and test adequately the procedure written in Exercise 3 or 4. What date should be used in conjunction with this testing program to establish with reasonable certainty that the procedure is written correctly?

10. The procedure described in Exercise 2 to calculate the number of days elapsed between two given calendar dates is also useful in other applications such as interest calculations on deposits and loans. Write a driving program to test adequately the procedure written for Exercise 2. What data should be used to be reasonably sure the procedure will always do what it is supposed to do?

11. Write a program to test the procedure that calculates the fines on overdue books. Design data to test it.

12. Exercise 9 in Section 2.1 describes a tuition rebate policy for the Enlightened Corporation. Write and fully refine a program that tells the Enlightened Corporation its total tuition rebate for employees. To a large extent, the program allgradeptavgs in this section and the previous section can be used as a model for the general structure of the desired program. If Exercise 9 in Section 2.1 was done previously, the program written for that exercise may be adapted to form the key procedure in this program.

13. Consider the version of the gradepoint average program written using procedures in this section. From the viewpoints of ease of reading and ease of writing, compare it with the version of the gradepoint average program written in the previous section without using procedures.

14. Compare this section's version and last section's version of the gradepoint average program from the viewpoint of ease of making modifications and improvements.

2.3 While-Loops

For all the care lavished on the gradepoint average programs in the previous two sections, there remain three places in the program allgradeptavgs where the use of for-loops makes the input more difficult to prepare and less flexible than one would like. In each of these cases, use of the more general *while-loop*, introduced in this section, will improve the program and make it easier to use.

The problem with a for-loop is that the upper bound on the for-variable—in other words, the number of iterations of the for-loop—must be known to the program *before the loop is entered.* We used three different solutions to this problem in the program allgradeptavgs of Section 2.2, none of which is entirely satisfactory.

First, there is the for-loop to read the letters of a student's name.

```
for i := 1 to namelength do
  read (name [i])
```

Because the value of the constant namelength is 30, we require all students to have 30-character names, or, failing that, to add blanks to their names until they reach 30 characters.

Second, there is the for-loop to read all the letter grades for one student; echos are omitted to emphasize the essential loop structure.

```
readln (nrcourses);
for course := 1 to nrcourses do
   readln (lettergrade [course], credit [course]);
```

This is slightly better than requiring all students to take precisely the same number of courses. The flexibility is there at the price of having the preparer of the input file count how many courses each student takes and enter this count as an additional item in the input file.

The third awkward for-loop occurs in the main program.

```
const
   nrstudents = 1037;
begin
for student := 1 to nrstudents do
   process one student's gradepoint average;
end.
```

The flexibility is still there, but now a constant declaration *in the program* must be changed if a new student matriculates or an existing student leaves South Mountain College. Worse yet, someone in the registrar's office must count the approximately 1037 student registration cards to determine *precisely* how many students registered this semester. Besides being time consuming, this is simply not the kind of operation people are good at. Anyone who has tried to count the cards in a standard deck of playing cards realizes how hard it would be to handle more than a thousand cards without miscounting. The computer, on the other hand, directed by a while-loop, is very good at counting, and it should be programmed to perform this task for the user.

This is not to say that for-loops are bad and that all you have learned about them should be forgotten; it is only that for-loops are too rigid for some purposes. The only way a computer can stop executing a for-loop and proceed to the rest of the program is to complete the prescribed number of iterations, and this number must be known before the loop is started. When it is known, as for example in the loops to convert letter grades to number grades or to calculate the gradepoint average, the for-loop is the most natural, efficient, and clearest way to program the calculation.

The use of a while-loop, on the other hand, allows selective termination of the loop at any time whatsoever during the execution of the loop. It also provides a means for testing later in a program to determine what condition caused termination of the loop. The while-loop is the most flexible loop construction needed to write any Pascal program. No more complex loop construct is used in any program in this book. A related loop construct of almost equal power, the *repeat-until-loop,* is also introduced in this section.

Signalling the End of Input Data

The reason the input for-loops in the programs gradeptavg and allgradeptavgs in the preceding two sections need to know how much input data to expect is the need to know when to stop short of reading an input item that isn't there. For example, an attempt to read one too many letter grades might read the first letter of the next student's name as a letter grade. An alternative to counting the number of course grade entries in advance is to place a final entry in the input file which has the final appearance of a legitimate course grade entry, but which contains obviously ridiculous information. This phony entry can serve as a signal that there are no more actual letter grades for that student in the input file. For example, a phony entry with a letter grade of ''Z'' and course credit of −9 credits is not likely to be mistaken for a valid grade entry by persons with normal intelligence and some familiarity with college grading practice. Moreover, a computer can read such an entry *using the same read statement* as for ordinary grade entries. A simple test to see if the letter grade is ''Z'' would suffice to distinguish this entry as a *termination signal* for the grade data of a student.

Reading Input With a While-Loop

A *while-loop* is a loop that is repeated as long as some specified condition is true. To illustrate how a while-loop is used, we rewrite the procedure readinput of the previous section that reads all of the input for one student, so that it stops after reading a termination signal entry following all the real grade entries instead of stopping on the basis of a user-supplied count of the number of courses taken. The while-loop in the rewritten procedure readinput is repeated as long as there are more course grades to be read. It retains its original name so that its procedure declaration can be substituted directly into the program allgradeptavgs. When the phony course grade ''Z'' is read, signalling the input data for that student, the *while-condition* becomes false and the loop is not repeated. Since the number of courses taken by a student, nrcourses, is used by later procedures, we also have the computer count how many real letter grades there are as they are read in.

```
procedure readinput; { for one student }

  const
    signal = 'Z';

  var
    morecourses : boolean;
    letter : char;
    number : integer;

  begin
  for i := 1 to namelength do
    read (name [i]);
  readln;
  writeln (name); { echo }
```

```
{ read and count letter grades }
nrcourses := 0;
morecourses := true;
writeln ('Input data:    grade   credit');
while (morecourses) and (nrcourses < maxcourses) do
  begin
  readln (letter, number);
  if letter = signal then
    morecourses := false
  else
    begin
    writeln (letter :17, number :8);
    nrcourses := nrcourses + 1;
    lettergrade [nrcourses] := letter;
    credit [nrcourses] := number;
    end; { else }
  end; { while-loop }
end; { readinput }
```

The condition "morecourses" is a boolean variable that takes on only the values true or false. Both the constant and variable declarations could have been put with the other declarations at the top of the program allgradeptavgs if we had shown that part of the program. However, it is permissible to put the declarations where they are shown; in fact, it is preferable in this case, as we will indicate in Chapter 4. Just before the while-loop is entered, the boolean variable morecourses is given the value true. When the termination signal entry is recognized, the boolean variable morecourses is set to false, the rest of the loop body is not executed, and the loop is not repeated.

Boolean Variables and Constants

A variable may be declared to be type boolean by listing the variable in the "var" part of a declaration followed by the keyword "boolean". The keyword "boolean" designates a type, just as "integer" and "real" do. A boolean variable may be assigned only one of two values, true or false. This value may be a boolean constant or computed as the result of evaluating a more general boolean expression. Boolean expressions, as they occur in if-tests, were discussed in Section 1.5. More generally, they are the expressions involving boolean variables and constants, comparisons, and the boolean operators "and", "or", and "not". The precise description of the syntax of the allowed boolean expressions is given in the syntax charts in Appendix C.

The While-Statement

The while-statement provides a second method of constructing a group of statements that can be executed repeatedly. The form of a while-statement is shown in Figure 2.3.1. The statement following the keyword "do" is executed repeatedly as long as the condition given by the boolean expression is true. The statement may, of course, be a compound statement, so that the body of the loop may be as complicated as needed. The boolean expression is tested *only just before the body of the loop is executed*. This has two consequences of interest. First, it is possible for the statement that makes up the body of the loop to be executed zero times if the condition is false when the while-statement is first executed. Second, if variables are changed in the middle of the loop so that the condition becomes false, this does not cause the loop to terminate immediately. Execution of the loop terminates only when the condition is tested prior to beginning execution of the loop the next time. This second problem is handled in the programs in this book by putting the rest of the body of the loop in an else-clause that is not executed if the condition terminating the loop is changed in the middle of the loop.

$\langle$WHILE_STATEMENT$\rangle$:

→ while → $\langle$EXPRESSION$\rangle$ → do → $\langle$STATEMENT$\rangle$ ⟶

Figure 2.3.1   While-statement syntax chart.

A Recipe

A while-loop is a good model for many ordinary events. Consider, for example, the following instructions to put the finishing touches on a pot of soup.

```
recipe final preparation for soup;
  begin
  delicious := false; { initial condition }
  while not delicious do
    begin
    stir;
    taste;
    if taste is just right then
      delicious := true
    else
      add a pinch of salt;
    end; { while-loop }
  serve;
  end.
```

Having completed all the other preparations for the soup, the chef wishes to add just the right amount of salt. On each iteration of the loop, the soup is stirred and tasted. If the taste is delicious, the chef stops cooking and serves the soup. Otherwise, the chef adds a pinch more salt and repeats the process.

Aside from the fact that the recipe final preparation for soup is executed by a chef, rather than by a computer, there is another important difference between it and the procedure readinput written in this section. The condition for exiting from the while-loop in the recipe is based on monitoring an internal process, the taste of the soup, while the exit condition in readinput is based on waiting for an external signal following all the real data cards.

Endless Loops

There is an ever-present danger in writing a while-loop that the condition might always be satisfied. For example, execution of the loop in the program endlessloop1 never terminates because the while-test is always satisfied.

```
program endlessloop1 (output);
  var
    hellstemp : real;
  begin
  hellstemp := 100;
  { until hell freezes over }
  while hellstemp >= -273 do
    begin
    this;
    that;
    theotherthing;
    end;
  { As long as the procedures this, that, and theotherthing do what
    one usually does in hell, and do not alter its temperature,
    it does not matter what comes next because the loop never
    ends.  }
  end.
```

The programming problem of an endless loop is cleared up by adding the following statement inside the loop.

```
hellstemp := hellstemp - 1;
```

The result is a program hellfreezesover that does not contain an endless loop.

```
program hellfreezesover (output);
  var
    hellstemp : real;
  begin
  hellstemp := 100;
  { until hell freezes over }
  while hellstemp >= -273 do
    begin
    hellstemp := hellstemp - 1;
    this;
    that;
    theotherthing;
    end;
  { No longer an endless loop.
    The rest of the program tells what
    to do when hell freezes over. }
    .
    .
    .
  end.
```

The for-loop does not have the same potential for creating endless loops, at least in theory. The number of iterations of a for-loop is specified in the heading of the for-statement before the loop execution is begun, and the loop execution ends when the specified number of iterations is completed. However, if the number of iterations specified is a very large number, it might be highly unlikely that the execution can be completed before the computer requires repairs or routine servicing, or if still larger, in the computer's or the programmer's lifetime.

When using a while-loop, it is important to design an exit condition that ultimately will be satisfied. If the chef in the soup example likes soup very salty, then it might be a long time before the soup is served. However, a much worse thing could happen. The chef's palate might be so delicate (or the pinches of salt so large) that, adding the critical pinch of salt would transform the taste from not salty enough all the way to too salty, bypassing in its haste the desired condition of being delicious. The soup might even be too salty before the tasting begins. If this chef were to execute the recipe as written, he or she would be obliged to go on adding pinch of salt after pinch of salt forever, because the taste would never be delicious and the loop would never be terminated. It would be better to stop the loop execution either if the taste is delicious or if the soup is already too salty. In general, one must beware of exit tests that are too discriminating.

Multiple Exit Conditions

It is permissible to put a compound condition after the keyword "while" in a while-statement. For example, it is possible to continue execution of a loop while at least one of several conditions is true or to continue execution of a loop only until one of several conditions becomes false. By using boolean variables to name the conditions, it is possible to test later in the program to see which of the possible conditions actually caused the termination of the loop in the current execution. The recipe final preparation for soup 2 incorporates these improvements.

```
recipe final preparation for soup 2;
  begin
  delicious : = false;
  toosalty : = false;
  while not (delicious or toosalty) do
    begin
    stir;
    taste;
    if taste is just right then
      delicious : = true
    else if taste is too salty then
      toosalty : = true
    else
      add a pinch of salt;
    end; { while-loop }
  if delicious then
    tell waiter to recommend soup to customers
  else
    tell waiter to serve soup only if customer insists;
  end.
```

Counting Cards

One of the practical problems that motivates changing some of the for-loops in the gradepoint average programs in the previous two sections to while-loops in this section is the difficulty people have in counting large numbers of cards. Computers, on the other hand, are very good at repetitive tasks and can be programmed to count cards quickly and accurately. We now develop a counting program uncluttered by the need to store the input data in an array.

To be specific, suppose that one has a deck of computer punchcards that must be counted, and that each card has a number between -5000 and $+5000$ punched into it. These numbers could represent withdrawals from and deposits into a savings account, or any number of other things, but the interpretation of the data is irrelevant to the mere counting of the number of cards. Behind the deck of cards to be counted, we place a termination signal card punched with the number 9999. Since this is too large a number to be a valid piece of data it is recognizable as a termination signal. The number zero, which is often used as a termination signal in other applications, cannot be used in this program, because zero is allowed as a valid piece of data. Note: If your computer system does not accept input data on punched cards, as many current computers do not, think of a computer punchcard as synonymous with a line in the input file.

The general structure of the program countcards is clearly a loop involving many repetitions of the step of counting one card. Because we do not know in advance how many cards there will be, a for-loop cannot be used. Thus the loop must be written as a while-loop, stopping when the termination signal card is reached.

```
program countcards (input, output);
  begin
  initialize;
  while morecards do
    begin
    examine the next card;
    if it is the termination signal card then
      morecards := false
    else
      count that card;
    end; { while-loop }
  print the number of cards;
  end.
```

In the light of past experience, we have included an initialization step, because almost every loop needs one, and we have made sure that there is a reasonable way to terminate execution of the loop, in this case after examining the termination signal card. It is important not to count the termination signal card.

The refinement process in this program starts by chipping away at the most easily refined statements. All that is needed to refine the statement

```
print the number of cards
```

is a name for the variable that holds this value. Although other choices are equally appropriate, we choose cardcount and refine the statement to

```
writeln ('There are ', cardcount, ' cards in the deck.')
```

With this choice of a variable name, the statement

```
count that card
```

is refined to

```
cardcount := cardcount + 1
```

We must also remember to declare cardcount to be type integer.
    To refine the statement

```
examine the next card
```

one must know that the only way a computer can physically handle a card or input line is by reading it. So reading the card must be a prelude to any examination or counting of the card. In this application, the card has one number on it, so this number can be read as a value of the variable information. Choosing the name signal for the termination signal, one can refine the two lines

```
examine the next card
if it is the termination signal card then
```

to the Pascal program lines

```
readln (information);
echo the input data
if information = signal then
```

    To refine the initialization step, we look at the almost completely refined program with all details supplied but the initialization, and we hand simulate the execution of the program to see what initialization is needed.

```
program countcards (input, output);
  { declarations are needed here }
  { every step is refined except the initialization
      and the echoing of the input data }
  begin
  initialize;
  while moredata do
    begin
    readln (information);
    echo the input data;
    if information = signal then
      moredata := false
    else
      cardcount := cardcount + 1;
    end; { while-loop }
  writeln ('There are ', cardcount, ' cards in the deck.');
  end.
```

The first step after the initialization, the while-statement, allows the computer to execute the body of the loop and to read and to test input cards *only* if the condition moredata is true. Thus the initialization section must set the boolean variable moredata to true to begin the loop. A value for the variable information is then read from the first data card. Suppose the value is +3456, for the sake of continuing the simulation. The if-test on the next line cannot be performed unless the computer has a value for the quantity signal. Thus a constant declaration setting signal = 9999 must be a part of the program's declaration section. It is better to use a constant for the termination signal instead of putting the particular termination signal 9999 in the if-test to make it easier to modify this program to handle situations where the number 9999 is a valid piece of data. In general, it is a good idea to choose a termination signal that is so different from any legitimate input value that most errors in preparing the data cards could not prevent its recognition.

In continuing the simulation, since the first value of information is 3456, the if-test is not satisfied, and the computer must increase cardcount by one. However, cardcount does not yet have a value, so one must be assigned in the initialization. Since we want the value of cardcount to be one after this first card is counted, the initial value of cardcount must be zero. Counting processes are used often in computer programming, so it would not be at all surprising for an experienced programmer to know from the very start that exactly this form of initialization is necessary, and write only the final form of the initialization down on paper. However, it is more typical to refine the initialization statement last, as we are doing here. Further simulation, using data cards with the values −76, 0, +5000, and 9999, discloses no further problems, so the final program is the following.

```
program countcards (input, output);

  const
    signal = 9999;

  var
    cardcount, information : integer;
    morecards : boolean;

  begin
  cardcount : = 0;
  { loop to read and count cards }
  morecards : = true;
  while morecards do
    begin
    readln (information);
    writeln ('Input data  information: ', information);
    if information = signal then
      morecards : = false
    else
      cardcount : = cardcount + 1;
    end; { while-loop }
  writeln ('There are ', cardcount :1, ' cards in the deck.');
  end.


run countcards
```

```
Input data  information:        462
Input data  information:      -1234
Input data  information:       3189
Input data  information:          0
Input data  information:       5000
Input data  information:       -500
Input data  information:         -1
Input data  information:       9999
There are 7 cards in the deck.
```

Refining the initialization statement last has numerous counterparts in daily life. For instance, in taking a vacation, packing your clothes is an initialization step that precedes the main experience. Of course, in planning the vacation (that is, programming it), you decide on the main events before you refine the packing step by determining what clothes to bring and how to put them into your suitcase.

Preparing Input Data

Many a correctly written while-loop fails during execution because the input data has not been prepared correctly. For example, consider the procedure readinput, paraphrased to emphasize the relevant steps.

```
procedure readinput;
  begin
  nrcourses := 0;
  morecourses := true;
  while (morecourses) and (nrcourses < maxcourses) do
    begin
    readln (letter, number);
    if letter = signal then
      morecourses := false
    else
      begin
      echo the input data;
      nrcourses := nrcourses + 1;
      lettergrade [nrcourses] := letter;
      credit [nrcourses] := number;
      end; { else }
    end; { while-loop }
  end; { readinput }
```

The important point is that precisely the same statement

```
readln (letter, number)
```

is used to read the real course grade entries as is used to read the termination signal entry. Thus the input data for the termination signal entry must contain a value for the number of credits, even though only the letter grade is tested to determine whether a real grade or a signal entry has been read. If the input file omits a value for the number of credits in the termination signal entry, the computer will probably search ahead trying to find one in the next group of data, or report an out-of-data error or a mistaken data type when it tries to interpret the next student's name as a number of credits. Most important, all this happens *before* the if-test in the next statement is attempted, so the execution probably will terminate with an error message or proceed with incorrect values.

The same problem can arise when we use a while-statement and a termination signal to rewrite the main loop that runs through all the students. The main program is easy to modify, and we do so without further fuss; only the preparation of the input data to accompany the modified program is tricky.

```
{ main program modified to use a termination signal }

const
   signalname = 'zzzzzzzzzzzzzzzzzzzzzzzzzzzzzz';

var
   morestudents : boolean;
      .
      .
      .

morestudents := true;
while morestudents do
   begin
   { process one student's gradepoint average }
   readinput; { modified to use signal }
   if name = signalname then
      morestudents := false
   else
      begin
      convertletterstonumbers;
      calculategpa;
      printoutput;
      end; { else }
   end; { while-loop }
end. { allgradeptavgs with 2 levels of termination signals }
```

The boolean variable morestudents controls repetition of the while-loop. If a real student's name and grades are read by the procedure readinput, then that student's gradepoint average is computed as before. If, however, the name read is the signal name consisting of 30 z's, then the condition morestudents is set to false and no further processing takes place. The difficult part is the preparation of the input file so that the program execution does not terminate with an error message in the procedure readinput *before* the if-test in the main program recognizes that the signal name has been read. As the program now stands, this means that the fake name that indicates a termination signal must be followed by a complete set of fake course grades and credits, including the signal entry "Z −9", which indicates that there are no more course grades for that student. The shortest input sequence that would serve to terminate the "while morestudents" loop is the following.

```
zzzzzzzzzzzzzzzzzzzzzzzzzzzzzz
Z −9
```

Repeat-Until-Loops

In ordinary English, it means the same thing when we say to execute a loop *while some condition is true* as to say to execute the loop *until the condition becomes false*, or *until the negation of the condition becomes true*. The choice of description is largely a matter of taste and whether the condition or its negation is more natural to talk about. Pascal also offers a loop structure based on the "repeat-until" construction that can do almost, but not quite, everything a while-loop can do, with almost equal ease. We now give one example to indicate what some of the programs in this section would look like using repeat-until-loops; it is the program countcards rewritten with the while-loop replaced by a repeat-until-loop.

```
program countcards (input, output);
{ uses repeat-until-loop }

  const
    signal = 9999;

  var
    cardcount, information : integer;
    outofcards : boolean;
  begin
  cardcount : = 0;
  { loop to read and count cards }
  outofcards : = false;
  repeat
    readln (information);
    writeln ('Input data  information: ', information);
    if information = signal then
      outofcards : = true
    else
      cardcount : = cardcount + 1;
    until outofcards;
  writeln ('There are ', cardcount :1, ' cards in the deck.');
  end.
```

Little is changed except to shift attention from the boolean condition variable morecards in countcards to its negation, the boolean variable outofcards in countcards2. The syntax of a repeat-until-loop shown in Figure 2.3.2 is uncharacteristic of Pascal in that the body of the loop is a sequence of statements sandwiched between the keywords "repeat" and "until" rather than a single statement that may be compound. Thus the keywords "begin" and "end" that ordinarily appear in loops that are more than one statement long may be omitted in a repeat-until-loop.

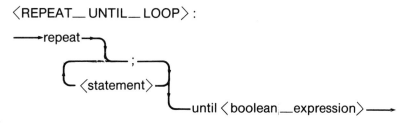

Figure 2.3.2   Repeat-until-loop syntax chart.

Repeat-until-loops are the opposite of while loops in another major respect. Whereas the boolean condition that controls repetition of a while-loop is tested only just before each iteration of the loop body, the boolean condition that controls repetition of a repeat-until-loop is tested only after the completion of each iteration of the loop body. In particular, the body of a repeat-until-loop is always executed at least once because no test for completion is made until after the first iteration is complete.

We do not use repeat-until-loops at all in the rest of the book because we believe that one good way to do everything is enough. Other reasons to avoid the repeat-until-loop are its syntactic peculiarities mentioned above and the fact that the termination condition appears at the end of the loop where it is more difficult to find.

Comparison of Loop Constructs

There are three major loop constructs in Pascal: the for-loop, the while-loop, and the repeat-until-loop. We now show with a few simple examples how the latter two loop structures differ but little from each other, while the for-loop is the more natural construct for an entirely different class of programs.

In the first group of programs, we want to find the first positive integer whose square exceeds 1000. A while-loop provides a clear program.

```
program testsquares1 (output);
  var
    n : integer;
  begin
  n := 0;
  while n * n <= 1000 do
    n := n + 1;
  writeln (n :1, ' is the smallest number ',
      'whose square exceeds 1000.');
  end.
```

```
run testsquares1
```

```
32 is the smallest number whose square exceeds 1000.
```

For this example, a repeat-until-loop is equally clear.

```
program testsquares2 (output);
  var
    n : integer;
  begin
  n := 0;
  repeat
    n := n + 1;
    until n * n > 1000;
  writeln (n :1, ' is the smallest number ',
      'whose square exceeds 1000.');
  end.
```

```
run testsquares2
```

```
32 is the smallest number whose square exceeds 1000.
```

Notice that the boolean condition in both a while-test and a repeat-until-test may be any boolean expression involving comparison operators as well as the boolean operations ''and'', ''or'', and ''not''. There is no completely satisfactory way to write this program using a for-loop.

On the other hand, when the loop limits are known in advance, the for-loop provides a natural program and both the while-loop and the repeat-until-loop are slightly awkward. For comparison, all three programs below print a table of squares from 1 to 10.

```
program squares1 (output);
  var
    n : integer;
  begin
  writeln ('number  square');
  for n := 1 to 10 do
    writeln (n :4, n * n :8);
  end.
```

```
run squares1
```

```
number  square
   1       1
   2       4
   3       9
   4      16
   5      25
   6      36
   7      49
   8      64
   9      81
  10     100
```

```
program squares2 (output);
  var
    n : integer;
  begin
  writeln ('number  square');
  n := 1;
  while n <= 10 do
    begin
    writeln (n :4, n * n :8);
    n := n + 1;
    end; { while-loop }
  end.
```

```
program squares3 (output);
  var
    n : integer;
  begin
  writeln ('number   square');
  n := 1;
  repeat
    writeln (n :4, n * n :8);
    n := n + 1;
    until n > 10;
  end.
```

Execution printouts are not shown for squares2 and squares3 because they duplicate that of squares1. Notice that both the while-loop and the repeat-until-loop require an explicit initialization

```
n := 1
```

and incrementation

```
n := n + 1
```

statements as well as their termination test expressions

```
while n <= 10    and    until n > 10
```

A for-loop is preferable for this application, because it condenses these details into the heading.

Exercises

---

1. The program countcards in this section reads a deck of computer cards and counts how many cards there are. Write a computer program to read two decks of computer cards and determine whether the two decks have the same number of cards. If your computer does not use punched cards for input, substitute "sequence of input values" for "deck of cards" in this problem.

2. Redesign the program avgofscores in Section 1.3 so that the computer does not need to be told in advance the number of students in the class. Instead, let the computer count the number of scores as they are read from the input cards. What is an appropriate signal value to punch into the card that follows the last real test score? The sample data used in the execution in Section 1.3 may be used to test the program, since their averages already have been calculated.

3. Rewrite the procedure readinput so that when the termination signal letter grade is read, the computer does not try to read a number of credits to go along with it. Instead execution of the procedure readinput should terminate without further action. Hint: Read a letter grade and a number of credits in separate read statements.

4. Rewrite the program allgradeptavgs so that as soon as the termination signal name is read, no further input is attempted. Hint: Break the procedure readinput into two procedures readname and readgrades.

5. A rabbit is 10 meters away from a carrot patch. It hops half the distance to the carrot patch and is then 5 meters away. It then hops half the remaining distance and is 2 1/2 meters away. The rabbit continues to hop half the distance. Write a program to calculate the number of hops the rabbit must take until it reaches the carrot patch. Does the execution of this program ever halt? (This is a tricky question!)

6. The number 10 is the square root of the number 100 because $10 \times 10 = 100$. If one guessed that the square root of 100 is 10, this could be verified because $100 / 10 = 10$, the original guess. If, however, the guess were too low, such as 9, the quotient $100 / 9 = 11.11111$ would be too high. If the guess were too high, perhaps 11, then the quotient $100 / 11 = 9.090909$ would be too low. In either case, the average of the guess and the quotient would be a much better guess than either. Write a program to use this method, sometimes called Newton's method, to calculate an approximate value for the square root of 100, printing all the guesses along the way. Stop the program after printing a final answer if the new guess is equal to the quotient of 100 and the new guess. In testing the program, try first guesses of 9, 10, 11, and 1.

7. Modify the program written for Exercise 6 to find an approximate value for the square root of 2. Use 1 as the initial guess.

8. Write a program, based on the method in Exercise 6, to find an approximate value for the square root of any number from 1 to 100 supplied as input. The number need not be an integer. Use an initial guess of 10 in all cases.

9. Modify the square root program for Exercise 6, 7, or 8 so that the process of testing a guess by division and making a new guess which is the average of the old guess and the quotient is never done more than 10 times. Hint: Keep a running count of the number of iterations of the process and add a second condition done10times to the while-test in the heading of the loop, as was done in the recipe final preparation for soup 2 in this section.

10. Each card of a deck of computer punchcards contains a number from -5000 to $+5000$. Write a computer program to read the deck of cards and count how many of them contain positive numbers, how many contain negative numbers, and how many contain the number 0.

11. Modify either the program countcards in this section or the program written for Exercise 10 so that, if a number outside the range -5000 to 5000 for valid data is encountered in the input data, but the number is not the termination signal value 9999, the following actions will be taken. The number on the invalid data card will be printed along with the position of the card in the deck, for example, 327th card. The invalid card should not be counted. Then the program execution will continue to count the rest of the cards.

2.4 Simulating Population Changes

The example in this section shows how to write a program that differs in two major ways from the programs written previously. First, the program execution consists of far more calculation than input. In fact, there are no read statements and only a scant handful of constants and variables assigned values in the initialization section. In contrast, programs like the payroll programs in this chapter and the averaging programs in Chapter 1 specify a fixed amount of calculation for each piece of input data. Thus the length of the program execution is directly dependent on the amount of input data.

Second, the number of iterations of the loop in the example in this section is neither fixed in advance nor directly tied to the amount of input data. Termination of the loop is determined by continually testing the value of a variable whose values cannot be predicted before the program is run. In programming terms, the loop structure of the example in this section closely resembles that of the soup preparation recipes in the previous section.

Population Density Of New Jersey

The problem is to predict the population of a state, say, New Jersey, at some time in the future. Of course, the predictions must be based on reliable information about the current population of New Jersey and, equally important, on some reasonable assumptions about how the population is likely to continue to grow in the future. The predictions can be only as accurate as the starting data and the assumptions about the growth rate. The programming method is called "computer simulation". Further discussion of the techniques, uses, and pitfalls of computer simulation are found in Chapter 7.

The most accurate information about the population of New Jersey is contained in the national census taken every 10 years by the Bureau of Census. In 1960, the population of New Jersey was 6,066,782 and, in 1970, the population had grown to 7,168,164. These numbers are the starting data of the simulation. The program poppredict is written in this section to investigate what would happen if the same population growth rate as occurred over the 10-year period 1960-1970 were to continue every 10 years into the future. This would be the case if there were no major changes in the birthrates, death rates, and immigration patterns into and out of New Jersey during the period of the simulation.

It is interesting to note that the computer punchcard was invented for use by the Bureau of the Census because the data from the 10-year census was taking longer that 10 years to tabulate. Computers were not available to help in the work until over half a century later, but now it is impossible to tabulate all the data collected in a census without their aid.

Because it is difficult for a person to visualize a million or more people, to give a clear, intuitive understanding of the meaning of the predicted populations, the program calculates the average number of square feet that will be available for each person in New Jersey during the years simulated. The average number of square feet per person can be compared to an easily visualized area such as 100 feet by 100 feet = 10,000 square feet. The additional piece of data required for this calculation, the area of New Jersey, is 7836 square miles, of which 7521 square miles are above mean high water. The number of square feet of dry land in New Jersey is calculated by multiplying 7521 square miles by 5280 squared, because there are 5280 feet in a mile. Rather than multiplying this out by hand, it can be left for the computer to do as part of the program.

The number of square feet per person in New Jersey is estimated every 10 years by dividing the number of square feet in New Jersey by the predicted number of people in New Jersey in that year. No allowance is made in the model for changes in land area due to an approaching ice age or sanitary landfill. The prediction of future populations will stop when (and if) there is less than 1 square foot of land per person in New Jersey.

The Population Prediction Program

There is now sufficient information available to write a first version of the program poppredict to solve this problem. The main part of the program consists of a loop executed once for each 10-year period. This time the procedure initialize is used from the start, because we know that there will be several initial calculations including calculating the area of New Jersey in square feet.

```
program poppredict (output);
  initialize;
  while NJ not very crowded do
    begin
    advance time by ten years
    calculate predicted population for this year
    print data for this year
    if space per person < 1 sq. ft. then
      confirm that NJ is very crowded
    end; { while-loop }
```

Keeping Track of Time

The advance of time can be recorded by a variable named year. With this choice of variable name, advancing time by 10 years is accomplished by executing the statement

```
year := year + 10
```

As usual, a variable like year that is changed within a loop requires some initialization before entering the loop. It must also be declared. For reasons explained later, the initialization step for the variable year, included in the procedure initialize, is

```
year := 1960
```

Predicting the Population

The population prediction for each 10-year period is based on the assumption that the rate of population growth for each decade is the same as for the decade from 1960 to 1970. First, this growth rate must be calculated in the initialization procedure. Then it is used in each repetition of the loop to predict the new population at the end of a 10-year period. The following statements calculate the population growth rate for the base period 1960-1970.

```
baseincrease := pop1970 - pop1960;
growthrate := baseincrease / pop1960;
```

It is also clear that the two constant declarations

```
pop1960 = 6066782.0
pop1970 = 7168164.0
```

must be included for the calculation of the growth rate. With the growth rate calculated before entering the loop, the population prediction step may be refined into the statements

```
popinc := pop * growthrate;
pop := pop + popinc;
```

Since these two statements change the value of the variable pop on each iteration of the loop, an initial value must be given to that variable before the loop is entered. Corresponding to the initial value of 1960 for the variable year, the initial value for pop must be the 1960 population. Thus the following statement is included in the procedure initialize.

```
pop := pop1960
```

Calculating the Population Density

Once the population has been predicted, the average number of square feet available per person may be calculated for any year of the simulation by the statement

```
sqftperson := sqft / pop
```

Writing this statement should remind the programmer that part of the procedure initialize must establish a value for the variable sqft. The program step that does the standard conversion to different units

```
sqft := sqmiles * 5280 * 5280;
```

resembles a step in the program meterstoinches in Section 1.2. The quantity sqmiles is established as 7521 using a constant declaration.

Incorporating all these details, we obtain the following refinement of the program poppredict. Unlike what was done in the refinement process for the program payroll, the first program in this chapter, we do not write down a new, complete refinement each time a single statement of the program poppredict is refined. This does not represent a basic difference in method, but rather an increased familiarity with the method, and consequently an increased ability to see what is going on without writing every intermediate step out in full. It is still perfectly permissible to write each refinement out in full as it is done. It only takes more paper.

```
program poppredict (output);

  const
    sqmiles = 7521.0;
    pop1960 = 6066782.0;
    pop1970 = 7168164.0;

  var
    baseincrease, growthrate, pop, popinc,
        sqft, sqftperson : real;
    year : integer;
    njcrowded : boolean;

  procedure initialize;
    begin
    sqft := sqmiles * 5280 * 5280;
    baseincrease := pop1970 - pop1960;
    growthrate := baseincrease / pop1960;
    year := 1960;
    pop := pop1960;

    { print heading }
    writeln;
    writeln ('  Year           Population        Sq. ft. per person');
    writeln;
    end; { initialize }

  begin
  initialize;
  njcrowded := false;
  while not njcrowded do
    begin
    year := year + 10;
    popinc := pop * growthrate;
    pop := pop + popinc;
    sqftperson := sqft / pop;
    { columns indicators used to align columns }
    writeln (year :6, pop :23, sqftperson :15:2);
    if sqftperson < 1 then
      njcrowded := true;
    end; { while-loop }
  end.


run poppredict
```

Year	Population	Sq. ft. per person
1970	7.168164000000000e + 06	29250.65
1980	8.469494227894788e + 06	24756.31
1990	1.000707189126018e + 07	20952.53
2000	1.182378606588190e + 07	17733.19
2010	1.397031204041224e + 07	15008.50
2020	1.650652484906324e + 07	12702.46
2030	1.950316942131110e + 07	10750.74
2040	2.304383393564216e + 07	9098.90
2050	2.722728142192162e + 07	7700.86
2060	3.217020464992600e + 07	6517.63
2070	3.801048114869335e + 07	5516.20
2080	4.491101915195606e + 07	4668.64
2090	5.306430174816929e + 07	3951.31
2100	6.269775598931430e + 07	3344.19
2110	7.408009672399423e + 07	2830.36
2120	8.752882210922584e + 07	2395.48
2130	1.034190698801699e + 08	2027.42
2140	1.221940814139222e + 08	1715.91
2150	1.443775654711751e + 08	1452.26
2160	1.705883064890283e + 08	1229.12
2170	2.015574249075736e + 08	1040.27
2180	2.381487709885030e + 08	880.43
2190	2.813830209893864e + 08	745.15
2200	3.324661478304914e + 08	630.66
2210	3.928230604127866e + 08	533.76
2220	4.641373499197371e + 08	451.75
2230	5.483982517832456e + 08	382.34
2240	6.479561332672901e + 08	323.59
2250	7.655880544357439e + 08	273.87
2260	9.045752312570882e + 08	231.79
2270	1.068794561596038e + 09	196.18
2280	1.262826767111213e + 09	166.04
2290	1.492084167560823e + 09	140.52
2300	1.762961651643237e + 09	118.93
2310	2.083015055541734e + 09	100.66
2320	2.461171924851141e + 09	85.19
2330	2.907980538863710e + 09	72.10
2340	3.435904143478939e + 09	61.02
2350	4.059668600048027e + 09	51.65
2360	4.796673147443680e + 09	43.71
2370	5.667475735121598e + 09	37.00
2380	6.696366465017562e + 09	31.31
2390	7.912045137825316e + 09	26.50
2400	9.348421803080194e + 09	22.43
2410	1.104556264353236e + 10	18.98
2420	1.305080757823728e + 10	16.07
2430	1.542009075870002e + 10	13.60
2440	1.821950079189365e + 10	11.51
2450	2.152712421089526e + 10	9.74
2460	2.543522361477103e + 10	8.24
2470	3.005281123458064e + 10	6.98

2480	3.550868971235763e + 10	5.90
2490	4.195504491232623e + 10	5.00
2500	4.957169098196046e + 10	4.23
2510	5.857108607429995e + 10	3.58
2520	6.920425863970359e + 10	3.03
2530	8.176780959457786e + 10	2.56
2540	9.661218568504812e + 10	2.17
2550	1.141514548221573e + 11	1.84
2560	1.348748560610575e + 11	1.55
2570	1.593604463984455e + 11	1.32
2580	1.882912250509853e + 11	1.11
2590	2.224741849841269e + 11	0.94

The names of the variables in the population prediction program are self-explanatory. However, a few of them have to be modified slightly from the most natural English phrases to meet the requirements of Pascal and to prevent them from being overly long. For example, pop1960 was chosen because 1960population does not start with a letter. Also, the characters ''sqft/person'' mean the quotient of a variable called sqft and one called person and cannot be used as a variable name.

The constants pop1960 and pop1970 and the variable pop are all type real because their values exceed the maximum integer values allowed on some computers. Notice that numerical constants in a program cannot contain commas.

Checking the Population Prediction Program

The population prediction program has a nice check built into it. The 1970 population is the first one actually calculated by the program, as written, during the first execution of the loop. The value calculated by the prediction scheme can be compared to the actual 1970 population, the constant 7168164 assigned to the variable pop1970. This check is the reason why the variable year is initialized to 1960 and the variable population is initialized to the 1960 population 6066782. The program would work as well if the initialization of year were 1970 and the initial value for pop were 7168164, the 1970 population. Only then, the first year for which the program predicts the population would be 1980, and the programmer would not have this useful check on its predictions.

A second check is provided by the fact that the population in 2590, for example, can be obtained by multiplying the 1960 population 63 times by the factor (1 + growthrate), once for each decade between 1960 and 2590. Thus the population prediction for 2560 is

```
pop1960 * (1 + growthrate) to the 63rd power
```

a number that can be obtained either by using an electronic calculator or logarithms, or by writing another simple program for a computer. Methods of raising a number to a power are described in Sections 2.5 and 2.6.

Exit Tests

The termination condition for the loop in the program poppredict is designed to carry the prediction to an absurd extreme, but it is carefully written to avoid an endless loop. An average of only 1 square foot per person is obviously so crowded that something would have to change in the assumption about the growth rate before this unfortunate state is reached. However, the form of the test is

```
if sqftperson < 1 then
```

rather than the equality test

```
if sqftperson = 1 then
```

because, as the execution output shows, it is unlikely that the quantity sqftperson will ever be exactly equal to any predetermined number. Only under special circumstances (as when all the numbers involved in the calculation are small integers and no division is used) is an equality test likely to work. Otherwise, exact equality is rarely obtained, and the result is an endless loop. Section 2.7 considers roundoff error and its effect on equality test in more detail.

Ensuring Termination of a While-Loop

Even with the inequality test for loop termination, it is hard to predict how many iterations will be required before the termination condition is satisfied, if indeed it ever will be. As a safeguard, suppose one is willing or allowed to print at most 200 lines of population predictions before quitting, even if the termination condition is not satisfied. Some combination of a for-loop and a while-loop such as

```
{ not Pascal }
for year := 1970 to 3960 in steps of 10 while not njcrowded
```

would be just the thing to have in this situation. Pascal does not have such a statement, but the same effect can be achieved by having a termination condition that depends upon the value of the variable year as well as the size of the population. The while-statement heading becomes

```
while (not njcrowded) and (year < 3960) do
```

In this revised program, there are two possible reasons that the loop might terminate. One is that after 200 or fewer iterations, the calculations will show that New Jersey is very crowded, that is, the area per person is less than 1 square foot. In this case the boolean variable njcrowded will be changed from its initial value false to true, so when the while-test is made prior to the next execution of the loop, it will be false and the loop will not be executed again.

The other possibility is that New Jersey does not become crowded by the year 3960 (but this is hardly likely). In this case, the loop will execute 200 times with both parts of the while-condition always remaining true, after which the expression (year < 3960) becomes false and the statement following the while-loop will be executed. In this case the boolean variable njcrowded will still have the value false after the loop is executed 200 times.

It is also appropriate to print a different message at the end depending upon whether the loop was terminated due to overcrowding in New Jersey or it was terminated after executing 200 times. This can be accomplished be adding the following statement at the end of the program.

```
if njcrowded then
  writeln ('New Jersey is very crowded; better move to New Mexico.')
else
  writeln ('New Jersey is not overcrowded in the year 3960.');
```

Exercises

---

1. Modify the program poppredict so that it predicts the future populations of your home state. An almanac or atlas should be consulted to provide the required census and area data.

2. The stopping criterion of less than 1 square foot per person used in the program poppredict is obviously absurd. Choose a more reasonable stopping value in the following way. Take the area (in square feet) of the plot of land on which you or your family lives and divide it by the number of people living there. Use this number of square feet per person as the stopping criterion in a modification of either the program poppredict as written for New Jersey, or as modified in Exercise 1 for your home state. Let the computer do whatever additional arithmetic is needed in the procedure initialize.

3. Use the built-in function round, described in Sections 2.2 and 2.6, to ensure that the populations predicted by the program poppredict are always whole numbers. (Who ever heard of 0.227894787 of a person?) How much difference does this make in the predictions?

4. Suppose a person has a very long shopping list but only a limited amount of money. The items on the list appear in order of priority. Write a program that tells a computer to first accept as input the amount of available money and then the prices of the various items on the list until all the money is spent. The computer should then print the number of items the person can purchase.

5. Suppose a person has a shopping list and enough money to buy everything on it. Write a program that directs a computer to first accept as input the amount of available money and then the prices of the various items. A price of zero is to be regarded as a signal that there are no more items, after which the remaining amount of money is to be printed.

6. Suppose a person has a shopping list but does not know whether there is enough money to pay for everything on it. Write a program that directs a computer to first accept the amount of money available and then the prices of the various items either until all the money runs out, in which case it should print out the number of items that can be purchased, or until a price of zero is entered indicating the end of the list, in which case it should print out the amount of money remaining after everything on the list has been purchased.

7. In testing for a certain disease, a specimen is taken that will contain an average of 20 individual disease bacteria if the disease is present. The specimen is then placed in a nutrient dish and incubated to promote growth. Under these conditions, the population of the disease bacteria is found to double every 37 minutes. It is estimated that a colony of between 1 and 2 million bacteria is needed before a positive identification can be made. Write a computer program that simulates the population growth of the bacteria colony and determines how long the bacteria culture should be incubated. The final answer should be converted to hours.

2.5 Using The Value of a For-Variable

Quite frequently, the successive values taken on by a variable follow a simple pattern, such as 1, 2, 3, 4, 5, 6, 7, 8, 9, 10, or 7, 6, 5, 4. Because these sequences occur so often in programming, there is a simple means of assigning successive values to a variable in Pascal. These are precisely the kinds of values assumed by a for-variable during execution of a for-loop.

Counting Forward

As the first example of the use of a for-variable in a loop, the program tennumbers tells a computer to print the numbers from 1 to 10. The only variable in the program, number, is declared to be type integer.

```
program tennumbers (output);
  var
    number : integer;
  begin
  for number := 1 to 10 do
    write (number :3);
  writeln;
  end.
```

```
run tennumbers

  1   2   3   4   5   6   7   8   9 10
```

The for-loop in this program consists of the heading and the body, which is a single write statement. The for-statement directs the computer to execute the write statement 10 times, once for each value of the variable number from 1 to 10. For each repetition of the body of the for-loop, the for-variable—that is, the variable named "number" in the for-statement that heads the block—takes on a new value.

During execution of the program tennumbers, the for-variable number first assumes the value 1, which is printed, as directed by the write command. After the body of the for-loop is executed using the value 1 for the for-variable number, the for-loop body execution is repeated using the value 2 for number. Thus, on the second iteration, the write command causes the number 2 to be printed. Then the for-loop body is executed again, this time using the value 3 for the for-variable number. Thus, on the third iteration, the write statement causes the value 3 to be printed, and so forth. Finally, on the tenth iteration, when the value of the for-variable number is 10, the write statement causes the number 10 to be printed; but no further repetition occurs, because the for-statement heading the loop specified that 10 is the highest value of the for-variable number. Execution of the for-loop is complete and execution of the program is completed by executing the writeln command to cause the unfinished line to be printed.

A Table of Squares and Square Roots

A structurally minor modification of the program tennumbers can produce a program sqrandsqrt to print a table of squares and square roots of numbers from 1 to 10. This program uses the built-in functions sqr (square) and sqrt (square root) described at the end of the next section.

```
program sqrandsqrt (output);
  var
    number : integer;
  begin
  writeln ('Number' :10, 'Square' :10, 'Square root' :15);
  for number := 1 to 10 do
    writeln (number :10, sqr (number) :10, sqrt (number) :15:3);
  end.
```

```
run sqrandsqrt
```

Number	Square	Square root
1	1	1.000
2	4	1.414
3	9	1.732
4	16	2.000
5	25	2.236
6	36	2.449
7	49	2.646
8	64	2.828
9	81	3.000
10	100	3.162

Eleven lines of output are printed by the program sqrandsqrt. The first writeln command that prints the heading of the columns is executed only once, because it is not within the for-loop. To make it easier for a person to see which instructions are to be repeated, the authors always indent the body of a for-loop. After the headings are printed, the writeln command within the for-loop prints a number, its square, and its square root, for each value of the variable number from 1 to 10.

There are three reasonable ways to decide what spacing must be used in the writeln command that prints the column headings. One is to run the program without printing the column heading or with a rough approximation of the proper position of the column headings, then to count how many spaces must be inserted or removed to position each heading directly over its column of numbers. The second method is to calculate where the column headings must start to be properly positioned over their respective columns, based on the formatting for the three numbers. If this method misses by a few spaces, as it so often does in practice, the first method can be used to improve the positioning. We recall that blank spaces written between an opening apostrophe and its paired closing apostrophe are perfectly usual characters in a character string, and are printed as blanks whenever the string is printed. The third method for ensuring that columns line up properly is to use the columns indicator with three character strings when printing the headings as described in Section 1.2; this is the method used in the program sqrandsqrt.

Counting Backward

In Pascal, it is possible to have a for-variable count backwards. Thus it is possible to print the complete words to the popular camp song "Ninety-Nine Bottles of Beer on the Wall" using a for-loop with the keyword "downto". Note that "downto" is a single keyword; no space is permitted within the keyword. The program beer to print the verses is given below, and the music is given in Figure 2.5.1.

```
program beer (output);
for n := 99 downto 1 do
   begin
```

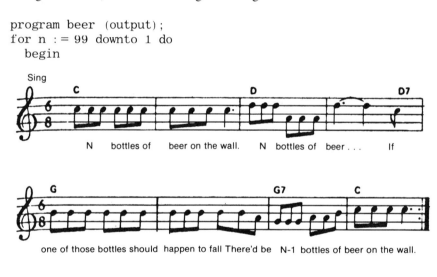

```
      end { of for-loop }
```

Figure 2.5.1   A musical for-loop for a 5-mile hike.

```
program beer (output);
  var
    n : integer;
  begin
  for n := 99 downto 1 do
    begin
    writeln;
    writeln (n :1, ' bottles of beer on the wall.');
    writeln (n :1, ' bottles of beer.');
    writeln ('If one of those bottles should happen to fall,');
    writeln ('There''d be ', n - 1 :1, ' bottles of beer on the wall.');
    end; { verse-loop }
  end.
```

```
run beer

99 bottles of beer on the wall.
99 bottles of beer.
If one of those bottles should happen to fall,
There'd be 98 bottles of beer on the wall.

98 bottles of beer on the wall.
98 bottles of beer.
If one of those bottles should happen to fall,
There'd be 97 bottles of beer on the wall.

97 bottles of beer on the wall.
97 bottles of beer.
If one of those bottles should happen to fall,
There'd be 96 bottles of beer on the wall.
        .
        .
        .

1 bottles of beer on the wall.
1 bottles of beer.
If one of those bottles should happen to fall,
There'd be 0 bottles of beer on the wall.
```

A short name n is chosen for the for-variable to make it easier to sing the program listing. The execution printout shown is abbreviated after three full verses, with the last verse also given to show how the loop ends. In practice, it is rarely reached, except by scouts on a 5-mile hike.

Note that the last line of each verse of the song contains an apostrophe. Apostrophes are used to delimit the character string within the program, so the apostrophe in ''there'd'' would normally be taken as the end of the character string. To avoid this difficulty, each apostrophe in a character string is represented by two apostrophes.

In the last verse of the song, shown in the abbreviated sample execution, and in the next to last verse, not shown, the computer printout continues to use the word ''bottles'', even though there is only one bottle of beer left on the wall. All too frequently, the users of computers see this violation of the rules of English grammar in their printouts, so much so that it has come to be recognized as a trademark or characteristic of a computerized operation. This need not happen.

The grammar shown is incorrect not because a computer is incapable of producing correct grammar, but because it is easier to write a program that allows the computer to err in these two cases than it is to write a program that treats all cases properly. What happens in the program beer is that the convenience of the programmer has taken inappropriate precedence over the convenience of the user of the program. For this application, it is not too difficult to correct the grammar of the last verses. (Two ways to do it are described in Exercises 12 and 13.) In many applications, the programmer should work just a little bit harder to produce a program more congenial to the eventual user.

Variable Limits for a For-Loop

For users who do not need or want all the lyrics of the popular camp song printed, the modified program anybeer allows a choice of which verses to print. The starting value and the stopping value need not be constants, but may also be given as the values of variables or other expressions. Of course, if a variable is used in specifying the starting value or stopping value for a for-variable, then it must be assigned a value before the for-loop is reached.

```
program anybeer (input, output);
  var
    first, last, n : integer;
  begin
  read (first, last);
  writeln ('Input data  first: ', first :1);
  writeln ('             last: ', last :1);
  for n := first downto last do
    begin
    writeln;
    writeln (n :1, ' bottles of beer on the wall.');
    writeln (n :1, ' bottles of beer.');
    writeln ('If one of these bottles should happen to fall,');
    writeln ('There''d be ', n - 1 :1, ' bottles of beer on the wall.');
    end;
  end.
run anybeer

Input data  first: 83
            last: 81

83 bottles of beer on the wall.
    .
    .
    .
```

For-Loops That Are Executed No Times

Sometimes, the body of a for-loop is executed no times at all. For one example, the body of a for-loop headed by

```
for n := 1 to 0 do
```

is never executed. Although there might seem to be no reason to write such a for-statement, a for-loop whose body goes unexecuted can occur meaningfully in practice when either the lower limit or the upper limit is a variable. For instance, the loop

```
for n := 1 to numberofentries do
  print the nth entry;
```

could be used to print all the entries in some collection. The convention that a for-loop may sometimes be executed no times at all is a tremendous convenience to programmers, because it enables this same for-loop to do exactly what is wanted, even when the number of entries happens to be zero. That is, the loop body is executed no times when there are no entries to print.

Counting By Twos

In Pascal, the differences between successive values of a for-variable must always be 1 or -1, as they have been in the previous examples. However, it is possible to achieve the effect of differences that are not 1 or -1, as is illustrated by the following two programs. The output from only one of these programs is shown, because both programs produce the same output.

```
program countbytwos1 (output);
  var
    m : integer;
  begin
  for m := 1 to 5 do
    write (2 * m :3);
  writeln;
  end.
```

```
program countbytwos2 (output);
  var
    n : integer;
  begin
  n := 2;
  while n <= 10 do
    begin
    write (n :3);
    n := n + 2;
    end; { loop }
  writeln;
  end.
```

```
run countbytwos1

  2  4  6  8 10
```

The first of these programs preserves the flavor of a for-loop headed by the non-Pascal statement

```
for n := 2 to 10 in steps of 2 { not Pascal }
```

which is convenient to use for planning programs, but, of course, must be refined to valid Pascal statements for execution. In the program countbytwos1, the role of the variable n (which does not appear) is played by 2 * m.

The second of these programs converts the for-loop to a while-loop. Since the while-statement heading

```
while n <= 10 do
```

tests only for completion of the for-loop, the programmer must supply a separate initialization statement

```
n := 2
```

before the loop and a separate incrementing statement

```
n := n + 2
```

within the loop to do the three jobs done by a for-statement.

Calculating a Mortgage Table

Nearly everyone who buys a house needs a mortgage in order to borrow some of the money for its purchase. A bank provides the needed money when the house is purchased, and the homeowner repays the bank in equal monthly installments over a relatively long period of time. What a prospective homeowner needs to know before buying a house and taking out a mortgage on it is how much the equal monthly payments are going to be. Neither the homeowner nor the bank wants to enter into a mortgage agreement where the monthly payments are more than the homeowner can afford to pay. Table 2.5.1 shows the basic form of a useful table of monthly payment amounts, keyed to the interest rate. For a $20,000 mortgage, the monthly payment is doubled, for a $30,000 mortgage, it is tripled, etc. A different table is needed if the duration of the mortgage is other than 25 years.

Table 2.5.1   Monthly Payments on a 25-Year Mortgage of $10,000 for a Few Possible Interest Rates.

Annual Interest Rate (%)	Monthly Payments ($)
11	98.01131
11.25	99.82395
11.5	101.6469
11.75	103.4798
12	105.3224

A Formula for Mortgage Installments

The formula for the amount a of the equal monthly installment on a mortgage of p dollars is

$$a = p * i * c / (c - 1)$$

where p = principal = amount borrowed
    i = monthly interest rate = annual interest rate / 12
    n = number of monthly payments = number of years * 12
    c = (1 + i) raised to the nth power

The derivation of this formula is of no immediate interest from a programming point of view, although persons who can derive the formula can check that no errors have been made in copying it. *A programmer does not need to know how a formula is derived—only how to program it.* Although some scientists and other people do their own programming, it is more frequently the case that a specialist who derives a formula turns the task of generating values from the formula over to a professional programmer. The programmer needs only to know how to write a program to calculate the formula

and for which values of the variables answers are desired. Simple curiosity and the
need to anticipate at least some of the answers for debugging purposes may lead a programmer to find out more about a formula than the bare minimum.

Incrementing Variables By a Value Other Than One

The program mortgage1, given below in preliminary form, again illustrates a situation in which a variable is to be incremented by a value different from one each time a
loop is executed. The intended values of the interest rate are every quarter of a percent
from the lowest interest rate specified by the user to the highest rate. Pascal does not
permit a for-variable to be incremented by any values other than plus or minus one;
therefore, some other means must be used to set and increment the value of the interest
rate. The program mortgage1 uses a while-loop patterned on the program count-
bytwos2.

```
program mortgage1 (input, output);
{ unrefined version }
  begin
  read values for the following:
      principal = the amount borrowed,
      years = the number of years mortgage runs,
      lowest = the lowest percentage rate,
      highest = the highest percentage rate;
  print table headings;
  rate : = lowest;
  while rate <= highest do
    calculate the monthly payment;
    write rate and payment;
    increase rate by 0.25;
  end.
```

In the refined version of this program, the formula for calculating the monthly payments is as recognizable as typography allows, because most of the original variable
names in the formula are retained in the program. Longer variable names could be
made more self-documenting, but they would make the formula longer and less readable. Often a programmer must choose between giving a long variable name that completely describes what values are assigned to a variable and a shorter name that is more
convenient to use. In this case, we have chosen the short variable names of the original
formula, except for the variable principal that appears in an input echo or prompt. The
original formula given earlier might be appended as documentation to a copy of the program. Note that a loop is used to raise $1 + i$ to the nth power.

```
program mortgage1 (input, output);

  const
    increment = 0.25;

  var
    years, n, power : integer;
    principal, lowrate, highrate,
        rate, annualrate, i, c, payment : real;
```

```
procedure readvalues;
  begin
  read (principal);
  writeln ('Input data  principal: ', principal :1:2);
  read (years);
  writeln ('Input data  years: ', years :1);
  n := 12 * years;
  read (lowrate);
  writeln ('Input data  lowrate: ', lowrate :1:2);
  read (highrate);
  writeln ('Input data  highrate: ', highrate :1:2);
  end; { readvalues }

procedure printheadings;
  begin
  writeln;
  writeln ('Table of monthly payments on a ', years :1,
      '-year mortgage of $', principal :1:2);
  writeln;
  writeln ('Annual interest rate (%)' :30, 'Monthly payments' :20);
  writeln;
  end; { printheadings }

begin
readvalues;
printheadings;
rate := lowrate;
while rate <= highrate do
  begin

  { calculate the monthly payment }
  annualrate := rate / 100;
  i := annualrate / 12;

  { calculate c := 1 + i to the nth power }
  c := 1;
  for power := 1 to n do
    c := c * (1 + i);

  payment := principal * i * c / (c - 1);
  writeln (rate :30:2, payment :20:2);
  rate := rate + increment;
  end; { while-loop }
end.


run mortgage1

Input data  principal:  25000.00
Input data  years: 20
Input data  lowrate:  11.00
Input data  highrate:  13.00
```

Table of monthly payments on a 20-year mortgage of $ 25000.00

Annual interest rate (%)	Monthly payments
11.00	258.05
11.25	262.31
11.50	266.61
11.75	270.93
12.00	275.27
12.25	279.64
12.50	284.04
12.75	288.45
13.00	292.89

A Second Method For Stopping the Mortgage Calculations

If termination of the loop that calculates one mortgage payment is desired when the monthly payment exceeds some upper limit specified by the borrower, the while-condition may be changed to the one in the program mortgage2. In this program, the loop terminates when the monthly payment exceeds some maximum specified by the user as part of the input data. A boolean variable paymentok is used to terminate the loop when the payment gets too large. As with the program mortgage1, the loop will also terminate when the mortgage payment for the highest interest rate has been calculated, if the maximum payment has not been exceeded.

```
program mortgage2 (input, output);
{ unrefined version }
  begin
  read the values for:
      principal = the amount borrowed,
      years = the number of years mortgage runs,
      lowest = the lowest percentage rate,
      highest = the highest percentage rate,
      limit = the borrower's limit on monthly payments;
  print table headings;
  rate := lowest;
  paymentok := true;
  while (rate <= highest) and (paymentok) do
    calculate the monthly payment;
    if payment > limit then
      paymentok := false
    else
      write rate and payment;
      increase rate by 0.25;
  end.
```

Since the details of refining the mortgage2 are nearly identical to those of refining the program mortgage1, they are left as an exercise. The sample execution shows input data for which the loop is terminated because the monthly payment exceeds the maximum. The monthly payment on a 25-year mortgage of $30,000.00 at 9 percent is $251.76, which exceeds the borrower's upper limit on monthly payments of $250.00.

If the borrower's limit on monthly payments were raised to $275.00 without changing any of the other input data, the resulting program execution (not shown) would terminate when the variable rate reached the upper limit of 10 percent because, even at 10 percent, the monthly payment on a 25-year mortgage of $30,000.00 is $272.61, which does not exceed the borrower's increased limit on monthly payments.

```
run mortgage2

Input data   principal:   30000.00
Input data   years: 25
Input data   lowrate:   8.00
Input data   highrate:   10.00
Input data   maxpayment:   250.00


Table of monthly payments on a 25-year mortgage of $ 30000.00


        Annual interest rate (%)    Monthly payments

                8.00                    231.54
                8.25                    236.54
                8.50                    241.57
                8.75                    246.64
```

Debugging An Endless Loop

When a variable that is to be incremented each time a loop is executed has a starting value, stopping value, and step size that are constants, it is easy to verify that the loop will be executed the proper number of times and then terminate if all the proper steps are included in the program. It is still possible to make mistakes such as the one in the following program statements.

```
n := 2;
while n <= 10 do
  compute;
```

Unless the procedure compute changes the value of n, it will always be 2 and the loop will never terminate.

When variables are used for the starting value, stopping value, or step size, a mistake is harder to see. The program endlessloop2 tries to find the sum of the even numbers from 0 to 10, inclusive, but it does not succeed because a programming error turns its loop into one like the preceding example. The nondescriptive variable names used in endlessloop2 help to conceal the error, showing what poor choices they are.

```
program endlessloop2 (output);
{ contains a programming error that
  creates an endless while-loop }
  const
    x = 0;
    y = 10;
    z = 2;
  var
    sum, n : integer;
  begin
  sum : = 0;
  n : = z;
  while n <= y do
    begin
    sum : = sum + n;
    n : = n + x;
    end; { while-loop }
  writeln ('The sum is ', sum :1);
  end.
```

```
run endlessloop2
```

```
Execution terminated-- 50000 statements executed
```

The exact nature of the error message varies from installation to installation, and some computer systems may even allow the program to run forever. It is essential for users of such systems to learn how to interrupt a program execution and to do so as soon as reasonable hope for normal program termination is lost. In any event, the writeln statement in the program endlessloop2 is never executed, because the step size x by which the variable n is incremented has a value of zero and the condition in the while statement is always true. The intended correct program is obtained by exchanging the values assigned to the variables x and z. It is doubtful that this particular error could have passed unnoticed if the variable names had been the more self-explanatory names smallest, largest, and stepsize.

The Use Of Input Echoes In Debugging

Suppose one wants to find the sum of the numbers 0, 2, 4, 6, ..., 100. Since the difference between successive numbers in this sequence is constant, it is natural to use a loop to compute the sum and increment a variable by 2 each time through the loop. However, one also expects to have to find the sums of other sequences with constant differences (arithmetic progressions), and thus a slightly more general program is written that can find the sum of any sequence of values whose successive terms differ by a constant. The plan—to read values for the smallest number in the sequence, the largest number in the sequence, and the constant difference, and then to compute the sum using a loop—is simple enough that the completed program and sample execution are given now without further ado. Remember that the columns indicator :1 causes each quantity to be printed using only as many columns as the number requires.

```
program sumofanyprog (input, output);
  var
    smallest, largest, difference,
        sum, n : integer;
  begin
  read (smallest, largest, difference);
  writeln ('Input data  smallest: ', smallest :1);
  writeln ('                largest: ', largest :1);
  writeln ('                difference: ', difference :1);
  sum : = 0;
  n : = smallest;
  while n <= largest do
    begin
    sum : = sum + n;
    n : = n + difference;
    end; { while-loop }
  writeln ('The sum of the terms of the arithmetic progresion is ',
      sum :1);
  end.
```

```
run sumofanyprog

Input data  smallest: 2
                largest: 100
                difference: 0
Execution terminated-- 50000 statements executed
```

Fortunately, the computer system being used does not allow this program execution to go on forever, chewing up valuable and expensive minutes of computer time. However, no answer at all is printed, so something is amiss. The sample execution is not a complete waste for two reasons. First, meaningful names have been used for the variables of the program and, second, the echo of input data provided allows us to look at what the values of some of these variables are when they are read in from input data cards. When the echoes of input data are compared to the program listing, it is not difficult to see that a value of zero for the variable difference spells trouble.

Since the input data contains only values, and not the names of the variables to which these values are to be assigned, one might guess that what has probably happened is that the three data values have been prepared in the wrong order. The intended values are smallest: 0, largest: 100, and difference: 2. With less descriptive variable names such as x, y, and z as in the program endlessloop2, the error might have been harder to spot and, without an echo of the input data, the error would have been *impossible* to spot from the execution printout. This is one of the reasons why the authors always recommend inserting a programmer-supplied echo of input data. Similarly, if this program is run interactively from a computer terminal with appropriate input prompting messages, it is less likely that the user will muddle the input data in this way.

Selective Printing For Program Verification

Since the reversal of the order of the input data fully explains the endless loop that occurred in the sample execution of the program sumofanyprog, one would hope that placing the data in the correct order is all that is necessary to ensure correct computer execution. However, the programmer, having grown somewhat more cautious, might ask this question: "Suppose the program execution now prints an answer, as there is good reason to believe it will. What reason is there to believe that the answer is correct?"

Certainly, the apparent correctness of the program listing is one bit of evidence, but more convincing proof can be obtained by selectively printing the value of some of the variables during the execution of the program. This selective printing could show, if the execution is correct, that the calculation is progressing exactly as anticipated. On the other hand, if for some reason the program execution still contains an error, the selective printing might help pinpoint the error. The program sumwithdebug is designed to provide evidence of the correctness of the program execution, or to provide information helpful in locating an error, should there be one, without printing an excessive number of lines of output.

```
program sumwithdebug (input, output);
  var
    smallest, largest, difference,
       sum, n : integer;
  begin
  read (smallest, largest, difference);
  writeln ('Input data  smallest: ', smallest :1);
  writeln ('              largest: ', largest :1);
  writeln ('              difference: ', difference :1);
  sum := 0;
  writeln ('Initial sum is ', sum :1);
  n := smallest;
  while n <= largest do
    begin
    sum := sum + n;
    { the if-statement is for debugging purposes }
    if n <= 10 then
       writeln ('n = ', n :1, ' sum = ', sum :1);
    n := n + difference;
    end; { while-loop }
  writeln ('The sum of the terms of the arithmetic progression is ',
     sum :1);
  end.

run sumwithdebug
```

```
Input data    smallest: 0
              largest: 100
              difference: 2
Initial sum is 0
n = 0 sum = 0
n = 2 sum = 2
n = 4 sum = 6
n = 6 sum = 12
n = 8 sum = 20
n = 10 sum = 30
The sum of the terms of the arithmetic progression is 2550
```

Not only is the answer printed, but the progress of the computation is monitored as far as n = 10. Since everything seems correct up to that point, and since the echo of input data for the stopping value seems correct, there is reason to believe that the answer is correct. Exercise 23 discusses what would happen if the reversal of the input data had not been corrected, and why the selective printing would provide ample indication of the exact nature of the original error. For the programmer who is still skeptical about whether the loop terminates correctly, another write command, selectively executed for values of n greater than 96, would provide additional confirmation of a correct execution.

Variables Whose Upper Limit Is Not Attained Exactly

Treated as a collection of English languages phrases, the unrefined loop control heading

```
for n := start to finish  in steps of stepsize { not Pascal }
```

carries with it an implication that, after a sufficient number of steps, the variable n will finally take on the value finish for the last iteration of the loop. However, there are two important reasons why this does not always happen for the standard while-loop refinement of this construct.

```
n := start;
while n <= finish do
  begin ...; n := n + stepsize end;
```

1. Because of minor differences between computer arithmetic and ordinary arithmetic, the values actually computed for the variable n can sometimes differ from the intended values by just enough to prevent equality between the final value of n and the value of finish. For example, since $1/3 + 1/3 + 1/3 = 1$, but $0.3333333 + 0.3333333 + 0.3333333 = 0.9999999$, a loop controlled by the statements

   ```
   { while-loop refinement of
     for n := 1/3 to 1 in steps of 1/3 }
   n := 1/3;
   while n <= 1 do
     begin ...; n := n + 1/3; end;
   ```

is unlikely to produce a final value for n of exactly one in actual computer execution. Much greater detail on this topic, called *roundoff error*, can be found in Section 2.7.

2. In some programs, the programmer never intends the upper limit to be reached exactly. Often, although it may be easy to describe a criterion to distinguish between the last desired value of a variable and the first excluded value, it may be more difficult to write a formula to express the last desired value exactly. For example, if one wants to print all multiples of 13 that are less than or equal to 500 using a loop, it might not be obvious what the last desired multiple of 13 is. However, as shown in the program multiples, it is unnecessary to know the final value in advance.

```
program multiples (output);
  const
    limit = 500;
    factor = 13;
  var
    multiple : integer;
  begin
  multiple : = factor;
  while multiple <= limit do
    begin
    writeln (multiple :4);
    multiple : = multiple + factor;
    end; { loop }
  end.
run multiples

   13
   26
   39

    .
    .
    .

  481
  494
```

For debugging purposes, the abbreviated execution printout shown above (minus the three dots) could be generated by changing the unconditional writeln statement to the following if-statement:

```
if (multiple <= 40) or (multiple >= 480) then
  writeln (multiple :4);
```

Exercises

---

1. Write a program to print a table of the numbers from 1 to 10 and their cubes.

2. Write a program to print all multiples of 3 from 3 to 30.

3. Write a program to print the numbers from 1 to 10 in 2 columns, with the odd numbers in the left column and the even numbers in the right column. Hint: Use the statement

```
writeln (n, n + 1)
```

4. Write a program to print the numbers from 1 to 100 in 10 lines, with the number from 1 to 10 on the first line, the numbers from 11 to 20 on the second line, and so on.

5. Write a program to print the numbers from 1 to 100 on 10 lines, with the numbers from 1 to 10 going down the first column, the numbers from 11 to 20 going down the second column, and so on.

6. If the price of an imported cheese is $3.85 per pound, write a program to print the cost of any number of ounces of the cheese from 1 ounce to 2 pounds. There are 16 ounces in a pound.

7. If pickled herring sells for $4.17 per pound, write a program using a while-loop that determines the largest whole number of pounds of pickled herring that can be purchased for less than $17.00. How many people will this feed if each person eats 2 ounces of pickled herring?

8. Use the built-in function trunc, introduced in Section 2.6, to write a more efficient program for the application in Exercise 7.

9. Write a program that determines the largest whole number whose square is less than 100,000.

10. The polynomial $x * x - 2$ has the value 0 for some value of x between 1 and 2. Write a program to print out the values of the polynomial $x * x - 2$ for values of x between 1 and 2 at intervals of $1/100$.

11. Write a program that computes the value of the polynomial $x * x - 2$ for values of x between 1 and 2 at intervals of 0.0001 and prints the largest of these for which the polynomial has a negative value. (This is not the most efficient way to approximate the square root of 2. See Exercises 6 and 7 in Section 2.3, and the program sqrtof2 in the chapter review, Section 2.8.)

12. When the program beer in this section is run, the first 97 verses of the output are in grammatically acceptable English, but the last two verses contain the unacceptable phrase, ''1 bottles of beer on the wall''. Produce an improved version of this program by stopping the for-loop at n = 3 and writing separate write commands for the last two verses.

13. An alternative way of correcting the grammar of the last two verses of the printout produced by the program beer is to use a character-valued variable bottles which is assigned the value ''bottle '' if the number of bottles for that line of the printout is one, or is assigned the value ''bottles'' if the number of bottles is different from one. Then, for example, the first line of any verse can be printed by the statement

```
writeln (n, ' ', bottles, ' of beer on the wall.')
```

Write a program to correct the grammar of the program beer by this method. Run the resulting program, perhaps starting at n = 10 instead of n = 99, unless you are on a 5-mile hike.

14. The method used in Exercise 12 to improve the grammar of the program beer may be thought of as excluding the difficult case from the main loop and handling it by separate statements. The method used in Exercise 13 may be thought of as keeping the difficult cases within the main loop at the expense of providing greater variation in the possible executions of the body of the main loop. Discuss the relative merits of these two ways of making the program beer use correct grammar.

15. Write a program to print the numbers from 1 to 10 in one column and the numbers from 10 backwards to 1 in another column to the right of the first. Hint: The sum of the two numbers on any line is 11.

16. Rewrite the program mortgage1 in this section using a for-loop in which the for-variable k takes on the values 1, 2, 3, ..., 25, 26 and the annual interest rate is computed as (k + 19) / 400.

17. Compare the program mortgage1 with the modifications made in it for Exercise 16 on the basis of program readability. (The printed output produced by each program, if written properly, is the same.)

18. Actual banking practice for treating the fractions of a cent in the monthly payment is to increase any fraction of a cent, no matter how small, to the next larger penny, so that the final payment will be a few cents less than the other payments rather than a few cents more. Use the built-in function round, introduced in Section 2.6, to modify any one of the mortgage programs in this section to calculate the monthly payments in this way.

19. Refine the initial version of the program mortgage2 following the pattern of the refinement of the mortgage1.

20. Hand simulate the execution of the program sumwithdebug using the original data that caused an endless loop in the sample execution of the program sumofanyprog. Would the selective printing of values for the variables sum and n help pinpoint the exact nature of the error?

21. Insert write commands into the program endlessloop2 that would help a programmer to determine the reason the loop does not terminate. As the program endlessloop2 now stands, the only printed output is the error message saying that the execution time limit has been exceeded.

22. Write a program to list all the odd numbers starting with 3 that do not exceed the square root of 271. You may use the built-in function sqrt described in the next section.

23. Write a program to test whether the number 271 is divisible by either the number 2, or by any odd number starting with 3 but less than the square root of 271. Hint: One integer a divides another integer b if and only if

    b mod a = 0

    where mod is the integer operator described in Section 2.6 that finds the remainder when b is divided by a. If an integer divisor of 271 is found, print it and the quotient. Otherwise, print a statement saying that no divisors have been found.

24. Why would the name fivehundred be inappropriate for the constant 500 in the program multiples? Hint: Recall the purposes of constant declarations given in Section 1.2.

2.6   Computer-Assisted Instruction; Built-In Functions

Educational theorists emphasize the value of immediate reinforcement of correct
responses in improving rates of learning. Yet the average classroom teacher has too
many students to give each one an immediate pat on the back for a right answer or to
correct a wrong answer, except on an occasional basis. For some types of learning, a
computer terminal can be programmed to provide greater individual attention to the
student than a classroom teacher, while still retaining far greater flexibility in instruction than a textbook or workbook. This section discusses how to write an interactive
program to conduct a drill on the addition of numbers and how to modify that program to conduct drills on the other arithmetic operations. Such drills are one aspect
of what is called ''computer-assisted instruction''.

In order to present the student with a more varied selection of problems during
the computer-assisted arithmetic drills, a random number generating function is used
so that the problems are never the same twice. Built-in functions are described in this
section, as well as the ''nesting'' of loops, one within another. Also, a new statement, the case-statement, is introduced.

Teaching Addition: A Dramatization

The interactive addition drill described here is intended for a young school child.
The child sits at a computer terminal, and someone starts the program running. The
first few times it might be an older person, perhaps a teacher, who explains what to
do, but thereafter the child might be able to do it alone. The session opens with a
mutual introduction.

```
Computer:              Hello.  I'm a computer.
                       What's your name?
Child types name:      Jessica
Computer:              Nice to meet you, Jessica.
                       Today we are going to do
                       twenty addition problems.
```

Then, as it promises, the computer poses 20 problems, each requiring the addition
of two one-digit numbers. For each problem, the child has three chances to give a
correct answer before the computer provides the correct answer and goes on the the next
problem. When the child replies correctly on the first try, the dialogue for that problem
might look something like this:

```
Computer:              Please tell me, Jessica,
                       how much is 5 and 2?
Child types answer:    7
Computer:              Correct, Jessica.  Very good.
```

When the child makes one or two mistakes before giving the right answer, the
problem printout might look like this:

```
Computer:                      Please tell me, Jessica,
                               how much is 7 and 8?
Child types answer:            19
Computer:                      That's not right, Jessica.
                               Please try again.
Child types another answer:    15
Computer:                      Correct, Jessica.  Very good.
Computer:                      Please tell me, Jessica,
                               how much is 8 and 8?
Child types answer:            18
Computer:                      That's not right, Jessica.
                               Please try again.
Child types another answer:    15
Computer:                      That's not right, Jessica.
                               Please try again.
Child types a third answer:    16
Computer:                      Correct, Jessica.  Very good.
```

An example of printout when the child does not give the right answer in the three allowed tries might be the following:

```
Computer:                      Please tell me, Jessica,
                               how much is 9 and 6?
Child types answer:            13
Computer:                      That's not right, Jessica.
                               Please try again.
Child types another answer:    16
Computer:                      That's not right, Jessica
                               Please try again.
Child types a third answer:    19
Computer, getting impatient:   Still wrong, Jessica.
                               The right answer is 15.
```

At the conclusion of the drill, the computer tells the child how many of the 20 problems were answered correctly before the three chances ran out. For example, the computer might print

```
Computer:         You answered 18 out of 20 correctly.
                  That is very good.
                  This was fun.  Goodbye, Jessica.
```

Interactive Dialog

Computer-assisted instruction is the first application in this book that absolutely requires interactive execution. It simply makes no sense to execute a computer-assisted instruction program when the student is not present. Interactive execution calls for a different sequence of input and output operations than used in previous noninteractive programs. While a noninteractive program reads data from a previously prepared input file and echoes it in the output file, an interactive program prints an *input prompt* before each read statement, telling the user what information is expected by the next read statement.

An interactive program has the ability to check input data for correctness or feasibility and to allow the user to make immediate corrections. In the addition drill dramatization, the student has three chances to get the problem right before the computer supplies the correct answer. The use of the student's name in the computer's responses and input prompts adds a nice personal touch to the dialog.

Figure 2.6.1   Even a small child can operate a computer terminal.

A Simpler Teaching Program: One Problem, One Chance

Before working out a nested loop structure to conduct the intended addition drill with 20 problems, it may be helpful to consider a less ambitious program simpledrill that poses only one problem and allows only one chance. This program illustrates the essential features of problem posing and interactive dialog without excessive superstructure. The first version leaves two steps unrefined: reading the student's name and posing the problem.

```
program simpledrill (input, output);
{ one problem, one chance }
{ unrefined version }

  var
    studentname : packed array [1..20] of char;
    x, y, answer : integer;
```

```
begin
writeln ('Hello, I''m a computer. What''s your name?');
write ('Please type your name: ');
read the student's name into the array studentname;
writeln ('Nice to meet you, ', studentname);
writeln ('Today we are going to do an addition problem.');
pose a problem, that is, choose two integers x and y;
writeln ('Please tell me, ', studentname);
writeln ('how much is ', x :1, ' and ', y :1, '?');
write ('Type the answer: ');
read (answer);
if answer = x + y then
  begin
  writeln ('Correct, ', studentname);
  writeln ('Very good.');
  end
else
  begin
  writeln ('That''s not right, ', studentname);
  writeln ('The answer is ', x + y :1);
  end;
end.
```

Recognizing End of Line in Input Data

It is unrealistic to expect every student to have a name that is exactly 20 characters long, and it is inconsiderate to require a student to add blanks at the end of the student's name to make the typed input exactly 20 characters. Besides, it is all too likely that the student would miscount the blanks and perhaps enter 19 or 22 characters instead of the required 20 characters.

Just as the programs in Section 2.3 use a while-loop and a termination signal to read an unspecified amount of input data and let the computer do the counting, the procedure readname that reads the student's name uses a while-loop and the built-in function eoln to read only as many letters as there are in the student's name. As a preliminary step, the procedure readname initializes each character of studentname to blank so that the characters not typed will be blanks. The constant declaration

```
const
  maxnamesize = 20;
```

is placed in the main program to make it easier to change this value everywhere it occurs, in case a maximum length of 20 for names turns out to be inappropriate. This declaration also makes the program more readable because the constant name maxnamesize means more to a reader of the program than the numeral 20.

```
procedure readname;
  begin
  for letter := 1 to maxnamesize do
    studentname [letter] := ' ';
  letter := 0;
  while not eoln (input) and (letter < maxnamesize) do
    begin
    letter := letter +1;
    read (studentname [letter]);
    end; { loop }
  readln;
  end; { readname }
```

The new feature in the procedure readname is the built-in function eoln. The value of eoln (input) is true whenever the input file is at the end of a line, as indicated by a carriage return, and is false otherwise. For the file named ''input'', the parentheses and the name of the file may be omitted.

Now to explain the procedure readname: First the entire student name is set to blanks. Then the while-loop is executed. Each execution of the statement

```
read (studentname [letter])
```

assigns the next character typed as the value of the appropriate letter of studentname. When the user types an end-of-line character, the value of the built-in function eoln (input) becomes true, and the while-loop is terminated.

The reader is warned that there is a great deal of confusion and disagreement about how interactive input should work in Pascal. On some systems, a different sequence of operations must be used to read a line of characters from a terminal. On many of these systems, whenever the end-of-line condition is true, a readln statement should be executed to skip the end-of-line character and to turn the condition off before the first character in the next line is read.

A Debugging Trick

Since one complicated new feature has been used to refine the readname step of the program simpledrill, we temporarily cheat on the refinement of the pose-the-problem step so that the procedures already written may be tested. It is a standard debugging practice to replace an unwritten step by an oversimplified, but functional refinement that allows the rest of the program execution to proceed after a fashion. The simple-minded refinement

```
x := 3;  { temporary refinement to }
y := 4;  { pose one fixed problem   }
```

is adequate for present purposes. This new version of the program simpledrill and a sample execution are given below.

```
program simpledrill (input, output);
{ one problem, one chance }
{ temporarily poses only the problem 3 + 4 = ? }
```

```
const
  maxnamesize = 20;

var
  studentname : packed array [1..maxnamesize] of char;
  x, y, answer : integer;
  letter : integer;

procedure readname;
  ... end; { readname }

begin
writeln ('Hello, I''m a computer. What''s your name?');
write ('Please type your name: ');
readname;
writeln ('Nice to meet you, ', studentname);
writeln ('Today we are going to do an addition problem.');
x := 3; { temporary refinement to  }
y := 4; { pose one fixed problem }
writeln ('Please tell me, ', studentname);
writeln ('how much is ', x :1, ' and ', y :1, '?');
write ('Type the answer: ');
read (answer);
if answer = x + y then
  begin
  writeln ('Correct, ', studentname);
  writeln ('Very good.');
  end
else
  begin
  writeln ('That''s not right, ', studentname);
  writeln ('The answer is ', x + y :1);
  end;
end.
```

```
runi simpledrill

Hello, I'm a computer. What's your name?
Please type your name: David
Nice to meet you, David
Today we are going to do an addition problem.
Please tell me, David
how much is 3 and 4?
Type the answer: 7
Correct, David
Very good.
```

Varying the Problems By Using the Function Randominteger

Looking ahead to a drill with 20 problems, the method of generating a problem used in simpledrill simply will not do; it can only generate one problem, the addition of

3 and 4. If the same sequence of problems is presented to a child in every drill, the child might memorize the sequence of correct answers instead of learning how to add. For this reason, the sequence of problems should be as varied as possible. Some Pascal systems have a built-in function that can be used to generate random problems, but even on Pascal systems that do not have such a function built in, if the function definition statements given in the next subsection are copied into the procedure declaration part of a program after the variable declarations, the function randominteger may be used as though it were built in.

For any two integers r and s, the value of the expression

```
randominteger (r, s)
```

is one of the integers from r to s, although exactly which one it will be cannot be predicted in advance. For instance, the value of the expression

```
randominteger (0, 9)
```

could be any one of the integers 0, 1, 2, ..., 9. The likelihood that any one of these possibilities will be the computed value is the same as the likelihood that any other one will be. The user does not know in advance which of these 10 possible values will occur when the computer evaluates the expression

```
randominteger (0, 9)
```

The user only knows that each possible value has a 1/10 chance of occurring. Moreover, each time the expression is evaluated, a completely new and independent choice is made for the random integer from the complete set of possibilities.

The problem posing step of simpledrill may now be refined as

```
x : = randominteger (0, 9);
y : = randominteger (0, 9);
```

Properties of Random Integers

In two consecutive evaluations of a random integer generating function, the second random integer is neither necessarily the same as nor necessarily different from the first. In fact, about 1/10 of the time they are the same, and about 9/10 of the time they are different. This property is illustrated by the program randomdigits that chooses a random integer from zero to nine, 50 consecutive times. The reader is advised not to pay too much attention to the definition for the function randominteger, which uses the integer operators div and mod, not described until late in this section, and which is supposed to be a secret anyway so that the random integers cannot be predicted in advance.

```
program randomdigits (output);

  var
    i, j, seed : integer;
```

```
function randominteger (r, s : integer) : integer;
{ generates an integer in the interval [r..s] }
{ uses and changes the global variable seed }
  const
    maxseed = 10000;
    multiplier = 201;
    adder = 3437;
  begin
  seed := (multiplier * seed + adder) mod maxseed;
  randominteger := r + seed * (s - r + 1) div maxseed;
  end; { randominteger }

begin
seed := 1;
for i := 1 to 10 do
  begin
  for j := 1 to 5 do
    write (randominteger (0, 9) :5);
  writeln;
  end; { for-loop }
end.
```

run randomdigits

3	4	3	8	2
2	0	6	9	9
7	2	4	4	1
6	8	7	4	8
0	9	5	9	0
9	5	9	9	8
3	6	7	5	0
2	2	0	5	7
7	4	8	0	9
6	0	1	0	6

Evaluation of the same expression randominteger (0, 9) in the write statement of the program randomdigits results in all 50 of the above random digits. Not every one of the 10 digits occurs exactly the same number of times in the above table, but surprising as it may seem at first sight, this is to be expected. Suppose, to make an analogy, that an experiment consisted of tossing a coin 8 times. The probability of obtaining exactly 4 heads and 4 tails is not a virtual certainty, but actually is less than 1/3. This may be verified either analytically by those who know how to compute combinatorial probabilities, or empirically by performing the experiment of tossing 8 coins a large number of times. To further illustrate why an exactly equal number of heads and tails in the coin tossing experiment, or exactly 5 repetitions of each digit in the random number table, is not the most reasonable or the most probable occurrence, imagine what a scrupulously fair coin would do in an experiment consisting of 5 coin tosses. Would it have to show up heads 2 1/2 times?

Programmer-Defined Functions: A Look Ahead

If the function randominteger is not available in the Pascal system one is using, it is still possible to run the program simpledrill modified for random problem generation if one adds the following programmer-defined function randominteger as a part of the program in exactly the same manner that a procedure would be added. A complete description of the Pascal facility to accept and use functions written by the programmer appears in Section 4.3.

```
function randominteger (r, s : integer) : integer;
{ generates an integer in the interval [r..s] }
{ uses and changes the global variable seed }
  const
    maxseed = 10000;
    multiplier = 201;
    adder  = 3437;
  begin
  seed := (multiplier * seed + adder) mod maxseed;
  randominteger := r + seed * (s - r + 1) div maxseed;
  end; { randominteger }
```

There are two important rules for using the function randominteger. Both of its *arguments*, the two numbers in the parentheses, should be integers, and the second integer should be at least as large as the first.

A program using the function randominteger must contain a declaration of the integer variable seed and a statement initializing the variable seed to some value between 1 and maxseed. For different initial values of the variable seed, different sequences of random numbers will be generated.

Pseudorandom Numbers (Optional Reading)

A word of explanation to curious persons is in order. Computers don't really generate random numbers. They fake it. For most purposes, the important thing is that the collection of numbers generated has the same properties as a truly random collection, not that the collection generated is actually random.

Suppose, for example, that randominteger (1, 73) is computed 7,300 times. The numbers produced would appear to be random, for our simple purposes, if each of the integers 1 to 73 is generated approximately 100 times, that is, approximately 1/73 of the time, and if there is no discernible pattern in the numbers generated. Of course, each will not occur exactly 100 times, but perhaps one number will occur 84 times, another will occur 107 times, and so on.

The function randominteger generates "random" numbers by keeping a number called the *seed*. Each time a new random number is to be produced, the seed is multiplied by multiplier and adder is added to the result. Then all but the last four digits of the seed are discarded by taking the remainder (modulus) when the seed is divided by 10,000. Next the interval 0 to 9999 is divided into $s - r + 1$ parts, one for each possible random number, yielding an integer from 0 to $s - r$. Then the value of r is added to this number to get an integer from r to s.

With the variable seed initialized to the value 1, the first ten values produced by randominteger (1, 100) are

37   47   32   90   22   29   9   63   92   94

It is no easy matter to decide whether the function randominteger does a good job of behaving like a true random generator, but it is entirely adequate for the present purpose of getting different problems for a small child.

Twenty Problems, Three Chances Each

Now that the use of the function randominteger to pose varied addition problems in a sequence the child cannot guess has been explained, and now that the simple drill program has shown how the playscript can be converted into computer terminal dialogue, it is time to write the intended program teachadd. Its initial form is the following.

```
program teachadd (input, output);
  begin
  initialize;
  make mutual introduction of computer and child;
  for problem := 1 to 20 do
    begin
    pose an addition problem;
    while (not answerok) and (chance <= 3) do
      evaluate and process the answer, possibly terminating
              the loop before three chances in case the answer
              is correct by setting answerok to true;
    if answerok then
      give the child a pat on the back
    else
      give the child the correct answer;
    end; { while-loop }
  evaluate the child's total performance and say goodbye;
  end.
```

The basic loop structure of the program teachadd is a while-loop nested within a for-loop. The outer for-loop poses and evaluates 20 problems, including for each problem an execution of the inner while-loop that permits up to three chances. Outside the for-loop, and only executed once, are the mutual introduction, the initialization, and the evaluation of the total drill performance.

As is often the case when programs are written for two similar applications, some of the program steps in an early version of the second program already have been refined while writing the first program. When the refined steps from the previous program are used again in the new program, the computer can understand these instructions. For example, the refinement of the mutual introduction is adapted easily from the mutual introduction in the program simpledrill:

```
{ make mutual introduction of computer and child }
writeln ('Hello, I''m a computer. What''s your name?');
writeln ('Please type your name: ');
readname;
writeln ('Nice to meet you, ', studentname);
writeln ('Today we are going to do twenty addition problems.');
```

The posing of a random addition problem can use the same refinement in the program teachadd as in the program simpledrill.

```
{ pose an addition problem }
x := randominteger (0, 9);
y := randominteger (0, 9);
writeln;
writeln ('Please tell me, ', studentname);
writeln ('How much is ', x :1, ' and ', y :1, '?');
```

Nested If-Statements

Forging ahead, we refine the while-loop that gives the child up to three chances to give the correct answer. The printed output produced by this loop must conform to the playscript at the beginning of the section in case the child gives one or more incorrect answers.

```
{ allow the pupil three chances to answer correctly }
chance := 1;
answerok := false;
while (not answerok) and (chance <= 3) do
  begin
  writeln ('Type the answer: ');
  read (answer);
  if answer = x + y then
    answerok := true
  else
    if chance < 3 then
      begin
      writeln ('That''s not right, ', studentname);
      writeln ('Please try again.');
      end;
  chance := chance + 1;
  end; { while-loop }
```

The most notable programming technique in this refinement is the nesting of one if-statement within another if-statement, a technique that has been in eclipse since the less readable programs in Section 1.5 that include credit for bonus questions in a test score. The else-clause of the outer if-statement is itself an if-statement, this time with no else-clause. The writeln statement terminates both of the if-statements. Notice that if the problem is not answered correctly on the third try, then nothing is printed and the while-loop is completed because this is the largest value for the variable chance specified in the while-statement.

Another if-statement that adapts readily from the program simpledrill is the statement that either congratulates the child for giving a correct answer or scolds the child for missing it three times.

```
{ either acknowledge answer correct or tell correct answer }
if answerok then

  begin
  right : = right + 1;
  writeln ('Correct, ', studentname);
  writeln ('Very good.');
  end
else
  begin
  writeln ('Still wrong, ', studentname);
  writeln ('The correct answer is ', x + y :1);
  end;
```

Evaluating the Drill Performance

Following the playscript, we give only a very simple kind of evaluation of the child's performance on the 20-question drill, consisting of a summary of how many questions the child got right and an opinion of how good or bad a performance this represents. Ideally, the opinion should be expressed in a positive manner and should take into account the pupil's age and past experience with arithmetic, among other factors, and the programmer might well consult a specialist in elementary education for guidance.

The evaluation of the child's performance given in the program teachadd is only a sample of what can be done.

```
{ evaluate child's performance and say goodbye }
if right = 20 then
  opinion : = 'excellent.              ';
if (18 <= right) and (right < 20) then
  opinion : = 'very good.              ';
if (16 <= right) and (right < 18) then
  opinion : = 'good.                   ';
if (14 <= right) and (right < 16) then
  opinion : = 'fair.                   ';
if right < 14 then
  opinion : = 'not as well as I hoped.  ';
writeln ('You answered ', right :1, ' out of 20 correctly.');
writeln ('That is ', opinion);
if right < 16 then
  writeln ('You need more practice.');
writeln ('This was fun.  Goodbye, ', studentname);
```

This sample evaluation procedure has five options, based on the number of problems the child answered correctly within the three allotted chances. Just as in the program incometax1 in Section 1.5, the various options are described in such a manner that they are clearly mutually exclusive. This is important because, in all cases, each of the five if-tests is performed, and it is intended that only one of the then-clauses contained in the first five if-blocks is to be executed. The character string constants assigned to opinion are all padded with blanks so that they have exactly the same length, 25, the declared length of the character string opinion. The effect of the student evaluation is shown in the sample execution of the program teachadd, now fully refined.

```
program teachadd (input, output);

  const
    maxnamesize = 20;


  var
    studentname : packed array [1..maxnamesize] of char;
    opinion : packed array [1..25] of char;
    x, y, answer : integer;
    seed, letter : integer;
    numberright, problem, chance : integer;
    answerok : boolean;


  function randominteger (r, s : integer) : integer;
      ... end; { randominteger }


  procedure readname;
      ... end; { readname }


  begin
  seed := 1;
  { make mutual introduction of computer and child }
  writeln ('Hello, I''m a computer. What''s your name?');
  writeln ('Please type your name: ');
  readname;
  writeln ('Nice to meet you, ', studentname);
  writeln ('Today we are going to do twenty addition problems.');


  { computer poses 20 problems, allowing the child up to
    three chances on each before telling the numberright answer }
  numberright := 0;
  for problem := 1 to 20 do
    begin
    { pose an addition problem }
    x := randominteger (0, 9);
    y := randominteger (0, 9);
    writeln;
    writeln ('Please tell me, ', studentname);
    writeln ('How much is ', x :1, ' and ', y :1, '?');
```

```
{ allow the pupil three chances to answer correctly }
chance : = 1;
answerok : = false;
while (not answerok) and (chance <= 3) do
  begin
  writeln ('Type the answer: ');
  read (answer);
  if answer = x + y then
    answerok : = true
  else
    if chance < 3 then
      begin
      writeln ('That''s not right ', studentname);
      writeln ('Please try again. ');
      end;
  chance : = chance + 1;
  end; { while-loop }



{ either acknowledge answer correct or tell correct answer }
if answerok then
  begin
  numberright : = numberright + 1;
  writeln ('Correct, ', studentname);
  writeln ('Very good. ');
  end
else
  begin
  writeln ('Still wrong, ', studentname);
  writeln ('The correct answer is ', x + y :1);
  end;
end; { for-loop }


{ evaluate child's performance and say goodbye }
if numberright = 20 then
  opinion : = 'excellent.              ';
if (18 <= numberright) and (numberright < 20) then
  opinion : = 'very good.              ';
if (16 <= numberright) and (numberright < 18) then
  opinion : = 'good.                   ';
if (14 <= numberright) and (numberright < 16) then
  opinion : = 'fair.                   ';
if numberright < 14 then
  opinion : = 'not as well as I hoped. ';
writeln ('You answered ', numberright :1, ' out of 20 correctly.');
writeln ('That is ', opinion);
if numberright < 16 then
  writeln ('You need more practice. ');
writeln ('This was fun.  Goodbye, ', studentname);
end.
```

```
runi teachadd
```

```
Hello, I'm a computer. What's your name?
Please type your name: Jessica
Nice to meet you, Jessica
Today we are going to do twenty addition problems.


Please tell me, Jessica
How much is 3 and 4?
Type the answer: 7
Correct, Jessica
Very good.
         .
         .   (18 more problems)
         .
Please tell me, Jessica
How much is 5 and 7?
Type answer: 12
Correct, Jessica
Very good.


You answered 19 out of 20 correctly.
That is very good.
This was fun.   Goodbye, Jessica
```

The Case-Statement

The programs teachadd in this section and incometax1 in Section 1.5 show that it is not uncommon to have a situation in which there are more than two alternatives, only one of which is to be executed. The solution employed in both these programs is to have several consecutive if-statements, each of which is executed, but to design the if-tests so that the conditions are mutually exclusive, thereby guaranteeing that only one then-clause is executed. The case-statement allows several alternatives, only one of which is to be executed. For example, the case-statement at the top of page 173 could replace five if-statements of the program teachadd.

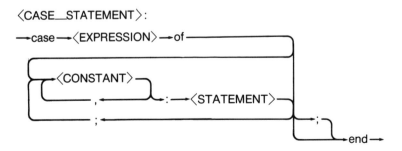

Figure 2.6.2   Case-statement syntax chart.

```
{ evaluate child's performance and say goodbye }
case numberright of
  20 :
    opinion := 'excellent.              ';
  18, 19 :
    opinion := 'very good.              ';
  16, 17 :
    opinion := 'good.                   ';
  14, 15 :
    opinion := 'fair.                   ';
  0, 1, 2, 3, 4, 5, 6, 7, 8, 9, 10, 11, 12, 13 :
    opinion := 'not as well as I hoped. ';
  end; { case }
```

Syntax of the case-statement is shown in Figure 2.6.2. Its description is a bit more complicated than the if-statement, but is not more difficult to write. It consists of a case-heading containing the keyword "case" followed by an expression and the keyword "of". This is followed by any number of cases, each of which is a list of constants followed by a colon and a statement. Any statement in a case may, of course, be compound. The entire case-statement ends with the keyword "end". This is one of the few situations in Pascal in which the keyword "end" is not paired with the keyword "begin". In the case-statement, it matches the keyword "case".

When the case-statement is executed, the expression in the case heading is evaluated. Then the case is selected which is headed by the constant that is the same as the value of the expression just computed. The statement in that case is executed, completing execution of the entire case statement. If there is no constant that is the value of the expression in the case heading, that is an error.

Each constant heading a case must be the same type as the expression in the case heading. This type must not be real.

The difference between a sequence of if-tests in separate if-statements and a case-statement with several cases is that, in the latter case, only one test is made, based on the value of the expression in the case heading. For this reason, the case-statement takes less execution time than the five if-statements that it replaces in the program teachadd. Also, the resulting program is easier to understand.

Teaching Other Arithmetic Operations

It isn't hard to modify the program teachadd into other programs that teach multiplication, subtraction, and division. Once the details of the problem posing step for these other arithmetic operations are straightened out, the minor changes needed follow naturally, both in the while-loop that allows up to three chances and in the final if-statement that either acknowledges or reveals the correct answer.

Although modifying the program teachadd to teach, instead of addition, the multiplication of small integers is sufficiently easy to leave as an exercise, there is a slight difficulty in making the modification needed to obtain a program that conducts a drill on subtraction, namely, that there are good reasons to begin with proper subtraction, avoiding problems in which the difference is negative. If the variables x and y are randomly selected integers from 0 to 9, then the "subtrahend" y might be larger than the "minuend" x. The following while-loop is an inefficient way to obtain a proper subtraction problem.

```
{ pose a proper subtraction problem, inefficiently }
proper : = false;
while not proper do
  begin
  x : = randominteger (0,9);
  y : = randominteger (0,9);
  if x - y >= 0 then
    proper : = true;
  end; { while-loop }
writeln ('Please tell me, ', studentname);
writeln ('how much is ', x :1, ' minus ', y :1, '?');
```

The inefficient part is waiting for the computer to generate values for the variables x and y so that their difference is not negative. Since there is a better than even chance that a random value for y will be less than or equal to a random value for x, the waiting time ordinarily will be imperceptibly short to the child sitting at a terminal. Thus it is not a terrible way to generate a proper subtraction problem. Nonetheless, choosing the value for y as a random integer from 0 to x instead of from 0 to 9 always guarantees a nonnegative difference the first time. This method is used in the second way of generating a subtraction problem.

```
{ pose a proper subtraction problem, second way }
x : = randominteger (0, 9);
y : = randominteger (0, x);
writeln ('Please tell me, ', studentname);
writeln ('how much is ', x :1, ' minus ', y :1, '?');
```

Persons acquainted with elementary probability theory may recognize that, while precisely the same 55 proper subtraction problems can be posed by either of the two methods described so far, the frequency of occurrence of a given problem is not the same for both methods. When the first method is used, each of the 55 possible proper subtraction problems is equally likely to occur, so each occurs about 1/55 of the time. When the second method is used, however, the problem of finding the difference zero minus zero is the most likely to occur, because whenever the variable x is assigned the value zero, the variable y necessarily will be assigned the value zero also. Since the minuend x is assigned the value zero about 1/10 of the time, zero minus zero will occur as the subtraction problem about 1/10 of the time. Another method of generating the same 55 proper subtraction problems by swapping unsuitable values for x and y is discussed in Exercise 4.

Uniformly Distributed Proper Subtraction Problems

A slightly different approach to generating proper subtraction problems ensures that each occurs with the same frequency. With this new approach, instead of assigning random values to the minuend and the subtrahend, we assign random values to the subtrahend and the difference. The minuend is obtained as the sum of the subtrahend and the difference, the standard way of checking a subtraction problem.

```
{ pose a proper subtraction problem, third way }
subtrahend := randominteger (0, 9);
difference := randominteger (0, 9);
minuend := subtrahend + difference;
writeln ('Please tell me, ', studentname);
writeln ('how much is ', minuend :1, ' minus ', subtrahend :1, '?');
```

This third way permits the minuend to be as large as 18, while the subtrahend may be only as large as 9. For a pupil who has had experience with the addition of one-digit numbers, this third way might have the desirable effect of reinforcing the notion that subtraction is the inverse operation of addition. This third way may easily be modified to provide a highly satisfactory method for posing drill problems involving division of integers without remainder. Modifying the rest of the program teachadd so that it might be used in a subtraction drill based on this third way of obtaining a proper subtraction problem is left as an exercise.

The Integer Operators Div and Mod

When working with integers, it is sometimes inconvenient that the quotient of two integers is not an integer. For example, when the net weight of a 50 ounce jar of apple sauce is quoted in other units, it is not listed as 50 / 16 = 3.125 pounds, but as 3 pounds 2 ounces. The integer operators div and mod provide a simple and convenient way to calculate these quantities as shown in the program ouncestopounds. The number 16 in this program is assigned as the value of the constant ouncesinapound.

```
program ouncestopounds (input, output);

  const
    ouncesinapound = 16;

  var
    totalounces, pounds, ounces : integer;

  begin
  read (totalounces);
  pounds := totalounces div ouncesinapound;
  ounces := totalounces mod ouncesinapound;
  writeln (totalounces :1, ' oz = ',
      pounds :1, ' lb(s) ',
      ounces :1, ' oz.');
  end.
```

```
run ouncestopounds

50 oz = 3 lb(s) 2 oz.
```

The value of the expression 50 div 16 is 3 (pounds), the integer part of the exact quotient 50 / 16 = 3.125 pounds. The value of the expression 50 mod 16 is 2 (ounces), the remainder after 48 of the 50 ounces have been accounted for to make the 3 pounds.

In general, the value of the expression n div d is the integer part of the quotient n / d, and the remainder n mod d is given by the formula

n mod d = n − d * (n div d)

Teaching Division With Remainder

In the computer-assisted drill on division suggested earlier in this section, care is to be taken so that the dividend in each problem is an exact multiple of the divisor, thereby guaranteeing that the quotient will be an integer. After exact integer division without remainder is mastered, the child can progress to division of integers with remainder. First, the function randominteger is used to pose an appropriate problem. Then the integer operators div and mod are used to calculate the correct answers for the quotient and remainder to check against the child's responses.

```
{ pose an integer division problem }
divisor := randominteger (1, 9);
dividend := randominteger (0, 10 * divisor - 1);
writeln;
writeln ('Please tell me, ', yourname);
writeln ('How much is ', dividend :1, ' divided by ', divisor :1, '?');
rightquot := dividend div divisor;
rightrem := dividend mod divisor;

{ allow the pupil three chances to answer correctly }
chance := 1;
answerok := false;
while (not answerok) and (chance <= 3) do
  begin
  writeln ('Input data  quotient: ');
  read (quotient);
  writeln ('Input data  remainder: ');
  read (remainder);
  if (quotient = rightquot) and (remainder = rightrem) then
    answerok := true
  else
    if chance < 3 then
      writeln ('Incorrect.  Please try again.');
  chance := chance + 1;
  end; { while-loop }
```

In posing the division with remainder problem, the dividend is chosen to be any nonnegative integer less than 10 times the divisor, so that the quotient is always less than 10. Another way of doing this, by choosing appropriate random integers for the divisor, quotient, and remainder and then calculating the dividend, is left as an exercise. To illustrate how the operators div and mod are used to compute the correct answers in the computer, we show part of a sample execution.

```
runi teachdiv

Hello, I'm a computer. What's your name?
Input data  your name:
Nice to meet you, Lisa
Today we are going to do twenty division problems.

Please tell me, Lisa
How much is 18 divided by  4?
Input data  quotient: 2
Input data  remainder: 4
Incorrect.  Please try again.
Input data  quotient: 4
Input data  remainder: 2
Correct, Lisa
Very good.
```

Since the value of dividend is 18 and the value of divisor is 4, the correct quotient is 18 div 4 = 4, the whole number of times 4 goes into 18. The correct remainder is 18 mod 4 = 2, the remainder when 18 is divided by 4.

Built-In Functions and Procedures

Several commonly used functions and procedures are built into all Pascal language processors. These are called *built-in functions and procedures*. Other functions and procedures added by the designers of the language processor also are called built in. Many of the built-in functions and procedures that are standard in Pascal are discussed in the remainder of this section. Others are introduced in appropriate later sections. It makes no difference who built a particular function or procedure into a language. All a programmer needs to know to use a built-in function or procedure is its name and what it is supposed to do. We consider first the Pascal built-in function for rounding numbers.

Rounding

The familiar process of rounding a number to the nearest integer is performed by the built-in function round. The value to be rounded must be type real and the result is type integer. For example,

```
round (1.234) = 1
round (1.543) = 2
round (-2.76) = -3
round (0.000) = 0
```

The built-in function round can be used to perform rounding to any arbitrary precision. For example, the value of the following expression is x rounded to the nearest 1/100.

```
round (x / 0.01) * 0.01
```

As described in Section 2.7, one may expect minor peculiarities with rounding when the computer representation of the precision is not exact. For example, the value assigned to x by the statements

```
onethird := 1/3;
x := round (1.0  / onethird) * onethird
```

is often calculated as 0.9999999 instead of 1.000000, because 1/3 is best represented by 0.3333333 and three times 0.3333333 is 0.9999999 and not 1.000000. Although rounding to the nearest tenth or hundredth on a binary computer has a similar peculiarity, in many computer systems, there may be no noticeable effect on the output unless further arithmetic is done on a rounded quantity before printing. Section 2.7 treats the subject of roundoff error in more detail.

The Integer Part of a Number

The integer part of a real number is obtained by truncation, that is, eliminating the fraction, if any. The integer part of a whole number is that number itself. The Pascal built-in function trunc produces a type integer value that is the integer part of its real argument. For instance,

```
trunc (4.73)  = 4
trunc (3.14159)  = 3
trunc (17.0)  = 17
trunc (-5.6)  = -5
trunc (2/3)  = 0
```

For positive numbers that are not whole numbers, the integer part of the number is less than the number, but for negative numbers that are not whole numbers, as the fourth example shows, the integer part is algebraically greater than the number.

Absolute Value

The *absolute value* of a number x is the number x itself if x is positive or zero, but the absolute value of a negative number x results from changing the sign of x to positive. Algebraically, this means that the absolute value of a negative number x is equal to the positive number -x. The built-in function abs is used to obtain absolute values in Pascal. The argument of the function must be either integer or real and the result will be the same type as that of the argument. For example,

```
abs (6.75)  = 6.75
abs (0)  = 0
abs (-13.8)  = 13.8
abs (-9)  = 9
```

Square and Square Root

The *square* of a number x is x multiplied by itself, that is, x * x. The Pascal built-in function sqr computes the square of an integer or a real number. The result has the same type as the argument. For example,

```
sqr (4)  = 16
sqr (-3.2)  = 10.24
```

The *square root* of a nonnegative number x is the unique nonnegative number y such that y * y = x. However, computer language square root functions are burdened with the problem that for most computer-representable numbers x, including integers, there is no computer-representable number y whose square is exactly equal to x. For example, the best possible seven-significant-digit decimal approximation to the square root of 2 is the number 1.414214, but the square of 1.414214 is equal to 2.000001237796, which is represented in seven significant decimal digits as 2.000001 and not 2. This phenomenon is not restricted to seven-digit computers nor to decimal computers. Even if a computer were to permit more digits of precision, roundoff error would still cause minor inconsistencies in a computer square root function.

The built-in Pascal function sqrt assigns the best possible approximate square root to a nonnegative number. The programmer should be prepared for an error message and possible program termination if the square root of a negative number is called for. The argument of the function sqrt must be integer or real, and the result is always real. In this regard, it behaves like the division operator (/).

Parity of an Integer

The built-in function odd produces a boolean value true or false that indicates whether an integer is odd or even. For example,

```
odd (33)  = true
odd (0)  = false
odd (2 * trunc (x))  = false
```

Scientific Functions

Table 2.6.1 lists the standard scientific functions available as Pascal built-in functions. Each of these functions has one argument that must be type integer or real. The result is always real.

Table 2.6.1   Some scientific built-in functions.

Pascal name	Description
ln	natural logarithm
exp	exponential (e to a power)
sin	sine
cos	cosine
arctan	arctangent

End-Of-Line and End-Of-File Built-In Functions

The built-in function eoln returns a boolean value that indicates whether or not a file of characters is positioned at the end of a line. If the argument is omitted, it is assumed to be the standard input file named "input". This function was used in the procedure readname in the teaching programs of this section.

Similarly, the function eof returns a boolean value that indicates whether or not a file is positioned at the end. This function provides an alternative method of exiting from a loop when all of the input data has been processed. Both the eoln and the eof built-in functions are used in the program copytext. The input file for this program looks exactly like the output file. There is no termination signal in the input data.

```
program copytext (input, output);

  var
    onecharacter : char;

  begin
  while not eof do
    begin
    while not eoln do
      begin
      read (onecharacter);
      write (onecharacter);
      end;
    readln; { skip over end-of-line character }
    writeln;
    end;
  end.

run copytext

The built-in function eoln has the value true
whenever the next character awaiting reading on
the file is an end-of-line character such as
a carriage return.  Otherwise, its value is false.
It may be used to terminate variable length
character strings in input data.
```

Exponentiation

It is possible to use the fact that x to the power p is mathematically equivalent to the Pascal expression exp (p * ln (x)) to raise any positive quantity to any power. The program raise shows some examples of calculating exponentiations in this manner.

```
program raise (output);
  begin
  writeln ('2 to the 10th power = ',
      round (exp (10 * ln (2))) :1);
  writeln ('14.7 to the -7.2 power = ',
      exp (-7.2 * ln (14.7)) :10);
  writeln ('The population of NJ in 2590 will be ',
      6066782.0 * exp (63 * ln (1 + 0.181543)) :10);
  end.
```

```
run raise

2 to the 10th power  =  1024
14.7 to the -7.2 power =    3.94e-09
The population of NJ in 2590 will be    2.22e+11
```

Other Built-In Functions

The other standard Pascal built-in functions are ord (ordinal position), chr (character with ordinal position), succ (successor), and pred (predecessor). These are used with character data and programmer-defined data types and are described in Sections 4.3 and 5.1.

Built-In Procedures

Pascal has four built-in procedures for input and output named ''read'', ''readln'', ''write'', and ''writeln''. These procedures have been discussed in previous sections. There are also two built-in procedures for the dynamic allocation of storage for data structures. These procedures are named ''new'' and ''dispose'' and are discussed in Section 6.6.

The Purpose of Built-In Functions and Procedures

Built-in functions and procedures are augmentations of a computer language to improve its convenience to users. Some functions and procedures are built into the language by the designer of the compiler for that language. Others might be added by a local computer center. It makes no difference who builds a particular function or procedure into a language, except that the programmer can rely on the standard ones being available with any Pascal system. All a programmer needs to know to use a built-in function or procedure is its name and what it is supposed to do.

In Chapter 4, we see that the individual programmer can also define functions to be used in much the same way as built-in functions. Several important reasons for having built-in functions and procedures are given below.

1. For some functions such as ln, the meaning and use of the function might be known and understood by users, but there are special computational problems in producing the most accurate function values that are known only to specialists in numerical analysis.

2. Some functions and procedures can be programmed only by accessing certain machine operations that may not be available to the programmer in Pascal. The integer part of a number and the input/output procedures are in this category.

3. Some functions and procedures are used by so many programmers that even though they could be programmed by each programmer who needs them, it is more efficient to have them programmed once and for all and built in.

4. Some built-in functions can be used to improve the readability of programs, even though other means exist for writing equivalent expressions. For example, the expression sqr (2 * x + 1) might be used instead of the mathematically equivalent expression (2 * x + 1) * (2 * x + 1) to make a program easier to write and easier to read.

Exercises

---

1. Write an arithmetic teaching program that poses five problems, each giving three chances to add a one-digit number to a two-digit number.

2. Write a program that teaches multiplication.

3. Modify the program teachadd in this section to conduct a drill on proper subtraction problems. (Some of the modifications are described in detail in the section.)

4. One cannot obtain a proper subtraction problem (i.e., with a difference greater than or equal to 0) by choosing two random integers from 0 to 9 for x and y and then asking for the difference x − y because almost half of the time the random integer chosen for y will be greater than the random integer chosen for x. However, it is possible to modify this procedure to pose proper subtraction problems by swapping the values of x and y in case the value of y is the larger of the two. Incorporate this method of generating proper subtraction problems into a program that teaches proper subtraction of one-digit numbers.

5. Revise the evaluation procedure of the program teachadd so that it tells the pupil how many problems were answered correctly on the first try, how many correctly on the second try, how many correctly on the third try, and how many were not answered correctly.

6. Modify the assigning of an opinion to describe the child's performance in the program teachadd to take into account the more detailed record keeping described in Exercise 5. One way is to assign three points for each problem answered correctly on the first try, two points for each problem answered correctly on the second try, one point for each problem answered correctly on the third try, and no points for problems still not answered correctly. Then the expression of opinion may be based on this weighted total of correct answers.

7. Revise the program teachadd so that, after an incorrect answer, it gives the pupil a hint saying whether the correct answer is higher or lower.

8. A neighboring entry of a product in the multiplication table is an entry one vertical position above or below the correct product, or an entry one horizontal position to the right or left of the correct product. Thus the neighboring entries of 7 x 8 = 56 are 6 x 8 = 48, 8 x 8 = 64, 7 x 7 = 49, and 7 x 9 = 63. A common error in multiplication is to give a neighboring entry as the answer instead of the correct product. Write a multiplication teaching program that recognizes when a neighboring entry has been given mistakenly as the answer and informs the student of this fact. For example, if the pupil gives 48 as the answer to 7 x 8, then the computer might print

```
No, Josh.   48 is 6 times 8.
Please try again.
```

9. An alternative way of generating integer division problems with remainder is to select the divisor, the quotient, and the remainder randomly and then to calculate the dividend by the formula

```
dividend := divisor * quotient + remainder
```

Write a program that teaches integer division with remainder using this method to generate problems. Both the divisor and the quotient should be less than 10, and the divisor must not be 0. Recall also that, in division with remainder, the remainder is always less than the divisor and may be 0 if the divisor divides the dividend exactly. Be careful in your program to use different variable names for the correct answers and the student's responses, which may or may not be correct.

10. Modify the program teachadd so that the computer does not reply in the same fashion if the child answers correctly on the second or third tries as it does when the student answers correctly on the first try. Also, modify the computer's replies to incorrect answers on the first two tries so that they are different. The program teachadd already replies differently for a third incorrect answer.

11. For each of the following three expressions, determine all possible values.

```
 2 * randominteger (0, 5)
randominteger (0, 10)
randominteger (0, 5) + randominteger (0, 5)
```

12. Which two of the three expressions in Exercise 11 are the most nearly alike? How does the other expression differ from these two?

13. Which of the following relationships are always true?

```
sqrt (sqr (x)) = x  for all x
sqr (sqrt (x)) = x  for all x >= 0
```

14. Rewrite the following two expressions using the integer operator mod. Assume n is type integer.

```
n - (n div 100) * 100
not odd (n)
```

15. An integer larger than one is called *prime* if there is no way to express it as a product of two positive integer factors unless the number itself is one of the factors. Write a program that divides a positive integer n, supplied as input, by as many of the numbers 2, 3, 4, ..., n − 1 as you think necessary to decide whether or not n is prime.

16. Prove that, if a positive integer is not prime (see Exercise 15), then the smaller of the two integers that factor the given number must lie between 2 and the square root of the given number. Use this fact in a program to test whether a number n supplied as input is prime.

17. Prove that, in deciding as in Exercises 15 and 16 whether an integer is prime, there is no need to divide by any even number except 2. Use this fact in a program to test whether a number is prime.

18. A proper divisor of a positive integer n is any exact divisor of n except n itself. (One is considered a proper divisor of any positive integer.) Write a program that lists all the proper divisors of a number n supplied as input.

19. A positive integer is called *perfect* if it equals the sum of its proper divisors (see Exercise 18). For example, the numbers 6 and 28 are perfect because

$$6 = 1 + 2 + 3$$
$$28 = 1 + 2 + 4 + 7 + 14$$

Write a procedure to decide whether a positive integer is perfect. Write a program to find the smallest perfect number greater than 28.

20. Write a program whose purpose is to find the smallest perfect odd number (see Exercise 19). Do you know whether the execution of your program is certain to terminate?

21. Evaluate the expression

    x + abs (x)

    for the following values of x: -2, -1.5, -1, -0.5, 0, 0.5, 1, 1.5, and 2.

22. Do the following two expressions always have the same value for any value of the variable x?

```
abs (x)
sqrt (sqr (x))
```

23. Write a program to conduct a vocabulary drill in the form of multiple-answer questions. For example, a question might be

    Please tell me, Pam, what is the meaning of apathy?
    (a) boredom (b) laziness (c) sloth (d) disinterest (e) I don't care what the meaning is

    Give 10 questions and allow the student to answer with either the letter (a to e) of the correct answer or the correct answer itself. Evaluation of the drill should be similar to that of teachadd.

24. Modify the vocabulary drill program in Exercise 24 so that, whenever the student gives an incorrect answer, the computer gives the definition of the student's answer and an explanation of why it is not the correct answer.

2.7   Roundoff

The subject of roundoff, or as it is less charitably called "roundoff error", occupies a curious position in an introduction to computer programming. On the one hand, it appears to be one of those annoying practical details that prevent a perfectly reasonable looking program from doing exactly what it seems to say it should. Yet, unlike most other details which are often specific to one language or computer installation, roundoff is not a characteristic of any one computer language or any one computer. It is a characteristic of the computational process itself.

To illustrate what roundoff is, and how likely it is to occur in actual computations, we give two simple examples. Readers who have access to a computer for running programs already may have noticed roundoff phenomena in their program executions. For example, using any computer or hand calculator, try the calculation

    (1 / 3) * 3

Chances are the computed answer is something like 0.9999999 instead of 1. The difference is *roundoff error*. If the previous calculation comes out exactly to 1, as it does on some hand calculators and computer systems, try calculating

    ((1 / 3) * 3) − 1

Even fewer computers or hand calculators obtain exactly 0 as the answer for this calculation.

Our point of view toward roundoff is that it is a special and practical problem, but one that is so important and so pervasive that, like debugging, it simply cannot be ignored if one wants to write real programs. Since roundoff refuses to confine itself to advanced mathematical and scientific applications, even the beginning programmer must be able to recognize when roundoff error has occurred and know how to apply first aid so that perfectly reasonable programs can be made to execute in a perfectly reasonable fashion.

Readers who have not yet encountered roundoff error in their programs, or who presently do not have access to a computer for running programs, might want to read only far enough into this section to find out what kinds of problems roundoff can cause in a computer program and then return to this section when the need arises. Other readers already may have discovered the need for an explanation of roundoff. After all, the two examples given above to illustrate the meaning of roundoff error use only programming features described in Section 1.1, the first section of the book.

In one major respect, this section differs from the rest of the book. The rest of the book emphasizes the similarity between ordinary usage and computer usage. This section emphasizes the differences between ordinary arithmetic and computer arithmetic. Precisely because it deals with things that do not happen quite as they might be expected to happen, this section requires closer and more careful reading than most other sections.

Storing Numbers

For every variable a program uses, the computer must reserve a certain portion of its memory to store its values. It does not matter whether the computer memory consists of tiny magnetic doughnut-shaped cores, or transistor circuits, or magnetic film, tape, drum, or disk, the principle is the same— a fixed number of units of the computer's physical hardware is reserved to store the values. For simplicity, our examples are based on a computer that stores the seven digits that make the largest contributions to the value of the number. This corresponds approximately to the behavior of many contemporary computers.

Nonrepresentable Numbers

Some numbers, like 123, can be represented exactly in seven (or fewer) digits. Others, like 1/3, cannot be so represented, although the seven-digit decimal value 0.3333333 is a very good approximation to the number 1/3. The difference between the two is only 1/30000000, so small as to be of no consequence whatsoever for most purposes. Moreover, the seven-digit value 0.3333333 is clearly the closest seven-digit value to the intended number 1/3.

Improving the Appearance of Printed Numbers

Many programs are not adversely affected by an error in the seventh significant digit. However, if an answer supposed to be $6.91 is printed as $6.909997, then it is both hard to read and misleading, because it appears that there is some significance in all of the digits printed. This phenomenon is illustrated by the program fabric.

```
program fabric (input, output);
  var
    cost, yards, price : real;
  begin
  read (yards, price);
  writeln ('Input data  yards: ', yards);
  writeln ('              price: ', price);
  cost := yards * price;
  writeln ('The cost is $', cost);
  end.
```

```
run fabric

Input data  yards:    1.3300000000000001e+00
            price:    4.3699999999999997+00
The cost is $    5.8120999999999998e+00
```

This difficulty can be avoided by using the columns and decimals indicators described in Section 1.2. Their use produces much nicer output as illustrated by the program nicer.

```
program nicer (input, output);
  var
    cost, yards, price : real;
  begin
  read (yards, price);
  writeln ('Input data  yards: ', yards :1:2);
  writeln ('              price: ', price :1:2);
  cost := yards * price;
  writeln ('The cost is $', cost :1:2);
  end.
```

```
run nicer

Input data  yards:   1.33
            price:   4.37
The cost is $ 5.81
```

Limiting the number of decimal places printed produces cleaner output. In commonly used programming languages, this problem also is handled by two techniques in addition to specifying the form of the printed output. In some languages, such as Cobol and PL/I, it is possible to specify that a variable always is to be rounded to a certain number of decimal places when it is calculated. In Pascal, one may use the built-in function round discussed in Section 2.6.

How A Small Roundoff Error Can Cause Big Trouble

In spite of the fact that a roundoff error might be very small, it can create a serious problem, as in the program listofprices.

```
program listofprices (input, output);
  var
    price, yards, cost : real;
  begin
  read (price);
  writeln ('Input data  price: ', price :1:2);
  writeln ('Yards' :25, 'Cost' :20);

  { a while-loop refinement of the non-Pascal statement
    for yards := 1/3 to 3 in steps of 1/3 }
  yards := 1/3;
  while yards <> 3 do
    begin
    cost := round (yards * price * 100) / 100;
    writeln (yards :25:16, cost :20:2);
    yards := yards + 1/3;
    end; { while-loop }
  end.
```

run listofprices

Input data price: 2.75
Yards	Cost
0.3333333333333333	0.92
0.6666666666666667	1.83
1.0000000000000000	2.75
1.3333333333333333	3.67
1.6666666666666667	4.58
2.0000000000000000	5.50
2.3333333333333333	6.42
2.6666666666666666	7.33
2.9999999999999999	8.25
3.3333333333333333	9.17
3.6666666666666666	10.08
3.9999999999999999	11.00
.	.
.	.
.	.

The intended values for the variable yards are clearly 1/3, 2/3, ..., 3. However, in actual computer execution, the values for yards might be slightly different. If a computer that retains seven-decimal digits were used, the first value would be 0.3333333, the closest possible seven-digit approximation to the intended value 1/3. This value is only 1/30000000 too low. However, the next calculated value is likely to be 0.3333333 + 0.3333333 = 0.6666666, which is not the closest possible seven-digit approximation to the intended value 2/3. The value 0.6666667 is closer, although the difference between either approximation and the intended value 2/3 is still extremely small. The next computed value for yards might be a little further off the mark. Increasing the computed value 0.6666666 by the step size of 0.3333333 might give a new value for yards of 0.9999999, which differs by 0.0000001 from the intended value 1. The point is that successive computed values stray ever farther from the intended values, so that eventually their difference is detectable by while- and if-tests.

When the program listofprices was run on a nondecimal machine, (see sample output above), the computed value for 1/3 was close enough to 1 to print as 1 to 16 decimal places, but a fatal problem had occurred by the time the value of yards was increased to where the intended value was 3. The computed value for yards was more than 0.000000000000001 too low. More importantly, the while-loop failed to terminate.

Even when the while-test failed, the difference between the computed and the intended values was very small. This difference is called *roundoff error*. In this example the largest roundoff error encountered so far was 1/10000000000000000. In most cases, it takes a rather large number of arithmetic operations to produce a significant roundoff error.

In executing a loop, however, a more subtle problem arises-- How does the computer know when to stop? The stopping value for yards in the program listofprices is 3, which is 3.000000000000000 to 16 decimal places. The computed values for yards are 0.3333333333333333, 0.6666666666666667, ..., 2.6666666666666667, and 2.9999999999999999, none of which is exactly equal to 3.000000000000000. Yet the programmer clearly does not intend the loop to continue to the next calculated value for yards of 3.3333333333333333, which is nearly 3 1/3.

This is precisely the kind of annoying detail that most programmers would prefer not to have to cope with, because it does not correspond to any comparable difficulty in the original problem. In the absence of roundoff error, the loop in the program listofprices would work properly and print the correct number of lines of output. However, in this case, there is some slight roundoff, and the value of the variable yards is never exactly equal to 3. Thus the while-condition yards $<>$ 3 is always true, and the loop never terminates. The failure of this loop to terminate is another instance of violating an important principle of prudent programming, already flagged for special attention in Section 2.3: *Avoid writing a test for equality of two quantities* if there is the slightest chance that one or both of the quantities, or even any of the preliminary calculations leading up to these quantities, can result in roundoff error. In practice the only truly safe numbers are relatively small integers exactly representable on all machines, and even these have been known to fail equality tests on occasion.

How To Avoid Tests For Equality

One substitute for a test for equality is a test for approximate equality. Instead of testing whether two quantities x and y are equal, one might test whether they are close to each other; that is, whether the difference between them is a small number. Since it may not be known which is larger, it is the absolute value of the difference that must be tested, as in the statement

```
if abs (x - y) < 0.001 then ...
```

In the program listofprices, a simpler test suffices. Rather than comparing the absolute values of the difference between yards and 3 to 0.001, the simpler test

```
while yards < 3000.1 do ...
```

can be made, since yards is increasing and will be greater than 3 + 0.001 = 3.001 for the first time during the program execution, when its value should be exactly equal to 3 1/3.

Another Way To Avoid Roundoff Error

The last general method given here to reduce roundoff error eliminates the cumulative roundoff that comes from adding an approximation to the step size during each iteration of a loop. The program accurateprices also uses the technique of calculating in advance the number of times the loop is to be executed, thereby minimizing the possibility that the loop executes the wrong number of times because of roundoff error.

```pascal
program accurateprices (input, output);


   var
      price, yards, cost : real;
      fewest, most, step : real;
      numberofprices, iteration : integer;


   begin
   read (price);
   writeln ('Input data  price: ', price :1:2);
   writeln ('Yards' :25, 'Cost' :20);
   fewest := 1/3;
   most := 3;
   step := 1/3;
   numberofprices := round (1 + (most - fewest) / step);
   for iteration := 1 to numberofprices do
      begin
      yards := fewest + (iteration - 1) * step;
      cost := yards * price;
      writeln (yards :25:16, cost :20:2);
      end; { for-loop }
   end.
```

```
run accurateprices

Input data  price:  2.75
                   Yards                    Cost
         0.3333333333333333                0.92
         0.6666666666666667                1.83
         1.0000000000000000                2.75
         1.3333333333333333                3.67
         1.6666666666666667                4.58
         2.0000000000000000                5.50
         2.3333333333333333                6.42
         2.6666666666666667                7.33
         3.0000000000000000                8.25
```

A Comparison of Two Methods

The extent of the roundoff error problems created by the repeated addition of a step size to a variable increases dramatically as the number of steps becomes larger and as the value for the variable becomes larger. This is seen by comparing the values printed by executing both the programs yards1 and yards2.

```
program yards1 (output);
  var
    yards : real;
    iteration : integer;
  begin
  iteration := 1;
  yards := 1000;
  while yards < 2000.1 do
    begin
    writeln (iteration, yards :20:13);
    yards := yards + 1/3;
    iteration := iteration + 1;
    end; { while-loop }
  end.

run yards1

        1   1000.0000000000000
        2   1000.3333333333333
        3   1000.6666666666667

              .

              .

              .

     2998   1999.0000000000274
     2999   1999.3333333333607
     3000   1999.6666666666941
     3001   2000.0000000000274

program yards2 (output);
  var
    yards, fewest, most, step : real;
    numberofsteps, iteration : integer;
  begin
  fewest := 1000;
  most := 2000;
  step := 1/3;
  numberofsteps := round (1 + (most - fewest) / step);
  for iteration := 1 to numberofsteps do
    begin
    yards := fewest + (iteration - 1) * step;
    writeln (iteration, yards :20:13);
    end; { for-loop }
  end.
```

```
run yards2
```

```
       1    1000.0000000000000
       2    1000.3333333333333
       3    1000.6666666666667
            .
            .           *
            .
    2998    1999.0000000000000
    2999    1999.3333333333333
    3000    1999.6666666666667
    3001    2000.0000000000000
```

Although the last three decimal places have been eroded by roundoff in the running of the program yards1, the computer used carries the binary equivalent of so many decimal digits that it would take billions of iterations in this range of numbers to fail the generous tolerance of the while-test. The values shown in the printout for yards2 are accurate to the number of places printed.

Table 2.7.1   A Comparison of Two Methods For Resisting Roundoff Error in a For-Variable.

Values of the for-variable yards

Iteration	Intended value	yards1 value	yards2 value
1	1000	1000	1000
2	1000 1/3	1000.333	1000.333
3	1000 2/3	1000.666	1000.667
4	1001	1000.000	1001
5	1001 1/3	1001.332	1001.333
6	1001 2/3	1001.665	1001.667
7	1002	1001.998	1002
8	1002 1/3	1002.331	1002.333
.	.	.	.
.	.	.	.
2997	1998 2/3	1997.668	1998.667
2998	1999	1998.001	1999
2999	1999 1/3	1998.334	1999.333
3000	1999 2/3	1998.667	1999.667
3001	2000	1999	2000
3002		1999.333	
3003		1999.666	
3004		1999.999	

However, on a machine that rounds all numbers to the seven most significant decimal digits, the results shown in Table 2.7.1 are quite different. The loop in yards1 results in three too many steps. The loop in yards2 produces the correct number of steps, and the values of the variable yards are the best possible seven-digit representations, properly rounded from the intended values. This is why the method used in yards2 is highly recommended when there are difficulties with roundoff error.

What Every Programmer Should Know About Roundoff Error

The systematic study of roundoff error is a very complicated affair and is not pursued further in this book. What every programmer needs to know about roundoff error is at least the following.

1. It can happen.

2. It almost never happens to small integers, which are usually immune to roundoff error.

3. Properly handled, it is rarely fatal to the intended calculation.

4. When roundoff problems develop, the first-aid measures of this section usually can cure the problem.

5. In those few cases where the first-aid measures fail, the reduction of roundoff error is a major component of the problem, and the services of an expert should be sought.

Binary Computers, A Postscript

A great many contemporary computers, probably the majority of them, do their internal arithmetic using a number system based on the number 2 instead of the ordinary base 10 decimal number system. In such a number system, called a *binary number system*, the place values of the integer places from right to left are 1, 2, 4, 8, 16, 32, ..., the powers of 2 instead of the usual decimal place values of 1, 10, 100, 1000, ..., the powers of 10. The places to the right of the binary point are worth successively 1/2, 1/4, 1/8, 1/32, ..., as compared to the place values of 1/10, 1/100, 1/1000, ..., for the places to the right of the decimal point in the ordinary number system.

Binary number representations tend to be long and monotonous and are not at all felicitous for human usage. For example, the decimal number 650 is represented in binary as 1010001010, and the decimal number 100 is represented in binary as 1100100. For this reason, when computer languages are implemented on a binary computer or on a computer using number systems based on 8 (''octal'') or 16 (''hexadecimal''), which are closely related to the binary number system, the user is still allowed to communicate with the computer using ordinary decimal numbers. The conversion of all input numbers from decimal notation into binary, and the reconversion from binary to ordinary decimal notation of all numbers to be printed or written as output in any other fashion for human use, are done automatically by the computer system. In fact, the user might not even know that the computer is binary.

The reason for mentioning binary computers at this point is the curious fact that, although 1/10 can be represented exactly in one significant decimal digit as 0.1, it cannot be represented exactly in binary, no matter how many significant digits are used. Just as the true decimal representation for 1/3 is 0.3333333333..., never ending, the true binary representation for 1/10 is 0.0001100110011001100..., without termination. In both cases, retaining the fixed number of significant places a particular computer's hardware is designed to handle results in a small but significant roundoff error. Thus 1/10 is represented exactly on every decimal machine but is never represented exactly on any binary machine. A tell-tale sign is that the expressions 10 * (1/10) and 1/10 + 1/10 + 1/10 + 1/10 + 1/10 + 1/10 + 1/10 + 1/10 + 1/10 + 1/10 are computed as exactly 1 on a decimal machines and usually as 0.9999999 on binary machines.

Besides the fact that there are many common decimal fractions exactly representable in ordinary decimal notation but not exactly representable in binary computers, the problems caused by roundoff error and their solutions are pretty much the same for binary computers as for decimal computers. Small integers are exactly representable in binary notation, as they are in decimal notation, provided they are small enough to fit in the number of binary digits provided by the computer's circuits. Of course, since binary number representations tend to be longer than decimal number representations, the number of binary digits (sometimes called ''bits'') provided on a given binary computer is usually sufficiently large that the size of the numbers that can be represented is roughly comparable to those representable on decimal machines. The programs for the decimal-to-binary and the binary-to-decimal conversions for input and output, which are supplied when a programming language is implemented on a binary computer, are usually reliable, and in some languages they can be made to do the rounding of the output to the desired number of decimal digits.

In summary, it is generally conceded that users want to communicate with computers using ordinary decimal numbers, even if the computer happens to be a binary machine. In most computer languages, it is perfectly possible to do so, and perhaps the only surprises encountered are related to the fact that numbers like 1/10 cannot be represented exactly in a binary computer.

Exercises

1. Perform the calculation (1 / 7) * 7 by hand, rounding the intermediate answer and the final answer to seven significant digits. (This involves calculating eight digits and then rounding to seven.) Is the answer equal to 1?

2. Perform the calculation (2 / 7) * 7 by hand, rounding the intermediate answer and the final answer to seven significant digits. Would a seven-decimal-digit computer call this answer equal to 2 in an if-test?

3. What significant difference is there between the calculations for Exercise 1 and for Exercise 2 that causes one to compute the exact answer and the other to show roundoff error?

4. Perform the calculations for Exercises 1 and 2 on a desk calculator or computer. Still better, perform them on several different calculating devices. Do all of them show roundoff error in the calculation for Exercise 1? Do any of them show roundoff error in the calculation for Exercise 2?

5. Perform the calculation (1 / 7) * 7 by carrying 14 digits throughout the calculation and rounding the final answer to seven significant digits. How does this computation differ from that for Exercise 1?

6. A well-known fact of ordinary arithmetic, called the Associative Law, says that, for any three numbers a, b, and c,

   a + (b + c) = (a + b) + c

   Test whether this law holds in computer arithmetic using the values a = 5.326451, b = 6.954603, and c = 1.719843. Be sure to round each intermediate result so that it retains no more than seven significant digits.

7. In ordinary arithmetic, the expression

   (a + b) − a

   is exactly equal to b. Keeping seven significant digits in all intermediate and final results, what is the size of the roundoff error that occurs when a = 12345 and b = 0.1234567 in the expression above? Why is the roundoff error so large compared to the size of b?

8. In the calculation and comparisons for Exercise 7, try different values for a and b. In particular, find values for a and b such that the number of significant digits remaining from b is only one; find values such that all seven significant digits of b remain; and find values for a and b such that only four significant digits of b remain in the final answer.

9. The calculation for Exercise 6 shows roundoff error in addition, and the calculation in Exercise 7 shows roundoff error in subtraction. Which operation has the greater potential for roundoff error disasters?

10. The Associative Law of Multiplication says that in ordinary arithmetic

    x * (y * z) = (x * y) * z

    for any numbers x, y, and z. Find three computer-represented numbers such that this equality fails on a seven-digit machine. Hint: Try making the first significant digit of x * y small and the first significant digit of y * z large. (The same calculation may be tried on a three-digit machine to save arithmetic done by hand.) Does multiplication have the same potential for roundoff disaster as addition or subtraction?

11. Calculate the sum

    0 + 1/3 + 2/3 + 1 + ... + 19 2/3 + 20

    using a computer. Be sure to print the computer approximations to each of the numbers added to form the sum. How does the answer compare to the exact answer 610?

12. Calculate the sum

    20 + 19 2/3 + 19 1/3 + 19 + ... + 1/3 + 0

    using a computer. Be sure to print the computer approximations to each of the numbers added to form the sum. How does this answer compare to the exact answer 610?

13. Theoretically, the sums in Exercises 11 and 12 are formed by the same numbers added in reverse order. In the computer output for Exercises 11 and 12, are the same numbers actually added in both sums? Explain any differences.

14. Compute the sums in Exercises 11 and 12 using the technique introduced in the program yards2 in this section to minimize the roundoff error in the calculation. Are the same numbers now used in both sums? Are the sums equal to each other or to the exact answer 610?

15. Why is roundoff error not a problem for the interest rate in the mortgage programs in Section 2.5?

16. Would roundoff be expected in the interest rate in the mortgage programs in Section 2.5 if the monthly payments were calculated for interest rates in steps of 1/10 percent?

17. Which of the simple calculational programs in Section 1.1 could be subject to roundoff error if slightly different numbers were used, and how much roundoff error might be expected?

18. In some computer languages, when the quotient of two quantities of type integer is written, the computed answer is the integer part of the quotient. (Pascal uses the integer operator div to indicate a truncated division of integers.) Using this convention for arithmetic on integers, compute the values of the two expressions

$$(6 * 4) / 3 \quad \text{and} \quad 6 * (4 / 3)$$

that are computed to seven significant digits in this section. Worse yet, compute the value of the expression

$$(1 / n) * n$$

for n = 1, 2, 3, and so on. It is a common programming error to believe that these expressions are evaluated in the usual arithmetic manner in languages that compute the quotient of two integers as an integer.

19. Are the values of the following two expressions equal (a) in ordinary arithmetic? (b) in computer arithmetic on a seven-digit decimal computer that rounds to the last digit? (c) on a binary computer?

$$10 * (7 / 5) \quad \text{and} \quad (10 * 7) / 5$$

21. In the absence of roundoff error, as the number n grows larger, the value of the expression

$$(1 + 1/n) \text{ to the nth power}$$

gets closer and closer to the important mathematical constant e = 2.718281828459045.... Using either a desk calculator or a computer, calculate the value of this expression for values of n in the following sequences:

(a) 2, 4, 8, 16, 32, 64, 128, 256, 512, 1024, 2048, 4096, 8192, ...,
(b) 3, 6, 12, 24, 48, 96, 192, 384, 768, 1536, 3072, 6144, 12288, ...,
(c) 10, 100, 1000, 10000, 100000, ...,

This formula, which is closely related to compound interest formulas, is especially sensitive to roundoff error for large values of n, so the answers may differ considerably depending on the machine used.

2.8   Chapter Review

The three principal topics in Chapter 2 are *loops*, *subroutines*, and the method of *successive refinements*, or *top-down programming*, as it is sometimes called. Loops and subroutines are structural elements in a computer program, but refinement is a technique of planning and writing computer programs by not looking at all the details at once.

Loops

A *loop* is a sequence of instructions that can be executed more than once in a single execution of a program that contains the loop. There are three basic types of loop structures in Pascal, the for-loop, the while-loop, and the repeat-until-loop, each named after the keyword in the statement that is used to form that type of loop block. The repeat-until-statement introduced in Section 2.3 is rarely used in this book because it is very similar to the while-statement. The for-loop, introduced in Section 1.3 and discussed in more detail in Sections 2.1 and 2.5, is used when the values of a variable in successive repetitions of a loop differ from each other by the same fixed increment and it is known that the loop will execute a fixed number of times. The while-loop, introduced in Section 2.3, is the most general form of a loop in Pascal, in the sense that any for-loop can be rewritten as an equivalent while-loop with no essential change in the execution of the program.

While-Loops

The *while-statement* gives the programmer the most flexibility when writing a loop. The number of repetitions of the loop does not need to be known before the loop is begun, and the loop execution can be terminated before the start of any iteration of the loop body. For example, the program sqrtof2 repeatedly takes the average of a number called before and the quantity 2 / before, stopping when there is no further change. The answers happen to stabilize to the square root of 2, which explains the text of the message printed, but this does not have to be known to follow the program execution.

```
program sqrtof2 (output);
  var
    before, after : real;
    equal : boolean;
  begin
  before := 1;
  writeln ('Starting value = ', before :1:16);
  equal := false;
  while not equal do
    begin
    after := (before + (2 / before)) / 2;
    writeln ('Next value = ', after :1:16);
    if before = after then
      equal := true
```

```
     else
       { prepare for next iteration }
       before : = after;
     end; { while-loop }
   writeln ('The square root of 2 is ', after :1:16);
   end.
run sqrtof2

Starting value =  1.0000000000000000
Next value =  1.5000000000000000
Next value =  1.4166666666666667
Next value =  1.4142156862745098
Next value =  1.4142135623746899
Next value =  1.4142135623730951
Next value =  1.4142135623730951
The square root of 2 is  1.4142135623730951
```

Each time through the loop, a new value for the variable after is calculated as the average of the value of the variable before and the quotient 2 / before. Only when the new value of after is equal to the previous value before is the if-test successful and the while-loop terminated.

Endless Loops

Although it did not happen in the displayed execution of the program sqrtof2, it is by no means obvious in advance that the if-test in this program couldn't fail every time through the loop, because the values of the variables before and after keep changing. Programs similar to sqrtof2 have been known to oscillate between the two nearest approximations to the square root. This would be disastrous, because only if two consecutive values are equal and the if-test succeeds can the repetition be stopped.

Experienced programmers are extremely suspicious of tests based on equality of computed quantities, unless all the computed numbers are small integers and no division operations are used. The program endlessloop3 shows a perfectly reasonable looking while-test that nevertheless fails on many computers used by the authors, because the number 1/3 cannot be represented exactly in a computer.

```
program endlessloop3 (output);
  var
    sum : real;
  begin
  sum : = 0;
  while sum <> 3 do
    begin
    sum : = sum + 1/3;
    writeln ('The sum is now ', sum :22:16);
    end; { while-loop }
  end.
```

```
run endlessloop3
```

```
The sum is now      0.3333333333333333
The sum is now      0.6666666666666667
The sum is now      1.0000000000000000
The sum is now      1.3333333333333333
The sum is now      1.6666666666666667
The sum is now      2.0000000000000000
The sum is now      2.3333333333333333
The sum is now      2.6666666666666666
The sum is now      2.9999999999999999
The sum is now      3.3333333333333333
The sum is now      3.6666666666666666
                         .
                         .
                         .
```

Testing to see whether the sum exceeds 3, or whether the sum is within some predetermined tolerance of 3, say between $3 - .001$ and $3 + .001$, are safer criteria to stop a loop from executing indefinitely. *Tests for equality are to be avoided whenever possible*.

For-Loops

Many programming applications require a sequence of values for a variable that consists of a consecutive set of integers, either counting up or counting down. Because this situation is so common, Pascal has a feature called a *for-statement*. The program countto4 shows an example of a for-loop and its relationship to the while-loop in Pascal.

```
program countto4 (output);
  var
    count : integer;
  begin
  for count := 1 to 4 do
    writeln ('Count = ', count :1, ' in the for-loop');
  writeln;
  count := 1;
  while count <= 4 do
    begin
    writeln ('Count = ', count :1, ' in the while-loop');
    count := count + 1;
    end; { while-loop }
  end.
```

```
run countto4
```

```
Count = 1 in the for-loop
Count = 2 in the for-loop
Count = 3 in the for-loop
Count = 4 in the for-loop
```

```
Count = 1 in the while-loop
Count = 2 in the while-loop
Count = 3 in the while-loop
Count = 4 in the while-loop
```

The general forms of a for-statement are

```
for variablename := start to stop do
  statement
```

```
for variablename := start downto stop do
  statement
```

If the value of the expression stop precedes the value of the expression start (in the indicated order or direction), the statement that forms the body of the for-loop is not executed. Otherwise, the for-variable variablename is assigned the value of the expression start for the first iteration of the loop, and then the value of the for-variable is increased by one for each subsequent iteration. If the keyword "to" is replaced by the keyword "downto", then the value of the for-variable is decreased by one for each iteration of the loop. The for-variable must be type integer, character, boolean, or a programmer-defined data type described in Section 4.3. *The for-variable must not be type real.* The expressions start and stop must be the same type as the for-variable. A for-loop terminates after it has been executed with the for-variable having the value of the expression stop. The Pascal language does not specify what value a for-variable will have upon completion of a for-loop.

The Case-Statement

The case-statement is used when one of several alternative computational sequences is to be selected on the basis of one value. It has two advantages over a sequence of if-statements: the resulting program is easier to read and the execution is slightly faster. The following program fragment illustrates the major features of the case-statement.

```
program cases (input, output);

  var
    lettergrade : char;

  begin
  read (lettergrade);
  write (lettergrade);
  case lettergrade of
    'A', 'B', 'C', 'D', 'P':
      writeln (' is passing');
    'F':
      writeln (' is failing');
    'W', 'I':
      writeln (' does not count toward gradepoint average');
    end; { case }
  end.
```

The cases may be of any scalar data type except real. Integer and character types are common, as are user-defined scalar data types described in Section 4.3. The computational alternatives are statements, which include null statements, simple statements, and compound statements. Only one alternative is executed each time the case-statement is executed.

Refinements of a Program

The methodology of writing programs recommended by the authors is first to write the essential procedures of the solution of a problem in the most convenient terms, often involving terminology from the original application, and then to refine these program steps until an executable program is obtained, perhaps after many such refinements. Meaningful statements are written as though a computer could understand them, and then refined into a succession of simpler steps if the computer cannot. Whenever possible, structural elements from the target language, such as loop constructions and if-statements, are introduced into a program in preference to equally meaningful directions to the computer that cannot be converted as easily into the target language for the final executable program.

This method of writing programs is sometimes called "top-down" programming, because the highest level of organization of the program is attended to first, and the nitty-gritty details are saved for last. It is often possible and quite reassuring to write every version of a program as a correct and complete set of steps for solving the problem. The first broad outline, every one of the refinements, and the final executable program itself should each be comprehensible to anyone or to any computer that understands the terminology or keywords used at that stage. This is also of great practical value in proving the correctness of programs.

Procedures

When writing a program from the top down, one often writes instructions as though a computer could understand them. Using procedures, it is possible to augment Pascal so that meaningful instructions not included in the language originally can be made into executable steps. For example, the program bigger

```
program bigger (input, output);
{ first version }
  begin
  read two numbers;
  print the larger;
  end.
```

can be refined into Pascal using the procedures readtwonumbers and writethelarger to refine the executable statements.

```
program bigger (input, output);

  var
    first, second : integer;
```

```
procedure readtwonumbers;
  begin
  read (first, second);
  writeln ('Input data  first: ', first :1);
  writeln ('            second: ', second :1);
  end; { readtwonumbers }

procedure writethelarger;
  begin
  if first > second then
    writeln (first :1, ' is larger.')
  else
    writeln (second :1, ' is larger.');
  end; { writethelarger }

begin
readtwonumbers;
writethelarger;
end.
```

```
run bigger

Input data  first: 42
            second: -127
42 is larger.
```

In Pascal, a variable name used in a procedure means the same quantity as when the same variable name is used in the main program that *calls* the procedure, unless the variable is redeclared within the procedure as described in Chapter 4. A program calls a procedure—that is, instructs the computer to execute the procedure—by means of a statement that consists of the procedure name itself.

Some of the time, a programmer is saved the trouble of writing the steps of a useful procedure, because it is supplied with the computer system or added to the computer system at the local installation. Or it can be found previously written by another programmer. However, even if all the details of a subroutine must be supplied by the programmer who uses it, there is still an advantage to using the calling program-procedure approach. Since the procedure removes the lower levels of detail from the calling program, some of the clarity of earlier refinements can be preserved as the calling program is refined into executable form. Types of subroutines more general that those used in this chapter are found in Chapter 4.

Integer Operators Div and Mod

If candy bars sell for 27 cents each, it might be amusing to know that one can buy 3.703704 candy bars for $1.00, but is is probably more useful to know that one can buy 3 candy bars and have 19 cents change from the dollar. The integer operators div and mod may be used for such calculations. The value of the expression 100 div 27 is 3, the integer part of the quotient 100 / 27 = 3.703704, and the value of the expression 100 mod 27 is 19, the remainder from 100 after the largest possible integral multiple of

27, that is, $81 = 3 \times 27$ has been subtracted. In general, the operations div and mod are related by the formula

$$n \bmod d = n - (n \operatorname{div} d) * d$$

Built-In Functions and Procedures

In most computer languages, the most common operations, such as the usual arithmetic operations addition, subtraction, multiplication, and division, are written using special symbols for each operation. Other useful operations are made available in the form of built-in functions. For example, the built-in function round is useful in producing satisfactory output. Other built-in functions include trunc, abs, sqr, sqrt, odd, eof, eoln, and several scientific functions.

Roundoff Error

Some numbers, such as the small integers 2 and 135, can be represented exactly in a computer's memory. Others, like 1/3 and 1/7, can be represented only approximately. The difference between the way computer calculates and stores an answer and the exact answer is called *roundoff error*. For example, the computer representation 0.3333333 for 1/3 differs from the exact value by 1/30000000.

Normally, the roundoff error in computed quantities is quite small compared to the size of the quantities. However, even a small roundoff error can upset the workings of an if-test or while-test that examines the possible equality of two computed quantities. For example, the following if-statement often fails to execute in the obvious manner because of roundoff error.

```
if (1 / 3) * 9 = 3 then
  writeln ('That''s what I thought.')
else
  writeln ('Curses!  Foiled again by roundoff error.')
```

Thus an important principle of prudent programming is to *avoid writing if-tests or while-tests for equality of numerical quantities if at all possible*. A possible exception to this policy occurs when all the quantities throughout the calculation are small integers and division is not used.

The sensitivity of some tests to roundoff error sometimes can cause problems in the execution of a loop, because failure of the test prevents recognition of the terminating condition. Even if one expects the upper limit of some variable in a loop to be reached exactly, it is safer to base termination of the loop on exceeding the upper limit rather than reaching it exactly. Section 2.7 describes two ways of modifying a loop so that it resists roundoff error problems, and these changes can be made if the execution of the original loop is unsatisfactory.

Binary Computers

Many, if not most, contemporary computers use a number system based on the number 2 instead of the ordinary decimal system based on the number 10. Although the user still may communicate with the computer by supplying input and receiving output written in decimal notation, the internal calculations and the memory configuration of the computer are based on binary representations of numbers. Unfortunately, numbers such as 1/10, 1/100, 1000, ..., cannot be represented exactly in binary and thus are subject to roundoff error. Besides the fact that some numbers, such as 123.456, that appear to be exactly representable, are in fact subject to roundoff error in binary computers, the use of a binary computer differs but little from the use of a decimal computer. The user may even be unaware of which type of computer is being used to run a program.

3

ARRAYS, LISTS, AND TABLES

Many programming applications require the processing of a number of different pieces of information of the same kind. In a payroll program, for instance, the wage rates of the various employees may differ, but each is the same kind of information—that is, a wage rate—and each is processed in the same way by the payroll program.

The loop structures introduced in Chapter 2 are well suited to the type of repetitive processing most applications require. But the variables are limited. Specifically, in none of the programming applications in the first two chapters is it necessary to have more than one piece of information of each kind available at one time. In the average of test scores programs in Chapter 1, only the next score and the most recent value of the running total are needed. Previous scores and older values of the running total need not be saved. In a payroll program, the name, social security number, hourly wage rate, and number of hours worked would be needed to process the pay of one employee, but once that employee's pay has been processed, this information is never used again. It might be replaced by similar information for the next employee.

Since a simple variable can have only one value at a time, the applications in the first two chapters are restricted. In those applications only one piece, or at most a small number of pieces, of data of each kind are needed at one time in the computation. As soon as all, or at least a large portion, of the data of some kind must be *simultaneously available* during the execution of a program, as in the searching, sorting, merging, and table look-up applications in this chapter, the language feature *arrays* is needed.

A variable with one subscript is called a *list*, and a variable with two subscripts is called a *table*, corresponding closely to the ordinary English meaning of these words. In Pascal, both lists and tables are called *arrays*. Lists of numbers are searched, sorted, and merged in Sections 3.2 to 3.4, while tables of printable characters are used to construct computer graphics in Section 3.5. The use of lists and tables allows some of the natural organization of the data for a problem to be mirrored in a computer program. More complex types of data organization in a computer program are treated in Chapter 6.

3.1 Lists, Subscripts, and Index Variables

In ordinary usage, a *list* is a sequence of values, usually all representing data of the same kind, or otherwise related to one another. A list of students registered for a particular course and a list of all students enrolled at a college are examples. The roster of active players on an athletic team and the names of all the presidents of the United States are also lists. So are grocery lists and lists of entrants in a jousting tournament. Popular synonyms for the same concept are ''one-dimensional array'' and ''vector''. Sometimes the phrase ''linear list'' is used to distinguish it from the more general list structures that are beyond the scope of this discussion.

In Pascal, a collection of values of the same type is called an *array*, a keyword that must be used in the variable declaration for such a collection. Except in variable declarations, where no synonyms are permitted, we will refer to a one-dimensional array as a *list*. This section is concerned mainly with introducing the programming techniques associated with lists, including the concepts of subscripts and index variables. Two-dimensional arrays of values often are called *tables* or *matrices*. Higher dimensional arrays are permitted in Pascal, but they are not treated in this book.

A Credit Card Checking Application

As an example of a problem concerned with a list, suppose that a company maintains a computerized list of credit cards either that have been reported lost or stolen or that are greatly in arrears in payments. The company needs a program to determine quickly whether a given credit card, presented by a customer wishing to charge a purchase, is on this list of credit cards that can no longer be honored.

In ordinary usage, a list has a first item, a second item, and so forth, up to a last item. The only type of computer list of immediate concern to us has the same structure. For example, in the credit card checking application, suppose that a company has a list of 8262 credit cards reported lost or stolen, as illustrated in Table 3.1.1, mercifully shortened by ellipses.

Since each of the 8262 numbers in the list must be retained simultaneously in the computer's main memory for efficient searching, each number must be assigned as the value of a variable with a different name so that the computer can be instructed to compare individually each account number of a lost or stolen card against the account number of the card offered in payment for goods and services.

Table 3.1.1   List of the Account Numbers of Credit Cards Reported Lost or Stolen.

Account number of 1st lost credit card	2718281
Account number of 2nd lost credit card	7389056
Account number of 3rd lost credit card	1098612
Account number of 4th lost credit card	5459815
Account number of 5th lost credit card	1484131
.	.
.	.
.	.
Account number of 8262nd lost credit card	1383596

Subscripts

It is possible to use Pascal variable names

```
accountnumberof1stlostcreditcard
accountnumberof2ndlostcreditcard
accountnumberof3rdlostcreditcard
        .
        .
        .
accountnumberof8262ndlostcreditcard
```

corresponding to the descriptive names in the left column of Table 3.1.1 with the blanks removed. Unfortunately, the Pascal language does not recognize the intended relationship between these variable names. (Some Pascal systems might even consider them all to be the same name, because the first 15 characters of all the names are the same.) Even the shorter variable names

```
numberof1stlostcard
numberof2ndlostcard
        .
        .
        .
numberof8262ndlostcard
```

whose relationship to each other is still perfectly clear to a person, do not bear any more relationship to one another in Pascal than do any 8262 variable names chosen at random. The form used for designating the items in a Pascal list is the following:

```
numberoflostcard [1]
numberoflostcard [2]
numberoflostcard [3]
        .
        .
        .
numberoflostcard [8262]
```

This seemingly minor modification of otherwise perfectly acceptable variable names opens up a new dimension of programming capabilities. All the programs in this chapter, and a large number of the programs in succeeding chapters, cannot be written without this form. The numbers in square brackets that specify the location of an item within a list are called *subscripts*, a name borrowed from mathematical usage. Although mathematical subscripts are usually written below the line (hence the name "subscript"), such a form of typography is impossible on most computer input devices. A substitute notation, enclosing the subscript in brackets or parentheses, is adopted in most computer languages. It is customary to read the expression x [3] as "x sub 3", just as if the number 3 were written below the line.

Why Use Subscripts?

The advantage of this method of naming the quantities over using the nearly identical variable names numberof1stlostcard, numberof2ndlostcard, ..., numberof8262ndlostcard springs from the following programming language capability:

The subscript of an array variable may itself be a variable, or even a more complicated expression.

The consequences of this simple statement are much more profound than would appear at first sight. In fact, it is one of the most important principles in modern computer programming. This entire chapter, and much of the rest of this book, is devoted to exploring some of the uses of this facility.

For a start in describing the uses of a subscript that is itself a variable, the two statements

```
i := 1;
write (numberoflostcard [i])
```

produce exactly the same output as the single statement

```
write (numberoflostcard [1])
```

namely, 2718281, the account number of the first lost credit card on the list. Similarly, the account numbers of the first three lost credit cards may be written by the statements

```
i := 1;
write (numberoflostcard [i]);
i := 2;
write (numberoflostcard [i]);
i := 3;
write (numberoflostcard [i])
```

The effect is the same as executing the three statements

```
write (numberoflostcard [1]);
write (numberoflostcard [2]);
write (numberoflostcard [3])
```

Based on the data in Table 3.1.1, the sample output in both cases would be

2718281 7389056 1098612

In fact, the entire list of account numbers of lost credit cards can be written by the procedure printlostcards.

```
procedure printlostcards;
  var
    { i must be an integer from 1 to 8262 }
    i : 1..8262;
```

```
begin
for i := 1 to 8262 do
  writeln (numberoflostcard [i]);
end; { printlostcards }
```

```
2718281
7389056
1098612
       .

       .

       .
1383596
```

The sample output resembles Table 3.1.1 without the names. The important thing to keep in mind when following the execution of the procedure printlostcards is that, each time the writeln command is executed, there is a different value for the subscript i, and consequently a different item in the list is printed.

Index Variables

A variable used to indicate which item in a list is being referenced is called an *index*. The variable subscript i in the procedure printlostcards is such an *index variable*. Traditionally, the name ''i'' is a very popular one for index variables, partly because it is the first letter in the word ''index'', and partly because the letter ''i'' is commonly used in mathematics for a variable subscript. The names ''j'' and ''k'' are popular also.

Local and Global Variables

The declaration of the variable i in the procedure printlostcards is new in two respects. First, it is the first time we have declared a variable in a procedure. We do so here because the calling program for the procedure printlostcards is not shown, but this placement of the declaration for i has other virtues, and it is where an experienced programmer would place it.

The variable i is used by the procedure printlostcards in a way that does not concern the calling program. The value of i before starting the procedure printlostcards has no effect on the execution of the procedure printlostcards, which initializes i to 1 in the for-loop, and the value of i upon completion of printlostcards is undefined. The variable i is declared in the procedure printlostcards because its meaning is *local* to that procedure. The full import of local variables is described in Section 4.1. A variable declared in the main program is called *global*. Its value is known everywhere in the program.

Subrange Types

The second new feature of the declaration for i is that it has a new kind of type, a *subrange type*. In this case, the expression 1..8262 indicates that the permissible values for i are precisely those integers that lie in the range 1 to 8262 inclusive. The values for i are a subrange of the integers because the lower bound 1 and the upper bound 8262 are both integer constants.

A declaration of a subrange type for a variable looks like an ordinary type declaration, except that the type is replaced by two constants with two periods between them. A variable declared to have values in a subrange of a type may be used any place a variable of that type may be used; however, a variable of a subrange type must assume values that are within the subrange. In the procedure printlostcards, for example, the variable i must never assume any values except the integers 1, 2, 3, ..., 8262. Many debugging Pascal compilers provide execution-time error messages if such a variable assumes a value outside its declared subrange.

It is possible to declare the values of a variable to be a subrange of characters or a subrange of a programmer-defined type as discussed in Section 4.3. It is even permissible to declare a subrange of boolean values, although this usually isn't very useful. A variable must not be declared to be a subrange of real values.

For example, with the following declarations, the variable x may assume any two-digit positive, negative, or zero value, uppercaseletter may have a value that is any single upper case letter of the alphabet, and digit may be any single character that is a decimal digit. Although their declarations are similar, the values of the variable digit must be characters and the values of the variable number must be integers.

```
var
  x : -99..99;
  uppercaseletter : 'A'..'Z';
  digit : '0'..'9';
  number : 0..9;
```

In subrange declarations, it is good programming practice to use names of constants in place of the constants themselves in all but the simplest cases. Thus in the example above, the constant 99 probably should be given a name so that the declaration of x may appear as

```
const
  limit = 99;
var
  x : -limit..limit;
```

Array Declarations

The name of an array must obey the same rules as an ordinary variable name. Each array must be declared in the variable declaration section of the program. In a declaration of an array, the keyword "array" is followed by the range of subscripts of the array in brackets, followed by the keyword "of", and ending with the type of each element of the array. For example,

```
var
  x, y : array [1..9] of real;
  yesno : array ['a'..'z'] of boolean;
  picture : array [0..5, 0..9] of char;
```

declares that x and y are lists of 9 real values, that yesno is a list of 26 boolean values yesno ['a'], yesno ['b'], yesno ['c'], ..., yesno ['z'], and that picture is a table of 60 characters arranged in 6 rows and 10 columns, with the rows numbered from 0 to 5 and the columns numbered from 0 to 9. This declaration implies that a subscript for x or y must be an integer expression with a value from 1 to 9, that a subscript for yesno must be a character expression whose value is a lower case letter, and that picture must always be used with two subscripts, the first of which must have an integer value from 0 to 5, and the second of which must have an integer value from 0 to 9.

In Pascal, a character string is simply a list of characters. Often the keyword "packed" is attached to a character string declaration to indicate that the characters are to be packed in memory as densely as possible in order to save space. For example, the following declaration allows the variable name to store character strings of exactly 20 characters, including trailing blanks.

```
var
   name : packed array [1..20] of char;
```

A list of character strings may be declared in a form such as the following.

```
var
   stringlist : array [1..17] of array [1..8] of char;
```

In this example, the variable stringlist is a list of 17 character strings, each of length 8. The equivalent form of declaration

```
var
   stringlist : array [1..17, 1..8] of char;
```

portrays the list of character strings as a table of characters, a conceptually different but equivalent structure. Experienced Pascal programmers would ordinarily define a new data type consisting of strings of length 8, as described in Section 3.3), and declare a list of character strings as follows.

```
type
   string8 = array [1..8] of char;
var
   stringlist : array [1..17] of string8;
```

Variable Length Lists

It is clearly absurd to assume that a company will always have exactly 8262 credit cards reported lost or stolen. However, Pascal requires fixed constant limits for the range of subscripts in an array declaration. The way around this restriction is to declare a constant maxquantityofcards of say 10000 to be used as the upper bound in array and subscript range declarations and a variable actualquantityofcards, whose current value would be 8262 for the data of Figure 3.1.1, to control the actual processing.

In this light, we rewrite the procedure printlostcards and show the relevant declarations in the main program that uses the procedure printlostcards, defining everything in terms of the single constant maxquantityofcards. In the main program, there would be declarations

```
const
  maxquantityofcards = 10000;
var
  actualquantityofcards : 1..maxquantityofcards;
  numberoflostcard : array [1..maxquantityofcards] of integer;
```

and the procedure itself would be rewritten as follows.

```
procedure printlostcards;
  var
    i : 1..maxquantityofcards;
  begin
  for i := 1 to actualquantityofcards do
    writeln (numberoflostcard [i]);
  end; { printlostcards }
```

With the availability of subrange declarations, very few variables need to be declared to be type integer. It is a good programming practice to specify the expected range of any integer quantity as a subrange type, whenever it is possible to do so.

Use of an Array When a Simple Variable Will Do

Some programs may be written either with or without arrays. For example, the averaging programs in Section 1.3 are written using simple variables. However, they also may be written using an array for the test scores. For comparison, we write a new version avgofscores2, without using an array, that counts the number of scores as well as averaging them.

```
program avgofscores2 (input, output);

  const
    signal = 9999;

  var
    enrollment : integer;
    outofdata : boolean;
    sum, nextscore : real;

  begin
  enrollment := 0;
  sum := 0;
  outofdata := false;
  while not outofdata do
    begin
    read (nextscore);
    if nextscore = signal then
      outofdata := true
    else
      begin
      writeln ('Input data  nextscore: ', nextscore :7:2);
      sum := sum + nextscore;
```

```
      enrollment : = enrollment + 1;
      end; { else-clause }
   end; { while-loop }
 writeln;
 writeln ('There are ', enrollment :1, ' test scores.');
 writeln ('Average test score = ', sum / enrollment :1:2);
 end.
```

This program shows a typical use of the simple variables nextscore and sum in a loop. On each iteration, a new value of the variable nextscore is read, and except when the termination signal card is read, a new value of the running total sum is computed. Of course, the previous values of these variables are lost.

In contrast, the preliminary version of the program avgofscores3 cannot be refined without using an array, because all the test scores are stored simultaneously in the computer's memory after the reading step.

```
program avgoftestscores3 (input, output);
{ preliminary version }
  read all the test scores
  calculate the average
  print the results
```

In refining the program avgofscores3, the programmer must recognize that the role filled by the simple variable nextscore in the program avgofscores and avgofscores2 now requires a list score [1..maxenrollment]. The simple variable nextscore is retained as a buffer for holding the next score while it is determined whether this score value is the termination signal. The variable sum does not need to be a list, because only one value for sum is needed at a time.

```
program avgofscores3 (input, output);
  const
    maxenrollment = 100;
    signal = 9999;

  var
    enrollment : 0..maxenrollment;
    i : 1..maxenrollment;
    outofdata : boolean;
    sum, nextscore : real;
    score : array [1..maxenrollment] of real;

  begin
  enrollment : = 0;

  { read all the test scores }
  outofdata : = false;
  while (not outofdata) and (enrollment < maxenrollment) do
    begin
    read (nextscore);
    if nextscore = signal then
      outofdata : = true
```

```
  else
    begin
    writeln ('Input data  nextscore: ', nextscore :7:2);
    enrollment := enrollment + 1;
    score [enrollment] := nextscore;
    end; { else }
  end; { while-loop }

{ check for more than 100 scores in data }
if not outofdata then
  begin
  read (nextscore);
  if nextscore <> signal then
    begin
    writeln ('The input data consists of more than ',
        maxenrollment :1, ' scores.');
    writeln ('Only the first ', maxenrollment :1,
        ' have been used.');
    end;
  end;

{ calculate the average }
sum := 0;
for i := 1 to enrollment do
  sum := sum + score [i];

{ print the results }
writeln;
writeln ('There are ', enrollment :1, ' test scores.');
writeln ('Average test score = ', sum / enrollment :1:2);
end.
```

The difference between these two programs is twofold. First, the reading of the scores and the calculating of the sum can be separate loops when the test scores are stored in a list. The calculation of the sum is particularly clear when it is done separately from the reading. For this problem, the increase in computer time needed for separate loops is a sufficiently cheap price to obtain clarity. Second, the program using a list requires more memory locations for storing values. When a computer with thousands of memory locations is used, this may be of no consequence. However, when a programmable desk calculator is used, there may not be enough room to run the program using subscripts. This is probably why many programmable desk calculators do not have the instructions needed to implement arrays.

The program vectorsum further illustrates the reading and printing of lists.

```
program vectorsum (input, output);

  const
    size = 3;

  var
    i : 1..size;
    a, b, c : array [1..size] of integer;
```

```
begin
write ('Input data  a :  ');
for i := 1 to size do
  begin
  read (a [i]); write (a [i] :1, ' ');
  end;
writeln;
write ('Input data  b :  ');
for i := 1 to size do
  begin
  read (b [i]); write (b [i] :1, ' ');
  end;
for i := 1 to size do
  c [i] := a [i] + b [i];
writeln; writeln;
write ('The vector sum is ');
for i := 1 to size do
  write (c [i] :1, ' ');
writeln;
end.
```

```
run vectorsum

Input data  a :  1 4 9
Input data  b :  5 12 13

The vector sum is 6 16 22
```

Keeping Track of the Size of a List

Since the programmer must always declare one fixed size for each array, it is necessary to keep track of the actual number of values that have been put in the array at any time during execution of the program. This is usually done by using a variable declared to have values in the subrange of the integers from 0 to the declared size of the list. Examples are the variable enrollment in the program avgofscores3 and the variable actualquantityofcards in the final version of the procedure printlostcards.

Program Testing and Debugging

Since the programs written in this chapter are longer and more complex than those written in previous chapters, program testing and, if necessary, debugging become more important. A major asset in program verification and debugging is a clear and readable program and, other things being equal, a program written using successive refinements tends to have a clearer structure than one that is written all at once. Moreover, before supplying details, an earlier refinement can be hand-simulated to see whether the basic structure of the program is correct, with the programmer "executing" those instructions not sufficiently refined for a computer.

As a program becomes longer, it is helpful to divide it up into procedures that can be written and tested independently. When this is done carefully, large sections of coding can be certified as being unlikely places to look for any bugs that might materialize when all the parts of a program are put together. It is extremely important to localize the source of a program error to a small enough section of the program so that careful rereading of the program, coupled with hand simulation, stands a reasonable chance of locating the error. Selectively placed write statements can help locate the source of an error by providing verification that some steps did what they were supposed to do, and by providing information about what the other steps did when they didn't do what they were supposed to do. Sometimes it is important to execute the debugging write statements only for certain values of the variables to avoid inundation in a sea of output paper, resulting from tracing parts of the program that are known to be correct.

Ultimately, debugging reduces to a programmer recognizing that either the intended program steps do not provide a correct solution to the problem, or that the computer language statements the computer is executing are not a faithful representation of the intended method of solving the problem. A clear understanding of the problem and the program written to solve it are the programmer's most important assets. Other debugging methods supplement these with information.

Exercises

1. A sprinter wants to make a neat listing of his times in the 100-meter dash. Write a program that accepts as input the times to the nearest 1/10 second for 10 trials in this event and makes a neat listing of them with the trial numbers in the left column and the times in the right column. Notes: (a) This program does not require the use of an array, but use one anyway. (b) Programmers who like to experiment with fancy output might want to use the columns indicator and digits indicator described in Section 1.2.

2. The sprinter in Exercise 1 would like the listing of his times printed with the most recent one first. Modify the program written for Exercise 1 so that it prints the tenth trial and its time first, and the first trial and its time last. The input data are still in the same order as in Exercise 1.

3. The sprinter in Exercise 1 would like to know his average time for the sequence of 10 trials. Modify the program for Exercise 1 so that after printing the list of times it prints the average time.

4. Modify the program for Exercise 2 so that, after printing the list of trials and times with the most recent first, it also prints the average of the five more recent times, followed by the average of the five less recent times.

5. A chess player who specializes in endgame combinations likes to keep track of the number of moves it takes her to win. Write a program that first reads as input the number of games she played in a month, then reads as input the number of moves it took her to win each of these games, and then prints the average number of moves it took her to win a game during the month. Note: Again this does not require an array, but the modification in the next exercise does.

6. The chess player in Exercise 5 also likes to play fast. Modify the program for Exercise 5 so that, after it reads the complete list of the number of moves in a game, it then reads as input a list of the time it took her to win each of these games and

prints as output three columns of numbers: the number of moves, the time for the game, and the average time per move in that game.

7. An author enjoys dreaming about which of his overdue bills he will pay when his royalty check arrives. He receives 43 cents for each of the first 1500 copies that sell in a year and 57 cents for each copy thereafter. Write a program that accepts as input a list of the number of copies sold during each of the 12 months of the year and prints as output the author's royalties for the year. Use an array, even though it isn't absolutely necessary.

8. The first edition of the book written by the author in Exercise 7 has been in print for 5 years (60 months). Write a program that reads as input the numbers of copies sold for each of the 60 months and calculates the author's royalties two ways. First, compute the royalties based on a calendar year; that is, compute the royalties for the first 12 months as in Exercise 7, then for the next 12 months, and so on, and finally compute the total royalties for the 5 years. Second, compute the royalties on a July 1 to June 30 basis. That is, treat the first 6 months as a separate year for royalty purposes, then compute the royalties for the next 12 months, and so on. The final 6 months are also treated as a separate year. Finally compute the total for the four whole years and two half years.

9. An amateur pianist, in training to play Chopin's "Minute Waltz" in less than 60 seconds, practices the piece between 25 and 40 times at a sitting. Write a program that reads as input a list of the times in seconds it takes the pianist to play the piece, followed by a termination signal, and prints as output the times for the last 10 performances of the waltz, followed by the average time for these 10 performances.

10. Write a program that reads a list of data and prints out the odd-numbered items, list [1], list [3], and so on, followed by the even-numbered items. Place headings before each of these two output lists to identify them.

11. Write a program that reads two lists and prints them side by side in two columns. Assume that both lists are the same length and that the length is read in as input before either list is read.

12. Write a program that reads two lists of possibly different lengths and prints them side by side in two columns. The reading of each list should be terminated by the reading of a termination signal.

13. Write a program that accepts as input a list and a number n and then extracts the first n items of the list as a new list, printing the result.

14. Write a program that reads as input a list of data and two numbers start and finish and then extracts the items of the original list with subscripts between start and finish, inclusive, as a new list. The program should also print the new list.

15. Write a program that reads as input a list and a number n and then deletes the first n items in the list. The program should also print the result.

16. (Mathematical) Write a procedure to compute the inner product of two vectors of dimension 3. Use it in a program to compute the length of a vector of dimension 3.

17. Write a program that reads as input a list and a number n and then "rotates" the list forward n locations. Thus, if the list is

    10 20 30 40 50 60 70 80

after rotating it forward three locations, the list will be

    40 50 60 70 80 10 20 30

18. (Mathematical) Write a program to compute the angle between two vectors of dimension 3.

3.2   Searching A List: Credit Cards

The previous section describes the appropriate terminology and some of the Pascal rules concerned with lists and subscripts. This section makes a start toward illustrating the power of lists and subscripts as they are used in meaningful programs. The application throughout this section is that of checking a given credit card account number against a list of account numbers of lost or stolen cards. Increasingly more efficient programs are presented here and compared.

When a customer presents a credit card in payment for goods or services, it is desirable to determine quickly whether it can be accepted or whether it previously has been reported lost or stolen or cancelled for any other reason. The programs in this section perform such an investigation. Companies that issue their own credit cards usually include such a card verification program in their combined charging, billing, and inventory control systems. Independent credit card companies offer a verification service, often by telephone, to the businesses that accept their credit cards.

Pascal Files

Between runs of a credit card checking program, the complete list of account numbers of cancelled cards is stored in computer-readable form on a magnetic disk. A read statement used to obtain information from a permanent file is similar to a read statement used to read data from punched cards, from a terminal, or from a prepared input file, except that it contains an initial argument specifying the name of the file to be read. For instance, if the variable cardfile is declared to be a file of characters, the statement

```
read (cardfile, actualnumberofcards)
```

tells the computer to read a value from the file named "cardfile" and to assign that value to the variable actualnumberofcards. Since many different files may be used by the same program, naming the particular file wanted is mandatory in any input or output statement that does not use the default files named input and output.

A *file* is a sequence of values, all of the same type. For the time being, we will consider only files of characters, which have the same format as the default files input and output. The name of such a file may be declared by a statement such as the following:

```
var
  cardfile : file of char;
```

The file names input and output are automatically declared to be files of characters in every Pascal program. That is, every program is treated as if it contained the declaration

```
var
  input, output : file of char;
```

These names are also special in that any input or output statement that does not contain a file name is assumed to specify either the file named input or the file named output.

All file names, including input and output, that are used by a Pascal program must appear within the parentheses of the program heading. The name of any file except input that is used for input in a Pascal program should appear as the argument of a reset procedure command before it is used. The procedure reset positions the file at its initial point in preparation for the first read command. For example, the statement

```
reset (cardfile)
```

appears in each of the credit card checking programs of this section prior to the first execution of a read statement for that file. Any Pascal file, except the one named output, that is used for output should appear as the argument of a rewrite command. The procedure rewrite removes all data from the file, if there is any, and prepares the file for writing. Pascal files will be discussed in much more detail in Chapter 6.

Sequential Search Through an Unordered List

The first and simplest strategy for checking a given credit card is simply to search from beginning to end through the list of cancelled credit cards, card by card, either until the given account number is found in the list, or until the end of the list is reached without finding that account number. In the program cardcheck1 to implement this strategy, the sequential search is accomplished by a while-loop that scans the list until the given account number is found in the list or all of the numbers have been examined.

It is good programming practice to put the searching part of the program in a procedure seqsearch (sequential search) because the other versions of the credit card program in this section can be obtained by simply rewriting the procedure and changing the main program only by changing the name of the procedure used. This style of programming is called *modular programming*.

When writing programs that read data to be entered from a terminal, it is a good idea to precede the read statement with a message to the user describing what information is expected. Such a message eases the user's task of supplying exactly the right information at exactly the right time during the execution of the program. Of course, printing such messages is more important when there is more than one kind of information to be entered.

There are two ways of exiting from the search loop. On one hand, when the credit card being checked is not in the list, the search loop is executed until the list is exhausted. On the other hand, when the card being checked is found in the list, the boolean variable found is set to true, causing the loop to terminate. The boolean variable found is tested subsequently to decide which of two output messages is appropriate.

```
program cardcheck1 (input, output, cardfile);

  const
    maxquantityofcards = 10000;

  var
    actualquantityofcards : 0..maxquantityofcards;
    i : 1..maxquantityofcards;
    presentedcard : integer;
    cancelledcard : array [1..maxquantityofcards] of integer;
    cardfile : file of char;
    found : boolean;

  procedure readcards;
    begin
    reset (cardfile);
    read (cardfile, actualquantityofcards);
    for i := 1 to actualquantityofcards do
      read (cardfile, cancelledcard [i]);
    end; { readcards }

  procedure seqsearch;
    begin
    i := 1;
    found := false;
    while (i <= actualquantityofcards) and (not found) do
      if presentedcard = cancelledcard [i] then
        found := true
      else
        i := i + 1;
    end; { seqsearch }

  begin
  readcards;
  write ('Enter card number to be checked: ');
  read (presentedcard);
  seqsearch;
  write ('Credit card #', presentedcard :1);
  if found then
    writeln (' cannot be accepted.')
  else
    writeln (' is acceptable.');
  end.
```

```
runi cardcheck1

Enter card number to be checked: 3572065
Credit card #3572065 is acceptable.

runi cardcheck1

Enter card number to be checked: 2718281
Credit card #2718281 cannot be accepted.
```

The essential dilemma that previously had prevented the efficient programming of a sequential searching application is now solved by using a list. Each card number in the list can be referenced individually using cancelledcard [1], cancelledcard [2], cancelledcard [3], and so on, yet the single expression cancelledcard [i] may refer to any one card, because the value of the index variable i may be the location in the list of any particular card.

Improving the Efficiency

The basic strategy of the program cardcheck1 is to check a credit card account number, supplied as input, against each account number, in turn, in the list of cancelled cards, either until a match is found or until the list is exhausted. Since most credit cards offered in payment for purchases or services represent the authorized use of active, valid accounts, by far the most usual execution of the program cardcheck1 terminates when the list is exhausted and the computer prints the message that the credit card presented is acceptable.

The number of comparisons a program must make before accepting a credit card is some measure of the efficiency of that program. For example, when searching for an acceptable credit card in a list of 10,000 cancelled credit cards, the program cardcheck1 always makes 10,000 comparisons. The actual elapsed computer time for the search section of the program depends on the time it takes the computer to make one comparison and to prepare to make the next comparison.

Sequential Search of an Ordered List

The disorder of the list of cancelled cards is the reason so many comparisons are needed before a presented card is accepted. If the list of cancelled credit cards is maintained in order of increasing card number, then some improvement is possible. The program cardcheck2 presumes that the list is in increasing order.

```
program cardcheck2 (input, output, cardfile);

  const
    maxactualquantityofcards = 10000;

  var
    actualquantityofcards : 0..maxactualquantityofcards;
    i : 1..maxactualquantityofcards;
    presentedcard : integer;
    cancelledcard : array [1..maxactualquantityofcards] of integer;
    cardfile : file of char;
    found, futile : boolean;

  procedure readcards;
      ... end; { readcards }

  procedure seqsearch2;
    begin
    i := 1;
    found := false;
```

```
   futile := false;
   while (i <= actualquantityofcards) and (not found) and (not futile) do
     if presentedcard <= cancelledcard [i] then
       if presentedcard = cancelledcard [i] then
         found := true
       else
         futile := true
     else
       i := i + 1;
 end; { seqsearch2 }

begin
readcards;
write ('Enter card number to be checked: ');
read (presentedcard);
seqsearch2;
write ('Credit card #', presentedcard :1);
if found then
  writeln (' cannot be accepted.')
else
  writeln (' is acceptable.');
end.
```

```
runi cardcheck2

Enter card number to be checked: 4629076
Credit card #4629076 is acceptable.
```

For the same input data, the output of the program cardcheck2 would be identical to that produced by the program cardcheck1, but the execution times are not identical. Before accepting a presented account number, cardcheck1 always must search the entire list, but cardcheck2 stops as soon as it reaches a number in the list of cancelled account numbers that is larger than the presented number.

Roughly speaking, the average number of comparisons needed for an acceptance by cardcheck2 is about half the list size, plus one additional comparison on the way out to determine whether the last entry examined was exactly the account number of the credit card being checked. For a list of 10,000 cancelled cards, it would take an average of 5001 comparisons, instead of 10,000 for cardcheck1.

To a limited extent, this increased efficiency in the checking program is counterbalanced by some additional computer time needed to maintain the list of cancelled credit cards in increasing order. Nevertheless, almost any increase in the efficiency of the checking program results, in practice, in an increase in the efficiency of the entire operation.

Multilevel Search

Still greater efficiency is possible if one imitates the procedure of looking up a word in a dictionary. One hardly searches through every word in the dictionary starting at "aardvark" when one hopes to find the word "zebra". Most dictionaries have the first and last words defined on a page printed at the top of that page, for easy visibility. There is no point in searching through all the words on a page if a glance at the top of the page confirms that the correct page has not yet been reached. For this purpose, 10,000 entries in a list of cancelled credit cards might be divided arbitrarily into 100 ''pages'' of 100 entries each.

The basic strategy of the program cardcheck3 is a two-level search, first for the correct page, and second for the correct entry (if there is one) on that page. Both the page search loop and the entry-by-entry search loop here are modelled on the search loop of cardcheck2, except that the page search loop does not have to check for exact agreement with the credit card number being presented.

```pascal
program cardcheck3 (input, output, cardfile);

  const
    maxquantityofcards = 10000;
    pagesize = 100;

  var
    actualquantityofcards : 0..maxquantityofcards;
    i, firstonpage, lastonpage : 1..maxquantityofcards;
    presentedcard : integer;
    cancelledcard : array [1..maxquantityofcards] of integer;
    cardfile : file of char;
    entryfound, futile, pagefound : boolean;

  procedure readcards;
    ... end; { readcards }

  procedure twolevelsearch;
    { the list of cancelled credit cards must be in
      increasing order by account number for this
      procedure to work }

    begin
    { search for the correct page }
    { each page has pagesize entries }
    pagefound := false;
    lastonpage := pagesize;
    while not pagefound do
      if lastonpage > actualquantityofcards then
        begin
        firstonpage := lastonpage - (pagesize - 1);
        lastonpage := actualquantityofcards;
        pagefound := true;
        end
      else
        if presentedcard <= cancelledcard [lastonpage] then
          begin
          firstonpage := lastonpage - (pagesize - 1);
          pagefound := true;
          end
```

```
      else
         lastonpage := lastonpage + pagesize;
    { end of while-loop }

  { search the page sequentially to see if
      the presented card is there }
  entryfound := false;
  futile := false;
  i := firstonpage;
  while (i <= lastonpage) and (not entryfound) and (not futile) do
    if presentedcard <= cancelledcard [i] then
      if presentedcard = cancelledcard [i] then
        entryfound := true
      else
        futile := true
    else
      i := i + 1; { end of while-loop }
  end; { twolevelsearch }

begin
readcards;
write ('Enter card number to be checked: ');
read (presentedcard);
twolevelsearch;
write ('Credit card #', presentedcard :1);
if entryfound then
  writeln (' cannot be accepted.')
else
  writeln (' is acceptable.');
end.
```

Efficiency of a Multilevel Search

No sample execution output for the program cardcheck3 is given, because it would look identical to the output of cardcheck1 and to the output of cardcheck2. The speed of execution, however, is quite different. At the very worst, if the credit card presented is the last card in a list of 10,000 cancelled cards, the program cardcheck3 must scan through 100 pages and through 100 entries on the last page, and then make one final comparison for equality, a total of 201 comparisons. On the average, only half the pages must be checked, and only half the comparisons on the selected page are needed before a conclusion is reached. Thus the average number of comparisons of account numbers made by cardcheck3 is about 101, as compared to 5001 for cardcheck2 and 10,000 for cardcheck1. The extra time spent writing the longer program cardcheck3 is quickly repaid in savings of computer time required for running the credit card checking program.

It is easy to see how a four-level search program could reduce the maximum number of comparisons to scan a list of 10,000 entries to $10 + 10 + 10 + 10 + 1 = 41$, with the average number of comparisons roughly half of that. The 10,000 entries are divided arbitrarily into blocks of 1000, then the correct block of 1000 is divided into subblocks of 100, then the correct block of 100 is divided into subblocks of 10, and finally the correct block of 10 is searched sequentially to see if the presented card is there. There are no new programming ideas in the writing of a program cardcheck4 to implement this four-level searching algorithm, so it is left as an exercise. A comparison of the efficiencies of cardcheck4 with the other programs of this section appears at the end of the section.

Binary Search

The number of comparisons required by the one-level, the two-level, and the four-level search procedures seems to indicate that, in spite of increasing the number of levels that must be checked, if the maximum number of comparisons on any one level is reduced, the total number of comparisons is reduced. Thus the ultimate in searching efficiency might be achieved by reducing the number of alternatives on each level to 2, even though the number of levels increases. This leads to an extremely efficient search procedure called a *binary search*. In fact, if the first alternative on any level is incorrect, then the second alternative must be correct. Thus only one test is needed on each level. With the use of such a binary search, it is possible to search a list of over 10,000 entries in only 15 comparisons, 14 comparisons to reduce the alternatives down to one entry, plus 1 more comparison to test that entry.

Surprisingly, the program cardcheck5 (listed later) to implement the binary search strategy has fewer statements than the program cardcheck3, which implements the much less efficient two-level search strategy. It is not necessary to write 14 successive loops for the binary search, because what is done at each level is sufficiently repetitive to form the only loop of the program. In order to clarify the details of a binary search, two examples are now provided.

EXAMPLE 1.

Table 3.2.1 shows how a binary search is used to seek the number 2415495 in a list of 16 numbers. The numbers are given in increasing order in the first column. The presented number 2415495 is not in the list, but this fact plays no role in the search procedure until the very last step.

As a first step in binary searching, the list is divided in half. An asterisk follows the eighth number in column 1 because it is the last entry in the first half of the list. Since the given number 2415495 is less than (or equal to) the eighth entry 2989957, the second half of the list can be eliminated from further consideration. Column 2 shows only the first half of the original list, entries 1 through 8, retained as the segment still actively being searched.

The procedure is repeated. An asterisk follows the fourth entry in column 2 because it is the last entry in the first half of the segment of the list still actively being searched. Since the given number 2415495 is greater than the fourth number 1627547, this time it is the first half of the active segment that is eliminated and the second half (entries 5 through 8 of the original list) that is retained. This is shown in column 3 of Table 3.2.1.

In the next stage, the second remaining number 2202646, which was the sixth entry in the original list, is marked with an asterisk because it is the last entry of the first half of the segment still being searched. Since this number is exceeded by the given number 2415945, the second half of the segment in column 3 (entries 7 and 8) is retained as the active segment in column 4. The seventh entry of the original list, the number 2718281, is the last entry of the first half of the remaining list of two entries and thus is marked with an asterisk in column 4 to indicate its role as a comparison entry. Since the given number 2415495 is less than this, the other entry (the eighth original entry) is discarded, and column 5 shows that after four comparisons, only the seventh entry 2718281 remains.

Table 3.2.1   Binary search for the number 2415495 in a list of 16 numbers. An asterisk denotes the last entry of the first half of the segment still under active consideration.

Before any comparisons	After 1 comparison	After 2 comparisons	After 3 comparisons	After 4 comparisons	Given number
1096633	1096633				
1202604	1202604				
1484131	1484131				
1627547	1627547*				
2008553	2008553	2008553			
2202646	2202646	2202646*			
2718281	2718281	2718281	2718281*	2718281 <>	2415495
2980957*	2980957	2980957	2980957		
3269017					
4034287					
4424133					
5459815					
5987414					
7389056					
8103083					
8886110					

Since only one entry remains, a test for equality is made between the given number 2415495 and the one remaining entry 2718281. They are not equal. Thus the given number is not in the list. Note that the previous comparison of these two numbers was only to determine whether the given number was less than or equal to the seventh entry.

EXAMPLE 2.

Table 3.2.2 shows how the binary search works for the number 7389056, which is found in the list of 16 numbers.

As before, the first column lists the original numbers with an asterisk following the last number of the first half of the list, the eighth entry. The number 7389056 is greater than the eighth entry, so the second half of the list (entries 9 to 16) is retained in column 2. A comparison of the given number 7389056 with the last entry of the first half of the segment remaining in column 2, the twelfth original entry 5459815, eliminates entries 9 through 12.

A comparison with the fourteenth entry, followed by an asterisk in column 3, eliminates the fifteenth and sixteenth entries. One more comparison of the given number 7389056 against the thirteenth entry, followed by an asterisk in column 4, eliminates that entry and leaves only the fourteenth entry 7389056. The final test for equality of the given number and the only remaining candidate in the list yields success, and it can be reported that the given number is the fourteenth entry in the list.

It is most convenient when programming a binary search to use a list size that is an exact power of 2, that is 2, 4, 8, 16, 32, ... This avoids fractions when the size of the list segment still under consideration is halved repeatedly. Since the smallest power of 2 greater than 10,000 is 2 to the fourteenth power, which is 16,384, it takes the same number of comparisons to perform a binary search on a list of 16,384 entries as on a list of 10,000 entries. The program cardcheck5 does a binary search on a list of 16,384 entries. Actually, because the integer operator div is used to prevent fractional parts when locating the last element of the first half of the list segment still under active consideration, this binary search procedure applies to a list of arbitrary length.

Table 3.2.2   Binary search for the number 7389056 in a list of 16 numbers. An asterisk denotes the last entry of the first half of the segment still under active consideration.

Before any comparisons	After one comparison	After two comparisons	After three comparisons	After four comparisons	Given number
1096633					
1202604					
1484131					
1627547					
2008553					
2202646					
2718281					
2980957*					
3269017	3269017				
4034287	4034287				
4424133	4424133				
5459815	5459815*				
5987414	5987414	5987414	5987414*		
7389056	7389056	7389056*	7389056	7389056 =	7389056
8103083	8103083	8103083			
8886110	8886110	8886110			

```
program cardcheck5 (input, output, cardfile);

  const
    maxquantityofcards = 16384;

  var
    actualquantityofcards : 0..maxquantityofcards;
    i, onlyremaining : 1..maxquantityofcards;
    beginning, ending, endoffirsthalf : 1..maxquantityofcards;
    presentedcard : integer;
    cancelledcard : array [1..maxquantityofcards] of integer;
    cardfile : file of char;
    found : boolean;

  procedure readcards;
      ... end; { readcards }

  procedure binarysearch;
    { The variables, beginning, ending, and endoffirsthalf
      refer to the part of the list still under consideration.
      Initially, this is the whole list. }
    begin
    beginning := 1;
    ending := actualquantityofcards;
```

```
while beginning <> ending do
  begin
  endoffirsthalf := (beginning + ending - 1) div 2;
  if presentedcard <= cancelledcard [endoffirsthalf] then
    ending := endoffirsthalf
  else
    beginning := endoffirsthalf + 1;
  end; { while-loop }

{ The only remaining location is beginning ( = ending ) }
onlyremaining := beginning;
found := presentedcard = cancelledcard [onlyremaining];
end; { binarysearch }

begin
readcards;
write ('Enter card number to be checked: ');
read (presentedcard);
binarysearch;
write ('Credit card #', presentedcard :1);
if found then
  writeln (' cannot be accepted.')
else
  writeln (' is acceptable.');
end.
```

The number of comparisons required in the binary search can be counted easily. With one comparison, the original list of 16,384 is cut down to 8192. A second comparison leaves only 4096 candidates. A third leaves 2048; a fourth 1024; a fifth 512; a sixth 256; a seventh 128; an eighth 64; a ninth 32; a tenth 16; an eleventh 8; a twelfth 4; a thirteenth 2; and finally a fourteenth comparison leaves only 1 candidate. The fifteenth and final comparison determines whether that candidate is the credit card being searched for or not. Thus, whether the presented credit card is in the list or not, the number of comparisons is always 15.

When the number of entries is less than 16,384, the number of candidates at each stage never exceeds the number of candidates for an original list size of 16,384. Thus 15 comparisons suffices for binary searching all lists of length up to 16,384 (= 2 to the 14th power), although sometimes even fewer are required.

Table 3.2.3   Comparison of Five Search Procedures Based on a 10,000-Entry List.

Search Method	Program Name	Comparisons Minimum	Maximum	Average
Sequential search (unordered)	cardcheck1	10,000	10,000	10,000
Sequential search (ordered)	cardcheck2	2	10,001	5,001.5
Two-level sequential search	cardcheck3	3	201	102
Four-level sequential search	cardcheck4	5	41	23
Binary search	cardcheck5	15	15	15

Table 3.2.4   Comparison of Five Search Procedures Based on a 100,000-Entry List.

Search Method	Program Name	Minimum	Comparisons Maximum	Average
Sequential search (unordered)	cardcheck1	100,000	100,000	100,000
Sequential search (ordered)	cardcheck2	2	100,001	50,001.5
Two-level sequential search*	cardcheck3	3	634	318.5
Four-level sequential search**	cardcheck4	5	73	39
Binary search***	cardcheck5	18	18	18

* Based on 316 * 317 = 100,172 entries
** Based on 18 * 18 * 18 * 18 = 104,976 entries
*** Based on 2 to the 17th = 131,072 entries

Comparison of the Efficiency of the Search Procedures

Table 3.2.3 summarizes the number of comparisons required by each of the programs in this section to check a credit card against a list of 10,000 (or in the case of the binary search, 16,384) cancelled credit cards. For each program and search method, the minimum, maximum, and average number of comparisons is given for the most likely circumstance that the presented credit card is acceptable and is not to be found in the list.

The information in Table 3.2.3 shows the clear superiority of binary searching over all the other methods, even those whose programs are much more complicated. This superiority even increases as the list becomes longer, because it takes the binary search only one additional comparison to search a list with twice as many entries, 32,768, two additional comparisons to search 65,536 entries, and only three additional comparisons to extend the length of the list that can be searched to 131,072 entries.

The other searching methods cannot begin to match this feat, as shown in Table 3.2.4. Perhaps surprisingly, only the very slowest of the searching procedures is implemented by a program shorter than the binary search, and then not very much shorter. Binary search techniques are recommended, therefore, for searching all ordered lists, except possibly very short lists.

Suggested Reading

Donald E. Knuth, ''Algorithms'', *Scientific American*, April 1977, pp. 63-80. This article describes searching methods, both those in this section and others.

Exercises

---

1. Write a program to read as input a number and a list of four numbers and to determine whether the value of the single number is found in the list. The program should print its conclusion, either ''yes'' or ''no''.

2. Modify the program for Exercise 1 so that it also prints out the location in the list where the value of the single number is found.

3. As in Exercise 1, write a program to read as input a single number followed by an ordered list of four numbers and to determine whether the value of the single number is found in the list, but this time do it by a binary search. Do not write the search as a loop, because the number of alternatives is small.

4. Write a program to read a list of numbers and to produce a new list consisting of all the numbers found in the original list, but without duplicates. Hint: One way to do this is to copy a number into the new list if and only if no previous number in the original list is equal to it, and this can be determined by a search for equality.

5. Write a program that reads two lists and forms their "union"; that is a new list without duplicates consisting of all the numbers found in at least one of the two original lists. Hint: One way is to combine the lists without removing duplicates and then to use the program written for Exercise 4 to eliminate the duplicates.

6. Write a program that reads as input three lists of names of people who signed three circulating copies of a petition and produces a combined list, without duplicates, of all persons who signed the petition and a count of the number of such people.

7. Write a program that reads as input two lists and prints only those values that appear in both lists.

8. Write a program to read as input two lists and to print only those values that appear in exactly one of the two given lists.

9. Write a program that reads as input two lists and produces a third list whose values are the locations in the second list where the items of the first list are found. The length of the resulting list is the same as the length of the first list. If an item from the first list is not found in the second list, the corresponding entry in the resulting list should be zero. If an entry from the first list is found two or more times in the second list, the corresponding entry in the resulting list is the location of the first such occurrence.

10. Write a program to read two lists and to determine whether every element of the first list is also an element of the second list.

11. Write a program to read as input a list of numbers and to produce as output two lists, the first consisting of all the original numbers without duplication, and the second of the frequency of occurrence of these numbers. Print the two lists in side-by-side columns.

12. Write a program to read a list of test scores and to compute the "mode", the test score that occurs most frequently in the list. Hint: Use the program written for Exercise 11. Note that the mode is more difficult for a computer to find than the average or "mean". For people, it is often the other way around.

13. Write a program to read the first 10,000 digits of the number pi into a list and to determine whether the sequence of digits 1234567 ever occurs in those 10,000 digits. Note: Write a more general program to test whether the elements of any first list occur in order as elements of a second list, and test the program to find whether the digits 123 ever appear in order within the first 30 digits of pi.

14. Write a program to further test the more general program written for Exercise 13 by generating 10,000 random integers from 0 to 9, and testing to see whether the sequence of digits 1234567 ever occurs within the 10,000 random digits.

15. The information in Table 3.2.4 about the comparative speed of the two-level search program of 100,000 items is based on 316 pages of 317 entries each. How many comparisons would be necessary (minimum, maximum, and average) if the two-level searching procedure were based on 1000 pages of 100 entries each? Can you formulate a general principle about minimizing the number of comparisons in a two-level search?

16. Write a program cardcheck4 based on a four-level searching procedure.

3.3 Finding The Smallest Element In A List; Sorting

The credit card checking programs in the previous section search unordered and ordered lists of cancelled credit cards to determine whether a particular number is in the list. This section presents another kind of searching application, searching an unordered list to find the smallest element. (If the list is ordered, then finding the smallest element is very easy.) The program developed to search for the smallest element in an unordered list is employed subsequently as the basis for several programs to sort the entire unordered list into increasing order.

A second theme emphasized in this section is that of program testing. The programs written in this chapter are not completely obvious to most beginners, partly because understanding the concept of a subscript requires some practice and partly because the programs involve nontrivial ways of processing data. It becomes increasingly important, therefore, for a programmer to know how to test a program to be sure that it does what it is supposed to do.

A third theme is while-loops. As illustrated by the credit card checking programs in the previous section, while-loops are essential for sequential scanning. Searching for the smallest element in an unordered list also requires sequential scanning.

Earned Run Averages for Baseball Pitchers

In baseball, a pitcher's earned run average (ERA) is roughly the average number of runs per game scored against him and his team while he is pitching, not counting "unearned" runs scored because of fielding errors, which do not have a direct bearing on the pitcher's ability as a pitcher. While a low earned run average for a particular pitcher does not guarantee that his team will win the games he pitches, it certainly makes that outcome more likely. For this reason, newspapers and sports periodicals frequently publish lists of names of pitchers in ascending order of earned run average, so that the best pitcher in this regard appears first.

The program smallestera tells the computer to read data on pitchers and their earned run averages and to print out the name and earned run average for the pitcher with the smallest earned run average. Input data for the program consist of one line for each pitcher in the league, containing the pitcher's name and his earned run average, and a "trailer line" containing a termination signal. Data for the first sample execution are based on a memorable American League season.

Lists of Character Strings

The main part of the program smallestera resembles the program avgofscores3 in Section 3.1 in that both of them read all the data before the main processing is done. In choosing the names of the variables, the abbreviation "era" is used sometimes instead of the full phrase "earnedrunaverage", to keep the variable names from becoming too long. A new feature of this program is that the list pitcher has values that are character strings, that is, the names of the pitchers.

```
program smallestera (input, output);

  const
    maxnumberofpitchers = 1000;
    sizeofname = 20;
    signal = 'Aaron Gross

  type
    listindex = 1..maxnumberofpitchers;
    nameindex = 1..sizeofname;
    nametype = packed array [nameindex] of char;

  var
    location, locsofar : listindex;
    letter : nameindex;
    i, numberofpitchers : 0..maxnumberofpitchers;
    name : nametype;
    pitcher : array [listindex] of nametype;
    era : array [listindex] of real;
    smallest, smallsofar : real;
    outofdata : boolean;

  procedure readeradata;
    begin
    i := 0;
outofdata := false;
while (i < maxnumberofpitchers) and (not outofdata) do
    begin
    for letter := 1 to sizeofname do
      read (name [letter]);
    writeln ('Input data  name: ', name);
    if name = signal then
      outofdata := true
    else
      begin
      i := i + 1;
      pitcher [i] := name;
      readln (era [i]);
      writeln ('Input data  era: ', era [i] :1:2);
      end; { else-clause }
    end; { while-loop }
numberofpitchers := i;
end; { readeradata }
```

```
procedure findsmallest;
  begin
  smallsofar := era [1];
  locsofar := 1;
  for i := 2 to numberofpitchers do
    if era [i] < smallsofar then
      begin
      smallsofar := era [i];
      locsofar := i;
      end; { if-statement and for-loop }
  smallest := smallsofar;
  location := locsofar;
  end; { findsmallest }

{ ---------- main program -----------}
begin
readeradata;
findsmallest;
writeln ('Out of ', numberofpitchers :1, ' pitchers,');
writeln ('the best earned run average is ', smallest :1:2);
writeln ('pitched by ', pitcher [location]);
end.
```

The name "Aaron Gross" is used to terminate reading of the data. A termination signal of "***" is safer, but programmers need to have some fun. Actually, Aaron Gross converted from pitcher to catcher at an early age and never pitched an inning of major league baseball, so his name cannot be confused with real data for this program. Baseball fans remember him best as a termination signal.

The basic strategy of the search is to examine each earned run average in turn and to remember it if it is the smallest encountered so far, or to forget it if it is not. The location where the smallest earned run average so far is found is also remembered so that the pitcher's name may be printed out at the end.

Type Declarations

In Pascal, it is possible to declare a name to be a programmer-defined data type. These new data types can then be used in variable declarations in the same way that the ordinary Pascal types real, integer, char, boolean, and subranges may be used.

The first uses of this type declaration will be to give names to combinations of standard Pascal types, such as arrays and subranges. For example, the type declaration

```
type
  nameindex = 1..sizeofname;
```

indicates that nameindex is a type that is the same as the subrange 1..sizeofname, which is the same as 1..20 in the program smallestera. The type declaration

```
nametype = packed array [nameindex] of char;
```

declares nametype to be a type that consists of character strings of length 20. Note that the type nameindex can be used in place of the subscript range 1..20 in the declaration.

Once a type has been declared, any variable can be declared to be that type. For example, in the program smallestera,

```
var
  name : nametype;
  pitcher : array [listindex] of nametype;
```

declares name to be a character string of length 20 and pitcher to be an array of 1000 character strings, each of length 20.

Type declarations must be placed after constant declarations and before variable declarations. Note that the equals sign (=) is used to separate the type name from its declaration. Type declarations will be used later to define completely new data types with constants that can be specified by the programmer. See Section 4.3.

Handling Ties

Before running this program, we make one improvement. In case of ties, the program smallestera locates and prints only the earliest of the equal entries. Since it makes little sense to ignore the other equally good pitchers, the following lines may be added to smallestera to print their names also.

```
for i := location + 1 to numberofpitchers do
  if era [i] = smallest then
    writeln ('and ', pitcher [i]);
```

This loop is another reason to find the location of the smallest earned run average in the list as well as its value. Incorporating these instructions to handle ties into the program smallestera results in the program smallestera2. The sample execution of the program smallestera2 has been reduced to reasonable size by using an alphabetical listing of only the best 10 pitchers in one season. The full execution, using all 122 pitchers who pitched in 12 or more games, is quite similar but much longer.

```
program smallestera2 (input, output);
    .

    .

    .
    { ---------- main program ----------}
    begin
    readeradata;
    findsmallest;
    writeln ('Out of ', numberofpitchers :1, ' pitchers,');
    writeln ('the best earned run average is ', smallest :1:2);
    writeln ('pitched by ', pitcher [location]);
    for i := location + 1 to numberofpitchers do
      if era [i] = smallest then
        writeln ('and ', pitcher [i]);
    end.
```

```
run smallestera2
```

```
Input data   name:  Vida Blue
Input data   era:   3.01
Input data   name:  Bert Blyleven
Input data   era:   3.00
Input data   name:  Steve Busby
Input data   era:   3.08
Input data   name:  Dennis Eckersley
Input data   era:   2.60
Input data   name:  Ed Figueroa
Input data   era:   2.90
Input data   name:  Catfish Hunter
Input data   era:   2.58
Input data   name:  Rudy May
Input data   era:   3.06
Input data   name:  Jim Palmer
Input data   era:   2.09
Input data   name:  Frank Tanana
Input data   era:   2.63
Input data   name:  Rusty Torrez
Input data   era:   3.06
Input data   name:  Aaron Gross
Out of 10 pitchers,
the best earned run average is   2.09
pitched by Jim Palmer
```

Program Testing

It is easy enough to check from the echoes of input data provided in the sample execution of smallestera2 above that the correct smallest earned run average is found and printed. However, before adopting this program for regular use, additional checking should be done using different data to reduce greatly or to eliminate the likelihood that the program runs correctly only because of some special property of this first batch of data. For instance, one should be especially suspicious of the testing data if the smallest earned run average turns out to be either the first one in the list or the last one in the list. These represent very special circumstances the program cannot depend on, but in which even an incorrect program might obtain the right answer. Since the pitcher with the smallest earned run average in the sample execution is the eighth pitcher out of 10, the data used are suitable on this account. Of course, for a complete testing of the program, test data should also be used in which the smallest earned run average does come first or last, because programs also can fail when the data have special properties. These tests are not shown here, in order to save space.

There is however, one eventuality allowed for in the program but not tested by the data given, the possibility of ties. Since the actual historical data do not oblige us with a tie for the smallest earned run average, ficticious pitchers are manufactured to help test the tie feature. The career histories of two of them are of particular importance:

Carl Curveball was a reliable southpaw with a lot of stuff and good control. His career ended abruptly when he was traded to Mexico City and found that is curveball wouldn't curve in the thinner air.

Fireman Fink holds the major league record for appearances as a relief pitcher in a single season, at 162, not counting the playoffs and the World Series. His team did not make the playoffs or the World Series.

```
run smallestera2

Input data   name:  Vida Blue
Input data   era:   3.01
Input data   name:  Bert Blyleven
Input data   era:   3.00
Input data   name:  Steve Busby
Input data   era:   3.08
Input data   name:  Carl Curveball
Input data   era:   2.09
Input data   name:  Dennis Eckersley
Input data   era:   2.60
Input data   name:  Ed Figueroa
Input data   era:   2.90
Input data   name:  Fireman Fink
Input data   era:   2.09
Input data   name:  Catfish Hunter
Input data   era:   2.58
Input data   name:  Rudy May
Input data   era:   3.06
Input data   name:  Jim Palmer
Input data   era:   2.09
Input data   name:  Frank Tanana
Input data   era:   2.63
Input data   name:  Rusty Torrez
Input data   era:   3.06
Input data   name:  Aaron Gross
Out of 12 pitchers,
the best earned run average is  2.09
pitched by Carl Curveball
and Fireman Fink
and Jim Palmer
```

After examining this somewhat fanciful execution, one would have good reason to believe that the program smallestera2 could handle correctly the case of ties if that situation ever came up in real data.

A Uniform Main Program for Sorting

Sorting data is a very common and very important programming application. In the credit card checking application in Section 3.2, for instance, all the efficient programs require the list of lost or stolen credit cards to be sorted previously into increasing order.

In recognition of the need for sorting in many different applications, the sorting programs presented in this chapter use general variable names, such as list and sortedlist, that fit many different circumstances. All the sorting programs in this chapter are refinements of the program dosort.

```
program dosort
   read all the data
   sort the data
   write the sorted list
```

When adapting any of these sorting programs to an application, such as those suggested in the exercises, variable names specific to the application may be substituted for the more general variable names used here. Chapter 4 introduces the full power of passing arguments to a procedure, a construction that saves the programmer the trouble or rewriting to make such variable name substitutions, so that the same sorting procedure may be used intact with many different calling programs.

Every sorting program in this chapter calls the same procedure readlist to read all the data. This procedure employs a loop whose execution is stopped by the reading of a termination signal at the end of the valid data. The major difference between this program and the program countcards in Section 2.3 is that readlist places the information from the data into a list, as well as counting the number of data items. An index variable counts the number of items as well as controlling where in the list the data are placed.

```
procedure readlist;
   begin
   i := 0;
   outofdata := false;
   while (i < maxlistsize) and (not outofdata) do
      begin
      read (datum);
      writeln ('Input data  datum: ', datum);
      if datum = signal then
         outofdata := true
      else
         begin
         i := i + 1;
         list [i] := datum;
         end; { else-clause }
      end; { while-loop }
   listsize := i;
   end; { readlist }
```

The procedure writelist is called to write the sorted list produced by the first sorting program to be considered. It employs a simple for-loop, and introduces no new features or methods.

```
procedure writelist;
   begin
   writeln;
```

```
writeln ('The sorted list is as follows:');
writeln;
for i := 1 to listsize do
  writeln (sortedlist [i]);
end; { writelist }
```

Testing the Input and Output Procedures

It is possible to test the input procedure readlist and the output procedure writelist without doing the sort in between. Since the sorting procedure is slightly more complicated than these procedures, it would be nice to know before checking the sorting procedure that the input and output procedures cannot contribute any errors that might be attributed falsely to the sorting procedure. A test program testio accomplishes this testing merely by copying the input list, without sorting, into the output list sortedlist. To avoid possible confusion, it writes a disclaimer that the output list remains unsorted.

```
program testio (input, output);

  const
    maxlistsize = 1000;
    signal = 9999;

  type
    listindex = 1..maxlistsize;
    number = -signal..signal;

  var
    i, listsize : 0..maxlistsize;
    datum : number;
    list, sortedlist : array [listindex] of number;
    outofdata : boolean;

  procedure readlist;
    ... end; { readlist }
  procedure writelist;
    ... end; { writelist }

  { ----- test read and write procedures ----- }
  begin
  readlist;
  sortedlist := list;
  writeln;
  writeln ('*** This an I/O test program only. ***');
  writeln ('*** The data have not been sorted yet. ***');
  writelist;
  end.
```

```
run testio

Input data  datum:        256
Input data  datum:        -37
Input data  datum:          8
Input data  datum:         45
Input data  datum:       9999

*** This an I/O test program only. ***
*** The data have not been sorted yet. ***

The sorted list is as follows:

      256
      -37
        8
       45
```

Assignment of Arrays

The statement that is used in the program testio to copy the values from the array list to the array sortedlist is a single assignment statement. One array may be assigned to another provided they are both declared to be the same type. An array assignment was used previously in the program smallestera to set the values of character strings, which are actually arrays of characters.

Sorting by Finding the Smallest Element Remaining in a List

One of the major ideas in programming is to use existing programs or parts of existing programs as building blocks to construct more complicated programs. A procedure to find the smallest element in a list, for example, is now used as a building block for a program to write the entire list in increasing order. All that is required is to "cross out" the smallest element from the list after it has been placed in the new, sorted list. Then, a second use of the same procedure to find the smallest element finds the second smallest original element, which may then be placed second in the sorted list. Repeated application of the strategy of "crossing out" the smallest element, and then using the previously written procedure to find the new smallest remaining element, ultimately produces a sorted list consisting of all the original items, but in increasing order.

The sorting procedure sort1 repeatedly uses a procedure findsmallest to locate the smallest remaining element in the list. That smallest remaining element is then recorded in the sorted list and subsequently "crossed out" by replacing it with a number too large to be plausible data, so that it will not be found by the next application of the procedure findsmallest. The current procedure findsmallest is the procedure findsmallest in the earned run average example, with its variable names changed to conform to the greater generality of the current program. (The procedure readeradata corresponds to the procedure readlist.)

```
procedure findsmallest;
  begin
  smallsofar := list [1];
  locsofar := 1;
  for i := 2 to listsize do
    if list [i] < smallsofar then
      begin
      smallsofar := list [i];
      locsofar := i;
      end; { if and for-loop }
  smallest := smallsofar;
  location := locsofar;
  end; { findsmallest }
procedure sort1;
  begin
  for locinsortedlist := 1 to listsize do
    begin
    findsmallest;
    sortedlist [locinsortedlist] := smallest;
    { cross out the smallest entry just found }
    list [location] := bignumber;
    end; { for-loop }
  end; { sort1 }
```

If execution speed is important, a small amount of time could be saved by using the same variables smallsofar and locsofar after the search as during the search. However, the sorting procedure sort1 is by no means the most efficient sorting procedure possible, only one of the simplest. Thus, improved clarity of variable names is preferred in this case to increased execution speed. Accordingly, the last two instructions of the procedure findsmallest introduce two new variables, smallest and location, to reflect the fact that the search has been completed.

Testing Individual Procedures

One might verify by hand that the procedure sort1 sorts a list into increasing order, assuming that the procedure findsmallest supplies correct values for the variables smallest and location. Verification that the procedure findsmallest works properly might also be done by hand. Since findsmallest is a separate procedure, it can be checked further using the small test program testfind, that runs independently of the procedure sort1.

```
program testfind (output);
  .
  .
  .
  { ----- test findsmallest procedure ----- }
  begin
  list [1] := 45; list [2] := 27; list [3] := 32;
  list [4] := 24; list [5] := 43;
  listsize := 5;
  findsmallest;
```

```
writeln ('The smallest is ', smallest :1);
writeln ('The location in the list is ', location :1);
end.
```

```
run testio

The smallest is 24
The location in the list is 4
```

More Program Testing

In the test program testfind, the values for the list are assigned by program steps to save the trouble of preparing input data. If more extensive testing is desired, the procedure readlist may be used to facilitate the reading of data to test findsmallest. The program morethorough illustrates this idea. Only one sample run is shown for this program, but it may be used as often as needed with different sets of test data, until the programmer is convinced that findsmallest works correctly for all possible data.

```
program morethorough (input, output);
   .
   .
   .
{ more thorough test of findsmallest procedure }
begin
readlist;
findsmallest;
writeln ('The smallest is ', smallest :1);
writeln ('The location in the list is ', location :1);
end.
```

```
run morethorough

Input data  datum:           81
Input data  datum:           35
Input data  datum:            0
Input data  datum:           14
Input data  datum:           -3
Input data  datum:           45
Input data  datum:          -27
Input data  datum:           36
Input data  datum:           12
Input data  datum:         9999
The smallest is -27
The location in the list is 7
```

The computer correctly recognizes that the number -27 is less than all positive numbers and less than the negative number -3. The echoes of input data that appear in the output are produced by the procedure readlist, which must be supplied along with the program morethorough to create a complete executable program.

Fitting All The Procedures Together

The program dosort1 combines several procedures that have been checked more or less independently of each other, with favorable results in each case. The program dosort1 itself must now be tested to see whether its way of combining the procedures actually provides a program for sorting data. The sample test run shown uses the same data previously used to test the procedure findsmallest, in order to guarantee that at least the first call to findsmallest will work correctly, thereby permitting a test of what happens after the first time.

```
program dosort1 (input, output);

   const
     maxlistsize = 1000;
     signal = 9999;
     bignumber = signal;

   type
     listindex = 1..maxlistsize;
     number = -signal..signal;

   var
     i, listsize : 0..maxlistsize;
     locsofar, location, locinsortedlist : listindex;
     datum, smallsofar, smallest : number;
     list, sortedlist : array [listindex] of number;
     outofdata : boolean;

   procedure readlist; ... end; { readlist };
   procedure writelist; ... end; { writelist }
   procedure findsmallest; ... end; { findsmallest }
   procedure sort1; ... end; { sort1 }

   { ---------- main program ---------- }
   begin
   readlist;
   sort1;
   writelist;
   end.

run dosort1

Input data  datum:         81
Input data  datum:         35
Input data  datum:          0
Input data  datum:         14
Input data  datum:         -3
Input data  datum:         45
Input data  datum:        -27
Input data  datum:         36
Input data  datum:         12
Input data  datum:       9999
```

The sorted list is as follows:

```
-27
 -3
  0
 12
 14
 35
 36
 45
 81
```

Doubling the Sorting Speed While Saving Space As Well

The procedure sort1 is based on two key ideas. One is to use a search procedure to find the locations of the smallest remaining item. The other is to form a sorted list by transferring items there one at a time, in ascending order, from an unsorted list. "Crossing out" numbers in the unsorted list by replacing them with very large dummy numbers is more of an incidental trick than a key idea. In fact, the "crossing out" trick is unnecessarily expensive in both time and space.

Toward the end of the execution of sort1, when very few of the original numbers remain in the unsorted list, the search procedure spends most of its time examining and bypassing the dummy numbers, hardly productive labor. Moreover, the space occupied by the dummy numbers ultimately becomes as great as the space occupied by the whole original list.

Another sorting method, considered next, preserves both of the key ideas of sort1. However, by using an interchange instead of "crossing out", it saves both time and space. In order to illustrate this interchange method, we now describe its effect on the same list supplied as input in the sample execution of the program testio.

256 −37 8 45 (original list)

As a first step in sorting by the interchange method, the smallest item is located by searching the original list in its entirety. For the original list of this example, it is the number −37 at location 2. The smallest item is then interchanged with the first item of the original list, as shown below. A vertical bar is drawn immediately after the first item in order to separate it from the remaining items.

−37 | 256 8 45

The second smallest item cannot be to the left of the vertical bar, because that is where the smallest item is. Thus the second smallest item of the original list is the smallest item to the right of the bar, and it can be found by searching the three locations to the right. This time the search locates the number 8 at location 3 of the list. This item, the second smallest item in the original list, is now interchanged with the item at location 2, yielding the following rearrangement of the list.

−37 8 | 256 45

This time the bar separates the two smallest items from the remaining items. The two items to the left of the bar are in increasing order. The two items to the right are not ordered. To find the third smallest item of the original list, it is sufficient to search the items to the right of the bar, because the third smallest is the smallest of those two items.

The third smallest item of the original list is the number 45, at location 4 of the list. The interchange method of sorting now requires that it be exchanged with whatever number is at location 3 of the list as shown below.

-37 8 45 | 256

Once again, the vertical bar separates an initial segment of the list, sorted into ascending order. With each step, the sorted initial segment grows and the unsorted final segment shrinks. When the final segment disappears, the list is completely sorted. Indeed, when the unsorted final segment has length one, as it does above, the list is completely sorted because the last number must be the largest number of the original list.

Because the unsorted final segment is constantly shrinking, it takes less and less time to find subsequent items to append to the sorted initial segment. By way of contrast, the search time for every item using the method of the procedure sort1 remains the same as the search time for the first item. Because of the reduced search time, this interchange method is about twice as fast as the "crossing out" method. The program dosort2 calls the procedure sort2 to apply this interchange method of sorting. The procedure writelist is changed slightly to make a procedure writelist2, because the sorted list is now formed in place of the original list instead of in a different list called sortedlist.

```
program dosort2 (input, output);

  const
    maxlistsize = 1000;
    signal = 9999;
  type
    listindex = 1..maxlistsize;
    number = -signal..signal;

  var
    i, listsize, numbersorted : 0..maxlistsize;
    locsofar, location : listindex;
    datum, smallsofar, smallest : number;
    list : array [listindex] of number;
    outofdata : boolean;

  procedure readlist; ... end; { readlist }
  procedure writelist2; ... end; { writelist2 }

  procedure findnextsmallest;
    begin
    smallsofar := list [numbersorted + 1];
    locsofar := numbersorted + 1; ;
    for i := numbersorted + 2 to listsize do
      if list [i] < smallsofar then
```

```
        begin
        smallsofar := list [i];
        locsofar := i;
        end; { if-statement and for-loop }
    smallest := smallsofar;
    location := locsofar;
    end; { findnextsmallest }

  procedure sort2;
    begin
    for numbersorted := 0 to listsize - 2 do
      begin
      findnextsmallest;
      { interchange smallest found with
        first item after sorted segment }
      list [location] := list [numbersorted + 1];
      list [numbersorted + 1] := smallest;
      end; { for-loop }
    end; { sort2 }

  { ---------- main program ---------- }
  begin
  readlist;
  sort2;
  writelist2;
  end.


run dosort2

Input data  datum:         81
Input data  datum:         35
Input data  datum:          0
Input data  datum:         14
Input data  datum:         -3
Input data  datum:         45
Input data  datum:        -27
Input data  datum:         36
Input data  datum:         12
Input data  datum:       9999

The sorted list is as follows:

      -27
       -3
        0
       12
       14
       35
       36
       45
       81
```

Suggested Readings

Donald E. Knuth, *The Art of Computer Programming*, Vol. 3, *Sorting and Searching*, Addison-Wesley, Reading, Mass., 1973.

William A. Martin, "Sorting", *Computing Surveys*, Vol. 3, pp. 147-174, 1971.

Robert P. Rich, *Internal Sorting Methods Illustrated with PL/I Programs*, Prentice-Hall, Englewood Cliffs, N.J., 1972.

Nicklaus Wirth, *Algorithms + Data Structures = Programs*, Prentice-Hall, Englewood Cliffs, N. J., 1976, Chapter 2.

Exercises
---

1. Write a program to read a list of baseball players and their batting averages and to print the name and the batting average of the player with the highest batting average. Be sure your program can handle ties.

2. Modify the program for Exercise 1 so that, instead of a batting average for each player, the program reads the number of times the player officially came to bat in the season and the number of hits the player got. The batting average is the quotient of these numbers, that is, the number of hits divided by the number of times at bat.

3. Using the procedure sort1 as a model, write a program that starts to sort a list by finding the largest number in the list, putting it at the end of the sorted output list, and then "crossing out" the largest number by replacing it with a very small number. Then the process is repeated to find the largest remaining number in the list, and so on.

4. Test the program for Exercise 3 using the same data used in this section to run the program morethorough.

5. Modify the procedure sort2 so that it can sort the list of pitchers and earned run averages used in the programs smallestera and smallestera2. Be sure that whenever two earned run averages are swapped, the names of the pitchers corresponding to them are also swapped.

6. Using the program written for Exercise 5, write a program modelled on the program dosort2 that can read a list of pitchers and their earned run averages and print them out in increasing order.

7. Hand simulate the execution of the procedure sort1, starting with a list whose values are 45, 32, 16, 32, 45. This is an important type of data to test, because the equality of two or more list items might upset the execution or the procedure findsmallest.

8. Write a program to test whether a list of names of persons is sorted into alphabetical order.

9. Write a program to read the list of credit cards maintained in the applications in Section 3.2 and sort them into increasing order. The input program readcards

used to read the list from disk for the program cardcheck1 can be used to read the list for this program. A similar procedure, using the statements

```
rewrite (cardfile);
write (cardfile, actualquantityofcards);
for i := 1 to actualquantityofcards do
  write (cardfile, cancelledcard [i]);
```

may be used to put the sorted list back onto a disk. The sorted list should also be printed.

10. A different way to remove an item from a list is to move all the items with larger subscripts frontward one location. Write a program to sort a list by finding the smallest element, copying it into the sorted list, and then removing it from the unsorted data by this method, repeating these steps until the list of unsorted data is empty.

11. Modify the program readlist used in this section so that the termination signal is not set by the program but is read instead as the first item of data. Thus the valid data of the list are sandwiched between two termination signals, which act like a pair of parentheses.

12. What are the advantages of the program written for Exercise 11 over the original program readlist?

13. Write a program to decide what number occurs most frequently in a sorted list of numbers containing duplications.

14. Write a program that reads a list of numbers and prints out the following list derived from it:

    location of smallest
    location of second smallest
    location of third smallest

    .
    .
    .

    location of largest

15. Write a program that reads a list of numbers and prints out the following list derived from it:

    location of largest
    location of second largest
    location of third largest

    .
    .
    .

    location of smallest

16. The *median* of a list of numbers is defined to be that item in the list that has as many items greater than the item as less than it, if there is an odd number of items. If there is an even number of items in the list, the median is the average of the two middle items. Write a program to read a list of numbers and print the median. Hint: Sort the list first.

17. Prove that to sort a list of nine items the procedure sort1 requires 72 comparisons. How many comparisons does sort1 take for a list of length n?

18. Prove that to sort a list of nine items the procedure sort2 requires 36 comparisons. Now many comparisons does sort2 take for a list of length n? Contrast this answer to your answer for Exercise 17.

19. Use the test data in Exercise 7 to see how sort1 handles ties.

20. What season are the earned run average data from?

3.4   Merging and Merge Sorting

Merging is the process of amalgamating two or more ordered lists into a combined list which is again in order. For example, a large company might obtain a complete list of all its employees, in alphabetical order, by merging the separate alphabetical order lists for its branch offices. Usually, as for this example, the use of a merging program presupposes some prior sorting. It is possible to merge many lists together at once but, for the sake of simplicity, the programs described here merges only two lists at a time.

Surprisingly, perhaps, it is possible to turn the tables on the ordinary relationship between sorting and merging—that is, to use repeated merging as the basis for a sorting method. Such a sort, called a *merge sort*, is extremely efficient.

An Illustration of the Merging Process

One characteristic of the merging process is that, although both of the lists to be merged are scanned sequentially, the index variables move *asynchronously* through the two lists in response to the data encountered, rather than in a preset pattern. Consider, for instance, the following merging of two lists.

    List A: 1 3 4 7
    List B: 2 4 5 10 11 12

The input lists, known as lista and listb, are both equipped with index variables, which are initialized to the first locations in those lists, as now shown by an arrow pointing to the item in the list at the position of the index variable. Initially, the combined list, known as mergedlist, has no values at all, also as now shown.

    List A: =>1 3 4 7
    List B: =>2 4 5 10 11 12
    Merged List:

The merging process begins with a comparison of the items indicated by the arrows in the input lists, that is, the numbers 1 and 2 in the example. The smaller of these two items is copied into the first location of the output list, and its index is increased by one to refer to the next item in its list, while the other index remains fixed, as now shown.

    List A: 1 =>3 4 7
    List B: =>2 4 5 10 11 12
    Merged List: 1

The next step is again a comparison of the two items indicated by the indices of the input lists, this time, the numbers 3 and 2 in the example. The smaller of these two items is copied onto the end of the output list and, as before, its index is increased by one, while the other index remains fixed. This yields the following situation.

List A: 1 =>3 4 7
List B: 2 =>4 5 10 11 12
Merged List: 1 2

At each subsequent step, the two items indicated by the arrows are compared. The smaller of the two is copied onto the end of the output list, and its index increased. This continues until one of the two input lists is exhausted. At this point, the example will have the following configuration.

List A: 1 3 4 7 =>
List B: 2 4 5 =>10 11 12
Merged List: 1 2 3 4 4 5 7

The position of the arrow beyond the end of list A shows that lista has run out. However, there remain three items in listb to be copied onto the end of the merged list. In any merging of two lists, as soon as all the items from one input list have been copied into the output list, the remaining items in the other list are copied without further comparisons into the output list to complete the merging. For this example, the following final result is obtained.

List A: 1 3 4 7 =>
List B: 2 4 5 10 11 12 =>
Merged List: 1 2 3 4 4 5 7 10 11 12

The number 4 occurs in both input lists and, accordingly, it is copied twice into the output list. When the items indicated by the two indices are equal, it doesn't matter which is copied first.

Asynchronous Index Variables

In the procedure merge to do the process just described, not only are there index variables aindex and bindex for the two input lists, but also there is an index variable mergeindex for the output list. Both aindex and bindex move asynchronously in response to the data. Therefore, it is better to represent the asynchronism naturally in the program, as shown, rather than to make the indices into nested for-variables. Whenever an entry is copied from lista into mergedlist, the index variable mergeindex is increased along with aindex. Whenever an entry is copied from listb into mergedlist, the index variable mergeindex is increased as well as bindex.

Since the management of the indices in the procedure merge is completely the responsibility of the programmer, explicit tests are written to determine whether the indices are still within meaningful ranges. In particular, whenever aindex is increased, it is immediately tested to see whether it has run off the end of lista. Similarly, whenever bindex is increased, it is immediately tested.

```
procedure merge;
  begin
  aindex := 1;
  bindex := 1;
  mergeindex := 1;
  while (aindex <= listasize) and (bindex <= listbsize) do
    if lista [aindex] <= listb [bindex] then
      begin
      { copy smaller entry from lista into merged list }
      mergedlist [mergeindex] := lista [aindex];
      aindex := aindex + 1;
      mergeindex := mergeindex + 1;
      end { if-clause }
    else
      begin
      { copy smaller entry from listb into merged list }
      mergedlist [mergeindex] := listb [bindex];
      bindex := bindex + 1;
      mergeindex := mergeindex + 1;
      end; { else-clause and while-loop }

  if (aindex > listasize) then
    copyb
  else
    copya;
  end; { merge }
```

Although the procedures copya and copyb clearly involve exactly the same steps, they cannot be combined into one procedure at this time because the names of the list and the index for the list to be copied are different in the two procedures. The use of procedures with explicit arguments, introduced in Chapter 4, would provide a convenient way of combining these two procedures into one.

The Merging Program

The program domerge provides management for the merging of two lists. It reads the two lists and the number of entries in them as input. Then domerge calls merge as a procedure to merge them. The program domerge would work correctly even when supplied with two empty lists.

```
program domerge (input, output);

  const
    maxlistsize = 1000;
    maxmergedsize = 2000;

  type
    listindex = 1..maxlistsize;
    mlistindex = 1.. maxmergedsize;
```

```
var
  lista, listb : array [listindex] of integer;
  mergedlist : array [mlistindex] of integer;
  aindex, bindex, i : listindex;
  mergeindex, j : mlistindex;
  listasize, listbsize : 0..maxlistsize;
procedure copya;
  begin
  for i := aindex to listasize do
    begin
    mergedlist [mergeindex] := lista [i];
    mergeindex := mergeindex + 1;
    end; { for-loop }
  end; { copya }

procedure copyb;
  begin
  for i := bindex to listbsize do
    begin
    mergedlist [mergeindex] := listb [i];
    mergeindex := mergeindex + 1;
    end; { for-loop }
  end; { copyb }

procedure merge;
  ... end; { merge }

{ ---------- main program ---------- }
begin
read (listasize);
writeln ('Input data  listasize: ', listasize :1);
for i := 1 to listasize do
  begin
  read (lista [i]);
  writeln ('Input data  lista [', i :1, ']: ', lista [i]);
  end;
read (listbsize);
writeln ('Input data  listbsize: ', listbsize :1);
for i := 1 to listbsize do
  begin
  read (listb [i]);
  writeln ('Input data  listb [', i :1, ']: ', listb [i]);
  end;
merge;
writeln;
writeln ('The merged list is as follows:');
for j := 1 to listasize + listbsize do
  writeln (mergedlist [j]);
end.
```

```
run domerge

Input data   listasize:  4
Input data   lista [1]:           1
Input data   lista [2]:           3
Input data   lista [3]:           4
Input data   lista [4]:           7
Input data   listbsize:  6
Input data   listb [1]:           2
Input data   listb [2]:           4
Input data   listb [3]:           5
Input data   listb [4]:          10
Input data   listb [5]:          11
Input data   listb [6]:          12

The merged list is as follows:
        1
        2
        3
        4
        4
        5
        7
       10
       11
       12
```

Sorting By Repeated Merging

Merging can be used as a building block to construct a very efficient sorting method, far faster than the method of the procedures sort1 and sort2 in the previous section. To gain an understanding of this efficient method, called a *merge sort*, let us consider a list of 16 items to be sorted into increasing order.

Skipping for the moment to the end of a merge sort execution, suppose that, by some unspecified previous program steps, the 16 items were arranged into two lists of 8 items each, both sorted into increasing order. Then the only remaining task would be to merge the two lists of 8 items into the final combined list of 16 items. Such ease of completing the task serves to motivate the pursuit of the magical previous program steps that yield the two sorted lists of length 8.

Accordingly, despite possible uncertainty that there really is a pot of gold at the end of this particular rainbow, we reapply our reasoning to the problem of producing the two sorted sublists of length 8. Suppose, in this regard, that it is possible to obtain four sorted sublists, each of length 4. Then two of them can be merged to obtain one sorted sublist of 8 items, and the other two can be merged to form the other sorted sublist of 8 items.

If, somehow, the original 16 items were organized into eight sorted lists of 2 items each, then the merging method could merge them in pairs to produce four sorted lists of 4 items each. A satisfying conclusion is now reached by pushing the line of reasoning just one more step. If 16 sorted lists, each 1 item long, were available, then they might be merged in pairs to form the eight sorted lists of length 2. But the pot of gold is now at hand, because a list 1 item long is always already sorted into increasing order.

As a concrete example of merge sorting, presented now in forward order, consider its application to a scrambled list of the numbers 1 to 16. As shown below, the first step is to merge the lists of length 1 in pairs to obtain eight sorted lists of length 2.

```
Unmerged segments    13| 5|10| 3| 4|12|16| 2| 7|11| 9| 6|14|15| 1| 8
Merged segments       5 13| 3 10| 4 12| 2 16| 7 11| 6  9|14 15| 1  8
```

In the second stage of the procedure, the sublists of length 2, which are the merged results of the first stage, become the unmerged segments for the second round of merging. As shown below, these sublists of length 2 are merged in pairs to give four sorted sublists of length 4. It is important that the results of each round of merging are sorted sublists, because the next round of merging cannot be done on unsorted lists.

```
Unmerged segments    5 13| 3 10| 4 12| 2 16| 7 11| 6  9|14 15| 1  8
Merged segments      3  5 10 13| 2  4 12 16| 6  7  9 11| 1  8 14 15
```

The segments of length 4 that are produced as merged lists during the second round of merging are next considered as the unmerged segments for the third round of merging shown below. The merged lists that are produced by this third round of merging are of length 8 and are in increasing order.

```
Unmerged segments    3 5 10 13| 2  4 12 16| 6 7 9 11| 1  8 14 15
Merged segments      2 3  4  5 10 12 13 16| 1 6 7 8  9 11 14 15
```

One more round of merging, consisting of a single merge of the two sorted sublists of length 8, produces the entire list in increasing order. As shown below, the merged segments from the third round become the unmerged segments for the fourth and final round of merging.

```
Unmerged segments    2 3 4 5 10 12 13 16| 1  6  7  8  9 11 14 15
Merged segments      1 2 3 4  5  6  7  8  9 10 11 12 13 14 15 16
```

The unrefined procedure mergesort shown here implements the method just described. It is designed as a procedure to be called by a program that reads as data the list to be sorted and prints as output the sorted list.

```
procedure mergesort;
{ listsize must be a power of two for this
    procedure to work properly }
{ calling program should pad end of list
    with high values, if necessary }
  sortedsegmentlength := 1;
  while sortedsegmentlength <> listsize do
    begin
    merge all sorted segments in pairs
    double the value of sortedsegmentlength
    end;
```

The first refinement of the procedure mergesort specifies in more detail the extent of the sorted segments that are merged in pairs. Actual merging of the segments is delegated to a procedure mergesegments called by the procedure mergesort.

```
procedure mergesort;   { first refinement }
  { listsize must be a power of two
      for this procedure to work properly }
  { calling program should pad the end of the
      list with high values if necessary }
  begin
  sortedsegmentsize := 1;
  while sortedsegmentsize <> listsize do
    begin
    { merge all sorted segments in pairs }
    startofleftsegment := 1;
    endofleftsegment := sortedsegmentsize;
    startofrightsegment := sortedsegmentsize + 1;
    endofrightsegment := 2 * sortedsegmentsize;
    while startofleftsegment < listsize do
      begin
      mergesegments;
          { merge list [startofleftsegment..endofleftsegment]
          with list [startofrightsegment..endofrightsegment]
          and place the merged list in
          list [startofleftsegment..endofrightsegment] }
      startofleftsegment := startofleftsegment + 2 * sortedsegmentsize;
      endofleftsegment := endofleftsegment + 2 * sortedsegmentsize;
      startofrightsegment := startofrightsegment + 2 * sortedsegmentsize;
      endofrightsegment := endofrightsegment + 2 * sortedsegmentsize;
      end; { while-loop for merging pairs of segments }
    sortedsegmentsize := 2 * sortedsegmentsize;
    end; { while-loop }
  end; { mergesort }
```

The most straightforward way to refine the procedure mergesegments is to use an auxiliary list (mergedlist) for the result of merging two segments, and then to copy the merged result back into the proper positions in the list named "list". Further refinement is left as an exercise.

Comparison of Sorting Efficiencies

As with searching techniques, one measure of sorting efficiency is the number of comparisons needed to sort a list into increasing order. A major portion of the execution time in any sorting program is spent making the comparisons that enable the program to put the list in order.

The simpler sequential sorting procedure used in sort1 scans the list to find the smallest entry and "crosses it out" by replacing it with a very large number. This search requires $n - 1$ comparisons if there are n items. Since n passes are required to put the list in order, the total number of comparisons made in sort1 is given by the formula $n * (n - 1)$.

The interchange sorting procedure used in sort2 is similar to that of sort1, except that, when the smallest entry is found, it is removed by an interchange that shortens the unsorted part of the list. Thus, although the number of comparisons needed to find the smallest entry in the list is $n - 1$, the number of comparisons needed to find the second smallest is only n − 2, and so on. The total number of comparisons made in sort2 is given by the formula n * (n − 1) / 2, exactly half that for sort1.

The number of comparisons in merge sorting depends upon the order of the input data, because merging of two of the segments of the input list does not require the full maximum number of comparisons if one segment runs out early. Thus two numbers of comparisons are given in Table 3.4.1 for merge sorting, the minimum number of comparisons and the maximum number of comparisons. If the number n of items to be sorted is a power of 2, say n = 2 to the kth power, then the maximum number of comparisons required by a merge sort is given by the formula n * (k − 1) + 1. The minimum number of comparisons is given by the formula (n / 2) * k. The number k in these formulas corresponds to the number of doublings of the length of the initial one-element sorted segments needed before the entire list is sorted. The number k is readily recognized as the base 2 logarithm of n.

The comparisons are summarized in Table 3.4.1. The clear superiority of a merge sort over sequential sorting procedures is evident before the number of data items grows very large, and becomes more pronounced as the quantity of data increases.

Table 3.4.1 Number of comparisons in sorting procedures.

Number of Data Items	Comparisons Sort1	Comparisons Sort2	Maximum Comparisons Merge Sort	Minimum Comparisons Merge Sort	Efficiency Merge Sort vs. Sort2
4	12	6	5	4	1.20
8	56	28	17	12	1.65
16	240	120	49	32	2.45
32	992	496	129	80	3.84
64	4032	2016	321	192	6.28
128	16526	8128	769	448	10.57
256	65280	32640	1793	1024	18.20
512	261632	130816	4097	2304	31.93
1024	1047552	523776	9217	5120	56.83
2048	4192256	2096128	20481	11264	102.35
4096	16773120	8386560	45057	24576	186.13
8192	67100672	33550336	98305	53248	341.26
16384	268419072	134209536	212993	114688	630.11

Exercises

1. Write a program to read as input a list of numbers and to place the positive numbers from the input in one list and the negative numbers from the input in a second list. The program should then print the two resulting lists. A number zero in the input data should be used as a termination signal. Hint: The two indices for the resulting lists move asynchronously in response to the input data.

2. Modify the program for Exercise 1 so that the final printing of the two resulting lists is side by side in two columns. Be sure to provide for the possibility that one of the resulting lists will be longer than the other.

3. Write a program that merges three lists by first merging two lists and then merging the result with the third list.

4. Write a program that merges three lists at one time.

5. Write a program that "interleaves" two lists read as input; that is, if the two lists are called a and b, it forms the list

a [1], b [1], a [2], b [2], a [3], b [3], ...

If one list becomes exhausted, the program should copy the remainder of the other list.

6. Write a program that "shuffles" a deck of cards as follows. The cards in the deck are represented by the numbers from 1 to 52 and are placed in a list in that order. Then the list is broken into two sublists of 26, and the two sublists are interleaved as in Exercise 3. Repeat the process of breaking the list in half and interleaving the two halves 100 times.

7. Write a program that "randomly interleaves" two lists as follows. Before copying each item into the resulting list, a random integer from 1 to 2 is chosen. If the integer is 1, the element copied will come from the first list. If the random integer is 2, the element copied will come from the second list.

8. Use the random interleaving method in Exercise 7 to randomly shuffle a card deck 100 times.

9. Show that in executing a merge sort, the ith segment of length $j = 2$ to the kth power extends from location $(i - 1) * j + 1$ to location $i * j$.

10. Refine the procedure mergesort.

11. Modify the procedure mergesort so that it can handle list sizes that are not exact powers of 2 by determining the next larger power of 2 that is greater than or equal to the given list length and padding the end of the list with a sufficient number of values that are very large numbers to bring the list size up to a power of 2.

12. Modify the procedure mergesort to handle list sizes that are not exact powers of 2 by modifying the stopping values in the merging procedure and in the loop that selects the pairs to be merged, so that the indices never exceed the given list size.

13. Place additional write statements in the procedure merge to produce output tracing the execution that resembles the hand simulation of merging shown in this section.

14. Hand simulate the merge sorting procedure using 16 playing cards or 16 computer cards with numbers written on them.

15. Modify the procedure merge so that it checks the input data to see if the two lists are in order. One way to do this: Whenever the index in one of the two lists is increased, the new smallest element in that list is compared to the old smallest element just copied. If the new one is smaller, it is an error, and an error message should be printed; then additional new elements from that list should be scanned until one at least as big as the previous one is found.

16. A transaction for a savings account is either a deposit or a withdrawal. Write a savings account program that does three things. First, it accepts a list of transactions encoded such that the positive numbers in the input data are deposits and the negative numbers are withdrawals. Second, it creates from this transaction list two more lists, one a list of deposits and the other a list of withdrawals. Third, it prints the list of deposits and the list of withdrawals.

17. Modify the program for Exercise 16 so that the list of deposits and the list of withdrawals are printed side by side, as in the following example.

```
Deposits  Withdrawals
 376.08    121.46
  14.11     38.42
   8.39
  93.47
```

3.5   Tables and Computer Graphics

A variable with two subscripts is called a *table*. The first subscript is often called the *row number*, and the second subscript the *column number*. After elementary examples involving a multiplication table and a telephone rate table, this section concentrates on tables used in computer graphics, including visual image processing.

Multiplication Table

One of the tables most familiar to many persons is the multiplication table. Each entry is the product of its row number and its column number. The program printtable produces a copy of the multiplication table.

```pascal
program printtable (output);
  var
    multtable : array [1..10, 1..10] of 1..100;
    row, column : 1..10;
  begin
  for row := 1 to 10 do
    for column := 1 to 10 do
      multtable [row, column] := row * column;
  { print table }
  for row := 1 to 10 do
    begin
    for column := 1 to 10 do
      write (multtable [row, column] :6);
    writeln;
    end;
  end.
run printtable
```

```
 1    2    3    4    5    6    7    8    9   10
 2    4    6    8   10   12   14   16   18   20
 3    6    9   12   15   18   21   24   27   30
 4    8   12   16   20   24   28   32   36   40
 5   10   15   20   25   30   35   40   45   50
 6   12   18   24   30   36   42   48   54   60
 7   14   21   28   35   42   49   56   63   70
 8   16   24   32   40   48   56   64   72   80
 9   18   27   36   45   54   63   72   81   90
10   20   30   40   50   60   70   80   90  100
```

In Pascal, there are several different ways to declare a table. One is to declare the variable multtable to be an array of arrays, as in the following declaration.

```
var
   multtable : array [1..10] of array [1..10] of 1..100;
```

A variation of this would be to declare a type called rowtype and then define multtable to be an array [1..10] of rowtype. This is the right way to do things if it is important to have other variables declared to be rowtype so that, for example, an assignment statement can assign the value of one row to another. This is what was done to declare a list of character strings in the programs to find the smallest earned run average for pitchers in Section 3.3. A third variation would be to define a second type called table to be an array of rows, then declare multtable to be type table.

```
   rowtype = array [1..10] of 1..100;
   table = array [1..10] of rowtype;
var
   multtable : table;
```

If it is not necessary to name or manipulate any of the components of the table except the individual elements, then the declaration in the program printtable is suitable. It is simply an abbreviation of the first method mentioned above.

As shown in the assignment and write statements of the program printtable, two subscripts are written within brackets, just like one subscript. The second subscript must be separated from the first by a comma. If the table multtable is considered an array of rows, then the ith row of multtable may be referenced as multtable [i]. The jth element in the ith row may be referenced by the form multtable [i][j] as well as the form multtable [i, j]. As illustrated, it is quite common in programs that deal with tables to have a for-loop for the columns nested within a for-loop for the rows.

A Telephone Rate Table for Long-Distance Calls

Another elementary example involving a table is calculating the billing charges for a long-distance telephone call. The rates depend upon the time of the day the call is placed. To encourage use of the telephone company's facilities and equipment during underutilized hours, the rates in effect during peak daytime hours are usually reduced somewhat in the evening, and further reduced at night. Table 3.5.1 is a simplified version of such a telephone rate table, giving the charge for the initial 3 minutes of direct-dialed long-distance calls from Fun City to selected garden spots on the eastern seaboard. Weekend and holiday rates are omitted to further simplify the program phonecharges written to compute the long-distance telephone charges based on this table.

If a call lasts 3 minutes or less, then the customer pays the 3-minute basic rate. If the call runs overtime, there is an overtime charge proportional to the basic rate. The full charge before tax is the sum of the basic rate and the overtime charge. A tax of 10 percent is added on, and the resulting amount is rounded to the nearest whole cent for printing.

Table 3.5.1 Telephone Charges for the Initial 3 Minutes of Direct-Dialed Long-Distance Calls Placed from Fun City.

	Code for City	Day, Code 1	Evening, Code 2	Night, Code 3
Hoboken	1	.65	.45	.25
Paramus	2	.70	.50	.25
Peapack	3	.80	.55	.30
Piscataway	4	.70	.50	.25
Secaucus	5	.60	.40	.20
Tenafly	6	.60	.40	.20
Weehauken	7	.65	.45	.25

```
program phonecharges (input, output, ratefile);

  const
    nrofcities = 7;
    nrofrates = 3;
    basictime = 3.0;
    taxrate = 0.10;

  var
    citycode : 1..nrofcities;
    ratecode : 1..nrofrates;
    rate : array [1..nrofcities, 1..nrofrates] of real;
    basiccharge, overtime, chargebeforetax, cost, duration : real;
    ratefile : file of char;

  begin
  { read nrofrates from ratefile }
  reset (ratefile);
  for citycode := 1 to nrofcities do
    for ratecode := 1 to nrofrates do
      read (ratefile, rate [citycode, ratecode]);

  { read data pertinent to charges for this call }
  read (citycode, ratecode, duration);
  writeln ('Input data  citycode: ', citycode :1);
  writeln ('            ratecode: ', ratecode :1);
  writeln ('            duration: ', duration :1:2);

  { calculate the charge }
  basiccharge := rate [citycode, ratecode];
  if duration <= basictime then
    overtime := 0
  else
    overtime := duration - basictime;
  chargebeforetax := basiccharge + overtime * (basiccharge / basictime);
  cost := chargebeforetax * (1 + taxrate);
  { print charge to customer }
  writeln ('Charge for this call:  $', cost :1:2);
  end.
```

```
run phonecharges

Input data   citycode: 3
             ratecode: 2
             duration:  19.00
Charge for this call:  $ 3.83
```

Tables of Characters

There is no reason why the values in a table must be numeric. The program blockofasterisks "computes" and prints a 9 x 20 rectangle of asterisks, a simple graphic. Recall that when characters are printed, no extra blanks are inserted between them.

```pascal
program blockofasterisks (output);

  const
    nrofrows = 9;
    nrofcolumns = 20;
    asterisk = '*';

  var
    block : array [1..nrofrows, 1..nrofcolumns] of char;
    row : 1..nrofrows;
    column : 1..nrofcolumns;

  begin
  { fill block with asterisks }
  for row := 1 to nrofrows do
    for column := 1 to nrofcolumns do
      block [row, column] := asterisk;

  { print block of asterisks }
  for row := 1 to nrofrows do
    begin
    for column := 1 to nrofcolumns do
      write (block [row, column]);
    writeln;
    end; { for row }
  end.
```

```
run blockofasterisks

********************
********************
********************
********************
********************
********************
********************
********************
********************
```

Superposition: Printing a Confederate Flag

The fundamental principle in printing more complicated graphics is to decompose them into simple shapes. In applying this principle, a programmer may make good use of superposition. The program printflag uses the superposition of shapes to produce a small facsimile of a Confederate flag.

```pascal
program printflag (output);

  const
    nrofrows = 17;
    nrofcolumns = 48;
    star = '*';
    blank = ' ';

  var
    row : 1..nrofrows;
    column, startcol, stopcol : 1..nrofcolumns;
    flag : array [1..nrofrows, 1..nrofcolumns] of char;
  begin
  { start with a block of stars }
  for row := 1 to nrofrows do
    for column := 1 to nrofcolumns do
      flag [row, column] := star;

  { superimpose a block of blanks in the middle,
       leaving a border of stars }
  for row := 3 to nrofrows - 2 do
    for column := 4 to nrofcolumns - 3 do
      flag [row, column] := blank;

  { diagonal bar from upper left to lower right }
  startcol := 4;
  for row := 3 to nrofrows - 2 do
    begin
    for column := startcol to startcol + 5 do
      flag [row, column] := star;
    startcol := startcol + 3;
    end;

  { diagonal bar from upper right to lower left }
  stopcol := nrofcolumns - 3;
  for row := 3 to nrofrows - 2 do
    begin
    for column := stopcol - 5 to stopcol do
      flag [row, column] := star;
    stopcol := stopcol - 3;
    end;

  { print the flag }
  for row := 1 to nrofrows do
```

```
      begin
      for column := 1 to nrofcolumns do
        write (flag [row, column]);
      writeln;
      end; { for row }
   end.
```

run printflag

```
************************************************
************************************************
********                                ********
***    ******                  ******   ***
***      ******              ******     ***
***        ******          ******       ***
***          ******      ******         ***
***            ************             ***
***              ******                 ***
***            ************             ***
***          ******      ******         ***
***        ******          ******       ***
***      ******              ******     ***
***    ******                  ******   ***
********                                ********
************************************************
************************************************
```

Plotting a Histogram

Another type of computer graphic easily produced on a printer is a histogram, also called a frequency distribution bar graph. Suppose, for example, that at a liberal arts college the registrar reports that there were 5281 A's, 6003 B's, 6717 C's, 3118 D's, 2644 F's, and 241 grades of ''incomplete'' given out in the fall semester. The program grades plots a vertical bar graph in which the height of each bar is proportional to the number of letter grades of that type given out. This makes it easier to see the general characteristics of the grade distribution pattern.

```
program grades (input, output);

  const
    letters = 6;
    nrofrows = 20;
    nrofcolumns = 36;
    star = '*';
    blank = ' ';
    line = '_____';

  type
    rowtype = packed array [1..nrofcolumns] of char;
```

```
var
  histogram : array [1..nrofrows] of rowtype;
  allblank : rowtype;
  frequency : array [1..letters] of 0..10000;
  percent : array [1..letters] of real;
  letter : 1..letters;
  row : 1..nrofrows;
  column : 1..nrofcolumns;
  numberofgrades : 0..60000;
  barheight, topofbar : 0..21;

begin
{ initialize allblank to all blanks }
for column := 1 to nrofcolumns do
  allblank [column] := blank;

{ read grade frequencies and calculate total number of grades }
{ 1, 2, ..., 6 represent grades A, B, C, D, F, INC }
numberofgrades := 0;
writeln ('Input data  frequency:');
for letter := 1 to letters do
  begin
  read (frequency [letter]);
  write (frequency [letter]);
  numberofgrades := numberofgrades + frequency [letter];
  end; { for }
writeln;

for letter := 1 to letters do
  begin
  percent [letter] := 100 * (frequency [letter] / numberofgrades);
  barheight := round (percent [letter] / 5);

  { row 1 is at top of graph }
  topofbar := 21 - barheight;
  for column := 6 * letter - 5 to 6 * letter - 1 do
    begin

    { blank out part above bar }
    for row := 1 to topofbar - 1 do
      histogram [row] [column] := blank;

    { fill in bar with stars }
    for row := topofbar to nrofrows do
      histogram [row] [column] := star;
    end; { for column }

  { put blanks between bars }
  for row := 1 to nrofrows do
    histogram [row] [6 * letter] := blank;
  end; { for letter }
```

```
writeln;
writeln (line);
writeln ('      Letter Grade Distribution');
writeln;

{ print the nrofrows that are not all blank }
for row := 1 to nrofrows do
  if histogram [row] <> allblank then
    writeln (histogram [row]);

writeln (line);
writeln (' A      B      C      D      F      INC');
writeln;
writeln ('Vertical scale:   1 line = 5%');
writeln;
write ('Percents: ');
for letter := 1 to letters do
  write (percent [letter] :7:2);
writeln;
end.

run grades

Input data  frequency:
     5281        6003        6717        3118        2644        241
```

```
_____

        Letter Grade Distribution

         *****
       ***** *****
 ***** ***** *****
 ***** ***** ***** *****
 ***** ***** ***** ***** *****
 ***** ***** ***** ***** *****
_____

   A      B      C      D      F     INC

Vertical scale:   1 line = 5%

Percents:    22.00  25.01  27.98  12.99  11.01   1.00
```

The first step in plotting this histogram is to obtain a total number of grades for the college during that semester. Next, each frequency is divided by the total number of grades to obtain the proportion of the total for each letter grade, and then multiplied by 100 to obtain the percentage. In the program grades, each bar is five columns wide, with one blank between the bars. Each 5 percent of the total distribution is plotted as a bar one line high. Rounding of the computed bar heights is necessary because, in the printed output, the height of each bar must be an integer. For a different distribution, a programmer might make different decisions about the size and scale of the histogram.

Figure 3.5.1 Graphic display terminals produce complex images as combinations of lines, points, and curves. Using the same generating techniques as for printer graphics, much finer detail is possible on a television-type display screen. The light pen shown may be used for graphic input by transmitting its coordinates to a computer.

Plotting a Graph

Many computer installations have special graph plotting equipment that can be directed by a computer. At installations that have an incremental plotter or a television-type display tube, there is usually available a collection of graphics procedures written in popular computer languages so that a programmer can write the calculation part of a program in a usual computer language and call the appropriate graphics procedure to display the answers. Besides general graphics procedures, there are also specialized graphics procedures designed for specific applications such as architectural drawing, contour mapping, and so on. (See Figure 3.5.1.)

Rather than use specialized equipment, the program parabola uses the printer to plot a graph of the function y = x * x. Even with graphics procedure packages designed for specialized plotters, one way to draw a graph is first to locate the points on the graph, as is done in the program parabola, and then to call a graphics procedure to plot the points and draw lines between them.

```
program parabola (output);
  put blanks everywhere
  put minus signs on the x-axis
```

```
put vertical lines on the y-axis
put a plus sign at the origin
for each column in the graph
  convert the column number to an x value
  calculate y = x * x
  convert y value to row number
  put an asterisk in the correct row and column in the graph
print the graph
```

Before the program parabola can be refined, it is necessary to specify in more detail what is wanted. One important detail is the selection of a range for the variables x and y. A decision is made to graph the region of the plane with both x and y coordinates between -1 and $+1$. Since the x and y coordinates include both positive and negative values, a decision is made to use both positive and negative subscripts for the array used to create the picture. Then a decision is made to use 20 columns for each unit distance in the x direction, and only 10 lines per unit distance in the y direction, because the spacing between lines is somewhat greater than that between successive characters on the same line. Thus the range of subscripts is from -20 to $+20$ for column numbers, and from -10 to $+10$ for row numbers. The program parabola can now be refined as shown.

```
program parabola (output);

  const
    rowmax = 10;
    colmax = 20;
    blank = ' ';
    star = '*';
    bar = '|';
    plus = '+';
    minus = '-';

  type
    rowindex = -rowmax..rowmax;
    colindex = -colmax..colmax;

  var
    row : rowindex;
    column : colindex;
    graph : array [rowindex, colindex] of char;
    x, y : real;

  procedure putblankseverywhere;
    begin
    for row := -rowmax to rowmax do
      for column := -colmax to colmax do
        graph [row, column] := blank;
    end; { putblankseverywhere }
```

```
procedure putminusonxaxis;
  begin
  for column := -colmax to colmax do
    graph [0, column] := minus;
  end; { putminusonxaxis }

procedure putbarsonyaxis;
  begin
  for row := -rowmax to rowmax do
    graph [row, 0] := bar;
  end; { putbarsonyaxis }

procedure putplusatorigin;
  begin
  graph [0, 0] := plus;
  end; { putplusatorigin }

procedure putstarsoncurve;
  begin
  for column := -colmax to colmax do
    begin
    x := column / colmax;
    y := x * x;
    row := round (rowmax * y);
    if abs (row) <= rowmax then
      graph [row, column] := star;
    end; { for }
  end; { putstarsoncurve }

procedure printthegraph;
  begin
  writeln ('Graph of the function y = x * x, ',
    ' -1 <= x <= 1, -1 <= y <= 1');
  writeln;
  for row := rowmax downto -rowmax do
    begin
    for column := -colmax to colmax do
      write (graph [row, column]);
    writeln;
    end; { for row }
  end; { printthegraph }
  { ----- main program ----- }
  begin
  putblankseverywhere;
  putminusonxaxis;
  putbarsonyaxis;
  putplusatorigin;
  putstarsoncurve;
  printthegraph;
  end.
```

```
run parabola

Graph of the function y = x * x, -1 <= x <= 1, -1 <= y <= 1
```

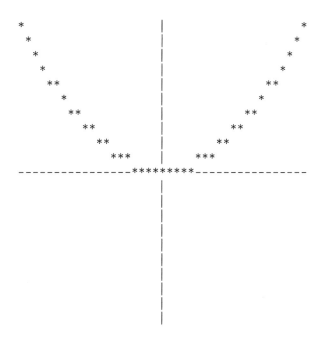

The smoothness of the graph is limited only by how close together points may be plotted. Using a microcomputer that displays 280 columns across and 192 rows vertically on a 12-inch video monitor, the authors have produced very good results. The major changes in the program are to increase the number of columns from 41 to 280, the number of rows from 21 to 192, and to replace assignments to the array element graph [row, column] with calls to a built-in procedure that displays a dot of a specified color on the screen in that row and column. The syntax and even the name of this procedure vary from machine to machine, but all Pascal systems that support screen graphics have such a procedure.

The graphs of other functions are easily obtained by minor modifications of the program parabola. For example, the graph of the cubic equation y = x * x * x over the same range of x and y values can be obtained merely by changing two lines, the line that computes the y value and the line that prints the description of the function on the output above the graph. Only the sample execution printout of the resulting program cubic is shown, because the program itself is so similar to the previous program. Modifications in the range of x and y values are discussed in the exercises.

```
run cubic
```

Graph of the function y = x * x *x, -1 <= x <= 1, -1 <= y <= 1

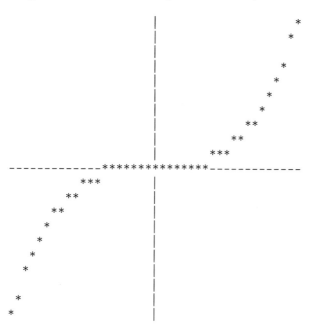

Visual Image Processing

When equipped with special hardware for input and output, a computer can be programmed to process visual images. At one end of the spectrum, this includes the printing of "computer portraits" of the kind that can be found at shopping malls, science museums, and amusement parks. At the other end of the spectrum, it includes the synthesis, enhancement, and analysis of photographs transmitted back to Earth from space probes. The special hardware needed for input, called a "video digitizer", scans one frame of a television camera image and converts the light intensity at each image point in the picture to an integer that encodes the intensity. For the sake of further discussion, we assume that the digitizer encodes light intensity as an integer from 0 to 9, with 0 meaning the brightest possible image point and 9 the darkest possible image point.

Matching the input hardware, a computer used for image processing usually has a television-type cathode ray tube (CRT) for display and the associated circuits for converting a table of digitized light intensities into visual intensities on the screen. However, the image on a CRT is not permanent unless photographed. Thus a second form of visual output, the printed page, is used during debugging of programs and whenever the lower cost and greater ease of handling printed output outweighs the loss in image quality. The program videoimage uses a digitizer for input but a printer for output. Of course, if no digitizer is available for program testing, the digitized image data can be simulated by hand and read from another input device.

```
program videoimage (input, output);
{ intitial version }
   read a table of digitized light intensities from the video digitizer
   convert each digitized light intensity to a printable character
       of appropriate print density
   print the resulting image
```

The refined version of the program videoimage is broken into three procedures representing the phases of the process, the input, the conversion of digits to characters, and the output. An echo of the input data is inserted to make it possible to check the execution of the program.

To complete the refinement of the procedure writeimage, 10 printable characters are chosen to represent the 10 possible digitized light intensities. Since no print character fills more than a small fraction of the space in which it is printed, it is not possible to obtain really dark image points in the printed output. The following 10 printable characters form a progression from very light to as dark as possible for a single character:

```
.   :   -   =   +   !   &   $   %   @
0   1   2   3   4   5   6   7   8   9
```

Refinement of the procedure printimage is now straightforward.

```
program videoimage (input, output);

   const
     nrofrows = 12;
     nrofcolumns = 24;
     maxintensity = 9;

   type
     rowindex = 1..nrofrows;
     colindex = 1..nrofcolumns;
     shadeindex = 0..maxintensity;

   var
     digitizedimage : array [rowindex, colindex] of shadeindex;
     printableimage : array [rowindex, colindex] of char;
     characters : array [shadeindex] of char;
     row : rowindex;
     column : colindex;

   procedure readimage;
     begin
     for row := 1 to nrofrows do
       for column := 1 to nrofcolumns do
         read (digitizedimage [row, column]);
     end; { readimage }

   procedure writedigits;
   begin
   for row := 1 to nrofrows do
```

```
    begin
    for column := 1 to nrofcolumns do
      write (digitizedimage [row, column] :3);
    writeln;
    end; { for row }
  end; { writedigits }

procedure convertimage;
  begin
  for row := 1 to nrofrows do
    for column := 1 to nrofcolumns do
      printableimage [row, column] :=
          characters [digitizedimage [row, column]];
  end; { convertimage }

procedure writeimage;
  begin
  writeln;
  for row := 1 to nrofrows do
    begin
    for column := 1 to nrofcolumns do
      write (printableimage [row, column]);
    writeln;
    end; { for row }
  end; { writeimage }

{ ----- main program ----- }
begin
characters := '.:-=+#&$%@';
readimage;
writeln ('Digitized image points:');
writedigits;
convertimage;
writeimage;
end.
```

The next phase is testing the program. If a video digitizer is not available, simulated input data can be read from a more usual input device. The test data for the sample execution shown for videoimage are based on a small section of a picture of Deimos, the smaller satellite of Mars, transmitted to Earth by the Viking I space probe orbiting Mars. The region chosen shows a small circular crater about 10 kilometers in diameter, with a raised rim. The original computer-generated photograph from which the input data are derived shows the entire disk of Deimos, using approximately three times as many scan lines in the vertical direction as the sample execution does for the same region. To view the printed output of the program videoimage, the printed image must be far enough away so that the individual print characters cannot be recognized as characters. At that distance, they appear as varying shades of white and gray, and an image may be seen. The main problems with the sample execution are the lack of a truly dark print character and the small number of points used to form the image. The crater is seen more distinctly when a larger region is shown in the same detail.

```
run videoimage
```

Digitized image points:

4	4	4	4	4	4	4	4	3	3	3	2	2	1	1	1	1	1	1	0	0	0	0	0
4	4	4	4	4	4	4	3	2	2	2	2	1	0	0	0	0	0	1	1	1	0	0	0
4	4	4	4	4	4	3	2	8	8	8	8	9	9	9	9	9	0	0	0	1	1	0	0
4	4	4	4	3	6	6	7	7	7	7	7	7	7	7	8	8	9	9	0	0	1	1	1
4	4	4	3	5	6	6	6	5	6	6	6	6	6	6	7	7	8	9	9	1	1	3	3
5	4	4	4	5	6	6	5	5	5	6	6	6	6	6	5	7	7	7	7	4	5	4	
5	5	5	5	4	4	6	6	5	6	6	6	6	6	6	5	5	5	6	6	7	5	6	6
5	5	5	5	3	4	4	4	4	6	4	4	4	4	6	6	6	6	6	4	5	6	6	6
5	5	5	5	2	1	1	1	2	2	3	4	4	4	4	4	4	4	5	6	6	6	7	
5	5	5	5	8	1	1	1	1	1	1	2	1	2	2	2	3	3	5	6	6	6	7	8
5	5	5	5	7	6	8	8	1	1	1	1	1	1	2	2	5	6	6	6	6	7	8	8
5	5	5	5	5	5	6	6	8	8	8	8	8	8	6	6	6	6	6	6	7	7	8	8

```
++++++++====--::::::......
+++++++=----:.......:::...
++++++=-%%%%αααα...::..
++++-&&$$$$$$$%%α..:::
+++-#&&&#&&&&&&$$%α:: ==
#+++#&&###&&&&&&&#$$$$ +#+
####++&&#&&&&&&###&&$#&&
####=++++&++++&&&&& +#&&&
####-:::--=++++++++#&&&$
####%::::::-:---==#&&&$%
####$&%%:::::::--#&&&&$%%
######&&%%%%%%&&&&&&$$%%
```

Image Enhancement

The processing of the video image done by the program videoimage consists of nothing more than a conversion from one form of representation to another. When a video camera and digitizer are available, this is all that is needed to print computer portraits. The subject sits before the video camera and a selected frame of the video image is digitized and printed. However, once the image is digitized, the stage is set for computer enhancement of the image to reveal details more clearly, to reduce the amount of static or "snow" in the image, and to perform other modifications of the image difficult or impossible to obtain photographically.

For example, details can sometimes be seen more clearly if the image is converted into a "high-contrast" image. What this involves is altering the digitized light intensities so that only the extreme intensities encoded as 0 and 9 are represented. The program hicontrast to do this results from adding a third procedure enhanceimage between the input and the output procedures of the program videoimage. In this procedure, all light intensities from 0 to 4 are changed to a light intensity of 0, the brightest intensity, and all light intensities from 5 to 9 are changed to a light intensity of 9, the darkest intensity.

```
program hicontrast (input, output);

  const
    nrofrows = 12;
    nrofcolumns = 24;
    maxintensity = 9;
    threshold = 4;

  type
    rowindex = 1..nrofrows;
    colindex = 1..nrofcolumns;
    shadeindex = 0..maxintensity;

  var
    digitizedimage : array [rowindex, colindex] of shadeindex;
    printableimage : array [rowindex, colindex] of char;
    characters : array [shadeindex] of char;
    row : rowindex;
    column : colindex;


  procedure readimage; ... end; { readimage }
  procedure writedigits; ... end; { writedigits }
  procedure convertimage; ... end; { convertimage }
  procedure writeimage; ... end; { writeimage }


  procedure enhanceimage;
  { changes all intensities 0..threshold to 0 }
  { changes all intensities threshold+1..maxintensity to maxintensity }
    begin
    for row := 1 to nrofrows do
      for column := 1 to nrofcolumns do
        if digitizedimage [row, column] <= threshold then
          digitizedimage [row, column] := 0
        else
          digitizedimage [row, column] := maxintensity;
    end; { enhanceimage }


{ ----- main program ----- }
begin
characters := '.:-=+#&$%@';
readimage;
writeln ('Digitized image points:');
writedigits;
enhanceimage;
writeln;
writeln ('Modified digitized image points:');
writedigits;
convertimage;
writeimage;
end.
```

```
run hicontrast
```

Digitized image points:
```
4  4  4  4  4  4  4  4  3  3  3  2  2  1  1  1  1  1  1  0  0  0  0  0
4  4  4  4  4  4  4  3  2  2  2  2  1  0  0  0  0  0  1  1  1  0  0  0
4  4  4  4  4  4  3  2  8  8  8  8  9  9  9  9  9  0  0  0  1  1  0  0
4  4  4  4  3  6  6  7  7  7  7  7  7  7  7  8  8  9  9  0  0  1  1  1
4  4  4  3  5  6  6  6  5  6  6  6  6  6  6  7  7  8  9  9  1  1  3  3
5  4  4  4  5  6  6  5  5  5  6  6  6  6  6  6  5  7  7  7  7  4  5  4
5  5  5  5  4  4  6  6  5  6  6  6  6  6  6  5  5  5  6  6  7  5  6  6
5  5  5  5  3  4  4  4  4  6  4  4  4  4  6  6  6  6  6  4  5  6  6  6
5  5  5  5  2  1  1  1  2  2  3  4  4  4  4  4  4  4  4  5  6  6  6  7
5  5  5  5  8  1  1  1  1  1  1  2  1  2  2  2  3  3  5  6  6  6  7  8
5  5  5  5  7  6  8  8  1  1  1  1  1  1  2  2  5  6  6  6  6  7  8  8
5  5  5  5  5  5  6  6  8  8  8  8  8  8  6  6  6  6  6  6  7  7  8  8
```

Modified digitized image points:
```
0  0  0  0  0  0  0  0  0  0  0  0  0  0  0  0  0  0  0  0  0  0  0  0
0  0  0  0  0  0  0  0  0  0  0  0  0  0  0  0  0  0  0  0  0  0  0  0
0  0  0  0  0  0  0  0  9  9  9  9  9  9  9  9  9  0  0  0  0  0  0  0
0  0  0  0  0  9  9  9  9  9  9  9  9  9  9  9  9  9  9  0  0  0  0  0
0  0  0  0  9  9  9  9  9  9  9  9  9  9  9  9  9  9  9  9  0  0  0  0
9  0  0  0  9  9  9  9  9  9  9  9  9  9  9  9  9  9  9  9  9  0  9  0
9  9  9  9  0  0  9  9  9  9  9  9  9  9  9  9  9  9  9  9  9  9  9  9
9  9  9  9  0  0  0  0  0  9  0  0  0  0  9  9  9  9  9  0  9  9  9  9
9  9  9  9  0  0  0  0  0  0  0  0  0  0  0  0  0  0  0  9  9  9  9  9
9  9  9  9  9  0  0  0  0  0  0  0  0  0  0  0  0  0  9  9  9  9  9  9
9  9  9  9  9  9  9  9  0  0  0  0  0  0  0  0  0  9  9  9  9  9  9  9
9  9  9  9  9  9  9  9  9  9  9  9  9  9  9  9  9  9  9  9  9  9  9  9
```

```
. . . . . . . . . . . . . . . . . . . . . .
. . . . . . . . . . . . . . . . . . . . . .
. . . . . . .@@@@@@@@@. . . . . .
. . . . .@@@@@@@@@@@@@. . . .
. . . .@@@@@@@@@@@@@@@. . . .
@. . .@@@@@@@@@@@@@@@@.@.
@@@@. .@@@@@@@@@@@@@@@@@@
@@@@. . . . .@. . . .@@@@@.@@@@
@@@@. . . . . . . . . . . . .@@@@@
@@@@@. . . . . . . . . . . .@@@@@
@@@@@@@. . . . . . .@@@@@@@
@@@@@@@@@@@@@@@@@@@@@@@@
```

The data for the sample execution of hicontrast are the same data used in the sample execution of the program videoimage. In the high-contrast printout, many details are lost, but the details that remain are seen more clearly. The threshold between light and dark is critical in determining which details remain in the high-contrast printout. If, for example, instead of a threshold intensity of 4, intensities of 5 or less are considered light, and intensities of 6 or greater are considered dark, the appearance of the high-contrast printout could change considerably. It is a simple matter to program a computer to produce a high-contrast printout based on any threshold light intensity, particularly when the threshold is defined in a constant declaration. This and additional methods of image enhancement are discussed in the exercises.

Exercises
---

1. Write a program that reads values for a 3 x 5 table and prints the table with a column of row totals on the right, a row of column totals along the bottom, and the total of all entries in the lower right-hand corner. Label the row or totals, the column of totals, and the grand total appropriately.

2. Write a program that prints a trigonometry table showing the sine, cosine, and tangent of each of the angles 0, 1, 2, ..., 45 degrees. Hint: Use the built-in functions described in Section 2.6. For the built-in functions sin and cos, the argument must be converted to radians by multiplying by pi / 180. Also tan (x) = sin (x) / cos (x).

3. Write a program that reads a table with the same number of rows as columns and prints the *transpose* of that table, that is, the table whose first row is the first column of the original table, whose second row is the original second column, and so on.

4. Write a program that performs a horizontal reflection on a table, that is, exchanges its leftmost column with its rightmost column, its next to leftmost column with its next to rightmost column, and so on.

5. Write a program that performs a vertical reflection of a table.

6. Write a program that converts a matrix (table) into a list, row by row.

7. Write a program that converts a matrix (table) into a list, column by column.

8. For each day of the month, a shot putter keeps a list of the distance she achieved in each of her shot puts that day. Write a program that reads each of these lists of distances into a row of a table and computes the average distance for the month for first puts, the average distance for second puts, and so on.

9. Modify the program for Exercise 8 so that it also prints out the number of the put in which the shot putter has the greatest average distance.

10. Write a program to extract from a table all entries the sum of whose subscripts is a given number. Extract them in order of increasing column number.

11. Using the program written for Exercise 10, write a program that converts a table into a list by first taking all entries the sum of whose row and column is 2, then 3, then 4, and so on.

12. Write a program to print out a facsimile of a United States flag.

13. Write a program to accept up to 10 values for plotting in a histogram, followed by a termination signal. The program should count the number of bars, choose a scale in the vertical direction so that the largest bar is exactly 10 lines high, and plot the histogram.

14. Modify the program parabola to plot the graph of the equation y = 2 * x * x * x − x for −1 <= x <=1 and −1 <= y <= 1.

15. Modify the program parabola to plot the graph of y = x * x for −2 <= x <= 2, and −2 <= y <= 2. Be sure that the program is not confused by y values outside the region.

16. Modify the program parabola so that it uses only positive row and column numbers.

17. Write a program that accepts as input pairs of values (x, y) and plots on a graph all the pairs that precede a termination signal. For testing purposes, generate points for x = −1, −0.95, −0.9, ..., +1, and y = x * x.

18. Write a program that accepts the triple coordinates (x, y, z) of points in space and plots the points according to the following rules:

      row = round (4 * x − 10 * z)
      column = round (−10 * x + 20 * y)

For testing purposes use the eight corners of a cube, x = +−0.5, y = +−0.5, z = +−0.5. Draw the 12 edges by hand on the plotted graph.

19. Modify the program videoimage to use a threshold of 5 for the lighter areas, that is to convert any digitized intensity from 0 to 5 into an intensity of 0, and any intensity from 6 to 9 into an intensity of 9, and run the modification using the same input data used in this section with a threshold of 4.

20. Write a program to make a negative print of a video image. This means that all light intensity relationships are reversed. The brightest points in the video image are to be printed darkest, and the darkest points in the original image are to be printed lightest.

21. Simulate the effect of random interference or static in the transmission of the video picture to the computer by generating for each image point a random integer from 1 to 100. If the random integer is 96 or greater, then generate another random integer, this time from 0 to 9, and replace the actual digitized light intensity with this second random integer. Test your program using a completely uniform gray image with a digitized intensity of 4 at all points.

22. Use the static generator written and tested in Exercise 21 to put static into the picture of the crater on Deimos whose digitized intensities are given in this section.

23. Write a program that accepts as input three consecutive images of the same object, each of which has random interference noise, or static in it. Use an array with three subscripts. Process the three images to reduce static by averaging the three values for the light intensity at each point in the image. Be sure to round the average to the nearest integer before printing.

24. Use the random noise generator written for Exercise 21 to test the program for Exercise 23.

25. Write a program that accepts three successive images of the same object and tries to reduce the random static in the images by computing a digitized light intensity at each point as follows. If two or more of the digitized intensities agree, accept that value regardless of what the other one is. If one value is more than twice as far from the other two as they are from each other, then reject that value and aver-

age the other two. If all three are relatively close, take their average, rounding to the nearest integer to obtain a valid digitized intensity.

26. Test the program for Exercise 25 using the random static generator in Exercise 21.

27. Write a program to rotate the rows of a table given as input by an amount also given as input.

28. Write a program to rotate the columns of a table given as input by an amount also given as input.

29. Write a program that reads two tables of the same size and adds them together, entry for entry, to compute a third table to be printed.

30. The position of the pieces on a chess board may be described as an 8 x 8 table of integers such that negative numbers denote various kinds of white pieces and positive numbers denote black pieces. A zero denotes an empty position. Write a program to decide whether there is a white piece horizontally adjacent to a black piece.

31. Execute the program videoimage using the following table of digitized light intensities as input data:

```
3 3 3 3 3 3 3 9 9 9 9 9 3 3 3 3 3 3 3 3 3 3 3
3 3 3 3 3 3 3 9 9 9 9 9 9 3 3 3 3 3 3 3 3 3 3
3 3 3 3 3 3 3 9 9 9 9 9 9 3 3 3 3 3 3 3 3 3 3
3 3 9 9 9 9 3 3 9 9 9 9 9 0 0 3 3 3 3 3 3 3 3
3 9 9 9 9 9 9 9 9 9 9 9 0 0 0 0 3 3 3 3 3 3 3
9 9 9 9 9 9 9 0 0 9 0 0 0 9 0 9 3 3 3 3 3 3 3
3 9 9 9 9 9 0 0 0 0 0 0 0 9 0 9 3 3 3 3 3 3 3
3 3 3 3 3 3 0 0 0 0 0 0 0 9 0 9 0 0 9 9 3 3
3 3 3 3 3 3 3 0 0 0 9 0 0 0 0 0 0 0 9 9 3 3 3
3 3 3 3 3 3 3 3 3 0 6 9 0 0 0 0 0 0 0 3 3 3 3
3 3 3 3 3 3 3 9 9 9 6 6 9 0 9 0 0 0 0 3 3 3 3
3 3 3 3 3 3 3 9 3 9 9 9 9 9 9 9 9 3 3 3 3 3 3
```

32. Modify the program grades so that one asterisk is printed for each percentage point. For this case, the top row of each bar of the histogram may have from one to five asterisks, rather than always having five asterisks.

3.6   Chapter Review

Information frequently presents itself in the form of lists and tables. The principal advantage of using an array instead of several simple variables to refer to the entries in a list or in a table derives from the fact that the subscript of an array may be variable.

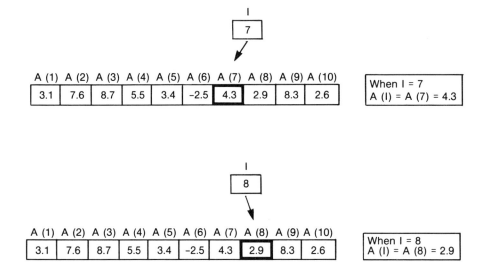

Figure 3.6.1   The effect of changing the value of the subscript I on the array element A[I].

The Subscript of an Array May Be a Variable

For example, if the value of the variable i is 7, then the expression a [i] is a reference to the quantity a [7]. If, however, the value of the subscript i is changed to 8, then the expression a [i] becomes a reference to a [8]. Figure 3.6.1 illustrates why a variable used as a subscript is called an *index variable*.

Using the subscript of an array as the for-variable in a for-loop permits a natural way of processing a list, item by item, from beginning to end. This is illustrated by the read and write statements in the program copyalist.

```
program copyalist (input, output);
  var
    i : 1..4;
    a, b : array [1..4] of 0..9;
  begin
  write ('Input data  a: ');
  for i := 1 to 4 do
    begin
    read (a [i]);
    write (a [i] :2);
    end; { for }
  writeln;
  b := a;
  write ('List b: ');
  for i := 1 to 4 do
    write (b [i] :2);
  writeln;
  end.
```

```
run copyalist

Input data  a:  9 7 2 5
List b:  9 7 2 5
```

Range of Subscripts

When the name of an array is written without a subscript, as in the statement

```
b := a
```

of the program copyalist, it refers to the entire list, from the lowest subscript to the highest subscript. When one array is assigned to another or two arrays are compared, they must be declared to be the same type.

Negative and zero subscripts are permitted in Pascal. Also, characters and programmer-defined data types described in Section 4.3 may be used as subscripts. Examples of these kinds of subscripts appear in Section 4.3.

Searching a List

One common form of list processing is searching a list, either for an exact match of a given value or for the next higher value in the list. Some simple methods of searching a list are *sequential,* considering each item in the list, from front to back, either until a match is found or until it can be determined that no match will be found by further searching. All efficient searching methods discussed in this chapter require a sorted list, so that some items in the list can be dismissed without testing them individually.

Faster searching programs can be written to organize the list into regular intervals, called *pages,* and to compare the given item with only one item per page instead of comparing it with every item in the list. After the correct page is found, a sequential search of that page only is used to locate the given item, if it is there. The two searches together, first for the correct page, and second within that page, take considerably less time than an item-by-item search of the entire list. Multilevel searches with more than two levels further decrease running time, at the expense of added program complexity.

Binary Searching

The most efficient searching procedure for locating an item in a sorted list is a binary search. The basic idea of a binary search is to compare the given item either to the middle item in the list, if the list has an odd number of items, or to one of the middle two items, if the list length is even. This one comparison enables the program to exclude either the first half or the second half of the list from further consideration. The process of testing against the middle item and eliminating half the remaining list is then repeated using only the half of the original list that could still contain the given item. After a very small number of repetitions of this halving process, there is only one item left in the sublist still under consideration and, if that item is not the one the program is looking for, then the given item is not in the list.

Finding The Smallest Element In A List

Another purpose in searching a list is to seek the smallest element. Since the list is presumably not in increasing order (in which case the task of finding the smallest element would be trivial), each item in the list must be examined. At any point in such a search, the computer must retain the value of the smallest element found so far and, for some applications, its location. Whenever a smaller entry is encountered later in the search, it becomes the new smallest value so far. After all items have been examined, the smallest one in the list has been found.

Sorting a List

If the smallest element in a list is "crossed out" of the list, then a second application of a program to find the smallest element in the list will find the second smallest element of the original list. If that element, too, is "crossed out", a third application will find the third smallest element of the original list. Repeating this process a sufficient number of times produces the elements of the original list, one at a time, in increasing order. This method and an elementary improvement upon it are presented in this chapter. A much faster sort is described also.

Merging Lists

Merging two or more lists means combining them to form a *merged list* with the same characteristics as the original lists. Usually, this means that the given lists are already arranged in order, and the merged list will be in order. As described in Section 3.4, a merging procedure can be used as a building block for a very efficient sorting procedure called a *merge sort*.

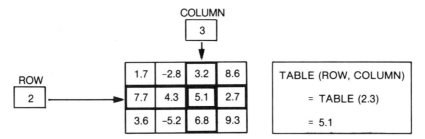

Figure 3.6.2   Referencing an entry in a table.

Doubly Subscripted Arrays

An array with two subscripts is often called a *table* or a *matrix*. By analogy with the terminology ordinarily used for tables, the first subscript is called the *row number*, and the second subscript is called the *column number*. Figure 3.6.2 shows how these two values serve to locate an entry.

Computer Graphics

The values of the individual entries in a list or table need not be numeric. Character strings are as acceptable as values in an array as they are of a simple variable. Many computer graphics techniques rely on forming the image to be displayed as a table of characters.

4

PROCEDURES WITH EXPLICIT ARGUMENTS; FUNCTIONS

When the purpose of a procedure is so specialized that it pertains to only one main program, it is often convenient to use the same variable names in the procedure as in the main program, which is exactly what has been done for all procedures prior to this chapter. Some programming processes, however, occur in many different contexts, and it would certainly save a programmer's time if the same procedure could be used to perform that process for all the different main programs applying to those contexts.

For example, the procedure findsmallest in Section 3.3 is designed to find the smallest value in a list named era, and it cannot be used as it stands to find the smallest value in a list of any other name. When, later in Section 3.3, as a step in sorting, it is necessary to find the smallest value in a list named list, the procedure findsmallest is rewritten because nearly every line of the procedure findsmallest uses a variable name that must be changed. This section presents a way for one procedure to do both jobs in instances like this, or better yet, many similar jobs, at considerable saving of programming effort. After carefully testing that a procedure works in the first context for which it is needed, it can be used in the other contexts as well.

Neither rewriting a procedure for each new application nor always using the same variable names regardless of the application is a good way to write programs. Procedures with *explicit arguments* offer a convenient way out of this impasse. When a procedure has explicit arguments, the variable names used in the calling program do not have to agree with those in the procedure for proper execution, thereby permitting both sets of variable names to be chosen appropriately. Pascal, like most programming languages, includes conventions for what is called the *passing of arguments* that enable a procedure to act on variables in a calling program, even though the names of the variables in the calling program are different from the names in the procedure. Thus, when a procedure has explicit arguments, its variable names do not have to be changed for each new application.

A *function* is a construction closely resembling a procedure. When the purpose of a programming process is to obtain a single value, that process may be written as a function rather than as a procedure. Generating a random number is an example of such a process. Arguments may be passed to functions as well as to procedures.

In writing a procedure, a programmer must take care that the procedure execution does not alter the values of any variables in the calling program other than the ones it is supposed to. A technique called *localization of procedure variables* helps to avoid undesirable side effects. The same technique is used on variables in a function.

4.1   Procedures With Explicit Arguments

This section describes how to write and use procedures with explicit arguments. It introduces extremely useful procedures named swap and readlist that reappear several times in this book. The section also contains a discussion of localization of procedure variables, a technique for guaranteeing that a procedure does not create undesirable side effects by accidentally reusing a variable name already used in the calling program.

Swapping the Values of Two Variables

The purpose of the procedure swapintegers presented here is to exchange two integer values, a fairly common programming operation. Although the program swapintegers contains only three executable statements, there is a good deal of merit in keeping these three lines from continually cluttering up the many programs that need this common operation. The procedure swapintegers is written with explicit arguments because, even in this section, the names of the variables whose values the procedure swapintegers must exchange in one program are different from the names of the variables it must exchange in another program. In fact, one easily imagines circumstances where swapintegers is used to exchange the values of several different pairs of variables in the same program. In each case, the names of the variables whose values are to be exchanged are passed to the procedure swapintegers, which actually does the exchanging.

```
procedure swapintegers (var a, b : integer);
  begin
  temporary := a;
  a := b;
  b := temporary;
  end; { swapintegers }
```

Dummy Arguments

The listing for the procedure swapintegers looks like the listings of procedures in previous chapters, except for one thing. In the title line, the procedure name swapintegers is followed by a list

(var a, b : integer)

of variable declarations enclosed in parentheses. The variables a and b in that list are called the *dummy arguments* of the procedure swapintegers.

Section 2.6 presents three ways to pose a proper subtraction problem to a child. The procedure swapintegers facilitates the design of a fourth method, used by the program propersubtraction. This example shows how dummy arguments are different from ordinary variables.

```
program propersubtraction (input, output);

  var
    x, y, answer : integer;
    seed : integer;
    temporary : integer;

function randominteger (r, s : integer) : integer;
{ generates an integer in the interval [r..s] }
{ uses and changes the global variable seed }
  const
    maxseed = 10000;
    multiplier = 201;
    adder = 3437;
  begin
  seed := (multiplier * seed + adder) mod maxseed;
  randominteger := r + seed * (s - r + 1) div maxseed;
  end; { randominteger }

  procedure swapintegers (var a, b : integer);
    begin
    temporary := a;
    a := b;
    b := temporary;
    end; { swapintegers }

  begin
  seed := 1;
  x := randominteger (0, 9);
  y := randominteger (0, 9);
  if y > x then
    swapintegers (x, y);
  writeln ('Please tell me, how much is ',
      x :1, ' minus ', y :1);
  writeln ('Input data  answer: ');
  readln (answer);
  if answer = x - y then
    writeln ('Correct.  Very good.')
  else
    writeln ('Incorrect.  The answer is ', x - y :1);
  end.


runi propersubtraction


Please tell me, how much is 4 minus 3
Input data  answer: 1
Correct.  Very good.
```

program propersubtraction (input, output;

.
.
.

begin   ⌠procedure swapintegers

  seed := 1;   x y
                                             (var a̸ b̸ : integer);
  x := randominteger (0, 9);   begin
  y := randominteger (0, 9);
  if y > x then   x
    swapintegers (x, y);   <----------------->   temporary := a̸;
  writeln ('Please tell me, how much is ',
    x :1, 'minus ', y :1);   x   y
  writeln ('Input data answer: ');   a̸ := b̸;
  readln (answer);
  if answer = x − y then   y
    writeln ('Correct. Very good.')   b̸ := temporary;
else   end; {swapinteger}
  writeln ('Incorrect. The answer is ', x − y :1);
end.

Figure 4.1.1   Supplying arguments to a procedure.

For the sake of discussion, suppose that in executing the first two statements of the program propersubtraction, the computer assigns to the variable x the randomly generated integer 3 and assigns to the variable y the randomly generated integer 4.

Since 4, the value of y, is greater than 3, the value of x, the computer executes the then-clause

```
swapintegers (x, y)
```

During execution of the procedure swapintegers, it is as if every occurrence of the dummy argument a in swapintegers were replaced by the variable x, and every occurrence of the dummy argument b in swapintegers were replaced by the variable y. Figure 4.1.1 shows this replacement. Thus, in executing the statement

```
temporary := a
```

of the procedure swapintegers, the computer assigns to the variable temporary the value 3 of the variable x in the program propersubtraction, just as if the statement were written

```
temporary := x
```

In executing the statement

```
a := b
```

of the procedure swapintegers, the computer assigns to the variable x the value 4 of the variable y, as though the statement were written

```
x := y
```

Finally, the value 3 that is saved as the value of the variable temporary is assigned to the variable y by the statement

```
b := temporary
```

as though it were written

```
y := temporary
```

Supplied Arguments

The variables x and y in the statement

```
swapintegers (x, y)
```

are known as the *supplied arguments* of the procedure call. From the above description of the way in which the computer executes a procedure with arguments, it is clear that there is no need for the supplied arguments to have the same names as the dummy arguments. Whatever the names of the dummy arguments, during the execution of the procedure, it is always as if the names of the supplied arguments were copied in place of the dummy arguments. This is why the supplied arguments are declared in the calling program to have the same types as declared for the dummy arguments in the procedure heading.

Local Variables

Having used the procedure swapintegers in the program propersubtraction, it is easy to envision additional uses and, indeed, others appear later in the book. The calling program for swapintegers does not use any of the same variable names as swapintegers, and one might wonder whether this is a necessary restriction.

The answer is that it would not matter if a calling program happened to use variables whose names coincided with those of the dummy arguments a and b of swapintegers. When swapintegers is called, it is executed as if the supplied arguments were written in place of the dummy arguments. That would leave no opportunity for the execution of swapintegers to affect calling program variables named a or b, unless those variables were supplied arguments.

On the other hand, if the calling program had a variable named temporary (see Exercise 4), execution of swapintegers could change its value, because the procedure swapintegers also has a variable named temporary. Fortunately, if a programmer desires to have a procedure affect nothing in the calling program except the supplied arguments, there is a way to realize this desire. It is called *localization* of the variables of a procedure. The following version of the procedure swapintegers, which is used in place of the previous version in all future applications, localizes the variable temporary.

```
procedure swapintegers (var a, b : integer);
   var
      temporary : integer;
```

```
begin
temporary : = a;
a : = b;
b : = temporary;
end; { swapintegers }
```

The declaration in this version of the procedure swapintegers

```
var
   temporary : integer;
```

tells the computer that whenever the variable temporary appears in the procedure, it is to be regarded as a private variable for that procedure, and not as a variable in the calling program that happens to have the same name. In general, it is a good programming practice to declare procedure variables locally within the procedure, unless there is a compelling reason to do otherwise.

The declaration section of a procedure may contain all of the kinds of declarations that can occur in a program. Thus a procedure may contain declarations of constants and types as well as declarations of variables. Indeed, since a procedure is a declaration, procedures may contain declarations of other procedures. All constants, types, variables, and procedures that are declared within a procedure are local to that procedure.

The program local illustrates how some of these concepts work. Note that two variable or constant names in different procedures may not only have different values, but may have different data types as well. In the program local, the variable temporary is a character, but it is type integer in the procedure swapintegers. A name could represent a simple variable in the main program and an array in a procedure called by the program. Note also that although the dummy arguments a and b of the procedure swapintegers have the same names as constants in the calling program local, the values of the constants a and b in the main program are unaffected by execution of the procedure swapintegers.

```
program local (output);

  const
    a = 1;  b = 2;

  var
    c, d : integer;
    temporary : char;

  procedure swapintegers (var a, b : integer);
    var
      temporary : integer;
    begin
    temporary : = a;
    a : = b;
    b : = temporary;
    end; { swapintegers }
```

```
begin
temporary := 'x';
c := 3;  d := 4;
swapintegers (c, d);
writeln (temporary :2, a :2, b :2, c :2, d :2);
end.
```

```
run local

 x  1  2  4  3
```

Compatibility of Supplied Arguments With Dummy Arguments

For a procedure call to be correct, the calling program must supply the same number of arguments as specified in the procedure heading. In addition, the data type of each supplied argument and its corresponding supplied argument must agree in the sense that the supplied argument must be assignable to the dummy argument. For example, if the dummy argument is type char, then the supplied argument could be type char or a subrange of type char. One consequence of this rule is that a different procedure must be written to swap two real values, since swapintegers swaps two integer values. The procedure swapreals is the same as swapintegers except that all variables in swapreals are declared to be type real.

```
procedure swapreals (var a, b : real);
  var
    temporary : real;
  begin
  temporary := a;
  a := b;
  b := temporary;
  end; { swapreals }
```

To avoid writing a different procedure, perhaps called swapchars, to swap two characters, and additional procedures to swap two strings of length 7 or two 4 x 5 arrays of real values, it is possible to use a programmer-defined data type to write a procedure that will swap two quantities of any type. The procedure swap illustrates how this is done.

```
procedure swap (var a, b : datatype);
  var
    temporary : datatype;
  begin
  temporary := a;
  a := b;
  b := temporary;
  end; { swap }
```

Responsibility for declaring the type datatype is thereby transferred from the procedure swap to the calling program in which swap is declared. A program that uses the procedure swap must contain a declaration of the type named datatype and the values to be swapped must be declared to be of that type. For example, if the procedure swap is to be used to swap integer values, then the program calling swap must contain the type declaration

```
type
  datatype = integer;
```

Scope of a Declaration

Any declaration made at the head of a procedure or program, including constant declarations, type declarations, variable declarations, and procedure declarations, applies to all parts of the procedure or program in which it is declared. In particular, this means that any such declaration applies not only within the procedure in which it is declared, but also in all procedures declared within that enclosing procedure (unless explicitly overridden by another declaration of the same name in the enclosed procedure).

Every constant, type, variable, or procedure used in a Pascal program must be declared in at least one procedure or program that encloses the references to it. According to this scope rule, the declaration that is in force at any given place in a program is the declaration for that name made in the smallest procedure or program that encloses the given place in the Pascal source program.

Scope rules for declarations allow selective sharing of constants, variables, types, and procedures between associated procedures. However, not all consequences of the scope rules are beneficial. If it is necessary to swap quantities of two different data types within the same program, then two different swapping procedures must be used because only one type declaration for datatype can contain the procedure swap in its scope.

An Array as an Argument

There is no restriction that an argument of a procedure must be a simple variable. One or more arguments might be a list or a table. The purpose of the procedure readlist is to create a list from data given as input. The procedure readlist reads data, adding each item to the list until stopped by a termination signal. The procedure is similar to the one with the same name in Section 3.3, except that dummy arguments and local variables are used.

```
procedure readlist (var list : listtype;
                    maxlistsize : listsizetype;
                    signal : listdatatype;
                    var numberofelements : listsizetype);
  var
    datum : listdatatype;
    i : listsizetype;
    moredata : boolean;

  begin
  moredata := true;
```

```
i := 0;
while (i < maxlistsize) and (moredata) do
  begin
  read (datum);
  writeln ('Input data  datum: ', datum);
  if datum = signal then
    moredata := false
  else
    begin
    i := i + 1;
    list [i] := datum;
    end; { else }
  end; { while-loop }
if moredata then
  numberofelements := maxlistsize
else
  numberofelements := i;
end; { readlist }
```

Declaring the variable i to be local is important. If the localization of the variable i were omitted, and if the calling program also contained a variable named i, then executing the procedure readlist would affect the value of the variable i in the calling program. The programmer-defined data types listtype, listsizetype, and listdatatype are used in the procedure readlist to allow the calling program to decide what type of data is to be stored in the list and what subscript bounds will apply to the array list.

Writing a Driver to Test a Procedure

In order to test the procedure readlist, it is necessary to have a calling program supply arguments for list, maxlistsize, signal, and numberofelements. A program written for the special purpose of testing a procedure is commonly called a *driver*, but the term "driver" is sometimes loosely applied to just about any calling program that supplies arguments. The program testreadlist is written expressly to test the procedure readlist.

```
program testreadlist (input, output);

  const
    maxlistsize = 9;
    signal = -1;

  type
    listdatatype = integer;
    listtype = array [1..maxlistsize] of listdatatype;
    listsizetype = 0..maxlistsize;

  var
    i : 1..maxlistsize;
    actuallistsize : listsizetype;
    evennumbers : listtype;
```

```
procedure readlist (var list : listtype;
                    maxlistsize : listsizetype;
                    signal : listdatatype;
                    var numberofelements : listsizetype);
   ... end; { readlist }

begin
readlist (evennumbers, maxlistsize, signal, actuallistsize);
for i := 1 to actuallistsize do
  write (evennumbers [i]);
writeln;
end.
```

```
run testreadlist

Input data  datum:          2
Input data  datum:          4
Input data  datum:          6
Input data  datum:         -1
              2         4         6
```

From the execution printout shown for testreadlist, it is reasonable to suppose that the procedure readlist works correctly. In particular, it does not include the termination signal in the list. A cautious programmer might design a few additional tests.

Declaration of Dummy Arguments

In declaring a dummy argument of a procedure in the procedure heading, it is necessary to make two choices. One is the type of the dummy argument, and the other is whether to precede the declaration with the keyword var to indicate that the value of the argument may be changed by the procedure.

In a procedure heading, the declared type of a dummy argument must be a one-word type name only. This rule means that programmer-defined data types are not just stylistically desirable; they are mandatory when a dummy argument is a composite type such as an array or subrange type. This is yet another instance of Pascal's design philosophy of making a necessity out of virtue.

A complete description of the effect of inclusion or omission of the keyword var in the declaration of a dummy argument would be quite lengthy. The following rules suffice for most purposes. A dummy argument is declared as var (variable) if the procedure contains a means of changing its value by reading, assignment, or another procedure call. The supplied argument also must be a variable and must be declared to be the same type. Neither constants nor expressions more complicated than a single variable name may be supplied arguments for dummy arguments declared as var (variable).

Dummy arguments whose values are not changed by executing the procedure should be declared as constant by omitting the keyword var in the procedure heading. Constants and expressions of all kinds (including a single variable) may be supplied arguments for constant dummy arguments. The types of the supplied arguments must be such that their values can be accepted by variables of the declared types of the dummy arguments.

A further general rule is that the procedure that results from simultaneously replacing every occurrence of each dummy argument in the procedure with its supplied argument must make sense. In particular, the first supplied argument for the procedure readlist must be a list and the second, third, and fourth arguments must not be lists.

Constants as Supplied Arguments

Constants may be supplied to a procedure as arguments, subject to the same replacement rule as variables; that is, the program that results from simultaneously replacing every occurrence of each dummy argument in the procedure by its corresponding supplied argument must be executable. For example, the single statement

```
readlist (numbers, arraysize, -1, numberofnumbers)
```

could do the same job for the program readlist as the two statements

```
signal := -1;
readlist (numbers, arraysize, signal, numberofnumbers);
```

In addition, signal could be the name of a constant, as in testreadlist, as well as a variable.

On the other hand, the procedure call

```
swapintegers (2, 3)
```

is a mistake, because replacement of the dummy arguments a and b of the procedure swapintegers by the supplied arguments 2 and 3, respectively, changes the perfectly reasonable statements

```
temporary := a;
a := b;
b := temporary
```

into the statements

```
temporary := 2;
2 := 3;
3 := temporary
```

The first of these three resulting statements makes sense, but the other two are nonsense, since one does not alter the value of a constant.

The way to avoid this problem is to follow the rule that a constant must not be supplied as an argument to a dummy argument that is declared to be variable. Expressions, too, may be used as supplied arguments, provided that it makes sense when they are substituted for the corresponding dummy arguments. As with constants, they should be supplied as arguments only to dummy arguments that are not variable. The procedures swap and readlist do not provide meaningful examples of expressions as supplied arguments. Section 4.3 provides a more detailed discussion of the use of expressions as supplied arguments.

Swapping Items in a List

Either or both of the arguments supplied to any of the swapping procedures may be individual items from a list or from a table, because replacing occurrences of the dummy arguments by such subscripted entries makes perfectly good sense. That is, it results in program steps the computer can execute. For instance, the program tryreversal supplies two arguments with subscripts to the procedure swapintegers. The "purpose" of the program tryreversal is to read a list of numbers and then to reverse the list and print the result. The printout shows that tryreversal does not succeed. We suggest trying to diagnose the error before reading the explanation given.

```
program tryreversal (input, output);
{ Read a list, reverse it, and print the result. }
{ Why does this program seem to accomplish nothing? }
{ Try to determine the programming error. }

  const
    maxlistsize = 9;
    maxdata = 9999;
    signal = -maxdata;

  type
    listdatatype = -maxdata..maxdata;
    listtype = array [1..maxlistsize] of listdatatype;
    listsizetype = 0..maxlistsize;
    datatype = listdatatype; { for swap }


  var
    i : 1.. maxlistsize;
    numberofv : listsizetype;
    v : listtype;

procedure readlist (var list : listtype;
                    maxlistsize : listsizetype;
                    signal : listdatatype;
                    var numberofelements : listsizetype);

  var
    datum : listdatatype;
    i : listsizetype;
    moredata : boolean;

  begin
  moredata := true;
  i := 0;
  while (i < maxlistsize) and (moredata) do
    begin
    read (datum);
    writeln ('Input data  datum: ', datum);
```

```
      if datum = signal then
        moredata := false
      else
        begin
        i := i + 1;
        list [i] := datum;
        end; { else }
      end; { while-loop }
  if moredata then
    numberofelements := maxlistsize
  else
    numberofelements := i;
  end; { readlist }

  procedure swap (var a, b : datatype);
    var
      temporary : datatype;
    begin
    temporary := a;
    a := b;
    b := temporary;
    end; { swap }

  begin
  readlist (v, maxlistsize, signal, numberofv);
  writeln ('Original list: ');
  for i := 1 to numberofv do
    write (v [i] :5);
  writeln;
  for i := 1 to numberofv do
    swap (v [i], v [numberofv - i + 1]);
  writeln ('Reversed list: ');
  for i := 1 to numberofv do
    write (v [i] :5);
  writeln;
  end.


run tryreversal

Input data   datum:           2
Input data   datum:           3
Input data   datum:           5
Input data   datum:           7
Input data   datum:          11
Input data   datum:          13
Input data   datum:       -9999
Original list:
    2    3    5    7   11   13
Reversed list:
    2    3    5    7   11   13
```

It is evident from the execution printout of tryreversal that something is the matter, because the "reversed list" is not the reverse of the original list. In proofreading the program for possible errors, what might stand out as most suspicious is the subscript numberofv − i + 1 in the statement that calls the procedure swap.

Since the procedure readlist discards the termination signal, the number of elements in the list v in the sample execution is 6. (Like any other list read by the procedure readlist, the list v has the number 1 for its lower bound.) It follows that when the for-variable i has the value 1, the expression numberofv − i + 1 has the value 6. Thus the first time the procedure swap is called, it is asked to exchange the arguments v [1] and v [6], exactly what is supposed to happen. When the number 2 is the value of the for-variable i, the value of the expression numberofv − i + 1 is 5. Hence, the second time swap is called, it is asked to exchange the values of v [2] and v [5], again the exchange wanted.

Thus careful scrutiny of the suspicious looking expression has produced nothing but evidence of its correctness. Accordingly, it is time to look elsewhere. Since the supposedly reversed list is still in the original order, perhaps there is doubt whether the for-loop of the program tryreversal is even executed. To investigate, we resort to programmed *tracing,* another standard tool in a programmer's debugging repertoire, generally employed when hand simulation does not locate the mistake easily.

A Debugging Trace

Inserting a debugging trace into a program makes the computer print the successive values of critical variables as those values occur during a program execution. To monitor the execution of the for-loop, we insert a writeln-statement immediately after the procedure call, thereby obtaining the following modified loop.

```
for i := 1 to numberofv do
  begin
  swap (v [i], v [numberofv - i + 1]);
  writeln (v [1], v [2], v [3], v [4], v [5], v [6], ' i = ', i :1);
  end; { for i }
```

After changing the program name to trywithdebug, it is rerun, using the same test data.

```
run trywithdebug
```

```
Input data  datum:            2
Input data  datum:            3
Input data  datum:            5
Input data  datum:            7
Input data  datum:           11
Input data  datum:           13
Input data  datum:        -9999
Original list:
    2    3    5    7   11   13
            13         3         5         7        11         2   i = 1
            13        11         5         7         3         2   i = 2
            13        11         7         5         3         2   i = 3
            13        11         5         7         3         2   i = 4
```

13	3	5	7	11	2	i = 5
2	3	5	7	11	13	i = 6

Reversed list:

2   3   5   7   11   13

The six trace lines in the execution printout of the program trywithdebug reveal the source of the problem. The first of these six lines

13   3   5   7   11   2   i = 1

shows that, after one iteration of the for-loop, the first and last numbers are exchanged. The second of the six trace lines

13   11   5   7   3   2   i = 2

indicates that, after two iterations of the for-loop, the second and the next to last numbers have been exchanged.

The third trace line

13   11   7   5   3   2   i = 3

demonstrates that, after the third iteration of the for-loop, the list is in reverse order. The fourth, fifth, and sixth trace lines, however, indicate that the fourth, fifth, and sixth iterations of the for-loop undo the achievements of the first three iterations by exchanging elements of the list back into their original locations.

Choice of Test Data

The choice of test data is often quite important in successful debugging. The test data used so far in sample executions of the reversing program possess several simple but important virtues. First, the input list is in increasing order, to make it easy to see whether all or part of the list is reversed. Second, the number of items in the list is small enough that the entire execution may be hand simulated or traced, if necessary, but not so small that the program execution is trivial.

In this instance, virtue is rewarded. The test data uncover the existence of a programming error, and the debugging trace gives enough additional information to attribute the source of the error to swapping each pair of values twice. The correction that suggests itself is to limit the for-loop to half as many iterations as before.

An alert programmer might immediately notice potential trouble in trying to halve the number of iterations of the for-loop. That is, if the number of elements in the input list were odd, then the proposed number of exchanges would not be an integer. The corrected program reversealist resolves this problem by truncating, if necessary, to obtain an integer, using the integer operator div. The execution printouts for the two sample runs indicate that the corrected program works, both for an input list of even length and for an input list of odd length.

```
program reversealist (input, output);
{ Read a list, reverse it, and print the result. }

  const
    maxlistsize = 9;
    maxdata = 9999;
    signal = -maxdata;
```

```
type
  listdatatype = -maxdata..maxdata;
  listtype = array [1..maxlistsize] of listdatatype;
  listsizetype = 0..maxlistsize;
  datatype = listdatatype; { for swap }

var
  i : 1.. maxlistsize;
  numberofv : listsizetype;
  v : listtype;

procedure readlist (var list : listtype;
                        maxlistsize : listsizetype;
                        signal : listdatatype;
                        var numberofelements : listsizetype);
  ... end; { readlist }

procedure swap (var a, b : datatype);
  ... end; { swap }

begin
readlist (v, maxlistsize, signal, numberofv);
writeln ('Original list: ');
for i := 1 to numberofv do
  write (v [i] :5);
writeln;
for i := 1 to numberofv div 2 do
  swap (v [i], v [numberofv - i + 1]);
writeln ('Reversed list: ');
for i := 1 to numberofv do
  write (v [i] :5);
writeln;
end.
```

```
run reversealist

Input data   datum:          2
Input data   datum:          3
Input data   datum:          5
Input data   datum:          7
Input data   datum:         11
Input data   datum:         13
Input data   datum:       -9999
Original list:
    2    3    5    7   11   13
Reversed list:
   13   11    7    5    3    2


run reversealist

Input data   datum:         17
Input data   datum:         19
```

```
Input data  datum:          23
Input data  datum:          29
Input data  datum:          31
Input data  datum:        -9999
Original list:
    17    19    23    29    31
Reversed list:
    31    29    23    19    17
```

To prove that a program works, one should test all the essentially different possible executions. In addition, if any test reveals an error, one should make a correction in the program and retest the resulting program with the same test data that were improperly processed by the previous program version. It seems sufficient to test the program reversealist for one input list of even length and one input list of odd length, as representatives of the only two essentially different cases.

Tests using randomly generated data are sometimes a valuable extra precaution because they can disclose possibilities not anticipated by the programmer. However, test cases carefully constructed by the programmer to tax all capabilities of the program usually are more productive in detecting errors.

Why Write Procedures

Removing integral portions of a computational process from the main program and encoding them as procedures often makes it easier to understand the flow of the main program. If such a portion might be reused in other computational processes, then encoding it as a procedure with explicit arguments makes it possible for the variable names to make sense both in the procedure and in all the programs that call it. Once a procedure has been tested thoroughly, it may be used in many applications without the extensive debugging frequently needed for new programs.

Using A Procedure to Assist In Tracing

In debugging a complicated program, sometimes the trace takes the form of a procedure. If it seems advisable to record the values of variables at several different locations in the program, and if more than one program statement is needed to take such a snapshot, then a programmer might design a tracing procedure, giving it a name such as snapshot. The procedure call

```
snapshot
```

could be inserted at the critical program locations. For example, the debugging writeln statement of trywithdebug could be replaced by this procedure call and the following procedure snapshot.

```
procedure snapshot;
  var
    j : 1..maxlistsize;
  begin
  for j := 1 to numberofv do
    write (v [j]);
  writeln ('  i = ', i :1);
  end; {snapshot }
```

Sometimes it is helpful if the tracing procedure is coded with explicit arguments in order to enable it to record, when called from one program location, information that is slightly different from what it records elsewhere. This is a special instance of a program containing several statements that call the same procedure.

Some Pascal systems have built-in tracing features. A programmer using such a system should learn both how to use the built-in feature and how to design a trace.

Exercises

---

1. Following the suggestions of Exercises 5, 6, 7, and 8 of Section 2.1, write a payroll program, but use procedures with arguments.

2. Inserting an item at location k of list of length n means increasing the list length to n + 1, moving the values in locations k, k + 1, k + 2, ..., n to locations k + 1, k + 2, k + 3, ..., n + 1, respectively, and storing the value of the new item at location k. Write a program that accepts as input a list of integers, a location in the list where a value is to be inserted, and a value to be inserted at that location; it then should insert the value at the prescribed location and print out the new list. Does it help to use the procedure swap?

3. Write a procedure

   ```
   insert (var list : listtype;
        location : listindextype;
        newitem : listdatatype;
        var numberofelements : listsizetype);
   ```

   that inserts a new item in a list at a specified location as described in Exercise 2.

4. The purpose of the program largestof4 (not an example of good programming techniques) is to determine the maximum of four numbers supplied as input. Hand simulate its executions for each of these cases:

   a) the variable temporary of the procedure swap is local

   b) the variable temporary is global

   Enter as input the numbers 23, 7, 14, and 3.

   ```
   program largestof4 (input, output);
   { designed to illustrate the need for local variables }
   { not the best way to find the largest of four numbers }

      type
        datatype = integer;

      var
        n1, n2, n3, n4, temporary, largest : datatype;

      procedure swap (var a, b : datatype);
        ... end; { swap }
   ```

```
begin
read (n1, n2, n3, n4);
writeln ('Input data  n1: ', n1);
writeln ('             n2: ', n2);
writeln ('             n3: ', n3);
writeln ('             n4: ', n4);
{ set temporary = larger of n1 and n2 }
if n1 >= n2 then
  temporary := n1
else
  temporary := n2;
{ make sure that n3 is not less than n4 }
if n3 < n4 then
  swap (n3, n4);
{ now pick the larger of temporary and n3 }
if n3 > temporary then
  largest := n3
else
  largest := temporary;
writeln (largest :1, ' is the largest.');
end.
```

5. A simple rotation of a list of length n is obtained by transferring the values at lo-cations 1, 2, ..., n − 1 into locations 2, 3, ..., n, respectively, and transferring the value at location n into location 1. This is something like a kindergarten snack line operated so that the child who is at the end of the line on one day moves to the front of the line the next day, causing everyone else to move back by one po-sition. Write a procedure that performs the simple rotation of a list supplied as ar-gument.

6. A "random transposition" in a list of length n is obtained by generating two ran-dom integers i and j from 1 to n and exchanging the value of the list item at loca-tion i with the value of the list item at location j. Write a procedure that shuffles a list of n numbers by performing n random transpositions.

7. A permutation of a list of distinct values is called a "derangement" if no value ends up in the same location it started in. A list of 10 distinct items is to be shuf-fled by the method in Exercise 6. Write a program that shuffles the list

    1 2 3 4 5 6 7 8 9 10

100 times and counts the number of such shufflings that result in derangements.

8. Write a program that performs random transpositions (Exercise 6) on a list of numbers until it is deranged (Exercise 7) and counts the number of random tran-spositions required.

9. The operation of transposing a table is defined in Exercise 3 in Section 3.5. Write a program that accepts a table of integers as input, uses the procedure swap to transpose the table, and then prints the transposed table. For the sake of simpli-city, it is permissible to restrict the shape of the table so that the number of rows equals the number of columns.

10. Suppose that the value of the integer variable i is 1, that the value of a [1] is 2, and that the value of a [2] is 3. The array a is also type integer. What are the

values of these variables after execution of the following statement? Test your answer on a computer, if possible.

```
swapintegers (i, a [i])
```

11. Write a procedure

```
drop (var list : listtype;
      n, maxlistsize : listsizetype;
      var numberofelements : listsizetype);
```

that drops the first n elements from a list of the specified size containing the designated number of elements.

Exercises 12 to 16 are concerned with starting to develop a computer program to play chess. The position of the pieces on the chessboard may be described as an 8 x 8 table of integers, using the following representation.

```
 0 empty square
-1 white pawn       1 black pawn
-2 white rook       2 black rook
-3 white knight     3 black knight
-4 white bishop     4 black bishop
-5 white queen      5 black queen
-6 white king       6 black king
```

Assume that the white pieces start in rows 1 and 2 and that the black pieces start in rows 7 and 8.

12. Write a program to decide which black pieces (and their locations) the white king can capture in a single move. Use one procedure to find the location of the white king and another procedure to test the positions surrounding the king.

13. Write a program to decide whether there is a black knight on the board in position to capture a white bishop. Use one procedure to find all black knights and another to check all possible captures.

14. Write a program to calculate the maximum number of squares that any black rook can move.

15. Write a program to decide whether the black king is in check.

16. Write a program to decide whether black or white is closer to graduating a pawn.

4.2   Nested Procedure Calls

It is certainly permissible and frequently desirable for one procedure to call another. The expression *nested procedure calls* describes the situation in which the main program calls a procedure and that procedure, in turn, calls another procedure. As a practical illustration of the nesting technique, this section presents another sorting method.

How the Initial Order of the Data Can Affect Sorting

Recalling that Chapter 3 presents three different methods for sorting, one might by surprised that sorting is here again the topic of discussion. Sorting by computer is required in many different circumstances, and no one method is best for all of them. If it is known from experience or from theoretical considerations that some starting arrangements are more likely than others in a particular situation, one might choose a method different from the one that works best for the case in which all starting arrangements are equally likely.

As one example of a starting arrangement of data to be sorted, consider the pile of examination answer booklets that students leave for an instructor of a large lecture class to grade. In order to return them with as little confusion as possible, the instructor might sort them into alphabetical order by student name. In the absence of inferences drawn from a careful sociological study of the correlation between student names and the tendency to complete examinations early or aggressiveness in rushing to the pile of answer booklets when the examination is over, it is probably best to assume that all starting arrangements are equally likely.

On the other hand, when a bank returns the monthly collection of cancelled checks from a personal account, it is likely that the order in which they are returned is reasonably close to the order in which they were written. If the checks are numbered consecutively, it is quite unlikely that they will be returned in reverse order, or in such an order that all the odd-numbered checks precede all the even-numbered checks, for example. Since checks are usually deposited soon after they are received, it may be expected that nearly all the checks written early in the month will arrive at the bank before the checks written late in the month. Most commercial banks return cancelled checks to the account holder in the order in which the payees present them for payment, a possibly useful fact in sorting them back into the order in which they were written.

The Bubble Sort

A sorting method that works well when the data to be sorted are not too far out of order is the *bubble sort*. Like the program sort2, the interchange sort described in Section 3.3, it creates an initial segment of properly positioned items and extracts from the unsorted final segment something it can append to the sorted initial segment. It extracts and appends repeatedly until everything is transferred from the final unsorted segment to the sorted initial segment, at which time the list is fully sorted. Whereas the interchange sort always extracts one item at a time from the unsorted segment to append to the sorted segment, the bubble sort sometimes transfers several items per pass (i.e., per iteration of the main loop). Therefore the program bubblesort, which performs a bubble sort, is sometimes capable of greater efficiency than sort2.

```
procedure bubblesort (var list : listtype;
                          sizeoflist : listsizetype);
{ sorts the list into ascending order }
```

```
var
  sortedsegmentsize : listsizetype;

procedure bubbleprocess;
  ... end; { bubbleprocess }

begin { bubblesort }
sortedsegmentsize := 0;
while sortedsegmentsize < sizeoflist do
  bubbleprocess;
end; { bubblesort }
```

When the procedure bubblesort is called by some other program, it calls the procedure bubbleprocess, which does the most interesting part of the work. The nesting of procedure calls goes even a step further when the procedure bubbbleprocess calls the procedure swap. Before examining the listing of the procedure bubbleprocess, however, it is important to have a full understanding of the fundamental step of this clever sorting method.

The Bubble Process

Using the bubble process on a list begins with a comparison of the last value in the list to its immediate predecessor. If the last value is less than the preceding value, then those two values exchange locations. After this first comparison and possible exchange, the value of the next-to-last item is compared to its immediate predecessor. If it is less, then those values are exchanged. After this second comparison and possible exchange, the third-from-last value is compared to its immediate predecessor. If necessary, an exchange is performed so that the lesser of these two items precedes the greater. This comparison and possible exchange sequence continues to the front of the list.

Thinking of the front as the "top", one might consider smaller numbers to be moving upward as bubbles move in water; hence the name "bubble process". For illustration, consider the following list of eight numbers.

8 13 2 17 6 5 15 9

The bubble process begins by comparing the last number, 9, to its immediate predecessor, 15. Since $9 < 15$, those two values exchange positions, resulting in the new list ordering

8 13 2 17 6 5 9 15

The bubble process continues by comparing the next-to-last number, now 9, to its immediate predecessor, 5. Since $5 < 9$, no exchange occurs at this point. However, when it is subsequently observed that the third-from-last number, 5, is less than its immediate predecessor, 6, those two values exchange locations, resulting in the reordering

8 13 2 17 5 6 9 15

Next, the number 5 bubbles past the number 17, yielding the ordering

8 13 2 5 17 6 9 15

but after its comparison to the number 2, its new immediate predecessor, the number 5, stays fixed.

Since the number 2 is smaller than either of the two numbers 8 and 13 that precede it, the number 2 bubbles past both of them, yielding the ordering

2 8 13 5 17 6 9 15

as the net result of applying the bubble process once to the original list of numbers.

From the completed illustration it should be clear that a minimum achievement of a first application of the bubble process is to move the smallest value to the front of the list.

Reiterating The Bubble Process

Reapplying the bubble process to the final result of the first application produces the following sequence of list orderings.

2 8 13 5 17 6 9 15	order before second application begins
2 8 13 5 6 17 9 15	order after 6 bubbles past 17
2 5 8 13 6 17 9 15	order after 5 bubbles past 13 and 8

Since the first number, 2, in the list is known to be the smallest as a result of the first application of the bubble process, it is not really necessary to compare 5 to 2. In any case, this reapplication of the bubble process results in movement of the second smallest number, 5, to the second location in the list.

A Third Application of the Bubble Process

Reapplying the bubble process to the final result of the second application generates list reorderings in the following sequence.

2 5 8 13 6 17 9 15	order before third application begins
2 5 8 13 6 9 17 15	order after 9 bubbles past 17
2 5 6 8 13 9 17 15	order after 6 bubbles past 13 and 8

If it is remembered that the initial segment

2 5

consists of the two smallest values in ascending order, there is no need to make comparisons involving either of them. On this third application, the third smallest number, 6, moves into the third location in the list.

A Fourth Application of the Bubble Process

A fourth application of the bubble process results in a list completely sequenced into ascending order, as now detailed.

2 5 6 8 13 9 17 15	order before fourth application begins
2 5 6 8 13 9 15 17	order after 15 bubbles past 17
2 5 6 8 9 13 15 17	order after 9 bubbles past 13

The list is now in order.

If a list of eight numbers is originally in descending order, it takes seven applications of the bubble process and the same number of comparisons as required by the interchange sort of Section 3.3 to arrive at a list in ascending order. If the original list is already in ascending order, it does not take any applications of the bubble process to arrive at a list in ascending order. For any given number between 0 and 7, it is not difficult to construct a list of eight values that requires precisely the given number of iterations of the bubble process to put the list in ascending order.

Knowing When to Stop Bubbling

If no exchanges occur on a given iteration of the bubble process, then the list is in ascending order, because no value is less than its immediate predecessor. In the above example of sorting a list of eight items with the bubble process, four iterations are sufficient to put the list in order. On a fifth iteration, there would be no exchanges, so it would then be known that the list is in order.

The way in which the bubble process is applied here involves remembering not merely whether any exchanges take place during an iteration of the bubble process, but more precisely the location nearest to the front of the list that is involved in an exchange on that iteration. The value in that location at the end of the iteration is less than all the values in later locations. Moreover, it is known that all the values from that location forward are in ascending order, because no further exchanges occurred during the iteration.

Interplay Between the Procedures Bubblesort and Bubbleprocess

The program bubblesort begins its work by setting the initial value of the variable sortedsegmentsize to zero, corresponding to the fact that, at the outset, the unsorted final segment is the entire list and the initial sorted segment is empty. It then calls the procedure bubbleprocess over and over again. Each time it is called, the procedure bubbleprocess uses the bubble process to transfer one or more items from the unsorted final segment to the sorted initial segment, thereby modifying the values of the variables in the argument list of bubblesort. The procedure bubbleprocess also changes the value of the variable sortedsegmentsize so that it equals the size of the newly augmented initial segment.

```
procedure bubbleprocess;

  type
    datatype = listdatatype;

  var
    lowestexchloc, j : listsizetype;

  { lowestexchloc = 0 means no exchanges
    so far for this iteration }

  procedure swap (var a, b : datatype);
    ... end; { swap }
```

```
begin { bubbleprocess }
lowestexchloc := 0;
for j := sizeoflist downto sortedsegmentsize + 2 do
  if list [j] < list [j - 1] then
    begin
    swap (list [j], list [j - 1]);
    lowestexchloc := j - 1;
    end; { if and for j }

{ determine new length of sorted initial segment }
if (lowestexchloc = sizeoflist - 1) or
    (lowestexchloc = 0) then
  sortedsegmentsize := sizeoflist
else
  sortedsegmentsize := lowestexchloc;
end; { bubbleprocess }
```

The computer's first step in executing the procedure bubbleprocess is to assign the starting value zero to the local variable lowestexchloc (lowest exchange location). If at the time of the execution of the final if-test the value of lowestexchloc is still zero, then it signals that during the iteration of the bubble process no exchanges took place, implying that the list is completely sorted. Observe also that, if at the time of the final if-test, the value of lowestexchloc is

sizeoflist − 1

it means that only the last two items in the list were exchanged during the iteration. The procedure bubbleprocess correctly infers that such an occurrence means the resulting list is sorted.

After an iteration of the bubble process, the initial sorted segment sometimes extends past the exchange location nearest the front of the list. Both the third and the fourth iterations in the illustrative example for eight items previously described are instances of this possibility. However, in an execution of the procedure bubbleprocess, unless the value of the variable lowestexchloc is equal to one less than the size of the list, the computer does not know how many additional items belong to the sorted initial segment. Since it is inefficient to try to find out after every iteration, the computer adopts the safe value, lowestexchloc for the variable sortedsegmentsize.

Hand simulation of the procedure bubblesort presents some evidence that it works correctly. Table 4.2.1 shows the values of the critical variables sortedsegmentsize and lowestexchloc the moment before execution of the if-test inside the for-loop of the procedure bubbleprocess. The rows in the table marked by asterisks show the values of those variables the moment after completion of the for-loop of bubbleprocess.

Efficiency of the Bubble Sort

Table 4.2.1 has a separate row, without asterisk, for each comparison step in the application of the bubble process to the supplied list. There are 16 comparison steps in

Table 4.2.1   Hand Simulation of Bubblesort Showing Values of Key Variables Before Each Comparison*

List Locations							Sorted Segment Size	Lowest Exchange Location	J
1	2	3	4	5	6	7			
5	14	4	25	36	11	8	0	0	7
5	14	4	25	36	8	11	0	6	6
5	14	4	25	8	36	11	0	5	5
5	14	4	8	25	36	11	0	4	4
5	14	4	8	25	36	11	0	4	3
5	4	14	8	25	36	11	0	2	2
*4	5	14	8	25	36	11	0	1	no value
4	5	14	8	25	36	11	1	0	7
4	5	14	8	25	11	36	1	6	6
4	5	14	8	11	25	36	1	5	5
4	5	14	8	11	25	36	1	5	4
4	5	8	14	11	25	36	1	3	3
*4	5	8	14	11	25	36	1	3	no value
4	5	8	14	11	25	36	3	0	7
4	5	8	14	11	25	36	3	0	6
4	5	8	14	11	25	36	3	0	5
*4	5	8	11	14	25	36	3	4	no value
4	5	8	11	14	25	36	4	0	7
4	5	8	11	14	25	36	4	0	6
*4	5	8	11	14	25	36	4	0	no value

*The rows marked by asterisks show the values of the variables the moment
after completion of the for-loop of bubbleprocess.

all. On the other hand, the interchange sort in Section 3.3 would need 6 comparisons to
find the smallest element, 5 comparisons to find the second smallest, 4 to find the third
smallest, and so on, for a total of

$$6 + 5 + 4 + 3 + 2 + 1 = 21$$

comparisons.

The reason for the difference is that, in the interchange sort, the sorted initial segment grows at a rate of one value for each iteration of the main loop, while in the bubble sort, the sorted initial segment sometimes grows by more than one item. If the supplied list is very close to the correct order to begin with, then the bubble sort may require even fewer comparisons than the merge sort. Ordinarily, however, the merge sort is faster. As we mentioned in Section 3.4, while the number of comparisons required is not a complete indicator of the efficiency of a sorting method, it is ordinarily a good one.

Passing Arguments Through Several Levels of Procedure Calls

The procedure bubblesort may be called by any program that requires the sorting of a list. For instance, the program bubblescores is designed to sort examination scores. In running the program bubblescores, the computer must execute a nest of procedure calls three deep.

```
program bubblescores (input, output);

  const
    maxlistsize = 100;
    signal = -999;

  type
    listdata = integer;
    listindex = 1..maxlistsize;
    listtype = array [listindex] of listdata;
    listsizetype = 0..maxlistsize;

  var
    testscores : listtype;
    numberofscores : listsizetype;
    i : listindex;

  procedure readlist (var list : listtype;
                      maxlistsize : listsizetype;
                      signal : listdatatype;
                      var numberofelements : listsizetype);
    ... end; { readlist }


  procedure bubblesort (var list : listtype;
                        sizeoflist : listsizetype);
  { sorts the list into ascending order }

    var
      sortedsegmentsize : listsizetype;

    procedure bubbleprocess;

      type
        datatype = listdata;

      var
        lowestexchloc, j : 0..maxlistsize;

      { lowestexchloc = 0 means no exchanges
        so far for this iteration }

      procedure swap (var a, b : datatype);
        ... end; { swap }

      begin { bubbleprocess }
      lowestexchloc := 0;
      for j := sizeoflist downto sortedsegmentsize + 2 do
        if list [j] < list [j - 1] then
```

```
          begin
          swap (list [j], list [j - 1]);
          lowestexchloc := j - 1;
          end; { if and for j }

     { determine new length of sorted initial segment }
     if (lowestexchloc = sizeoflist - 1) or
         (lowestexchloc = 0) then
       sortedsegmentsize := sizeoflist
     else
       sortedsegmentsize := lowestexchloc;
     end; { bubbleprocess }

  begin { bubblesort }
  sortedsegmentsize := 0;
  while sortedsegmentsize < sizeoflist do
    bubbleprocess;
  end; { bubblesort }

{ ---------- main program ---------- }
begin
readlist (testscores, maxlistsize, signal, numberofscores);
if numberofscores > 1 then
  bubblesort (testscores, numberofscores);
writeln ('These are the scores in ascending order: ');
for i := 1 to numberofscores do
  write (' ', testscores [i] :1);
writeln;
end.


run bubblescores

Input data  datum:       95
Input data  datum:       80
Input data  datum:      100
Input data  datum:       73
Input data  datum:       85
Input data  datum:     -999
These are the scores in ascending order:
 73 80 85 95 100
```

It is specifically permitted to pass a supplied argument through several levels of procedure calls. In executing the main program statement

```
bubblesort (testscores, numberofscores)
```

the supplied argument testscores, a list, is passed to the procedure bubblesort to replace the dummy argument list. The procedure bubblesort, in turn, calls the procedure bubbleprocess, which is written without explicit arguments because it is so special-purpose that no other procedure is likely to call it. It therefore shares all variables, including dummy variables, with the enclosing procedure bubblesort. The procedure bubbleprocess contains the statement

```
swap (list [j], list [j - 1])
```

that becomes, in effect

```
swap (testscores [j], testscores [j - 1])
```

In the execution of that procedure call statement, therefore, the dummy arguments a and b of swap are replaced by list [j] and list [j − 1] of bubbleprocess. The variable j is local to bubbleprocess, but the variable list is inherited from the enclosing procedure bubblesort, where it is a dummy argument replaced by the supplied argument testscores from the main program. Thus the dummy arguments of swap are replaced by supplied arguments that originate three levels up. Under certain conditions, an argument might be passed through many levels of procedures calls.

For the sample run whose execution printout is shown, the variable j has the value 4 the first time this call to swap is executed. Accordingly, the procedure swap exchanges the values of the list entries testscores [4] and testscores [3], and the numbers 100 and 73 exchange locations. The two list components whose values are affected by this exchange are declared back in the main program three levels up.

Nested Procedure Declarations

Declarations of procedures may be nested as well as their calls. For example, since the only place that the procedure bubbleprocess is called is within the procedure bubblesort, the declaration of the procedure bubbleprocess is included within the procedure bubblesort. According to the scope rules for names described in Section 4.1, this means that all variables, types, constants, etc., declared in or applicable to the procedure bubblesort automatically are applicable within the enclosed procedure bubbleprocess. Variables, types, constants, and procedures declared in the main program bubblescores are applicable in all of its declared procedures, that is, in readlist and bubblesort, through which they become applicable to bubbleprocess and ultimately to swap.

Exercises

1. Hand simulate execution of the interchange sort in Section 3.3 for the supplied list 8, 13, 2, 17, 6. How many comparisons are required?

2. Prove that for any supplied list of length n the interchange sort in Section 3.3 always requires $n * (n − 1) / 2$ comparisons.

3. Hand simulate the execution of the procedure bubblesort for the list 92, 12, 56, 76, 43, 46, 18. How many comparisons occur?

4. Prove that for any supplied list of length n the procedure bubblesort never requires more than $(n * n − n) / 2$ comparisons. Tell how to construct a list that forces the procedure bubblesort to make this number of comparisons.

5. Construct an example of a list of length nine that requires exactly five iterations of the bubble process to attain ascending order.

6. Recalling the discussion of merging in Section 3.4, write a procedure with three list arguments that merges the first two lists together and sets the third list equal to the result of that merge.

7. Hand simulate a merge sort, as described in Section 3.4, for the list 16, 14, 12, 10, 8, 6, 4, 2. How many comparisons are needed? Does the number of comparisons depend on the list values or only on the list size?

8. A list whose length is not a power of 2 can be extended by adding on (very large) extra entries until the length is a power of 2. If each extra entry is a number as large as any number in the original list, one can merge sort the extended list and discard the extra entries from the end of the list to obtain a sorted copy of the original list. Write a program that does this.

9. Prove that for any list whose length n is a power of 2, the number of comparisons needed by a merge sort is less than n * log2 (n), where log2 is the logarithm to the base 2. Hint: First prove that the number of comparisons needed to merge two lists of length m is less than 2m. A stronger bound is n * (log2 (n)) − n + 1.

10. A *sinking sort* is the "opposite" of a bubble sort. In a sinking process, the first two values of a list are compared and exchanged, if necessary, so that the larger of the two is second. Then the second and third values are compared and exchanged, if necessary, so that the larger follows the smaller. Reiteration of this comparison and possible exchange down to the end of the list establishes a terminal segment of length 1 or more whose values are in increasing order and each of them greater than or equal to all the values in the initial segment. Repeated application of the sinking process results in a sorted list. Write a procedure for a sinking sort.

11. Hand simulate the execution of the procedure stinkingsort for a list of five items supplied in decreasing order. How many comparisons are required? Contrast your answer to the results for Exercises 2 and 4. Do you think that the name of the program is appropriate? Why or why not?

```
procedure stinkingsort (var list : listtype; listsize : listindex);

{ sorts the list into ascending order }

  type
    datatype = listdatatype;

  var
    i : listindex;
    listsorted, outoforder : boolean;

  procedure swap (var a, b : datatype);
    ... end; { swap }

  begin { stinkingsort }
  listsorted := false;
```

```
      while not listsorted do
      begin
      outoforder := false;
      i := 1;
      while (i < listsize) and (not outoforder) do
        if list [i] > list [i + 1] then
          outoforder := true
        else
          i := i + 1;
      if outoforder then
        swap (list [i], list [i + 1])
      else
        listsorted := true;
      end; { outer while-loop }
end; { stinkingsort }
```

12. Write a program to sort a list of numbers into decreasing order.

13. A list of 8262 credit card numbers is in increasing order. A list of 10 additional credit card numbers, not in order, is to be added on. The final list is to be in order.

   (a) Estimate how many comparisons are needed to first sort the short list and then to merge it with the long list.

   (b) Estimate how many comparisons are needed first to append the short list to the end of the long list and then to bubble sort the result.

   (c) Estimate how many comparisons are needed first to append the short list to the end of the long list and then to merge sort the result.

4.3 Functions; Enumerated Data Types

A *function* is a construction that looks a lot like a procedure, but is used like a built-in function to compute a single value. It is a programmer's way of augmenting a language to include functions that are not built in. Like a procedure, a function has a title line that might list some dummy arguments, followed by a body of statements. The title line contains a declaration of the type of value returned by the function as well as declarations of any dummy arguments. Like a procedure, a function is executed as if supplied arguments were copied in place of the dummy arguments. One difference, however, is that a procedure is called *explicitly* by a procedure call statement, while a function is called *implicitly* whenever the computer executes a program statement that uses the function's name. This section describes how to write a function and how to convert an existing program into a function.

Exponentiation

   Our first example of a function is concerned with raising an integer to a power that is a nonnegative integer. The function intpower computes this value and returns it to the calling program. The driver program testintpower tests the function intpower.

```
program testintpower (output);

  function intpower (number, exponent : integer) : integer;

    var
      value, i : integer;
    begin
    value : = 1;
    for i : = 1 to exponent do
      value : = value * number;
    intpower : = value;
    end; { intpower }

  begin
  writeln (intpower (2, 10));
  end.
```

```
run testintpower
```

```
    1024
```

The function intpower has two explicit arguments, number and exponent, both declared to be type integer in the title line

```
function intpower (number, exponent : integer) : integer;
```

By means of the type specifier integer following the argument list, the title line also declares that the value of the function intpower is type integer. In order to protect any possible calling program from unexpected side effects, the function intpower declares that its variables value and i are local.

Assigning A Function Value

Most of the assignment statements in the function intpower are executed exactly as if they were in a procedure. The first assignment statement assigns the constant 1 to the local variable value. Each time the second assignment statement is executed, the expression on the right of the assignment symbol is evaluated using the first supplied argument, 2, in place of the dummy argument number, and the resulting value is assigned to the variable value on the left of the assignment symbol. The last assignment statement

```
intpower : = value
```

however, is a form of assignment called a *function value assignment*, found only in functions. The difference is that the name on the left of the assignment is the function name, not a variable. This instruction is executed by evaluating the expression on the right of the assignment symbol and assigning it as the function value. The name of the function must not be used as a variable in the program; in particular, once assigned, its value must never be used in an expression within the function. However, the value of a function may be assigned more than once during execution of a function. The last value assigned is the one returned to the calling program.

```
                        2        10
function intpower (number,   exponent   : integer) : integer;

   var
      value, i : integer;

   begin
   value := 1;
                        10
   for i := 1 to exponent  do

                              2
      value := value * number;
   intpower := value;
   end; { intpower }
```

Figure 4.3.1 Supplying arguments to a function program.

Returning a Function Value to the Calling Program

When the execution of the function is completed, the function value is returned to the calling program, and the computer continues with the execution of the calling program. Suppose, for example, that a program includes the calling statement

```
writeln (intpower (2, 10))
```

As illustrated in Figure 4.3.1, the value 2 is supplied to the function intpower to replace the dummy argument number, and the value 10 is supplied to replace the dummy argument exponent. The loop in the function intpower is executed 10 times, each time multiplying value by 2. That value is 2 to the 10th power (1024) when the loop is completed. The final assignment statement assigns 1024 as the value of the function.

Since execution of the function is now completed, the function value is returned to the calling program, and execution of the calling program resumes. In this case, the computer completes execution of the writeln statement that called intpower by printing the function value just calculated.

A function program is declared in exactly the same manner as a procedure. Function and procedure declarations may be mixed in any order. Execution of any program that calls an available function program proceeds exactly as if the function were built in.

What Day of the Week is New Year's Day?

The program newyearsday calculates the day of the week on which the new year began or will begin, for every year in the twentieth century. As a precaution, when the computer reads a year as input, the program newyearsday checks that the year is an integer from 1901 to 2000, inclusive.

```
program newyearsday (input, output);
   read (year);
   if year is from 1901 to 2000 then
      initialize jan 1 day to Tuesday { for the year 1901 }
```

```
calculate the day of Jan 1 for the year input
    by advancing jan 1 day by one for each year
    and one additional day for each leap year
convert the day to a character string and print it
else
  print an error message
```

Advancing of Calendar Dates and Days of the Week

The advancing of New Year's Day by 1 day of the week per ordinary year may be explained as follows. Division of the number of days in an ordinary calendar year, 365, by the number of days in a week, 7, yields a quotient of 52 weeks and a remainder of 1 day. If New Year's Day of an ordinary year falls on a Thursday, for example, the remainder of 1 day will push New Year's Day of the following year to a Friday. After 52 weeks of an ordinary year beginning on a Monday, the day of the week will again be a Monday. The remainder of 1 day, the last day of the year, will cause the subsequent New Year's Day to be a Tuesday.

A leap year of 366 days has 52 whole weeks and two extra days. It follows that, if New Year's Day of a leap year falls on a Wednesday, the year after it will fall on a Friday. Leap year causes New Year's Day to advance 2 days of the week.

A similar progression occurs for other fixed dates in the calendar year. In successive years a fixed calendar date advances 1 day of the week unless a February 29 intervenes, in which case it advances 2 days.

Some Background Information For Calendar Computations

The twentieth century began on January 1, 1901, a Tuesday, and will end on December 31, 2000. Some confused persons mistakenly believe that it began in 1900 and will end in 1999, but that would be inconsistent with the fact the the first century began in the year 1 (there never was a year 0) and the fact that every century is 100 years long.

The only additional information one needs to understand the calculations employed by the program newyearsday is which years of the twentieth century are leap years. Although most calendar years are 365 days long, the earth requires nearly 365 1/4 days to orbit the sun. In order to compensate for the extra fraction of a day beyond 365, nearly every fourth year is designated a leap year, during which the calendar is lengthened to 366 days by adding one day to February's normal 28.

It was arbitrarily decided long ago that, if the number 4 evenly divides the year number, or equivalently, if it evenly divides the last two digits of the year number, then the year is a leap year, except for one special case, the last year of a century. Although the year number of the last year of any century is always divisible by 4, such a year is not a leap year unless its year number is also divisible by 400. for example, the years 1800 and 1900 were not leap years, and the years 2100, 2200, and 2300 will not be leap years. On the other hand, 2000 and 2400 will be leap years.

The reason for this complication in the last year of a century is that the earth's orbiting time is about 365.24219879 days, a shade under 365 1/4 days, and the general goal of the rule for designating leap years is to keep the average length of the calendar year nearly equal to the earth's orbiting time.

Fortunately for the program newyearsday, it is not necessary to know the reasoning behind the assignment of leap years. What one must know is simply that a year of the twentieth century is a leap year if and only if its year number is divisible by 4.

Testing the Executable Refinement of the Program Newyearsday

The execution printouts for the executable refinement of the program newyearsday show that it is being tested with years whose starting dates are verified easily. An almanac is a likely source of calendars for the past few years and the next few years.

```
program newyearsday (input, output);

  const
    daysinweek = 7;

  type
    day = (sun, mon, tue, wed, thu, fri, sat);
    string9 = packed array [1..9] of char;

  var
    dayname : array [day] of string9;
    year : integer;
    numberofleapyears : 0..24;
    advances : 0..6;
    i : 1..6;
    jan1day : day;

  function nextday (givenday : day) : day;
    begin
    if givenday = sat then
      nextday := sun
    else
      nextday := succ (givenday);
    end; { nextday }

  begin
  dayname [sun] := 'Sunday   ';
  dayname [mon] := 'Monday   ';
  dayname [tue] := 'Tuesday  ';
  dayname [wed] := 'Wednesday';
  dayname [thu] := 'Thursday ';
  dayname [fri] := 'Friday   ';
  dayname [sat] := 'Saturday ';
  read (year);
  writeln ('Input data  year: ', year);
  if (year >= 1901) and (year <= 2000) then
    begin
    numberofleapyears := (year - 1901) div 4;
    advances := (year - 1901 + numberofleapyears) mod daysinweek;
    jan1day := tue; { 1901 Jan 1 was a Tuesday }
    for i := 1 to advances do
      jan1day := nextday (jan1day);
    writeln ('New Year''s Day, ', year :1,
        ', was or will be ', dayname [jan1day]);
    end { if }
```

```
    else
      writeln ('The year must be an integer ',
          'from 1901 to 2000.');
    end.
```

```
run newyearsday
```

```
Input data  year:        1981
New Year's Day, 1981, was or will be Thursday
```

```
run newyearsday
```

```
Input data  year:        1984
New Year's Day, 1984, was or will be Sunday
```

The variable numberofleapyears is assigned a value equal to the number of occurrences of February 29 between New Year's Day, 1901, and New Year's Day of the
given year. The variable advances is then assigned as its value the total number of advances of New Year's Day from 1901 to the given year. Since each 7 advances return
the day of the week to the same day it was, the variable advances is reduced mod 7 to
shorten the for-loop that follows.

For example, the number of leap years from 1901 to 1981 is 20, the result of dividing 80 by 4. The number of advances, therefore, is 100, one day's advance for each
of the 80 years from the base date January 1, 1901, to the objective date January 1,
1981, plus one additional day's advance for each of the 20 leap years between those
two dates. If the day of the week is advanced 7 times, there is no change, so the
number of advances made is the remainder when the actual number of advances is divided by 7. For 1981, this is 100 mod 7 = 2, so the day of the week is advanced from
Tuesday to Thursday. In the second sample execution, the number of occurrences of
February 29 between New Year's Day, 1901, and New Year's Day, 1984, is also 20,
the integer part of (1984 − 1901) / 4. The number of advances therefore is 103, the
sum of 83 and 20. Thus the day of the week is advanced 103 mod 7 = 5 times from
Tuesday to Sunday.

Enumerated Data Types

It is possible for the programmer to define a completely new data type by
enumerating all the names of constants for the type. In Pascal, these new types are
called *enumerated data types*.

In the program newyearsday the type day is an enumerated data type with possible
values the constants sun, mon, tue, wed, thu, fri, and sat. Any variable declared to be
type day can be assigned a value consisting of one of these constants. However, a variable that has an enumerated data type cannot be read or written.

The values of an enumerated data type are considered to be ordered by their appearance in the type declaration. Thus, for our enumerated type called day,

sun < sat
thu >= tue

are both true expressions.

It doesn't make any sense to apply arithmetic operators such as + and mod to enumerated data type values, but there are three built-in functions whose argument may be an enumerated data type. The built-in function ord (ordinal) returns an integer 0, 1, 2, ... indicating the position in the declaration of an enumerated data type value. In our example,

ord (sun) = 0
ord (mon) = 1

ord (sat) = 6

The function ord may also be used with an argument of type char or boolean. The use of the function with an argument of type char is described in Section 5.1. For a boolean argument,

ord (false) = 0
ord (true) = 1

For an enumerated data type, the built-in function succ (successor) gives the next value in the enumeration of values in the type declaration. This function is not defined for the largest (last) value. In our example,

succ (sun) = mon
succ (mon) = tue

succ (fri) = sat

and succ (sat) is not defined.

The built-in function pred (predecessor) gives the value preceding its argument. It is not defined for the first value of an enumerated data type. Thus pred (sun) is not defined, but

pred (mon) = sun
pred (tue) = mon

pred (sat) = fri

Some relationships that hold between the functions ord, pred, and succ are

pred (succ (x)) = x, unless x is largest
succ (pred (x)) = x, unless x is smallest

ord (x) + 1 = ord (succ (x)), unless x is largest
ord (x) − 1 = ord (pred (x)), unless x is smallest
x < y if and only if ord (x) < ord (y)

The function nextday used in the program newyearsday declares the enumerated data type day for both its argument and its returned value. For any day of the week in the enumerated type day, the value of the function nextday is the same as the value of the built-in function succ, except that nextday (sat) = sun, while succ (sat) is not defined.

It is possible to have a subrange of an enumerated data type. For example,

```
type
  workday = mon..fri;
```

declares workday to be an enumerated data type that is a subrange of the type day. Variables declared to be type workday could then assume only the values mon, tue, wed, thu, or fri.

Enumerated data types and subranges of enumerated data types may be used as subscripts. For example,

```
var
  temperature : array [day] of real;
  dowjones : array [workday] of real;
```

could be used to declare an array temperature to record a temperature for each day of the week and to declare an array dowjones to record the Dow Jones stock market indicator for each work day of the week. With this declaration dowjones [fri] would be the week's closing average.

A for-variable may be an enumerated data type. For example, if d is a variable declared to be type day or workday, then

```
for d := mon to fri do
  write (dowjones [d]);
```

writes the Dow Jones average for each day of the work week.

Expressions as Supplied Arguments

In general, a supplied argument to a function or procedure may be an expression. With a built-in function, the only restriction is that the function value be defined for the value of the supplied argument. However, in order for a procedure call or a call to a programmer-defined function to be executed when an expression is supplied as an argument, it is necessary that it makes sense to substitute the expression itself for each occurrence of the corresponding dummy argument. In particular, a dummy argument that receives an expression as a supplied argument should not be declared as a variable. For instance, the following calls to the function intpower are both executable, because the substitutions they specify all make sense is y type integer.

```
write (intpower (y + 5, 4))
write (intpower (2 * y, y div 4))
```

Comparison of Functions and Procedures

A function listing looks so much like a procedure listing that one might wonder why both structures are included in a programming language. The reason is largely a matter of tasteful usage.

In mathematical usage, a function f assigns a value f (x) or f (x1, x2, ..., xn) to each allowable value of its argument x or list of arguments x1, x2, ..., xn. The job of a function is to compute, for a supplied argument (or list of supplied arguments), a single value and to return that value for use in the calling program. By way of contrast, a procedure might be used to accomplish any part whatever of the whole program.

The guiding principle in deciding whether to isolate a part of the whole program as a function or as a procedure is that, if its purpose is to produce a single value, then usually a function is used. Otherwise a procedure is used. Beyond this guiding principle, however, there are some important conventions to be obeyed in writing functions.

Avoidance of Side Effects

The most important convention for writing functions is that a function should have no side effects. A statement like

```
jan1day : = nextday (jan1day)
```

tells the computer to calculate the value of the function nextday and assign this value to the variable jan1day. If there were any other effect of executing this statement, a person reading the program in which the statement is contained would be totally unaware of it. Therefore, if execution of a function caused side effects, it would be very difficult to determine the behavior of a program that calls that function.

Particularly, execution of a function should not change the values of its dummy arguments, nor should it change the value of any variables that are not local to the function. Accordingly, the dummy arguments of a function should never be declared variable, even though this is permitted in Pascal, and all variables used in a function should be declared local. If other effects on the calling program are necessary or desirable, the programmer should write a procedure instead of a function. These rules are violated once in this book in order to write the function randominteger, which is traditionally written as a function although it changes the value of the global variable named seed.

Any effect of a procedure on a calling program not related to the procedure's stated computational purpose is a side effect and also should be avoided. However, procedures commonly are used to achieve numerous effects on the calling program, including changing the values of some variables in the calling program. For example, the entire point of the procedure swap is to change the values of its arguments. Thus such a change in the arguments is not a side effect. On the other hand, changing the value of a calling program variable that happens to be named temporary is a side effect, readily avoided by localizing the procedure variable temporary.

Converting a Main Program Into a Function Program

Sometimes a programmer discovers that a process originally written as a main program is so useful that it should be converted into a function. Two fundamental steps in such a conversion are transmuting the input into arguments and turning the output into a function value. It is frequently appropriate to generalize the variable names. To avoid side effects, all variables except for the arguments should be localized. As an illustration, we now convert the program cardcheck1 in Section 3.2 into a function locinunsortedlist (location in unsorted list).

```
function locinunsortedlist
        (entry : listdatatype;
        list : listtype;
        lowestsubscript, highestsubscript : listindex;
        signalformissing : augmentedlistindex)
        : augmentedlistindex;

  var
    i : listindex;
    entryfound : boolean;

  begin
  entryfound : = false;
  i : = lowestsubscript;
  while (i <= highestsubscript) and (not entryfound) do
    if entry = list [i] then
      entryfound : = true
    else
      i : = succ (i); { this permits enumerated data types }

  if entryfound then
    locinunsortedlist : = i
  else
    locinunsortedlist : = signalformissing;
  end; { locinunsorted }
```

The input variable presentedcard of the program cardcheck1 is converted into the dummy argument entry. The input variable cancelledcard, which is a list, is converted into the dummy argument list. The variable i is declared within the function to make it local. Since the subscripts for the more general list argument list need not run from 1 to quantityofcards as they did in the program cardcheck1, the function locinunsortedlist has two additional arguments, lowestsubscript and highestsubscript. Whereas the program cardcheck1 prints messages as output, the function locinunsortedlist returns either a location in the list searched or a signal to indicate that the entry was not found. The calling program can use the returned value to print whatever is appropriate or for any other purpose. The program cardcheck1withfunction shows what a calling sequence for this function looks like. Its execution output is the same as the program cardcheck1.

```
program cardcheck1withfunction (input, output, cardfile);

  const
    maxquantityofcards = 10000;
    signalformissing = 0;
```

```
type
  listdatatype = integer;
  listindex = 1..maxquantityofcards;
  listtype = array [listindex] of listdatatype;
  listsizetype = 0.. maxquantityofcards;
  augmentedlistindex = signalformissing..maxquantityofcards;

var
  cancelledcard : listtype;
  presentedcard : listdatatype;
  actualquantityofcards : listsizetype;
  loc : augmentedlistindex;
  cardfile : file of char;

procedure readcards;
  ... end; { readcards }

function locinunsortedlist
        (entry : listdatatype;
        list : listtype;
        lowestsubscript, highestsubscript : listindex;
        signalformissing : augmentedlistindex)
        : augmentedlistindex;
  ... end; { locinunsortedlist }

begin
readcards;
write ('Enter card number to be checked: ');
read (presentedcard);
loc := locinunsortedlist (presentedcard, cancelledcard,
        1, actualquantityofcards, signalformissing);
write ('Credit card #', presentedcard :1);
if loc = signalformissing then
  writeln (' is acceptable. ')
else
  writeln (' cannot be accepted. ');
end.
```

The procedure readcards, used here exactly as it appeared in Section 3.2, also should be generalized to have explicit arguments. This is left as an exercise.

Arguments Outside the Intended Function Domain

Functions and procedures ordinarily are not equipped to handle the most ill-conceived possibilities for supplied arguments. It is a serious mistake to attempt to pass to a function or procedure a supplied argument that is incompatible with the corresponding dummy argument. For instance, supplying character strings to the function intpower won't work.

Even if a supplied argument is of the correct type, its value might still be outside the function domain. If, for example, the supplied argument to the built-in function log were -1, the function could not produce a value, because the logarithm of a negative number is not defined. Many computer systems would terminate execution of the program if this were attempted.

When a supplied argument is of the right type, and when its value is not a total shock to the system, it is still possible that the value might represent something of a nonstandard case. Under such circumstances, the function may return a special, recognizable signal instead of doing the usual calculations and returning their result.

For instance, the function locinunsortedlist is designed to handle the possibility that the value of the entry supplied as the first argument is not to be found in the list supplied as the second argument. The specific signal to be used to report that an entry cannot be found in the list must be supplied as a fifth argument, because what is a recognizable signal value to one calling program might be a valid location in the list supplied by another calling program.

Although the inability to find a particular entry in a list might be a disaster for one calling program, it might be merely a mild setback for another, and possibly a routine occurrence for a third calling program. Returning the special signal value enables the calling program to react according to its individual needs. The calling program is free either to test for the signal value or to continue computing without testing, at its own possible peril.

The burden of screening the values of supplied arguments does not always fall completely on the function or on the procedure. Sometimes the calling program screens them itself in order to avoid meaningless computations or possible program termination.

Style Rule: Avoid Reassigning a Function Value

Although a function program may contain arbitrarily many function value assignment statements, during a single execution of the function program only one of them should be executed. It is essential, however, that at least one function value assignment be executed during a function call, for otherwise, the function might return no value at all or a value unrelated to the present supplied arguments. For instance, it might return the function value computed for the supplied arguments in the previous call, or perhaps still worse, the garbage left by another program or programmer.

A function program is easier to read when not more than one function value assignment is made during a single function execution. In reading the function program listing, when one encounters a function value assignment, it is then possible to relax briefly and to conclude that at least one case of the computation is finally settled.

Another Conversion of a Main Program Into a Function

In order to have a fast searching method available for sorted lists that arise later, we now convert the program cardcheck5 in Section 3.2 into a binary search function named location. Since the program cardcheck5 was written with an eye toward eventual conversion into a general-purpose function, only the most minor modifications are necessary to enable it to search a list of arbitrary length, not just length 16,384. Of course, the names of the variables are generalized to reflect the program's increased versatility.

```
function location
        (entry : listdatatype;
        list : listtype;
        lowestsubscript, highestsubscript : listindex;
        signalformissing : augmentedlistindex)
        : augmentedlistindex;

{ binary search on a sorted list }
{ The indices beginning, ending, and endof1sthalf
     refer to the segment of the list still
     under active search. }

    var
        beginning, ending, endof1sthalf, onlyremaining : listindex;

    begin
    beginning := lowestsubscript;
    ending := highestsubscript;
    while beginning <> ending do
        begin
        endof1sthalf := (beginning + ending - 1) div 2;
        if entry <= list [endof1sthalf] then
            ending := endof1sthalf
        else
            beginning := endof1sthalf + 1;
        end; { while-loop }
    onlyremaining := beginning; { it also equals ending }
    if entry = list [onlyremaining] then
        location := onlyremaining
    else
        location := signalformissing;
    end; { location }
```

Nesting Procedure Calls Inside Function Calls and Vice Versa

It is permissible for a function to call a procedure. Conversely, it is permissible for a procedure to call a function. Supplied arguments pass through several levels of such mixed calls in the same manner as through several levels of procedures, described in the previous section. Similarly, it is permissible to nest function *declarations* within procedure declarations and vice versa.

Exercises

---

1. Write a function named average to find the average of a list of numbers supplied as the argument.

2. Write a function named even that returns the boolean value true if the supplied argument is an even integer or the value false if the supplied argument is an odd integer.

3. Write a program to test the function even for Exercise 2.

4. The quantity n!, called *n factorial*, is the number 1 if n = 0, and is the product

$$n * (n - 1) * (n - 2) * \ldots * 3 * 2 * 1$$

   if n is a positive integer. When n is a positive integer, the quantity n! is the number of ways of arranging n different items in a row. Write a function factorial that returns the function value n! if the argument n is a nonnegative integer, and the value −1 to signal an improper supplied argument otherwise.

5. Write a function listminimum to which a calling program supplies as argument a list of numbers and obtains in return the smallest number in that list.

6. Write a function locofmin that returns not the minimum number itself but the location of the minimum number in a list supplied as an argument.

7. Convert the program cardcheck3 in Section 3.2 into a function that uses a two-level search to find the location of a supplied argument entry in a supplied argument list.

8. Write a function remainder that works exactly the same as the operator mod.

The function oneyearinterest calculates the total interest accumulating in 1 year for a savings account that pays interest monthly. The initial amount and the annual rate are supplied as arguments. Exercises 9 to 12 are concerned with diagnosing and curing possible side-effects of the poorly written function.

```
function oneyearinterest
         (principal : real;
          var rate : real)
          : real;
{ causes possible undesirable side effects }

  begin
  balance : = principal;
  { convert annual interest rate to a monthly rate }
  rate : = rate / 12;
  for month : = 1 to 12 do
    balance : = balance + balance * rate;
  oneyearinterest : = balance - principal;
  end; { oneyearinterest }
```

9. Hand simulate the execution of the driver program oneyeartest1 for the function oneyearinterest to find the undesirable side effect. What is it?

```
program oneyeartest1 (output);
{ one year's compound interest on $1000 at 5% and 6%
        annual rate, compounded monthly }

const
  principal = 1000;
```

```
var
  rate, balance : real;
  month : 1..12;

function oneyearinterest ...end; { oneyearinterest }

begin
rate := 0.05;
writeln ('One year''s compound interest on $1000');
writeln ('    at 5%, compounded monthly = ',
    oneyearinterest (principal, rate) :1:2);
rate := rate + 0.01;
writeln ('One year''s compound interest on $1000');
writeln ('    at 6%, compounded monthly = ',
    oneyearinterest (principal, rate) :1:2);
end.
```

10. Hand simulate the execution of the driver program oneyeartest2 for the function oneyearinterest to find the undesirable side effect. What is it?

```
program oneyeartest2 (output);
{ interest accumulated for different starting amounts }

var
  rate, balance : real;
  month : 1..12;

function oneyearinterest ..end; { oneyearinterest }

begin
writeln ('Deposit' : 20, 'Interest at 10%' :20);
balance := 100;
while balance <= 500 do
  begin
  rate := 0.10;
  writeln (balance :20:2,
      oneyearinterest (balance, rate) :20:2);
  balance := balance + 100;
  end; { while-loop }
end.
```

11. Write a calling program (to replace oneyeartest2) on which the function oneyearinterest has no side effects.

12. Rewrite the function oneyearinterest so that it has no side effect on any calling program.

13. The *median* of a list of numbers is the middle value, if the list has odd length, or the average of the two values closest to the middle, if the list has even length. Write a function median to calculate the median of a list of numbers. Hint: One method, but not the most efficient one, is to call a sorting procedure.

14. Write a function that returns as its value the character string 'SORTED ' if a list of numbers supplied as argument is in ascending order, and the character string 'UNSORTED' otherwise.

15. Hand simulate the execution of the function illdefined for the supplied arguments −3.14, 8, and 6.4. Why is this function ill-defined? What kind of remedy is needed to make it well?

```
function illdefined (a, b, c : real) : boolean;
  begin
  if b <= a then
    illdefined := false;
  if (b > a) and (b <= c) then
    illdefined := true;
  end; { illdefined }
```

16. Write a function that accepts as arguments a month name, a number representing the day of the month, and a year number in the twentieth century and returns the number (from 1 to 366) of the day in the year on which the given date occurred. Hint: The function needs to include a list of the number of the days in the various months and a leap year test.

17. Write a program that calculates for any date in the twentieth century the day of the week on which it has occurred or will occur. Hint: Refer to Exercise 16 and to the program newyearsday.

18. Unfortunately, there is no built-in function that is the inverse of the function ord. For the enumerated type day in the program newyearsday, write a function called dayofweek that gives the nth day for any value of its argument n, from 0 to 6. That is

    dayofweek (0) = sun
    dayofweek (1) = mon

                .

                .

                .

    dayofweek (6) = sat

19. Modify the function intpower so that its value is −1 if the exponent supplied is negative.

20. Modify the procedure readcards of Section 3.2 into a procedure with explicit arguments that reads values for a list from any file of char by first reading the actual number of data entries and then reading all of the data entries from the file.

4.4 Recursion

It is permissible for a procedure or function to call itself, or even for a procedure to call another procedure which calls the first one. The names and values of the arguments it supplies to itself may differ from the ones supplied in the original call. The effect of a procedure or function calling itself is as if a second copy were created and the usual substitution rules applied to the passing of arguments to the second copy.

Printing a List Backward

The first example of a recursive program is a procedure to write a list backward, a task that could just as easily be accomplished without recursion. However, in its simplicity, writebackward clearly illustrates the two basic principles of recursive programming:

1. Reduction of the problem to an instance of the problem that is simpler in some sense

2. A direct, nonrecursive path through the procedure to handle the "simplest" cases

```
procedure writebackward (list : listtype; sizeoflist : listsizetype);

  begin
  if sizeoflist > 0 then
    begin
    write (list [sizeoflist]);
    writebackward (list, sizeoflist - 1);
    end; { if }
  end; { writebackward }
```

The idea of the procedure writebackward could be described simply as follows:

```
if the list isn't empty then
  write the last element of the list and then
  write the rest of the list backward
```

If the list is empty, there is nothing to be done.

The driver program testbackward uses the procedure readlist from Section 4.1 to provide a list as input for the procedure writebackward to write backward.

```
program testbackward (input, output);

  const
    maxlistsize = 100;
    signal = -1;

  type
    listdatatype = integer;
    listindex = 1..maxlistsize;
    listtype = array [listindex] of listdatatype;
    listsizetype = 0.. maxlistsize;

  var
    inputlist : listtype;
    numberofentries : listsizetype;

  procedure readlist (var list : listtype;
                      maxlistsize : listsizetype;
                      signal : listdatatype;
                      var numberofelements : listsizetype);
  ... end; { readlist }
```

```
procedure writebackward (list : listtype; sizeoflist : listsizetype);

  begin
  if sizeoflist > 0 then
    begin
    write (list [sizeoflist]);
    writebackward (list, sizeoflist - 1);
    end; { if }
  end; { writebackward }
  begin
  readlist (inputlist, maxlistsize, signal, numberofentries);
  write ('Reversed list: ');
  writebackward (inputlist, numberofentries);
  writeln;
  end.
```

```
run testbackward
```

```
Input data  datum:          2
Input data  datum:          3
Input data  datum:          5
Input data  datum:          7
Input data  datum:         11
Input data  datum:         -1
Reversed list:      11    7    5    3    2
```

A Recursive Exponentiation Function

A second example shows how a simple recurrence relation is implemented as a recursive function. In mathematics, nonnegative integral powers of a number are defined by the following recurrence relations.

$$x^0 = 1$$

$$x^n = x * x^{n-1} \text{ for } n > 1$$

The recursive function simplepower implements this recursive relation exactly. A preliminary test prevents function evaluations for negative powers which would never reduce to the nonrecursive path in this simple version of the function. See Exercise 1 for ways to treat negative powers.

```
function simplepower (x : real; n : integer) : real;

  begin
  if n <= 0 then
    simplepower := 1
  else
    simplepower := x * simplepower (x, n - 1);
  end; { simplepower }
```

The function program features a nonrecursive assignment

```
simplepower := 1
```

in case the power n = 0 and a recursive assignment

```
simplepower := x * simplepower (x, n - 1)
```

for higher powers. All function evaluations for nonnegative integral powers reduce in a finite number of steps (in fact, exactly n steps) to the nonrecursive case, x to the zero power = 1, so that recursion ultimately ends. For pedagogical purposes, writeln statements are inserted at the beginning and end of the recursive function simplepower to trace the execution sequence.

```
program testsimplepower (output);

  function simplepower (x : real; n : integer) : real;

    begin
    writeln ('Entering simplepower to compute ',
        x :11, ' to the power ', n :1);
    if n <= 0 then
      simplepower := 1
    else
      simplepower := x * simplepower (x, n - 1);
    writeln ('Leaving simplepower evaluation of ',
        x :11, ' to the power ', n :1);
    end; { simplepower }

  begin
  writeln (simplepower (2, 10) :11);
  end.
```

```
run testsimplepower
Entering simplepower to compute    2.000e+00 to the power 10
Entering simplepower to compute    2.000e+00 to the power 9
Entering simplepower to compute    2.000e+00 to the power 8
Entering simplepower to compute    2.000e+00 to the power 7
Entering simplepower to compute    2.000e+00 to the power 6
Entering simplepower to compute    2.000e+00 to the power 5
Entering simplepower to compute    2.000e+00 to the power 4
Entering simplepower to compute    2.000e+00 to the power 3
Entering simplepower to compute    2.000e+00 to the power 2
Entering simplepower to compute    2.000e+00 to the power 1
Entering simplepower to compute    2.000e+00 to the power 0
Leaving simplepower evaluation of    2.000e+00 to the power 0
Leaving simplepower evaluation of    2.000e+00 to the power 1
Leaving simplepower evaluation of    2.000e+00 to the power 2
Leaving simplepower evaluation of    2.000e+00 to the power 3
Leaving simplepower evaluation of    2.000e+00 to the power 4
Leaving simplepower evaluation of    2.000e+00 to the power 5
```

```
Leaving simplepower evaluation of    2.000e+00 to the power 6
Leaving simplepower evaluation of    2.000e+00 to the power 7
Leaving simplepower evaluation of    2.000e+00 to the power 8
Leaving simplepower evaluation of    2.000e+00 to the power 9
Leaving simplepower evaluation of    2.000e+00 to the power 10
   1.024e+03
```

Recursion As Top-Down Programming

The recursive function program simplepower in this section and the nonrecursive function program intpower in Section 4.3 both calculate a number raised to a nonnegative integral power by repeated multiplication. However, there is a significant difference in approach evident in the program listings. The nonrecursive function intpower uses a for-loop to calculate x to the power zero, which is 1, x to the first power, which is x, x to the second power, x to the third power, and so on until x to the power n is calculated. This is bottom-up programming. In contrast, the recursive function program simplepower addresses the stated task, calculating x to the power n, and describes how to do this task in terms of the simpler task of calculating x raised to the power n − 1. It so happens that the simpler task may be accomplished by the same function program, which is what makes this example recursive, but the principle of writing a program to handle the highest-level task and letting the details take care of themselves later is a perfect example of top-down programming.

A More Efficient Power Function

Repeated multiplication is not the most efficient method for raising a number to a nonnegative power. For example, raising 2 to the 16th power requires 15 multiplications to obtain the answer 65,536. On the other hand, repeated squaring can produce the answer with 4 multiplications: 2 squared is 4; 4 squared is 16; 16 squared is 256; and 256 squared is the answer 65,536.

In general, it is a fact that any number raised to an even power may be calculated as the square of that number raised to half the power. Odd powers may be obtained by one additional multiplication.

The recursive function program power, shown below with a driver program testpower, implements the recurrence relationships. Recall that n div 2 is the integer part of the quotient n/2, and that odd (n) is true if n is odd and false if n is even.

```pascal
program testpower (input, output);

  var p : real;

  function power (x : real; n : integer) : real;
    begin
    writeln ('Entering function power to calculate ',
        x :11, ' raised to the power ', n :1);
    if n <= 0 then
      power := 1
    else if odd (n) then
      power := x * sqr (power (x, n div 2))
```

```
   else
      power := sqr (power (x, n div 2));
   writeln ('Leaving function power to calculate ',
      x :11, ' raised to the power ', n :1);
   end; { function power }
begin
p := power (2, 10);
writeln ('2 to the 10th power = ', p :11);
p := power (1.181543, 63);
writeln ('The population of NJ in 2590 will be ',
   6066782.0 * p :11);
end.
```

```
run testpower
```

```
Entering function power to calculate    2.000e+00 raised to the power 10
Entering function power to calculate    2.000e+00 raised to the power 5
Entering function power to calculate    2.000e+00 raised to the power 2
Entering function power to calculate    2.000e+00 raised to the power 1
Entering function power to calculate    2.000e+00 raised to the power 0
Leaving function power to calculate     2.000e+00 raised to the power 0
Leaving function power to calculate     2.000e+00 raised to the power 1
Leaving function power to calculate     2.000e+00 raised to the power 2
Leaving function power to calculate     2.000e+00 raised to the power 5
Leaving function power to calculate     2.000e+00 raised to the power 10
2 to the 10th power =    1.024e+03
Entering function power to calculate    1.182e+00 raised to the power 63
Entering function power to calculate    1.182e+00 raised to the power 31
Entering function power to calculate    1.182e+00 raised to the power 15
Entering function power to calculate    1.182e+00 raised to the power 7
Entering function power to calculate    1.182e+00 raised to the power 3
Entering function power to calculate    1.182e+00 raised to the power 1
Entering function power to calculate    1.182e+00 raised to the power 0
Leaving function power to calculate     1.182e+00 raised to the power 0
Leaving function power to calculate     1.182e+00 raised to the power 1
Leaving function power to calculate     1.182e+00 raised to the power 3
Leaving function power to calculate     1.182e+00 raised to the power 7
Leaving function power to calculate     1.182e+00 raised to the power 15
Leaving function power to calculate     1.182e+00 raised to the power 31
Leaving function power to calculate     1.182e+00 raised to the power 63
The population of NJ in 2590 will be    2.225e+11
```

In the first example, 2 raised to the 10th power is to be calculated as the square of 2 raised to the 5th power. A second copy of the function program power is created and delegated the task of calculating 2 to the 5th power. The second copy of power decides that 2 to the power 5 will be calculated as 2 times the square of 2 to the power 5 div 2 = 2. A third copy of power is created to calculate 2 raised to the power 2. The third copy decided that 2 raised to the power 2 is the square of 2 raised to the power 1 and creates a fourth copy of power to calculate 2 raised to the power 1. The fourth copy decides to calculate 2 to the power 1 as 2 times the square of 2 raised to the power 0 and creates a fifth copy to calculate 2 raised to the power 0. The fifth copy has more immediate success, assigning a value of 1 to power and returning this value to the fourth copy which squares it and multiplies by 2 to get the value 2 for 2 to the power 1. This value 2 is returned to the third copy which squares it to get the value 4 for 2 raised to the power 2 to return to the second copy. The second copy squares 4 and multiplies the result by 2 to get the value 32 for 2 to the power 5. The value 32 is returned to the first copy where it is squared to get the final answer 1024, which is returned to the calling program testpower for printing.

The Towers of Hanoi

According to legend, there is a temple in Hanoi which contains a ritual apparatus consisting of 3 posts and 64 gold disks of graduated size that fit on the posts. When the temple was built, all 64 gold disks were placed on the first post with the largest on the bottom and the smallest on the top as shown schematically in Figure 4.4.1. It is the sole occupation of the priests of the temple to move all the gold disks systematically until all 64 gold disks are on the third post, at which time the world will come to an end.

There are only two rules that must be followed:

1. Disks must be moved from post to post one at a time.
2. A larger disk may never rest on top of a smaller disk on the same post.

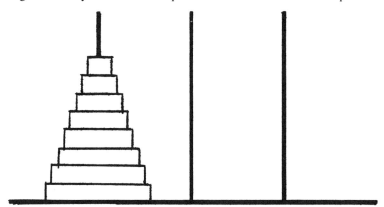

Figure 4.4.1   The towers of Hanoi.

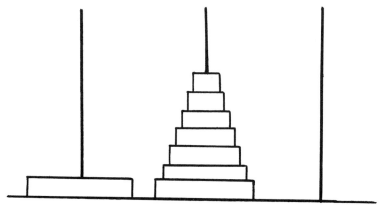

Figure 4.4.2   Locations of the disks when the largest disk is to be moved.

A smaller version of this apparatus with only eight disks made of plastic is sold as a recreational puzzle. The sequence of moves necessary to solve the simpler puzzle is not obvious, and often takes hours to figure out. We propose to write a simple recursive procedure hanoi to print complete directions for moving any number of disks from one post to another. It is extremely difficult to write a nonrecursive procedure to print these directions.

The recursive procedure hanoi is based on the following top-down analysis of the problem. Suppose n disks are to be moved from a starting post to a final post. Because the largest of these n disks can never rest on a smaller disk, at the time the largest disk is moved, all n − 1 smaller disks must be stacked on the free third post as shown in Figure 4.4.2.

For the number of disks n > 1, the algorithm has 3 steps.

1. Legally move the top n − 1 disks from the starting post to the free post.

2. Move the largest disk from the starting post to the final post.

3. Legally move the n − 1 disks from the free post to the final post.

The middle step involves printing a single move instruction. The first and third steps represent simpler instances of the same problem, simpler in this case because fewer disks must be moved. The first and third steps therefore may be handled by recursive procedure calls. In case n = 1, only the second step should be executed, and this provides a nonrecursive path through the procedure for the simplest case. The Pascal procedure hanoi, its test program testhanoi, and a sample execution output for 4 disks is shown.

```
program testhanoi (input, output);

   type
     smallnumber = 0..64;
     postnumber = 1..3;

   var
     numberofdisks : smallnumber;

   procedure hanoi (numberofdisks : smallnumber;
                    startingpost, goalpost : postnumber);
      const
        allposts = 6;

      var
        freepost : postnumber;

      begin
      freepost := allposts - startingpost - goalpost;
      if numberofdisks > 1 then
        hanoi (numberofdisks - 1, startingpost, freepost);
      writeln ('Move disk ', numberofdisks :1,
           ' from post ', startingpost :1,
           ' to post ', goalpost :1);
```

```
  if numberofdisks > 1 then
    hanoi (numberofdisks - 1, freepost, goalpost);
  end; { hanoi }

begin
read (numberofdisks);
writeln ('Input data  numberofdisks: ', numberofdisks :1);
writeln;
hanoi (numberofdisks, 1, 3);
end.


run testhanoi

Input data  numberofdisks: 4

Move disk 1 from post 1 to post 2
Move disk 2 from post 1 to post 3
Move disk 1 from post 2 to post 3
Move disk 3 from post 1 to post 2
Move disk 1 from post 3 to post 1
Move disk 2 from post 3 to post 2
Move disk 1 from post 1 to post 2
Move disk 4 from post 1 to post 3
Move disk 1 from post 2 to post 3
Move disk 2 from post 2 to post 1
Move disk 1 from post 3 to post 1
Move disk 3 from post 2 to post 3
Move disk 1 from post 1 to post 2
Move disk 2 from post 1 to post 3
Move disk 1 from post 2 to post 3
```

Dangers of Recursive Programming

The power of recursive programming brings with it two entirely new types of dangers, exponential execution time and infinite recursive descent. For example, each call to the recursive procedure hanoi specifying a number of disks n > 1 generates two recursive calls to hanoi at the next level to move n − 1 disks. Thus when the testing program testhanoi executes 1 call to hanoi to move 4 disks, the procedure hanoi executes 2 recursive calls, each to move 3 disks. These calls produce 4 recursive calls, each to move 2 disks, which in turn produce 8 recursive calls, each to move 1 disk. These last calls produce no further recursion.

The total number of calls to the recursive procedure hanoi produced by one call of it in the main program for moving 4 disks is

$$1 + 2 + 4 + 8 = 15 = 2 \text{ to the 4th power} - 1$$

Looking at examples with different numbers of disks, it is not hard to convince oneself, or for the mathematically inclined to prove by induction, that in general one main program call to hanoi for n disks produces exactly 2 to the nth power − 1 total calls to hanoi, approximately 2 raised to the power that is the number of disks. This is the meaning of *exponential execution time:* the number of steps in an execution is approximately proportional to 2 raised to the power that is one of the supplied arguments. The danger of exponential execution time is that 2 raised to a power increases exceedingly rapidly, so that procedures that work rapidly for small values of their arguments may take a very long time to execute for only slightly larger values of their arguments. It is left as an exercise to calculate how long it would take to move all 64 disks, and how many recursive calls and pages of output the procedure hanoi would use to print the directions.

The recursive procedure hanoi cannot be blamed for producing exponential execution time. Exponential execution time is inherent in the Towers of Hanoi problem because the expected number of line of output, one for each call to the procedure hanoi, is itself exponential. Thus no program could print the expected output in less than 2 to the nth power steps because the number of lines of output is just one less than that number.

Fibonacci Numbers

In the next example, exponential execution time is not inherent, but is introduced by careless use of recursion. The Fibonacci sequence

1, 1, 2, 3, 5, 8, 13, 21, 34, ...,

arises in such diverse applications as the number of petals in a daisy, the maximum time it takes to recognize a sequence of characters, and the most pleasing proportions for a rectangle, the "golden section" of Renaissance artists and mathematicians. It is defined by the relations

$$f(1) = 1$$
$$f(2) = 1$$
$$f(n) = f(n-1) + f(n-2) \quad \text{for } n > 2$$

Starting with the third term, each Fibonacci number is the sum of the two previous Fibonacci numbers. Naive incorporation of this recurrence relation in a recursive function program

```
function fibonacci (n : integer) : integer;
  begin
  if n <= 2 then
    fibonacci := 1
  else
    fibonacci := fibonacci (n - 1) + fibonacci (n - 2);
  end; { fibonacci }
```

produces an exponential execution time disaster for moderately large n. Like the recursive procedure hanoi, each call to the function fibonacci produces two recursive calls to fibonacci, one to calculate fibonacci $(n - 1)$ and one to calculate fibonacci $(n - 2)$. Table 4.4.1 shows the first 20 Fibonacci numbers and the number of recursive calls to the function fibonacci to calculate them. Taking the last two ratios $13529/8361 = 1.618...$ and $8361/5167 = 1.6180339...$, it is clear that the number of recursive calls does not quite double each time, but more than doubles each two times.

Table 4.4.1   Fibonacci numbers and number of recursive calls to calculate them.

n	fn	cn	n	fn	cn
1	1	1	11	89	177
2	1	1	12	144	287
3	2	3	13	233	465
4	3	5	14	377	465
5	5	9	15	610	1219
6	8	15	16	987	1973
7	13	25	17	1597	3193
8	21	41	18	2584	5167
9	34	67	19	4181	8361
10	55	109	20	6765	13529

On the other hand, a simple for loop to calculate Fibonacci numbers

```
f [1] := 1;
f [2] := 1;
for i := 3 to n do
  f [i] := f [i - 1] + f [i - 2];
```

requires only $n - 2$ additions, but requires instead an array with at least n elements. (This poses something of a problem in Pascal since each array must be declared to be a fixed size.) Exponential execution time is clearly not inherent in the calculation of Fibonacci numbers. See Exercise 6 for ways to write a recursive program to calculate Fibonacci numbers without exponential execution time.

An even worse execution time disaster happens in the next program. The factorial function (denoted n! in mathematics) is defined by the recurrence relations

$$0! = 1$$
$$n! = n * (n - 1)! \text{ for } n > 0$$

In an effort to trace the various levels of recursive calls, a writeln statement is inserted in the recursive function program factorial to print the answer before returning from a successful execution of the function program.

```
program testfactorial (output);

  function factorial (n : integer) : integer;
    begin
    if n <= 0 then
      factorial := 1
    else
      factorial := n * factorial (n - 1);
    writeln ('Completion of factorial execution-- ',
        n :1, '! = ', factorial (n) :1);
    end; { factorial }

begin
writeln ('3! = ', factorial (3) :1);
end.
```

The writeln statement disguises a recursive call from within factorial to itself with *the same value for the dummy argument n.* This recursive call is not for a simpler instance of the same problem; it is for the same instance of the same problem. Thus one level of recursion follows another indefinitely without any simplification of the problem leading to a nonrecursive path through the function.

This execution time disaster, called *infinite recursive descent,* may be guarded against by carefully checking that there is at least one nonrecursive path through a procedure or function, and that each recursive call that does appear in the procedure or function supplies changed values for the dummy arguments in such a way that after a finite number of nested recursive calls, a nonrecursive path is taken.

Exercises

---

1. The recurrence relations

   x to the zero power = 1
   x to the nth power = x * (x to the n − 1 power)   for n > 0
   x to the nth power = (x to the n − 1 power) / x   for n < 0

   define x to the nth power for all integers n. Modify the function program simplepower to calculate x to the nth power for any integer power n.

2. What execution time problems could develop if the test for n < 0 were removed from the function program simplepower? Explain.

3. Modify the function program power to handle negative powers also.

4. Axiomatic developments of the nonnegative integers define addition recursively by the relations

   a + 0 = a   for all a
   a + b = succ (a + pred (b))   for all a, and for b > 0

   Write a recursive function sum (a, b) based on these recurrence relations and test it on the sum 5 + 3.

5. In axiomatic developments of the nonnegative integers, multiplication is defined by the recurrence relations

   a × 0 = 0
   a × b = a + a × pred (b)   for b > 0

   Write a recursive function program product (a, b) based on these relations. Use the recursive function sum written in Exercise 4 to do the addition. Test your program with the product 5 x 3.

6. Define a Fibonacci sequence as any sequence of numbers satisfying the recurrence relation

   f [n] = f [n − 1] + f [n − 2]

The usual Fibonacci sequence, 1, 1, 2, 3, 5, 8, ..., is specified by the additional conditions that f [1] = f [2] = 1. Other Fibonacci sequences, for example 1, 3, 4, 7, 11, ..., are generated by other starting values. Define a a Fibonacci triple (a, b, n) as a first term, a second term and a number of terms in a Fibonacci sequence and the value v (a, b, n) of a Fibonacci triple as the value of the nth term f [n] in the Fibonacci sequence starting with f [1] = a and f [2] = b. Values of Fibonacci triples satisfy the recurrence relations

$$v (a, b, 1) = a$$
$$v (a, b, 2) = b$$
$$v (a, b, n) = v (b, a + b, n - 1) \quad \text{for } n > 2$$

Write a recursive function program to calculate the nth term in the usual Fibonacci sequence based on these relations.

7. In the recursive program for Fibonacci numbers written in Exercise 6, how many calls are necessary to calculate f [10], f [20], f [n]?

8. For positive integers a and b, the greatest common divisor of a and b satisfies the following recurrence relationship.

$$\text{gcd } (a, b) = b \qquad \text{if } a \bmod b = 0$$
$$\text{gcd } (a, b) = \text{gcd } (b, a \bmod b) \quad \text{if } a \bmod b <> 0$$

Write a recursive function program gcd (a, b) using these recurrences. Test the program by finding gcd (24, 36), gcd (16, 13), gcd (17, 119), and gcd (177, 228).

9. Modify the function factorial so that the value computed by the function is printed correctly just prior to leaving the function.

10. (Very difficult) Write a program to print instructions for the Towers of Hanoi without using recursion. It is not fair if you fake recursion using the advanced data structure technique of stacks or using level of recursive call subscripts on variables.

4.5   Chapter Review

Reusing a procedure (after carefully testing to see that it works) is an excellent way to save programming effort. To reap the full advantage of the principle of reusing a procedure that works, however, it is often necessary to write the procedure with *explicit arguments*. Without explicit arguments, each time a procedure is reused, the calling program must use exactly the same variable names. Function programs, similar but not identical in structure to procedures, are used for calculating a single value and returning it for use in the calling program.

Dummy Arguments and Supplied Arguments

The arguments a and b of the procedure swap are called *explicit*, because they are specified explicitly in the title line. They are also called *dummy arguments*, because they stand for the variables in the calling program whose values are to be exchanged, and they are never used without first being replaced by *supplied arguments* from the calling program.

```
procedure swap (var a, b : datatype);
  var
    temporary : datatype;
  begin
  temporary : = a;
  a : = b;
  b : = temporary;
  end; { swap }
```

The names a and b of the dummy arguments do not matter, because when some other program calls swap with a statement

```
swap (this, that)
```

the procedure swap is executed as if every occurrence of the first dummy argument a were replaced by the first supplied argument this and every occurrence of the second argument b were replaced by the second supplied argument that. Thus the execution exchanges the values of the variables this and that in the calling program.

A function is called as if it were a built-in function. For example, the statement

```
writeln (intpower (-2, 3))
```

in a calling program supplies the arguments -2 and 3 to the function intpower, whose execution produces the function value -8, which is returned to the calling program that prints the result.

```
program testintpower (output);

  function intpower (number, exponent : integer) : integer;

    var
      value, i : integer;

    begin
    value : = 1;
    for i : = 1 to exponent do
      value : = value * number;
    intpower : = value;
    end; { intpower }

  begin
  writeln (intpower (2, 10));
  end.
```

Just like a procedure, a function is executed as if every occurrence of each dummy argument were replaced by the corresponding supplied argument.

Compatibility of the Supplied Arguments With the Dummy Arguments

In order for a call to a procedure or to a function to be executed, it is necessary that the supplied arguments be compatible with the dummy arguments. First, the number of supplied arguments must agree with the number of dummy arguments. Second, it must make sense when the supplied arguments replace the dummy arguments. Supplying a list and a table as arguments to the function intpower, for example, makes no sense, because the function intpower expects two simple integer arguments.

Either constants or expressions may be supplied arguments, providing that the corresponding dummy arguments are not declared variable. The same rules apply to both procedures and functions. It is not a good programming practice to assign a value to a dummy argument that is not declared to be variable.

Localization of Variables

Inclusion of the declaration

```
var
  temporary : datatype;
```

in the procedure swap ensures that, if a calling program has a variable named temporary, the value of that variable will not be affected by the execution of swap. Thus the declaration for the variable temporary protects calling programs from suffering undesirable undesirable side effects. Similarly, the declaration

```
var
  value, i : integer;
```

in the function intpower protects its calling programs from side effects, in case one of them should happen to contain a variable named value or a variable named i.

Rules for Writing Functions

Any evidence of a function's behavior besides the return of a function value to the calling program is a side effect and is undesirable. Execution of a function should not change the values of the supplied arguments or any other variables in the calling program.

A function program may contain more than one function value assignment statement, but to make the program more readable each function value assignment should represent an end of the calculation. Once a function value is assigned, it should not be changed on the same function call. Neglecting to assign any function value at all for some combination of values of the supplied arguments is an extremely serious error.

For some values of supplied arguments, the usual computation of a function or procedure is either impossible or makes little sense. If the calling program does not screen the arguments before supplying them, the function program has two choices. If the error is considered severe and unrecoverable, the function program can direct the computer to print an error message and to terminate execution of the calling program. Otherwise, the function program can return a recognizable signal value for the calling program to test.

Testing Procedures and Functions

A procedure or a function cannot be executed without supplied arguments to replace its dummy arguments. Therefore, in order to test a procedure or a function, one writes a "driver" program that provides the procedure or function with supplied arguments. The name "driver" is loosely applied to any calling program.

Programmer-Defined Data Types

A programmer may define a new data type called an *enumerated data type* by listing its constants in a type declaration. An ordering of values is implied by the order of the constants in the declaration. This ordering is used by the relational operators, the built-in functions ord (ordinal), pred (predecessor), and succ (successor), and a for-variable of the enumerated data type. It is possible to declare a subrange of an enumerated data type and to use an enumerated data type for subscripts of an array. The value of an enumerated data type must not be read or written.

Recursion

In Pascal, a procedure or function may call itself. The effect is as though an entirely new copy of the procedure or function is created, including entirely new storage spaces for all local variables, and the new copy of the procedure or function is called by the old copy.

A recursive procedure must have at least one nonrecursive path through the procedure and all recursive calls must be for "simpler" instances of the same procedure in the sense that after a finite number of such recursive calls, a nonrecursive path is always reached.

5

CHARACTER DATA

Many programming applications are concerned with information appearing in the form of written text, rather than as numbers. Such text may represent names, places, responses to a survey, literary works, and so on. Most programming languages have special features for the manipulation of character data.

One such feature, used often in the preceding four chapters, is that a variable or array element may be assigned a value consisting of a single character or a string of characters. This chapter provides a systematic study of character data processing techniques, devoting particular attention to their applications in word processing, text analysis, and cryptography.

5.1 Processing Character Data

In a computer program, a piece of written text is called a *character string*. This emphasizes the fact that the computer treats a character string as a sequence of individual characters, and it does not "understand" the meaning of the text these characters represent. Character strings have been used in this book from the very first section, to retain messages and identifying information that are printed out but not processed in any other way. This section reviews such simple use of character strings and presents some computer programs in which the character strings themselves are the center of interest. There is a discussion of the facility for comparing character strings and the treatment of variable length character string input.

Character String Declarations

A character string variable in a Pascal program is declared to be an array of type character. Thus, a character string variable of length seven is declared as an array of seven characters as in the following example.

```
var
  string7 : packed array [1..7] of char;
```

The only effect of the optional keyword "packed" is to indicate that as many characters as possible should be stored together in the computer's memory. However, in some Pascal systems, operations can be performed on packed arrays of characters that cannot be done with ordinary arrays of characters. Therefore, all strings in this book will be declared as packed arrays of characters. Figure 5.1.1 indicates the difference between a packed array and an ordinary array.

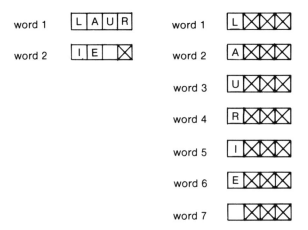

Figure 5.1.1   Packed (left) and Unpacked (right) Storage of the Character String 'Laurie   '.

Character String Constants

As a program might contain numeric constants, such as −4.23, 7, or 0.0031, it also might contain character string constants, such as 'love', 'Good morning.', or 'bG7*5 Ad'. In a program, a character string constant is always enclosed in apostrophes, sometimes referred to as "single quotes". This makes it easy for the computer to tell the difference, for example, between the character string constant 'yesterday' and the variable yesterday, or between the character string constant '14' and the integer constant 14. Even a character string constant that could not possibly be regarded as anything else is enclosed in apostrophes when it appears in a program.

When a character string constant appears in a write or writeln statement, execution of that statement causes printing of the constant itself and not any "meaning" of it. This may be recalled, for instance from the program calc1version2 (calculation 1, version 2) reprinted from Section 1.1. The character string constant '84 + 13 = ' is printed verbatim while the arithmetic expression 84 + 13 is evaluated before printing the result, 97.

```
program calc1version2 (output);
  begin
  writeln ('84 + 13 = ', 84 + 13);
  end.
```

```
run calc1version2
```

```
84 + 13 =          97
```

The point of repeating this example is to reemphasize that enclosing a numeric expression in apostrophes identifies it as character data, so that it is not evaluated as a numeric expression.

Assigning Values to Character Variables

A variable that has been declared to be a character string may be assigned a value that is a character string of *exactly* the declared length. For example, in the program teachadd in Section 2.6, the variable opinion is given a character string value by the execution of one of five assignment statements. Close examination will show that each possible value for the variable opinion is padded at the end with sufficient blanks to make it of length 25, the declared length of the character string opinion.

A two-dimensional array named flag is used by the program printflag in Section 3.5 to print a picture of a Confederate flag. In this case, the value of each entry of the array is either a single blank—that is, the character string ' ', or an asterisk—that is, the character string '*'.

Assigning written text to a variable provides an alternative to executing write statements containing different messages, as shown by the program testsign.

```
program testsign (input, output);

  var
    number : real;
    sign : packed array [1..8] of char;

  begin
  read (number);
  if number > 0 then
    sign := 'positive'
  else if number = 0 then
    sign := 'zero    '
  else
    sign := 'negative';
  writeln (number :1:5, ' is ', sign);
  end.


run testsign

 -2.30000 is negative
```

Length of a Character String

The *length* of a character string is the number of characters in the string. The length of a Pascal character string must be greater than zero. Each blank occurring in the string is counted in its length. The length of a character string that may be assigned to a character variable must be exactly the length declared for that variable. For instance, three different character strings may be assigned as the value of the variable sign in the program testsign. Each of the three has length eight, the declared length of sign.

Input and Output of Character Strings

In standard Pascal, the characters of a character string must be read one at a time. Thus it is common to use a for-loop to read a character string, as shown in the following example.

```
var
  name : packed array [1..namelength];
  i : 1..namelength;
  ...
for i := 1 to namelength do
  read (name [i]);
```

Many Pascal systems have extensions to read whole strings. However, details vary considerably and descriptions of the local extensions should be obtained from the instructor or system manuals.

On the other hand, it is permissible to put the name of a character string in a write or writeln statement to indicate that the entire string is to be printed, as illustrated by the statement

```
writeln (name);
```

Variable Length Input

Even more so than for numeric arrays, words, names, and other character string input data tend to be variable in length. The standard technique for coping with variable length input, a programmer-defined termination signal, may be used with character input. For example, if the input data is a sentence, the period (.) at its end is a suitable termination signal. The procedure readsentence, shown below with a driver program testreadsentence, implements this method of representing variable length input. The terminating period is the last character read into the array, and the rest of the array is filled with blanks.

```
program testreadsentence (input, output);

  const
    maxlength = 40;
    blank = ' ';
    period = '.';

  var
    sentence : packed array [1..maxlength] of char;

  procedure readsentence;

    var
      i : 0..maxlength;
      endofsentence : boolean;
      lengthofsentence : 0..maxlength;
```

```
begin
i := 0;
endofsentence := false;
while (i < maxlength) and (not endofsentence) do
  begin
  i := i + 1;
  read (sentence [i]);
  endofsentence := (sentence [i] = period);
  end; { while }
lengthofsentence := i;
for i := lengthofsentence + 1 to maxlength do
  sentence [i] := blank;
end; { readsentence }

begin { driver program }
readsentence;
write ('Input sentence -->');
write (sentence);
writeln ('<--'); { to show the end of the trailing blanks }
end.
```

```
run testreadsentence

Input sentence -->Variable-length input is common.          <--
```

Using the Functions Eof and Eoln With Test Files

The standard input file input and the standard output file output are also sequences
of characters. As we describe in more detail in Chapter 6, files, unlike arrays, do not
have fixed length. They end when there is no more data in them, a condition called
end-of-file. The built-in function eof has the value true when every character of the file
input has already been read, and the value false whenever unread characters remain in
the file. It may be tested as a termination signal for the file input.

For example, the procedure readtextfile will read all of the characters in the file input (provided there are no more than maxlength characters) into a character string variable named inputfile.

```
procedure readtextfile;

  begin
  i := 0;
  while (i < maxlength) and (not eof (input)) do
    begin
    i := i + 1;
    read (inputfile [i]);
    end; { while }
  end; { readtextfile }
```

A file of characters is also called a *text file*. Pascal automatically supplies the following type and variable declarations for every program.

```
type
  text = file of char;
var
  input, output : text;
```

All other text files must be declared explicitly in a Pascal program.

Quite often, an input file will need several termination signals. For example, a paragraph of input text may be divided into individual lines of input text, each with its own termination signal. The built-in function eof (end-of-file) cannot handle this situation because a file can have only one end-of-file. Text files such as the standard file input support another built-in function eoln (end-of-line), ideally suited to this situation.

Besides the usual printable characters such as letters, numerals, punctuation marks, and printable special characters such as the asterisk and percent sign, the character (char) data type includes some special characters with no printable equivalents. Some of these correspond to special keys on an input/output terminal such as backspace, carriage return, line feed, or carriage return without line feed; on some output terminals, one of them will produce an audible signal (beep or bell) when transmitted for printing.

In each Pascal system, a small group of these characters, usually including carriage return, line feed, and one or more characters with no external equivalents, are designated *end-of-line characters*. The built-in function eoln has the value true when the next character awaiting reading in the file input is an end-of-line character; otherwise, it has the value false.

The built-in procedure read can read an end-of-line character into a character string array. If it is desired to skip over an end-of-line character, the built-in procedure readln is used. Under direction of the procedure readln, after enough characters have been read to satisfy the input list, subsequent characters in the file input are skipped over until the next end-of-line character has been passed over. A subsequent read or readln statement will start with the character after that end-of-line character. Often, the procedure readln is used without an input list to skip over an end-of-line character.

The program readparagraph illustrates two levels of termination signals. The entire paragraph is terminated by the end-of-file, and each line of the paragraph is terminated by an end-of-line character. The procedure readline (or minor modifications of it) will be used many times in this chapter to provide convenient input of variable-length character data.

```
program readparagraph (input, output);

  const
    maxlength = 50;

  type
    stringindex = 1..maxlength;
    stringlength = 0..maxlength;
    string = packed array [stringindex] of char;

  var
    line : string;
```

```
procedure readline (var line : string);

   const
     blank = ' ';

   var
     i : stringlength;

   begin
   i := 0;
   while (i < maxlength) and (not eoln (input)) do
     begin
     i := i + 1;
     read (line [i]);
     end; { while-loop }
   readln (input);
   if i < maxlength then
     for i := i + 1 to maxlength do
       line [i] := blank;
   end; { readline }

 begin
 while not eof (input) do
   begin
   readline (line);
   writeln (line);
   end; { while }
 end.
```

```
run readparagraph
```

```
    The programmer-supplied procedure readline
is a valuable extension to the language Pascal.
It allows the user to type variable-length
character input followed by an end of line
character such as carriage return.  The
procedure readline fills the rest of the fixed
length array line with blanks to facilitate
further character string processing in Pascal.
```

In preparing the input file for the sample run of the program readparagraph, the paragraph was entered exactly as in ordinary typing. The first 5 characters of the input were blank characters to create paragraph indentation, each line was followed by a carriage return, there were no apostrophes or ''single quotes'' surrounding the paragraph or its individual lines, and no line was extended with blanks to make a full 50 characters before the carriage return was pressed.

Many Pascal systems provide a built-in procedure similar or identical to readline as an extension to the standard language. Details vary considerably; inquire of your instructor or computer center.

Comparison of Character Strings

In Pascal the comparison operators

$$< \quad > \quad <= \quad >= \quad = \quad <>$$

may be used to compare two character strings of *exactly the same length*. The ordering of strings is an extension of the ordinary lexicographic (i. e., dictionary) ordering of words. If two strings are both words, and if one word precedes the other in a dictionary, then the string corresponding to the word that appears earlier is "less then" the string that appears later. Thus

'aardvark   ' < 'bananas   ' < 'crepuscular' < 'diaphanous '

Lexicographic order does not take meaning into account. Thus, although for numbers, the relationship

$$1 < 2 < 3 < 4$$

is correct, for strings the relationship

'four ' < 'one ' < 'three' < 'two '

is correct. Worse yet, as character strings,

'11' < '2 '

String ordering is an extension of ordinary lexicographic ordering in several ways. First, strings include nonsense words as well as words with meaningful content. Second, strings need not be single words. Third, strings may include a lot of characters not found in dictionary words, such as the special symbols $, (, and *. There is an American Standard Code for Information Interchange (abbreviated ASCII), which specifies an ordering for characters. The Extended Binary Coded Decimal Interchange Code (EBCDIC) is also used widely, and it too specifies an ordering. The ASCII and EBCDIC orderings do not agree. See Tables 5.1.1 and 5.1.2.

Table 5.1.1   The collating sequence for a selection of printable ASCII characters.

blank ! " # $ % & ' ( ) * + , - . /
0 1 2 3 4 5 6 7 8 9 : ; < = > ? @
A B C D E F G H I J K L M N O P Q R S T U V W X Y Z [\ ] ^ _ `
a b c d e f g h i j k l m n o p q r s t u v w x y z { | } ~

Table 5.1.2   The collating sequence for a selection of printable EBCDIC characters.

blank] . < (+ ! & [$ *) ; ^ - / , % _ > ? : # @ ' = "
a b c d e f g h i j k l m n o p q r s t u v w x y z
A B C D E F G H I J K L M N O P Q R S T U V W X Y Z
0 1 2 3 4 5 6 7 8 9

Two computers that both run Pascal programs will sort some character strings differently if one uses ASCII and the other used EBCDIC. Fortunately, they agree to the extent that all the letters are in alphabetical order and all the numerals are in the correct order. Most of the programs in this book will work correctly using either code.

In Pascal, as in most other programming languages, comparison of a character string to a number is not permitted. Comparing a string, say 'ABC', to the string '123' is acceptable, since the string '123' is different from the number 123. Although permissible, such comparisons should be used with great caution because the result of this comparison may depend upon the collating sequence being used. (See Tables 5.1.1 and 5.1.2 and Exercise 13.)

The Built-In Functions Ord and Chr

It is possible to determine the code being used on any particular computer by executing the following program.

```
program chars (output);
  var
    code : 0..127;
  begin
  for code := 0 to 127 do
    begin
    write (code :6, chr (code) :2);
    if code mod 8 = 7 then
      writeln;
    end; { for-loop }
  end.
```

run chars

0	1	2	3	4	5	6	7
8	9	10					
11	12	13	14	15			
16	17	18	19	20	21	22	23
24	25	26	27	28	29	30	31
32	33 !	34 "	35 #	36 $	37 %	38 &	39 '
40 (	41)	42 *	43 +	44 ,	45 -	46 .	47 /
48 0	49 1	50 2	51 3	52 4	53 5	54 6	55 7
56 8	57 9	58 :	59 ;	60 <	61 =	62 >	63 ?
64 @	65 A	66 B	67 C	68 D	69 E	70 F	71 G
72 H	73 I	74 J	75 K	76 L	77 M	78 N	79 O
80 P	81 Q	82 R	83 S	84 T	85 U	86 V	87 W
88 X	89 Y	90 Z	91 [	92 \	93]	94 ^	95 _
96 '	97 a	98 b	99 c	100 d	101 e	102 f	103 g
104 h	105 i	106 j	107 k	108 l	109 m	110 n	111 o
112 p	113 q	114 r	115 s	116 t	117 u	118 v	119 w
120 x	121 y	122 z	123 {	124		125 }	126 ~	127

The value of the built-in function chr is the character whose code or position in the collating sequence is the integer that is the argument of chr. For example, on a computer that uses the ASCII code, chr (65) = 'A', chr (66) = 'B', etc.

The program chars will take some experimentation to run. You must determine if the computer uses the 128-character ASCII character set (as shown) or the 256-character EBCDIC character set, or some other character set of another size. Also, the output is bound to look peculiar in places, because some characters do not print and some, such as line feed, cause the format of the printed page to change. The sample output shown is typical; it was produced on the VAX 11/750 computer using the ASCII character code. The output device used for computer-controlled typesetting also modified the spacing.

The built-in function ord used previously in Section 4.3 may be used with an argument of type char. It produces an integer that represents the position of that character in the collating sequence of the computer being used. Thus for each character c, the value of chr (ord (c)) = c; for each integer n that represents the ordinal of a character, that is n = 0 to 127 for ASCII or n = 0 to 255 for EBCDIC, ord (chr (n)) = n.

Language Translation

It may be recalled that the procedure seqsearch (sequential search) in Section 3.2 searches an unordered list of integers. The elementary language translation program germantoenglish now uses the string comparison facility to search an unordered list of character strings.

```
program germantoenglish (input, output);
  establish German vocabulary, English vocabulary;
  begin
  while there are still more words do
    begin
    read a German word;
    if the German word is 'halt' then exit from loop;
    look for the German word in the German vocabulary;
    if it is there then
      retrieve the corresponding English word
    else
      respond that the word is not in the German vocabulary;
    end; { while-loop }
  end.
```

The scope of the present translator is only the conversion of the German names of the digits 0, 1, 2, ..., 9 into their correct English equivalents. Supplying the character string 'halt' as input causes the translating process to terminate. If the vocabularies were larger, then the searching method should be somewhat faster than a sequential search, but for the limited case, the following Pascal refinement of the program germantoenglish is adequate.

```
program germantoenglish (input, output);

  const
    wordlength = 6;
  type
    digit = 0..9;
    word = packed array [1..wordlength] of char;
    vocabulary = array [digit] of word;
```

```
var
  germanvocab, englishvocab : vocabulary;
  germanword, englishword : word;
  morewords, wordfound : boolean;
  i : 1..wordlength;
  d : digit;

begin
{ establish vocabularies }
germanvocab [0] := 'null  '; englishvocab [0] := 'zero  ';
germanvocab [1] := 'eins  '; englishvocab [1] := 'one   ';
germanvocab [2] := 'zwei  '; englishvocab [2] := 'two   ';
germanvocab [3] := 'drei  '; englishvocab [3] := 'three ';
germanvocab [4] := 'vier  '; englishvocab [4] := 'four  ';
germanvocab [5] := 'funf  '; englishvocab [5] := 'five  ';
germanvocab [6] := 'sechs '; englishvocab [6] := 'six   ';
germanvocab [7] := 'sieben'; englishvocab [7] := 'seven ';
germanvocab [8] := 'acht  '; englishvocab [8] := 'eight ';
germanvocab [9] := 'neun  '; englishvocab [9] := 'nine  ';

morewords := true;
while morewords do
  begin
  for i := 1 to wordlength do
    read (germanword [i]);
  readln;
  writeln ('Input data  germanword: ', germanword);
  if germanword = 'halt  ' then
    morewords := false
  else
    begin

    { search for German word }
    wordfound := false;
    for d := 0 to 9 do
      if germanword = germanvocab [d] then
        begin
        wordfound := true;
        englishword := englishvocab [d];
        end; { if-statement and for-loop }

    if wordfound then
      writeln ('English equivalent of ', germanword,
          ' is ', englishword)
    else
      writeln ('══ German word not in dictionary ══');

    end; { else }
  end; { while }
end.


run germantoenglish
```

```
Input data   germanword: acht
English equivalent of acht    is eight
Input data   germanword: zehn
=== German word not in dictionary ===
Input data   germanword: null
English equivalent of null    is zero
Input data   germanword: halt
```

The input data for the program germantoenglish must consist of German words for the digits, written one per line. There must be at least six characters on each line, which means that trailing blanks must be written after any words that are shorter than six letters. This awkward and inconvenient form of input is used to emphasize the fundamental one-character-at-a-time nature of character string input in standard Pascal. A more reasonable program would use the procedure readline given earlier in this section to allow the user to enter the German words without trailing blanks.

Exercises

---

1. What is the value of each of the following expressions?

   ```
   chr (ord ('*'))
   chr (ord ('a') + 1)
   ord ('7') - ord ('0')
   ```

2. Write a program entitled namethebabygirl that accepts as input a list of first names and a list of middle names and prints as output a list of all combinations. Thus, if the suitable first names are Barbara, Henrietta, and Elizabeth, and the suitable middle names are Bonnie, Estelle, and Ann, then the possible combinations are Barbara Bonnie, Barbara Estelle, Barbara Ann, Henrietta Bonnie, Henrietta Estelle, Henrietta Ann, Elizabeth Bonnie, Elizabeth Estelle, and Elizabeth Ann.

3. Write a program that accepts as input three letters and prints a output every possible ordering of the three letters.

4. Write a program that sorts four character strings supplied as input.

5. Write a program that tests whether an eight-letter word supplied as input is in a list of passwords and prints "okay" if it is or "try again" if it is not.

6. Write a program that accepts a person's birthday as input and prints as output the name of the person's astrological sign.

7. Write a program that converts a letter on the telephone dial into the corresponding digit. For instance, the letters "A", "B", and "C" should all be converted to the numeral 2. The program should print error messages for letters that are not on the dial.

8. The alphabetical order of the German names for the digits is acht, drei, eins, funf, neun, null, sechs, sieben, vier, zwei. Write a program that accepts the vocabulary of German digit names and their English equivalents in the alphabetic order of the

German names, and uses the more efficient search method of the function program location in Section 4.3 to do language translation. Note that the same function cannot be used because of the requirement for agreement of data type of supplied and dummy arguments.

9. Design a program for a two-way language dictionary that can convert either a German digit name to its equivalent or an English digit name to its German equivalent.

10. Write a program to form a four-word sentence according to the following rules.

    (a) The first word is "The".

    (b) The second word is either "boy" or "dog".

    (c) The third word is either "likes" or "chases".

    (d) The fourth word is either "cats" or "hamburger".

    (e) When there is a choice in the selection of a word, each of the possibilities should be equally likely.

Be sure that there is at least one blank between words and a period at the end of the sentence.

11. Write a program that lists in lexicographic order all eight sentences that can be written by the program for Exercise 10.

12. Mark Twain wrote in "The awful German language" (in *A Tramp Abroad*, Harper & Brothers, New York, 1893) that he heard a California student in Heidelberg say, in one of his calmest moods, that he would rather decline two drinks than one German adjective. Write a program to help this California student by providing the strong declension of a German adjective supplied as input.

13. Compare the two character strings 'ABC' and '123' using the ASCII and the EBCDIC collating sequences given in Tables 5.1.1 and 5.1.2. Which string comes first (i.e., collates low) in ASCII? Which in EBCDIC?

14. Modify the program germantoenglish to use the procedure readline so that the user may enter variable-length input words.

15. Using the program germantoenglish as a model, write a small telephone directory assistance program that, given the name of a friend or acquaintance, will print the telephone number of that friend or acquaintance.

5.2 Word Processing and Text Editing

Since the invention of movable type, people have been concerned with the problem of producing a clean, error-free copy of a manuscript. In typed copy, a small number of typographic errors can be corrected cleanly by erasing, whiting out, or using some new "miracle" technologies for lifting the errant character from the page. The problems begin when a sentence, or sometimes even just a long word, must be inserted in the middle of a paragraph. When the insertion is long enough that the rest of the text must be moved down to make room for it, an entirely new copy of the page or document must be typed, introducing new typographic errors, and the process starts over again. Even with movable type, moving a partial line is a tricky process, involving redistributing the blank characters (spacers), and with linotype slugs (type), each line is one piece of metal, so the rest of the paragraph must be reset.

In recent years, an increasing share of document preparation is being done by computer-assisted methods called *word processing* or *text editing*. Major newspapers and books, including this one, are prepared using computer text editing systems. Small, special-purpose computers supporting text editing programs similar to the ones written in this section (with additional features, of course) are sold for office use as *word processors* or *intelligent typewriters*.

Some students, at installations with interactive terminals, have been using text editors from the very beginning to prepare programs and input files. This section will give such students a glimpse of one way that such a text editor might be written. For students with no previous experience with text editors or word processors, the sample executions will shed some light on how a word processor might be used.

Some Editing Tasks

A text editing program can be broken into a supervisory main program that communicates with the user and individual subroutines, each of which performs one type of editing task. The text editing program editor2 written in this section can maintain a copy of a document and perform the following editing operations:

1. Clear the system of all lines from the previous document.
2. Enter a new line of the document.
3. Delete a line of the document.
4. Replace an existing line of the document with a new line.
5. Print the most recent version of the document, or selected parts of it.
6. Locate and print all lines containing a given word, phrase, or other sequence of characters.
7. Replace all occurrences of a given word, phrase, or string of characters with another substitute word, phrase, or string of characters.
8. Renumber the lines of the document without changing the text itself.
9. Save the most recent version of the document for later use.
10. Recall the most recently saved version of the document.

A sophisticated text editing system performs many additional operations as well, such as inserting extra blanks in order to align the right margin, centering lines to be used as titles or displayed formulas, setting tab stops for tables, lists, and paragraph indentation, and maintaining more than one document at a time. Suggestions are given in the exercises of this section as to how some of these improvements might be implemented. The 10 editing operations listed above are reasonably adequate for many purposes, and illustrate the basic principles of text editing and word processing.

A Program for a Simple Text Editor

As an introduction to the general structure of text editing programs, a very simple text editing program editor is written first. It allows only the operations 1 to 5 and does operations 9 and 10 automatically. In a basic decision about how the text will be stored, we require every line of the document to have a unique line number, with the lines of the document being saved in order of increasing line number. This is the way it is done in many commercially available text editors. Since each line of the document is already an array of characters, the whole document becomes an array of arrays of characters, or more simply, an array of character strings, one for each line.

The following declarations show the basic strategy for storing the document in the computer's memory.

```
const
  maxlength = 50;
  maxlines = 500;

type
  string = packed array [1..maxlength] of char;

var
  linenumber : array [1..maxlines] of integer;
  document : array [1..maxlines] of string;
```

The program editor1 is designed to recall automatically the most recent version of the text, created when the program was used last. Then, requests are processed until the request "Stop" is given. Finally, before terminating, the program editor1 always saves the most recently updated version of the document for later use. The values of variables and lists created in the computer's main memory during the execution of a program usually cannot be expected to remain unchanged in the main memory between runs of a program because space in the computer's main memory usually is too scarce and expensive to reserve for data which is at least temporarily not being used. A text file saveddocument, similar in use to the standard text files input and output, is used to save the most recent version of the document on a less expensive auxiliary storage device such as magnetic disk or tape between runs.

```
program editor1 (input, output, saveddocument);
{ a very simple editor }

  begin
  get most recent version of document from permanent file saveddocument;
  morerequests := true;
  while (morerequests) do
    begin
    write ('Request: ');
    readline (request);
    if request = clearreq then
      begin
      double check that ''clear'' really was intended;
      erase all lines of the text now maintained;
      end { if clear }
    else if request = enterreq then
      enter the new line of text
    else if request = deletereq then
      delete line of text
    else if request = replacereq then
      replace a line of text
    else if request = printreq then
      print the entire document
    else if request = stopreq then
      morerequests := false
```

```
     else
       writeln ('Illegal request');
     end; { while-loop }
  save complete document with line numbers in file saveddocument;
  end.
```

Double Checking Before Clearing

As long as each section of the program maintains the working copy of the document in the proper format, with the line numbers in increasing order and the count of the number of lines correctly computed, the design of the text editor can be completely modular. The main program editor1 has the responsibility for initiating the dialog with the user and finding out which kind of request the user wants performed next. It then turns further processing of that request over to a specialized procedure which continues the dialog and finishes processing the request. Each specialized procedure for processing a request can be written completely independently of the other procedures of the text editor. This assumes, of course, that each one leaves the saved copy of the document in good order. With such modularity, it is very easy first to construct a very simple text editor that executes a limited number of operations, and later to add additional operations on the text by appending additional specialized procedures to a working program.

In creating a new document with our simple editor, the first request issued must be "clear". Accordingly, we refine this section of the program first.

```
procedure cleardocument;

  const
    yes = 'yes                                      ';

  var
    answer : string;

  begin
  writeln ('Are you sure you want to destroy the entire document?');
  writeln ('If so, confirm by answering "yes".');
  readline (answer);
  if answer = yes then
    numberoflines := 0
  else
    writeln ('No action taken.');
  end; { cleardocument }
```

The reason for double checking a "clear" request is that clearing the entire working text is a very serious step, and its accidental use could destroy thousands of lines of text and waste many hours of work entering the text. It is perfectly reasonable to be even more careful than editor1 and allow a "clear" request to be processed only upon presentation of a closely guarded password or authorization code.

Entering a New Line

The refinement of the procedure enternewline is equally easy, with all of the hard work pushed off into the procedures locate and insertline. The procedures are given here after the procedure enternewline in a top-down fashion, although in the finished Pascal program they would appear either before it or within it. In fact, the procedure insertline will be contained within the procedure enternewline because it is used only during an execution of enternewline.

```
procedure enternewline;

  var
    newlinenumber : integer;
    newtext : string;

  begin { enternewline }
  if numberoflines = maxlines then
    writeln ('Request cannot be processed; document is full.')
  else
    begin
    write ('New line number: ');
    readln (newlinenumber);
    locate (newlinenumber);
    if indocument then
      begin
      writeln ('Request not processed;');
      writeln ('Line number ', newlinenumber :1,
            ' is in document already.');
      writeln ('This line reads:');
      writeln (document [location]);
      end { if }
    else
      begin
      write ('Text: ');
      readline (newtext);
      insertline;
      end; { else }
    end; { else }
  end; { enternewline }

procedure locate (number : integer);

  begin
  locate the first line of text with a line
      number equal to or greater than number;
  indicate if there is already a line with this number;
  end; { locate }
```

```
procedure insertline;

  begin
  numberoflines := numberoflines + 1;
  make room for new line by moving all lines
      following it down one location;
  insert new line number and new text into document;
  end; { insertline }
```

The location of the first line of the existing text with a line number equal to or greater than the value of newlinenumber can be determined by a procedure differing but little from the function location in Section 4.3 that searches for an entry in a table. For simplicity, we build the procedure locate using a sequential search algorithm. It is left as an exercise to rewrite the procedure locate to use the more efficient binary search algorithm. Both algorithms require the list of line numbers to be maintained in increasing order. If the linenumber being searched for is greater than all entries of the search list, or otherwise does not appear, then the value of the boolean variable indocument is set to false as a signal.

```
procedure locate (number : integer);

  var
    n : 0..maxlines;
    positionfound : boolean;

  begin
  positionfound := false;
  n := 0;
  while (n < numberoflines) and (not positionfound) do
    begin
    n := n + 1;
    positionfound := (linenumber [n] >= number);
    end; { while-loop }

  if not positionfound then
    begin
    location := numberoflines + 1;
    indocument := false;
    end { if }
  else
    begin
    location := n;
    indocument := (linenumber [n] = number);
    end; { else }
  end; { locate }

procedure insertline;

  var
    n : docindex;
```

```
begin
numberoflines := numberoflines + 1;
{ make room for new line by moving all lines }
{    following it down one location. }
{ this must be done from bottom to top to avoid overwritting }
for n := numberoflines downto location + 1 do
  begin
  linenumber [n] := linenumber [n - 1];
  document [n] := document [n - 1];
  end; { for-loop }
linenumber [location] := newlinenumber;
document [location] := newtext;
end; { insertline }
```

Using a Simple Text Editor

Before proceeding to similar refinements for the steps to delete a line, a sample execution is shown, using mainly the requests "clear" and "enter". Most of the session takes the form of a dialog in which the computer asks a question, and the user types a response followed by a carriage return. The procedure readline of the previous section allows all character string input to be variable in length instead of the full maxlength = 50 characters, a decided convenience when some responses are "yes", "no", or "enter".

Of particular interest in this session are the computer's actions when the user mistakenly attempts to use the line number 60 a second time, and when the user fails to give the only acceptable confirming response, "yes", after making the second request to clear the document.

```
run editor1

Request: clear
Are you sure you want to destroy the entire document?
If so, confirm by answering "yes".
Answer: yes
Request: enter
New line number: 10
Text: Eighty-seven years ago, our
Request: enter
New line number: 20
Text: forefathers brought forth on
Request: enter
New line number: 30
Text: this continent, a new nation,
Request: enter
New line number: 40
Text: founded on democratic principles,
Request: enter
New line number: 50
Text: conceived in liberty, and dedicated
Request: enter
```

```
New line number: 60
Text: to the principle that all men are
Request: enter
New line number: 60
Request not processed;
Line number 60 is in document already.
This line reads:
to the principle that all men are
Request: enter
New line number: 70
Text: equal in the eyes of the law.
Request: clear
Are you sure you want to destroy the entire document?
If so, confirm by answering "yes".
Answer: I guess not
No action taken.
Request: print
        10 Eighty-seven years ago, our
        20 forefathers brought forth on
        30 this continent, a new nation,
        40 founded on democratic principles,
        50 conceived in liberty, and dedicated
        60 to the principle that all men are
        70 equal in the eyes of the law.
Request: stop
```

This sample execution gives some idea of what it is like to use this simple text editor. The most frequent request is usually ''enter'', by a large margin. Thus, better text editors have an ''enter multiple lines'' request that allows the user to specify the first line number of an insertion or addition to the text, and then automatically supplies line numbers for all subsequent lines.

One of the best features of even a simple text editor is the ability to produce a clean, complete, error-free copy of the most recent version of the document at any time. The back of an old envelope cannot do as well. The coding to produce such a printout is straightforward.

```
procedure printdocument;

  var
    n : docindex;

  begin
  if numberoflines = 0 then
    writeln ('Document is empty')
  else
    for n := 1 to numberoflines do
      writeln (linenumber [n] :10, ' ', document [n]);
  end; { printdocument }
```

Deleting a Line

The coding required to delete a line is quite similar to that required to enter a line. The line with the given line number must be located, deleted, and all subsequent lines must be moved up one location in the array document. The procedure locate is used to search for the line of text with line number equal to the line number to be deleted. The value of the boolean variable indocument distinguishes between an exact match and locating the next higher line number.

```
procedure deleteline;

  var
    oldlinenumber : integer;

  procedure removeline;

    var
      n : docindex;

    begin
    numberoflines := numberoflines - 1;
    for n := location to numberoflines do
      begin
      linenumber [n] := linenumber [n + 1];
      document [n] := document [n + 1];
      end; { for-loop }
    currentindex := location;
    end; { removeline }

  begin { deleteline }
  write ('Line number to be deleted: ');
  readln (oldlinenumber);
  locate (oldlinenumber);
  if indocument then
    removeline
  else
    writeln ('There is no line number ', oldlinenumber :1);
  end; { deleteline }
```

The following sample execution of editor1 shows the effect of the requests "delete" and "print" on the version of the document that was saved at the conclusion of the last sample execution shown previously.

```
run editor1

Request: print
         10 Eighty-seven years ago, our
         20 forefathers brought forth on
```

```
            30 this continent, a new nation,
            40 founded on democratic principles,
            50 conceived in liberty, and dedicated
            60 to the principle that all men are
            70 equal in the eyes of the law.
Request: delete
Line number to be deleted: 40
Request: enter
New line number: 70
Request not processed;
Line number 70 is in document already.
This line reads:
equal in the eyes of the law.
Request: delete
Line number to be deleted: 70
Request: enter
New line number: 70
Text: created equal.
Request: print
            10 Eighty-seven years ago, our
            20 forefathers brought forth on
            30 this continent, a new nation,
            50 conceived in liberty, and dedicated
            60 to the principle that all men are
            70 created equal.
Request: stop
```

Saving the Document Between Runs

In the sample execution, the previous version of the document does not have to be reentered. It is automatically saved at the end of each execution and recalled automatically at the start of the next execution of editor1. Saving the document is accomplished by writing it onto a text file saveddocument. The first line in the text file saveddocument will contain the number of lines in the document, and subsequent lines will come in pairs, one line with an integer-valued line number in the document, and the second line with the complete text corresponding to that line number. The procedure savedocument implements this operation.

```
procedure savedocument;

  var
    n : docindex;

  begin
  rewrite (saveddocument);
  writeln (saveddocument, numberoflines :1);
  for n := 1 to numberoflines do
    begin
    writeln (saveddocument, linenumber [n] :1);
    writeln (saveddocument, document [n]);
    end; { for-loop }
  end; { savedocument }
```

The only additional facts one must know about text files other than the standard files input and output is that a read, readln, write, or writeln statement for such a file has a first argument which is the name of the file, followed by the usual list of items for input or output. Thus, the first argument in each writeln statement, the variable saveddocument, is not an item to be written, but the name of the text file into which the remaining items are to be written.

File names are variables in Pascal. Except for the standard text files input and output, they must be declared as shown. The built-in procedure reset positions a text file at its beginning for reading. The procedure rewrite does the same for writing. These procedures are performed automatically for the standard files input and output.

The procedure fetchdocument that restores the internal arrays linenumber and document at the start of each execution to the exact values they contained at the conclusion of the previous execution is equally easy, merely reversing the steps of the procedure savedocument.

```
procedure fetchdocument;

  var
    n : docindex;
    i : stringindex;

  begin
  reset (saveddocument);
  readln (saveddocument, numberoflines);
  for n := 1 to numberoflines do
    begin
    readln (saveddocument, linenumber [n]);
    for i := 1 to maxlength do
      read (saveddocument, document [n] [i]);
    readln (saveddocument);
    end; { for-loop }
  end; { fetchdocument }
```

The subscripts of the array document require some explanation. Recall that the variable document is an array of type string, and that a ''string'' is an array of type character. Thus the first subscript, n, refers to the nth line in the array document, and the second subscript, i, refers to the ith position within that string considered as an array of characters. It is also permissible to write both subscripts within the same set of brackets as document [n, i], which has the same meaning.

Replacing an Existing Line

In the sample execution, the line 70 was replaced by first deleting it and then entering its replacement as a new line using the request ''enter''. This method is wasteful of both the user's and the computer's time. The procedure replaceline simply locates the line to be replaced and substitutes a new line.

```
procedure replaceline;
  var
    oldlinenumber : integer;
    newtext : string;
```

```
begin
write ('Line number to be replaced: ');
readln (oldlinenumber);
locate (oldlinenumber);
if indocument then
  begin
  write ('Replacement text: ');
  readline (newtext);
  document [location] := newtext;
  currentindex := location;
  end { if }

else
  writeln ('There is no line number ', oldlinenumber :1);
end; { replaceline }
```

The next sample execution shows the use of the request "replace".

```
run editor1

Request: replace
Line number to be replaced: 20
Replacement text: fathers brought forth on
Request: print
        10 Eighty-seven years ago, our
        20 fathers brought forth on
        30 this continent, a new nation,
        50 conceived in liberty, and dedicated
        60 to the principle that all men are
        70 created equal.
Request: stop
```

It is clear from this execution that it is a convenience to be able to change a single word in a line instead of having to replace the entire line as is required so far by editor1. This feature, which involves a deeper understanding of the processing of character strings to extract and replace substrings (i.e., parts) of a character string, is included in the better text editor, editor2, described later in this section. First, we collect all of the procedures in one place to give a complete listing of the program editor1. The complete text of the procedures is not repeated.

```
program editor1 (input, output, saveddocument);
{ a very simple text editor }

  const
    maxlength = 50;
    maxlines = 500;
    clearreq   = 'clear                                             ';
    enterreq   = 'enter                                             ';
    deletereq  = 'delete                                            ';
    replacereq = 'replace                                           ';
    printreq   = 'print                                             ';
    stopreq    = 'stop                                              ';
```

```
type
  stringindex = 1..maxlength;
  stringlength = 0..maxlength;
  docindex = 1..maxlines;
  string = packed array [stringindex] of char;

var
  linenumber : array [docindex] of integer;
  document : array [docindex] of string;
  numberoflines : 0..maxlines;
  saveddocument : file of char;
  request : string;
  location : docindex;
  morerequests, indocument : boolean;

procedure fetchdocument;
  ... end; { fetchdocument }

procedure savedocument;
  ... end; { savedocument }

procedure readline (var line : string);
  ... end; { readline }

procedure locate (number : integer);
  ... end; { locate }

procedure cleardocument;
  ... end; { cleardocument }

procedure enternewline;
  ... end; { enternewline }

procedure deleteline;
  ... end; { deleteline }

procedure replaceline;
  ... end; { replaceline }

procedure printdocument;
  ... end; { printdocument }

begin { ----- main program ----- }
fetchdocument;
morerequests := true;
while morerequests do
  begin
  write ('Request: ');
  readline (request);
  if request = clearreq then
    cleardocument
  else if request = enterreq then
    enternewline
```

```
      else if request = deletereq then
         deleteline
      else if request = replacereq then
         replaceline
      else if request = printreq then
         printdocument
      else if request = stopreq then
         morerequests := false
      else
         writeln ('Illegal request');
      end; { while-loop }
   savedocument;
   end. { editor1 }
```

A Slightly Better Text Editor

Text editors grow by adding operations and convenience features. We show how to print a single line and how to locate and change any sequence of words or characters *within a line*. Users of commercial text editors will realize that editor2 still has a long way to go, but it now includes some powerful operations.

The basic structure of editor2 is the same as that of editor1. All changes are accomplished by adding further requests and procedures to handle them. All requests and procedures written for editor1 are retained as part of editor2.

Suppose that a writer has entered the beginning of a playscript and now wants to make a few changes before continuing. The first thing to do is print what is already there.

```
run editor2

Request: print
        100 Scene 1:  A typical soap opera coffee shop.
        110 Time:  Midmorning.
        120
        140       As the scene opens, John and Mary are seated
        150 stage left.  Mary toys nervously with a cup of
        160 coffee.  John stares absently at the ceiling.
        170       Joan enters stage right, sees Mary, and
        180 quickly takes a seat with her back to Mary.
        190       After a few moments, George enters stage
        200 left, looking rather more cheerful than either
        210 John or Mary.
```

Finding and Changing a Word or Phrase

Suppose now that the writer wants to have John toy nervously with the cup of coffee and Mary stare at the ceiling. The request "find" can be of use in this situation. It is designed to find and print the next line of the document (in the order of ascending line number) that contains a given phrase, word, or string of characters. The sample execution below shows how this request can be used in conjunction with the request "change" to make such changes.

```
Request: find
Text to be found: toys nervously
        150 stage left.  Mary toys nervously with a cup of
Request: change
Text to be changed: Mary
Replacement text: John
        150 stage left.  John toys nervously with a cup of
Request: find
Text to be found: John
        160 coffee.  John stares absently at the ceiling.
Request: change
Text to be changed: John
Replacement text: Mary
        160 coffee.  Mary stares absently at the ceiling.
Request: stop
```

The request "find" is used to locate the line containing the phrase "toys nervously" so that replacement can take place selectively. The writer does not want to change "Mary" to "John" everywhere in the playscript, only in the stage directions where she "toys nervously" with a cup of coffee. Once this change is made, the writer guesses that the reverse substitution of "Mary" for "John" is to be made in the next line, line number 160. The "find" request locates this next occurrence and "Mary" is changed to "John" in the next line.

Printing a Single Line

Each time a change is made, the computer prints out the new line using the procedure print1. The procedure can also be executed by typing the request "print1".

```
procedure print1;

  begin
  if numberoflines = 0 then
    writeln (empty)
  else
    writeln (linenumber [currentindex] :10, ' ',
             document [currentindex]);
  end; { print1 }
```

The procedure print1 prints the line designated by the variable currentindex. In editor2, this variable is set to 1 by the improved version of the procedure fetchdocument and is set to the appropriate value by each of the procedures enternewline, deleteline, replaceline, and find.

Substrings

The requests "find" and "replace" operate on character strings in a more detailed way than any previous usage. for the first time, selected parts of a character string are examined and modified, instead of reading, moving, writing, or comparing a character string as a whole.

A *substring* of a character string is any consecutive sequence of characters in the string. For example, 'J', 'ne D', and 'oe' are substrings of the character string 'Jane Doe', but 'J Doe' is not a substring. Every string is regarded as a substring of itself. The following table indicates all the substrings of the character string 'then'.

Length 1:   't'   'h'   'e'   'n'
Length 2:   'th'   'he'   'en'
Length 3:   'the'   'hen'
Length 4:   'then'

In Pascal, neither a character string constant nor a declared character string variable can have length 0. However, the mathematical concept of the *empty character string* of length 0, consisting of no characters at all, is sometimes useful. For example, one way to delete a word or phrase from a document is to replace it with the empty character string.

Since Pascal has no built-in features for reading, writing, moving, or comparing substrings of a character string, all processing of substrings is done character by character using the fact that each individual character in a string can be referenced by using its position in the string as a subscript. Before proceeding to the coding to implement requests of "find" and "change", we develop two utility functions, trimlength and position, that make the processing of substrings easier.

Trim Length of a Character String

It is a nuisance that the length of a character string variable is always the same regardless of its value. A definition of length that is suitable for many applications is the length of the substring that includes all characters up to and including the last nonblank character. For example, although the character string constant 'Yes   ' has length 7, including 4 trailing blank characters, its *trim length,* as we call it, is 3. Similarly, the constant 'No, sir! ' has length 10, but its trim length is 8. Only the 2 final blank characters are omitted from the trim length count. The blank character between the words is counted in the trim length because a nonblank character appears later in the string.

The function trimlength written below nicely complements the procedure readline because the procedure readline adds blanks at the end of the characters read from the input file. Of course, the function trimlength gets fooled if the last characters of a string were supposed to be blanks, but this is a small price to pay for its convenience.

```
function trimlength (s : string) : stringlength;

  const
    blank = ' ';

  var
    position : stringlength;
    letterisblank : boolean;

  begin
  position := maxlength;
  letterisblank := true;
```

```
while (position >= 1) and (letterisblank) do
  if s [position] <> blank then
    letterisblank := false
  else
    position := pred (position);
trimlength := position;
end; { trimlength }
```

Finding the Position of One String in Another

There are numerous reasons for wanting to know if one string is contained as a substring in another. We might want to know if a particular letter is in a word or if a certain word is in a sentence. The function position tells us even more than that; it tells us where to find the first instance of one character string as a substring of another. For example

position ('monkey   ', 'on   ', 1) = 2

because the substring 'on' begins at the second letter of the string 'monkey', and

position ('monkey   ', 'key   ', 1) = 4

because the substring 'key' begins at the fourth letter of 'monkey'. Because character string variables are declared with a fixed length in Pascal, both the text that is the first argument and the substring that is the second argument of position are considered as extending only up to their respective trim lengths. The full string 'on   ' is not found as a substring of 'monkey   ' at all because the 8 trailing blanks of the former are not found in the latter.

The third argument, 1, is the position in 'monkey   ' where the search is to start. For example

position ('banana   ', 'ana   ', 1) = 2

because characters 2 to 4 of 'banana' are 'ana'. Even though characters 4 to 6 of 'banana' are also 'ana', the function position reports the starting position of the leftmost occurrence. If locating the other occurrence of 'ana' in 'banana' is desired, the search may be started in position 3 of 'banana'. Thus

position ('banana   ', 'ana   ', 3) = 4

If the second argument is not a substring of the first argument, rather than calling it an error and halting, a signal value of 0 is used, in agreement with the convention adopted for the function location in Section 4.3. For instance

position ('monkey   ', 'off   ', 1) = 0

A program that calls the function position can test for the signal value zero if desired.

```
type
  stringindex = 1..maxlength;
  stringlength = 0..maxlength;
  string = packed array [stringindex] of char;
```

```
function position (text, substring : string;
                   startsearch : stringindex;)
                 : stringlength;

  var
    firststart, laststart : stringindex;
    lengthtext, lengthsubstring, i : stringlength;
    startposition : stringlength;
    stringfound, match : boolean;

  begin
  lengthtext := trimlength (text);
  lengthsubstring := trimlength (substring);
  if lengthsubstring > lengthtext then
    position := 0
  else
    begin
    laststart := lengthtext - lengthsubstring + 1;
    stringfound := false;
    startposition := startsearch - 1;
    while (startposition < laststart) and (not stringfound) do
      begin
      startposition := startposition + 1;

      { see if substring can be found at startposition }
      match := true;
      i := 0;
      while (i < lengthsubstring) and (match) do
        begin
        i := i + 1;
        match := (substring [i] = text [startposition + i - 1]);
        end; { match }

      stringfound := match;
      end; { while }

    if stringfound then
      position := startposition
    else
      position := 0;
    end; { else }
  end; { position }
```

Locating a Character String in a Document

With the function position doing most of the work, it is easy to implement the request "find".

```
procedure find;
  var
    newindex : docindex;
    textfound : boolean;
    text : string;
```

```
begin
if numberoflines = 0 then
  writeln ('Document is empty')
else
  begin
  write ('Text to be found: ');
  readline (text);
  newindex := (currentindex mod numberoflines) + 1;
  textfound := false;
  while (newindex <> currentindex) and (not textfound) do
    if position (document [newindex], text, 1) > 0 then
      textfound := true
    else
      newindex := newindex mod numberoflines + 1;
  if textfound then
    begin
    currentindex := newindex;
    print1;
    end
  else
    writeln ('Text not in document');
  end; { else }
end; { find }
```

Replacing a Substring

Replacing a substring with a substitute string is easy as long as the substitute has exactly the same length as the substring it replaces. For instance, the lines

```
name := 'John X. Public';
initial := 'Q';
name [6] := initial
```

tell the computer to change the value of the variable name from 'John X. Public' to 'John Q. Public'. If more than one character is to be changed, a loop must be used, as illustrated by the four lines

```
name := 'John Xavier Public';
newmiddle := 'Quincy';
for letter := 1 to 6 do
  name [5 + letter] := newmiddle [letter]
```

that direct the computer to change the value of the variable from 'John Xavier Public' to 'John Quincy Public'.

The complications start when the replacement string is not the same length as the substring it replaces. If the replacement string is longer, then all characters following the substring it replaces must be moved to the right to make room. Also, it is possible that some characters at the end will be lost because there is not room for them. If the replacement string is shorter, all characters following the replaced substring must be moved to the left, and blank characters written to replace the last few characters of the string this movement produces. These steps appear in the procedure change.

```
procedure change (var line : string;
                       text1, text2 : string);

  var
    p, length1, length2 : stringlength;
    i : stringindex;
    newline : string;

  begin
  p := position (line, text1, 1);
  if p > 0 then
    begin
    length1 := trimlength (text1);
    length2 := trimlength (text2);
    for i := 1 to p - 1 do
      newline [i] := line [i];
    for i := 1 to length2 do
      newline [p + i - 1] := text2 [i];
    if length1 <= length2 then
      for i := p + length2 to maxlength do
        newline [i] := line[i + length1 - length2]
    else
      begin
      for i := p + length2 to maxlength - length1 + length2 do
        newline [i] := line [i + length1 - length2]
      for i := maxlength - length1 + length2 + 1 to maxlength do
        newline [i] := blank;
      end; { else }
    end; { if }
  line := newline;
  end; { replace }
```

Some further sample execution may clarify how the new operations of editor2 are used. In this execution, the writer decides to change the name of the character "John" to "Fred" in the playlet, and then to go on with the story. This having been done successfully, the writer slips into old habits when writing the continuation of the playlet and the name "John" is mistakenly typed for the character in the continuation. Fortunately, the text editor comes to the rescue, and the operation "find" helps detect this mistake so it can be corrected.

```
run editor2

Request: find
Text to be found: John
      140       As the scene opens, John and Mary are seated
Request: change
Text to be changed: John
Replacement text: Fred
      140       As the scene opens, Fred and Mary are seated
Request: find
Text to be found: John
      150 stage left.   John toys nervously with a cup of
```

```
Request:  change
Text to be changed: John
Replacement text: Fred
        150 stage left.   Fred toys nervously with a cup of
Request:  find
Text to be found: John
        210 John or Mary.
Request:  change
Text to be changed: John
Replacement text: Fred
        210 Fred or Mary.
Request:  find
Text to be found: John
Text not in document
Request:  enter
New line number: 310
Text: He advances to their table.
Request:  enter
New line number: 320
Text: George:   Feeling better this morning, Mary?
Request:  enter
New line number: 330
Text:        Both John and Mary stare intently into
Request:  enter
New line number: 340
Text: their coffee cups, pointedly ignoring him.
Request:  find
Text to be found: John
        330       Both John and Mary stare intently into
Request:  change
Text to be changed: John
Replacement text: Fred
        330       Both Fred and Mary stare intently into
Request:  find
Text to be found: John
Text not in document
Request:  print
        100 Scene 1:   A typical soap opera coffee shop.
        110 Time:   Midmorning.
        120
        140      As the scene opens, Fred and Mary are seated
        150 stage left.   Fred toys nervously with a cup of
        160 coffee.  Mary stares absently at the ceiling.
        170      Joan enters stage right, sees Mary, and
        180 quickly takes a seat with her back to Mary.
        190      After a few moments, George enters stage
        200 left, looking rather more cheerful than either
        210 Fred or Mary.
        310 He advances to their table.
        320 George:   Feeling better this morning, Mary?
        330      Both Fred and Mary stare intently into
        340 their coffee cups, pointedly ignoring him.
Request:  stop
```

Exercises

---

1. Use the text editing operations available in editor1 to convert the most recent version of the text shown in the sample executions of editor1 into an appropriate portion of the Gettysburg Address.

2. Convert the text in the sample executions of editor1 into the appropriate portion of the Gettysburg Address using the operations available in editor2.

3. If both Exercises 1 and 2 have been done, use the results as the basis of comparison of the ease of use of the two text editors.

4. Modify editor2 to provide for a request to print a selected range of lines.

5. Modify editor2 to provide for a request to change all occurrences of a particular substring in the current line to another given substring.

6. Modify editor2 to provide for a request to change all occurrences of one substring to another substring throughout the entire document.

7. Modify editor2 so that if a line number is typed as a request, it becomes the current line and is printed.

8. Modify editor2 so that a request consisting of a blank line (that is, a carriage return) causes the next line to be printed and to become the current line.

9. Modify editor2 so that any of the print requests can specify that line numbers are not printed. Under what circumstances might this capability be useful?

10. Write a procedure centerline (var text : string) that rearranges the characters of an input string line so that there is at most one more blank character at the right of the string than there is at the left. For simplicity, you may assume that the first character of the string text is not a blank.

11. Using the procedure center of Exercise 10, write the program steps necessary to add a request ''center'' to editor2. The current line should be centered.

12. Adapt the binary search algorithm used in the function location of Section 4.3 to the procedure locate in this section.

13. Write a procedure alignmargins (var : text : string) that spreads out the nonblank characters of the character string text by inserting blanks between the words of text until the first and last characters of the text are nonblank. The numbers of blanks between different pairs of consecutive words should differ by at most one from each other, so that the resulting spacing is as nearly uniform as possible.

14. Modify the procedure alignmargins of Exercise 13 so that if the first characters of the line are '@P', the left margin is not to be aligned. Instead, the first nonblank character following the '@P' should be indented 5 spaces as a paragraph indentation, and blanks inserted evenly so that the last character of the text becomes nonblank.

15. Modify editor2 to allow requests that align the current line, align all lines of the document, and align the portion of the document within a selected range of line numbers. See Exercise 4.

16. Modify editor2 to allow requests to delete a selected range of lines.

17. The sample execution of the program editor2 shows a playlet with the characters Joan and Mary playing principal roles. Using the operation "change", interchange the roles that Joan and Mary play. Hint: See how the procedure swap in Section 4.1 accomplishes an interchange and adapt that technique to this situation.

18. Write a program that lists all substrings of length 3 of the character string supplied as input. No substring should extend beyond the last nonblank character of the input string.

19. Write a program that lists all substrings of all possible lengths of a character string supplied as input. No substring should extend beyond the last nonblank character of the input string.

20. Write a function reverse (s : string) : string that returns a value consisting of a character string that is the reverse of the supplied argument. That is, it contains the characters of the string s in reverse order. All trailing blanks should remain at the right end of the string. For example reverse ('until ') = 'litnu ' for strings of length 7.

21. Write a program border that accepts as input any character string whose length is 20 characters and surrounds it with a rectangle of asterisks. There should be one blank before and one blank after the nonblank characters of the string. A sample execution of the program border might be

    run border

    Input data title: PAYROLL REPORT

    * * * * * * * * * * * * * * * * *
    * PAYROLL REPORT *
    * * * * * * * * * * * * * * * * *

22. Add two operations "copy" and "move" to editor2. "Copy" should insert a second copy of the current line after a specified line number. "Move" should work the same way, except that the original set of lines is deleted after they are copied. Try to use as many previously written procedures as possible.

23. In the "move" operation of Exercise 22, the total number of lines is the same after the operation as it was before. Program the "move" operation so that the minimum number of lines is moved. Hint: Use a temporary string to hold the line being moved.

24. Write a procedure deblank (var s : string) that moves all of the blanks in the string s to the end. After this is done, trimlength (s) will be one less than the position of the first blank in the string.

25. Modify editor2 to accept a request "renumber" that renumbers the lines of the document 10, 20, 30, ...

5.3   Text Analysis

There are numerous reasons for examining text in minute detail, word by word and letter by letter. One of the reasons is to determine the authorship of an historical or literary work. Such quantities as the average length of a word or the frequency of the usage of certain letters can be an important clue. Computers have been useful in studying text from this viewpoint.

Success has been reported distinguishing certain ancient Greek authors by the fraction of time common pronouns are used in the genitive form. Several measures, including distribution of word lengths and distribution of sentence lengths, have given confirming evidence that of the 14 epistles attributed to St. Paul, only 4 have a common author. An unfinished Jane Austin novel, completed in conscious imitation of her style by an anonymous admirer, easily is recognized as having two authors by the frequency of occurrence of certain pairs of words. In the forensic field, attempts have been made to determine authorship of confessions presented in evidence, but denied by the alleged confessor.

Average Word Length

In order to compute the average length of a word of a given text, it is necessary to determine both the total number of letters in the text and the total number of words. The most direct way that comes to mind is used by the program avgwordlength1 (average wordlength, version 1).

```
program avgwordlength1 (input, output);
  begin
  initialize word count and letter count to zero;
  read text;
  start scan at leftmost character of the text;
  while end of text is not yet reached do
    begin
    locate the beginning and end of a word;
    if no more words then exit the loop;
    increase the letter count by the number of letters in the word;
    increase the word count by 1;
    end;
  writeln ('Average word length = ', letter count / word count);
  end.
```

After reading in the text, the computer starts to look for the first word at the extreme left. Blanks, commas, and other nonletters are passed over to find the beginning of a word. Then letters are counted until the first nonletter such as a blank or punctuation signals the end of the word. These steps are repeated for each word in the text. Each time it locates a word, the computer increases the letter count by its length and the word count by one.

Sets

The refinement of avgwordlength1 is so straightforward that we take this opportunity to introduce a new feature. Almost uniquely among major programming languages, Pascal allows the value of a variable to be a *set* or a collection of elements of a fixed *base type*. For example, the variable alphabet is declared to be a set of characters.

```
var
  alphabet : set of char;
```

The specific collection of characters we assign to alphabet turn out to be the set of uppercase and lowercase letters.

```
alphabet := ['a'..'z'] + ['A'..'Z']
```

This gives only a hint of how sets may be defined using brackets to enclose a list of elements, subrange descriptions, and the operation +, meaning set union.

The advantage of set notation in the current application is the *set membership relation* denoted by the keyword "in". The test

```
if text [scanloc] in alphabet then
```

is a shorter and clearer way to test for an alphabetic character than the alternative test

```
if (('a' <= text [scanloc]) and (text [scanloc] <= 'z')) or
   (('A' <= text [scanloc]) and (text [scanloc] <= 'Z')) then
```

Moreover, the set membership version executes extremely rapidly in most implementations of Pascal. The only catch is that to achieve this efficiency, the Pascal standards allow Pascal processors to restrict the size of the base type for a set variable so that a set of type char may not be available on all systems. In that case, the set membership test simply is refined to the longer form for execution.

```
program avgwordlength1 (input, output);
{ computes the average wordlength in a line of text }

  const
    maxlength = 50;

  type
    stringindex = 1..maxlength;
    stringlength = 0..maxlength;
    string = packed array [stringindex] of char;

  var
    text : string;
    scanloc : 0..maxlength;
    wordstart, wordend : stringindex;
    wordcount, lettercount, wordlength : 0..maxint;
    morewords : boolean;
    alphabet : set of char;

  procedure locatebeginning; { of a word }

    var
      beginningfound : boolean;
```

```
begin
beginningfound := false;
while (scanloc < maxlength) and (not beginningfound) do
  begin
  scanloc := scanloc + 1;
  beginningfound := (text [scanloc] in alphabet);
  end; { while }
wordstart := scanloc;
morewords := beginningfound;
end; { locatebeginning }

procedure locateend; { of a word }

  var
    endfound : boolean;

  begin
  endfound := false;
  while (scanloc < maxlength) and (not endfound) do
    begin
    scanloc := scanloc + 1;
    endfound := not (text [scanloc] in alphabet);
    end; { while }
  if endfound then
    wordend := scanloc - 1
  else
    wordend := maxlength;
  end; { locateend }

procedure readline (var line : string);

  const
    blank = ' ';

  var
    i : stringlength;

  begin
  i := 0;
  while (i < maxlength) and (not eoln (input)) do
    begin
    i := i + 1;
    read (line [i]);
    end; { while-loop }

    readln (input);
    if i < maxlength then
      for i := i + 1 to maxlength do
        line [i] := blank;
    end; { readline }
```

```
begin { main program }
alphabet := ['a'..'z'] + ['A'..'Z'];
wordcount := 0;
lettercount := 0;
readline (text);
write ('Input data  text: '):
writeln (text);

scanloc := 0;
morewords := true;
while (scanloc < maxlength) and (morewords) do
  begin
  locatebeginning; { of the next word }
  if morewords then
    begin
    locateend; { of the word }
    wordlength := wordend - wordstart + 1;
    lettercount := lettercount + wordlength;
    wordcount := wordcount + 1;
    end; { if }
  end; { while }
writeln ('Average wordlength = ', lettercount / wordcount :1:3);
end.  { avgwordlength1 }


run avgwordlength1

Input data  text: Never mind the whys and wherefores.
Average wordlength =  4.833


run avgwordlength1

Input data  text: I computed the average word length.
Average wordlength =  4.833
```

The sample execution printouts of the program avgwordlength1 might suggest that to use average word length as a test for authorship, one should have a fairly large sample of text. In any case, average word length is no absolute criterion for deciding authorship. Nor is it an absolute indicator of artistic merit.

Modification for a Large Quantity of Text

If the amount of text is very large, then the computer might not have enough memory to hold it all at one time. Also, in some Pascal systems, there is a maximum length for character strings. For these reasons, it may be desirable to modify the program avgwordlength1 so that it reads the text one line at a time, rather than all at once. The program avgwordlength2 incorporates such a modification. Most of the main pro-

gram avgwordlength1 is split into two procedures, initialize and scanoneline. Scanning
stops when a signal line of three asterisks is read.

```
program avgwordlength2 (input, output);
{ computes the average wordlength of many lines of text }

  const
    maxlength = 50;

  type
    stringindex = 1..maxlength;
    stringlength = 0..maxlength;
    string = packed array [stringindex] of char;

  var
    text, signal : string;
    scanloc : 0..maxlength;
    wordstart, wordend : stringindex;
    wordcount, lettercount, wordlength : 0..maxint;
    morewords, outofdata : boolean;
    alphabet : set of char;

procedure initialize;

  const
    blank = ' ';

  var
    i : stringindex;

  begin
  alphabet := ['a'..'z'] + ['A'..'Z'];
  wordcount := 0;
  lettercount := 0;
  for i := 1 to 3 do
    signal [i] := '*';
  for i := 4 to maxlength do
    signal [i] := blank;
  outofdata := false;
  end; { initialize }

procedure locatebeginning; { of a word }

  var
    beginningfound : boolean;

  begin
  beginningfound := false;
  while (scanloc < maxlength) and (not beginningfound) do
```

```
      begin
      scanloc : = scanloc + 1;
      beginningfound : = (text [scanloc] in alphabet);
      end; { while }
    wordstart : = scanloc;
    morewords : = beginningfound;
    end; { locatebeginning }

procedure locateend; { of a word }

    var
      endfound : boolean;

    begin
    endfound : = false;
    while (scanloc < maxlength) and (not endfound) do
      begin
      scanloc : = scanloc + 1;
      endfound : = not (text [scanloc] in alphabet);
      end; { while }
    if endfound then
      wordend : = scanloc - 1
    else
      wordend : = maxlength;
    end; { locateend }

procedure readline (var line : string);

    const
      blank = ' ';

    var
      i : stringlength;

    begin
    i : = 0;
    while (i < maxlength) and (not eoln (input)) do
      begin
      i : = i + 1;
      read (line [i]);
      end; { while-loop }
    readln (input);
    if i < maxlength then
      for i : = i + 1 to maxlength do
        line [i] : = blank;
    end; { readline }

procedure scanoneline;

    begin
    scanloc : = 0;
```

```
      morewords : = true;
      while (scanloc < maxlength) and (morewords) do
        begin
        locatebeginning; { of the next word }
        if morewords then
          begin
          locateend; { of the word }
          wordlength : = wordend - wordstart + 1;
          lettercount : = lettercount + wordlength;
          wordcount : = wordcount + 1;
          end; { if }
        end; { while }
      end; { scanoneline }

  begin { main program }
  initialize;
  while not outofdata do
    begin
    readline (text);
    write ('Input data  text: ');
    writeln (text);
    if text = signal then
      outofdata : = true
    else
      scanoneline;
    end; { while }

  writeln ('Average wordlength = ', lettercount / wordcount :1:3);
  end.  { avgwordlength1 }


run avgwordlength2

Input data   text: One of the important uses
Input data   text: of the character manipulation
Input data   text: capability of computers is
Input data   text: in the analysis of text.
Input data   text: ***
Average wordlength =  4.944
```

Frequency of Occurrence of Letters

There are two basic ways to count the number of occurrences of each letter of the alphabet in a given text. Both ways use 27 counters, one for each letter of the alphabet and one to count all the other characters. A function uppercase (letter : char) : char is used to convert all the lowercase letters in a text into the corresponding capital letters.

One way to tabulate letter frequencies in a line of text is first to scan it for all occurrences of the letter "A", then to scan it for all occurrences of the letter "B", and so on through the alphabet. This requires 26 scans of the whole line. This method is embodied in the program lettercount1.

```
program lettercount1 (input, output);
  begin
  initialize;
  while more text do
    begin
    read line of text;
    if line = '***' then exit from loop;
    for letter := 'A' to 'Z' do
      scan line of text, counting occurrences of that letter;
    calculate the number of nonletters and increment nonletter total;
    repeat for the next line;
    end;
  print the counts;
  end.
```

The second way to count letter frequencies in a line of text is to begin with the first symbol of the text, to decide which of the 27 counters to increment, to continue with the second letter of the line of text, to see which counter to increment this time, and so on through the text. This second way is implemented by the program lettercount2.

```
program lettercount2 (input, output);
  begin
  initialize;
  while more text do
    begin
    read a line of text;
    if line = '***' then exit the loop;
    for each character in the line do
      if the character is a letter
     increment the appropriate letter count
      else
     increment the nonletter count;
    repeat for next line of text;
    end;
  print the counts;
  end.
```

By the method of the program lettercount1, the text must be scanned completely once for each letter of the alphabet. By the method of the program lettercount2, the text is scanned just once. Thus the second program executes considerably faster than the first one and so only the program lettercount2 is refined.

For-Variables and Subscripts of Type Character

The data type character has a natural order induced by the collating sequence (ASCII, EBCDIC, etc.) in effect for the Pascal system. We have used this ordering in previous sections to compare, search, and sort character strings. Now, for the first time, in the program lettercount2, we exploit the ordering of the character data type to define subscripts and for-variables of type character. The 27 counters in this program are named count ['A'], count ['B'], ..., count ['Z'], and count ['@'] for all other characters. Taking advantage of the fact that in the ASCII collating sequence, '@' is the predecessor of 'A', we initialize all counts to zero with the for-loop

```
for i := '@' to 'Z' do
  count [i] := 0;
```

A similar loop is used to print the final total letter frequencies.

```
for i := 'A' to 'Z' do
  writeln (i :10, count [i] :10);
```

Any data type for which the built-in functions succ (successor) and pred (predecessor) are defined may be used in this way for subscripts and for-variables. In particular, one may use the following types: integer, subrange of integer, character, subrange of character, boolean, and enumerated data. Type real must not be used for subscripts.

```
program lettercount2 (input, output);

  const
    maxlength = 50;
    blank = ' ';
    other = '@'; { '@' = pred ('A') in ASCII }

  type
    stringindex = 1..maxlength;
    stringlength = 0..maxlength;
    string = packed array [stringindex] of char;
    letterorother = other..'Z';

  var
    line, signal : string;
    count : array [letterorother] of 0..maxint;
    outofdata : boolean;
    i : stringindex;

  procedure initialize;

    var
      i : letterorother;
      j : stringindex;

    begin
    for i := '@' to 'Z' do
      count [i] := 0;
    for j := 1 to 3 do
      signal [j] := '*';
    for j := 4 to maxlength do
      signal [j] := blank;
    outofdata := false;
    end; { initialize }
```

```
procedure readline (var line : string);
   ... end; { readline }

function trimlength (s : string) : stringlength;
   ... end; { trimlength }

function uppercase (letter : char) : char;

   var
     uppercaseshift : integer;

   begin
   uppercaseshift := ord ('A') - ord ('a');
   uppercase := chr (ord (letter) + uppercaseshift);
   end; { uppercase }

procedure docounting;

   var
     i : stringindex;
     c : char;
     index : letterorother;

   begin
   for i := 1 to trimlength (line) do
     begin
     c := line [i];
     { decide which counter to increment }
     if c in ['A'..'Z'] then
       index := c
     else if c in ['a'..'z'] then
       index := uppercase (c)
     else
       index := other;
     count [index] := count [index] + 1;
     end; { for-loop }
   end; { docounting }

procedure printcounts;

   var
     i : letterorother;

   begin
   writeln;
   writeln ('Letter' :10, 'Frequency' :10);
   for i := 'A' to 'Z' do
     writeln (i :10, count [i] :10);
   writeln ('other' :10, count [other] :10);
   end; { printcounts }

begin { main program }
initialize;
```

```
while not outofdata do
  begin
  readline (line);
  write ('Input data  line: ');
  for i := 1 to trimlength (line) do
    write (line [i]);
  writeln;
  if line = signal then
    outofdata := true
  else
    docounting;
  end; { while-loop }
printcounts;
end.
```

```
run lettercount2
```

Input data line: ONE OF THE IMPORTANT TEXT ANALYSIS
Input data line: TECHNIQUES (TO DETERMINE AUTHORSHIP)
Input data line: IS TO MAKE A FREQUENCY COUNT OF LETTERS
Input data line: IN THE TEXT.
Input data line: ***

Letter	Frequency
A	6
B	0
C	3
D	1
E	15
F	3
G	0
H	5
I	7
J	0
K	1
L	2
M	3
N	8
O	8
P	2
Q	2
R	5
S	6
T	16
U	4
V	0
W	0
X	2
Y	2
Z	0
other	20

Palindromes

Another aspect of text analysis is searching for patterns. Perhaps the text repeats itself every so often, or perhaps the lengths of the words form an interesting sequence of numbers. One pattern for which we search here is called a *palindrome,* which means that the text reads the same from right to left as from left to right. The word "radar" is a palindrome, for example. Liberal palindromers customarily relax the rules so that punctuation, spacing, and capitalization are ignored. To liberal palindromers, the names "Eve", "Hannah", and "Otto" are all palindromes, as is the sentence

"Able was I ere I saw Elba."

something Napoleon might have said, except that he preferred speaking French.

The program palindrome satisfies the most conservative palindromers. As the two sample runs show, it accepts the string

"NAT SAW I WAS TAN"

as a palindrome, but it rejects the string

"MADAM I'M ADAM"

One of the exercises involves writing a procedure that excises from a string everything but the letters and another exercise deals with writing a program using this procedure that applies a more liberal palindrome test.

```pascal
program palindrome (input, output);

  const
    maxlength = 50;
    blank = ' ';

  type
    stringindex = 1..maxlength;
    stringlength = 0..maxlength;
    string = packed array [stringindex] of char;

  var
    text : string;
    i, j : stringindex;
    mismatch : boolean;

  procedure readline (var line : string);
    ... end; { readline }

  function trimlength (s : string) : stringlength;
    ... end; { trimlength }

  procedure writeout (c : char);
    begin
    if c = blank then
      writeln ('blank')
    else
      writeln (c);
    end; { writeout }
```

```
begin
readline (text);
write ('Input data  text: ');
for i := 1 to trimlength (text) do
  write (text [i]);
writeln;

i := 1;
j := trimlength (text);
mismatch := false;
while (i < j) and (not mismatch) do
  if text [i] <> text [j] then
    mismatch := true
  else
    begin
    i := i + 1;
    j := j - 1;
    end; { else }

if not mismatch then
  writeln ('Palindrome')
else
  begin
  writeln ('Not a palindrome');
  write ('Character ', i :1, ' from the left is ');
  writeout (text [i]);
  write ('Character ', i :1, ' from the right is ');
  writeout (text [j]);
  end; { else }
end.
```

```
run palindrome

Input data  text: NAT SAW I WAS TAN
Palindrome
```

```
run palindrome

Input data  text: MADAM I'M ADAM
Not a palindrome
Character 5 from the left is M
Character 5 from the right is blank
```

Readings

A. Q. Morton, Literary Detection: *How to Prove Authorship and Fraud in Literature and Documents,* Charles Scribner's Sons, 1979. (Reviewed in *Scientific American,* Vol. 241, No. 5, Nov. 1979, p. 39.)

Exercises

1. Modify the program lettercount2 so that it prints only the tallies for letters that occur in the text.

2. Write a procedure that excises everything from a string supplied as input except the letters.

3. Write a procedure that converts every lowercase letter in a string supplied as input into the corresponding capital letter. Hint: use the function uppercase.

4. Use the procedures for Exercises 2 and 3 to create a more liberal test for palindromes than the program palindrome.

5. Write a program that determines the percentage of the letters in a text that are vowels.

6. Using the methods of this section, analyze all the plays of William Shakespeare to determine if they were all written by one person. Was that person Sir Francis Bacon?

7. Write a program that determines the proportion of words in a text supplied as input that end with the substring ''ing''.

8. Write a program ppick to count the number of words in a sentence starting with the letter ''p'' (either capital or lowercase). Test it on the following sentence: ''In his popular paperback, *Party Pastimes People Prefer,* prominent polo player Paul Perkins presents pleasing palindromes.''

9. Write a program alliteration that determines which letter of the alphabet starts the most words in a sentence and then counts the maximum number of consecutive words starting with that letter.

10. Write a program that counts the maximum number of consecutive words in a sentence starting with the same letter.

11. Write a program that counts the number of double letters in a string. For example, ''aa'' is a double letter.

12. Write a program that counts the number of double characters in a string. for example, ''**'' and ''zz'' are double characters.

13. Write a program that determines the proportion of a text that does not consist of letters.

14. Write a program to examine a text and determine the ratio of the number of letters from the first half of the alphabet to the number of letters from the second half of the alphabet.

15. Write a program that counts the number of two-letter prepositions in a given text.

16. A two-letter string is called a *digraph*. Write a program that makes a digraph frequency count. That is, it should determine the number of occurrences of each consecutive letter pair. The following table gives the digraph frequency count for the text ''HOW NOW, BROWN COW?''. Ignore all characters but letters.

BR	1
CO	1
HO	1
NC	1
NO	1
OW	4
RO	1
WB	1
WN	1

17. Write a program that determines the frequency of each word of a given text supplied as input.

18. Find the order of frequency of occurrence of the letters of the alphabet in English text. (Suggestion: Go to the library for such information.) Compare the published letter frequencies with a run of lettercount2 using a typical page from a work of fiction or a 1500-word article from a newspaper or magazine.

5.4   Cryptography

The encoding and decoding of messages is called *cryptography*. The character data processing capability of computers makes them well suited to such tasks. There is a lot more to cryptography than secrecy but, for simplicity, the present examples pertain to elementary secrecy codes.

Substitution Encoding

One method for encoding messages begins with the designation of a substitute letter for each letter of the alphabet. Then every time a letter occurs in the message to be encoded, it is replaced by its substitute. The encoded message is called a *cryptogram*. To avoid ambiguity, no letter is permitted to substitute for more than one other letter. It is usually understood in puzzle cryptograms that no letter can substitute for itself, but this restriction is unimportant. Table 5.4.1 shows the substitution code used in our illustrations.

Table 5.4.1   A substitution table.

| letter | A B C D E F G H I J K L M N O P Q R S T U V W X Y Z |
| substitute | T F H X Q J E M U P I D C K V B A O L R Z W G N S Y |

Suppose the message "THE ENEMY IS RETREATING IN DISARRAY" is to be encoded according to Table 5.4.1. To do this encoding by hand, first write the message on a piece of paper. Below each "A" in the message, write the letter "T". Below each "B" write the letter "F". Below each "C" write an "H". And so on. In general, below each letter of the message, write whatever letter appears in the substitution table immediately below the message letter. The result of this procedure for the message of interest here is the following.

Original message   THE ENEMY IS RETREATING IN DISARRAY
Encoded message   RMQ QKQCS UL OQROQTRUKE UK XULTOOTS

If a message is known to be encoded according to Table 5.4.1, then it may be decoded by inverting the encoding procedure. First write the encoded message on a piece of paper. Below each "T" of the encoded message, write the letter "A". Below each "F" write the letter "B". Below each "H" write a "C". And so on. In general, below each letter of the encoded message, write whatever letter appears in the substitution table immediately above the encoded letter. The following is an example.

Encoded message   RMQ FUORMXTS BTORS JVO PVLMZT UL T LZOBOULQ
Decoded message   THE BIRTHDAY PARTY FOR JOSHUA IS A SURPRISE

A Program to Encode by Substitution

The program encodesub (encode by substitution) tells how to encode a message by the substitution method just described. First the computer reads the code alphabet, corresponding to the second line of the substitution table. Then it reads the message to be encoded. Next it encodes the message. Finally, it prints the result.

```
program encodesub (input, output);

  const
    maxlength = 50;

  type
    stringindex = 1..maxlength;
    stringlength = 0..maxlength;
    string = packed array [stringindex] of char;
    letter = 'A'..'Z';

  var
    message : string;
    code : packed array [letter] of letter;
    i : stringindex;
    ltr : letter;

  procedure readline (var line : string);
    ... end; { readline }

  begin
  write ('Alphabet:           ');
  for ltr := 'A' to 'Z' do
    write (ltr);
  writeln;
  for ltr := 'A' to 'Z' do
    read (code [ltr]);
  readln;
  write ('Input data  code: ');
  for ltr := 'A' to 'Z' do
    write (code [ltr]);
```

```
writeln;
readline (message);
write ('Input data  message: ');
for i := 1 to maxlength do
  write (message [i]);
writeln;

{ replace each letter of the message by
      the corresponding code letter }
for i := 1 to maxlength do
  if message [i] in ['A'..'Z'] then
    begin
    ltr := message [i];
    message [i] := code [ltr];
    end; { if }

writeln ('Encoded message:      ', message);
end.
```

```
run encodesub
```

```
Alphabet:           ABCDEFGHIJKLMNOPQRSTUVWXYZ
Input data   code: TFHXQJEMUPIDCKVBAOLRZWGNSY
Input data   message: THE ENEMY IS RETREATING IN DISARRAY.
Encoded message:      RMQ QKQCS UL OQROQTRUKE UK XULTOOTS.
```

The program encodesub uses the string named "code" to store the corresponding code letter for each letter of the alphabet. Character one of the message to be encoded in the sample run above is the letter "T". Thus on the first iteration of the main loop, the value of the variable ltr is 'T'. The value of code ['T'] is 'R', so the first letter of the message is changed from "T" to "R". Character two of the message is the letter "H" and the value of code ['H'] is 'M', so the second letter of the message is changed from "H" to "M". The loop continues through the rest of the message. Using input data for which the correct output has already been calculated is a good way to test a program.

A Program to Decode by Substitution

The program decodesub (decode by substitution) tells how to decode a message previously encoded by the substitution method. Its structure is much like that of the encoding program; however, it uses another string called "decode" instead of the variable code to determine which characters are to be substituted. The characters in the string decode are related to those in the string code by

decode [code [ltr]] = ltr

for each letter of the alphabet.

```
program decodesub (input, output);

  const
    maxlength = 50;

  type
    stringindex = 1..maxlength;
    stringlength = 0..maxlength;
    string = packed array [stringindex] of char;
    letter = 'A'..'Z';

  var
    message : string;
    code, decode : packed array [letter] of letter;
    i : stringindex;
    ltr : letter;

procedure readline (var line : string);
  ... end; { readline }

begin
write ('Alphabet:           ');
for ltr := 'A' to 'Z' do
  write (ltr);
writeln;
for ltr := 'A' to 'Z' do
  read (code [ltr]);
readln;
write ('Input data  code: ');
for ltr := 'A' to 'Z' do
  write (code [ltr]);
writeln;

{ set up decoding string }
for ltr := 'A' to 'Z' do
  decode [code [ltr]] := ltr;
readline (message);
write ('Input data  message: ');
for i := 1 to maxlength do
  write (message [i]);
writeln;

{ replace each letter of the message by
      the corresponding decode letter }
for i := 1 to maxlength do
  if message [i] in ['A'..'Z'] then
    begin
    ltr := message [i];
    message [i] := decode [ltr];
    end; { if }
```

```
    writeln ('Decoded message:        ', message);
    end.
```

```
run decodesub
```

```
Alphabet:            ABCDEFGHIJKLMNOPQRSTUVWXYZ
Input data   code:  TFHXQJEMUPIDCKVBAOLRZWGNSY
Input data   message:  RMQ FUORMXTS BTORS JVO PVLMZT UL T LZOBOULQ
Decoded message:       THE BIRTHDAY PARTY FOR JOSHUA IS A SURPRISE
```

A Combined Program for Encoding or Decoding

The programs encodesub and decodesub have differences in their comments and other details, but there is only one difference that really matters. Whereas the encoding program uses the string code to find the character to substitute for the one in the message, the decoding program uses the string decode. Thus it easy to write a program that does either encoding or decoding by simply selecting one of the two strings. In the program encodeordecode, this is done by reading a request for encoding or decoding and selecting the proper string with a case-statement.

```
program encodeordecode (input, output);

  const
    maxlength = 50;
    encoderequest =
        'ENCODE                                        ';
    decoderequest =
        'DECODE                                        ';

  type
    stringindex = 1..maxlength;
    stringlength = 0..maxlength;
    string = packed array [stringindex] of char;
    letter = 'A'..'Z';

  var
    message, request : string;
    code, decode : packed array [letter] of letter;
    i : stringindex;
    ltr : letter;

  procedure readline (var line : string);
    ... end; { readline }

  begin
  write ('Alphabet:          ');
  for ltr := 'A' to 'Z' do
    write (ltr);
  writeln;
```

```
for ltr := 'A' to 'Z' do
  read (code [ltr]);
readln;
write ('Input data  code: ');
for ltr := 'A' to 'Z' do
  write (code [ltr]);
writeln;

{ set up decoding string }
for ltr := 'A' to 'Z' do
  decode [code [ltr]] := ltr;
readline (request);
write ('Input data  request: ');
for i := 1 to maxlength do
  write (request [i]);
writeln;
if (request <> encoderequest) and
   (request <> decoderequest) then
  writeln ('Request must be "ENCODE" or "DECODE"')
else
  begin
  readline (message);
  write ('Input data  message: ');
  for i := 1 to maxlength do
    write (message [i]);
  writeln;

  { replace each letter of the message by
      the corresponding encode or decode letter }
  for i := 1 to maxlength do
    if message [i] in ['A'..'Z'] then
      begin
      ltr := message [i];
      case request [1] of
        'E' : message [i] := code [ltr];
        'D' : message [i] := decode [ltr];
        end; { case }
    end; { if }
  end; { else }

writeln ('Rewritten message:    ', message);
end.
```

```
run encodeordecode

Alphabet:            ABCDEFGHIJKLMNOPQRSTUVWXYZ
Input data  code:    TFHXQJEMUPIDCKVBAOLRZWGNSY
Input data  request: DECODE
Input data  message: RMQ FDZQ FVTR LTUDL TR LZKLQR
Rewritten message:    THE BLUE BOAT SAILS AT SUNSET
```

Puzzle Solving

Many newspapers have a daily cryptogram, because cryptograms make amusing puzzles. Of course, the newspaper does not print the substitution table. The point of the puzzle is for the reader to work out the substitution table by trial and error, using a knowledge of English text.

For example, a one-letter word must be either "A" or "I". A three-letter word is likely to be "THE", particularly if it begins a sentence. And one letter of any two-letter word must be a vowel.

The frequency of the letters in the code message can be an important clue, because some letters like "E" and "R" occur for more often in English text than other letters like "Z" and "Q". Moreover, certain other pairs such as "CH" and "GR" are more likely than certain other pairs such as "BH" and "GW". Consequently, knowing one letter helps to determine the letters next to it.

There are 26 x 25 x 24 x ... x 3 x 2 = 4.0e26 different possible substitution tables. Slightly more than a third of these replace every letter by some letter other than itself. Despite this large number of possibilities, the clues mentioned above and the use of context makes substitution cryptograms sufficiently easy to solve that they are not often employed to encode confidential information. Text analysis programs of the sort discussed in the previous section can be quite helpful to the amateur cryptanalyst in "breaking" substitution codes.

Increment Coding

A particularly simple kind of substitution encoding is called *incrementing*. Table 5.4.2 gives an example of an increment substitution table.

Table 5.4.2   A substitution table with increment 18.

letter	A B C D E F G H I J K L M N O P Q R S T U V W X Y Z
substitute	S T U V W X Y Z A B C D E F G H I J K L M N O P Q R

An arbitrary substitute is selected for the letter "A". Then the substitute for the letter "B" is the letter of the alphabet that follows the substitute for "A". Thus, in Table 5.4.2, the letter "T" is the substitute for "B". The substitute for the letter "C" is the letter of the alphabet that follows the substitute for "C". When it becomes necessary to do so, we regard the alphabet as a cycle and take "A" for the letter that follows "Z".

The letter "A" is first in the alphabet. Its substitute "S" is nineteenth. Thus, in a sense, the letter "A" is pushed forward 18 letters. The letter "B" is second in the alphabet, and its substitute "T" is twentieth. Thus the letter "B" is also pushed forward 18 letters. Indeed, every letter of the alphabet is pushed forward 18 by the encoding process, provided we regard the alphabet as a cycle. The number 18 is called the *increment* for the substitution code in Table 5.4.2.

To encode or decode messages by Table 5.4.2, one does not even need a copy of the table, only the increment 18. For example, to encode the letter "G", we first observe that it is seventh in the alphabet. Since 7 + 18 = 25, the substitute for "G" is "Y", the twenty-fifth letter of the alphabet. To encode the letter "N", we observe that it is fourteenth in the alphabet. Since 14 + 18 = 32, the substitute for "N" is the thirty-second letter of the alphabet. If the alphabet is regarded as a cycle, the identity of this mysterious thirty-second letter is obtained by subtracting 26, the number of letters in the alphabet, from 32. Since $32 - 26 = 6$, the substitute for "N" is "F", the sixth letter. In general, the location in the alphabet of the substitute for a letter is obtained by adding the increment to the location of the letter and subtracting 26 if necessary.

To decode a code letter, subtract the increment and, if the result is not positive, add 26. For instance, let us decode the letter "X" and "J". The letter "X" is twenty-fourth. Since $24 - 18 = 6$, it must be the substitute for "F", the sixth letter of the alphabet. The letter "J" is tenth. Since $10 - 18 = -8$, we must add 26 to obtain $-8 + 26 = 18$. Thus, "J" is the substitute for "R", the eighteenth letter of the alphabet.

An increment substitution cryptogram is very easy to solve, because as soon as one letter is guessed correctly the entire message can be decoded immediately. At most 25 guesses are needed. However, a modification of the increment substitution encoding method produces messages that are for more difficult to unravel than a substitution cryptogram.

Table 5.4.3 Encoding a message with the keyword "RAVEN"

messsage		keyword		encoded message	
D	4	R	18	V	22
O	15	A	1	P	16
I	9	V	22	E	5
T	20	E	5	Y	25
R	18	N	14	F	6
I	9	R	18	A	1
G	7	A	1	H	8
H	8	V	22	D	4
T	20	E	5	Y	25
T	20	N	14	H	8
H	8	R	18	Z	26
E	5	A	1	F	6
F	6	V	22	B	2
I	9	E	5	N	14
R	18	N	14	F	6
S	19	R	18	K	11
T	20	A	1	U	21
T	20	V	22	P	16
I	9	E	5	N	14
M	13	N	14	A	1
E	5	R	18	W	23

Keyword Encoding

Keyword encoding begins with the choice of a *keyword,* whose letter are used to provide increments. For example, suppose "RAVEN" is selected as the keyword.

Since "R" is eighteenth in the alphabet, it corresponds to increment 18. Observing that "A" is first, "V" is twenty-second, "E" is fifth, and "N" is fourteenth, we interpret the keyword "RAVEN" as a list

18, 1, 22, 5, 14

of five increments.

To encode a message with the keyword "RAVEN", we increment the first letter by 18, the second letter by 1, the third letter by 22, the fourth letter by 5, and the fifth letter by 14. Having reached the end of the keyword, we go back to the beginning and increment the sixth message letter by 18, the seventh by 1, the eighth by 22, the ninth by 5, and the tenth by 14. Having reached the end of the keyword again, we return again to the beginning. Table 5.4.3 shows the encoding of the message "DO IT RIGHT THE FIRST TIME" using the keyword "RAVEN".

In some rows of Table 5.4.3, the number for a letter of the encoded message is the sum of the two numbers to the left of it in the same row. In other rows, the number for a letter of the encoded message is 26 less than the sum of the two numbers to the left of it.

A program that encodes messages using a keyword must first determine the increment for each letter of the keyword and then keep track of which increment is to be used to encode each letter of the message. This is the idea behind the program keywordencoding.

```
program keywordencoding (input, output);

  const
    maxlength = 50;

  type
    stringindex = 1..maxlength;
    stringlength = 0..maxlength;
    string = packed array [stringindex] of char;

  var
    message, keyword : string;
    keylength, msglength, i : stringlength;
    c : stringindex;
    increment : array [stringindex] of 0..25;
    nextord : 0..256;

  procedure readline (var line : string);
    ... end; { readline }


  function trimlength (s : string) : stringlength;
    ... end; { trimlength }

  begin
  readline (keyword);
  keylength := trimlength (keyword);
  write ('Input data keyword: ');
  for c := 1 to keylength do
```

```
      write (keyword [c]);
   writeln;

   { convert keyword to increments }
   for c := 1 to keylength do
      increment [c] := ord (keyword [c]) - ord ('A') + 1;

   readline (message);
   write ('Input data  message: ');
   msglength := trimlength (message);
   for c := 1 to msglength do
      write (message [c]);
   writeln;
   { encode message }
   i := 0;
   for c := 1 to msglength do
      if message [c] in ['A'..'Z'] then
        { all nonletters remain unchanged }
        begin
        { obtain next increment }
        i := (i mod keylength) + 1;
        { find replacement letter }
        nextord := ord (message [c]) + increment [i];
        if nextord > ord ('Z') then
           nextord := nextord - 26;
        message [c] := chr (nextord);
        end; { if }

  write ('Encoded message:      ');
  for c := 1 to msglength do
     write (message [c]);
  writeln;
  end.

run keywordencoding

Input data   keyword: RAVEN
Input data   message: DO IT RIGHT THE FIRST TIME
Encoded message:      VP EY FAHDY HZF BNFKU PNAW
```

Keyword Decoding

Modifying the program keywordencoding to do keyword decoding is very simple. The two statements below the comment

```
{find replacement letter}
```

that calculate the value of the variable nextord must be replaced by the statements

```
nextord := ord (message [c]) - increment [i];
if nextord < ord ('A') then
   nextord := nextord + 26;
```

so that the increment is subtracted during decoding to cancel the effect of adding the increment during encoding. The keyword decoding program can be checked by trying it on the encoded message produced by the keyword encoding program. Another clever way to check the decoding program is shown in the second sample run.

```
program keyworddecoding (input, output);

  const
    maxlength = 50;

  type
    stringindex = 1..maxlength;
    stringlength = 0..maxlength;
    string = packed array [stringindex] of char;

  var
    message, keyword : string;
    keylength, msglength, i : stringlength;
    c : stringindex;
    increment : array [stringindex] of 0..25;
    nextord : 0..256;

  procedure readline (var line : string);
    ... end; { readline }


  function trimlength (s : string) : stringlength;
    ... end; { trimlength }

  begin
  readline (keyword);
  keylength := trimlength (keyword);
  write ('Input data  keyword: ');
  for c := 1 to keylength do
    write (keyword [c]);
  writeln;
  { convert keyword to increments }
  for c := 1 to keylength do
    increment [c] := ord (keyword [c]) - ord ('A') + 1;

  readline (message);
  write ('Input data  message: ');
  msglength := trimlength (message);
  for c := 1 to msglength do
    write (message [c]);
  writeln;

  { encode message }
  i := 0;
  for c := 1 to msglength do
    if message [c] in ['A'..'Z'] then
      { all nonletters remain unchanged }
```

```
      begin
      { obtain next increment }
      i := (i mod keylength) + 1;
      { find replacement letter }
      nextord := ord (message [c]) - increment [i];
      if nextord < ord ('A') then
        nextord := nextord + 26;
      message [c] := chr (nextord);
      end; { if }

  write ('Decoded message:      ');
  for c := 1 to msglength do
    write (message [c]);
  writeln;
  end.
```

```
run keyworddecoding
```

```
Input data   keyword: RAVEN
Input data   message: VP EY FAHDY HZF BNFKU PNAW
Decoded message:      DO IT RIGHT THE FIRST TIME
```

```
run keyworddecoding
```

```
Input data   keyword: RAVEN
Input data   message: RAVEN RAVEN
Decoded message:      ZZZZZ ZZZZZ
```

If the keyword is not known, then decoding a message is quite difficult. It is a big help to know the length of the keyword.

Suggested Reading

Martin Gardner, A new kind of cypher that would take millions of years to break, *Scientific American,* August 1977, pages 120-124.

Abraham Sinkov, *Elementary Cryptanalysis,* New Mathematical Library (Mathematical Association of America), 1966.

David Kahn, *The Code Breakers; The Story of Secret Writing,* Macmillan, New York, 1967.

Exercises

---

1. Use Table 5.4.1 to encode the message "CRYPTOGRAPHY IS EASIER IF YOU USE A COMPUTER".
2. Modify the program encodesub so that the blanks and other nonletter characters are excised from the encoded message.

3. Modify the program keywordencoding so that the usual spacing is suppressed, and instead the letters of the output message are grouped in fives. For example, the encoded message of the text would be

    VPEYF AHDYH ZFBNF KUPNA W

4. Decode the following cryptogram (just for fun).

    XIHH UAZ EJIMX NUYIY LI LEY OM LOY BUYYIYYOUM E NEJOK YXEVV
    GLOKL GOHH XAZM OMXU E YIZBIMX ABUM KUNNEMT. EHYU XIHH LON
    XLEX XLI BEYYGUZT LI OY XU AYI EX BLEZEUL'Y KUAZX OY: "HIX
    NS BIUBHI JU."

5. Modify the program keywordencoding so that it inputs a continuous text as a key-word, instead of repeating the same keyword over and over. The idea is to input lines of keyword alternately, say, from a newspaper or a book, with lines of message.

6. Modify the program keywordencoding so that it can do both encoding and decod-ing.

7. Decode the following cryptogram (more fun):

    QLHCADXIFAEXTFO FX EYD OBHD UK EYD AFEEAD HBO ZYU XCLO
    XEQBZ FOEL RUAW

8. A coding scheme that is completely different from both the substitution and key-word methods is permutation. Group the letters of the input message into fives, (or into larger groups if desired). Pick a reordering of the numbers from 1 to 5, say 4 1 5 3 2. Then permute each group of letters according to the reordering of the numbers. According to the sequence 4 1 5 3 2, the fourth letter in each group becomes first, the first becomes second, the fifth becomes third, the third be-comes fourth, and the second becomes fifth. For example, the message

    A THREE DOLLAR BILL IS PHONY

    is first grouped as

    ATHRE EDOLL ARBIL LISPH ONY

    and then permuted into

    RAEHT LELOD LALBR PLESI OYN

    Note that special handling of the last group is required if it does not contain the full five characters. Write a program that encodes messages according to this scheme.

9. Modify the program encodesub so that is inserts nonsense words at random between words of the encoded message. Use the following rule. After each word is encoded, obtain a random integer between 0 and 2. If it is 0, go directly to the encoding of the next word. Otherwise, generate a random integer from 1 to 26 and interpret it as the first letter of a nonsense word. The number 1 is interpreted as "A", 2 as "B", and so on. Now obtain another random integer between 0 and 2. If it is 0, leave the nonsense word at one letter and go on to encode the next word of the actual message. Otherwise, extend the nonsense word by another ran-dom letter, and so on.

10. What knowledge is needed to decode messages encoded by the scheme described in Exercise 9?

5.5   Chapter Review

Computer solutions to numerous problems in topics such as text analysis and cryptography depend on only a few special string processing features. This chapter shows how to develop from these Pascal programming language features a few fundamental string processing function programs and procedures that facilitate construction of programs for the applications.

Character String Variables and Constants

Just as variables or arrays may have numeric or boolean values, a variable may have a single character or a string of characters as its value. A character string variable in Pascal actually is an array of characters. Thus each character in the string may be referenced individually by using its position in the string as a subscript. For example, if the variable name has the character string value 'David', then name [1] = 'D', name [2] = 'a', name [3] = 'v', etc.

In the last analysis, all character string processing can be reduced to manipulation of the individual characters that comprise a string. However, Pascal has several built-in features that allow an entire character string to be processed at once. The price of using the special string processing features is usually that all the strings involved must have the same declared type.

Assignment of Values

For example, a character string variable or constant may be assigned as the value of a character string variable in one assignment, provided both strings have the same length. For variables, the length means the fixed declared length. For constants, one counts the number of characters, including blanks, between the opening and the closing single quote signs. Thus, the statements

```
var
  name, copy : packed array [1..7] of char;

name : = 'Michael';
copy : = name;
```

are permissible, but the statements

```
var
  name : packed array [1..7] of char;
  copy : packed array [0..6] of char;

name : = 'David';
copy : = name;
```

are both incorrect. The constant 'David' must be padded with two blanks, making it 'David ', before it can be assigned to the string name of length seven. In the second statement, although copy has the correct length, it has the wrong subscripts, so assignment cannot take place.

Input and Output of Character Strings

A write or writeln statement will accept a character string constant or variable in its output list, but read (in standard Pascal) accepts one character at a time. Fixed length character string input is done easily with a for-loop. For example, the loop

```
for i := 1 to 7 do
  read (name [i]);
```

reads a 7-character value for the string name. No apostrophes are used in the input file, unless an apostrophe is to be part of the character string name. The built-in boolean functions eof (end of file) and eoln (end of line) may be used to detect the end of variable-length character string input. The programmer-defined procedure readline, written in this chapter, provides one convenient way for a user to supply variable-length character string input for a fixed-length character string variable. Many Pascal systems provide nonstandard built-in procedures similar to readline.

Comparison of Character Strings

Character strings of the same length may be compared using the six comparison relations

= <> < > <= >=

If all characters are lowercase letters or blanks, one string is "less than" another string if it would appear first in ordinary lexicographic (dictionary) ordering. For strings containing mixed uppercase and lowercase letters or other nonalphabetic characters, their reported order depends on a collating sequence defining the order of all computer representable characters for that installation. The two most commonly used collating sequences, called ASCII and EBCDIC, do not agree on such details as whether uppercase letters follow lowercase letters or numerals. They do agree that both uppercase and lowercase alphabets are in alphabetical order and that the numerals are in numerical order. The built-in function ord tells the position of a character in the collating sequence and the built-in function chr tells what character has that ordinal position in the collating sequence.

Substrings

Any consecutive sequence of characters within a character string is called a *substring*. Every string is regarded as a substring of itself. In Pascal, a substring must be referenced one character at a time, treating each character as one element of the array of characters that constitute the character string.

Because character string variables have fixed declared length, they often have trailing blanks, especially when the data they hold is variable length. The programmer-defined function trimlength, developed in this chapter, may be used to isolate the substring obtained by excluding the trailing blanks. The trimlength of a character string is the position of the last nonblank character. For example,

trimlength ('Mr. Smith   ') = 9

Other substrings may be located using the programmer-defined function position (text, substring, startsearch) whose value is the position or subscript where its second argument starts as a substring of its first argument. Trailing blanks are ignored. For example,

position ('hubbub', 'ub   ', 1) = 2

because characters 2 to 3 of 'hubbub' are 'ub'. On the other hand, changing the starting position of the search to position 3 results in

position ('hubbub', 'ub   ',   3) = 5

because positions 5 to 6 of 'hubbub' are the leftmost occurrence of 'ub' as a substring of 'hubbub' starting at position 3 or later.

position ('hubbub', 'glub   ', 1) = 0

is a signal meaning 'glub' is not a substring of 'hubbub'.

Word Processing

A great deal of textual information is prepared and edited using computers, large and small. Letters, document, books, and newspapers are prepared using computers. At some computer installations, all programs and input files are entered in an interactive dialog between the user and the computer. What all these applications have in common is a text editing program used to manage the preparation of the text.

Details of the use of text editing programs differ widely, but most provide for the following manipulations of the data.

 (1) Erase the complete document
 (2) Enter one or more lines
 (3) Delete one or more lines
 (4) Replace a line
 (5) Print all or part of the document
 (6) Locate a sequence of characters in the document
 (7) Replace a word or other substring with a substitute
 (8) Renumber the lines of the document
 (9) Save the most recent version of a document
 (10) Recall a saved document for further editing

as well as many other operations. The sample executions of the text editors written in Section 5.2 give a preliminary idea of how a text editor is used. Facility in the use of a text editor comes with practice and experimentation to make good use of the full power built into many text editors.

6

FILES

A computer's memory may be divided into two parts, called *main memory* and *auxiliary memory*. Main memory is usually designed to provide the fastest possible access to stored information. Although main memory storage capacity has increased substantially, it still tends to be relatively scarce and relatively expensive per unit of information stored. Auxiliary memory, on the other hand, provides a larger storage capacity at substantially reduced cost per unit of information. Magnetic disk has been used extensively for this purpose over the last decade. However, the speed of storage or retrieval of information in auxiliary memory may be several orders of magnitude slower than that for main memory.

Operating systems treat the two types of memory differently. Most operating systems consider main memory a scarce resource, allocated to an actively executing program and withdrawn as soon as the execution is completed or suspended. In contrast, information stored in auxiliary memory ordinarily is retained indefinitely, providing a means for permanent or semipermanent storage of information between executions of the one or more programs that access it.

Most programming languages make another distinction between main memory and auxiliary memory. A piece of information is stored in main memory by making it the value of a variable, and it is retrieved for processing by referencing the name of that variable in a subsequent statement. Storage and retrieval of information in auxiliary memory use input and output statements resembling and extending the usual read and write statements.

When electronic digital computers first gained widespread acceptance as useful tools of business, there was a significant difference between business computing and scientific computing. A typical scientific calculation involved a vast number of arithmetic operations whose purpose was to produce a relatively small amount of data answering a specific question. Solving a complex system of equations to determine the future position of an orbiting satellite is an example of such a calculation. A typical business application was concerned with processing large amounts of data while doing only a very few simple calculations per item. A program that processes thousands of payroll records to produce paychecks and to retain cumulative information is an example of such an application.

These two types of computing were then considered so inherently different that computer manufacturers even produced two different types of machines, one for science and one for business. "Business computers" were designed with the brain of a dinosaur but excellent capabilities for handling input and output to auxiliary memory. "Scientific computers" had the fastest possible main memories and central processing (arithmetic and logical) units, but often far less sophisticated input and output. Different programming languages were invented: Fortran, primarily for science and engineering, and Cobol, primarily for business.

The distinction between business computing and scientific computing has now substantially faded. Business organizations use sophisticated mathematical techniques such as simulation to assist in management decisions. Conversely, a search by scientists for oil deposits may require the analysis of huge quantities of seismic data.

However, certain data processing problems are still more likely to occur in business applications than in scientific applications. The necessity for organizing data into a form amenable to efficient handling is a characteristic of business problems. This chapter is concerned with data organization and its implications for the programs used to process the data. Although the examples in this chapter are selected mostly from business, the methods described also apply to data organization problems in scientific applications.

When a large amount of data is collected, additional uses are frequently discovered for that data besides the ones originally envisioned. For example, employee data collected primarily to process paychecks might also be used by management to help make long-range economic forecasts or short-term staffing decisions. The information collected by the Bureau of the Census may be useful to economists, political scientists, and even intelligence agencies.

A collection of data that may be used by many computer programs is called a *data base*. Because the changes one program makes in a data base affect subsequent executions of other programs that access the data base, all programs of the system must be coordinated, and the needs of all programs of the system must be provided for in the design of the structure of the data base. This chapter shows how to create and maintain simple data bases in auxiliary memory and how to access them with one or more programs. It also deals with the special programming problems associated with storing large amounts of information and using two levels of memory, with locating specific pieces of information when needed, with minimizing input and output time, and with organizing data into structures that permit convenient processing and easily read programs.

6.1   Auxiliary Memory Devices

The two most widely used auxiliary memory devices are magnetic tape and magnetic disk. The operating characteristics of these devices influence both the way data must be organized for efficient use of these devices and the form of the input and output statements written to access them.

Magnetic Tapes

Magnetic tapes used to store data for computer processing are very similar to those used in sound recording systems. In fact, many computer systems use tape cassettes identical to those used in small audio cassette recorder/player systems. Cassettes can hold relatively small amounts of data. Larger amounts of data, up to 46 million alphabetic characters or 11 million numbers, can be stored on 10½-inch-diameter reels of tape up to 2400 feet long. Like the tapes for many home recording devices, computer tapes are composed of a flexible plastic base with a thin rust-colored coating of iron oxide, a material that can be magnetized.

Each computer character stored on the tape is represented by eight spots across the width of the tape, each of which is magnetized or not, depending on the particular representation or tape code used for each character. In addition, there is usually a ninth spot that is either magnetized or not so as to make the total number of spots magnetized (out of a possible nine spots) an odd number. A small speck of dust on the tape can cause one or more spots to be read incorrectly by the tape unit. However, a check (called a *parity check)* to see that an odd number of spots is magnetized provides a means of detecting faulty tapes or improperly recorded data. A tape such as the one just described is called a *nine-channel tape* or *nine-track tape,* since all the nine spots are magnetized or detected simultaneously as the tape passes the read or write heads of the tape unit.

A tape typically can have 1600 lines of spots recorded in each inch of its length. That is, two adjacent lines of spots are 1/1600 inch apart. Such a tape is said to have a *recording density* of 1600 bits per inch (abbreviated bpi).

There are materials that can be placed on a magnetic tape to make the magnetized spots visible so that a person can read the information on the tape. However, this is usually done only for demonstration purposes, or when all efforts to read the tape by machine fail. Figure 6.1.1 is a schematic representation of a small piece of magnetic tape with four characters of data, each represented by eight spots and a parity spot.

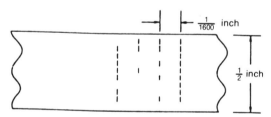

Figure 6.1.1 Schematic representation of data on magnetic tape.

Tape Units

Tape units or *tape drives* move the tape and read the data on the tape by sensing the magnetic flux created by the magnetized spots moving past a read head, and they record data onto a tape by magnetizing spots as the tape passes the write head. Actually, there are nine read heads in a row and nine write heads in a row to read or write simultaneously all nine bits of information representing one tape character. For comparison, stereophonic audio systems have two aligned tape heads, and quadraphonic audio systems have four aligned tape heads to record and play back the proper number of channels.

Typical computer tape units are capable of moving the tape at about 150 inches per second, as compared with a rate of 1⅞ to 15 inches per second for audio equipment. If 1600 characters are stored on each inch of a computer tape, then the tape unit can read or write

$$\frac{1600 \text{ characters}}{1 \text{ inch}} \times \frac{150 \text{ inches}}{\text{second}} = 240,000 \text{ tape characters per second}$$

Magnetic Disks

Magnetic disks use the same principles as magnetic tape to store data. The main difference is the shape of the material coated with iron oxide. The disk is coated on both sides with iron oxide and is not unlike a very thin phonograph record. The material recorded on the disk is organized into concentric circles, called *tracks,* around the center of the disk. The information is sensed and recorded by heads that are very close to the surface of the disk but do not touch it. Each head is movable so that it may be positioned to read or write on any of the tracks on a disk surface, as shown schematically in Figure 6.1.2. The head is shown positioned over track 2.

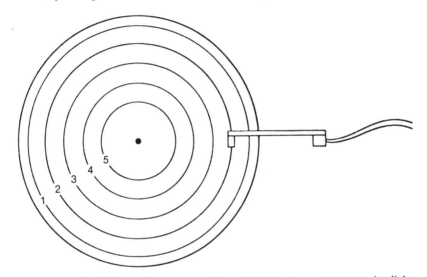

Figure 6.1.2   Schematic representation of the tracks on a magnetic disk.

Often several disks are placed on a shaft and rotated together at high speed. The surface of the rotating disk moving past the read/write head has the same electromagnetic effect as magnetic tape moving past the read/write head of a tape unit. Figure 6.1.3 is a schematic side view of a disk unit with three disks. Each disk surface used for recording has a separate read/write head.

One disk system in use has 11 disks on its shaft. The top surface of the top disk and the bottom surface of the bottom disk are not used to record information, so 20 surfaces are used. Each surface has 400 tracks, and each track has approximately 60,000 magnetizable spots. At 8 spots per alphabetic character, approximately 3 million characters can be recorded on each surface, so that a total of 60 million characters can be stored in the disk unit.

Disk Access Time

The amount of time required to read information from a magnetic disk depends upon the position of the read head. If the read head is positioned over the correct character or the correct disk track, reading can take place at the rate of

$$\frac{7500 \text{ characters}}{\text{revolution (track)}} \times \frac{40 \text{ revolutions}}{\text{second}} = 300,000 \text{ characters per second}$$

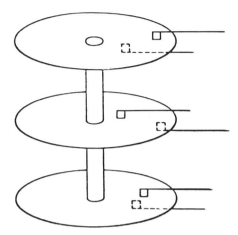

Figure 6.1.3 Schematic diagram of a disk unit with three disks.

a transfer rate comparable to that of tape units.

If, however, the read head is not correctly positioned, it must be moved to a position over the track containing the information to be read. The time required for this movement is typically a few milliseconds (a few thousandths of a second). There may be a further delay while the disk rotates into a position so that the desired information reaches the read head. A typical disk rotates at 2400 revolutions per minute, or 40 revolutions per second. Thus the delay might be anywhere from no time at all to 1/40 second in the unfortunate case that the information of interest passes the read head just before the read head is positioned at the correct track to read it. On the average, the delay is about half of 1/40 second, or 1/80 second, which is 12.5 milliseconds.

A statistic of interest is the average time it takes for the head to be positioned over the correct track and the disk to rotate to the correct position. This is called the *average access time*. A typical average access time for a magnetic disk is 25 milliseconds.

When To Use Auxiliary Memory

There are two main reasons for storing information in a computer's auxiliary memory rather than in its main memory. First, in most computer systems, storage space in main memory is relatively scarce, and expensive enough so that is is allocated only during the execution of a program and then withdrawn automatically by the operating system immediately upon conclusion of the execution. Storage space in auxiliary memory is far less expensive per unit of information. Consequently, information is stored in auxiliary memory for permanence. Second, many data files contain more information than can fit into a computer's main memory. Auxiliary memory devices usually have a greater capacity and are used to hold the overflow.

Virtual Memory

In some computer systems, auxiliary memory devices are used automatically to extend the apparent capacity of main memory. Information is transferred automatically from auxiliary memory into main memory when it is needed by a program, and then it is transferred back to auxiliary memory when the main memory space is needed for other information. These systems are said to have *virtual memory,* because, the system behaves as though main memory is available even when it is not. Programs for such a system often are written as if there were an unlimited amount of main memory available. However, most computer systems require explicit instructions when information is to be moved between main memory and auxiliary memory.

File Access

A group of values is called a *record,* and a collection of records stored on an auxiliary device is called a *file.* There are two basic ways to access a record in a file. One way is to read all the records that precede it, one at a time, until the computer reaches the desired record. This is called *sequential access.* It is generally well suited for circumstances where it is necessary to process all the records in a file during a single execution of a program, because then it is necessary to read every record in the file anyway. Such a program should be designed to process the records in the order in which they are stored in the file, so that it is necessary to scan the file only once. For instance, a computer program used by a department store to send advertising circulars to all its customers could use sequential access to a mailing list file.

The other way to access a file is called *direct access.* (Some persons call this "random access", even though there is nothing uncertain about it.) Direct access means the computer can retrieve any record from a file, no matter where it is stored in the file, without reading through the records that precede it. In particular, after one record is processed, the next record to be processed need not be one stored near it. All one needs to know is where to find the next record. Normally, a program uses direct access to a file when many of the records are not to be processed during a particular execution. For instance, a program that processes hospital claims should have direct access to the file of policyholders because, on a given execution, it processes only the records of policyholders who have actually been hospitalized, not the records for everybody who pays premiums.

Sequential-Access Input Statements

When a tape cassette or a tape reel is mounted on a tape unit, the only information on the tape readily available for reading is the information about to pass under the read heads. Thus information recorded on tape is read sequentially, in the order in which it appears on the tape. For example, in Pascal, the statement

```
read (numberfile, a, b, c)
```

may be used to read the next three numbers from a tape file called "numberfile" and to assign these three numbers as the values of the variables a, b, and c, respectively.

The read statement above looks like the ordinary read statement

```
read (a, b, c)
```

except for an extra first argument which is the name of a file. The two statements

```
read (a, b, c);
read (input, a, b, c);
```

are considered to be identical, because inclusion of the default file name "input" as a first supplied argument is optional. Each file used in a program, except the ones named "input" and "output", must appear in a variable declaration that indicates the type of each record in the file. For example, the file numberfile might be declared by

```
var
  numberfile : file of real
```

which indicates that each record of the file is a real number.

Text Files

All of the files in this book so far have been *text files,* which means they are files whose records are single characters. The files called "input" and "output" are assumed by every program to be text files, that is, they are predeclared by the Pascal system to have the form

```
var
  input, output : file of char
```

The individual records in a text file are single characters. However, the built-in procedures read and readln convert the characters of a text file into the data types of the arguments of the procedure. Similarly, the arguments of the procedures write and writeln are converted from their data type to single characters. All file names used by a program must appear within the parentheses of the title line of the program.

Sequential-Access Output Statements

Information may be recorded sequentially in a file using a write statement. For example, the statement

```
write (numberfile, a, b, c)
```

directs a computer to record the values of the variables a, b, and c, in sequence, as three records of the file named "numberfile" starting at the current position of the file. Values in the file before the current position are not affected by execution of this write statement. Whenever any values are written sequentially to a file, those values then become the last values in the file. All other information that was stored in the file after that point is discarded.

The Built-In Procedures Reset and Rewrite

The built-in procedure reset causes its argument, a file, to be positioned at its beginning point, so that the next read statement will read the first record of the file. For a file that is on tape, this is equivalent to rewinding the tape.

The built-in procedure rewrite also positions a file at its beginning point, but destroys the entire contents of the file in preparation for rewriting it. If there is no file with the given name, a new empty file is created.

Direct-Access Input and Output Statements

The operational characteristics of magnetic disk as auxiliary memory differ substantially from those of magnetic tape. For a typical disk unit, any one of the millions of characters of information stored in the disk unit may be accessed in the same average amount of time, a few thousandths of a second, as any other piece of stored information. This is quite different from magnetic tape where information directly under the read heads is accessible within a few millionths of a second, but information at the far end of the tape reel may take several minutes to read.

For this reason, a second type of auxiliary memory input and output statements, called *direct access* input and output, is provided for files stored on magnetic disk. Each record in a directly accessed disk file is assigned a *record number* by which it may be uniquely referenced at any time, regardless of which record is accessed immediately before it. For example, the statements

```
writedirect (realfile, 1, a, error);
writedirect (realfile, 3, d, error);
writedirect (realfile, 5, g, error);
writedirect (realfile, 2, j, error);
readdirect (realfile, 3, x, error)
```

direct a computer to write real values into the four records numbered 1, 3, 5, and 2 of a file named "realfile" and then to read the value just stored in record 3 as the value for the variable x. Thus, after these statements are executed, the value of the variable x is the same as the value of the variable d, and as the value stored in record 3 of the file "realfile". The value in record 4 (if any) of the file is unchanged by the execution of these statements, as are the values in any other record of the file except records 1, 2, 3, and 5. It is assumed that the variable realfile is declared to be type file of real and that a, d, g, j, and x are all declared to be type real.

The fourth supplied argument for the procedures readdirect and writedirect is a boolean variable that is set to true if an error occurs during the input or output operation and is set to false if no error occurs.

Unfortunately, the Pascal language does not contain the built-in procedures readdirect and writedirect for direct access input and output. These procedures must be supplied by the programmer, the instructor, or the computer center. Some systems do not support any form of direct access input and output and some systems have added features similar to (but probably not exactly like) the procedures described here. For computer systems that support direct access input and output, the procedures readdirect and writedirect are written in terms of the extensions to Pascal for direct access available on that computer system. For systems that do not support direct access, the procedures readdirect and writedirect given in Appendix D may be used to simulate direct access input and output for instructional purposes.

Card, Printer, And Terminal Files

Card and terminal input files, such as the file that is usually implied by the default file named "input", are sequentially accessed files. As described in Section 1.4, when a program is first submitted, many operating systems copy the standard input file onto a magnetic disk, if it is not already there, so that the input data may be accessed more rapidly when the program is run. This is normally of no concern to the programmer, except to emphasize the essential similarity between card input files and other sequentially accessed files.

Printer and terminal output files are also accessed sequentially. Because a program that uses only a few seconds of computational (central processing unit) time might generate several thousand lines of printed output, requiring several minutes to print, many operating systems first write the lines for printing as records in a magnetic tape or disk file. Then, when a printer with the correct forms is available for printing, the print file on magnetic tape or disk is copied onto paper. When no file name is specified in a write or writeln statement, the standard output file named ''output'' is implied.

Exercises

---

1. Write a program that reads 10 numbers sequentially from a text file named ''inputdata'' and prints the average of the numbers.

2. Modify the program avgofscores in Section 1.3 to accept the test scores from a text file called ''scores''.

3. A direct-access file named ''bankaccounts'' contains one record for each bank account. Each record consists of one number, the bank balance. For simplicity, assume that each balance is stored a record of the file whose record number is the same as the account number. Write a program that accepts as input from a terminal an account number and prints the bank balance for that account.

4. Assume that the sequential file named ''cardfile'' described in Section 3.2 is a file of integers whose first record contains the number of entries in a list of credit card numbers for accounts that have been cancelled, and the remaining records of the file each contain the number of one cancelled card. Write a program that reads this file, sorts the list into increasing order, and rewrites the file with the list of cancelled credit cards in increasing order.

5. How many characters can be read or written each second on a magnetic tape that can store 800 characters per inch if the tape moves at 120 inches per second?

6. What is the average access time for a magnetic disk system if the average time to position the read head is 20 milliseconds and the disk rotates 1000 times per minute?

6.2 Organization of Data

A principal benefit of adopting the top-down style for constructing a program is that the resulting organization of the various programming steps is easy to understand. The organization of the data to be processed also should be easy to understand. Frequently, the organization of the data imposes certain requirements on the program steps. In many cases, designing a structure for the data is as important as designing the program itself, particularly when the program is concerned with files in auxiliary memory.

Data Structures

In order to begin with a simple example, suppose that a person decides to computerize the entries in a little black book that gives information about various acquaintances and contacts. For each person in the book, there is a name, an address, a telephone number, and sometimes a few remarks. One way of organizing the data is to have four lists, one for each type of information. However, depending on how the information is to be processed, it might be more convenient to organize the data into natural groupings, one for each person in the black book.

A data structure for the information in one black book entry might be organized as shown in Figure 6.2.1. When the owner of the black book wishes to arrange by telephone a future meeting with someone, only the person's telephone number is needed. On the other hand, to send a letter the address is needed. The point is that different parts of the information may be needed for different purposes.

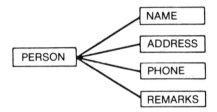

Figure 6.2.1   A data structure for a black book entry.

Figure 6.2.1 illustrates that the name of the entire structure is person and that it has four components, which are name, address, phone, and remarks. Sometimes, one or more components might be broken down into lower-level components. For instance, if the owner of the black book wanted to contact every acquaintance in a particular city, it would be helpful to have the component address broken down into lower-level components corresponding to the number, street, city, state, and postal zip code. This level of detail would enable a computer to scan the entries for city and state without having to look at the street address or zip code. For other reasons it might be convenient to subdivide each telephone number into a three-digit area code and a seven-digit local number. Figure 6.2.2 shows a finer structure for the same black book entry.

If there were a good reason, one might want to specify more detail for each person's name or for the remarks. Specifying too much detail, however, makes a program less efficient than specifying the right amount. The use of the information is what determines the right amount.

Refining Data Structures

The technique of successive refinements can be applied to the design of data structures as well as to the writing of programs. It is often a good idea to coordinate the refinement of the data structure with the refinement of the program. As more detailed steps of the program are written, the data structures used by those steps can be refined to the level of detail needed by the program.

The data structures shown in Figures 6.2.1 and 6.2.2 are called *tree structures* because of the analogy with the root, branches, and leaves of a tree lying on its side.

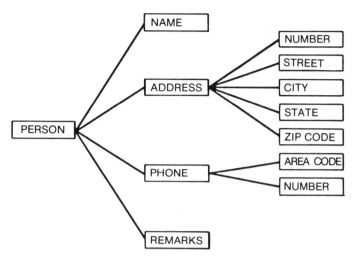

Figure 6.2.2 A finer data structure for a black book entry.

In both figures, the box labelled "person" is the root. The lines between boxes are the branches. Any box from which it is impossible to travel to the right is a leaf. Thus, in Figure 6.2.1, the components name, address, phone, and remarks are all leaves. In Figure 6.2.2, the components name and remarks are still leaves, but there is further branching from the nodes address and phone in Figure 6.2.2, so those nodes are not leaves. The components number, street, city, state, and zip code are all leaves for the component address, and the components area code and number are leaves for the component phone. As the data structure is refined, the tree grows by acquiring new leaves.

Data Structure Declarations

In Pascal, data structures like the ones shown in Figures 6.2.1 and 6.2.2 are called *records*. The same term is used for both data structures and the components of a file, because it is usually the case that the components of a file are data structures, although, in simple cases, the record of a file may consist of a single value, as in the examples discussed so far. A programmer communicates the form of a data structure to the computer by a *record declaration*. To declare the structure illustrated in Figure 6.2.1, the programmer writes the following data structure declaration for the type of the variable person.

```
type
  persontype = record
    name : string20;
    address : addresstype;
    phone : phonetype;
    remarks : string20;
    end; { persontype }
```

Such a declaration indicates that any variable of the type persontype consists of four components, name, address, phone, and remarks.

The type declaration for persontype is completed by making preceding declarations for the types string20, addresstype, and phonetype. If none of the components name, address, phone, or remarks will be subdivided further as in Figure 6.2.1, then the following declarations will serve.

```
type
  string20 = packed array [1..20] of char;
  string57 = packed array [1..57] of char;
  string12 = packed array [1..12] of char;

  addresstype = string57;
  phonetype = string12;
```

In order to permit immediate access to subgroupings within these components, the programmer should declare a more detailed data structure, such as the one shown in Figure 6.2.2. This is done by writing refined declarations for the data types of the components of the type persontype, as shown below. These refined type declarations are used in the declaration of persontype and so must precede the declaration of persontype.

```
type
  string2 = packed array [1..2] of char;
  string3 = packed array [1..3] of char;
  string5 = packed array [1..5] of char;
  string6 = packed array [1..6] of char;
  string8 = packed array [1..8] of char;
  string20 = packed array [1..20] of char;

  addresstype = record
    number : string6;
    street : string20;
    city : string20;
    state : string2;
    zipcode : string5;
    end; { addresstype }

  phonetype = record
    areacode : string3;
    number : string8;   { the 4th character is a hyphen }
    end; { phonetype }

  persontype = record
    name : string20;
    address : addresstype;
    phone : phonetype;
    remarks : string20;
    end; { persontype }
```

It is certainly possible to analyze the entire address as a character string (of length 57, which includes four separator characters between the five subfields, in this example) and to pick out the number, street, city, state, and zip code as substrings of the appropriate lengths, separated by blanks or punctuation. Using the more detailed data structure saves the programmer the trouble of doing this analysis.

A record type declaration consists of the variable name, an equals sign, and the keyword ''record'', followed by a list of declarations of the components of the record, each of which looks like a variable declaration. The declaration is terminated by the keyword ''end''. Any of the components of a record may themselves be records.

A component of a record may be an array, which is illustrated by the fact that all of the character strings in the black book entry are arrays. Conversely, it is possible to declare a variable to be an array of records, which is what we want to do, in order to be able to have all of the entries in the black book file stored in main memory at once. Thus, all programs for the black book example will use the variable person declared by

```
var
  person : array [1..100] of persontype;
```

Referencing Components of a Data Structure

A component of a data structure is referenced in a program by writing its full *path name,* which consists of all names from the root of the tree along the branch to the component. Successive names in a path are separated by a period (.). Any reference to a component that is part of an array must specify which element of the list or table is intended, unless the whole array is intended. For example,

```
person [13] . address . zipcode
```

is the zip code of the 13th person in the black book. Similarly, provided the variable newaddress has been declared to be of type addresstype, the statement

```
person [47] . address := newaddress
```

assigns the value of newaddress as the address of the 47th person in the black book. Assignment to a variable or component of record type is permitted as long as the right hand side has the same type as the left hand side.

One of the advantages of declaring a component to be a record is that one can still reference the entire record by a single name, instead of having to specify each part of the record. This is illustrated by the statement above that tells the computer to assign the entire address component newaddress to person [47] . address without having to have a separate assignment statement statement for the number, street, city, state, and zipcode components of the address.

Another example of full path name addressing for components of a data structure is the following statements that print the names and telephone numbers of all persons with area code 505.

```
{ print phone number of all persons with area code 505 }
for entry := 1 to numofpersons do
  if person [entry] . phone . areacode = '505' then
    writeln (person [entry] . name, person [entry] . phone . number);
```

Perhaps the most standard use of a little black book is to look up someone's telephone number. The instructions below tell the computer to print out the telephone number of a person whose name is the value of the variable persontobecalled. For simplicity of exposition, a sequential search is used. The procedure readline is borrowed from Section 5.1 and not relisted here.

```
{ procedure readline borrowed from Section 5.1 }
readline (persontobecalled);
{ look in black book for person to be called }
entryposition := 1;
personfound := false;
while (entryposition <= numofpersons) and (not personfound) do
  if person [entryposition].name = persontobecalled then
    personfound := true
  else
    entryposition := entryposition + 1;
if personfound then
  writeln ('The telephone number is ',
      person [entryposition] . phone . areacode, '/',
      person [entryposition] . phone . number);
else
  writeln (persontobecalled,
      ' is not in your little electronic black book.');
```

A Data Structure for Library Information

As another example of a collection of information with a natural tree structure, we consider a simple computerized cataloging system for a library. For each book in the library, there are two kinds of data. Some of the data serves to identify the book, and the rest of it tells about the status of the copies of it owned by the library.

To identify the book, it is necessary to specify the author, the title, the publisher, the year of publication, and the Library of Congress catalog number. In naming the publisher, it is also customary to tell the city in which the book was published. For instance, the following is a standard citation for a popular book on the oriental game of Go.

> Arthur Smith,
> *The Game of Go, Charles E. Tuttle Company,*
> Rutland and Tokyo, 1956, LCN 56-12653.

The library status information is comprised of the number of copies owned by the library, the number of copies out on loan, and the number of additional copies on order. It is appropriate to make the data structure booktype shown below. The Pascal type declarations are written from the bottom up because, to aid efficient compilation, each type must be declared above any line where it is used. The top-down tree structure is most easily seen by starting at the end with the declaration for the variable book, an array which represents the entire catalog.

```
type
  string9 = packed array [1..9] of char;
  string30 = packed array [1..30] of char;
```

```
publishertype = record
  company : string30;
  location : string30;
  end; { publishertype }
idtype = record
  author : string30;
  title : string30;
  publisher : publishertype;
  year : 0..1999;
  catalognumber : string9;
  end; { idtype }
copytype = record
  owned, borrowed, ordered : 0..99;
  end; { copytype }
booktype = record
  identification : idtype;
  copies : copytype;
  end; { booktype }

var
  book : array [1..numberofbooks] of booktype;
```

A Data Structure for Baseball Performance Records

A third example of a data structure is one that a baseball television announcer or news reporter might use to organize statistics on the players. The defensive component of a player's performance consists of the position played, the number of fielding chances, and the number of errors committed. Different kinds of data are kept for pitchers. The offensive component of a player's performance includes the number of times at bat, the number of hits, the number of runs scored, and the number of runs batted in. The hits have a finer classification as singles, doubles, triples, and home runs. The data structure declaration shown for the type playertype might be used.

```
type
  number = 0..999;
  hitstype = record
    singles, doubles, triples, homeruns : number;
    end; { hitstype }
  idtype = record
    name, team : string20;
    end; { idtype }
  defensetype = record
    position : string20;
    fieldingchances, errorscommitted : number;
    end; { defensetype }
  battingtype = record
    timesatbat : number;
    hits : hitstype;
    walks, runsscored, runsbattedin, strikeouts : number;
    end; { battingtype }
```

```
playertype = record
  identification : idtype;
  defensiveperformance : defensetype;
  battingperformance : battingtype;
  end; { playertype }
```

Files

A *file* is a collection of values, called records. The records in a file are often values of variables declared to be type record in the program, but can also be values of any other type. The values constituting a file are usually stored in some auxiliary memory, such as magnetic tape or magnetic disk, but also can be information on punched cards or on printed paper. All of the records in a file must be the same type, so in this regard a file is like an array. The main difference between a file and an array is that a file is stored on an auxiliary memory device and is accessed by read and write statements instead of by array subscripting. Other differences include the facts that some files, such as those on punched cards or magnetic tape, must be accessed sequentially, whereas any element of an array may be referenced at any time, and that the number of records in a file is not declared, whereas the number of elements in an array must be declared.

Exercises

---

1. Write statements to print the name and telephone number of all persons in the black book with zip code 91711.

2. Assume that a program uses the data structure player declared to be an array of playertype, a type declaration given in this section, and that values have been read in for the eight players (all but the pitcher) using the statement

   ```
   for i := 1 to 8 do
     read (playerfile, player [i])
   ```

   Write a procedure to print the name of each player with the player's position and the percentage of fielding chances that have produced errors.

3. Assume that a program uses a variable book, declared to be an array of booktype, a type declared in this section, and that values have been read in for 9437 books in the library using the statement

   ```
   for b := 1 to 9437 do
     read (bookfile, book [b])
   ```

   Write a procedure search (var there : string3) that sets there = 'yes' if the following book is in the library and sets there = 'no ' otherwise.

Walter S. Brainerd, Charles H. Goldberg, and Jonathan L. Gross, *Fortran 77 Programming,* Harper and Row, New York, 1978. LCN 78-18301.

4. Give a data structure type declaration suitable for use by the Internal Revenue Service to hold information on a taxpayer. The information should include name, address, social security number, wages reported by employers, dividends and interest paid to the taxpayer, income tax withheld, and social security contributions (FICA) withheld.

5. Design a suitable data structure type declaration for information on a college student to be used by the college registrar.

6. Using the record type declaration for Exercise 5, write statements to list all juniors with a gradepoint average of 2.8 or better.

7. Design a suitable data structure for information on each reservation made with an airline for a flight during the next year.

8. Design a suitable data structure for information on each flight to be made by an airline during the next year.

9. Using the data structure for Exercise 7 or 8, write statements that tell the computer to list all the passengers on a given flight.

10. Using the data structures for Exercise 7 or 8, write statements to determine if a given person has any reservation on any flight during the next year.

11. Design a data structure suitable for a bank to keep the information on a checking account.

6.3   Creating and Updating a File

The most important use of auxiliary memory is for permanent storage of information between runs of the programs that access it. In most computer systems, storage space in main memory is too valuable to be used to retain information that might not be accessed for several hours or days. Besides, when the computer is shut down for preventative maintenance or for the night, the contents of main memory are lost. In contrast, magnetic tapes and disks retain the information recorded on them indefinitely, unless explicit user action is taken to change or erase it. Even physically removing a tape or a disk from a computer does not change the information it contains.

This section continues the discussion of the computerized little black book of information on friends and acquaintances for which a data structure was developed in Section 6.2. The procedures given here for creating and updating a black book file illustrate in miniature the procedures used for creating and updating larger files.

The point of this section is the relationship and interplay between the permanent copy of a file in auxiliary memory and the highly transient copy of the same file created in main memory during execution of a program that accesses the file. Although the programs in this section use sequential-access input and output statements, the question of sequential versus direct access is effectively sidestepped, because the black book file is small enough to fit in its entirety in main memory, and it is always read or written as a whole. Sections 6.4 and 6.5 discuss applications where sequential and direct access must be treated differently because the entire file is not all in main memory at one time.

Creating a File

The first step in computerizing the little black book is to obtain file space for the data. This consists of requisitioning a region of auxiliary memory for the purpose and staking a claim to it. For a noncomputerized black book file, this may be likened to buying an empty black book. In general, securing file space is like taking a manila folder, attaching a label to it, and putting the empty folder into a filing cabinet.

When the black book file is being read by a program, there must be a way to determine when all of the entries have been read. Since all of the records of the file must be the same data type, there is no simple way to put the number of entries at the beginning of the file. We choose to put a termination signal record as the last entry in the file in preference to using the eof (end-of-file) built-in function discussed in Section 2.6. The program createblackbook uses the built-in procedure rewrite to create an empty file and then puts a record with all blank fields in the file as the last and only record of the file.

```
program createblackbook (input, output, blackbook);

  const
    blank20 = '                    ';

  type
    string2 = packed array [1..2] of char;
    string3 = packed array [1..3] of char;
    string5 = packed array [1..5] of char;
    string6 = packed array [1..6] of char;
    string8 = packed array [1..8] of char;
    string20 = packed array [1..20] of char;

    addresstype = record
      number : string6;
      street : string20;
      city : string20;
      state : string2;
      zipcode : string5;
      end; { addresstype }

    phonetype = record
      areacode : string3;
      number : string8;
      end; { phonetype }

    persontype = record
      name : string20;
      address : addresstype;
      phone : phonetype;
      remarks : string20;
      end; { persontype }
```

```
var
  signalperson : persontype;
  blackbook : file of persontype;
  answer : char;

begin
{ signalperson will contain blanks in all fields }
signalperson.name := blank20;
signalperson.address.number := '        ';;
signalperson.address.street := blank20;
signalperson.address.city := blank20;
signalperson.address.state := '  ';
signalperson.address.zipcode := '      ';
signalperson.phone.areacode := '    ';
signalperson.phone.number := '       ';
signalperson.remarks := blank20;

writeln ('This program will destroy any file named blackbook.');
writeln ('Do you wish to continue?');
writeln ('Enter answer:  "y" to continue, "n" to stop.');
read (answer);
if answer = 'y' then
  begin
  { create black book file }
  rewrite (blackbook);
  { put signalperson in file as only entry }
  write (blackbook, signalperson);
  end; { if }
end.
```

Most of the lines of the program createblackbook are concerned with declaring a natural data structure for the variable person and assigning blank values to its components. Then, the rewrite command tells the computer to set aside space in auxiliary memory for a new file, assuming one by that name does not exist already. If a file already in the computer's auxiliary memory has the name "blackbook", then the computer removes all the information from that file and is prepared to write new data into it. Therefore, it is important to know that a needed file is not being destroyed.

The With-Statement

It is something of a nuisance to have to write the full path name of a component of a record, especially when many such full path names start with the same record name. The *with-statement* allows a programmer the convenience of not repeating the initial part of a full path name. For example, all fields in the record signalperson of the previous example may be set to blank by the following with-statement.

```
with signalperson do
  begin
  name := blank20;
  address.number := '       ';
```

```
address.street := blank20;
address.city := blank20;
address.state := ' ';
address.zipcode := '      ';
phone.areacode := '    ';
phone.number := '            ';
remarks := blank20;
end; { with signalperson }
```

The scope (that is, the range of applicability) of a with-statement is the simple or compound statement that follows the keyword "do" in the heading of the with-statement. With-statements may be nested within each other, so that the preceding example may also be written as follows.

```
with signalperson do
  begin
  name := blank20;
  with address do
    begin
    number := '        ';
    street := blank20;
    city := blank20;
    state := '   ';
    zipcode := '       ';
    end; { with address }
  with phone do
    begin
    areacode := '     ';
    number := '            ';
    end; { with phone }
  remarks := blank20;
  end; { with signalperson }
```

Putting Records Into a File on the First Updating Run

Having reserved a storage location in auxiliary memory for the black book file, the next step is to put some entries there. To conserve programming effort, the same program used later to add or delete entries is used now to add the first entries to the empty black book file. Accordingly, the point of view used in writing the program updateblackbook is that there may already be several entries in the permanent copy of the black book file in auxiliary memory. After the program is written, one verifies that it works equally well in the present situation where the permanent copy of the black book file contains only the signal record written by the program createblackbook.

```
program updateblackbook (input, output, blackbook);
{ initial version }

  var
    person : array [entryindex] of persontype;
    blackbook : file of persontype;
    line : string;
```

```
begin
readblackbook;
{ requested changes are first made only in the
      main memory copy of the file }
morechanges : = true;
while morechanges do
  begin
  write ('Enter a request: ');
  readline (line);  { reads input into variable named line }
  if line = add then
    addnewentry
  else if line = delete then
    deleteentry
  else if line = done then
    morechanges : = false
  else
    writeln ('Update request must be "Add", "Delete", or "Done"');
  end; { while-loop }
writeblackbook;
end.
```

Before refining the program updateblackbook, which consists of filling in missing declarations and refining the called procedures, let us see how it is supposed to work during a program execution that places the following two entries in the file. Because the number of entries is expected to remain small enough that a computer could search through them all quickly, no effort is made to put them in alphabetical order.

Otis Quattlebaum
433 Out Way
Little Rock, AR 72901
501/555-4357
Likes Mexican food

Sara Hoshizaki
1134 Squid Street
Los Alamos, NM 87544
505/555-7272
QA expert

Suppose that the program createblackbook has been run to create the almost empty auxiliary memory file blackbook, and that the owner of the black book finally finds the time to start putting the entries into the file. As execution of the program updateblackbook begins, the copy of the file in auxiliary memory contains only the record for the signal person, in which all fields are blank, as represented in Figure 6.3.1. None of the elements of the array person nor any other variable in main memory has been assigned a value.

The program execution starts by faithfully copying the data in the first record of the auxiliary memory file blackbook into the first element of the array person. Since there are no information entries in the black book file at this time, the first entry is the

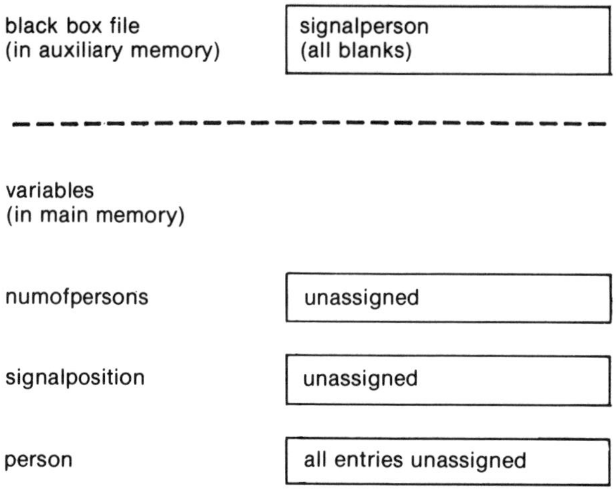

black box file   signalperson
(in auxiliary memory)   (all blanks)

- -

variables
(in main memory)

numofpersons   unassigned

signalposition   unassigned

person   all entries unassigned

Figure 6.3.1   Contents of the black book file (in auxiliary memory) and values (as yet unassigned) of the data structure person (in main memory) at the start of an execution of the program updateblackbook.

signal person, consisting of all blank fields. Thus the procedure readblackbook terminates after setting signalposition to 1 and numofpersons to 0. Figure 6.3.2 illustrates this stage of the program execution.

Next, suppose that ''Add'' requests for Quattlebaum and Hoshizaki entries are given. Each ''Add'' request causes execution of the procedure addnewentry that moves

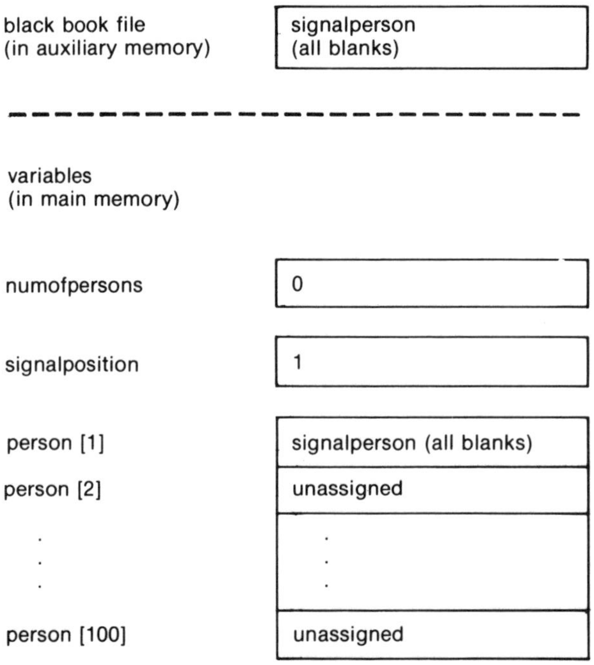

black book file   signalperson
(in auxiliary memory)   (all blanks)

- -

variables
(in main memory)

numofpersons   0

signalposition   1

person [1]   signalperson (all blanks)

person [2]   unassigned

     .   .
     .   .
     .   .

person [100]   unassigned

Figure 6.3.2   Contents of the black book file and values of the data structure person after reading contents of black book file from auxiliary memory into main memory.

the signal entry to the position in the array person with the next higher subscript (assuming there is any more room in the black book), increases the values of signalposition and numofpersons by one, and sets the value of entryposition to the position in the array person that was previously occupied by the signal person. Then it reads the complete data supplied for an entry and uses the data to assign values to components of the data structure person [entryposition]. What Figure 6.3.3 shows is that making this assignment does not change anything in the auxiliary memory file blackbook. Writing new records into the permanent copy of the black book file is a program step entirely separate from organizing the data for these records in main memory. Thus, in Figure 6.3.3, the variable numofpersons has been changed to 2 and signalposition has been changed to 3 by two executions of the procedure addnewentry.

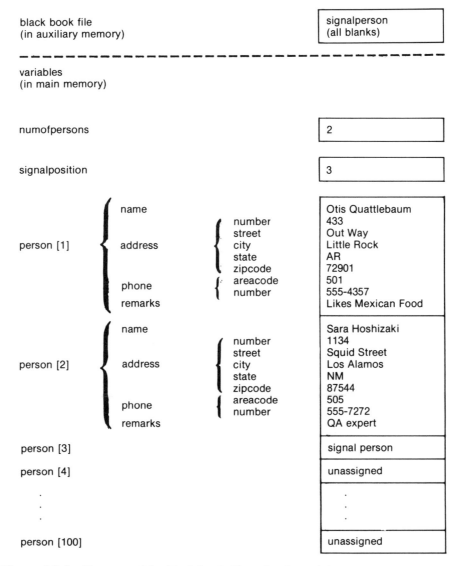

Figure 6.3.3   Contents of the black book file and values of the data structure person after data for the Quattlebaum and Hoshizaki entries are read.

After all intended additions to and deletions from the black book file have been entered and the request ''Done'' is given, a rewrite statement in the program instructs the computer to delete the contents of the auxiliary memory file blackbook in preparation for writing new entries into the file, after which the entire collection of entries is written from main memory into this permanent copy of the black book file. The last record written is the signal person. Repositioning the auxiliary memory file blackbook at its beginning and writing the values of person [1], person [2], and person [3] in it changes the values stored in auxiliary memory for the black book file but does not affect the values of any of the variables in main memory. Figure 6.3.4 shows all these values after the last statement of the program updateblackbook is executed. Although the main memory copy of the black book file is usually erased shortly after termination of the program execution, the auxiliary memory file blackbook is retained indefinitely, so that all the information is available for future use.

black book file (in auxiliary memory)	Otis Quattlebaum . . . Likes Mexican food
	Sara Hoshizaki . . . QA expert
	signalperson (all blanks)

- -

variables (in main memory)

| numofpersons | 2 |
| signalposition | 3 |

person [1]	Otis Quattlebaum . . . Likes Mexican food
person [2]	Sara Hoshizaki . . . QA expert
person [3]	signalperson (all blanks)
person [4]	unassigned
. . .	. . .
person [100]	unassigned

Figure 6.3.4   Contents of black book file and values of person after rewriting the auxiliary memory file. Values in main memory of person are lost after program termination, but values in the auxiliary memory file blackbook are retained for later use.

A Second Updating Run

Suppose that the program updateblackbook is run for a second time. At the beginning of the second run, the values in the auxiliary memory file blackbook are exactly as they were at the conclusion of the first run as illustrated by Figure 6.3.4. The values of person in main memory, however, have been lost in the interim. Starting from this more-or-less typical status of the black book file, a second hand simulation is done in conjunction with refining the called procedures. All the main program updateblackbook needs to be fully refined is complete definitions of the called procedures and a refining of the data structure declarations.

```pascal
program updateblackbook (input, output, blackbook);

  const
  blank20 = '                    ';
  maxentries = 100;
  add =      'Add                 ';  { padded with blanks to length 20 }
  delete = 'Delete              ';  { because string comparisons }
  done =     'Done                ';  { require equal length strings }
  maxlength = 20;  { maximum length of string read by readline }

type
  entryindex = 1..maxentries;
  stringindex = 1..maxlength;
  stringlength = 0..maxlength;
  string2 = packed array [1..2] of char;
  string3 = packed array [1..3] of char;
  string5 = packed array [1..5] of char;
  string6 = packed array [1..6] of char;
  string8 = packed array [1..8] of char;
  string = packed array [stringindex] of char;
  string20 = string;

  addresstype = record
    number : string6;
    street : string20;
    city : string20;
    state : string2;
    zipcode : string5;
    end; { addresstype }

  phonetype = record
    areacode : string3;
    number : string8;  { character 4 is a hyphen }
    end; { phonetype }

  persontype = record
    name : string20;
    address : addresstype;
    phone : phonetype;
    remarks : string20;
    end; { persontype }

var
  person : array [entryindex] of persontype;
  blackbook : file of persontype;
```

```
  entryposition, signalposition : entryindex;
  numofpersons : 0..maxentries;
  morechanges : boolean;
  line : string;

procedure readline (var line : string); ... end; { readline }
procedure readblackbook; ... end; { readblackbook }
procedure addnewentry; ... end; { addnewentry }
procedure deleteentry; ... end; { deleteentry }
procedure writeblackbook; ... end; { writeblackbook }

begin { ----- main program ----- }
readblackbook;
{ requested changes are first made only in the
      main memory copy of the file }
morechanges := true;
while morechanges do
  begin
  write ('Enter a request: ');
  readline (line);
  if line = add then
    addnewentry
  else if line = delete then
    deleteentry
  else if line = done then
    morechanges := false
  else
    writeln ('Update request must be "Add", "Delete", or "Done"');
  end; { while-loop }
writeblackbook;
end.
```

The procedure readblackbook directs the computer to read all the values in the black book file and assign them to elements of the array of data structures person. Reading terminates with the signal record. After the procedure readblackbook is executed, the contents of the auxiliary memory file blackbook and the value of person in main memory are identical to what they were at the termination of execution of the previous update run, as shown in Figure 6.3.4.

```
procedure readblackbook;

  var
    entryposition : entryindex;
    moreentries : boolean;

  begin
  reset (blackbook);
  moreentries := true;
  entryposition := 1;
  while moreentries do
```

```
  begin
  read (blackbook, person [entryposition]);
  if person [entryposition].name = blank20 then
    moreentries := false
  else
    entryposition := entryposition + 1;
  end; { while }
signalposition := entryposition;
numofpersons := signalposition - 1;
end; { readblackbook }
```

Suppose the first two requests are to add entries for persons named Peggee Franklin and Carole Hicke. This causes the procedure addnewentry to be executed twice.

```
procedure addnewentry;

  var
    i : stringindex;

  begin
  if signalposition = maxentries then
    writeln ('The black book is full.')
  else
    begin
    signalposition := signalposition + 1;
    numofpersons := numofpersons + 1;
    entryposition := numofpersons;
    { move signal person up one to make room
        for the new entry }
    person [signalposition] := person [entryposition];
    { obtain information for the new entry }
    with person [entryposition] do
      begin
      write ('Enter name: ');
      readline (name);
      write ('Enter house number: ');
      readline (line);
      for i := 1 to 6 do
        address.number [i] := line [i];
      write ('Enter street: ');
      readline (address.street);
      write ('Enter city: ');
      readline (address.city);
      write ('Enter state (2 letters): ');
      readline (line);
      for i := 1 to 2 do
        address.state [i] := line [i];
      write ('Enter zip code: ');
      readline (line);
```

```
  for i := 1 to 5 do
    address.zipcode [i] := line [i];
  write ('Enter area code: ');
  readline (line);
  for i := 1 to 3 do
    phone.areacode [i] := line [i];
    write ('Enter number: ');
    readline (line);
    for i := 1 to 8 do
      phone.number [i] := line [i];
    write ('Enter remarks: ');
    readline (remarks);
    end; { with person [entryposition] }
  end; { else }
end; { addnewentry }
```

Figure 6.3.5 shows the status of the auxiliary memory file blackbook and of the main memory variable person after the data are supplied for the Franklin and Hicke entries. The value of numofpersons is now 4 and the signal entry is now in position 5.

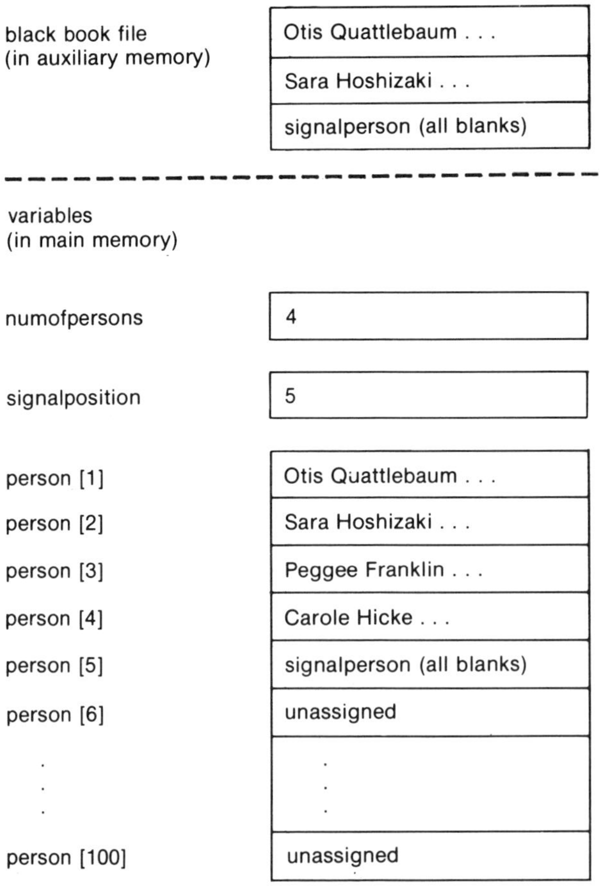

Figure 6.3.5   Contents of black book file and values of person after two more entries are added to the main memory copy of the file.

Deleting an Entry

Suppose that the next request is to delete the entry for Sara Hoshizaki. The procedure deleteentry, which is used to remove an entry, is a little more complicated than the procedure for adding a new entry, in spite of the fact that it is shorter, because in deleting an entry it is first necessary to locate the entry to be deleted. Because the black book file is small, and because the file is not kept in alphabetical order, the procedure deleteentry uses a sequential search modelled on the program cardcheck1 in Section 3.2.

```
procedure deleteentry;

  var
    name2delete : string20;
    entryposition : entryindex;
    namefound : boolean;

  begin
  write ('Enter name to be deleted: ');
  readline (name2delete);
  namefound := false;
  entryposition := 1;
  while (entryposition <= signalposition) and (not namefound) do
    if person [entryposition].name = name2delete then
      namefound := true
    else
      entryposition := entryposition + 1;
  if namefound then
    begin
    { move last person to position of
         person to be deleted }
    person [entryposition] := person [numofpersons];
    { move signal person forward one position }
    person [numofpersons] := person [signalposition];
    numofpersons := numofpersons - 1;
    signalposition := signalposition - 1;
    end { then }
  else
    begin
    writeln ('Cannot delete ', name2delete);
    writeln ('  It is not in the little black book');
    end; { else }
  end; { deleteentry }
```

Moving an Entire Structure in Main Memory

Once the entry to be deleted is located, there is still the problem of how to remove it. Merely obliterating (that is, blanking out) the data for Sara Hoshizaki would leave a gap at person [2] between the entries for Otis Quattlebaum and Peggee Franklin. To avoid this gap, the procedure deleteentry simply replaces the data for the entry to be deleted with the data for the last entry in the file (not counting the signal entry) and moves the signal entry into the position just vacated. As shown in Figure 6.3.6, this results in an apparent duplication of the signal person, but this has no effect on the program, because the value of numofpersons is now 3 and the value of signalposition is now 4, which will prevent any procedure from using the second signal entry or examining the first signal entry as an actual person entry.

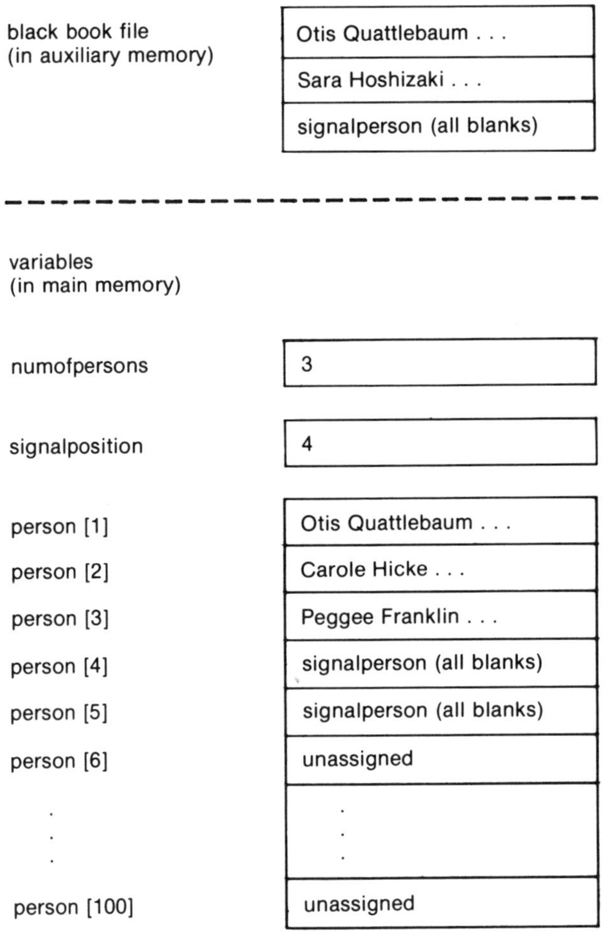

black book file (in auxiliary memory)	Otis Quattlebaum . . .
	Sara Hoshizaki . . .
	signalperson (all blanks)

- -

variables
(in main memory)

numofpersons	3

signalposition	4

person [1]	Otis Quattlebaum . . .
person [2]	Carole Hicke . . .
person [3]	Peggee Franklin . . .
person [4]	signalperson (all blanks)
person [5]	signalperson (all blanks)
person [6]	unassigned
.	.
.	.
.	.
person [100]	unassigned

Figure 6.3.6 Contents of black book file and values of person after the entry for Sara Hoshizaki is deleted. The duplicate entry for signalperson has no effect on the program because the values of numofpersons and signalposition are 3 and 4, respectively.

Although the statement

```
person [entryposition] := person [numofpersons]
```

is an assignment statement, it is a very powerful one because each entry in the array person is a data structure. Execution of this statement causes the value of each component of the variable person [numofpersons] to be assigned as the new value of the corresponding components of the variable person [entryposition], just as if the following nine simpler set statements were executed.

```
person [entryposition] . name : =
    person [numofpersons] . name
person [entryposition] . address . number : =
    person [numofpersons] . address . number
person [entryposition] . address . street : =
    person [numofpersons] . address . street
person [entryposition] . address . city : =
    person [numofpersons] . address . city
person [entryposition] . address . state : =
    person [numofpersons] . address . state
person [entryposition] . address . zipcode : =
    person [numofpersons] . address . zipcode
person [entryposition] . phone . areacode : =
    person [numofpersons] . phone . areacode
person [entryposition] . phone . number : =
    person [numofpersons] . phone . number
person [entryposition] . remarks : =
    person [numofpersons] . remarks
```

Values in main memory will be lost at the conclusion of the execution of updateblack-book, but values recorded in the auxiliary memory file blackbook preserve the information for future use.

Recopying the Updated File from Main Memory Into Auxiliary Memory

As shown in Figure 6.3.6, all the changes in the black book file requested during the second simulated execution have been made only in the main memory copy of the file. The updated copy of the black book file must be recopied into auxiliary memory if the changes are to be permanent. This is exactly what happens after the request "Done" is supplied. The while-loop is exited and the procedure writeblackbook is executed.

The most recent input/output operation performed with the auxiliary memory file blackbook was to read all the records of the file. Thus the file is positioned at its end-point, that is, after the last record. This is easily visualized if the file is stored on a reel of tape. The part of the tape containing the file has been read, and the tape is partly wound onto the take-up reel. The new file should be written starting at the beginning of the tape. Thus the tape should be rewound by a rewrite instruction before the updated version of the file is written on it by the procedure writeblackbook.

```
procedure writeblackbook;

  var
    entryposition : entryindex;

  begin
  rewrite (blackbook);
  for entryposition : = 1 to signalposition do
    write (blackbook, person [entryposition]);
  end; { writeblackbook }
```

Figure 6.3.7 shows that at the conclusion of the second simulated execution, the black book file in auxiliary memory contains entries for Otis Quattlebaum, Carole Hicke, and Peggee Franklin. The values of the array variable person in main memory are not changed by writing them into auxiliary memory. Main memory values are lost after program termination, but values saved in the records of the auxiliary memory file blackbook preserve all the relevant information for future use.

black book file (in auxiliary memory)	
	Otis Quattlebaum . . .
	Carole Hicke . . .
	Peggee Franklin . . .
	signalperson (all blanks)

- -

variables (in main memory)

numofpersons	3
signalposition	4
person [1]	Otis Quattlebaum . . .
person [2]	Carole Hicke . . .
person [3]	Peggee Franklin . . .
person [4]	signalperson (all blanks)
person [5]	signalperson (all blanks)
person [6]	unassigned
. . .	. . .
person [100]	unassigned

Figure 6.3.7 Contents of black book file and values of person after execution of the procedure writeblackbook. Values in main memory will be lost at the conclusion of the execution of updateblackbook, but values recorded in the auxiliary memory file blackbook preserve the information for future use.

A System of Programs

The programs createblackbook and updateblackbook in this section share a file blackbook in auxiliary memory and therefore may be thought of as part of a *system of programs*. Other programs of this system include the fragments in Section 6.2 to print all telephone numbers for persons in one area code, and to look up a person's telephone number. (These fragments must be furnished with data structure declarations and initialization statements, including a call to the procedure readblackbook to read the shared auxiliary memory file into main memory.) Although each program of a system of programs is technically a "main program" in the sense that is is not called by any other program, these programs must be coordinated with each other, because the values that one program writes into the shared file in auxiliary memory affect subsequent executions both of itself and of the other programs of the system.

On the other hand, the procedures readblackbook, addnewentry, deleteentry, and writeblackbook that are called by the program updateblackbook in this section form a *system of procedures*, that is, several procedures that may be called and executed during a single run of a main program. The most important difference between a system of programs and a system of procedures is that the programs of a system of programs can only pass information among themselves by writing it into one or more shared files in auxiliary memory, while the procedures of a system of procedures also can pass information by assigning it as the value of one or more variables in main memory.

Variant Record Types

It is sometimes inconvenient to require all records of a file to have the same format. For example, it might be desirable to preface the person records of the black book file with a title record giving the name of the file, the date it was last updated, and the number of entries, or it might be desirable to keep different performance statistics for pitchers than for baseball players who play other positions. An advanced Pascal feature, *variant record types*, allows the last field in a record to vary in structure.

The form of the variant part of a record resembles a case statement as shown in the example below, which builds on types already declared for the black book examples in this section.

```
type
  titleorperson = (titlerecord, personrecord);

  mixedtype = record
  case selectionfield : titleorperson of
    titlerecord : (filename : string20;
                   date : string7;
                   numofpersons : 0..maxentries);
    personrecord : (name : string20;
                    address : addresstype;
                    phone : phonetype;
                    remarks : string20);
  end; { mixedtype }

var
  blackbook : file of mixedtype;
  person : array [entryindex] of mixedtype;
  title : mixedtype;
```

Each record of type mixedtype has a component selectionfield, called the *tag field*, whose value determines what other fields will complete the record. If the value of selectionfield is titlerecord, the remaining components of the record are filename, date, and numofpersons. properly declared and enclosed in parentheses. If the value of selectionfield is personrecord, the remaining components of the record are name, address, phone, and remarks.

The variable declarations for the black book applications may now use the type mixedtype. Blackbook is a file of mixedtype because its first record is a title record and the remaining records are person records. The variable person is an array of mixedtype, even though we intend to put only person records into it. The variable title is of mixedtype, even though we intend to read only the title record into it.

The price of variants in a record type is a tag field that appears in every record. It may be examined if desired, or ignored if the variant used in a particular record is already known. In the black book example, components such as person (37) . name and title . date would ordinarily be referenced without examining the tag field. In other applications, the mixture of record formats in the input file might be sufficiently unpredictable that the tag field must be interrogated before processing a record.

A variant record type also may have a fixed part consisting of ordinary component declarations preceding the variant part. All variants of the record would include the fixed part as well as the tag field for the variant part.

Variant parts may be nested in two ways. First, the type of a component in a variant part may itself by a record type with a variant part, and second, the last field in the parenthesized list of fields in an alternative of a variant part itself may be a variant part constructed using the same case construction. The names of components must all be different, even if they appear in different alternatives of a variant record type.

Exercises

---

1. Design a data structure for records in a file on presidents of the United States. Each record must have at least the following information: name, dates of birth and death, and dates of office.

2. Write a program createpresidents that requisitions auxiliary memory space and writes a signal record into the file of of Exercise 1.

3. Write a program updatepresidents to update the file created for Exercise 2. Allowable update requests must include adding a new president, inserting a date of death, and changing dates of office.

4. For some applications, it is important that records in the file be sorted in alphabetical order or ordered by some other key such as social security number. Assume that the black book file is sorted in alphabetical order by name, that the names are written last name first, and that the file contains two records preceding the signal record, one for ''Hoshizaki, Sara'', and one for ''Quattlebaum, Otis'', in that order.

   Modify the procedure addentry so that each new entry is inserted in alphabetical order. When the appropriate place for a new entry is found, each entry to go after the new one (including the signal person) must be moved to the position with the next higher subscript, and this shifting must be done by moving the signal person first.

5. Modify the procedure deleteentry so that, when an entry is deleted, all entries after the one deleted are moved to the next lower position in the file. If the current entries in the file are in alphabetical order, this will keep them in alphabetic order in sequential positions starting at the first record of the file.

6. Assuming that the black book file is being maintained in alphabetical order using the procedures addnewentry and deleteentry as described in Exercises 4 and 5, and that the file initially consists of records for ''Hoshizaki, Sara'', ''Quattlebaum, Otis'', and the signal person, in that order, then draw figures corresponding to Figures 6.3.5 to 6.3.7 based on this starting status of the file and the following additional requests.

   Add Hicke, Carole...
   Add Franklin, Peggee...
   Delete Hoshizaki, Sara
   Done

7. Modify the program updateblackbook in this section to permit a ''Change'' request which modifies information for a person already listed in the black book. Use the procedures deleteentry and addnewentry that have been written already.

8. Write a program to create a data base containing information for a college registrar based on the data structure for Exercise 5 in Section 6.2.

9. Write a program to create a data base consisting of one record for each course offered by a college. To keep things manageable, assume that each course has only one section. Include information such as department, course number, number of hours credit, meeting time, and so on.

10. Using the variant record type mixedtype described at the end of this section, modify the procedures readblackbook and writeblackbook to handle a blackbook file headed by a title record containing the number of entries in the file. Also modify the procedures createblackbook and updateblackbook to process the title record properly. Do any other procedures in this section require modification because of the change in record format? Explain.

11. Ordinarily, different performance statistics are kept for pitchers than for baseball players who play other positions. Modify the data structure playertype given in Section 6.2 for keeping performance statistics on baseball players to include a variant part describing pitching performance.

6.4   Updating a Sequentially Accessed Inventory File

Although, when viewed at the level of individual Pascal statements, the black book file processing programs of the preceding sections use the built-in sequential access procedures read and write for input and output, when viewed at a higher level, they really use the programmer-defined procedures readblackbook and writeblackbook that read or write the entire black book file. The black book file is small enough to fit in its entirety in main memory, so it is simply read in its entirety into main memory by the procedure readblackbook at the beginning of each program execution and written in its entirety to auxiliary memory by the procedure writeblackbook at the conclusion of each execution. All other procedures of the system are insulated completely from the details of the file organization in auxiliary memory. They only see the file as an array of records in main memory.

An important side benefit of this division of responsibility among the procedures, a technique called *modularization,* is that if the file organization were to be changed, only the procedures readblackbook and writeblackbook would need to be modified. Modularized programs are easier to modify and easier to write by a group of programmers. In the next two sections, we discuss programming techniques used when the entire file is not kept in main memory. The major added complication of such programs is that they must not only process the records; *they must also arrange to have the correct records together in main memory for processing.* Sequential access is treated in this section because all Pascal systems support sequential access; direct access is treated in Section 6.5.

When to Use Sequential Access

In some inventory applications, such as a point of sale supermarket checkout and inventory system, the ''real time'' aspect of the situation (that is, the need to access quickly the price of each item) may dictate the choice of a direct-access device such as magnetic disk for the inventory master file. However, for many businesses, it is sufficient to update the inventory records once per day, once per week, or perhaps even less frequently. Unless the capability for rapid access to any record of the inventory file at any instant is required, an inventory system using magnetic tape for storage of files can often provide comparable or better processing speed and capacity at less cost than an equivalent system using magnetic disk.

This section focuses attention on some of the programming techniques used in processing sequentially accessed files. In particular, a program named updateand-reorder is considered in depth, both because it illustrates these techniques and because it is central to the inventory application. This program processes inventory transactions of two types, quantities shipped and quantities received, updating the records of the inventory master file appropriately. It also produces a list of items for reorder.

Principles of Program Design for Files Accessed Sequentially

The four main types of sequentially accessed files are tape files, disk files, interactive terminal files, and punched card files. Although these devices differ considerably in speed of data transmission, most of the techniques used in previous chapters in programs for card, terminal, or disk input apply equally well to programs for magnetic tape input. Some fundamental principles of program design for sequentially accessed file systems are described below in preparation for planning an inventory updating and reordering program.

1. *Input and output speeds usually determine execution speed.*

In inventory control, as in most business data processing, the amount of calculation required for each record is small. Thus the execution speed is basically determined by the information transmission rates of the input and output devices used. Since a typical magnetic tape unit can transmit several hundred times more information per second than a card reader, printer, or terminal, (approximately

1000 characters per second for an 800-card-per-minute card reader), the full speed of magnetic tape input and output ordinarily cannot be realized if there is extensive use of a card reader or printer in the same program.

2. *Tape files should not be backspaced nor their records rewritten.*

Although it might seem perfectly reasonable to update a record in a magnetic tape file by backspacing to the beginning of the record and rerecording the updated values for the record in the same part of the tape formerly occupied by the record before updating, there are several reasons why this must not be done.

(a) The fastest data transmission rates are obtained when the tape moves forward continuously without stopping or reversing direction.

(b) Frequent changes in the direction of tape travel tax the strength of the magnetic tape and the machinery of the tape drives, resulting in increased wear and tear and more frequent repair or replacement of equipment and tapes.

(c) Small mispositioning errors occur in backspacing a tape and overwriting a record, even with a record of exactly the same length. If repeated often enough, the location of the physical records on the tape may drift far enough that they are no longer readable.

For card files, backspacing is impossible without operator intervention, and ''erasing'' the information punched into a card and ''rewriting'' the card with updated information is impossible.

3. *When a sequentially accessed file is updated, it is rewritten in full on a different reel of tape.*

Since a tape should not be backspaced for rewriting, the only way to update a tape file is to write an entirely new and complete, updated version of the file onto another reel of tape. Although the records of a card file that are unchanged by an updating could be extracted and reused in the updated file, it is usually better to repunch the entire file, unless the proportion of records changed is small. To make a virtue out of necessity, it is observed that writing an entirely new copy of the file has several important advantages over making changes in the old copy.

(a) In many computer systems, the writing of a record into the new file can ''overlap'', that is, take place at the same time as the reading of a record from the old file. By the first principle, this usually reduces the total processing time.

(b) Saved older versions of the file can be used to analyze trends and make predictions.

(c) Previous versions of the file can be used to reconstruct the most recent version of the file in case of accidental loss or damage to the most recent version. Indeed, most systems that are primarily disk-oriented periodically dump disk files onto tape for precisely this reason.

4. *The records of an input tape or card file are best processed in the order in which they appear in the file.*

Since tape and card files usually are not backspaced, and since only a limited number of records is kept in main memory at one time, each record of an input tape or card file must be processed in turn, in a single beginning-to-ending scan of the file. When there is only one input file, as in the programs in previous chapters, or when there is only one sequentially accessed input file, this programming fact of life usually is not an undue hardship. The order of processing of records is determined by the order of the records in the sequentially accessed input file. However, when there are two or more sequentially accessed input files to be coordinated, as in the program updateandreorder in this section, *the records of all the sequentially accessed input files must be in the same order* for any reasonable type of processing to be possible. This usually is accomplished by sorting all sequentially accessed input files before they are accessed in the same program.

Coordinating Two Sequentially Accessed Input Files

With these principles in mind, one can design a program to update an inventory master file stored on magnetic tape. The same principles also are applicable to sequentially accessed files stored on magnetic disk. To achieve the fastest possible processing rates, all input and output is on magnetic tape, except for a (hopefully) small number of error messages. The two input files for this program are the inventory master file and a transaction file listing shipping and receiving transactions to modify the quantities recorded in the inventory master file. Since these two files must be coordinated, each record in the transaction file and each record in the inventory master file must have an item identification number or other key by which the kinds of records can be matched, and both files must be sorted on these identification numbers before the program execution starts.

It is no great problem to maintain the inventory master file in increasing order of item identification number. In fact, the programs for adding a new item to and deleting an existing item from a sequentially accessed inventory file maintained in sorted order are simpler than the corresponding programs for directly accessed files, and they are left as exercises.

There are several good ways to prepare a sorted transaction file. One is to sort the punched cards from which the transaction records are most often derived before copying them onto tape. Another is to put unsorted transaction records onto tape and then to sort the tape file before running the inventory updating and reordering program. In any event, the necessary step of sorting the transaction file must be considered in the total time and cost of running the inventory system.

Since the transaction file is always sorted before use, and since the inventory master file occasionally might be sorted, it is wise to design a termination signal that is unaffected by sorting the file. A good choice of termination signal is a trailer record with an item identification number higher than any actual item identification number, so that it remains at the end of the file when the file is sorted. Such a record is sometimes called a "nines record" when an identification number of all nines is the highest possible number. An item identification number of zero in the end of file record may not be satisfactory, because it could wind up at the beginning rather that the end of the file when the file is sorted.

Flow of Information in an Updating Program

Based on considerations just described, one way to design a tape-oriented inventory updating program is to have two input tape files, oldmasterfile and transactionfile, and two output tape files, newmasterfile and reorderfile. These names are just names of Pascal variables in the program; the names of the actual files used may change from one run to the next. Operating system commands are often used to assign names of actual files to the program names for the files. For example, if in one run the actual file used for oldmasterfile is inventory37, and the actual file used for newmasterfile is inventory38, then for the next run the actual file used for oldmasterfile might be inventory38 and the actual file used for newmasterfile might be inventory39. The details of associating a catalogued file name with a Pascal file variable vary too widely to describe here. A printer is used for the small number of error messages that might be necessary. Figure 6.4.1 depicts this flow of information. The rectangular box represents the program, the roundish shapes suggesting reels of tape represent files accessed sequentially, and the remaining box represents a printed output file.

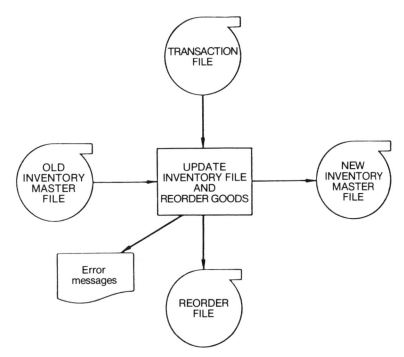

Figure 6.4.1   Flow of information through the program updateandreorder. Roundish shapes represent magnetic tapes.

An initial version of the program updateandreorder can now be written, in which each iteration of the main loop processes one transaction record. Normal termination of the loop occurs when all transactions records have been processed. However, a second possibility of terminating the loop early in case of severe error is provided also. The only error condition tested for explicitly in this version of the program is the possibility of transaction records out of sequence, which might happen if the transaction file is improperly sorted or not sorted at all before running the updating program. Other possibilities for error tests are discussed in the exercises.

```
program updateandreorder
      (oldmasterfile, transactionfile, newmasterfile,
       reorderfile, output);
{ initial version }
{ all files are accessed sequentially }

begin
initialize;
until all transactions processed or severe error encountered do
  begin
  read a transaction record from transaction file;
  if the transaction record is the end of file signal then
    confirm that all transactions are processed and exit loop
  else if transaction record is out of order then
    begin
    set error condition := 'transaction record out of order';
    confirm that severe error encountered and exit loop;
    end { else if }
  else
    begin
    find corresponding inventory record and update it;
    { save transaction id to determine if records are in order }
    set previous transaction id := transaction id;
    end; { else }
  end; { loop }

if all transactions processed then
  copy rest of old inventory file into updated new inventory file
else
  print an appropriate error message;
end.
```

Matching Inventory Records and Transaction Records

The most difficult problem in refining the program updateandreorder is finding the inventory record in the inventory master file that corresponds to a given transaction record, that is, the inventory record with an item identification number to match the item identification number in a transaction record. It is difficult both because there may be more than one transaction involving the same inventory item and because there may be no transaction at all for many of the items in the inventory. Thus, although the master file and the transaction file are sorted according to the same key, their entries might not match up one-to-one.

One solution to this problem is based on always having a copy of exactly one inventory record available in main memory at any time during program execution. (This means that the initialization step for the program must include the reading of the first inventory record.) Since the inventory master file is sorted into increasing order by item identification number, a new record is read from the inventory master file if and only if it is determined that the identification number for the transaction record just read is larger than the item identification number in the inventory record then in main memory.

Figure 6.4.2 illustrates the position and contents of the files oldmasterfile, transactionfile, and newmasterfile just after a transaction record has been read. The values in the shaded inventory record with item identification number 3 are also stored in main memory at that moment, as are the values in the shaded transaction record just read with item identification number 5. Both files are sorted in increasing order by item identification numbers.

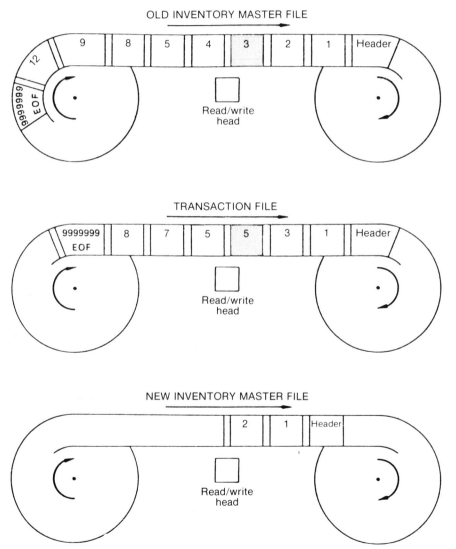

Figure 6.4.2   Positions of the tape files oldmasterfile, transactionfile, and newmaster-file just after a new transaction record has been read. Information from the shaded records also is available in main memory.

Since the item identification number, 5, of the current transaction record in main memory, is greater than 3, the current inventory record item identification number, the inventory master file must be advanced (and new records read) to reach the corresponding inventory record, which has item identification number 5. Before this can be done however, processing must be completed on the inventory record with identification number 3 currently in main memory. This file processing could not have been done earlier since the previous transaction identification number was 3, and only when the transaction record with identification number 5 is read is it certain that all updating transactions for item 3 have been processed. So, before reading the next inventory record, the updated inventory record for item 3 must be written into the new inventory master file and then checked to see if item 3 should be reordered. Only then should the next inventory record be read. This inventory record, as shown in the simulated tape file in Figure 6.4.2, has the item identification number 4, so the search for the corresponding inventory record must continue.

An important point that might be overlooked when first writing an updating program for sequentially accessed files is that, even though this new inventory record with item identification number 4 is not updated, it still must be rewritten into the updated inventory master file. This is because the new master file must contain the most recent information on *all* items kept in inventory, not just on the items whose information is changed. Finally, as shown in Figure 6.4.3, the next inventory master file record read has item identification number 5, so processing of the first updating transaction for item 5 then can be done in main memory.

What To Do If The Inventory Record Cannot be Found

Suppose a transaction record has an item identification number for which there is no corresponding inventory record, like the transaction record with identification number 7 in the simulated tape file in Figure 6.4.3. In the simulated example, this is discovered only after the inventory record with item identification number 5 is discarded because it it too low, and the next inventory record, with item identification number 8, is discovered to be too high. This lack of a corresponding inventory record is clearly an error, perhaps caused by faulty keypunching of the transaction item identification number, or else by a newly stocked item for which no record yet exists in the inventory master file. However, it is not an serious error, because it does not prevent correct processing of the other, correct transaction records. Thus printing an error message and proceeding is a reasonable way to handle a transaction record that has no corresponding inventory record.

On the other hand, a transaction record out of order is a serious error, because in that case, no following transaction records with lower item identification numbers can be processed. Their corresponding inventory records already will have been passed over and transcribed in the new (updated) inventory master file. Besides, if one transaction record is out of order, there is reason to believe that the sorting of transaction records was not done properly and that, most likely, many other transaction records are also out of order. In this case, it seems reasonable to terminate the program execution so that the transaction file can be sorted properly before running the updating program again. There are few further obstacles to refining the program updateandreorder completely, and most of them can be resolved by referring to Figures 6.4.2 and 6.4.3.

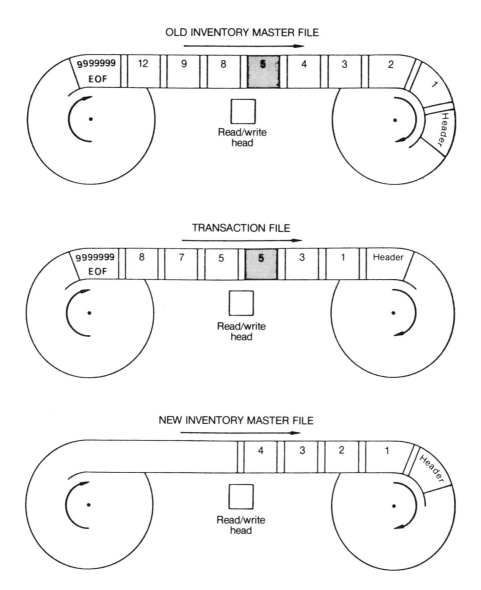

Figure 6.4.3 Positions of the tape files oldmasterfile, transactionfile, and newmastefile after the corresponding inventory record is found. Information from the shaded records also is available in main memory.

```
program updateandreorder
    (oldmasterfile, transactionfile, newmasterfile,
     reorderfile, output);

  const
    maxid = 9999;
    maxqty = 99999;
    deslength = 50;
    eofsignal = 9999;
```

```
type
  idtype = 0..maxid;
  qtytype = 0..maxqty;
  transtype = record
    id : idtype;
    kind : (received, shipped);
    quantity : qtytype;
    end; { transtype }
  invtype = record
    id : idtype;
    description : packed array [1..deslength] of char;
    qtyinstock, reorderpoint, reorderqty : qtytype;
    reordered : boolean;
    end; { invtype }

var
  transrecord : transtype;
  invrecord : invtype;
  previousid : idtype;
  oldmasterfile, newmasterfile : file of invtype;
  transactionfile : file of transtype;
  reorderfile : file of char;
  allprocessed : boolean;
  error : (none, unspecified, outoforder);

procedure initialize;
  begin
  reset (oldmasterfile);
  reset (transactionfile);
  rewrite (newmasterfile);
  rewrite (reorderfile);
  previousid := 0;
  error := none;
  read (oldmasterfile, invrecord);
  end; { initialize }

procedure checkreorder;
  begin
  with invrecord do
    if (qtyinstock < reorderpoint) and (not reordered) then
      begin
      writeln (reorderfile, id :9, reorderqty :9, description);
      reordered := true;
      end; { if and with invrecord }
  end; { checkreorder }

procedure updateinvrecord;
  begin
  case transrecord . kind of
    received :
```

```
    begin
    invrecord . qtyinstock : =
        invrecord . qtyinstock + transrecord . quantity;
    invrecord . reordered : = false;
    end; { received }
  shipped :
    invrecord . qtyinstock : =
        invrecord . qtyinstock - transrecord . quantity;
  end; { case }
end; { updateinvrecord }


procedure findandupdateinvrecord;

  var
    found, missing : boolean;

  begin
  found : = false;
  missing : = false;
  while (not found) and (not missing) do
    if invrecord . id < transrecord . id then
      { finish all summary processing of current inventory record }
      begin
      checkreorder;
      write (newmasterfile, invrecord);
      read (oldmasterfile, invrecord);
      end { if }
    else if invrecord . id = transrecord . id then
      found : = true
    else
      missing : = true;

  if found then
    updateinvrecord
  else
    writeln ('No inventory record found for transaction item ',
        transrecord . id :1);
  end; { findandupdateinvrecord }


procedure copyrestofoldmasterfile;
{ copy remaining records from old inventory master file
  into new inventory master file without updating }

  begin
  while invrecord . id <> eofsignal do
    begin
    write (newmasterfile, invrecord);
    read (oldmasterfile, invrecord);
    end; { while-loop }
```

```
      write (newmasterfile, invrecord);  { signal record }
      writeln (reorderfile, eofsignal :9, 0 :9, ' ' :deslength);
      end; { copyrestofoldmasterfile }

  procedure handleerrors;
    begin
    if error = outoforder then
      begin
      writeln ('Transaction file not sorted.');
      writeln ('Identification number: ', previousid :1,
               ' precedes ', transrecord . id :1);
      end { if }
    else
      writeln ('Unspecified error condition');
      writeln ('Severe error.  Execution terminated.');
    end; { handleerrors }

  begin { ---------- main program ---------- }
  initialize;
  allprocessed := false;
  while (not allprocessed) and (error = none) do
    begin
    read (transactionfile, transrecord);
    if transrecord . id = eofsignal then
      allprocessed := true
    else if transrecord . id < previousid then
      error := outoforder
    else
      begin
      findandupdateinvrecord;
      previousid := transrecord . id;
      end; { else }
    end; { while-loop }

    if allprocessed then
      copyrestofoldmasterfile
    else
      handleerrors;
    end.
```

Use of With-Statements

All of the data structure references in the procedure checkreorder refer to components of the record invrecord. The with-statement provides a very convenient tool in this case for clarifying the program by suppressing the duplicate references. In the procedure updateinvrecord, however, some references are to invrecord and some references are to transrecord, so a with-statement cannot be used.

Why Do Reorder Checking at the Same Time As Updating?

If the reordering of items low in stock is done by a separate program, an additional pass through the inventory master file is required. If a separate reordering run is done for each supplier, it will require a complete pass through the inventory master file for each supplier. Since execution time is spent largely on reading and writing files, it is more efficient to do both types of processing in one pass through the master file, if possible.

One principle of efficient programming for sequentially accessed files is to process information as soon as it becomes available. In the updating program, when an updated inventory record is written into the new inventory master file, all the information needed to decide if an item needs reordering is available in main memory. Thus a reorder list can be prepared at this time without further handling of the inventory master file.

One interesting feature of the reorder checking procedure is the reorder flag, implemented using a boolean variable. Normally, an item is reordered when the quantity in stock drops below the reorder point. However, once an item has been ordered, it should not be ordered again until the first order is received. The boolean field reordered of each inventory record keeps track of whether a reorder request has been placed. It is set to true whenever the sum of all transactions for an item in one updating run reduces the inventory of that item below the reorder point, and it remains true to prevent further reordering until a quantity of that item is received in a subsequent updating run. In a more sophisticated system, it might be desirable to issue a second or third order as the quantity on hand drops lower and lower.

Exercises

---

1. Hand simulate the execution of the program updateandreorder in this section from the beginning of the execution until the files are positioned as in Figure 6.4.2. Assume that no transaction record causes a reorder request. Draw a diagram similar to Figure 6.4.2 each time a record is read from one of the files.

2. Hand simulate the execution of the program updateandreorder starting from the situation depicted in Figure 6.4.2 and continuing until the situation depicted in Figure 6.4.3 is reached. Draw a new diagram similar to Figures 6.4.2 and 6.4.3 each time a record is read from one of the files.

3. Hand simulate the execution of the program updateandreorder starting from the situation depicted in Figure 6.4.3 and continuing to the end of the program execution. Assume that no transaction record causes a reorder request. Draw a diagram similar to Figure 6.4.3 each time a record is read from one of the files.

4. Write a program to add new records to and delete existing records from the sequentially accessed inventory master file in this section.

5. Write a program to merge two sorted files containing inventory transactions into a combined sorted file. Modify the program updateandreorder to use this file as input.

6. Write a program deleteitems that accepts a list of item identification numbers in increasing order as input and deletes the inventory records for those items from the sequentially accessed inventory master file in this section.

7. Write a program addnewitems that accepts as input a sorted file of complete inventory records for items not previously stocked and adds these new items to the

inventory master file in this section in the proper order. Hint: Review the discussion of merging in Section 3.4.

6.5   A System of Payroll Programs and Files

Since the mid-1960s, most payrolls have been processed by computer. Nearly everyone is familiar with the ubiquitous computer-printed paycheck and accompanying stub. This section describes a relatively complete system that provides a detailed paycheck stub with every paycheck and prints an annual report giving yearly company pay and tax totals. The key to such a system is retaining relevant information about each employee in an ''employee master file'' in auxiliary memory. Once established to serve the payroll system, this master file also might be used as an important source of personnel information for a management information system or for other company business.

Direct Versus Sequential Access

In the black book programs in Section 6.3, it does not matter whether the black book file is accessed sequentially or directly, because the file is always read as a whole from auxiliary memory, processed while the entire file resides in main memory, and finally rewritten as a whole into auxiliary memory. In the inventory programs of the previous section all files are accessed sequentially and a great deal of the planning was concerned with coordinating the processing of the input files. In this section the employee master file is accessed directly, mostly because this is easier and more nearly similar to accessing a list in main memory. Management inquiry programs referencing the same employee master file actually might require the instant, random access to any record, as provided by accessing the file directly. The organization of the file and many important details, especially in the updating programs, would be quite different if sequential access were used.

Since the language Pascal provides facilities only for accessing files sequentially, the procedures readdirect and writedirect are not built in, but must be programmer-defined procedures. One possible implementation of these procedures appears in Appendix D. These implementations are not efficient and should be used only for the purpose of learning how direct access files can be used. Many Pascal systems provide direct access read and write procedures. If they are available, they should be used instead of readdirect and writedirect, or the procedures readdirect and writedirect should be written using the locally available direct access facilities.

Programs and Files of the Payroll System

The most important program in the payroll system is the program weeklypayroll that calculates the weekly paycheck information. Input to this program consists of two files, a timecard file containing weekly information and the employee master file containing more permanent information. As output, this program produces a weekly summary report and a paycheck file containing all the information needed to print the paychecks with detailed check stubs. In addition, the program weeklypayroll updates the information kept in the master file for each employee who receives a paycheck that week.

Other programs of the payroll system include a program createempfiles to create the employee master file and an index file containing social security numbers used to locate records in the employee master file, a program updateempfiles to update them, a program paycheckprocessor to print the actual paychecks and stubs, a procedure done separately because different forms are required in the printer than for the weekly summary report, and a program prepareannualreport to prepare an annual report from the year-to-date totals stored in the master file. Figure 6.5.1 illustrates the flow of information between the various programs and files of the payroll system. This diagram depicts the flow of data between programs and files, and not the flow of control

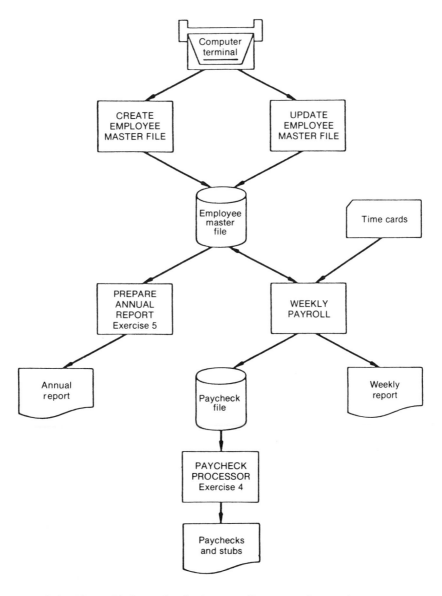

Figure 6.5.1   Flow of information in the payroll system. Rectangles represent programs and cylinders represent direct access files.

within a program. The rectangular boxes represent programs, and the other shapes suggest storage devices that contain data files. In particular, the cylinders are meant to suggest magnetic disk units.

The Weekly Payroll Program

Since the program weeklypayroll is the heart of the entire payroll system, it is that program that receives immediate attention. Although the following plan of action may not be feasible if the employee master file already has been established and a new payroll program is needed to process the existing file, it is best to design the programs and the data structures together. In the initial version of the program weeklypayroll below, both the data structures and the statements need refinement.

```
program weeklypayroll
     (employfile, indexfile, checkfile, timefile, output);

  var
    timecard : timetype;
    employeedata : employtype;
    paycheck : checktype;

  begin
  initialize;
  while moretimecards do
    begin
    read time card;
    if time card is a termination signal then
      moretimecards := false
    else if person described on the time card is an employee then
      begin
      read employee data from the employee master file;
      calculate information for paycheck and stub;
      update employee data record in main memory;
      write paycheck information into paycheck file;
      adjust totals for weekly payroll report;
      update permanent copy of employee data in master file;
      end { else if }
    else
      print an error message saying there is no such employee;
    end; { while-loop }

  write trailer record into paycheck file;
  print weekly payroll report;
  end.
```

It is reasonable to begin refinement by deciding what information is to be punched into the time cards, deferring refinement of the initialization step, as usual, until last. Each time card must contain a number of hours worked during the week past and enough identifying information to specify the employee unambiguously. The refined data structure timetype below meets these requirements.

```
type
  ssntype = packed array [1..11] of char;
timetype = record
  name : string;
  ssn : ssntype;
  hoursworked : real;
  end; { timetype }
```

Signalling the End of the Time Card File

Since the time card file is a card file, permitting only sequential access, its end may be signalled by a *trailer record* containing the special signal value of all z's for the name and '999-99-9999' for ssn (social security number) following all the actual time card records. The following statement refines the exit test for the main loop of the program weekly payroll.

```
if timecard . name = allzs then
  moretimecards := false
```

These values are chosen for the trailer record so that if the file is sorted either by name or by social security number, the trailer record will still be the last record. Of course, it is also possible to use the Pascal built-in function eof to test for the end of a sequentially accessed file instead of a programmer-defined trailer record.

Finding an Employee's Record in the Master File

If the value of timecard . name is not all z's, then the time card contains real data to be processed. The next step, in this, case is to find and retrieve from the corresponding record of the employee master file the permanent information for the employee specified. This will be easier if we design the employee master file to be accessed directly.

The problem now is to design a procedure whereby the record number of an employee record in the employee master file may be determined from the identifying information in a time card. One possibility is to use an employee's social security number as that employee's record number in the master file. However, only a small fraction of the billion possible nine-digit social security numbers correspond to employees of any one company, so there would always be great gaps in the record numbers.

In order to use record numbers that run consecutively from one to the number of employees in the company, one may construct an index. The form of the index adopted in this section for the employee master file consists of a list ssntable of employee social security numbers, in which the location of an employee's social security number is the same as the record number in the master file. That is, the first social security number in the index list ssntable matches the social security number in record 1 of the master file, the second social security number in the index list matches the social security number in record 2, and so forth. One may recall from Section 4.3 that the value of the function

```
locinunsortedlist (timecard . ssn, ssntable, 1, nrofemps, signalformissing)
```

is the location of the social security number timecard . ssn in the list ssntable, if that social security number is in the list; otherwise it is the value of signalformissing. The supplied arguments 1 and nrofemps tell how much of ssntable to search.

Although a sorted index list would permit a faster searching procedure, a sorted list is not used here because it would involve keeping the records of the master file sorted in the same order as the index, necessitating more complex and less efficient updating programs.

These decisions on the form of the index clear the last obstacle to refining the major if-block of the program weeklypayroll as shown below. Of course, for this refinement to work, the value of signalformissing must be initialized, and the ssntable must be read into main memory from the file indexfile at the beginning of an execution of the program weeklypayroll.

```
{ refinement of the major if-statement of the program weeklypayroll }
{ determine record number of corresponding employee master file record }
recnumber := locinunsortedlist (timecard . ssn, ssntable,
                                1, nrofssns, signalformissing);
if recnumber <> signalformissing then
  begin
  readdirect (employfile, recnumber, employeedata, error);
  if error then
    writeln ('read direct error for ', employeedata . ssn)
  else
    begin
    calculatepay;
    { the procedure calculatepay also updates the
      employee data record currently in main memory }
    write (checkfile, paycheck);
    adjusttotals;
    writedirect (employfile, recnumber, employeedata, error);
    if error then
      writeln ('Write direct error for ', employeedata . ssn);
    end; { else }
  end { if recnumber }
else
  begin
  writeln ('There is no record for ', timecard . name);
  writeln ('with social security number ', timecard . ssn);
  writeln ('in the index file.');
  end; { else }
```

Direct-Access Read and Write Statements

As described in Section 6.1, the statement

```
readdirect (employfile, recnumber, employeedata, error)
```

directs the computer to copy the information from record number recnumber of the employee master file employfile as the values of the data structure employeedata and to set the boolean variable error to true or false. In the process of making the paycheck calculations, some of the information in an employee data record, including the year-to-date

totals for pay and taxes, are changed in main memory to include amounts for the
current week. However, just as in the black book file updating program, these changes
do not become permanent until they are written into auxiliary memory.

In this weekly payroll program, there is never more than one employee's record in
main memory at one time, because reading another employee's record from the master
file in auxiliary memory replaces the values for the employee whose time card was
processed previously. Thus, soon after all the pay calculations for an employee are finished, to ensure permanence, the updated values for the employee's record must be
copied back into the master file in auxiliary memory by the following statement.

```
writedirect (employfile, recnumber, employeedata, error)
```

Refining the Data Structure Declarations

Before writing the procedure calculatepay, it is necessary to decide what information is to be kept in the employee master file and what information is to be written into
the paycheck file, and to declare data structures for their respective records.

The declaration below for the data structure employtype includes essential items
such as hourly pay rate and year-to-date totals, standard identifying information such as
name, address, and social security number, and other information whose purpose might
not be obvious at this time. This other information is used in other programs of the
payroll system, including modifications and additions to the system described in the exercises. In practice, these components might not be included in the data structure employtype until after the other programs are written, at which time the data structure declaration in the weekly payroll program must be enlarged, and, worse yet, the weekly
payroll program itself must be modified to process and update the newly added components. It is especially important, therefore, that the individual programs in a system
of programs that will be in operation for several years be written clearly and be easy to
read and modify, because over the lifetime of the system, they almost certainly will be
revised and modified several times as the system evolves. Programs that cannot be
modified easily soon become useless, and they must be replaced at great cost in time
and effort.

```
addresstype = record
  street, citystatezip : string;
  end; { addresstype }
paytype = record
  grosspay, incometax, fica, netpay : real;
  end; { paytype }
employtype = record
  name : string;
  ssn : ssntype;
  address : addresstype;
  department, skills : string;
  hourlyrate : real;
  yeartodate : paytype;
  status : string;
  dateoflastpaycheck : datetype;
  end; { employtype }
```

The components of the data structure checktype, on the other hand, are pretty much what one might expect. Some payroll systems also might include the employee's address, if paychecks often are mailed. Of course, if more elaborate pay calculations, including such items as pension contributions and health benefit deductions, are carried out, there will be more information for the check stub. The following declaration suffices for current purposes.

```
stubtype  = record;
  thisweek, yeartodate : paytype;
  end; { stubtype }
checktype = record
  name : string;
  date : datetype;
  stub : stubtype;
  end; { checktype }
```

The paycheck file consists of paycheck records containing the information of the data structure checktype, and a trailer record with the name consisting of all z's as a termination signal.

Pay Calculations

The calculations of gross pay proceed much as in the previous payroll program discussed in Section 1.6. After the gross pay is calculated, 11 percent is withheld as income tax, and 6.65 percent is withheld as the FICA deduction. These amounts are subtracted from the gross pay to give the employee's net pay, and then all these amounts for the current week are added to the corresponding year-to-date totals for the employee. Year-to-date totals also are entered in the checkstub data structure, along with the employee's name and the amounts for the current week. The date of the most recent paycheck is changed to make it possible to check for duplicate or missing time cards (left as an exercise). These steps are accomplished by the procedure calculatepay that appears below with the final version of the program weeklypayroll.

The remaining tasks are to write the paycheck and stub records for later printing onto bank check forms, to write the updated master file record into auxiliary memory so that the new information is retained after all time cards are processed, to update the weekly report totals and, after all time cards are processed, to print the weekly summary report. Adjustment of the weekly report totals is done by the procedure adjusttotals, which also appears below with the final version of the program weeklypayroll. This procedure uses four values for the summary totals, which must be initialized to zero at the beginning of the program weeklypayroll. The procedure printreport is straightforward. The refined program weeklypayroll may seem rather long to the beginner, but experienced programmers can see that this is because of the large number of details and not because any part of the program is difficult. This characteristic of bulky size without real complexity is typical of many operational file processing programs.

```
program weeklypayroll
    (employfile, indexfile, checkfile, timefile, output);
const
  maxlength = 30;
  maxnrofemps = 1000;
  signalformissing = 0;

type
  stringindex = 1..maxlength;
  stringlength = 0..maxlength;
  string = packed array [stringindex] of char;
  ssntype = packed array [1..11] of char;
  ssnloctype = 0..maxnrofemps;
  ssnindex = 1..maxnrofemps;
  tabletype = array [ssnindex] of ssntype;
  datetype = packed array [1..8] of char;


  timetype = record
    name : string;
    ssn : ssntype;
    hoursworked : real;
    end; { timetype }
  addresstype = record
    street, citystatezip : string;
    end; { addresstype }
  paytype = record
    grosspay, incometax, fica, netpay : real;
    end; { paytype }
  employtype = record
    name : string;
    ssn : ssntype;
    address : addresstype;
    department, skills : string;
    hourlyrate : real;
    yeartodate : paytype;
    status : string;
    dateoflastpaycheck : datetype;
    end; { employtype }
  stubtype = record;
    thisweek, yeartodate : paytype;
    end; { stubtype }
  checktype = record
    name : string;
    date : datetype;
    stub : stubtype;
    end; { checktype }
  empfiletype = file of employtype;
  filetype = empfiletype; { for readdirect and writedirect }
  fileindex = 0..maxnrofemps;
  recordtype = employtype;
```

```
var
  timecard : timetype;
  employeedata : employtype;
  paycheck : checktype;
  nrofemps : 0..maxnrofemps;
  ssntable : tabletype;
  payrolldate : datetype;
  allzs : string;
  moretimecards, error : boolean;
  total : paytype;
  employfile : empfiletype;
  indexfile : file of ssntype;
  checkfile : file of checktype;
  timefile : file of char;
  recnumber : ssnloctype;
  i : stringindex;
  j : 1..11;

function locinunsortedlist
            (entry : ssntype;
             table : tabletype;
             lower, upper : ssnindex;
             signalformissing : ssnloctype)
             : ssnloctype;
  var
    i : ssnloctype;
    found : boolean;

  begin
  i := lower - 1;
  found := false;
  while (i < upper) and (not found) do
    begin
    i := i + 1;
    found := (table [i] = entry);
    end; { while-loop }

  if found then
    locinunsortedlist := i
  else
    locinunsortedlist := signalformissing;
  end; { locinunsortedlist }

procedure readdirect (filename : filetype;
                      recordnumber : fileindex;
                      var recordname : recordtype;
                      var error : boolean);
  ... end; { readdirect }
procedure writedirect (filename : filetype;
                       recordnumber : fileindex;
                       recordname : recordtype;
                       var error : boolean);
  ... end; { writedirect }
```

```
procedure initialize;

  var
    i : 1..8;
    j : stringindex;

  procedure readssntable;
  { reads the index file into main memory }

    const
      lastssn = '999-99-9999';

    var
      moreemps : boolean;
      ssn : ssntype;

    begin
    reset (indexfile);
    moreemps := true;
    nrofemps := 0;
    while (moreemps) and (nrofemps < maxnrofemps) do
      begin
      read (indexfile, ssn);
      if ssn = lastssn then
        moreemps := false
      else
        begin
        nrofemps := nrofemps + 1;
        ssntable [nrofemps] := ssn;
        end; { else }
      end; { while-loop }
    end; { readssntable }

  begin { initialize }
  readssntable;
  for i := 1 to 8 do
    read (payrolldate [i]);
  write ('Input data  payrolldate: ');
  for i := 1 to 8 do
    write (payrolldate [i]);
  writeln;
  for j := 1 to maxlength do
    allzs [j] := 'z';
  rewrite (checkfile);
  with total do
    begin
    grosspay := 0;
    incometax := 0;
    fica := 0;
    netpay := 0;
    end; { with total }
  end; { initialize }
```

```
procedure calculatepay;
{ calculate grosspay }

  const
    regularhours = 40;
    otfactor = 1.5;
    inctaxrate = 0.11;
    ficarate = 0.0665;

  var
    regularpay, othours, otpay : real;

  begin
  with paycheck . stub . thisweek do
    begin
    if timecard . hoursworked <= regularhours then
      grosspay := employeedata . hourlyrate *
          timecard . hoursworked
    else
      begin
      regularpay := employeedata . hourlyrate * regularhours;
      othours := timecard . hoursworked - regularhours;
      otpay := otfactor * employeedata . hourlyrate * othours;
      grosspay := regularpay + otpay;
      end; { else }

    { calculate deductions and net pay }
    incometax := inctaxrate * grosspay;
    fica := ficarate * grosspay;
    netpay := grosspay - incometax - fica;

    { update employee year-to-date totals
      and enter in two places }
    employeedata . yeartodate . grosspay :=
        employeedata . yeartodate . grosspay + grosspay;
    employeedata . yeartodate . incometax :=
        employeedata . yeartodate . incometax + incometax;
    employeedata . yeartodate . fica :=
        employeedata . yeartodate . fica + fica;
    employeedata . yeartodate . netpay :=
        employeedata . yeartodate . netpay + netpay;
    end; { with paycheck . stub . thisweek }

  paycheck . name := employeedata . name;
  paycheck . stub . yeartodate := employeedata . yeartodate;
  paycheck . date := payrolldate;
  employeedata . dateoflastpaycheck := payrolldate;
  end; { calculatepay }

procedure adjusttotals;

  begin
  with paycheck . stub . thisweek do
```

```
      begin
      total . grosspay := total . grosspay + grosspay;
      total . incometax := total . incometax + incometax;
      total . fica := total . fica + fica;
      total . netpay := total . netpay + netpay;
      end; { with paycheck . stub . thisweek }
    end; { adjusttotals }

procedure printreport;

  begin
  with total do
    begin
    writeln ('Payroll totals for the week ending ', payrolldate);
    writeln ('Gross pay    $', grosspay :1:2);
    writeln ('Income tax   $', incometax :1:2);
    writeln ('FICA         $', fica :1:2);
    writeln ('Net pay      $', netpay :1:2);
    end; { with total }
  end; { printreport }

begin { ---------- main program ---------- }
initialize;
moretimecards := true;
while moretimecards do
  begin
  with timecard do
    begin
    for i := 1 to maxlength do
      read (name [i]);
    for j := 1 to 11 do
      read (ssn [j]);
    readln (hoursworked);
    writeln ('Input data  timecard:');
    writeln ('                    name: ', name);
    writeln ('                    ssn: ', ssn);
    writeln ('                    hoursworked: ', hoursworked :1:2);
    end; { with timecard }
  if timecard . name = allzs then
    moretimecards := false
  else
    begin
    recnumber := locinunsortedlist (timecard . ssn, ssntable,
                                    1, nrofemps,
                                    signalformissing);
    if recnumber <> signalformissing then
      begin
      readdirect (employfile, recnumber, employeedata, error);
      if error then
        writeln ('read direct error for ', employeedata . ssn)
      else
        begin
        calculatepay;
```

```
        { the procedure calculatepay also updates the
          employee data record currently in main memory }
        write (checkfile, paycheck);
        adjusttotals;
        writedirect (employfile, recnumber, employeedata, error);
        if error then
          writeln ('Write direct error for ', employeedata . ssn);
        end; { else }
      end { if recnumber }
    else
      begin
      writeln ('There is no record for ', timecard . name);
      writeln ('with social security number ', timecard . ssn);
      writeln ('in the index file.');
      end; { else }
    end; { else }
  end; { while-loop }

{ write trailer record into paycheck file }
with paycheck do
  begin
  name := allzs;
  with stub do
    begin
    with thisweek do
      begin
      grosspay := 0;
      incometax := 0;
      fica := 0;
      netpay := 0;
      end; { with thisweek }
    yeartodate := thisweek;
    end; { with stub }
  end; { with paycheck }

write (checkfile, paycheck);
printreport;
end.
```

Creating the Employee Master File

The procedure initialize reflects a decision that the index of social security numbers, one for each employee, is to be kept in a separate file named indexfile. Thus, when the master file, initially containing no employees, is created by executing the statement

```
rewrite (employfile)
```

the indexfile must also be created and a trailer record must be put in it to indicate that there are no employee data records. These functions are performed by the program createempfiles.

```
program createempfiles (input, output, employfile, indexfile);

  const
    maxlength = 30;

  type
    stringindex = 1..maxlength;
    stringlength = 0..maxlength;
    string = packed array [stringindex] of char;
    ssntype = packed array [1..11] of char;
    datetype = packed array [1..8] of char;
    addresstype = record
      street, citystatezip : string;
      end; { addresstype }
    paytype = record
      grosspay, incometax, fica, netpay : real;
      end; { paytype }
    employtype = record
      name : string;
      ssn : ssntype;
      address : addresstype;
      department, skills : string;
      hourlyrate : real;
      yeartodate : paytype;
      status : string;
      dateoflastpaycheck : datetype;
      end; { employtype }

  var
    employfile : file of employtype;
    indexfile : file of ssntype;

  begin
  rewrite (employfile);
  rewrite (indexfile);
  write (indexfile, '999-99-9999');
  end.
```

One may recall that the rewrite statement used in the program createempfiles tells the computer to create a new file if one of that name doesn't exist and, in any case, to leave it containing no data. For simplicity, we have omitted rigorous password checks.

Updating the Employee Master File

Another important program in the system of payroll programs is the one that keeps the employee master file up-to-date. The program must be able to add new employees, delete current employees, and make changes in an employee's address or hourly pay rate. Deleting an employee at this point only involves changing the person's employment status to ''terminated''. The employee data record for a terminated employee is not deleted from the master file at this time, because it will be needed at the end of the

year to prepare annual reports, even if the employee leaves the company and receives
no further weekly paychecks.

```
program updateempfiles
     (employfile, indexfile, input, output);

  const
    maxlength = 30;
    blank = ' ';
    maxnrofemps = 1000;
    signalformissing = 0;
    lastssn = '999-99-9999';
    add             = 'Add                        ';
    delete          = 'Delete                     ';
    changexaddress = 'Change address             ';
    changexrate    = 'Change hourly rate         ';
    done           = 'Done                       ';

  type
    stringindex = 1..maxlength;
    stringlength = 0..maxlength;
    string = packed array [stringindex] of char;
    ssntype = packed array [1..11] of char;
    ssnloctype = 0..maxnrofemps;
    ssnindex = 1..maxnrofemps;
    tabletype = array [ssnindex] of ssntype;
    datetype = packed array [1..8] of char;

    addresstype = record
      street, citystatezip : string;
      end; { addresstype }
    paytype = record
      grosspay, incometax, fica, netpay : real;
      end; { paytype }
    employtype = record
      name : string;
      ssn : ssntype;
      address : addresstype;
      department, skills : string;
      hourlyrate : real;
      yeartodate : paytype;
      status : string;
      dateoflastpaycheck : datetype;
      end; { employtype }
    empfiletype = file of employtype;
    filetype = empfiletype; { for readdirect and writedirect }
    fileindex = 0..maxnrofemps;
    recordtype = employtype;

  var
    employeedata : employtype;
    nrofemps : 0..maxnrofemps;
    ssntable : tabletype;
```

```
    allzs, request : string;
    ssnforchange : ssntype;
    nameforchange : string;
    allupdatesdone, error : boolean;
    indexfile : file of ssntype;
    employfile : empfiletype;
    recnumber : ssnloctype;
    i : 1..11;

function locinunsortedlist
              (entry : ssntype;
               table : tabletype;
               lower, upper : ssnindex;
               signal : ssnloctype)
               : ssnloctype;
  ... end; { locinunsortedlist }

procedure readdirect (filename : filetype;
                      recordnumber : fileindex;
                      var recordname : recordtype;
                      var error : boolean);
  ... end; { readdirect }

procedure writedirect (filename : filetype;
                       recordnumber : fileindex;
                       recordname : recordtype;
                       var error : boolean);
  ... end; { writedirect }

procedure readline (var line : string);
{ variable length character input procedure }
  ... end; { readline }

procedure readssntable;
{ reads the index file into main memory }
  ... end; { readssntable }

procedure writessntable;

  var
    i : ssnindex;

  begin
  rewrite (indexfile);
  for i := 1 to nrofemps do
    write (indexfile, ssntable [i]);
  write (indexfile, lastssn);
  end; { writessntable }
```

```
procedure getrecord;

  begin
  recnumber := locinunsortedlist (ssnforchange, ssntable,
                                  1, nrofemps, signalformissing);
  if recnumber <> signalformissing then
    begin
    readdirect (employfile, recnumber, employeedata, error);
    if error then
      writeln ('Read direct error for ', ssntable [recnumber]);
    end { if recnumber }
  else
    writeln ('social security number entered is not in master file.');
  end; { getrecord }

procedure addemployee;

  begin
  with employeedata do
    begin
    name := nameforchange;
    ssn := ssnforchange;
    readline (address . street);
    readline (address . citystatezip);
    readline (department);
    readline (skills);
    readln (hourlyrate);
    with yeartodate do
      begin
      grosspay := 0;
      incometax := 0;
      fica := 0;
      netpay := 0;
      end; { with yeartodate }
    status := 'active                       ';
    dateoflastpaycheck := '00-00-00';
    end; { with employeedata }
  nrofemps := nrofemps + 1;
  writedirect (employfile, nrofemps, employeedata, error);
  ssntable [nrofemps] := employeedata . ssn;
  end; { addemployee }

procedure deleteemployee;

  begin
  getrecord;
  if recnumber <> signalformissing then
    begin
    employeedata . status := 'terminated                   ';
    writedirect (employfile, recnumber, employeedata, error);
    end; { if }
  end; { deleteemployee }
```

```
procedure changeaddress;

  var
    addressforchange : addresstype;
  begin
  readline (addressforchange . street);
  readline (addressforchange . citystatezip);
  getrecord;
  if recnumber <> signalformissing then
    begin
    employeedata . address := addressforchange;
    writedirect (employfile, recnumber, employeedata, error);
    end; { if }
  end; { changeaddress }

procedure changerate;

  begin
  getrecord;
  if recnumber <> signalformissing then
    begin
    readln (employeedata . hourlyrate);
    writedirect (employfile, recnumber, employeedata, error);
    end; { if }
  end; { changerate }

begin { ---------- main program ---------- }
readssntable;
allupdatesdone := false;
while not allupdatesdone do
  begin
  readline (request);
  if request = done then
    allupdatesdone := true
  else
    begin
    readline (nameforchange);
    for i := 1 to 11 do
      read (ssnforchange [i]);
    readln;
    if request = add then
      addemployee
    else if request = delete then
      deleteemployee
    else if request = changexaddress then
      changeaddress
    else if request = changexrate then
      changerate
    else
      writeln ('Request not recognized');
    end; { else }
  end; { while-loop }
writessntable; { Note:  in the event an abnormal program termination
    occurs and this procedure call is not executed, the file indexfile
    will not be a complete index to the master file empfile. }
end.
```

Running a System of Programs

The programs in a system of programs like the payroll system in this section communicate with each other by writing information into and reading information from files in auxiliary memory. It is not possible to run the central program of this system, weeklypayroll, by itself. The programs that produce the input files for the program weeklypayroll must be run beforehand, and the programs that process the output files from the program weeklypayroll must be run afterward, in order to see what the program weeklypayroll does. The abbreviated sample executions below are designed to show the order in which the individual programs of the payroll system are run in normal use and how they pass information to each other. It may be useful while following the sequence of program executions to refer back to Figure 6.5.1, which shows the overall flow of information.

The First Day of System Operation

Suppose the payroll system in this section is to be put into operation for the first time. The employee master file and the associated index file are created by running the program createempfiles. The result is that the file employfile is empty and the file indexfile contains only a trailer record with the social security number '999-99-9999'. Next, the employee master file is updated by running the program updateempfiles. The following data would be provided as input.

Add
Aaron Aardvark
123-45-6789
111 Aleutian Avenue
Anchorage, Alaska 12345
Maintenance
Exterminator
4.25

Add
Barbara Banana
234-56-7890
222 Bucolic Byway
Beagle Bend, British Columbia
Food services
Waitress-Cashier
3.75

Add
Charles Canary
345-67-8901
333 Columbus Circle
Claremont, California 34567
Sales
None
4.50

Done

The result is a payroll master file with three employees in it, Aaron Aardvark, Barbara Banana, and Charles Canary, old friends of the authors. Year-to-date totals for each employee are all zero.

The First Execution of the Weekly Payroll Program

On the first Friday of the year, January 7, 1983, the first payroll is prepared using the new programs. First, the number of hours worked is calculated for each employee in the usual way (by hand, assuming a 5 p.m. quitting time on Friday), and four time cards are punched, one for each of the three employees and a trailer card with a name consisting of all z's for a termination signal at the end of the time card file. Then, with a time card file prepared and with the payroll master file containing all employee records available, the program weeklypayroll can be run.

```
run weeklypayroll

Input data   payrolldate: 83-01-07
Input data   timecard:
                         name: Aaron Aardvark
                         ssn: 123-45-6789
                         hoursworked: 50.00
Input data   timecard:
                         name: Barbara Banana
                         ssn: 234-56-7890
                         hoursworked: 40.00
Input data   timecard:
                         name: Charles Canary
                         ssn: 345-67-8901
                         hoursworked: 30.00
Input data   timecard:
                         name: zzzzzzzzzzzzzzzzzzzzzzzzzzzzzz
                         ssn: 999-99-9999
                         hoursworked: 0.00
Payroll totals for the week ending 83-01-07
Gross pay    $518.75
Income tax   $57.06
FICA         $34.50
Net pay      $427.19
```

The program weeklypayroll also updates the year-to-date totals for each employee, and it produces a paycheck file to be printed on bank check forms. Since everything seems to be working right, the bank check forms are put into the printer, and the program paycheckprocessor (Exercise 4) is run.

A Second Execution of the Weekly Payroll Program

The second weekly payroll is prepared on Friday, January 14, 1983 using the new payroll system of programs and files. To test alternatives in the programs, assume that Barbara Banana has quit to work in an ice cream parlor, and Dolores Donut has been hired to replace her. The four cards punched this week are the hours-worked cards for

Aaron Aardvark, Charles Canary, and Dolores Donut, and the trailer card with the signal of all z's. Assume that the program weeklypayroll is run next, under most circumstances, a perfectly reasonable thing to do.

```
run weeklypayroll

Input data    payrolldate: 83-01-14
Input data    timecard:
                          name:  Aaron Aardvark
                          ssn:  123-45-6789
                          hoursworked:  47.00
Input data    timecard:
                          name:  Charles Canary
                          ssn:  345-67-8901
                          hoursworked:  35.00
Input data    timecard:
                          name:  Dolores Donut
                          ssn:  456-78-9012
                          hoursworked:  42.00
There is no record for Dolores Donut
with social security number 456-78-9012
in the index file.

Input data    timecard:
                          name:  zzzzzzzzzzzzzzzzzzzzzzzzzzzzzz
                          ssn:  999-99-9999
                          hoursworked:  0.00
Payroll totals for the week ending 83-01-14
Gross pay    $372.12
Income tax   $40.93
FICA         $24.75
Net pay      $306.44
```

A subsequent spot check of the employee master file, perhaps using a program printemployfile that prints the entire contents of the employee master file, would show that the year-to-date totals for Aaron Aardvark and Charles Canary include the most recent amounts, that the year-to-date totals for Barbara Banana include only the amounts for the first week, and that Dolores Donut is nowhere to be found in the master file. The mistake is, of course, that her payroll record should have been added in an update run using the program updateempfiles before the most recent run of the program weeklypayroll. The paycheck records for Aaron Aardvark and Charles Canary are still good, so the program paycheckprocessor, should be run next to print their paychecks.

To rectify the oversight and to produce a paycheck for Dolores Donut, it is now necessary to update the master file to include a record for her and then to make a separate payroll run using only her time card. The input data for the update run would be as follows.

Add
Dolores Donut
456-78-9012
444 Decatur Drive
Dover, Deleware 45678
Food Service
Waitress-Cook
3.75

Delete
Barbara Banana
234-56-7890

Done

The lack of forethought in not running the program updateempfiles at the proper time creates the following extra work. One must pull the card for Dolores Donut and the trailer card from the deck of time cards. Next, the program weeklypayroll must rerun to produce a special payroll, complete with its own summary report, for Dolores Donut. Finally, the program processpaychecks must be rerun, including inserting the bank check forms in the printer, just to print one paycheck.

Annual Report

Although one could go on creating sample data for each week in the year, and indeed one should in a full-scale test of the system, it is possible to skip to the last workday of the year and run the yearly report program (Exercise 5). Of course, one doesn't actually have to wait for the end of the year. All the sample executions shown here could be run in one day. The yearly report, if run after the two weeks of payrolls simulated above, would show the company totals for the two weeks and payroll records for Aaron Aardvark, Barbara Banana, Charles Canary, and Dolores Donut. In particular, one would notice that the record for Barbara Banana is retained to the end of the year, although her employment status is shown as "terminated". After the annual report is printed, Barbara Banana's name and record are removed from the master file, and the year-to-date totals for everyone else are reset to zero in preparation for the new year. After a sufficiently profitable year, one could run a program (Exercise 9) to give everyone a 10 percent raise, effective for the first pay period of the new year.

Exercises

---

1. Modify the program weeklypayroll to check that the employee's name on the time card and the employee's name on the master file record containing the same social security number agree for each time card processed.
2. Modify the program weeklypayroll so that no more FICA withholdings are made when the year-to-date reaches $1975.05.

3. Test the result for Exercise 2 by running it with data so that the year-to-date FICA withholdings reach $1975.05.

4. Write a program processpaychecks that prepares paychecks and stubs using the information in the paycheck file. Be sure that each paycheck has a date as well as name and net pay.

5. Write a program prepareannualreport for the payroll system in this section that

   (a) prepares a report for each employee showing total gross pay, income tax withheld, FICA withheld, and net pay for the year.

   (b) prepares a summary for the company showing company yearly totals for gross pay, income tax withheld, FICA withheld, and net pay.

   (c) deletes from the employee master file the records for all employees whose employment status is "terminated".

   (d) resets all year-to-date totals to zero.

6. If someone runs the program updateempfiles but gives an incorrect social security number, no update is done. Modify the procedure getrecord to give three tries at entering a correct social security number. Make all updating input interactive.

7. Assuming that the program updateempfiles is run interactively, modify the procedure addemployee so that, if the user mistypes any part of the input information, there is an opportunity to correct only the mistyped information without reentering the correctly typed information.

8. Write a program maketimecardfile that reads a time card and checks the time card name and social security number against the employee master file. If the name and social security number are those of an active employee, then the time card is copied into a sequentially accessed disk file of timetype. If the social security number is found, but the names differ, the program should accept the time card, substituting the spelling of the name from the master file, but also should print an error message describing the problem. If the social security number is not found in the master file, the program should print an error message and reject the time card. Modify the program weeklypayroll to accept time card information from the file produced by this program.

9. Write a program that reads as input a department name and a percentage raise in hourly rates and gives each employee in the specified department the specified percentage raise, effective for the next payroll.

10. Using the date of the last pay period for which a check was issued that appears in the data structure employeedata, modify the program weeklypayroll so that it checks to see if a check has already been issued for an employee for that week. Print an error message if this duplication occurs and don't process the second time card for that employee.

11. Modify the program updateempfiles so that the master file records are maintained in order of increasing social security numbers. What advantage, if any, is there in doing this?

12. Modify the design of the payroll system so that it also contains a second index file allowing an employee's record to be located by the employee's name instead of

social security number. Modify the programs createempfiles and updateempfiles to include this name index file.

13. Using the modified version of the payroll system described in Exercise 12, write a program that can answer inquiries of the following sort: What is John Jones' hourly rate, or what is anybody else's? Design into the program a procedure to handle the case of several employees with the same name.

14. Write a program paycheckinquiry that can be used to determine whether or not a paycheck was issued to an employee specified as input for the last pay period. How could existing programs be used to remedy the situation if, by mistake, no paycheck had been issued?

15. Write a program that copies the current version of the employee master file onto magnetic tape for safekeeping, as insurance against failure of the disk unit on which the master file is stored or destruction of the master file due to incorrect input data or update requests.

16. Write a program that restores the employee master file to the previous values that were saved on magnetic tape by the program for Exercise 15.

6.6 Dynamic Data Structures; Pointers

One of the nice properties of a Pascal sequential file is that the programmer does not have to indicate a maximum size for it. However, the individual records that comprise the file tend to be difficult to access except in the original sequential order in which they were written. Insertions in the middle of a file also are difficult. On the other hand, an array must always be given a maximum size, but its elements may be accessed easily in any order the programmer desires. Insertions in the middle of an array are still time consuming, if not difficult, to program.

With Pascal pointers, a feature to be discussed in this section, it is possible to create a structure, a dynamic list, that has many of the properties of an array, yet has the desirable feature that no maximum size need be given, and that insertions and deletions can be made in the middle of the list without moving other items in the list.

Dynamic Lists

Suppose T is any Pascal data type other than a file; for example, T could be real, array of char, or record type. A *dynamic list of T* is a (possibly empty) sequence of items of type T. A dynamic list is much like an array of T except that a) it has no fixed maximum length, b) items in the dynamic list are not referenced using subscripts, and c) it is not a built-in data type in Pascal.

There is another way to look at a dynamic list of T. A dynamic list of T is either empty or it is a T followed by a dynamic list of T. Note that this is a recursive definition (see Section 4.4). It is of interest because it is often easy to process a dynamic list using a recursive program. Suppose, for example, that a program is needed to print all of the values in a list of integers. The first definition suggests an iterative procedure such as the following.

```
while not at the end of the list do
  print the next integer in the list
```

The recursive view of a dynamic list suggests a different (recursive) procedure to print all of the integers in a list.

```
if the list is not empty then
  begin
  print the first integer;
  print the remainder of the list;
  end
```

Of course, if the list is empty, there is nothing to do. If the dynamic list is not empty, then the treatment is recursive. The last statement of this preliminary version of the recursive procedure is a call upon the same procedure, but with an argument that is a list with one less element than the original list.

At first glance it might appear that the first (iterative) version of the procedure is simpler than the recursive version. However, you should reserve judgement until you examine executable Pascal procedures corresponding to these preliminary versions. The Pascal language features needed to implement dynamic lists tend to encourage the recursive view.

In Pascal, dynamic data structures can be implemented using the language feature called a pointer. A *pointer* is a variable whose value is the *location* in the computer memory of a particular value. The pointer is said to *point to* the value stored in that location.

A Pascal pointer variable may point to the location of a value of any Pascal type except file, including types integer, real, array of char, and record. However, once declared in a program, a pointer variable can point only to values of that one type for which it has been declared.

Declaration of Pointers

A Pascal pointer variable is declared by indicating the type of value to which it may point. For example,

```
var
  p1, p2 : ˆreal;
```

declares the variables p1 and p2 to be pointers to real values and

```
type
  a = array [1..9] of integer;
  pa = ˆa;
```

declares pa to be a type that is a pointer to an array of integers. In a variable or type declaration the caret (ˆ) before a type should be read as ''pointer to'' the type, so that p1 and p2 are declared to be ''pointers to type real'' and the type pa is declared to be ''pointer to type a'', that is, a pointer to an array of integers. Some computer output devices print the caret (ˆ) as an upward arrow, reinforcing the interpretation that it means ''pointer to something''.

The Use of Pointers

If p is a Pascal pointer, then p^ is the value of the object pointed to by p, that is, the value stored in the location that is the value of p. Note that this time the caret comes *after* the name of the pointer variable. For example, if p is declared to be type ^real, a pointer to a real, then

```
p^ := 5.6
```

assigns the value 5.6 to the the object pointed to by p. This object itself has no name other than p^. Similarly,

```
write (p^)
```

will cause the computer to print the value of the object pointed to by p; this value is 5.6 in our example.

So far it doesn't look as if pointers to values behave much differently than variables. Indeed, they are somewhat similar, but they have some very interesting properties that are different. In order to take advantage of these differences, it is important to keep in mind that the value of a pointer is some location in computer memory. Let us examine one of the consequences of this fact. Suppose p1 and p2 are pointers to a value of type real, declared by

```
var
  p1, p2 : ^real
```

Then suppose the following four statements are executed.

```
p1^ := 5.6;
p2 := p1;
p1^ := 3.7;
writeln (p2^)
```

What is printed? The effect of the first statement is to store the value 5.6 in the location pointed to by p1. It is convenient to picture the result of this statement by

p1 -->| 5.6 |

which represents the fact that the value of p1 is a location in which the real number 5.6 is stored. That is, p1 points to the real value 5.6.

The second statement assigns to p2 the value of p1. It does not assign 5.6 as the value of p2; it assigns the location of the value 5.6 to p2. The situation now can be pictured as

p1 -->
       | 5.6 |
p2 -->

Both p1 and p2 point to the same location in memory, which happens to contain the real value 5.6. Next, the real value 3.7 is stored in the location pointed to by p1. Since this is also the location pointed to by p2, both p1 and p2 now point to a location occupied by the real number 3.7. Thus the fourth statement prints the value 3.7. The situation is

p1 -->
```
      ┌─────┐
      │     │
      │ 3.7 │
p2 -->│     │
      └─────┘
```

Note that what happens is quite different from what would happen if p1 and p2 were real variables. The difference is that changing the value pointed to by p1 also has the effect of changing the value pointed to by p2, since in this case they both point to the same location. This property can be used very effectively in some situations.

Using Pointers to Construct Dynamic Lists

If *T* is any Pascal data type except file, we can represent a dynamic list of items of type *T* in terms of the record type node defined below.

```
type
  node = record
    info : T;
    link : ^node;
    end; { node }
```

As illustrated in the following diagram, each node in the dynamic list listname is a collection of memory locations containing an information (info) field of type *T* and a pointer field linking this node to the next node in the dynamic list. For this reason, a dynamic list also is called a *linked list*.

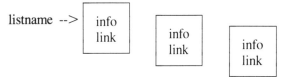

The variable listname also is of type ^node. It points to the first node in the dynamic list.

The Pointer Constant Nil

There is one constant that may be assigned to a pointer variable. It is named "nil" and is used to represent the fact that the pointer isn't pointing to anything. In particular, the link field in the last node of a dynamic list has the value nil because no node follows it, and an empty list is represented by assigning the value nil to the pointer variable listname.

A dynamic list of integers can be created using the types and variables in the following declarations.

```
type
  listtype = ^node;
  node = record
    number : integer;
    restoflist : listtype;
    end; { node }

var
  listofintegers : listtype;
```

The first declaration is an example of the only case in which a name (node) is used in a Pascal program prior to its definition. This exception is necessary because not only is the type node used in the definition of the type listtype, but also the type listtype is used in the definition of the type node.

The name of the link field in the record node has been changed to restoflist to emphasize the recursive view of a dynamic list, namely that it consists of one list item of the proper type followed by the rest of the list, which is itself a dynamic list. To declare a dynamic list of any other type T, simply replace the keyword "integer" by the name of the type T.

The Built-In Procedure New

Suppose we wish to construct a dynamic list of integers containing the numbers 23, -7, and 45. The Pascal *built-in procedure new* is used to create a new node in which to put the first integer 23. The procedure new has one argument, which must be a pointer. The procedure allocates space to store one object of the type pointed to by the pointer and sets the pointer so that it points to that location. The procedure new does not assign any values to the object pointed to by the pointer. In our case execution of the statement

```
new (listofintegers)
```

allocates storage in memory to hold a record of type node and then assigns that location to the pointer variable listofintegers. Thus the situation may be represented by the following diagram.

Note that the fields of the record have no values. The next task is to assign the integer 23 to the number field of the node. This is accomplished by the statement

```
listofintegers^ . number := 23
```

This may be read as "assign the value 23 to the number field of the node pointed to by listofintegers". Now the situation is

The pointer field of this first node should point to the second node containing the number −7. Of course, memory locations for the second node must first be allocated. This is accomplished by executing the statements

```
new (listofintegers^ . restoflist);
listofintegers^ . restoflist^ . number := -7
```

This situation is depicted by

listofintegers -->   23
                      ● --   -->   −7

Scanning from right to left, we may read the second of these statements as "assign the value −7 to the number field of the node pointed to by the restoflist field of the node pointed to by the variable listofintegers".

As one might readily imagine, the statements to put the third item in the list are going to become unreadably long. One solution is to introduce another variable that can point to any node.

```
var
  tempptr : ^node;
```

With this declaration, the previous two statements can be written more clearly as

```
new (tempptr);
tempptr^ . number := -7;
listofintegers^ . restoflist := tempptr
```

after which the situation can be represented by the following diagram.

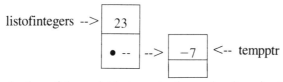

Introduction of the variable tempptr also makes it easier to add the third item to the list using a second temporary pointer tempptr2 and the statements

```
new (tempptr2);
tempptr2^ . number := 45;
tempptr^ . restoflist := tempptr2
```

The result is this list.

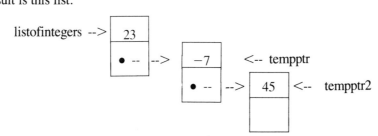

We complete the dynamic list by setting the last pointer to nil.

```
tempptr2^ . restoflist := nil
```

This allows a program to test for a nil pointer to see when it comes to the end of the list.

Note again that there is nothing in the declarations for a dynamic list that limits the size of the list. Integers can be added to this list until the computer runs out of storage space. To emphasize this fact, we show how to build a list of integers consisting of all the numbers in the input file up to but not including the first occurrence of some termination signal. Pascal statements needed to build this list are shown below. The resulting list is in the reverse of the order in which items are read; it is assumed that the order is not important in this example.

```
listofintegers := nil;
morenumbers := true;
while morenumbers do
  begin
  read (n);
  if number = signal then
    morenumbers := false
  else
    begin
    new (newnode);
    newnode^ . number := n;
    newnode^ . restoflist := listofintegers;
    listofintegers := newnode;
    end; { else }
  end; { while }
```

Suppose the input list consists of the numbers 23, −7, and 45, followed by the signal. After the while-loop is executed once, the situation is

listofintegers --> | 23 | <-- newnode
                    | nil |

As each of the statements in the else-clause for n = −7 is executed, the resulting situation is shown.

```
new (newnode);
```

listofintegers --> | 23 | | | <-- newnode
                    | nil | | |

```
newnode^ . number := n;
```

listofintegers --> | 23 | | −7 | <-- newnode
                    | nil | | |

```
newnode^ . restoflist := listofintegers;
```

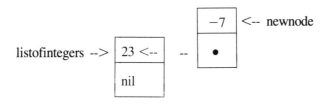

```
listofintegers := newnode;
```

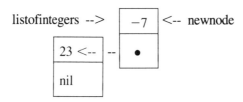

Inserting the third node for n = 45 proceeds similarly.

The order of the items in a dynamic linked list is determined solely by the array of linking pointers restoflist. Any other order or disorder that appears in a diagram has no relevance to the program execution because the program has no knowledge of or control over which memory locations are allocated by the built-in procedure new.

Printing a Dynamic List

The elements of a dynamic list can be printed with the help of a variable that points in turn to each of the members of the list.

```
procedure printlist (list : listtype);
{ iterative version }

  var
    p : listtype; { listtype = ^node }
  begin
  p := list;
  while (p <> nil) do
    begin
    write (p^ . number);
    p := p^ . restoflist;
    end; { while }
  end; { printlist }
```

The key step

```
p := p^ . restoflist
```

which moves the pointer p to point to the next node in the dynamic list corresponds to
the statement

```
i := i + 1
```

which might increment the subscript in a procedure to print the elements of a list stored
in an array.

The recursive procedure to print a dynamic list is based on the recursive definition
of a dynamic list. The procedure prints the first member of the list (if there is one) and
then calls itself to print the rest of the list.

```
procedure printlist (list : listtype);
{ recursive version }

  begin
  if list <> nil then
    begin
    write (list^ . number);
    printlist (list^. restoflist);
    end; { if }
  end; { printlist }
```

Sorting With a Dynamic List

One of the special features of a dynamic list is that the programmer need not
specify a maximum size for the list. Another important feature is that items may be inserted and deleted from any part of the list without moving large amounts of data. This
feature will be used to construct a program that sorts a list of numbers. This program
could be modified easily to sort inventory records of the kind described in Section 6.4
or any other file of records in which the correct order is determined by the value of one
of the fields in the record, such as the one named "id" in the inventory file.

The sorting procedure is quite simple. As each record is read from the input file, it
is inserted into a dynamic list of integers at the appropriate place to keep the list in ascending order according to its key field. Most of the time this involves inserting each
new integer between the next smaller and the next larger integers already in the list.
However, this level of detail is not necessary to write the first version of the program.

```
program sortlist (input, output);

  begin
  morenumbers := true;
  listofintegers := nil;
  while morenumbers do
    begin
    read a number;
    if number = termination signal then
      morenumbers := false
    else
      insert number at correct spot in listofintegers;
    end; { while-loop }
  print listofintegers;
  end.
```

In this simple case, the items to be sorted are just integers. Thus, the appropriate declarations for the dynamic list are

```
type
  listtype = ^node;
  node = record
    number : integer;
    restoflist : listtype;
    end; { node }
var
  n : integer;
  listofintegers : listtype;
```

The essential part of this program is inserting one number at the appropriate place in the sorted list of integers. One approach is to break the process into two steps: finding the correct spot to insert the number and then inserting it. However, if the recursive point of view is adopted, the insertion procedure can be broken into three simple cases.

1) If the list is empty, add the new record as the only item in the list.

2) If the new record belongs before the first record of the list, put it there.

3) If the new record belongs anywhere after the first number in the list, insert it properly into the remainder of the list. This is a recursive call.

```
procedure insert (var list : listtype);

  procedure putnewitemfirst;

    var
      newitem : listtype;

    begin
    new (newitem);
    newitem^ . number := n;
    newitem^ . restoflist := list;
    list := newitem;
    end; { putnewitemfirst }

  begin
  if list = nil then
    putnewitemfirst
  else if n < list^ . number then
    putnewitemfirst
  else
    insert (list^ . restoflist);
  end; { insert }
```

The complete refined program follows.

```
program sortlist (input, output);

   const
      signal = -999;

   type
      listtype = ^node;
      node = record
         number : integer;
         restoflist : listtype;
         end; { node }

   var
      n : integer;
      listofintegers : listtype;
      morenumbers : boolean;

   procedure insert (var list : listtype);
      ... end; { insert }

   procedure printlist (list : listtype);
      ... end; { printlist }

   begin
   morenumbers := true;
   listofintegers := nil;
   while morenumbers do
      begin
      read (n);
      writeln ('Input data  n : ', n :1);
      if n = signal then
         morenumbers := false
      else
         insert (listofintegers);
      end; { while-loop }

   writeln; writeln ('Sorted list:');
   printlist (listofintegers);
   writeln;
   end.
```

```
run sortlist

Input data  n :  265
Input data  n :  113
Input data  n :  467
Input data  n :  264
Input data  n :  907
Input data  n :  265
Input data  n :  -999
```

```
Sorted list:
      113         264         265         265         467         907
```

The Built-In Procedure Dispose

If the program sortlist included a loop to sort many different lists, the repeated use of the procedure new eventually would use up all of the available computer memory. The *built-in procedure dispose* is used to return all storage allocated for the list to the pool of available storage at the completion of each sorting loop.

If p is a pointer variable, then the statement

```
dispose (p)
```

deallocates the memory space reserved for the node pointed to by p. The memory space is then available for other use by the program, and any values contained in the node are lost. The values of p and all other pointers to the node p^ become meaningless because the node they point to no longer exists.

The programmer-defined recursive procedure disposeall deallocates all of the nodes of a dynamic list supplied as its argument.

```
procedure disposeall (var list : listtype);

  begin
  if list <> nil then
    begin
    disposeall (list^ . restoflist);
    dispose (list);
    end; { if }
  end; { disposeall }
```

For this procedure, it is critical that, to dispose a nonempty list, the procedure must first call itself recursively to dispose of the list consisting of everything after the first item, then use the built-in procedure dispose to return the storage of the first item to the pool of available storage. If the first item were disposed first, the value of its link field restoflist would be lost and there would be no pointer to the remainder of the list, which would be inaccessible for the remainder of the execution of the program. Of course, a temporary pointer variable could be used to save the value of the link field restoflist before a node is disposed. A non-recursive version of the procedure based on this strategy is discussed in Exercise 4.

Trees

Other more complicated dynamic data structures can be built using Pascal pointers. To conclude this section, we will consider briefly a structure that is one of the simplest ones except for dynamic lists. Using the recursive approach, if *T* is a Pascal data type, then a *binary tree of T* is empty or it is a node containing a *T* and links to two binary trees of *T*. The first node of a binary tree is called the *root,* and the two subtrees linked to that node are called the *left subtree* and the *right subtree* of the binary tree. More general tree structures do not restrict the number of subtrees to two.

One common use of trees in computer science is to represent expressions of a computer program. For example the Pascal expression (a + b) * (c + d) can be represented by the tree

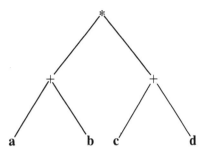

The root of this tree is the node containing the multiplication operator (*). Its two subtrees correspond to the two expressions (a + b) and (c + d) that are multiplied to form the complete expression. Each of the two subtrees is itself a binary tree with a plus sign (+) in the root node and only one node in each subtree.

The botanical analogies implied by the terminology are clearer if the tree diagram is turned upside down. The root is then at the bottom. Each node corresponds to a branching point of the botanical tree. Subtrees are branches emanating from a node. The term *leaf* is applied to a node with only empty subtrees. In this example, the nodes containing a, b, c, and d are leaves.

This tree would be implemented in Pascal using records consisting of a one-character operator (+, *, a, b, c, d in the example) and two pointers, one to the first operand (the left subtree) and one to the second operand (the right subtree). The type statements

```
type
  binarytreetype = ^node;
  node = record
    operator : char;
    leftsubtree, rightsubtree : binarytreetype;
    end; { node }
```

define a record organization suitable for constructing binary trees. In terms of this record structure, a more detailed picture of the tree above would be

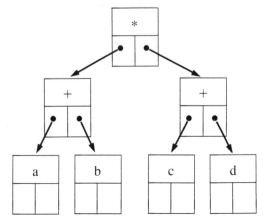

Sorting Using a Tree Structure

It is possible to use a tree to create an even more efficient program to sort a file. Suppose a file of integers contains the numbers 265, 113, 467, 264, 907, and 265. When the first number is read from the input file, a tree is created containing only one node, which contains the number.

treeofintegers --> | 265 |

When the next number is read, it is compared with the first. If it is less than the first number, it is placed as a node in the left subtree; if it is greater than or equal to the first number, it is placed in the right subtree. In our case, 113 < 265, so a node containing 113 is created and the left pointer of the node containing 265 is set to point to it.

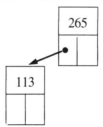

The next number is 467, so it is placed in the right subtree of 265.

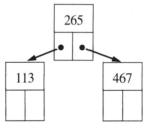

The next number is 264, so it is to be placed in the left subtree of 265. It is then compared with 113, the occupant of the top of the left subtree. since 264 > 113, it is placed in the right subtree of the one with 113 at the top yielding

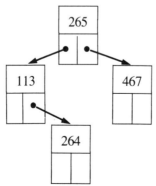

The next number 907 is larger than 265, so it is compared with 467 and put in the right subtree of the node containing 467.

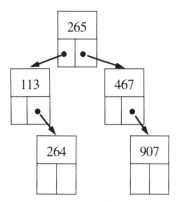

The final number 265 is equal to the number in the root node. An insertion position is therefore sought in the right subtree of the root. Since $265 < 467$, it is put to the left of 467. Notice that the two nodes with key 265 are not even adjacent, nor is the node with key 264 adjacent to either node with key 265. This doesn't matter.

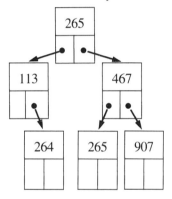

Printing the Tree in Order

Once the tree has been constructed, it is necessary to write out the numbers in the tree in the correct order. The correct order is to print all the numbers in the left subtree in order, then print the number in the top node, then print all the numbers in the right subtree in order. This procedure works because in the whole tree and in each subtree, all numbers in the left subtree are less than the number at the top and all numbers in the right subtree are larger than or equal to the number at the top. The procedure just described is, of course, recursive. Both the insert procedure and the print procedure are contained in the complete version of the program sortnumbers below. The output from the program is not shown because it is identical to the output from the previous program.

```
program sortnumbers (input, output);

  const
    signal = -999;

  type
    binarytreetype = ^node;
```

```
  node = record
    number : integer;
    leftsubtree, rightsubtree : binarytreetype;
    end; { node }

var
  n : integer;
  treeofintegers : binarytreetype;
  morenumbers : boolean;

procedure insert (var tree : binarytreetype);

  var
    newitem : binarytreetype;

  begin
  if tree = nil then
    begin
    new (newitem);
    newitem^ . number := n;
    newitem^ . leftsubtree := nil;
    newitem^ . rightsubtree := nil;
    tree := newitem;
    end { if }
  else if n < tree^ . number then
    insert (tree^ . leftsubtree)
  else
    insert (tree^ . rightsubtree);
  end; { insert }

procedure printtree (tree : binarytreetype);

  begin
  if tree <> nil then
    begin
    printtree (tree^ . leftsubtree);
    write (tree^ . number);
    printtree (tree^. rightsubtree);
    end; { if }
  end; { printtree }

begin { main program }
morenumbers := true;
treeofintegers := nil;
while morenumbers do
  begin
  read (n);
  writeln ('Input data  n :  ', n :1);
  if n = signal then
    morenumbers := false
  else
    insert (treeofintegers);
  end; { while-loop }
```

```
writeln; writeln ('Sorted list:');
printtree (treeofintegers);
writeln;
end.
```

Both for debugging purposes and to understand the sequence of procedure calls in a recursive program such as this, it is desirable to insert write statements into the principal recursive procedures to trace the execution. Inserting the following if-statement at the beginning of the procedure insert gives a good picture of what happens in that procedure.

```
if tree = nil then
  writeln ('found insertion place for ', n :1)
else if n < tree^ . number then
  writeln ('look to the left of ', tree^ . number :1)
else
  writeln ('look to the right of ', tree^ . number :1);
```

If even further prettying of the output is desired, an integer variable depth may be introduced to keep track of the current depth of recursive call, that is, the number of simultaneous executions of the procedure insert started but not yet completed. Each output line then can start with a number of dots proportional to the current depth of recursive call. Additional statements are

```
var
  depth : 0..999;
```

in the main heading,

```
depth := 0;
```

at the beginning of the main program,

```
var
  i : 0..999;
```

in the procedure insert,

```
depth := depth + 1;
for i := 1 to depth do
  write ('..');
```

before the added if statement at the beginning of the procedure insert, and

```
depth := depth - 1;
```

just before the end of the procedure insert. The resulting output is interpreted easily.

```
run sortnumbers

Input data  n : 265
..found insertion place for 265
Input data  n : 113
..look to the left of 265
....found insertion place for 113
Input data  n : 467
..look to the right of 265
....found insertion place for 467
Input data  n : 264
..look to the left of 265
....look to the right of 113
......found insertion place for 264
Input data  n : 907
..look to the right of 265
....look to the right of 467
......found insertion place for 907
Input data  n : 265
..look to the right of 265
....look to the left of 467
......found insertion place for 265
Input data  n : -999

Sorted list:
     113        264        265        265        467        907
```

Suggested Readings

Donald E. Knuth, *The Art of Computer Programming,* Vol. 1, *Fundamental Algorithms,* Chapter 2, ''Information Structures'', Addison-Wesley, Reading, MA, 1968.

Donald E. Knuth, ''Algorithms'', *Scientific American,* April 1977, pp. 63-80.

Niklaus Wirth, *Algorithms + Data Structures = Programs,* Prentice-Hall, Englewood Cliffs, NJ, 1976.

Exercises

1. Write a procedure that will merge two sorted dynamic lists.
2. Write a procedure that builds a dynamic list of integers in the same order as the input file. Hint: Use a pointer variable that always points to the last node of the dynamic list under construction. Test your procedure using the procedure printlist in this section.
3. Write a nonrecursive procedure to print a dynamic linked list.
4. Write a nonrecursive procedure to dispose all the nodes of a dynamic list. Hint: Use a temporary pointer to hold the link field of a node about to be disposed.
5. Write a recursive procedure to print a dynamic list backward, that is, last element first.
6. Write a nonrecursive procedure to print a dynamic list backward. Compare it with the recursive procedure written in Exercise 5.

7. A rough measure of the efficiency of the two sorting programs discussed in this section is the number of times the procedure insert is executed. Add a global variable count to each program and increase it by one each time the procedure insert is called. Print the value of count at the completion of the sort in order to compare the efficiencies of the sorts based on a dynamic list and a dynamic tree structure.

8. Modify the program sortnumbers to create a program that sorts the inventory master file of Section 6.4.

9. Write a nonrecursive procedure insert for use in the program sortlist to sort a dynamic list.

10. Try to write a procedure that will print the tree treeofintegers built in the program sortnumbers in this section in proper sorted order without using recursion.

11. A very efficient recursive partition sort called "quicksort" is programmed as follows. The first record in a dynamic list is compared to all records in the rest of the list. Those records with key fields less than that of the first record are put into a "low" dynamic list. Those records with keys equal to or greater than that of the first record are put into a "high" dynamic list. Then the "low" and the "high" dynamic lists are sorted by recursive calls to the same procedure. The original dynamic list is printed in sorted order by first printing the "low" list in sorted order, then the first test record, and finally the "high" list in sorted order. Write a Pascal program to implement quicksort and test it against input lists of various sizes. Under what circumstances does the number of key comparisons counted by your program appear to be proportional to n * log2 (n)? When is is proportional to n * n?

12. Reverse Polish notation (RPN) is used on some computers and calculators to represent arithmetic expressions. In reverse Polish notation, the two operands of a binary operation precede the operation symbol. For example, a + b is written ab+ and (a + b) * (c + d) is written ab+cd+*. Parentheses are never necessary in reverse Polish notation. Write a procedure that takes a binary tree representing an arithmetic expression as described in this section, and prints the reverse Polish notation form of the expression.

13. (Very hard) Write a procedure that reads Pascal arithmetic expressions as character string input and builds the binary tree corresponding to that arithmetic expression. In the unlikely event that you succeed, test your procedure using the reverse Polish notation procedure written for Exercise 12 or the procedure printtree in this section. Hint: Read David Gries, *Compiler Construction for Digital Computers* before attempting this exercise; arithmetic expression scans are an important part of any compiler.

6.7 Chapter Review

In addition to a main memory, most computers have a somewhat larger auxiliary memory consisting of devices such as magnetic tapes and disks. Information is stored in auxiliary memory using write statements and retrieved from auxiliary memory with read statements.

The basic unit of storage in auxiliary memory is the *record,* most concisely described as the body of information transcribed by one write statement. A collection of records is called a *file*.

Direct and Sequential Access to Auxiliary Memory Files

A magnetic computer tape is similar to an audio tape in several ways. First, both kinds of tape are coated on one side with magnetizable ferrous oxide. Both kinds of tape are mounted on a unit that can run the tape forward or backward. The operations called "recording" and "playing back" for an audio tape are called "writing" and "reading" for a computer tape. Moving from one part of the tape to another can be quite time consuming, even if one uses fast forward or fast rewind.

A magnetic computer disk, on the other hand, is something like a phonograph record. Just as one may select any band on a phonograph record and physically move the phonograph arm to it, thereby avoiding having to listen to everything that comes before, it is possible to select a track on a magnetic disk that contains the needed information and to instruct the computer physically to move the read/write head there very quickly. A magnetic disk is different from a phonograph record in that the information is stored magnetically rather than by cutting grooves in the record. Therefore it is possible to change what is recorded on a magnetic disk as often as one wants.

In the only type of file access for which there are built-in Pascal procedures, *sequential access,* the only record that may be accessed easily is the next record in the file, that is, the record stored immediately following the one last accessed. (Although rewinding is an allowable operation, it is used sparingly.) Card files, tape files, and terminal files are examples of sequentially accessed files. A typical card reader can read 800 per cards per minute, which is equivalent to approximately 1000 characters per second, while a typical tape unit can read approximately 240,000 characters per second at full operating speed. Read statements and write statements to access a file sequentially are buil into the language Pascal, as illustrated by the following examples.

```
write (sequentialfile, a);
read (sequentialfile, b)
```

In some auxiliary memory files, each record of the file has a unique *record number* by which it is referenced. One says that such files may be *accessed directly* by record number. The following statements are typical direct-access write and read statements, although the procedures readdirect and writedirect are programmer-written procedures and not built in.

```
writedirect (directfile, 7, a, error);
readdirect (directfile, n + 1, b, error);
```

The first statement writes the value of the variable a into record 7 of directfile. The second statement reads the value of record n + 1 of directfile and assigns the value to the variable b. The fourth argument, error, of the procedures readdirect and writedirect is a boolean variable whose value is set to true if an error occurred in attempting to read or write the indicated record; otherwise, it is set to false.

Since any record of a directly accessed file may be read or written at any time during the execution of a program, directly accessed files can be stored only on devices
like magnetic disk units that have a direct-access hardware capability. A typical magnetic disk unit can store 60 million characters and can retrieve any record stored in it in
an average of 1/40 second. By way of comparison, values stored in main memory may
be accessed in less that a millionth of a second on most computers.

Data Structure Declarations

In Pascal, certain types of hierarchical organizations of data can be incorporated by
means of a *data structure declaration* into the names of variables used to hold that data.
A typical data structure declaration might look like the one below for the variable computeraccount.

```
type
  nametype = packed array [1..namelength] of char;
  persontype = record
    name : nametype;
    password : packed array [1..8] of char;
    end; { persontype }
  projecttype = record
    name : nametype;
    accountnumber : 0..9999;
    end; { projecttype }
  accounttype = record
    project : projecttype;
    fundsremaining : real;
    person : persontype;
    end; { accounttype }

var
  computeraccount : accounttype;
```

The data structure described by this declaration is called a *tree structure*, where the
major name accounttype is regarded as the *root* of the tree, and the components that are
not further subdivided are called *leaves*. Values are assigned only to the leaves of a
data structure. For the data structure declared above, the full names of the five components that have values are the following:

```
computeraccount . project . name
computeraccount . project . accountnumber
computeraccount . fundsremaining
computeraccount . person . name
computeraccount . person . password
```

Periods are used to separate the parts of a name that derive from different *levels* of
the data structure declaration. However, it is possible to have a whole block of statements refer to components of the same structure. For example, within a block of statements headed by

```
with computeraccount do
```

the five names above can be abbreviated to

```
project . name
project . accountnumber
fundsremaining
person. name
person . password
```

Data structure declarations are essential for programs that read and write records or move groups of related data in main memory. For example, if the data structures computeraccount and currentuser are both declared to be type accounttype and accountfile is declared to be type file of accounttype, the following statements will tell a computer to read a record from the sequentially accessed file named accountfile, assign the values read to the leaves of the data structure computeraccount, and then copy all values in the data structure computeraccount as values of the corresponding components of the data structure currentuser.

```
read (accountfile, computeraccount);
currentuser := computeraccount
```

Systems of Programs and Files

Storage space in main memory is ordinarily too valuable and scarce to tie up with information that might not be accessed for several hours or days. In most computer systems, main memory space is allocated for variables only while a program is executing and is withdrawn immediately and automatically by the operating system at the conclusion of the program execution. Auxiliary memory space is usually less expensive and less scarce. Consequently, information stored in auxiliary memory usually is retained indefinitely, until the user erases it deliberately or replaces it with other information.

When information is stored permanently or semipermanently in auxiliary memory, many programs may access the same information. Programs that share a common file in auxiliary memory can communicate with each other by means of values stored in that shared file. The individual programs of such a *system of programs* cannot be designed independently but must be coordinated by a higher-level system design, because the values that one program of the system writes in a shared file affect subsequent executions both of itself and of other programs of the system.

Creating a Computer File

In order to read and process a file in auxiliary memory, a computer must be supplied either with a count of the number of records in the file or with an end-of-file signal following the last record to be processed. For files that fit entirely in main memory, a count of the number of records is easy to maintain. For sequentially accessed files, a termination signal in a *trailer record* is a natural way to indicate the extent or end of the file, as is the built-in function eof.

Creating a computer file consists of requisitioning the file space in auxiliary memory and perhaps writing a trailer record into the file. Often, a newly created file temporarily contains no records at all. In Pascal, an empty file named "f" is created by executing the statement

```
rewrite (f)
```

Maintaining a File In Auxiliary Memory

Since information stored in auxiliary memory ordinarily is retained at the conclusion of a program execution, while information stored in main memory is not, the cardinal rule for maintaining a permanent computer file is this: When a record of the file in main memory is altered, the resulting record must be written into auxiliary memory before the new values are lost at the conclusion of the program execution. A typical file processing procedure consists of reading records from one or more files from auxiliary memory into main memory, processing the information in the records in the main memory, and then writing the results back into auxiliary memory, either as updated records for the same files or as new output files.

Locating Records in a Directly Accessed File

Although each record of a directly accessed file can be retrieved by its record number, there is still the problem of determining which record number in the file corresponds to an entry described by any other means. For example, it might be desirable to locate an employee data record by the employee's name or social security number.

One solution used in this chapter is to maintain an *index* associating record descriptions with record numbers. For the employee master file in the payroll system of programs, a list of the social security numbers of all employees of a company is maintained so that the location of a social security number in this index list is the same as the record number of the corresponding employee record. A more flexible variant is to enlarge each index entry to include a reference, so that the record number for a given social security number is the value of the corresponding reference. In either case, the record number is found by looking up the social security number in an index. For better access to the information contained in a file, it is possible to have two or more indexes for the same directly accessed file. For instance, for a company's employee master file, a second list for locating record numbers from employee names also might be useful.

Programming for Sequentially Accessed Files

Programs for sequentially accessed files require especially careful planning, because the records of a sequentially accessed file are significantly less accessible than those of a directly accessed file. For a variety of reasons, it is inadvisable to backspace or rewrite the records of most sequentially accessed files, and so this operation is prohibited in the Pascal language. Thus, when a sequentially accessed file is updated, an entirely new, complete copy of the file is written, and when a sequentially accessed input file is read, its records are processed in essentially the order in which they appear in the input file. Also, if several sequentially accessed input files are to be coordinated for processing, each file must be sorted before processing is feasible. The reading of each file can then proceed in sequence of increasing value of the key on which the files are sorted, the only variation occurring when files containing fewer records with intermediate or repeated keys pause to allow the other files to catch up. The total execution time of many programs that use auxiliary memory quite often consists almost exclusively of the time it takes to read and write records during the execution. Such programs are called ''input/output bound''.

Dynamic Data Structures

Pascal permits a programmer to define *pointer data types* which can point to a location in memory reserved to hold a value of any Pascal type except file. Each pointer may point to only only one type. Pointers to array and record types are permitted, as well as pointers to simple types such as reals and integers. The declarations

```
type
  string = packed array [1..9] of char;
  stringpointer = ^string;

var
  p1, p2 : ^real;
  p : char;
  name : stringpointer;
```

define a new data type, stringpointer, which is a pointer to strings, that is, a pointer to arrays of characters. The variables p1 and p2 are declared to be pointers to locations in memory reserved for real values, the variable p points to character values, and the variable name points to strings, that is, it points to arrays of characters. The caret (^) in these declarations is read ''pointer to'' when it precedes a data type.

Memory locations pointed to by a pointer variable are allocated by the built-in procedure *new* and deallocated by the built-in procedure *dispose*. For example, the statements

```
var
  p1 : ^real;
  . . .
new (p1);
p1^ := 5.6;
dispose (p1)
```

allocate storage for a real number, make the pointer variable p1 point to the location allocated, place the value 5.6 in the location p1 points to, and then release the location for other use by the program. The expression p1^ means ''the location p1 points to''. Notice that the caret sign follows the pointer variable for this meaning. When a location is disposed, its value is lost. The value of the pointer variable p1 is meaningless because it no longer points to an allocated location.

A program may allocate as few or as many locations as it chooses. *Dynamic lists* with no fixed length may be constructed of building blocks called *nodes* of the following type.

```
type
  listtype = ^node;
  node = record
    info : T;
    link : listtype;
    end; { node }
```

The type T of the information (info) field in the record node may be any Pascal data type except file. It may be built-in or programmer-defined in an earlier type declaration. It may even be a record type or a pointer type.

Dynamic lists are constructed by making the link field of each node in the list point to the next node in the list. The link field of the last node in the list is assigned the pointer constant value *nil* meaning that it is not pointing to anything. A dynamic list is referenced by a pointer variable of type listtype which points to the first node of the list. When constructed this way, dynamic lists are called *linked lists*. The following diagram illustrates the linking information in a linked list of three nodes.

Insertions at the beginning and even in the middle of a linked list are relatively easy procedures and never involve moving previously allocated nodes. Everything is done by changing the link pointers.

A moderately efficient insertion sort is written in this section using a dynamic list to store the sorted data. The sorting method resembles how some people pick up a hand of cards. First one card is picked up. Then a second card is picked up and placed to the left or right of the first card depending on whether its value is less than or greater than or equal to the value of the first card. Subsequent cards are picked up one at a time and inserted in the proper place in the hand so that the cards picked up so far remain in ascending order. A *recursive definition of a dynamic list* as either empty or one node followed by a dynamic list of nodes helps simplify the insertion and printing procedures.

Trees

The simplest nonlinear dynamic data structure is a *binary tree*. It is defined recursively as either empty or one node, called the *root*, linked to two other binary trees, called the *left subtree* and the *right subtree*. No nonrecursive definition is attempted; most programs processing tree structures are recursive. Figure 6.7.1 shows a binary tree with nine nodes.

Each node of the tree in Figure 6.7.1 is represented in a Pascal program by a record of the type node defined below.

```
type
  binarytreetype = ^node;
  node = record
    info : integer;
    leftsubtree, rightsubtree : binarytreetype;
  end; { node }
```

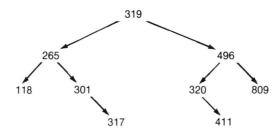

Figure 6.7.1 A binary tree used in sorting.

An entire binary tree is referenced by a pointer variable of type binarytreetype that points to the root node of the binary tree.

When used for sorting, sequence information obtained by comparison of the key fields in two records is represented by placing a new node with a smaller key field than the root node in the left subtree of that root and a new node with a key field greater than or equal to the key field of the root node in the right subtree of the root. Since each subtree is itself a binary tree, a short efficient recursive procedure is written to insert new nodes into a binary tree in a manner that preserves, or at least represents, the storage of records in sequence of increasing key fields.

A second recursive procedure, printtree, recovers the sequence information implicit in the tree by the simple expedient of first printing the left subtree in the proper sorted order, then printing the information in the root node, and finally printing the right subtree in sorted order. The joy of recursion is that the first and third steps of this procedure do not have to be refined further—they are simply recursive calls to the same procedure supplying as argument a variable pointing to the first node of the left or right subtree. The only other step in the procedure printtree is to do nothing if the tree is empty.

7

SIMULATION

In computer applications such as the weekly payroll of a large corporation, the computer performs almost the same calculations human clerks would do, only faster and probably more accurately. In other applications, however, the computer uses methods that generally would be unfeasible for pencil-and-paper implementation because of the large amount of computation. The concern of this chapter is simulation methods, which fall largely in the latter category. In a simulation program, the computer keeps track of the progress of each pertinent characteristic of the situation as it actually might occur.

This chapter illustrates how simulation techniques can be used to solve problems in population growth, ecology, gambling, queuing, and game playing. Some of the problems presented might be solved by conventional analytical methods, but the programming solutions presented here illustrate techniques applicable to much more difficult problems. Later sections of this chapter discuss "artificial intelligence", the simulation of intelligent behavior. One program enables the computer to learn to play a simple game against a human opponent. Another program enables the computer to create simple melodies.

One kind of simulation problem involves what are called *deterministic* simulations, in which no element of chance affects the values of the problem variables. A deterministic model is used in Section 2.4 to predict the future population density of the state of New Jersey, assuming that the growth rate in a recent decade will continue indefinitely. The correctness of the prediction depends heavily on the correctness of that assumption. The program poppredict (population prediction) in that section simulates the population growth in New Jersey until a certain population density is reached.

Another kind of simulation is called *probabilistic*, or *nondeterministic*. The programmer-defined function randominteger, introduced in the arithmetic teaching program in Section 2.6, permits a programmer to generate a random integer from 1 to 6. By interpreting the result as the outcome of the roll of a single die, it is possible to simulate dice games. The uncertainty of the result is the reason the simulation is called nondeterministic. A nondeterministic simulation is used in Section 7.2 to calculate the proportion of rolls in a fair dice game that come up either 7 or 11.

Even if it is impossible to predict with certainty the outcome of any particular occurrence of a random event, it may be possible to ascertain some facts about what will happen if the event is repeated many times. A typical nondeterministic simulation program simulates a random event many times, recording information about the entire sequence of events. A nondeterministic simulation is often called a Monte Carlo simulation, after the casino famed for its games of chance.

The key to writing simulation programs for either a deterministic or a probabilistic situation is to design a model that includes enough of the relevant information to represent the situation accurately, but that ignores unimportant details in order to keep the length of the calculation manageable. Most simulation programs compromise between a desire to take more factors into account, thereby better portraying the situation, and a desire to simplify the model, thereby reducing the program size, data requirements, and execution time.

7.1   Deterministic Models of Population and Water Pollution

Simple population growth is one of the least complicated forms of simulation, as demonstrated in Section 2.4 for the state of New Jersey. To review the basic ideas, this section begins with another population growth simulation, this time for Idaho. The model chosen for Idaho, like the one for New Jersey, is deterministic. The more variables that affect what is being studied, the more complex a model is needed for a simulation. A second problem considered in this section is concerned with ecology, and this particular problem requires a more complex deterministic model than the population growth problem.

Predicting the Population of Idaho

The population of the state of Idaho was 694,364 in the year 1970, and at that time the annual growth rate was 0.4 percent. Suppose we want to project the population for the year 1990.

In the program idaho, the variable population represents the population of Idaho, and the variable year represents the year. A for-loop is used to simulate the growth for the years 1971 to 1990. In order to print the predicted population only for the years 1980 and 1990, instead of for all years, the program idaho uses the integer operator mod, described in Section 2.6.

```
program idaho (output);

  const
    growthrate = 0.004;

  var
    population : real;
    year : 1971..1990;

  begin
  population := 694364.0;
  for year := 1971 to 1990 do
    begin
    population := population + growthrate * population;
    if year mod 10 = 0 then
      writeln (year :10, round (population) :15);
    end; { for-loop }
  end.
```

```
run idaho
```

```
        1980          722644
        1990          752076
```

Using a constant annual growth rate to project a future population is mathematically equivalent to projecting a future balance for a savings account that pays compounded interest and in which no deposits are made. Thus an alternative way to calculate the population of Idaho in 1990 is to use the formula

population := 694364.0 * power (1 + growthrate, 20)

where power is the function described in Section 4.4 that raises a real number to an integer power. Conversely, it is possible to calculate a future savings account balance by a deterministic simulation.

Deterministic simulation provides a natural way to solve many problems and is often easier to understand than any other method. A deterministic simulation program that solves a problem about water pollution provides a second illustration of the technique.

A Water Quality Problem

The residents of Mudville, located on the shore of Lake Sludge, notice that the quality of the water in their beautiful lake has deteriorated in recent years, and they make a special study of the situation producing some critical facts, illustrated in Figure 7.1.1.

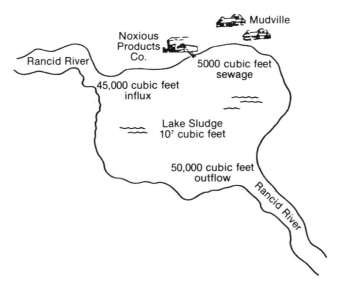

Figure 7.1.1   The environs of Mudville.

First, they observe that the volume of Lake Sludge is 10 million cubic feet, and that the lake is 0.5 percent polluted. That is, the quantity of polluting materials is

0.005 * 10,000,000 = 50,000 cubic feet

Second, the influx from the Rancid River, which is 0.2 percent polluted, is 45,000 cubic feet per day. Third, the town of Mudville puts into the lake daily 5000 cubic feet of sewage, of which 10 percent is concentrated polluting materials.

A Simulation of the Water Flow

A deterministic simulation which can calculate when the pollution level in the lake reaches 1 percent needs to record only one item of information, the amount of pollutants in Lake Sludge. That is the value of the variable lakegunk in the program pollute. The initial value of lakegunk is the current quantity of pollutants in the lake, which is 0.005 * 1,000,000 cubic feet. Each day, counted by the variable day, the value of lakegunk is increased by the quantity of pollutants coming from sewage and the influx of the Rancid River. The value of lakegunk is then decreased by the amount of pollutants that flow out of the lake. This calculation is repeated until the proportion of pollutants in the lake, lakegunk / lakevolume, is more than 1 percent.

In the program pollute, some simplifying assumptions have been made. 1) There is no loss of water by evaporation, so the amount of liquid flowing out of Lake Sludge is equal to the amount flowing in. 2) The pollutants in the lake are completely mixed, so that the proportion of pollutants leaving Lake Sludge via the river is the same as the proportion for the whole lake. The first simplification can be removed easily and is left for an exercise at the end of this section.

```
program pollute (output);

  const
    lakevolume = 1.0e7;        { cubic feet }
    riverinflux = 45000.0;     { cubic feet / day }
    sewageinflux = 5000.0;     { cubic feet / day }
    riverpollution = 0.002;
    sewagepollution = 0.10;
    initialpollution = 0.005;
    maxpollution = 0.01;
    maxdays = 10000;

  var
    lakegunk, rivergunk, sewagegunk : real;
    riveroutflow : real;
    day : 0..maxdays;
    toopolluted : boolean;

  begin
  rivergunk := riverpollution * riverinflux;
  sewagegunk := sewagepollution * sewageinflux;
  riveroutflow := sewageinflux + riverinflux;
  lakegunk := initialpollution * lakevolume;
  toopolluted := false;
  day := 0;
  while (day < maxdays) and (not toopolluted) do
    begin
    day := day + 1;
    lakegunk := lakegunk + rivergunk + sewagegunk;
```

```
      lakegunk := lakegunk - (lakegunk / lakevolume) * riveroutflow;
      if lakegunk / lakevolume > maxpollution then
        toopolluted := true;
      end; { while-loop }

    if toopolluted then
      writeln ('Mudville is doomed in ', day :1, ' days.')
    else
      writeln ('There is no danger to Mudville for at least ',
          maxdays :1, ' days.');
    end.
```

```
run pollute
```

```
Mudville is doomed in 271 days.
```

Testing Corrective Actions

If the Noxious Products plant were closed and sewage treatment facilities built, the town could reduce the pollutant level of the sewage going into the lake to 0.1 percent. If the septic tanks along the Rancid River were replaced by a sewer system, the pollutant level of the river would drop to 0.03 percent. If these actions could be implemented immediately, how long would it be before the pollution level of the lake dropped to 0.1 percent?

The program cleanup is similar to the program pollute. The pollutant levels of the water sources have been changed, and the simulation is stopped when lakegunk < 0.001 * lakevolume. Simply by changing the numbers in the program cleanup, it is possible to predict the effect on the lake of any other changes in the pollutant levels of the river or of the town's sewage.

```
program cleanup (output);

  const
    lakevolume = 1.0e7;
    riverinflux = 45000.0;
    sewageinflux = 5000.0;
    riverpollution = 0.0003;
    sewagepollution = 0.001;
    initialpollution = 0.005;
    minpollution = 0.001;
    maxdays = 1000;

  var
    lakegunk, rivergunk, sewagegunk : real;
    riveroutflow : real;
    day : 0..maxdays;
    cleanedup : boolean;

  begin
  rivergunk := riverpollution * riverinflux;
```

```
sewagegunk := sewagepollution * sewageinflux;
riveroutflow := sewageinflux + riverinflux;
lakegunk := initialpollution * lakevolume;
cleanedup := false;
day := 0;
while (day < maxdays) and (not cleanedup) do
  begin
  day := succ (day);
  lakegunk := lakegunk + rivergunk + sewagegunk;
  lakegunk := lakegunk - (lakegunk / lakevolume) * riveroutflow;
  if lakegunk / lakevolume < minpollution then
    cleanedup := true;
  end; { while-loop }

if cleanedup then
  writeln ('Pollutant level down to ', minpollution * 100 :1:1,
          '% after ', day :1, ' days.')
else
  writeln ('Pollutant level still not below ', minpollution * 100 :1:1,
          '% after ', maxdays :1, ' days.');
end.
```

```
run cleanup

Pollutant level down to  0.1% after 398 days.
```

The simulation technique illustrated in the program cleanup is being used to solve some very complex problems. In *American Scientist*, Walter Orr Roberts discussed a simulation program to model the weather system of the entire world.

> Not only will the model, when built and tested, permit experiments to re-fine weather and climate forecasting research, but also we anticipate, as sug-gested above, that such a model will permit experiments in global weather modification—safely in the model, and not in nature. We should be able, for example, to level the Rockies or rotate the earth backwards and see what the impact is on weather. Or more usefully and realistically, we hope to be able to simulate, for a few thousand dollars, cleaning up world air pollution, so that we may be able to evaluate the meteorological consequences of such a clean-up—giving us a handle to the value of so doing in the real world. This would be a very powerful decision-making aid. (Walter Orr Roberts, ''Man on a Changing Earth'', *American Scientist*, Vol. 59, No. 1, pp. 16-19, January-February, 1971.)

Exercises

---

1. The population of the United States in 1970 was 203.2 million. By 1980 it had increased 11.5 percent to 226.5 million. If it increases by 11.5 percent each decade, what will the population of the United States be in 2000? In 2050?

2. The town of Bettysburg had 10,324 residents in the year 2073. Every year there is a new baby born for each 173 residents and one death for every 211 residents. Every year exactly 47 new residents move to town, and 76 move away. Write a deterministic simulation that will determine the population in the year 2084.

3. Suppose the pollutant level of the Rancid River is reduced to 0.03 percent, but the residents of Mudville are not willing to close the Noxious Products plant because most of them would lose their jobs. Therefore the pollutant level in the town's sewage will be 1 percent, even after installation of a treatment facility. What will happen to the pollution level of the lake? Put a writeln statement in the simulation program that will display the pollution level of the lake only every 30 days.

4. Modify the Lake Sludge program pollute to reflect the assumption that 500 cubic feet of pure, unpolluted water evaporate each day and the flow of water out of the lake into the Rancid River is 49,500 cubic feet.

5. The individuals of certain species of birds may be any one of three genetic types: BB, Bb, or bb. Individuals of types BB and Bb have brown eyes, and those of type bb have blue eyes. Each year during mating season, mating between the members of each pair of genetic types produces a number of offspring, which is equal to 10 percent of the number of individuals in the smaller of the two groups. To illustrate, if there are 31 million BB adults and 22 million bb adults, they will produce 0.1 x 22 million = 2.2 million offspring. The genotype of each offspring is determined by selecting at random one of the genes (B or b) from each parent. Each of the four not necessarily distinct genotypes comprises one-fourth of the offspring generation. Each year, after the offspring are produced, 15 percent of the brown-eyed adults and 5 percent of the blue-eyed adults die. The new offspring become reproducing adults in 1 year.

   If the current population distribution is given by the following table

TYPE	POPULATION (MILLIONS)
BB	16.3
Bb	41.2
bb	75.6

   what will be the population of each type in 30 years?

6. A husband and wife plan to save money from their paychecks to make a down payment on a home. They intend to make monthly deposits of $800 in a savings account on which the bank pays monthly interest at the rate of 7/12 of 1 percent. (The bank advertises a nominal annual rate of 7 percent, but it actually pays somewhat more, because the interest is compounded monthly.) How many months will they need to accumulate $30,000?

7. A house is purchased for $75,000 with a down payment of $15,000. The $60,000 balance is borrowed at an interest rate of 12 percent per annum. Payments are to be made monthly, and from each payment is deducted the interest due for 1 month. The remainder of the payment is applied to reducing the principal. To the nearest dollar, how much should the payments be in order that the loan will be

repaid in 25 years? The payments are to be level, that is, the same amount each month. Try simulating with payments varying in size until the number of payments comes out right. Note: The formula for computing the correct monthly payment, given in Section 2.5, can be used to check the answer, but the point of this exercise is to simulate the steady decrease of the outstanding principal.

7.2   Probabilistic Simulation of Gambling Games

The problem of calculating the proportion of times that the roll of two fair dice results in a 7 or an 11 is posed in the chapter introduction. One way to solve this problem by a simulation is to take a pair of dice and roll them a large number of times, while recording the number of favorable outcomes. One might even use the results of a real dice game in progress, provided one is sure the dice are fair. An easier and faster way, however, is to have a computer probabilistically simulate the rolls of the dice, as described in this section.

Simulating the Throw of a Die

Since a die has six faces with one to six dots on a face, a computer can simulate the throw of one die by evaluating the function randominteger (1, 6). We introduced this function in Section 2.6. The value of the function represents the number of dots on the face of the die when it is rolled.

The program seven11 estimates the percentage of rolls of two dice that yield a 7 or 11. The variable wins records the number of *successes*, that is, the number of times the dice come up 7 or 11. The loop that simulates each trial roll of the dice is executed 1000 times. The trial is successful if the value of the variable dice, representing the total number of dots showing on the two dice, is 7 or 11, in which case the value of wins is increased by 1. The final percentage is (wins / 1000) * 100 = wins / 10.

```
program seven11 (output);

  const
    numberofrolls = 1000;

  var
    dice : 2..12;
    wins : 0..numberofrolls;
    i : 1..numberofrolls;
    seed : integer;

  function randominteger (r, s : integer) : integer;
  { generates an integer in the interval [r..s] }
  { uses and changes the global variable seed }
    const
      maxseed = 10000;
      multiplier = 201;
      adder = 3437;
```

```
  begin
  seed := (multiplier * seed + adder) mod maxseed;
  randominteger := r + seed * (s - r + 1) div maxseed;
  end; { randominteger }

begin
seed := 711;
wins := 0;
for i := 1 to numberofrolls do
  begin
  dice := randominteger (1, 6) + randominteger (1, 6);
  if (dice = 7) or (dice = 11) then
    wins := wins + 1;
  end; { for-loop }

writeln ('The percentage of rolls that are 7 or 11 is ',
      wins / numberofrolls * 100 :1:2);
end.
```

```
run seven11
```

```
The percentage of rolls that are 7 or 11 is  22.10
```

It would be incorrect for the program seven11 to use the statement

```
dice := 2 * randominteger (1, 6)
```

because this statement generates only one roll and doubles it, so that the result always would be even. The statement used in the program seven11 generates two random numbers that might be the same, but more often are not.

The program seven11 simulates the event of rolling two dice 1000 times. The problem of deciding how may times to simulate the event in order to obtain a good approximation to the true value is a difficult one. Ten times obviously is not enough, and a trillion simulations would require too much time on any computer.

One way to approach this problem is to run the program 3 or 4 times with some fairly small number of simulations of the event, but using different starting values for the seed. If the answers are all fairly close to each other, that is an indication that the number of simulations was sufficient. If the answers are quite different, then the number of simulations could be increased by a factor of 10 if there is sufficient computer time available to execute the program. One should not expect in rerunning the program seven11 to duplicate the answer 22.10 percent shown in the sample execution. The authors ran the dice program four more times (changing the initial value of seed each time) with the following results:

 21.80 percent 21.60 percent

 22.50 percent 22.80 percent

The true answer is $6/36 + 2/36 = 8/36 = 22.22$ percent. A method for calculating the true answer is discussed in Section 7.3.

Roulette

Roulette is a popular game in gambling casinos. Many interesting questions about the game can be answered by simple simulation programs, which will be Monte Carlo simulations because of the uncertainty of the result of spinning the roulette wheel.

When the roulette wheel is spun, a metal ball is allowed to drop onto it and to come to rest in one of 38 different positions numbered 1 to 36, 0, and 00. Half of the positions 1 to 36 are colored red and the other half black, as noted in Figure 7.2.1. Positions 0 and 00 are colored green. Before the wheel is spun, bets may be placed on "red", "black", "even", "odd", any individual number, or several different combinations of numbers. Figure 7.2.1 shows what the betting table looks like, how bets are made, and the amount paid to the winners. A winner who bets on a combination that pays 6 to 1 is paid $6 for each $1 bet and the amount bet is also returned.

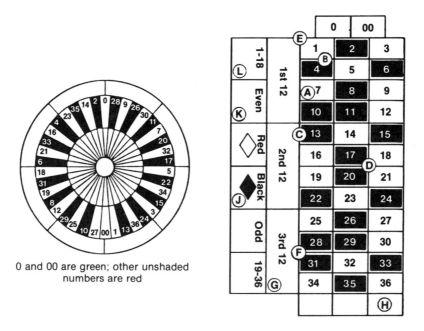

0 and 00 are green; other unshaded
numbers are red

A Single numbers . . . . pays 35 to 1
B Two numbers . . . . (split) . . . . pays 17 to 1
C Three numbers . . . . pays 11 to 1
D Four numbers . . . . pays 8 to 1
E Five numbers . . . . pays 6 to 1
F Six numbers . . . . pays 5 to 1
G Dozen . . . . pays 2 to 1
H Column . . . . pays 2 to 1
J Color . . . . pays even
K Odd or even . . . . pays even
L High or low . . . . pays even

Figure 7.2.1   A roulette wheel and its payoffs.

A Comparison of Two Betting Strategies; Computer-Assisted Decisions

Suppose a gambler enters a Las Vegas casino with $1000. She decides to play roulette, betting each time on the red. She is considering two different betting strategies.

1. Bet $1 each time.

2. Bet $1 on the first spin and on any spin following a win. On any spin following a loss, bet $1 more than the total losses since the last win, or whatever is left of the $1000, whichever is smaller.

If each bet takes a minute, how much money should the gambler expect to have after an hour using one of these strategies?

A Session Using the Fixed-Bet Strategy

The program roulettewithfixedbet simulates a 1-hour gambling session in which the gambler bets $1 each minute on the red. The information the program must record consists only of the amount of money in the gambler's possession and the number of bets that have been made.

```
program roulettewithfixedbet (output);
  begin
  start with $1000;
  for 60 bets do
    begin
    place bet;
    spin roulette wheel;
    if position is red then
      pay off;
    end; { loop }
  print the amount of money left;
  end.
```

In the more detailed version, the value of randominteger (1, 38) simulates the spin of the roulette wheel; the values 37 and 38 represent 0 and 00, respectively. This random value is assigned to the variable wheel and checked to see if it is one of the 18 red positions to determine if the gambler wins.

As seen in Figure 7.2.1, the red numbers on the roulette wheel do not follow a simple pattern, such as all even numbers or all odd numbers, so no simple formula suffices to decide if the value of wheel represents a red number or not. However, this test may be programmed easily in Pascal using the *set* construct and the *set membership relation*. A list of constants, all of the same type, enclosed in square brackets defines a set constant. The set membership operator "in" may be used to decide whether a specific value belongs to the set, that is, to decide whether a specific value appears in the list of values that define the set. In the program roulettewithfixedbet, the test to decide whether the random integer wheel represents a red number on the roulette wheel is written simply as

```
if wheel in [1, 3, 5, 7, 9, 12, 14, 16, 18, 19,
             21, 23, 25, 27, 30, 32, 34, 36] then
```

The variable money represents the amount of money in the gambler's possession and is initialized at $1000. The loop that simulates one bet is executed 60 times. The value of money is decreased by one when the bet is placed, and if the gambler wins, the variable money is increased by the $1 won plus the $1 bet.

```
program roulettewithfixedbet (output);

  const
    nrofbets = 60;

  var
    money, seed : 0..maxint;
    k : 1..nrofbets;
    wheel : 1..38;

  function randominteger (r, s : integer) : integer;
  { generates an integer in [r..s] }
  { uses and changes the global variable seed }
  ... end; { randominteger }

  begin
  seed := 83;
  { start with $1000 }
  money := 1000;
  { simulate nrofbets }
  for k := 1 to nrofbets do
    begin
    { place bet }
    money := money - 1;
    { spin wheel }
    wheel := randominteger (1, 38);
    { check if result is red }
    if wheel in [1,3,5,7,9,12,14,16,18,19,
                 21,23,25,27,30,32,34,36] then
      { pay off }
      money := money + 2;
    end; { for-loop }
  writeln ('The amount of money left is $', money :1);
  end.
```

```
run roulettewithfixedbet

The amount of money left is $996
```

The 1-hour gambling session is simulated only once by the program roulettewith-fixedbet. The program would have to be run many times in order to obtain a good estimate of what the average win or loss would be. Of course, a loss should be expected, since a bet on the red pays even money, but there are 20 losing positions and only 18 winning ones on the roulette wheel. Don't forget to change the initial value of seed for each simulation.

Sessions Using the Strategy to Recoup Losses

Sessions using the second gambling strategy are simulated by the program roulettewithvariablebet. The variable loss records the amount lost on the previous bets since the last win. For the first bet, and after any bet that is won, loss = 0. In the betting strategy simulated by the program, the amount of the bet is loss + 1 unless the gambler doesn't have that much money left. In that case, all that is left is bet. Thus the amount bet should be loss + 1 or money, whichever is smaller.

The program roulettewithvariablebet simulates any number of 60-minute betting sessions. The number of sessions (nrofsessions) is declared as a constant at the beginning of the program. The variable session counts the sessions simulated. After each session, the amount of money remaining in the gambler's possession is added to total, so that the average amount left can be printed after all the sessions have been simulated. The value of the variable total is set to zero initially. As might be expected, the sample execution printout shows that a gambler employing this strategy either wins a few dollars or loses a lot almost every time.

```
program roulettewithvariablebet (output);

  const
    nrofsessions = 25;
    nrofbets = 60;

  var
    money, total, seed : 0..maxint;
    session : 1..nrofsessions;

  function randominteger (r, s : integer) : integer;
    ... end; { randominteger }

  procedure dobetting;

    var
      loss, bet : 0..maxint;
      k : 0..nrofbets;
      outofmoney : boolean;

  begin
  outofmoney := false;
  { loss is amount lost since last win }
  loss := 0;
  k := 0;
  while (k < nrofbets) and (not outofmoney) do
    begin
    k := k + 1;
```

```
          { bet is previous loss + 1,
             but no more than gambler has left }
      if loss < money then
         bet := loss + 1
      else
         bet := money;

      { place bet }
      money := money - bet;
      if randominteger (1, 38) in
          [1, 3, 5, 7, 9, 12, 14, 16, 18, 19,
            21, 23, 25, 27, 30, 32, 34, 36]  then
         begin
         money := money + 2 * bet;
         loss := 0;
         end { if }
      else
         begin
         outofmoney := (money = 0);
         loss := loss + bet;
         end; { else }
      end; { while-loop }
  end; { dobetting }

begin
seed := 299;
total := 0; { total of amounts left after each session }
writeln ('Session' :20, 'Amount left' :20);
for session := 1 to nrofsessions do
   begin
   { start with $1000 }
   money := 1000;
   dobetting;
   writeln (session :20, money :20);
   { add amount left to total }
   total := total + money;
   end; { for-loop }
   writeln;
   writeln ('The average amount left is $',
            total / nrofsessions :1:2);
   end.

run roulettewithvariablebet
```

```
            Session        Amount left
                  1               1027
                  2               1027
                  3               1035
                  4               1025
                  5                902
                  6               1031
                  7               1029
                  8               1023
                  9               1028
                 10               1023
```

11	1030
12	1027
13	1024
14	515
15	1036
16	1022
17	1029
18	1024
19	1028
20	1030
21	1024
22	1034
23	1022
24	1031
25	0

The average amount left is $ 961.04

Exercises

---

1. Write a program that determines by simulation the percentage of times the sum of two rolled dice will be 2, 3, or 12.

2. Two dice are rolled until a 4 or 7 comes up. Write a simulation program to determine the percentage of times a 4 will be rolled before a 7 is rolled.

3. Write a simulation program to determine the percentage of times exactly 5 coins will be heads and 5 will be tails, if 10 fair coins are tossed simultaneously.

4. If the six sides of two dice each are marked with two, two, three, four, five, and six dots (that is, a dot is added to the side normally containing one dot), what percentage of rolls of the two dice will produce a total of 7?

5. Use the function randominteger to create a program which deals a five-card poker hand. Remember that the same card cannot occur twice in a hand.

6. A certain skier likes to have the snow 5 feet deep. He skis at a slope in New Hampshire where the snow begins falling as early as August 24. From August 24 to July 4 the percentage of days with snow is 25 percent. On a snowy day, there is always a deposit of exactly 2 feet. On other days, 4 inches of snow melt away. What percentage of skiing seasons will have a 5-foot accumulation by September 12? What percentage of days between August 24 and July 4 will there be 5 feet of snow on the ground?

7. Modify the program roulettewithvariablebet so that, after 60 minutes, the gambler continues either until she has more than $1000 or until she goes broke.

8. If $1 is bet for each spin of the roulette wheel, then determine which of the following bets results in the smallest average loss: single numbers, two numbers, six numbers, columns, odd, or even. See Figure 7.2.1 for the amount won on each type of bet.

9. If two cards are drawn from a standard deck of playing cards, what percentage of the time will the cards be an ace and a face card (10, jack, queen, or king)? When simulating the draw of the second card, remember that there are only 51 cards left in the deck, and that the same card cannot be drawn twice.

10. Suppose a gambler bets $1 on the following game. Two dice are rolled. If the result is odd, the bettor loses. If the result is even, a card is drawn from a standard deck. If the card is 1 (an ace), 3, 5, 7, or 9, the bettor wins the value of the card, otherwise he loses. What, on the average, will the bettor win (or lose) in this game?

11. Write a simulation program to determine which of the following is better to bet on.

    (a) three or more heads when four fair coins are tossed
    (b) a sum of 9 or more on the roll of two fair dice

12. Write a simulation program to find out the percentage of rolls of two dice that produce "doubles" (the same number on each die).

13. A man on a vacation in Las Vegas strikes up a conversation at a bar with a regular casino patron, Ms. Lisa Bet. The man says he would really like to return home and be able to tell his friends he won money from the gambling casino, but he knows that all of the games favor the house, so he is reluctant to play. Ms. Bet makes the following proposal: "Let me advise you while you are gambling. You must be willing to risk losing up to $100. I am so confident that you will win some money from the casino that I will pay you $200 if you do not win. If you do win money, you must pay me $100 for my advice." The man agrees, figuring that, if he wins, it will be worth $100 (less what he wins) to say that he "beat the house" and, if he loses the $100, he will get $200 from Lisa and be $100 richer. Ms. Bet takes the man to the roulette table and tells him to bet $1 each time on the red. If his wins ever exceed his losses, he is to stop. He also must stop if he loses $100.

    What are the expected winnings for (a) the man, (b) Ms. Bet, and (c) the casino? (These three numbers, treating losses as negative, must sum to 0.)

14. Find the answer to Exercise 13 if the strategy used is to bet each time on the red and always bet $1 more than the amount of money lost (or all that remains of the $100).

15. Each January 1 in Smogsville the air pollution index is 100. Smoggy days and clear days occur "randomly", the probability of each being 1/2. On a smoggy day, the index goes up 10 points. On a clear day the index decreases by 10 percent of its value. Simulate 10 years of 365 days each to estimate the probability that the pollution index will be greater than 105 on any given day. In this simulation, the air pollution index magically returns to 100 each January 1, regardless of what its value was the previous day.

7.3   Queues and Probability

The next example is typical of many simulation programs which solve problems concerning queues (waiting lines). Queues are involved in such things as the study of highway traffic flow, the scheduling of jobs in an industrial plant, and the people waiting for service from a bank teller.

A Waiting Line at the Bank

Suppose a bank teller can serve two patrons each minute. Also, suppose that in any minute, either zero, one, two, or three new arrivals may get in the line and each number is as likely as any other number; that is, during about one-fourth of the minutes of a typical day, no one gets in line, during one-fourth of the minutes of the day, one new person gets in line, and so on. The concise mathematical way of describing the way people arrive is to say that the probability of no arrivals is 1/4, the probability of one arrival is 1/4, and so on, or in standard notation, $Pr(0) = Pr(1) = Pr(2) = Pr(3) = 1/4$. The program queue estimates the average amount of time a customer must wait for service.

```
program queue (output);
  begin
  for day = monday to friday do
    begin
    start the day with an empty line, and other initialization;
    simulate the arrivals and service during a six-hour banking day;
    print day, number of patrons served that day,
     and average waiting time;
    end; { loop }
  end.
```

The main step within the loop is simulation of the arrivals and service during a 6-hour banking day. In this step, the computer must generate new arrivals and add them to the queue, it must decrease the length of the queue by the number of persons who are served, and it must keep track of the waiting time. After the bank entrance closes at 3 p.m., people already inside waiting in line must be served, and the computer program must not neglect this possibility. The refinement of the program queue calls the procedure simulatebankingday to do this main step.

```
program queue (output);

  var
    qlength, patrons, totaltime, seed : 0..maxint;
    day : (mon, tue, wed, thu, fri);

  function randominteger (r, s : integer) : integer;
    ... end; { randominteger }

  procedure simulatebankingday;

    const
      minutesperday = 360; { a six-hour banking day }

    var
      minute : 1..minutesperday;
      arrivals : 0..3;
```

```
begin
for minute := 1 to minutesperday do
  begin
  { generate number of arrivals
    in one minute and add to queue }
  arrivals := randominteger (0, 3);
  qlength := qlength + arrivals;
  patrons := patrons + arrivals;


  { serve 2 persons, if in line }
  if qlength >= 2 then
    qlength := qlength - 2
  else
    qlength := 0;
  { add person-minutes waited that minute }
  totaltime := totaltime + qlength;
  end; { for-loop }

{ end of banking day:
  serve persons already inside when bank entrance closes
  at the rate of two persons per minute
  until line is empty }
while qlength > 0 do
  begin
  if qlength >= 2 then
    qlength := qlength - 2
  else
    qlength := 0;
  totaltime := totaltime + qlength;
  end; { while-loop }
end; { simulatebankingday }


begin
seed := 1313;
for day := mon to fri do
  begin
  qlength := 0;
  patrons := 0;
  totaltime := 0;
  simulatebankingday;
  writeln;
  writeln ('On day ', ord (day) + 1 :1,
          ' the total number of persons served was ',
          patrons :1);
  writeln ('The average waiting time was ',
          totaltime / patrons :1:3, ' minutes');
  end; { for-loop }
end.
```

```
run queue
```

```
On day 1 the total number of persons served was 565
The average waiting time was 0.522 minutes

On day 2 the number of persons served was 523
The average waiting time was 0.314 minutes

On day 3 the number of persons served was 539
The average waiting time was 0.609 minutes

On day 4 the number of persons served was 546
The average waiting time was 0.505 minutes

On day 5 the number of persons served was 530
The average waiting time was 0.421 minutes
```

Before discussing the program queue in detail, some comments on the output are in order. In the 5 days simulated, the number of persons served varies less than 5% from the center of its range. We may have reasonable confidence that most simulated banking days will fall in this range. The average waiting time per person varies a little more from day to day, about 30% maximum from the center of its simulated range. Still, we would not expect many simulated days to have average waiting times of more than 1 minute. These particular simulations also show that the relationship between the number of persons served and the average waiting time is not as direct as one might imagine. More people were served in day 1 than in day 3, yet the average waiting time is smaller in day 1. It is not only the number of people served, but also the way their arrivals happen to be clustered that affects the average waiting time.

In the refinement of the program queue and the procedure simulatebankingday, the variable qlength stands for the length of the queue, the variable patrons accumulates the number of persons served during a whole day, and the variable totaltime is the sum of the number of person-minutes spent waiting by all the patrons in 1 day.

One way to calculate the total number of person-minutes spent in line is to add up the number of minutes spent in line by each of the patrons during a day. The procedure simulatebankingday uses another method, which is easier for this model. The method used is to add up the number of persons still waiting in line during each minute of the day.

Each of the 360 executions of the body of the for-loop in the procedure simulatebankingday represents the passing of 1 minute of the day. The queueing model is nondeterministic, because the number of new arrivals during a minute is uncertain.

Random Variables

The queuing example provides a framework within which to look a bit more carefully at some of the elementary principles of probability theory. Probability theory deals with random events, events whose outcome in general is uncertain. A *random variable* is a quantity whose value depends upon a random event. The number of arrivals in 1 minute, the number of patrons served in a day, and the average waiting time

are all random variables associated with the bank teller queuing problem. The number
of arrivals in 1 minute may be one of only four possible numbers, 0, 1, 2, or 3. The
average waiting time may be any positive number. It is easiest to discuss properties of
random variables that can assume only a finite number of different values, but similar
ideas also relate to other situations.

Suppose that a random event is repeated over and over many times, and suppose a
random variable X associated with the event can assume only the n possible values
v[1], v[2], ..., v[n]. There are numbers p[1], p[2], ..., p[n], one for each possible value
of X, which represent the fraction of times X has the value v[1], v[2], ..., v[n]. The
numbers p[i] are called *probabilities,* and the notation p[i] = Pr (X = v[i]) is used,
which reads "p[i] is the probability that the random variable X has the value v[i]". If,
in the queuing problem, the letter "A" represents the random variable whose value is
the number of customers arriving in a given minute, then

$$\text{Pr } (A = 0) = \text{Pr } (A = 1) = \text{Pr } (A = 2) = \text{Pr } (A = 3) = 0.25$$

This information is displayed in Figure 7.3.1.

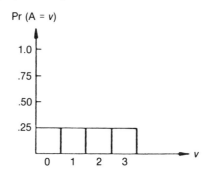

Figure 7.3.1   Probability distribution of the number of patrons arriving.

Sometimes Pr (X = v) is written more briefly as Pr (v), as was done earlier when
describing the probabilities associated with the number of persons arriving in one
minute in the queuing simulation.

Notice that the sum of the probabilities of any random variable must equal 1, and
that each probability must be a number between 0 and 1.

Generating Random Numbers with a Given Distribution

To simulate many different kinds of random occurrences, it is of interest to be able
to generate numbers which have a given probability distribution. Suppose it is known
from past experience that the number A of new customers arriving at the checkout
counter of a supermarket in any 1 minute has the distribution:

v	Pr (A = v)
0	0.273
1	0.324
2	0.116
3	0.214
4	0.073

A way to simulate arrivals of customers according to this distribution is to generate a single random number R, between 0 and 1. Since the random number R is equally likely to be at any particular value between 0 and 1, if the interval from 0 to 1 is divided into 5 subintervals, the probability that R will lie in a given subinterval is proportional to its length. Choosing as lengths for the 5 subintervals the 5 desired probabilities from the table (which add to 1.000), if $0 <= R < 0.273$, set A = 0; if $0.273 <= R < 0.597 = 0.273 + 0.324$ (i.e., R lies in the second subinterval whose length is 0.324), set A = 1; if $0.597 <= R < 0.713 = 0.273 + 0.324 + 0.116$, set A = 2; and so on. The function named "a" generates a value for the random variable A with the distribution given by the table. The data type smallinteger = 0..4 must be defined in a calling program because only a simple data type may appear in a function heading.

```
function a : smallinteger;

  var
    i : 0..4;
    pr : array [0..4] of real;
    r, cummulativepr : real;


  begin
  pr[0]:= 0.273; pr[1]:= 0.324; pr[2]:= 0.116; pr[3]:= 0.214; pr[4]:= 0.073;
  r := randomnumber (0, 1);
  i := 0;
  cummulativepr := pr [0];
  while (cummulativepr <= r) do
    begin
    i := i + 1;
    cummulativepr := cummulativepr + pr [i];
    end; { while-loop }
  a := i;
  end; { a }
```

The function a uses the function randomnumber that produces a random real number between any two real values. It differs from the function randominteger primarily in that its arguments are declared real and that real division is used in the last line.

```
function randomnumber (a, b : real) : real;
{ generates a real in (a..b) }
{ uses and changes the global variable seed }

  const
    maxseed = 10000;
    multiplier = 201;
    adder = 3437;

  begin
  seed := (multiplier * seed + adder) mod maxseed;
  randomnumber := a + seed * (b - a) / maxseed;
  end; { randomnumber }
```

Suppose the distribution is a little more complicated because the values of v are not simply 0, 1, 2, ... If the distribution of A is

v	Pr (A = v)
0	0.137
2	0.562
5	0.212
13	0.089

then a new list of v's can be added and the function program changed as follows.

```
function a : smallinteger;

  var
    i : 1..4;
    pr, v : array [1..4] of real;
    r, cummulativepr : real;

  begin
  pr[1]:= 0.137; pr[2]:= 0.562; pr[3]:= 0.212; pr[4]:= 0.089;
  v[1]:= 0; v[2]:= 2; v[3]:= 5; v[4]:= 13;
  r := randomnumber (0, 1);
  cummulativepr := pr [1];
  i := 1;
  while (cummulativepr <= r) do
    begin
    i := i + 1;
    cummulativepr := cummulativepr + pr [i];
    end; { while-loop }
  a := v [i];
  end; { a }
```

Using this example as a model, functions may be written to simulate any random variable that can assume a finite number of different values.

The queuing problem could be changed by specifying a different probability distribution for the random variable arrivals. It could be made more complex by also specifying a probability distribution for a random variable S, the number of customers served each minute. This would reflect the fact that different patrons require different amount of service time from the bank teller.

Accuracy of Data

There is one statement concerning simulations that is obvious, but nevertheless needs to be emphasized. It is the old "garbage in, garbage out" truism in a different guise. Any results of a simulation will have meaning only if the assumptions about the distributions of the random variables in the program are correct. In the queuing example, the average waiting times provided by the program are valid only if the distribution of arrivals is accurate. Often these distributions can be obtained by actual observation. Why not then simply have the observer record waiting times and forget the simulation? The answer is that, once the distribution of arriving customers is obtained, different types of service can be simulated by the program based on the same data. For example, the effect of having an additional teller can be simulated, avoiding the expense and inconvenience of actually performing the experiment.

There is another more subtle way in which meaningful answers depend upon input data. Input data usually are measured data (or even numbers whose values represent only intelligent guesses). What if their values are wrong by 2 percent? In some cases this kind of error may affect the answer by only a little bit. But there are cases in which a 2 percent error in the data can produce a 100 percent error in the results. This is true not only of simulation programs, but of any programs that use input data whose values are not known precisely. One way to check for this disastrous possibility is to change the input data by 2 percent and rerun the program. If the results are quite different with a 2 percent change in some of the input data, a more careful study of the whole problem is indicated.

Exercises

1. Let D be the random variable whose value is the sum of the dots on two fair dice which are rolled.

    (a) What is the probability that $D > 7$?

    (b) What is the probability that D is even?

2. When a roulette wheel is spun, what is the probability that the result will be

    (a) 00?

    (b) 0 or 00?

    (c) 1, 2, 3, 4, 5, or 6?

    (d) in the first column (in Figure 7.2.1)?

    (e) odd?

3. Write a function program that generates a random number A with the following distribution.

v	Pr(A = v)
−0.6	0.1
2.4	0.2
5.4	0.3
8.4	0.4

4. Write a function whose value is a random number r uniformly distributed between 0 and 1/2 one-third of the time and uniformly distributed between 1/2 and 1 two-thirds of the time.

5. Ten students are working at terminals connected to a central computer. Periodically they request service by hitting the SEND button, which transmits a command to the computer. The random variable S represents the time in seconds for each student between receiving an answer from the computer and issuing the next command. Let C be the random variable that represents the time required by the

computer to process each command. Suppose S and C have the following probability distributions:

s	Pr (S = s)	c	Pr (C = c)
3	0.02	1	0.44
4	0.03	2	0.41
5	0.02	3	0.12
6	0.01	6	0.02
12	0.02	7	0.01
13	0.05		
14	0.16		
15	0.11		
16	0.05		
27	0.13		
28	0.29		
20	0.11		

The computer processes the commands one at a time in the order received. If two commands are received in the same second, the one from the lowest-numbered terminal is processed first. What is the average response time of the system? That is, what is the average time between issuing a command and receiving an answer?

6. At a particular restaurant, the number A of diners arriving in any 5-minute period is given by the distribution

a	Pr (A = a)
0	0.63
1	0.11
2	0.21
3	0.01
4	0.04

If the number of patrons already in the restaurant is P when a new customer enters the restaurant, then the total time T needed to be served and to eat is given by the following table.

P	T
0	30
1	35
2	35
3	40
4	40
5	40
6	45
7	50
8+	60

There are no new arrivals whenever 15 or more diners are already in the restaurant. What is the average time a customer spends in the restaurant?

7. Write a Monte Carlo simulation program to compute an approximate value of pi (the ratio of the circumference of a circle to its diameter) by the following method. Generate 1000 points randomly distributed over the unit square whose corners are the points (0, 0), (0, 1), (1, 1), and (1, 0). Calculate the number N of points that lie inside the circle inscribed within the square with center at (1/2, 1/2) and radius 1/2. Since the area of the circle is Ac = pi * sqr (r) = pi / 4 and the area of the square As = 1, the proportion of points inside the circle should be Ac / As = pi / 4. Thus N / 1000 should be approximately equal to pi / 4 and pi should be given approximately by 4 * (N / 1000) = N / 250. Hint: A point (x, y) lies within the inscribed circle if and only if

$$\text{distance } [(x, y), (1/2, 1/2)] = \sqrt{(\text{sqr } (x - 0.5) + \text{sqr } (y - 0.5))}$$
$$\leqslant 1/2$$

8. Write a Monte Carlo simulation to find the area under any given curve y = f (x) between x = a and x = b as follows. Let m be a number larger than any function value f (x) for x between a and b. (See Figure 7.3.2.)

The proportion of randomly generated points in the (b − a)-by-m rectangle that fall within the shaded area should be approximately equal to the area under the curve (shaded) divided by the area of the rectangle, which is m * (b − a). A point (x, y) is in the shaded area if y <= f (x).

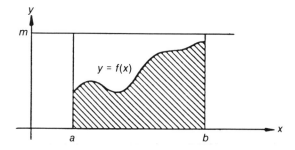

Figure 7.3.2 Area below the curve y = f (x).

7.4 Computer Game Playing

One of the most entertaining demonstrations is a computer simulation of the playing of a game. It is fair to say that the computer often does more than simulate playing the game, it actually plays the game, except that we usually expect an opponent actually to move the chess pieces, or to return the change due for a rent payment in Monopoly instead of merely printing what physical actions are to be taken. This section discusses a computer program to play a game called "matchsticks" against a human opponent. The next section describes how the computer can be programmed to *learn* to play this game so that its performance improves with experience.

How to Play Matchsticks

Two contestants begin a game of matchsticks by placing some matchsticks (or toothpicks, coins, beads, etc.) in a row. The players take alternate turns. On each turn a player removes one, two, or three matchsticks from the row. The player who removes the last matchstick is the winner.

Computer Representation of the Game

A consideration of primary importance in a computer program to play a game is the representation of the status of the game and of the rules of play. A position in the game of checkers, for example, might be an 8×8 table, each entry signifying whether a board location is occupied by a red checker, by a black checker, or is empty. The data types piece and board for this representation could be defined by

```
type
  piece = (red, black, empty);
  board = array [1..8, 1..8] of piece
```

Fortunately, computer representation of the positions and rules for matchsticks is easy. A position may represented faithfully by a single value, the number of matchsticks left. A legal move is a number, necessarily 1, 2, or 3, that does not exceed the number of matchsticks remaining. Other attempted moves are forbidden.

Playing Matchsticks Against the Computer

The program playmatchsticks enables the computer to play as many games of matchsticks against a human opponent as the person wants to play. The constant startingnumber is used to begin each game with a row of 20 matchsticks. The computer checks the legality of each of its opponent's moves and checks to see if a move by either player wins the game.

As directed by the program playmatchsticks, the computer selects its moves by generating a random integer from 1 to 3, but not exceeding the number of matchsticks left. Accordingly, it does not play very well. The human opponent always plays first against the program playmatchsticks.

```
program playmatchsticks (input, output);

  const
    startingnumber = 20;
    linelength = 3;
    yes = 'yes';

  var
    personfinished : boolean;
    response : packed array [1..linelength] of char;
    seed : integer;
```

```
procedure readresponse;
  ... end; { readresponse }

procedure playonegame;

  var
    nrofmatches : 0..startingnumber;
    personwins, computerwins : boolean;

  procedure makepersonmove;

    var
      legalmovemade : boolean;
      nrtoberemoved : integer;

    begin
    legalmovemade := false;
    while not legalmovemade do
      begin
      writeln ('How many do you want to remove?');
      write ('Input data  number to be removed: ');
      readln (nrtoberemoved);
      if (1 <= nrtoberemoved) and
          (nrtoberemoved <= 3) and
          (nrtoberemoved <= nrofmatches) then
        begin
        nrofmatches := nrofmatches - nrtoberemoved;
        writeln ('That leaves ', nrofmatches :1, ' matches.');
        legalmovemade := true;
        end { if }
      else
        begin
        writeln ('You can''t take ', nrtoberemoved :1, ' matches.');
        writeln ('Move again.  There are ', nrofmatches :1,
                  ' matches left.');
        end; { else }
      end; { while-loop }
    end; { makepersonmove }

  procedure makecomputermove;

    var
      nrtoberemoved, maxtoberemoved : 1..3;

    function randominteger (r, s : integer) : integer;
      ...    end; { randominteger }

    begin
    if nrofmatches > 3 then
      maxtoberemoved := 3
    else
      maxtoberemoved := nrofmatches;
    nrtoberemoved := randominteger (1, maxtoberemoved);
```

```
        nrofmatches := nrofmatches - nrtoberemoved;
        writeln ('I take ', nrtoberemoved :1, ' matches, ',
                 'leaving ', nrofmatches :1, '.');
        end; { makecomputermove }


  begin { playonegame }
  nrofmatches := startingnumber;
  write ('There are ', nrofmatches :1, ' matches.');
  writeln ('  You go first.');
  personwins := false;
  computerwins := false;
  while (not personwins) and (not computerwins) do
    begin
    makepersonmove;
    if nrofmatches = 0 then
      personwins := true
    else
      begin
      makecomputermove;
      if nrofmatches = 0 then
        computerwins := true;
      end; { else }
    end; { while }
  if computerwins then
    writeln ('I win.')
  else
    writeln ('You win.');
  end; { playonegame }


begin
seed := 13;
personfinished := false;
while not personfinished do
  begin
  playonegame;
  writeln ('Do you want to play again?');
  writeln ('Input data  response: ');
  readresponse;
  personfinished := (response <> yes);
  end; { while-loop }
end.



runi playmatchsticks

There are 20 matches.  You go first.
How many do you want to remove?
Input data  number to be removed: 3
That leaves 17 matches.
I take 2 matches, leaving 15.
How many do you want to remove?
Input data  number to be removed: 1
```

```
That leaves 14 matches.
I take 3 matches, leaving 11.
How many do you want to remove?
Input data   number to be removed:  4
You can't take 4 matches.
Move again.   There are 11 matches left.
How many do you want to remove?
Input data   number to be removed:  3
That leaves 8 matches.
I take 1 matches, leaving 7.
How many do you want to remove?
Input data   number to be removed:  0
You can't take 0 matches.
Move again.   There are 7 matches left.
How many do you want to remove?
Input data   number to be removed:  2
That leaves 5 matches.
I take 3 matches, leaving 2.
How many do you want to remove?
Input data   number to be removed:  2
That leaves 0 matches.
You win.
Do you want to play again?
Input data   response:  no
```

Exercises

---

1. Modify the procedure makecomputermove so that whenever the computer encounters a position with one, two, or three matchsticks left, it takes them all. Does this improve the computer's performance when playing against you?

2. Modify the procedure makecomputermove so that the computer bases its move on the person's previous move in the following manner. If the person takes 1, the computer takes 3. If the person takes 2, the computer takes 2. If the person takes 3, the computer takes 1. Does this improve the computer's performance when playing against you?

3. Make modifications in the program playmatchsticks and its procedure playonegame so that, instead of always starting with 20 matchsticks, the number at the start of a game is a random integer from 18 to 26.

4. Modify the program playmatchsticks so that it keeps running totals of the number of games won by the person and by the computer and prints them when the person signals to stop play.

5. A simplified game of NIM, played by two contestants, begins by placing one, two, and three objects, such as matches, in three rows as shown in Figure 7.4.1. Represent the status of the game by a three-digit number, each digit representing the number of matches in one row. The starting position is 123. Each player takes a turn by removing some or all of the objects from any single row. The player who removes the last object wins the game. Write a boolean function

Figure 7.4.1 Starting position for NIM.

legalmove (p1, p2) that determines if a move from position p1 to p2 is a legal move. For example,

```
legalmove (123, 121) = true
legalmove (121, 101) = true
legalmove (121, 110) = false {objects taken from two rows}
```

6. Write a program that plays the game of NIM described in Exercise 5.

7. Represent a position in the game of checkers by an 8 × 8 table of data type piece, where piece and board are defined by

```
type
  piece = (blackking, black, empty, white, whiteking);
  board = array [1..8, 1..8] of piece
```

Write a function program legalcheckersmove of four arguments that determines whether moving a piece from square (i1, j1) to square (i2, j2) is legal.

8. Write a program that plays checkers against a human opponent by randomly generating moves until one is legal.

9. The game of hexapawn is described by Martin Gardner in his article, "How to Build a Game-Learning Machine and Then Teach It to Play and to Win", in *Scientific American,* March 1962. It is played on a 3 × 3 board like that used for tic-tac-toe. The play starts with three pawns for each player, positioned as shown in Figure 7.4.2.

A player moves one pawn either straight ahead one place to an empty square or diagonally one place to a square occupied by an opponent's pawn, capturing that pawn (which is removed from the board). These moves are basic moves for the pawn in chess, hence the name "hexapawn". The arrows in Figure 7.4.3 show the four possible moves for player X from one position and the resulting board positions.

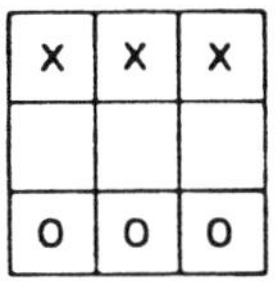

Figure 7.4.2   Starting positions for hexapawn.

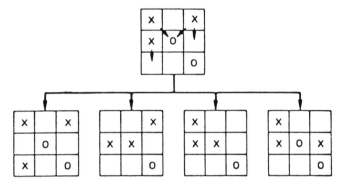

Figure 7.4.3   Some hexapawn moves.

The game is won by (a) moving into the third row, (b) capturing all the opponents pawns, or (c) leaving the opponent with no legal move. No draw is possible. Write a program to play hexapawn that permits the human player to move first.

10. The game of tic-tac-toe is played on a board with nine squares. Two players alternate by placing a mark (usually ''X'' or ''O'') in an empty square. The game is won by the player who places three of his or her marks in a straight line in a row, a column, or either diagonal. A winning position for player X is illustrated in Figure 7.4.4. Write a program that enables the computer to play tic-tac-toe against a human opponent. Let the computer move first.

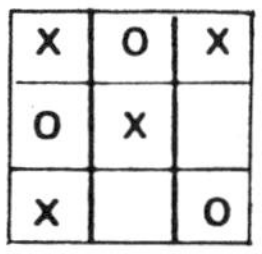

Figure 7.4.4   A winning tic-tac-toe position for player X.

7.5 Artificial Intelligence: A Program That Learns

Despite the great speed and high reliability of computers, there are many tasks that people can do faster and more accurately. For instance, a person can quickly pick out of a crowd of possibly hundreds of other persons the face of a friend or a relative. A person also can identify numerous acquaintances by their voices. A brief glance at a chess board is often sufficient for a master player to tell which side has the better position, even though the end is many moves away and the number of possible combinations is vast. A person frequently can understand the meaning of a written or spoken sentence even if it contains grammatical errors. A computer has substantial difficulty with each of these tasks. Indeed, some of these activities, so easy for a person, are unfeasible for a computer at present.

The theory of artificial intelligence is derived from the attempts that have been made to program a machine to perform tasks which seem to be easier for humans than for machines. An important aspect of many studies in artificial intelligence is the attempt to learn something about how humans perform these seemingly complex tasks by carefully analyzing the ways a machine can be programmed to perform them.

Game Playing

Computer programs that play games, such as the program playmatchsticks, provide the opportunity to study some of the aspects of artificial intelligence. The rules of most games are simple enough that a programmer can easily write a program to play a correct game. The goals of a game are simply defined, so that the success of a program can be measured easily. It also might seem to be an easy task to program a computer to play a perfect game of chess (for example) by allowing it to examine all possible moves and select one certain to lead to a win or draw. In principle, this could be done, but there are so many different moves in the game of chess that the fastest and largest computers are not capable of making an exhaustive analysis in a reasonable amount of time. Thus it is an interesting project to try to program a computer to play chess as well as the best human players.

One of the classic studies in artificial intelligence is a program written by Arthur L. Samuel which learned to play checkers. Samuel was able to defeat his program at first, but as the program acquired experience it was able to beat its creator consistently and go on to defeat some of the best checker players. Some techniques for programming a machine to learn are discussed in this section.

A Program that Learns to Play Matchsticks

While it might seem, at first, as if learning is something too ''biological'' for a computer, the program learnmatchsticks modifies its own behavior according to its experience. Winning a game reinforces its tendencies, and losing a game causes it to decrease the frequency of its behavior patterns on the path to the loss. The result is improved performance. Such behavior modification satisfies most definitions of learning.

In order to learn to play a better game of matchsticks, as instructed by the program learnmatchsticks, the computer keeps an important statistic in the list named success. For each position in the game, that is, for each possible number j of matches left, from zero up to the starting number of matches, the value of the list entry success [j] is the difference between the number of wins and the number of losses in all games in the learning session in which the computer left j matches by its move.

At the start of the learning session, the value of every entry in the list success is initialized to zero, corresponding to the absence of any experience so far. During each game of the learning session, the computer records each move played in the game. At the end of any game it wins, it increases by one the value of each entry in the list success corresponding to a move it played during the game. After a loss, the computer decreases by one the value of each entry in the list success corresponding to a move it played during the game.

At each of its turns, the computer uses the value of an entry success [j] as a measure of the desirability of a move leaving its human opponent with j matchsticks. In particular, the computer plays by selecting from all legal moves the one of greatest worth under this measure. Ties are resolved somewhat arbitrarily, by selecting the smaller move. The program learnmatchsticks resembles as closely as possible the program playmatchsticks in the previous section, and the procedure makepersonmove from that section is used without change.

```
program learnmatchsticks (input, output);

   const
     startingnumber = 20;
     maxmove = 3;
   yes = 'yes';

type
   positiontype = 0..startingnumber;

var
   movesingame, nrofmatches : positiontype;
   personfinished : boolean;
   personwins, computerwins : boolean;
   response : packed array [1..3] of char;
   matchesleft : array [positiontype] of positiontype;
   success : array [positiontype] of integer;
   seed : integer;

procedure readresponse; { reads 'yes' or 'no' response }
   ... end; { readresponse }

procedure playonegame;

   var
     nrofmatches, movenumber : positiontype;

   procedure makepersonmove;

     var
       legalmovemade : boolean;
       nrtoberemoved : integer;

     begin
     legalmovemade := false;
     while not legalmovemade do
       begin
       writeln ('How many do you want to remove?');
       write ('Input data  number to be removed: ');
       readln (nrtoberemoved);
       if (1 <= nrtoberemoved) and
          (nrtoberemoved <= maxmove) and
          (nrtoberemoved <= nrofmatches) then
```

```
          begin
          nrofmatches := nrofmatches - nrtoberemoved;
          writeln ('That leaves ', nrofmatches :1, ' matches.');
          legalmovemade := true;
          end { if }
        else
          begin
          writeln ('You can''t take ', nrtoberemoved :1, ' matches.');
          writeln ('Move again.  There are ', nrofmatches :1,
                      ' matches left.');
          end; { else }
      end; { while-loop }
    end; { makepersonmove }

procedure makecomputermove;

  var
    nrtoberemoved, bestmovesofar, move : 1..maxmove;

  begin
  move := 1;
  bestmovesofar := 1;
  while (move < maxmove) and (move < nrofmatches) do
    begin
    move := move + 1;
    if success [nrofmatches - move] >
        success [nrofmatches - bestmovesofar] then
      bestmovesofar := move;
    end; { while-loop }
  nrtoberemoved := bestmovesofar;
  nrofmatches := nrofmatches - nrtoberemoved;
  writeln ('I take ', nrtoberemoved :1, ' matches, ',
            'leaving ', nrofmatches :1, '.');
  end; { makecomputermove }

begin { playonegame }
nrofmatches := startingnumber;
write ('There are ', nrofmatches :1, ' matches.');
writeln ('  You go first.');
  movenumber := 0;
  personwins := false;
  computerwins := false;

  while (not personwins) and (not computerwins) do
    begin
    movenumber := movenumber + 1;
    makepersonmove;
    matchesleft [movenumber] := nrofmatches;
    if nrofmatches = 0 then
      personwins := true
    else
      begin
      movenumber := movenumber + 1;
```

```
      makecomputermove;
      matchesleft [movenumber] := nrofmatches;
      if nrofmatches = 0 then
        computerwins := true;
      end; { else }
    end; { while }

  if computerwins then
    writeln ('I win.')
  else
    writeln ('You win.');
  movesingame   := movenumber;
  end; { playonegame }

procedure modifyexperience;

  var
    move : positiontype;

  begin
  if computerwins then
    begin
    move := 0;
    while move < movesingame do
      begin
      move := move + 2;
      success [matchesleft [move]] :=
          success [matchesleft [move]] + 1;
      end; { while-loop }
    end { if }

  else if personwins then
    begin
    move := 0;
    while move < movesingame - 1 do
      begin                    .
      move := move + 2;
      success [matchesleft [move]] :=
          success [matchesleft [move]] - 1;
      end; { while-loop }
    end; { else }
  end; { modifyexperience }

begin { learnmatchsticks -- the main program }
seed := 13;

{ computer is initially completely inexperienced }
for nrofmatches := 0 to startingnumber do
  success [nrofmatches] := 0;

{ play as many games as human opponent desires }
personfinished := false;
while not personfinished do
```

```
begin
playonegame;
modifyexperience;
writeln ('Do you want to play again?');
writeln ('Input data  response: ');
readresponse;
personfinished := (response <> yes);
end; { while-loop }
end.
```

The graph in Figure 7.5.1 shows the results of one session between the computer and a human opponent who played each game to win if possible. Any time the computer won a game the human opponent avoided, if possible duplicating the moves which allowed the machine to win. This causes the computer to learn quite rapidly. A human opponent can delay the learning process by such tricks as letting the program win after it has made a poor move. This poor move is then recorded as a good one, and the program tries the move again until eventually it learns that it is a poor one. Of course, in order to retard the program's learning, the opponent must lose some games.

In Figure 7.5.1, a loss by the computer is represented by a downward sloping line. A win is indicated by an upward slope. The height of the line after any number of games thus represents the difference between the program's wins and the number of games won by its opponent.

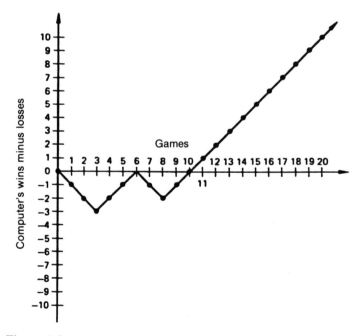

Figure 7.5.1   History of a learning session with a human opponent.

Heuristics

The program learnmatchsticks and Samuel's checkers program are examples of what often are called *heuristic* programs. To a computer scientist, a heuristic is an aid to decision making, often associated with learning. In the program learnmatchsticks, each possible number of matchsticks left is rated for its desirability as a situation after making a move, the particular rating used being the net number of wins minus losses in the past when this situation previously occurred. Samuel's checkers program uses a far more complex experience-influenced rating of checkers positions to make its moves. In both cases, the rating method is the heuristic.

Another example of a heuristic is the Goren point count used by some bridge players to estimate the value of their cards. Each ace counts 4 points, each king counts 3, and so forth. Points are added or subtracted for distributions of the suits and other factors. The point count is then used to help decide what bid to make.

The term "heuristic" usually is applied to procedures not fully guaranteed to find a "best" solution to a particular problem, or any solution at all. Even if Samuel's checkers program learned enough to defeat the best players, it still might not play perfectly; perhaps another program could beat it. Similarly, there is certainly no assurance that Goren's methods provide the optimal bidding strategy in bridge.

Suggested Readings

Edward A. Feigenbaum, "Artificial Intelligence: Themes in the Second Decade", *Proceedings of the IFIP Congress 1968, Edinburgh, Scotland*, pp. J10-J24, August 1968.

Edward A Feigenbaum and Julian A. Feldman, editors, *Computers and Thought*, McGraw-Hill, New York, 1963.

Martin Gardner, "How to Build a Game-Learning Machine and Then Teach it to Play and Win", Mathematical Games Department, *Scientific American*, Vol. 206, No. 3, pp. 138-152, March 1962.

Arthur L. Samuel, "Some Studies in Machine Learning Using the Game of Checkers", *IBM Journal of Research and Development*, Vol. 3, No. 3, pp. 210-219, July 1959.

Exercises

---

1. Modify the program learnmatchsticks so that it more fully uses its record of all moves made by both players in the following way. After each game, have it increase the success value of each move made by the winner and decrease the success value of each move made by the loser. Compare the learning rate of the new program with that of the old program.

2. If a human opponent plays poorly against the program learnmatchsticks, the program may learn to make wrong moves, allowing the opponent to win later games. Suppose 20 games are played against learnmatchsticks. Try to determine the maximum number that can be won by the program's opponent.

3. Write a program that learns to play hexapawn. (See Exercise 9 in Section 7.4.)

4. Write a program that learns to play tic-tac-toe. (See Exercise 10 in Section 7.4.) Let a draw have a value of $+1$, a win $+2$, and a loss -1.

5. Write a program that learns to play NIM. (See Exercise 5 in Section 7.4.)

6. Modify the program learnmatchsticks so that the record of the computer's experience is stored permanently in a file in auxiliary memory (tape or disk). At the beginning of each run, the modified program should play as well as it did at the end of the previous run.

7. Write a program replacing the human opponent in the program learnmatchsticks with a computer procedure that randomly selects a legal move as in the program playmatchsticks in Section 7.4. Compare the record of the learning program against this random opponent to the record shown in Figure 7.5.1 for learning against a human opponent.

8. Modify the program for Exercise 7 so that, after 100 games against a random opponent, the computer pits its learning program against a human opponent. How well does it play for this amount of experience?

9. Modify the program learnmatchsticks so that two learning programs are pitted against each other. How do the learning rates for play against another learning program compare to those for play against human opponents or random opponents?

10. Modify the program learnmatchsticks so that, in case of two or more moves having been equally successful in the past, the computer randomly selects among them. Does this modification have a noticeable effect upon the computer's play or its learning rate?

11. Modify the heuristic in the program learnmatchsticks so that a move made in a winning game counts as $+1$, but a move made in a losing game counts as -2 toward the experience array success, that is, success [j] = wins $- 2 *$ losses for games in which move j has been made. How does the learning rate with this modified heuristic compare with the learning rate for the old heuristic for play against random opponents? against human opponents?

7.6   Simulation of Creativity

Artistic creativity often is regarded as one of the highest forms of intellectual activity, even though there is disagreement as to what is "creative" and what is not. Computers, properly programmed, are capable of producing respectable works of art, music, and even poetry. This sort of activity may be viewed as an attempt to have a computer simulate creativity.

Creativity and Randomness

Many works of art produced by a computer depend extensively on a random number generator. Random numbers generated by a computer can represent notes, colors, or words. Rules specifying the distributions of generated numbers impose the artist's control over the form and structure of the work. For example, a program could be written so that it will produce only music whose structure and harmony is like that of music of the classical period. Another program could be written to generate only six-sided designs that look like snowflakes.

It is important to note that, in using even the simplest schemes for generating music, art, or poetry, the programmer probably will be somewhat surprised by the result produced by the program. This contradicts the intended meaning of the cliche,

"The computer only does exactly what it is told", which is true only in a very narrow sense.

A Program that Composes Music

A program to compose music is a combination of deterministic steps to provide the overall structure of the composition and some of the specific details, and random variations within this framework to simulate the spark of creativity. For example, one might write a program to print the opening motif of Beethoven's Fifth Symphony with the last note chosen at random instead of as Beethoven chose it, or one might write a program to generate random sequences of 12 tones, called random "tone rows", in which no note of the well-tempered scale is repeated.

The program composemelody writes a musical composition in two phrases. The first phrase consists of 10 notes in the range C below middle C to C above middle C with an eleventh note of middle C added to the end of the phrase. The second phrase is an exact repetition of the first phrase with the last note changed to the A below middle C. Numbers from −7 to 7 are used to represent the notes. The number 0 represents middle C. The numbers 1, 2, 3, 4, 5, 6, and 7 represent the notes D, E, F, G, A, B, and C above middle C, and −1, −2, −3, −4, −5, −6, and −7 represent B, A, G, F, E, D, and C below middle C. The program simply generates a sequence of notes without specifying length or volume. Primes are used to distinguish the lowest five possible notes from notes of the same name in the octave containing middle C. Lowercase letters are used for the three highest possible notes. The notes are generated by the following statements.

```
homewardtendency := distancefrommiddlec / 3;
randomvariation := randomnumber (-3, 3) + randomnumber (-3, 3);
newdistance := round (distancefrommiddlec -
            homewardtendency + randomvariation);
```

The scheme for generating the notes is somewhat arbitrary. The "homeward tendency" keeps the notes from straying too far from middle C, and the random variation is the sum of two random numbers to make values near the middle of the range of possible variations somewhat more likely than more extreme variations between successive notes. The resulting number is rounded to the nearest integer. If the number generated is either less than −7 or greater than 7, it is ignored and another note generated. The process continues until 10 acceptable notes are stored for printing in each of the two phrases. Although some computers can be hooked directly to a speaker to play the music generated, or hooked directly to an audio tape recorder to record the music, the program composemelody only prints the music and leaves its performance to others.

```
program composemelody (output);

  const
    melodylength = 10;
    maxnote = 7;

  type
    noteindex = 1..melodylength;
    noterange = -maxnote..maxnote;
```

```
var
  distancefrommiddlec : noterange;
  newdistance : integer;
  melody : array [noteindex] of noterange;
  i : noteindex;
  homewardtendency, randomvariation : real;
  noteinscale : boolean;
  seed : integer;

function randomnumber (r, s : integer) : integer;
  ... end; { randomnumber }

procedure printnote (note : noterange);
  begin
  if (note >= -2) and (note <= 4) { octave containing middle C } then
    write (chr (ord ('C') + note), ' ')
  else if note >= 5 { A above middle C } then
    write (chr (ord ('c') + note - 7), ' ')
  else if note <= -3 { G below middle C } then
    write (chr (ord ('C') + note + 7), ''' ');
  end; { printnote }

begin
seed := 299;
distancefrommiddlec := 0;
for i := 1 to melodylength do
  begin
  noteinscale := false;
  while not noteinscale do
    begin
    homewardtendency := distancefrommiddlec / 3;
    randomvariation := randomnumber (-3, 3) + randomnumber (-3, 3);
    newdistance := round (distancefrommiddlec -
                    homewardtendency + randomvariation);
    noteinscale := abs (newdistance) <= maxnote;
    end; { while-loop }
  melody [i] := newdistance;
  distancefrommiddlec := newdistance;
  end; { for-loop }

{ print melody }
for i := 1 to melodylength do
  printnote (melody [i]);
writeln ('C');
for i := 1 to melodylength do
  printnote (melody [i]);
writeln ('A');
end.

run composemelody

B C F' B D E D B F' G' C
B C F' B D E D B F' G' A
```

Figure 7.6.1 shows one way of scoring the melody generated by the program composemelody as a waltz for piano in the key of A minor.

Figure 7.6.1   A melody composed by a computer and scored for piano.

Suggested Readings

Martin Gardner, ''White and Brown Music, Fractal Curves, and One-over-f Fluctuations'', Mathematical Games Department, *Scientific American,* Vol. 238, No. 4, pp. 16-31, April 1978.

Lejaren A. Hiller, ''Music Composed with Computers—A Historical Survey'', in *The Computer and Music,* H. B. Lincoln (Ed.), Cornell University Press, Ithaca, N. Y., 1970.

Sally Y. Sedelow, ''The Computer in the Humanities and Fine Arts'', *Computing Surveys,* Vol. 2, No. 2, pp. 89-110, June 1970.

Douglas R. Hofstadter, *Godel, Escher, and Bach: An Eternal Golden Braid,* Basic Books, New York, 1979, pp. 127-134, 603-609, 619-627.

Exercises

---

1. As defined by Arnold Schonberg, a *tone row* is a sequence of the 12 tones of the well-tempered scale in which no note is repeated. Write a program to produce randomly generated tone rows.

2. Modify the program for Exercise 1 so that ascending intervals of 3 or 4 semitones and descending intervals of 8 or 9 semitones are preferentially chosen if the resulting notes have not been used already. This method has been used by some 12-tone composers to give a more tonal feeling to their music.

3. Write a program to produce pictures by printing X's on the output page. Some rules must be imposed concerning the way the X's are printed if the picture is to have some ''form''.

4. Write a program to produce rock-and-roll music. Hint: One way is to preselect the rhythmic pattern 4/4 time, and then to have the computer randomly select all accented notes of the melody from the notes of chords of C major, A minor, D minor seventh, and G seventh in successive half measures.

7.7   Chapter Review

Solving a problem by simulation begins with the formulation of a programming model incorporating the relevant features of the real process in which the problem originates. Ordinarily, the more accurate the representation, the more reliable the results of the simulation. For many problems, however, it is not worth the programming effort to capture every detail, nor the execution time to run such a program. Accordingly, many simulation programs deliberately compromise between utter faithfulness to the real process and computational simplicity.

A Deterministic Model for Predicting a Rabbit Population

Simulation is often used to make population predictions, as illustrated both in Section 7.1 by the model for the population of Idaho and in Section 2.4 for the population density in New Jersey. The technique is not restricted to human populations. For review of the basic idea, suppose we want to estimate the number of rabbits resulting from one newly born pair after 3 years, if its species has the following life cycle characteristics.

1. The rabbits live for about 4 years.

2. They first reproduce about 8 months after birth and tend to have a litter every 2 months thereafter until the age of 3 1/2.

3. They produce an average litter of 8, with males and females equally distributed, that is, four new pairs of rabbits.

For modeling purposes, it is convenient to take a 2-month interval as the basic unit of time and to allow pop [j] to stand for the rabbit population after j time intervals. The problem is to calculate pop [18]. Since the original pair of rabbits does not reproduce during the first 3 time units, it follows that

pop [0] = pop [1] = pop [2] = pop [3] = 2

For values of t from 4 to 18, we observe that

pop [t] = survivors [t] + newborns [t]

where survivors [t] denotes the number of rabbits surviving from the previous time period, and newborns [t] denotes the number of rabbits born just in time to be counted in pop [t]. Since this model is of such short duration that no rabbits die,

survivors [t] = pop [t − 1]

Also, the life cycle characteristics imply that

newborns [t] = 4 * pop [t − 4]

Thus

pop [t] = pop [t − 1] + 4 * pop [t − 4]

The following chart shows the rabbit population for the first 8 time units.

time t:	0	1	2	3	4	5	6	7	8
pop [t]:	2	2	2	2	10	18	26	34	74

A *deterministic* model is one whose behavior is independent of chance. The growth of a real-life rabbit population obviously depends on complicated variables such as the food supply, the presence of predators, and the health of the rabbits, which make it unlikely that future rabbit populations can be predicted exactly. Moreover, the stated life cycle characteristics are only averages. The actual reproduction processes are far less mechanistic. Nonetheless, in the absence of additional information, it is entirely appropriate to construct the deterministic model just presented. The program rabbits calculates the estimate of pop [18], the number of rabbits after 3 years, by deterministically simulating the reproduction process.

```
program rabbits (output);

  const
    maxtime = 18;

  type
    time = 0..maxtime;

  var
    pop : array [time] of integer;
    t : time;

  begin
  for t := 0 to 3 do
    pop [t] := 2;
  for t := 4 to maxtime do
    pop [t] := pop [t - 1] + 4 * pop [t - 4];
  writeln ('After ', maxtime div 6 :1, ' years there are ',
           pop [maxtime] :1, ' rabbits.');
  end.
```

```
run rabbits
```

```
After 3 years there are 20666 rabbits.
```

A Probabilistic Model for the Scheduling of Office Hours

If the data describing a process indicate the dependence of the process on chance, or the unpredictability of individual events within a generally predictable pattern preclude a deterministic model, then it is possible and often appropriate to design a *probabilistic* model whose behavior reflects the uncertainties of the process. Suppose, for example, that a college computer center wants to schedule sufficiently many office hours for its programming consultants that they can give help to at least 100 students a day. The center's past experience is that, about 1/10 of the time, a 5-minute conference is sufficient; about 2/10 of the time, a 10-minute conference is adequate; about 3/10 of the time, 15 minutes are needed; and about 4/10 of the time, 20 minutes are required. The program consultanthours is designed to simulate 10 days of consulting work and to print the number of hours needed on each of those days.

```
program consultanthours (output);
  begin
  initialize;
  for day := 1 to number of days do
    begin
    total consulting time = 0;
    for student := 1 to number of students do
      begin
      use given distribution to generate time needed by this student;
      increase total consultant time by the time needed by this student;
      end; { student for-loop }
    print total consultant time for the day;
    end; { day for-loop }
  end.
```

Repetition of Experiments

Typically, a program concerned with a probabilistic model simulates the behavior of the model a sufficiently large number of times to provide a general picture or an average result. One time might be insufficient because of the uncertainty. Even the 10 days of consulting work simulated might not be enough to give a general picture, in which case the program would be modified. In order to see whether the 10 days simulated were a representative sample, one might rerun the program consultanthours several times and compare the results.

Making Random Values Fit a Distribution

The only statements of the program consultanthours that need to be refined are the ones concerned with generating the amount of time a particular student needs and the initialization statement. The refined version of the program consultanthours shows both how to represent a probability distribution by intervals within the line segment (0, 1) and how to use that representation and the function randomnumber to make the random variable values assigned fit the distribution.

```pascal
program consultanthours (output);

  const
    nrofdays = 10;
    nrofstudents = 100;
    nroftimes = 4;
    dayfieldwidth = 20;
    timefieldwidth = 30;

type
  timeindex = 1..nroftimes;

var
  time, probability : array [timeindex] of real;
  day : 1..nrofdays;
  seed : integer;

procedure initialize;

  begin
  seed := 9999;
  time [1] := 5 / 60;
  time [2] := 10 / 60;
  time [3] := 15 / 60;
  time [4] := 20 / 60;
  probability [1] := 1 / 10;
  probability [2] := 2 / 10;
  probability [3] := 3 / 10;
  probability [4] := 4 / 10;
  { print column headers }
  writeln ('Day' :dayfieldwidth,
           'Total Consultant Hours' :timefieldwidth);
  writeln;
  end; { initialize }

procedure simulateoneday;

  var
    student : 1..nrofstudents;
    r, cummulativepr, totalconsultanttime : real;
    i : 0..nroftimes;

  function randomnumber (a, b : real) : real;
    ... end; { randomnumber }

  begin { simulateoneday }
  totalconsultanttime := 0;
```

```
for student := 1 to nrofstudents do
  begin
  { generate time required for this student-- time [i] }
  r := randomnumber (0, 1);
  i := 1;
  cummulativepr := probability [1];
  while cummulativepr <= r do
    begin
    i := i + 1;
    cummulativepr := cummulativepr + probability [i];
    end; { while-loop }
  totalconsultanttime := totalconsultanttime + time [i];
  end; { for-loop }
writeln (day :dayfieldwidth,
         totalconsultanttime :timefieldwidth:2);
end; { simulateoneday }

begin { main program consultanthours }
initialize;
for day := 1 to nrofdays do
  simulateoneday;
end.
```

run consultanthours

Day	Total Consultant Hours
1	25.17
2	24.17
3	25.42
4	25.83
5	24.58
6	26.00
7	24.00
8	25.58
9	25.08
10	23.75

APPENDIX A: PASCAL RESERVED WORDS

and	downto	if	or	then
array	else	in	packed	to
begin	end	label	procedure	type
case	file	mod	program	until
const	for	nil	record	var
div	function	not	repeat	while
do	goto	of	set	with

APPENDIX B: PREDECLARED IDENTIFIERS

Constants:

maxint   true   false

Types:

boolean   char   integer   real   text

Variables:

input   output

Functions:

abs	eof	odd	round	sqrt
arctan	eoln	ord	sin	succ
chr	exp	pred	sqr	trunc
cos	ln			

Procedures:

get	page	readln	rewrite	write
new	put	reset	unpack	writeln
pack	read	dispose		

APPENDIX C: PASCAL SYNTAX CHARTS

1. ⟨PROGRAM⟩:

2. ⟨BLOCK⟩:

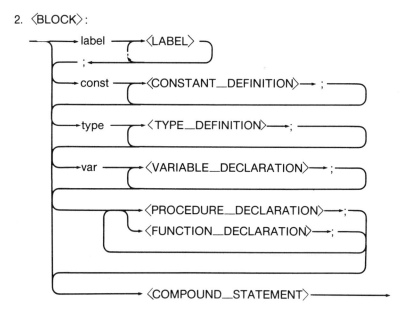

3. ⟨CONSTANT_DEFINITION⟩ :

→⟨IDENTIFIER⟩→ = →⟨CONSTANT⟩——→

4. ⟨TYPE_DEFINITION⟩ :

→⟨IDENTIFIER⟩→ = →⟨TYPE_DENOTER⟩——→

5. ⟨TYPE_DENOTER⟩ :

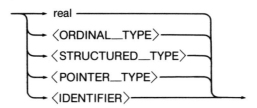

6. ⟨ORDINAL_TYPE⟩ :

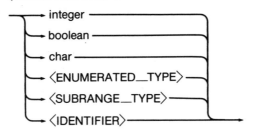

7. ⟨ENUMERATED_TYPE⟩ :

———→ (—→⟨IDENTIFIER_LIST⟩—→) ——→.

8. ⟨SUBRANGE_TYPE⟩ :

→⟨CONSTANT⟩—→.. →⟨CONSTANT⟩—→

9. ⟨STRUCTURED_TYPE⟩ :

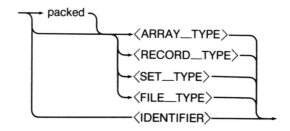

10. ⟨ARRAY_TYPE⟩:

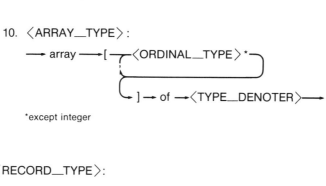

*except integer

11. ⟨RECORD_TYPE⟩:

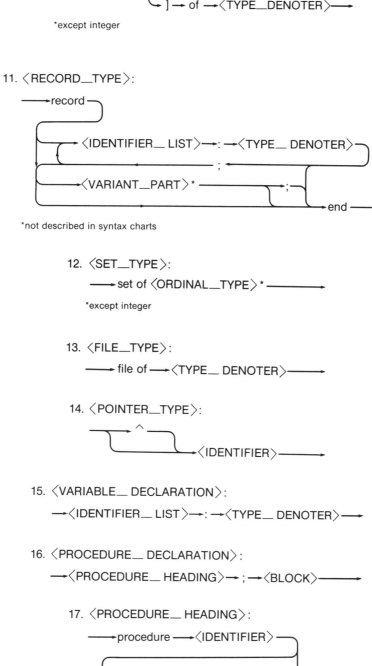

*not described in syntax charts

12. ⟨SET_TYPE⟩:

⟶ set of ⟨ORDINAL_TYPE⟩* ⟶

*except integer

13. ⟨FILE_TYPE⟩:

⟶ file of ⟶⟨TYPE_ DENOTER⟩⟶

14. ⟨POINTER_TYPE⟩:

15. ⟨VARIABLE_ DECLARATION⟩:

⟶⟨IDENTIFIER_ LIST⟩⟶: ⟶⟨TYPE_ DENOTER⟩⟶

16. ⟨PROCEDURE_ DECLARATION⟩:

⟶⟨PROCEDURE_ HEADING⟩⟶ ; ⟶⟨BLOCK⟩⟶

17. ⟨PROCEDURE_ HEADING⟩:

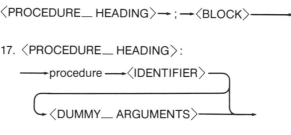

18. ⟨FUNCTION__ DECLARATION⟩:

→⟨FUNCTION__ HEADING⟩→; →⟨BLOCK⟩→

19. ⟨FUNCTION__ HEADING⟩:

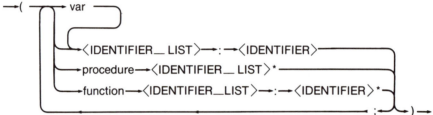

20. ⟨DUMMY__ARGUMENTS⟩:

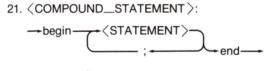

*Allows functions and procedures to be passed
as arguments; not discussed in text.

21. ⟨COMPOUND__STATEMENT⟩:

→begin→⟨STATEMENT⟩→
           ;   →end→

22. ⟨STATEMENT⟩

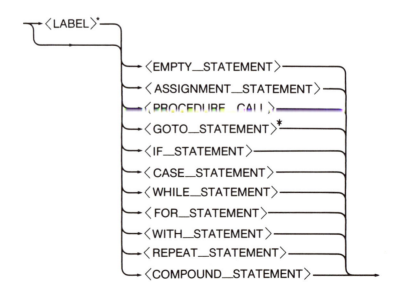

*not described in text

23. ⟨EMPTY_STATEMENT⟩:

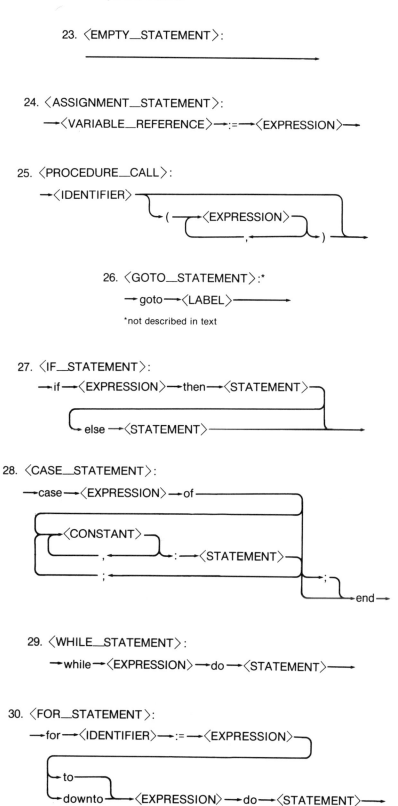

24. ⟨ASSIGNMENT_STATEMENT⟩:

→⟨VARIABLE_REFERENCE⟩→:=→⟨EXPRESSION⟩→

25. ⟨PROCEDURE_CALL⟩:

→⟨IDENTIFIER⟩

(→⟨EXPRESSION⟩ ,)

26. ⟨GOTO_STATEMENT⟩:*

→ goto →⟨LABEL⟩

*not described in text

27. ⟨IF_STATEMENT⟩:

→ if →⟨EXPRESSION⟩→ then →⟨STATEMENT⟩

else →⟨STATEMENT⟩

28. ⟨CASE_STATEMENT⟩:

→ case →⟨EXPRESSION⟩→ of

⟨CONSTANT⟩

, : →⟨STATEMENT⟩

;

; end →

29. ⟨WHILE_STATEMENT⟩:

→ while →⟨EXPRESSION⟩→ do →⟨STATEMENT⟩

30. ⟨FOR_STATEMENT⟩:

→ for →⟨IDENTIFIER⟩→:=→⟨EXPRESSION⟩

to
downto →⟨EXPRESSION⟩→ do →⟨STATEMENT⟩

31. ⟨WITH_STATEMENT⟩:

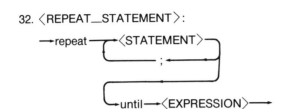

32. ⟨REPEAT_STATEMENT⟩:

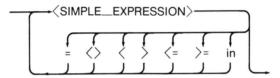

33. ⟨EXPRESSION⟩:

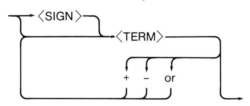

34. ⟨SIMPLE_EXPRESSION⟩:

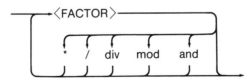

35. ⟨TERM⟩:

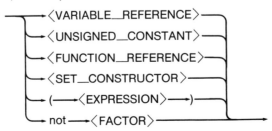

36. ⟨FACTOR⟩:

37. ⟨VARIABLE__REFERENCE⟩:

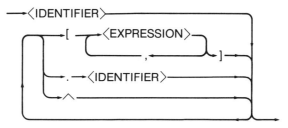

38. ⟨UNSIGNED__CONSTANT⟩:

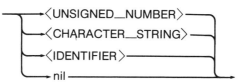

39. ⟨FUNCTION__REFERENCE⟩:

40. ⟨SET__CONSTRUCTOR⟩:

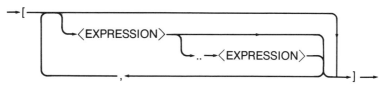

41. ⟨IDENTIFIER__LIST⟩:

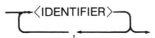

43. ⟨CONSTANT⟩:

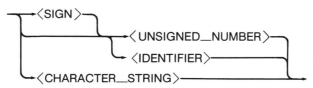

44. ⟨UNSIGNED_NUMBER⟩:

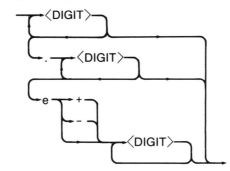

45. ⟨CHARACTER_STRING⟩:

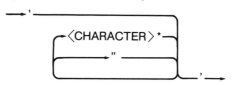

*The set of allowed characters is processor-dependent;
it does not include an apostrophe (').

46. ⟨LABEL⟩:*

*not discussed in the text

47. ⟨LETTER⟩:

48. ⟨SIGN⟩:

49. ⟨DIGIT⟩:

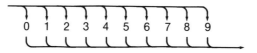

APPENDIX D: DIRECT-ACCESS I/O PROCEDURES

```
procedure readdirect (filename : filetype;
                      recordnumber : fileindex;
                      var recordname : recordtype;
                      var error : boolean);

   var
     i : fileindex;

   begin
   reset (filename);
   i := 0;
   while (i < recordnumber) and (not eof (filename)) do
     begin
     i := i + 1;
     read (filename, recordname);
     end; { while }
   error := (i < n);
   end; { readdirect }
```

```
procedure writedirect (filename : filetype;
                       recordnumber : fileindex;
                       recordname : recordtype;
                       var error : boolean);

   var
     i : fileindex;
     temprecord : recordtype;
     tempfile : filetype;

   begin
   error := (n = 0);
if not error then
   begin
   reset (filename);
   rewrite (tempfile);
   i := 0;
   while (i < recordnumber - 1) and (not eof (filename)) do
     begin
     i := i + 1;
     read (filename, temprecord);
     write (tempfile, temprecord);
     end; { while }
   if i < recordnumber - 1 then
     { add multiple copies of record to fill the gaps between
         the last existing record and the position of the new record }
     for i := i + 1 to recordnumber do
         write (filename, temprecord);
   else
     begin
     if not eof (filename) then { reads old copy of record to be written }
         read (filename, temprecord);
     write (tempfile, recordname); { write new copy }
     while not eof (filename) do
         begin
         read (filename, temprecord);
         write (tempfile, temprecord);
         end; { while-loop }
     rewrite (filename);
     reset (tempfile);
     while not (eof (tempfile) do
         begin
         read (tempfile, temprecord);
         write (filename, temprecord);
         end; { while-loop }
     end; { else }
   rewrite (tempfile);
   end; { if not error }
end; { writedirect }
```

APPENDIX E: PASCAL REFERENCE GUIDE

PROGRAM

program program name (file name 1, file name 2, . . . , file name n);

   const

      constant name 1 = constant 1;

      constant name 2 = constant 2;

      . . . ;

   type

      type name 1 = type 1;

      type name 2 = type 2;

      . . . ;

   var

      variable name 1.1, variable name 1.2, . . . , variable name 1.n1 : type 1;

      variable name 2.1, variable name 2.2, . . . , variable name 2.n2 : type 2;

      . . . ;

   procedure procedure name 1 (dummy argument declaration 1.1; . . .);

      . . . **end**; {procedure name 1}

   . . . ;

   function function name 1 (dummy arg. decl. 1.1; . . .): result type name;

      . . . **end**; {function name 1}

   . . . ;

   begin   main program

   statement 1;

   statement 2;

       .

       .

       .

   statement n

   end. {program name}

Notes: All files names except "input" and "output" must be declared as variable names (**var**). With only one other exception (recursive type definitions using pointer variables), all names must be declared in earlier lines than they are referenced.

NAME

A name consists of a letter followed by any number of letters or digits (no blanks).

Note: All Pascal identifiers (i.e., program names, file names, constant names, type names, procedure names, etc.) have this form.

CONSTANT
unsigned number
±unsigned number
constant name
±constant name
'xyz . . . w'

TYPE
Simple Type
  Enumerated Type
    (element name 1, element name 2, . . . , element name n)
  Subrange Type
    constant 1 . . constant 2
  Named Type
    type name
Pointer Type
    ⌃type name
Structured Type
  Array Type
    array [simple type 1, simple type 2, . . . , simple type n] **of** type
  Record Type
    record
      field name 1.1, field name 1.2, . . . : type 1;
      field name 2.1, field name 2.2, . . . : type 2;
      . . . ;
      case field name type name **of**
        constant 1.1, constant 2.1, . . . : (field name & type list 1);
        constant 2.1, constant 2.2, . . . : (field name & type list 2);
        . . . ;
      end   {record name}
  File Type
    file of type
  Set Type
    set of type name
    set of constant 1 . . constant 2
    set of (element name 1, element name 2, . . . , element name n)
Packed Type
    packed array type
    packed record type
    packed file type
    packed set type
    Notes: 1) Either the variant part (following **case**) or the fixed part (preceding
              case) of a record type may be omitted.
           2) The base type for a set type must be finite and unstructured. Pascal
              implementations are permitted to further restrict the size of the base
              type in the interest of efficient implementation.
           3) Packed types are implementation dependent.

PROCEDURE AND FUNCTION DEFINITIONS
Procedure Declaration

procedure procedure name (variable name 1.1.1, . . . : type name 1.1;
 . . . ;
 var variable name 2.1.1, . . . : type name 2.1;
 . . . ;
 function function name 3.1.1, . . . : type name 3.1;
 . . . ;
 procedure procedure name 4.1.1, . . . ;
 . . .);

const
 . . . ;
type
 . . . ;
var
 . . . ;
procedure or function declaration 1;
. . . ;
begin
statement 1;
statement 2;

 .

 .

 .

statement n
end; {procedure name}

Note: There are four kinds of dummy arguments, "by value" parameters that
 cannot return a value to the calling program, variable (**var**) parameters
 that can return values, and function and procedure dummy arguments
 whose corresponding supplied arguments are function or procedure
 names (some restrictions apply). Dummy arguments of all kinds may be
 mixed in any order.

Function Declaration

function function name (dummy arg & type list): result type name;
const
 . . . ;
type
 . . . ;
var
 . . . ;
procedure or function declaration 1;
. . . ;
begin
statement 1;
statement 2;

 .

 .

 .

statement n
end; {function name}

Notes: 1) Each execution path should have one function value assignment
statement of the form
    function name := expression
2) Dummy argument declarations for a function follow same rules
as dummy argument declarations for a procedure.

STATEMENT

Assignment Statement

variable := expression

Restrictions: 1) The type of the expression must be assignable to the type
of the variable. Usually they are identical types or have a base
type/subrange type relationship. Integer expression values
are assignable to real variables.
2) Arithmetic, boolean, and set variables allow unrestricted
expressions of assignable type.
3) Character string, pointer, and record variables allow only
simple expressions (i.e., variables, constants, or constant
names) of the corresponding types.
4) Function value assignments follow the rules for the
result type.

Conditional Statement

1) **if** boolean condition **then**
    statement
2) **if** boolean condition **then**
    statement 1
  else
    statement 2

Caution: A semicolon after **then** or **else** implies that the then-clause or else-
clause consists of an empty statement. A semicolon between
statement 1 and **else** is a syntax error.

Compound Statement

begin
statement 1;
statement 2;
   .
   .
   .
statement n
end

Comment

{ text of comment }

Note: May be placed anywhere a blank is permitted.

Empty Statement

Note: The empty statement has no characters at all. It explains why a semicolon may immediately precede **end** in a compound statement —
statement n, the last statement, is empty.

For Statement
    1) **for** variable name := expression 1 **to** expression 2 **do**
       statement
    2) **for** variable name := expression 1 **downto** expression 2 **do**
       statement

While Statement
    while boolean condition **do**
      statement
    Note: The while-condition is tested immediately before each execution of
         statement. If the while-condition is initially false, statement will not be
         executed at all. If some assignment within statement causes the while-
         condition to become false, the current execution of statement is still
         completed normally, and the while-condition is tested for exit
         before the next execution of statement begins.

Repeat-Until Statement
    repeat
      statement 1;
      statement 2;

        .
        .
        .

      statement n
      until boolean condition
    Note: The until-condition is tested only upon completion of statement n.
         Normal exit from a repeat-until-loop cannot occur before one complete
         execution of the statement sequence.

Case Statement
    case expression **of**
      constant 1.1, constant 1.2, . . . :
        statement 1;
      constant 2.1, constant 2.2 . . . :
        statement 2;
      . . . ;
      constant n.1, constant n.2, . . . :
        statement n;
      end { case statement }

With Statement
    with record variable 1, record variable 2, . . . **do**
      statement
    Note: Permits abbreviated names instead of full path names for subfields
         of the indicated record variables.

Procedure Call
    1) procedure name
    2) procedure name (supplied arg 1, supplied arg 2, . . .)
    Note: Supplied arguments are expressions with the type of the corresponding
         dummy arguments. For a variable (**var**) dummy argument, the supplied

argument must be a variable. Procedure or function dummy
arguments (not discussed in this book) require procedure or function
names as supplied arguments.

EXPRESSION
Arithmetic Expression
   1) unsigned number
      ±unsigned number
      arithmetic constant name
      ±arithmetic constant name
      arithmetic variable
      arithmetic function name (supplied argument 1, . . .)
   2) Combinations of arithmetic expressions using
      +   –   *   /
      div   mod   (integer types only)
      (   )
Boolean Expression, Boolean Condition
   1) true
      false
      boolean variable
      boolean function name (supplied argument 1, . . .)
   2) Combinations of boolean expressions using
      or   and   not
      (   )
   3) expression 1   comparison operator   expression 2

Expression Type	Comparison Operators
arithmetic	$<$ $>$ $=$ $<=$ $>=$ $<>$
boolean	all 6 (false $<$ true)
set	$=$ $<>$ $<=$ $>=$ (set inclusion)
character string	all 6 (must be same length and type)
pointer	$=$ $<>$
record	none
array, file	none except character strings

   4) element expression **in** set expression
   Note: The type of the element expression must be the same as the base type
         of the set expression.
Set Expression
   1) [   ]   (the empty set)
      [expression 1, expression 2, . . . , expression n]
      [expression 1.1 . . expression 1.2, exp 2.1 . . exp 2.2, . . .]
      [list of mixed element and subrange expressions]
   2) Combinations of set expressions using
      +   (set union)
      *   (set intersection)
      –   (relative complement)
      (   )
Character String Expression
      character string constant: 'char 1   char 2 . . . char n'
      character string constant name

character string variable: Has declared type
> **packed array** [simple type] **of char**

where
> simple type = (element name 1, . . . , element name n)
> > or constant 1 . . constant 2
> > or type name of previously defined simple type

Pointer Expression
> **nil**
> pointer variable name
> record variable . pointer field name

Record Expression
> record variable

VARIABLE

variable name
array variable [expression 1, expression 2, . . . , expression n]
record variable . field variable name
file variable ∧   (references the "file buffer"
                          which contains the next "unread"
                          component — usually a record —
                          in the file.)
pointer variable ∧   (has type that pointer variable
                          points to.)

BUILT-IN PROCEDURES

Input/Output
> 1) **read** (variable name 1, variable name 2, . . . , variable name n)
> 2) **read** (file name, variable name 1, variable name 2, . . . , variable name n)
>
> Note: When the file name is omitted, the standard file "input" is implied.
>
> 3) **write** (item 1, item 2, . . . , item n)
> 4) **write** (file name, item 1, item 2, . . . , item n)
> > where
> > item = expression
> > > expression: field width
> > > real expression: field width: number of decimal places
>
> Note: When the file name is omitted, the standard file "output" is implied.
>
> 5) **reset** (file name)
> > (positions file at start for reading)
>
> 6) **rewrite** (file name)
> > (erases file and positions file at start for writing)

Input/Output For Text Files Only
> 1) **readln**
> 2) **readln** (file name)
> 3) **readln** (file name, variable name 1, variable name 2, . . . , variable name n)
>
> Note: **readln** passes over next end of line character after reading.
>
> 4) **writeln**
> 5) **writeln** (file name)
> 6) **writeln** (file name, item 1, item 2, . . . , item n)
>
> Note: **writeln** writes an end of line character after other items.

File Buffer Procedures (not used in this book)
    1) **get** (file name)
    Note: **get** advances the file one component and assigns the values found there
          to the file buffer file name$^\wedge$.
    2) **put** (file name)
    Note: **put** appends the current contents of the file buffer (i.e., file name $^\wedge$)
          to file as next component.
      file name $^\wedge$ is the name of the file buffer, a
        variable with the same type as the base type of the file.
Dynamic Allocation Procedures
    1) **new** (pointer variable name)
    Note: **new** allocates storage for a node of the type pointed to by the pointer
          variable, and sets the pointer variable to point to this node.
    2) **dispose** (pointer variable name)
    Note: **dispose** releases storage for the node pointed to.

INDEX OF PROGRAMS

575

INDEX

W